CHURCHILL

CHURCHILL

Edited by Robert Blake and
Wm. Roger Louis

W·W·Norton & Company
New York   London

Manufacturing by The Courier Companies.

Printed in the United States of America.

ISBN 0-393-03409-7

W. W. Norton & Company, Inc., 500 Fifth Avenue, New York, N. Y. 10110
W. W. Norton & Company Ltd., 10 Coptic Street, London WC1A 1PU

1 2 3 4 5 6 7 8 9 0

PREFACE

THE time has come to take full measure of that extraordinary man who is perhaps the greatest figure in twentieth-century history. Now that the official biography by Martin Gilbert has been completed and now that most of the archives and collections of private papers of the period are accessible, it is possible to make a reassessment of Churchill's life and career. His reputation has grown to almost mythical proportions. Such is the admiration for him, especially in the United States, that it sometimes seems difficult to separate the legendary figure from the man. Can the subject be demythologized but treated fairly and judiciously? Or, to put it more modestly, what is the result when one takes a fresh look at his career and tries to make balanced judgements?

The opportunity to answer those questions was provided by a conference held at the University of Texas at Austin in March 1991. Each of the participants, most of them historians, spoke as an authority on at least one aspect of Churchill's career. It is unusual, perhaps, that a group of such experience and range could have been assembled. No-one knew what the outcome would be. No-one foresaw the delicate interplay of ideas about Churchill's motives or the controversial exchange of views on his policies. No-one fully anticipated the extent to which the debate would develop into an inquiry that at times was both critical and unflattering. And yet Churchill emerged from the conference as very much the same familiar figure, though with more nuances. In the mind's eye the statue of him did not change. But the features became more finely chiselled. As a historical figure he became more of a human being with remarkable flaws as well as overarching strengths. His achievement seemed greater than ever. These themes are apparent in the book. All in all, the book helps to provide a better understanding of how Churchill came to be, in A. J. P. Taylor's phrase, 'the saviour of his nation'.

The papers presented at the conference have been rewritten to create the book. Some of the participants at the conference did not write chapters but contributed significantly to the conference discussion that made the book possible. These include Winston S. Churchill, MP;

J. Roderick Heller III of Washington, DC; Donald Lamm of New York City; George Macatee of Dallas; Dr Hans Mark, Chancellor of the University of Texas System; Dr Harry Shukman of St Antony's College, Oxford; and Dr Frank Vandiver of Texas A&M. We regret that Martin Gilbert was unable to come to the conference. We are grateful to Dr Alaine Low for serving as the Conference Rapporteur. We thank Richard Ollard and David Reynolds for writing chapters for the book that did not form part of the original plan of the conference.

The principal sponsors of the Conference were the Kerr Chair of English History and Culture at the University of Texas and the Lyndon Baines Johnson Library. We wish to thank the Director of the Library, Harry J. Middleton, and his staff for the conference arrangements. Our especial thanks go to Marjorie Payne, the conference secretary, to Professor William R. Braisted, who assisted us in the preparation of the manuscript, and to Mary Bull, who prepared the index. We warmly thank those who helped to make the conference possible: Dr and Mrs Alfred B. Brady; Mr and Mrs Ollie Brown; Mr and Mrs Sam J. Brown; Mr and Mrs Creekmore Fath; Mr and Mrs Edwin Gale; Mr and Mrs Baine Kerr; Dr Damon Wells; and, above all, the President and staff of the Pennzoil Company. At the University of Texas we gratefully acknowledge support from the College of Liberal Arts; the Chancellor's Council; the Cline Visiting Professorship Endowment; the Macatee Fellowship Fund; the College and Graduate School of Business; the School of Law; the Division of Continuing Education; the LBJ School of Public Affairs; and the Harry Ransom Humanities Research Center.

R.B.
W.R.L.

CONTENTS

LIST OF PLATES

LIST OF CONTRIBUTORS

PAUL ADDISON is a Fellow of Edinburgh University and a former Visiting Fellow of All Souls College, Oxford. He is the author of *The Road to 1945: British Politics and the Second World War*; and *Now the War is Over*. He was an assistant to the late Randolph S. Churchill in editing the Churchill papers for publication. His latest book is *Churchill on the Home Front 1900–1955*.

STEPHEN AMBROSE is the Boyd Professor of History at the University of New Orleans. He is an editor of the *Eisenhower Papers*. His biographies include *The Supreme Commander: The War Years of General Dwight D. Eisenhower*; and *Eisenhower: The President*. He has recently published a biography of *Richard M. Nixon*. His other books include *Rise to Globalism*.

LORD BELOFF is Emeritus Professor of Government and Public Administration, and Emeritus Fellow of All Souls College, Oxford. His books include *The Foreign Policy of Soviet Russia*; *Wars and Welfare: Britain, 1914–1945*; and the two volumes of *Imperial Sunset: Britain's Liberal Empire 1897–1921* and *Dream of Commonwealth, 1921–1942*. He is a Fellow of the British Academy.

LORD BLAKE was Editor of the *Dictionary of National Biography* and Provost of Queen's College, Oxford. His books include *Disraeli*; *The Unknown Prime Minister: Bonar Law*; *The Conservative Party from Peel to Thatcher*; *A History of Rhodesia*; and *The Decline of British Power*. He is a former Chairman of the Rhodes Trustees and a Fellow of the British Academy.

DONALD CAMERON WATT is Stevenson Professor of International History at the London School of Economics. He was an editor of the *Survey of International Affairs*. His books include *Personalities and Policies*; *Succeeding John Bull*; and *How War Came*. He is the Official Historian of *The Central Organization of British Defence, 1945–1966*, and a Fellow of the British Academy.

DAVID CANNADINE, formerly a Fellow of Christ's College, Cambridge, is Professor of English History at Columbia University. His books include *Lords and Landlords: The Aristocracy and the Towns*; *The*

Pleasure of the Past; and *The Decline and Fall of the British Aristocracy.* He has recently edited a one-volume anthology of Churchill's speeches.

FIELD MARSHAL LORD CARVER served as British Chief of the Defence Staff, 1973–6. His books include *El Alamein*; *Tobruk*; *Harding of Petherton*; *The Apostles of Mobility*; *War since 1945*; *The Seven Ages of the British Army*; and *Twentieth Century Warriors.*

PETER CLARKE is a Fellow of St John's College, Cambridge, and Professor of Modern British History in the University of Cambridge. His books include *Liberals and Social Democrats*; *The Keynesian Revolution in the Making, 1924–36*; and *A Question of Leadership: Gladstone to Thatcher.* He is a Fellow of the British Academy and a regular contributor to the *Times Literary Supplement.*

GORDON A. CRAIG is J. E. Wallace Sterling Professor of Humanities Emeritus at Stanford University. He is the author of the Oxford history of *Germany: 1866–1945*; *The Germans*; and *Triumph of Liberalism: Zürich in the Golden Age.* He is a former President of the American Historical Association.

ROBIN EDMONDS served in the British Foreign Service and has been a Fellow of the Woodrow Wilson Center as well as a member of the Council of the Royal Institute of International Affairs. His books include *Soviet Foreign Policy*; and *Setting the Mould: The United States and Britain 1945–1950.* His study of Churchill, Roosevelt and Stalin, *The Big Three*, was published in 1991.

SARVEPALLI GOPAL is Emeritus Professor of Contemporary History at the Jawaharlal Nehru University, New Delhi, and Fellow of St Antony's College, Oxford. He is the author of the three-volume biography of *Nehru.* His other books include *The Viceroyalty of Lord Irwin*; *British Policy in India*; and *Modern India.* He is a former President of the India History Congress.

JOHN GRIGG is a biographer of Lloyd George. His volumes on this subject so far are *The Young Lloyd George*; *Lloyd George: the People's Champion*; and *Lloyd George: From Peace to War 1912–1916.* His other books include *1943: The Victory That Never Was*; and *Nancy Astor.* He is a Fellow of the Royal Society of Literature.

SIR HARRY HINSLEY was Master of St John's College, Cambridge, from 1979 to 1989. His publications include *Command of the Sea*; *Hitler's Strategy*; *Power and the Pursuit of Peace*; and *British Intelligence in the Second World War*. He is a former Editor of *The Historical Journal* and a Fellow of the British Academy.

SIR MICHAEL HOWARD, formerly Regius Professor of Modern History at Oxford, is now Robert A. Lovett Professor of History at Yale University. He is a Fellow of the British Academy. His books include *The Franco-Prussian War*; *The Mediterranean Strategy in the Second World War*; *The Continental Commitment*; *War and the Liberal Conscience*; and *Clausewitz*.

RONALD HYAM is a Fellow of Magdalene College, Cambridge. His publications include *Elgin and Churchill at the Colonial Office*; *The Failure of South African Expansion*; (with Ged Martin)·*Reappraisals in British Imperial History*; and *Britain's Imperial Century 1815–1914: A Study of Empire and Expansion*. He is an Editor of the *British Documents on the End of the Empire*.

LORD JENKINS OF HILLHEAD is Chancellor of Oxford University. He was a Labour MP from 1948 to 1977 and held Cabinet posts as Home Secretary and Chancellor of the Exchequer. He was founder and first Leader of the Social Democratic Party. Among his books are *Mr. Balfour's Poodle*; *Sir Charles Dilke: A Victorian Tragedy*; *Asquith*; *Baldwin*; *Truman*; and *European Diary*.

DOUGLAS JOHNSON is Professor of French History at the University of London. His works include *France and the Dreyfus Affair*; the *Concise History of France*; *The French Revolution*; and *Britain and France: Ten Centuries*. He is a Fellow of the Royal Historical Society.

R. V. JONES was one of Churchill's principal scientific advisers. He is Professor of Natural Philosophy Emeritus at the University of Aberdeen. In the 1939–45 war he served as Assistant Director of Intelligence. In the post-war Churchill government he was Director of Scientific Intelligence. His publications include *Most Secret War* and *Reflections on Intelligence*.

JOHN KEEGAN is Defence Editor of the *Daily Telegraph*. His books include *Six Armies in Normandy*; *The Face of Battle*; *The Mask of Command*; *The Nature of War*; *The Second World War*; and *The Price of Admiralty*. He is a Fellow of the Royal Society of Literature.

WARREN F. KIMBALL is Professor of History at Rutgers University. He is the author of *The Juggler: Franklin Roosevelt as Wartime Statesman* (1991); *The Most Unsordid Act: Lend-Lease*; *Swords or*

Plowshares?; and is the editor of *Churchill & Roosevelt: The Complete Correspondence*. He was the 1988–9 Pitt Professor of American History at Cambridge University.

WILLIAM ROGER LOUIS is Kerr Professor of English History and Culture at the University of Texas, and Fellow of St Antony's College, Oxford. His books include *Imperialism at Bay*; *The British Empire in the Middle East*; and *Leo Amery and the British Empire in the Age of Churchill*. In 1992 he received the Liberal Arts Student Council Award for Outstanding Undergraduate Teaching at the University of Texas.

RICHARD OLLARD has taught at the Royal Naval College, Greenwich, and for many years was a senior editor at William Collins. He is a past Vice-President of the Navy Records Society. His books include *Pepys: A Biography*; *Clarendon and His Friends*; *An English Education: A Perspective of Eton*; and *Fisher and Cunningham: A Study in the Personalities of the Churchill Era*.

ROBERT O'NEILL is Chichele Professor of the History of War and a Fellow of All Souls College, Oxford. He was Director of the International Institute for Strategic Studies from 1982 to 1987. His books include *The German Army and the Nazi Party 1933–39*; *Vietnam Task*; and *Australia in the Korean War*. He is the Armed Services Editor of the *Australian Dictionary of Biography*.

HENRY PELLING is a Fellow of St John's College, Cambridge. His publications include *Origins of the Labour Party*; *America and the British Left*; *The British Communist Party*; *Britain and the Second World War*; and *The Labour Governments 1945–51*. His biography of *Winston Churchill* was published in 1974. He holds an honorary degree from the New School for Social Research.

DAVID REYNOLDS is a Fellow of Christ's College, Cambridge. His publications include *The Creation of the Anglo-American Alliance, 1937–1941* (awarded the Bernath Prize, 1982); *An Ocean Apart: The Relationship between Britain and America in the Twentieth Century* (co-author); and *Britannia Overruled: British Policy and World Power in the Twentieth Century*.

SIR ROBERT RHODES JAMES was Conservative Member of Parliament for Cambridge, 1976–1992. He is a former Fellow of All Souls College, Oxford, and a present Fellow at Wolfson College, Cambridge. His biographies include *Lord Randolph Churchill*; *Lord Rosebery*; *Anthony*

Eden; and *Churchill: A Study in Failure 1900–1939*. He is the Chairman of the History of Parliament Trust.

NORMAN ROSE holds the Chaim Weizmann Chair of International Relations at the Hebrew University, Jerusalem. His books include *Vansittart: Study of a Diplomat*; *The Gentile Zionists*; *Lewis Namier and Zionism*; and *Chaim Weizmann: A Biography*. A Fellow of the Royal Historical Society, he is writing a one-volume biography of Churchill.

D. J. WENDEN was a Fellow of All Souls College, Oxford. He died in 1992. His books include *The Birth of the Movies* and *Battleship Potemkin: Film and Reality*. He was associate Editor of *The Historical Journal of Film, Radio and Television*. He was at work on a book on *Political Cinema in Britain, France and Germany*.

PHILIP ZIEGLER served in the British Foreign Service and as Editor-in-Chief at William Collins. His books include *Diana Cooper* and *The Sixth Great Power: Baring's*, as well as official biographies of King Edward VIII and Earl Mountbatten of Burma. He is a Fellow of the Royal Society for Literature and the Royal Historical Society.

ABBREVIATIONS

ADM	Admiralty Papers
BM	British Museum
CAB	Cabinet Papers
FO	Foreign Office Papers
HO	Home Office Papers
PREM	Papers of the Prime Minister's Office
PRO	Public Record Office
T	Treasury Papers

The official biography of Churchill (Randolph S. Churchill and Martin Gilbert, 8 vols., plus companion volumes), is referred to in the following way:

R. S. Churchill, *Churchill*   **Randolph S. Churchill,** *Winston S. Churchill* (London, 1966–7), i: *Youth, 1874–1900* (1966); ii: *The Young Statesman, 1901–1914* (1967); companion vol. ii (1969).

Gilbert, *Churchill*   **Martin Gilbert,** *Winston S. Churchill* (London, 1971–88), iii: *1914–16* (1971); companion vol. iii (1973); iv: *1917–22* (1975); companion vol. iv (1977); v: *1922–39* (1976); companion vol. v (1982); vi: *The Finest Hour* (1983); vii: *The Road to Victory* (1986); viii: *Never Despair, 1945–65* (1988).

Citations will take the following forms: R. S Churchill, *Churchill*, ii.32; Gilbert, *Churchill*, iii. 49; Gilbert, *Churchill*, companion vol. iii, part 2, pp. 36–7.

INTRODUCTION

WINSTON LEONARD SPENCER CHURCHILL was born on 30 November 1874 at Blenheim Palace, the elder of the two sons of Lord Randolph Churchill, who was the third son of the of the seventh Duke of Marlborough. Winston's mother was Jennie Jerome, daughter of Leonard Jerome of New York. Lord Randolph, after a brilliant early political career, made the fatal error of tangling with his leader, the Conservative Prime Minister Lord Salisbury, and resigned from the Chancellorship of the Exchequer in 1886, dying in 1895 from a disease of the brain. He regarded his son as useless, and Lady Randolph was equally unsympathetic. Such affection as Winston received came from his nanny, Mrs Anne Everest, to whom he was devoted. He was sent to Harrow, where he was unhappy, though his academic performance was not as bad as he later claimed. He was put in the 'army class', the dumping ground for less intelligent boys, and got into Sandhurst on the third attempt. He was commissioned in 1895 in the 4th Queen's Own Hussars, just after his father's death.

Money was a problem. Cavalry officers were supposed to have private means: Lord Randolph left only debts. The young Winston, perhaps because of the indifference shown by a father whom he adored, was intensely ambitious and anxious to prove himself. He needed fortune as well as fame and a political career was always his goal. At an early age he acquired a remarkable command of the English language, written and spoken. Eight months after he was commissioned he went as an observer of the Spanish–American war in Cuba and wrote modestly remunerated accounts of it for the *Daily Graphic*. For the next four years he combined, whenever he could, the role of serving officer and war correspondent, pulling every string with his family connections to get himself posted to the places that mattered: the North-West Frontier in 1897; and the Sudan in 1898, when he took part at Omburman in one of the last cavalry charges in the history of the British army. In 1899 he resigned his commission and stood unsuccessfully for Parliament as a Conservative in a by-election at Oldham. Later that year he went out to South Africa as the *Daily Telegraph*'s military correspondent. He was taken prisoner by the Boers after the derailment of the armoured train in which he was travelling near Colenso. He then made a dramatic escape that hit the headlines all over the world. Four books emerged from his military experiences, written in a style that blended Gibbon and Macaulay, whose works he had read avidly during his spare time in India. By writing and lecturing he had accumulated £10,000 by 1901—a sum worth having in those non-inflationary days.

He stood again for Parliament at Oldham in the general election of 1900. This time he succeeded, though he soon became uneasy about his party's policy. He may have been influenced by writing the life of his father, whose papers revealed how badly he believed he had been treated by the Conservative hierarchy. The party's split over free trade and protection gave Winston the occasion to move over to the other side in 1904. His name and fame made him certain of office in a Liberal government. He was appointed Parliamentary Under-Secretary at the Colonial Office in December 1905—a post all the more important since the Colonial Secretary, Lord Elgin, was in the House of Lords. In 1908 H. H. Asquith, who had succeeded Sir Henry Campbell-Bannerman as Prime Minister, offered him the position of First Lord of the Admiralty—a glittering prize which Churchill refused only because his uncle-by-marriage, Lord Tweedmouth, was the sitting tenant. He became President of the Board of Trade and was supported by David Lloyd George, the new Chancellor of the Exchequer. They struck up a close alliance and promoted a vigorous policy of social reform. Earlier that year he married Clementine Hozier by whom he had a son and four daughters, one of whom died as a child. It was a marriage of intense loyalty on both sides, occasionally interrupted by tiffs and rows: he could be inconsiderate and she was always worried by his extravagance, his passion for gambling, and his consumption of alcohol, which has been exaggerated but was in any view considerable.

In 1910 he became Home Secretary. His tenure was brief but marked by two episodes of some celebrity—the 'Siege of Sidney Street', when he appeared to be personally supervising the massive over-kill of a gang of anarchists in a house off the Mile End Road in London, and the dispersal of rioting Welsh miners on strike at Tonypandy in the Rhondda Valley, alleged forever afterwards to have involved the army, though it was in fact achieved by unarmed police.

In 1911 Asquith invited him for the second time to take on the Admiralty. It was a crucial moment in the 'Naval Race' with Germany. It was also the end of a major political crisis over the position of the House of Lords. Churchill had been almost as virulent as Lloyd

George in attacking the hereditary peerage. It is fair to say that Churchill's career ever since the Boer War had aroused a blaze of controversy. He was hated by the Conservatives as a turncoat, and he was distrusted by many 'respectable' Liberals as a brilliant but undependable adventurer. Asquith took a major risk in appointing him to this crucial post, but the fleet was ready when war broke out in 1914 and Churchill's role was vital. He held his post for four years, advised informally at first and officially after October 1914 by Admiral Sir John ('Jacky') Fisher, an eccentric anti-establishment figure to whom Churchill was instinctively attracted. Fisher wrecked him in the end by suddenly resigning at the height of the crisis over the Dardanelles expedition in 1915.

The fiasco of the Dardanelles was for the time being disastrous to Churchill. The ensuing political explosion caused a reconstruction of the government on a basis of coalition with the Conservatives. Their leader, Andrew Bonar Law, did not trust Churchill an inch and made his exclusion from the Admiralty a condition of joining. Shunted into a sinecure post Churchill soon resigned, serving for a time as a battalion commander on the Western Front. He was not included in Lloyd George's Cabinet in December 1916, again because of Conservative hostility. It was during these months of enforced leisure that he took up painting. In July 1917 the Prime Minister decided to bring him back as Minister of Munitions.

The Conservatives were furious but were not prepared to break up the government. Churchill ran his department with characteristic energy and iconoclasm. After the end of the war Lloyd George reconstructed his coalition government, and in January 1919 moved Churchill to the War Office with responsibility also for the Air Ministry. Among other activities Churchill pressed the Cabinet persistently and fiercely to use force to destroy Russian Bolshevism. War-weariness, Treasury economy, and left-wing propaganda worked against him. In February 1921 Lloyd George moved him to the Colonial Office. Less than two years later the coalition collapsed: Bonar Law became Prime Minister and won an overall majority for the Conservatives at the ensuing election in November 1922. Churchill lost his seat. He was in the political wilderness until October 1924 when he returned to the House of Commons, having by then abandoned the Liberal Party because of the support it had given to the short-lived Labour government of Ramsay MacDonald earlier that year. Amid general surprise Stanley Baldwin, who had succeeded Bonar Law, made

Churchill the Chancellor of the Exchequer. He held the office until the Conservative defeat in 1929. The return to the Gold Standard in 1925 and his militant attitude towards the General Strike of 1926 stamped him in the eyes of many as a reactionary. That impression was enhanced by his resignation in January 1931 from Baldwin's shadow Cabinet over his leader's mildly liberal policy towards Indian self-government. He was not included in Ramsay MacDonald's Conservative-dominated 'national government' of 1931, and his intemperate opposition to the India Bill confirmed his isolation from the mainstream of politics. It required a second World War to bring him back into the Cabinet.

For the next few years he devoted much of his spare time to writing works of both history and popular journalism. He had been doing so sporadically ever since his early days as a war correspondent. Financially he was successful. He probably made, in real terms, more money by his pen than any other non-fiction writer in the twentieth century. His volumes of memoirs of the First World War, published in the 1920s, were best-sellers and so were those he later wrote about the Second. His four-volume biography of the great Duke of Marlborough that came out in the 1930s also sold well, and during the same period he almost completed his *History of the English-Speaking Peoples*, though it was laid aside after 1939 and was not published until 1956–8. He also engaged in highly lucrative journalism. He needed the money. His style of life was expensive and his country house, Chartwell, which he bought in 1922 and largely rebuilt, was a constant drain on his resources.

Churchill was not a great historian, though he was an intelligent and readable one. He was interested more in war and politics than in social, economic, and scientific change, or in the history of ideas, literature, and art. He saw history as a pageant, a colourful drama. His attitude was highly personal, and his memoirs of both world wars have to be read in the light of what he said to one of his helpers, Sir William Deakin: 'this is not history, this is my case'. Like other prominent statesmen he was liable to claim a greater degree of foresight, consistency, and single-mindedness than the facts warrant. It is one of the purposes of this volume to disentangle, where necessary, retrospective legend from contemporary reality. This is not to denigrate Churchill, merely to point out that he, like all mortals, was not infallible and that memoirs written within ten years of the events cannot, and perhaps should not, reveal everything.

After his failure to block the India Bill, Churchill took up a cause that was to be far more advantageous for both his country and his career. He was the first figure of major political stature to discern the menace of the rise of Hitler and the threat of a resurgent Germany. The story of his battle against Neville Chamberlain and appeasement, and of his advocacy of rearmament from 1933 onwards, is too familiar to be repeated. He was very much a lone voice and he became highly unpopular—even more so when he spoke up for King Edward VIII during the abdication crisis at the end of 1936. He was shouted down in the House of Commons. He criticized the Munich agreement over Czechoslovakia in October 1938, which had been generally welcomed, and got into serious trouble with the Conservative constituency organization at Epping, his Parliamentary seat. But when Hitler dismembered Czechoslovakia on 15 March 1939 his warnings seemed vindicated. Even so Chamberlain did not bring him back into the government, for fear of provoking Hitler. It took the German invasion of Poland in September 1939 to convince the Prime Minister that appeasement was dead and that Churchill's talents must not be wasted. Churchill returned as First Lord of the Admiralty and a member of the War Cabinet.

In May 1940 the failure of the Norway campaign brought down Chamberlain, and Churchill succeeded him. There was nothing inevitable about this. The King as well as the retiring Prime Minister and the Conservative Party would have preferred Lord Halifax, the Foreign Secretary. The succession was Halifax's for the asking, but he decided to remain where he was. Seldom has a more crucial decision been made. It meant that Britain had at the head of its affairs the one statesman who, at precisely the moment of the Fall of France, could not only unite all parties by his eloquence but was prepared in the face of all the odds to continue a struggle which objectively seemed hopeless. It was this determination, unflagging energy, and infectious optimism that prevented a dictated peace. Counterfactual interpretations are speculative, but with Britain out of the way Hitler would almost certainly have conquered the Soviet Union, and Japan might not have risked Pearl Harbor. A defeated Russia and a humiliated Britain would have been more vulnerable victims. The United States might not have been drawn into the struggle. Hitler might have ruled a satellite empire from the Urals to the Atlantic. No doubt Churchill's contribution to the outcome, and more specifically to strategy, can be variously assessed. He was not always right and his ideas could be eccentric. What cannot be disputed is his contribution to morale. As he put it, he gave the roar to the British lion, and in those critical years 1940–1 his eloquence, however dated it may seem today, was of enormous importance. As Disraeli said, 'with words we govern men'. Churchill not only governed but inspired.

One should never forget that he was half-American. In the darkest days he cherished the belief that American help would be forthcoming sooner or later. Whether it would have been, but for the unpredictable Japanese attack on Pearl Harbor, is a moot point. Churchill carefully cultivated his relations with Franklin D. Roosevelt. The 'Former Naval Person' correspondence is famous. Churchill and Roosevelt by no means always agreed, but their friendship did much to oil the wheels of the Anglo–American war machine. Towards the end Roosevelt to some extent played off Churchill against Stalin. The 'Big Three' were becoming the 'Big Two-and-a-Half', and the American and Russian contributions soon dwarfed that of the British. When victory occurred in 1945 Churchill was emphatically the junior partner.

The general election that year brought a crushing defeat to the Conservatives. Should Churchill have retired? Many people said 'Yes'—privately if not publicly. No-one who knew him thought that he would, and he did not. He wrote his memoirs, made his famous 'Iron Curtain' speech at Fulton, Missouri, and waited upon events. The Conservatives narrowly lost in 1950 and narrowly won in 1951. Churchill held office from October 1951 for three and a half years. Late in July 1953 he suffered a stroke from which he made a remarkable recovery, though he was never to be quite the same again. He resigned in April 1955, four months after his eightieth birthday. He died on 24 January 1965. Dr Johnson said of Edmund Burke: 'If a man were to go by chance at the same time with Burke under a shed to shun a shower, he would say—"this is an extraordinary man."' Churchill in his valedictory speech about Lloyd George said: 'When the English history of the first quarter of the twentieth century is written it will be seen that the greater part of our fortunes in peace and war were shaped by this one man.' The first quotation, and the second (with a suitable adjustment of dates) could be applied equally well to Churchill himself.

In disentangling the myth from the reality, it is useful to bear in mind the phases of Churchill's life. For present purposes these phases may be thought of as the period up to the First World War followed by the one of wartime, 1914–18, and then the two decades of the 1920s and the 1930s. The wartime era 1939–45 was, of course, the most distinctive phase of his career. There followed a period in opposition and then his return to power in 1951–5. The following comments and questions suggest some of the general themes that spill over from one phase to another and, in this book, from one chapter to another.

What was it like to be an aristocratic adventurer in the late nineteenth century? Churchill often found himself at odds with others of his class. In the period before the First World War he helped to initiate social reforms that eventually laid the basis for the welfare state. He was detested by Tories who believed him to place ambition above party loyalty, and by Liberals who thought that he had only a superficial commitment to such measures as unemployment insurance, pensions for widows and orphans, and shorter working hours. In fact he did contribute substantially to progressive causes before 1914. His ideas not only on social reform but also on the British Empire and certain foreign issues, notably those concerning Germany and France, took shape long before the First World War.

In 1914 Churchill was one of the few members of the Cabinet with first-hand experience in battle. He became a scapegoat for the fiasco of attempting to force the Dardanelles, though he continued to regard his plan as one of the truly original strategic initiatives of the war. What were the lessons he learned from the First World War? How did his experience with Lloyd George contribute to his knowledge of the conduct of government during wartime? How is one to assess his ideas towards revolution in Russia and the peace with Germany?

The issues of the war carried over the decade of the 1920s. As Colonial Secretary how did he view the territorial settlement in the Middle East? The issue of Zionism? Later, as Chancellor of the Exchequer, he was by his own admission less successful than he might have wished, but he was certainly less inept than has often been supposed. He had clearly defined ideas about fiscal economy and policies to be pursued by the Bank of England and the Treasury. His domestic agenda continued to be finance and social reform, though it is debatable whether he ever developed a consistent policy. Coincidental themes that emerge in the phase of the 1920s are his habits of work, which were similar whether at the Colonial Office or the Treasury—or later in Downing Street.

In the 1930s Churchill saw himself as the saviour of Britain's Indian Empire. He made certain assumptions about India, as he did about Egypt, that can only be described as racist. His stand on India antagonized a large part of the public and his insistence on rearmament was unpopular. He was widely distrusted by many people, as he had been throughout the earlier parts of his career. Popular perceptions of Churchill changed in the 1930s, but by the end of the decade he was still regarded by many as a reactionary figure. Nor was his judgement always accurate. His estimates of numerical superiority of the German air force over the British air force were exaggerated. Would his programme of anti-appeasement have made any difference in view of the evidence now available on Hitler's plans for war?

What were the political circumstances that allowed Churchill to become Prime Minister in May 1940? What were the military circumstances? After the outbreak of war in 1939 he had underestimated the strength of the Japanese and misunderstood their intent. What assessment can be made of his grand strategy in Asia as well as in the Middle East and Europe? What conclusions may be drawn about his intervention in military operations? What of his technical grasp of military issues? Was his judgement generally good on the selection of military commanders? How influential was his actual relationship with Roosevelt? What was his estimate of Stalin? One theme to emerge from the wartime period is Churchill's grasp of scientific developments, and another, his remarkable use of secret intelligence.

In 1945 the electorate dismissed Churchill at his moment of greatest triumph. Might it indeed have been better for him to have retired in 1945? What does one make of him as Leader of the Opposition in the post-war period? Despite his scaremongering about a Labour Gestapo, he depended on Labour leaders to further some of his own aims, including a national health service and wider opportunities for education. He did not attempt to repeal Labour legislation after he returned to power in 1951. He demonstrated that there was greater agreement in domestic as well as foreign and imperial affairs than many of his opponents thought possible. Did he believe that Britain's fate ultimately lay in Europe? What of the Commonwealth? Did he remain truly convinced of the viability of the Anglo-American relationship?

Having taken Churchill apart, how is one to put him together again? There is general consensus in this book that Churchill will be remembered above all as a great war leader and as a great orator and writer. The book pays tribute to his stature, though sometimes the investigation is critical and the judgements are unflattering. The critical line of approach must not be misinterpreted as an attempt to diminish Churchill's reputation. On the contrary, when subjected to scrutiny in the light of the historical evidence, Churchill emerges with both his integrity and his greatness intact.

ROBERT BLAKE
ROGER LOUIS

1

Churchill and the Pitfalls of Family Piety

DAVID CANNADINE

WHEN in his early twenties, Winston Churchill was briefly the heir to one dukedom, and over half a century later, on his retirement from public life, he declined his sovereign's offer of another.[1] This double connection with the highest rank in the British peerage forcibly reminds us that Churchill himself was in many ways a quintessential patrician: in C. P. Snow's words, 'the last aristocrat to rule—not just preside over, rule—this country'. It was at Blenheim Palace that he took the two most important decisions of his life—'to be born, and to marry, and I never regretted either'. It was to Blenheim that he went with Clementine for the first part of their honeymoon, and it was to Blenheim that he regularly returned during the course of his subsequent career. Throughout his life, he regarded the Duke of Marlborough as the head of his family, and as the bearer of the greatest name in the land.[2] And it was in Bladon churchyard, within sight of his ancestral palace, that he was buried, beside his father, Lord Randolph Churchill, and Jennie, his mother.

In retrospect, Churchill liked to present himself as a deprived and disadvantaged child, further handicapped by a minimal education, who achieved renown in the world by his own unaided efforts. But while there can be no doubting his ambition and his application, it is also clear that in the early stages of his career he shamelessly exploited his aristocratic connections with single-minded purpose and success. As a soldier hungry for action and glory, he secured postings to the Indian frontier and the Sudan, thanks not merely to his own tireless lobbying, but also to that of his mother, who furthered his plans and guarded his interests 'with all her influence and boundless energy'.[3] When he began his political career as a Conservative candidate, his cousin, the Duke of Marlborough, helped to pay his election expenses.[4] And when he crossed the floor, he was invited to contest Manchester North-West thanks to the intervention of his uncle, Lord Tweedmouth, a senior

figure in the Liberal Party. In some senses, young Winston may indeed
have been a self-made man. But he was also, by birth and by connection, a member of Britain's charmed 'inner circle', and he early on
learned how to pull its strings to his own advantage.

Yet there was another side to Churchill's patrician family background which deserves more detailed exploration than it has so far
received. At the outset of his career, he certainly benefited from the
patronage and support of his ducal relatives and noble connections. But
in the much longer perspective of his ninety-year lifetime, the balance
tilted markedly the other way. Despite his own reverential feelings
towards them, too many of Churchill's ancestors and relatives were
tainted by unstable temperament, unsound judgement, financial
profligacy, and rhetorical (and also alcoholic) excess. And these were
also the very defects of character which censorious contemporaries
detected in Churchill himself. In explaining his 'failure' in the years
before 1940, the political consequences of this genealogically precarious
reputation should not be ignored.[5]

Although he took the greatest pride in his ducal blood, Churchill's
family and forebears were hardly those which any ambitious politician
would freely have chosen. The first Duke may have been a 'heaven-
born general', but he was also a man of dubious political and personal
morality. Indeed, most Victorians, brought up on Macaulay, regarded
him as disreputable and untrustworthy: he had betrayed James II and
conspired against William III, and he had pursued power and wealth
with unscrupulous and single-minded ardour.[6] Since then, the
Marlboroughs had been either unhappy or undistinguished or both.
Many of them had been unstable, depressive, and bad-tempered, and
the third, fourth, and fifth dukes were profligate even by the standards
of the late eighteenth and early nineteenth centuries. Indeed,
Gladstone's harsh words of 1882 expressed the generally held late
Victorian view: 'There never was a Churchill from John of
Marlborough down that had either morals or principles.'[7]

By the last quarter of the nineteenth century, the Marlboroughs were
heading rapidly and self-destructively downhill. But in marked contrast
to his predecessors, Churchill's grandfather, the seventh duke, who
inherited the title in 1857, was a pious and high-minded Victorian
nobleman, and his wife was the formidable Lady Frances Anne, daughter of the third Lord Londonderry. Nevertheless, the Marlboroughs
were far from rich, and the seventh duke inherited the estates in par-

lous condition. As a result, he was reluctantly compelled to disperse much of the patrimony he would have wished to safeguard. In 1862, he sold the family estates in Wiltshire and Shropshire, and twelve years later he parted with his Buckinghamshire holdings to Baron Ferdinand de Rothschild for £220,000. Heirlooms went the same way as ancestral acres. In 1875, the Marlborough gems were auctioned for 35,000 guineas, and during the early 1880s, the magnificent Sunderland Library was disposed of for £56,581, after special legislation had been obtained from Parliament.[8]

This process of dispersal was continued by the eighth Duke, Churchill's uncle, who succeeded in 1883, and soon parted with most of the magnificent collection of Blenheim Old Masters, for £350,000. But there the resemblance between father and son ended. For the eighth Duke was one of the most disreputable men ever to have debased the highest rank in the British peerage. As a youth he was expelled from Eton, and soon acquired a well-deserved reputation for being rude, erratic, profligate, irresponsible, and lacking in self-control. In 1876 his affair with the already married Lady Aylesford became a public scandal; and in 1881 he fathered by her an illegitimate child.[9] Two years later his first wife divorced him, and the new Duke's social disgrace was complete. In 1886 he figured prominently in the sensational divorce case featuring Lady Colin Campbell, his one-time mistress, and shortly after, he married a rich American, Lilian Hammersley, whose wealth enabled him to install electric light and central heating at Blenheim. He died, as he had lived, in the tradition of a Gothic villain, being discovered in his laboratory at Blenheim 'with a terrible expression on his face'.[10]

This was the unhappy state of affairs that 'Sunny' Marlborough, Churchill's cousin, sought to remedy during his long tenure as ninth duke, from 1892 to 1934. But he met with only very limited success. In politics, his career fizzled out: he held minor office in the last years of the Salisbury-Balfour governments, from 1899 to 1905; voted against the Parliament Bill in 1911, and by the inter-war years had become a paranoid and anti-Semitic reactionary.[11] In matrimony, he fared no better. His first marriage, to Consuelo Vanderbilt, was blatantly arranged for the money; they separated in 1906, and divorced in 1920. His second wife, Gladys Deacon, had previously been his mistress, but marriage soured their relationship, and they separated in 1931. In financial terms, the Vanderbilt millions enabled the duke to restore the gardens and terraces at Blenheim, but he died virtually insolvent. And in social terms, the Marlboroughs remained unacceptable. Neither King Edward VII nor King George V would receive him at court, and most duchesses refused to recognize his second wife.[12]

In the course of his short and tragic life, Churchill's father, Lord Randolph, was even more notorious. From his days as an Oxford undergraduate he had shown an unhealthy delight in gambling, in drinking, and in over-spending. His marriage to another American, Jennie Jerome, was accompanied by unseemly wrangles over money; by the early 1880s he was heavily in debt and in thrall to money-lenders and company promoters; and at the end of his life he owed the Rothschilds nearly £70,000. Like so many Churchills, only more so, his temperament was erratic and uncontrollable, and it seems almost certain that he contracted syphilis, which led to the general paralysis which slowly and humiliatingly killed him.[13] In society, the Churchills were publicly ostracized between 1876 and 1884, after Lord Randolph had impulsively taken his elder brother's part in the row with the Prince of Wales over the Aylesford scandal. And in politics, he was widely regarded as an unstable, unprincipled, and vituperative adventurer, whose abrupt resignation as Chancellor of the Exchequer in January 1887 merely confirmed the widely held view that he was an unscrupulous menace, so unbalanced as to be almost insane.[14]

Churchill's mother was no less unrespectable. Although renowned for her beauty, and much admired for her public loyalty to Lord Randolph during his last, pitiful years, she was as spendthrift, wayward, and irresponsible as her husband. Their marriage soon became one of convenience only, and it was widely known that she was having many affairs. After Lord Randolph's death, she showed no inclination to moderate her ways, and in 1898 was obliged to raise a loan of £17,000 to clear her debts. She briefly edited a magazine, the *Anglo-Saxon Review:* but it made no money. And she wrote her reminiscences: but on her own admission, they were 'interesting chiefly in what is left unsaid'.[15] In 1900, after a long affair, she married George Cornwallis-West. But he was twenty years younger than she was, scarcely older than Winston himself. In society, the union was widely condemned; it soon broke down, and it ended in divorce thirteen years later. Undaunted, she married her third husband, Montagu Porch, who was also twenty years her junior. Once again, her behaviour was generally regarded with derision, incredulity, and astonishment.[16]

By contrast, Churchill's wife, Clementine Hozier, whom he married in 1908. was high-minded, and endowed with much sounder judgement of men and events than her husband. But she had spent her early life in genteel poverty. Her father, Henry Hozier—who was probably not her father at all—was an unsavoury and unattractive character, who had divorced her mother, Blanche, and left the family pitifully short of money. And as the daughter of the Earl of Airlie, Blanche was herself descended from one of the more impoverished of Scotland's great families. Indeed, the household was so poor that Clementine could scarcely afford to take part in the expensive pageant of London high society, and before she met and married Winston, she earned money by giving French lessons at two shillings and sixpence an hour. To make matters worse, Blanche Hozier was not only an adultress, but also an incorrigible gambler, and this latter trait was inherited by Clementine's sister, Nellie, and by her brother, William. In 1921, after having resolved to give up gambling altogether, Bill Hozier committed suicide in a cheap Paris hotel.[17]

Churchill's younger brother, Jack, was inoffensive and self-effacing, and took no part in public affairs, and Winston remained close to him all his life. But he, too, became the subject of gossip that did not do his elder brother's reputation any good. In appearance, and in temperament, they were markedly unalike, and it was widely (but mistakenly) believed that Jack and Winston were only half-brothers, and that the fifth Earl of Roden was in fact Jack's father.[18] In an attempt to make some much-needed money, Jack took up a career as a stockbroker. But in the early twentieth century this was still thought by many to be an unsuitable career for a gentleman, and in 1907 Jack had to postpone his marriage to Lady Gwendeline Bertie, because her mother, the Countess of Abingdon, thought his financial resources inadequate. Nor was this the last time that Jack's profession got him into trouble. When Churchill became Chancellor of the Exchequer, it was mildly awkward that his brother dealt in stocks and shares. And during the Second World War, he was criticized for housing Jack in 10 Downing Street after his own London home had been bombed, and for keeping him as a permanent member of his Prime Ministerial entourage.[19]

But this was as nothing compared with the embarrassment that Churchill had been caused, during the 1930s, by three of his children, Randolph, Diana, and Sarah. They were ill-disciplined, rowed with their parents, and all became heavy drinkers. In 1932 Diana married John Bailey, son of Sir Abe Bailey, a South African mining magnate and friend of her father's. Both her parents were opposed to the marriage, and it ended in divorce three years later. In 1935 Diana married

Duncan Sandys, but they, too, were later divorced, and in 1963, she committed suicide. Her younger sister Sarah sought a career in the theatre, and in 1935 became a chorus girl in one of C. B. Cochrane's reviews. While working on the stage she fell in love with Vic Oliver, a twice-divorced, Austrian-born comedian, who was seventeen years her senior. Her parents were determined to prevent her marriage to this 'itinerant vagabond', but Sarah ran off to join Oliver in New York, and they were married on Christmas Day 1936.[20] On both sides of the Atlantic the publicity was extensive and adverse, and did Churchill no good in political circles. In the autumn of 1938, when the *Daily Telegraph* and other newspapers owned by the Berry brothers were pushing for his return to the Cabinet, the periodical *Truth* wickedly suggested that if Vic Oliver was also made a minister, the comedy turn would then be complete.[21]

But even Diana and Sarah seemed almost angelic compared to their rude, spoiled, unstable, headstrong, irresponsible, and argumentative brother, Randolph. He dropped out of Oxford University, took to drinking and gambling, got into debt, and became notorious as the most dangerous and boorish party guest in London. For a time, he was much attracted by the ideas of Oswald Mosley and the New Party, and later wrote a newspaper column in which he championed his father's views on India with a tactless fervour that can only have been counter-productive. Early in 1935 he stood at the Wavertree by-election as theunofficial Conservative candidate, on a Diehard platform, with the result that the Tory vote was split, and a safe seat was needlessly handed over to Labour. And in January 1936, he again stood unsuccessfully in a much-publicized by-election at Ross and Cromarty, against Malcolm MacDonald, who was not only in the Cabinet, but also the son of the former Prime Minister. Such ill-judged political action by his son did Churchill great damage in the eyes of the Tory leadership and the National government.[22]

Churchill's sense of clan loyalty extended well beyond his immediate relatives, to encompass those more distantly located on the twigs and branches of his broadly spreading family tree. One of Lord Randolph's sisters was Lady Cornelia Spencer-Churchill, who always took the greatest interest in Winston's career, 'not only for your dear father's sake, but also for you'. In 1868 she had married Ivor Guest, scion of the great dynasty of South Wales iron masters. But Guest was an incorrigible snob and social climber, so much so that he was widely known as 'the paying Guest'.[23] He was created Baron Wimborne in 1880 by Disraeli, but turned against the Tories in the 1900s. The ostensible reason was his loyalty to free trade, but a more likely explanation was rumoured to be his annoyance that his request for promotion to an earldom had been refused. In January 1910 he tried to get one of his sons, Freddie, elected for the local constituency of East Dorset, in the Liberal interest. But it was claimed that the Guests exerted undue influence on their tenants, and on petition the election was disallowed.[24]

Lord Wimborne's eldest son, another Ivor Guest, was thus Churchill's first cousin. Like his father, he was a shameless importuner: Asquith thought him 'very unpopular', and the general feeling about him was well expressed in the damning couplet: 'One must suppose that God knew best | when he created Ivor Guest.'[25] In 1900 he had been elected Conservative MP for Plymouth, but in 1906 he followed his father and his cousin into the Liberal Party. Actively helped by his 'friend and ally' Churchill, he sought promotion in the peerage and preferment in government. Asquith was distinctly unenthused, but in 1910 he gave Guest a peerage in his own right as Lord Ashby St Ledgers, and made him Paymaster General. But this did not satisfy him and, with Churchill's help, he continued to press his claims. Eventually, he accepted the Viceroyalty of Ireland in 1915. But he was not a success there, resigned three years later, consoled himself with a Viscountcy, and took no further part in public life. Clementine never approved of him, and Margot Asquith thought him a 'bounder'.[26]

Ivor Guest's younger brother, Freddie, was still more suspect. He was a snob, a playboy, and a lightweight (in 1919 he suggested that the best solution to any possible working-class unrest was to drug their tea), and he had a 'passion for begging and pushing'. He, too, left the Tories for the Liberals, but failed to get elected in 1906. Churchill thereupon appointed him one of his private secretaries, and in December 1910, he became MP for the family constituency of East Dorset at the second attempt. Thanks to his cousin's efforts, minor government office soon came his way, but it was only in 1917 that he became a significant (and sinister) political figure, when he was appointed Liberal Coalition Whip.[27] For the next five years, Guest was responsible for raising money for Lloyd George's personal fund. As a result he was closely involved in the sale of honours. During the dying months of the Coalition he succeeded his cousin as Secretary of State for Air, but he held no office thereafter. He was completely cynical about honours, probably knew more embarrassing secrets than any other man in public life, and was regarded by Viscount Gladstone as Lloyd George's 'evil genius'.[28]

Through his Marlborough grandfather's marriage to Lady Frances Anne, Churchill was also related to the Londonderry family. Between 1910 and 1914 the sixth Marquess took great exception to Churchill's championing of Irish Home Rule, and for most of the inter-war years Churchill and the seventh Marquess were not on the best of terms.[29] On at least two occasions, Churchill certainly put himself out for his relative: in 1919 when, as the newly appointed Secretary of State for Air, he gave him a junior job as Parliamentary Under-Secretary; and in 1928, when he successfully urged Baldwin to bring him into the Cabinet as First Commissioner of Works and Public Buildings. But for much of the 1920s Londonderry devoted himself to Ulster politics, a decision which Churchill thought unwise, and they did not see eye to eye over the General Strike. During the 1930s, they drifted still further apart. Churchill was a vehement critic of Londonderry as Secretary of State for Air, from 1931 to 1935, and found his admiration of Adolf Hitler incomprehensible.[30]

The final Marlborough connection, which was also much publicized during the inter-war years, was with a cadet branch, descended from the second son of the fourth duke: the Churchills of Wychwood. The first Viscount Churchill, who had inherited the estates in 1886, sold off most of the ancestral acres and heirlooms soon after, and spent his life as a professional courtier and businessman, eventually becoming Lord in Waiting to King Edward VII, and chairman of the Great Western Railway.[31] But he achieved greater notoriety because of his long-standing, and much-publicized, quarrel with his wife. Shortly before the First World War she took up spiritualism and theosophy, under the influence of a medium named Kathleen Ellis. Lord Churchill thereupon separated from his wife, and pronounced her insane. She fled to North Africa, along with her son, and Lord Churchill tried unsuccessfully to recapture them at gunpoint. (He eventually divorced her in a Scottish court in 1927.) During the First World War Lady Churchill returned to Paris, set up house with Kathleen Ellis, and forced her son to marry her friend. Having already broken with his father, the son now broke with his mother, ran away to America, smoked opium, went on the stage, and was (falsely) accused of stealing the Wimborne jewels.[32]

In addition to these more distant Marlborough relations, Churchill was also connected to another group of patrician families through his mother, Lady Randolph. Her eldest sister, Clare, married Moreton Frewen, the younger son of a Sussex squire, who inherited an Irish estate in 1890s. But the man who was thus Winston's uncle misman-aged his affairs so hopelessly, and so publicly, that he was nicknamed 'Mortal Ruin'. He spent his portion of £16,000 on a cattle ranch in Wyoming, but by 1887 had lost his entire investment. Thereafter, he was involved in a variety of preposterous schemes: to make axle grease for locomotives, to produce ice artificially, to extract gold from refuse-ore, and to cut down timber in Kenya.[33] All these enterprises lost him borrowed money, and he was regularly on the brink of bankruptcy. His elder brother's Sussex estate was mortgaged and the timber cut down; his own Irish property was laden with debt; and he even persuaded his children to mortgage their life interests as soon as they came of age. At his death, in 1924, he left less than £50 As Kipling put it, 'he lived in every sense except what is called common sense'.[34]

Lady Randolph's other sister, Leonie, married Sir John Leslie, a worthy and dutiful Irish baronet, whose family owned land in County Monaghan. Their eldest son, John Randolph, was thus Winston's cousin. In one guise, he was passionately attached to the Ascendancy, and wrote a series of books lovingly recalling the lost world of his childhood. He mourned the end of the old paternalism, the demise of the great Irish estates under the Land Acts, and the suicide of European civilization as a result of the First World War.[35] But even as he lamented the passing of his patrician heritage, he also deliberately rejected it. He 'deeply affronted the Anglo-Irish Ascendancy into which he had been born', by renouncing his right of succession to the family estates, by embracing Roman Catholicism, and by using Shane, the Irish form of his name. Even more to his relatives' dismay, he took up the cause of Irish Nationalism and, thanks to Churchill's intercession, was introduced to the Irish Nationalist politician John Redmond. In January 1910 he contested Londonderry City as an Irish Nationalist, and in 1916 he urged that the British government should not execute those who had taken part in the Easter Rising.[36]

Lady Randolph's remarkable matrimonial career brought two more tainted patricians into Churchill's family orbit. One of them was her second husband, George Cornwallis-West, heir to Ruthin Castle in Denbighshire, one of the oldest estates on the Welsh borders. But by the late nineteenth century it was sadly decayed, and his parents were very short of money. Under these circumstances, marrying the spend-thrift Lady Randolph was an extremely imprudent move, and by 1906

Cornwallis-West's finances were so precarious that Churchill was obliged to come to his stepfather's assistance.[37] In order to make some urgently needed money, Cornwallis-West mortgaged his reversionary interest in the Ruthin estates, and set up a small issuing house in the City. In 1914 he divorced Lady Randolph and married Mrs Patrick Campbell. In 1916 his business collapsed and he was declared bankrupt. And in 1920 he had to sell the family estates, to which he had succeeded three years before, to discharge his debts. Meanwhile, his marriage to Mrs Campbell had broken down, and he was obliged to eke out a living writing reminiscences, novels, and biographies. Mrs Campbell refused to grant him a divorce, and it was only on her death in 1940 that he could marry again. Shortly afterwards, he contracted Parkinson's Disease, and he committed suicide in 1951.[38]

Through his stepfather's sister, Constance Cornwallis-West, Churchill's family ties were strengthened with another flawed and fallen grandee: Bend Or, second Duke of Westminster.[39] In 1901 Constance became the first of Bend Or's wives, but the marriage was not a success. The son and heir the Duchess bore her husband died in 1909, and thereafter the couple went their separate ways. In 1919 they were divorced, amidst much adverse publicity, and three more marriages brought Bend Or neither happiness nor repose. He was obliged to resign the Lord Lieutenancy of Cheshire, and neither King George V nor King George VI would have anything to do with him. And this social ostracism only intensified his restless paranoia. He hated democracy, disliked Jews, voted against the Parliament Bill in 1910, and favoured a negotiated peace with Hitler. On his death in 1953, Henry Channon composed a damning epitaph: 'he was restless, spoilt, irritable . . .; his life was an empty failure . . .; he did few kindnesses, leaves no monument.'[40]

Clementine's aristocratic relatives were at least as unrespectable as those of her mother-in-law. Her sister, Nellie, who gambled and was generally considered rather 'fast', married Bertram Romilly, whose forebears were of illustrious lineage, but not rich. There were two children of their marriage, Esmond and Giles, who were thus Winston's nephews, and they regularly visited the Churchills' home, Chartwell, during the inter-war years. But in 1934 Esmond became newsworthy in a sensational manner, by running away from Wellington College. He declared himself a Communist, and began to publish a subversive periodical entitled *Out of Bounds*. Inevitably, the press had a field day, publishing sensational stories under such unfortunate but predictable headlines as 'Winston's Red Nephew'. To make matters worse, Esmond possessed both a Churchillian countenance and a Churchillian temperament, and it was widely rumoured that he was in fact Winston's illegitimate son. For the rest of the decade, he remained constantly in the news. In 1936 he went to Spain, and fought on the side of the pro-Republican forces. And in the following year, he eloped with his cousin, Jessica Mitford.[41]

But this was not the only connection between Clementine Churchill and the Mitfords. Her aunt, Clementina Ogilvy, had married Bertram Mitford, first Baron Redesdale. (Indeed, it was whispered in some quarters that Bertram was in fact Clementine's father.[42]) As a result, the Mitford children were frequent visitors to Chartwell, and Randolph showed a more than fleeting interest in Diana. But by the 1930s the family was in serious financial trouble, and four of the daughters were regularly hitting the headlines: Nancy embraced socialism, and began writing novels; Jessica preferred Communism and ran away with Esmond Romilly; Unity became a whole-hearted supporter of Hitler; and Diana, having divorced Bryan Guinness, married Sir Oswald Mosley. Once again, Churchill suffered because of these distant but definite connections. In the late 1930s, both the English and the German press made much of the fact that Winston and Unity were relatives. And it was more than mildly embarrassing to the new wartime Prime Minister that two of the first people to be interned under the Defence of the Realm Regulations in 1940 were Sir Oswald and Lady Mosley.[43]

Despite their dynastic delinquencies, Churchill's fierce loyalty to his extended family was one of his most endearing qualities. But it cannot have helped his reputation that so many of his relatives were so often in the newspapers for such unedifying reasons. In every generation, there were too many debts, too much gambling, too much drinking. Even by the relatively lax standards of the Edwardian era or the inter-war years, there was an above-average amount of infidelity, divorce, erratic behaviour, sexual scandal, social ostracism, and court disfavour. Thus described, the Churchills were a textbook case of a declining and degenerate dynasty: Lord Randolph might have stepped straight from the pages of Trollope's *The Way We Live Now*, the ninth duke was a character of almost Proustian pitifulness, and the headline-stealing antics of Diana, Sarah, and Randolph might have been taken from a less imaginative novel by Evelyn Waugh—with whom, appropriately enough, Randolph enjoyed a lifelong love–hate relationship. And this only reinforced the prevailing view that all the Churchills were unstable, unreliable, and untrustworthy: utterly devoid, as Gladstone had damningly observed, of either morals or principles.

In 1885 the fifteenth Earl of Derby had dismissed Lord Randolph as 'thoroughly untrustworthy: scarcely a gentleman and probably more or less mad'. Thirty years later, Derby's nephew described Lord Randolph's son in very similar words: 'he is absolutely untrustworthy, as was his father before him.' And he was not the first—or the last—man in public life to make such damning and damaging comparisons. When summing up Churchill's performance in his first ministerial job, at the Colonial Office, the Permanent Secretary observed that he was 'most tiresome to deal with, and will, I fear, give trouble—as his father did'.[44] Of course, with the passage of time, there were fewer who could remember Churchill's father. But by the 1930s, everyone knew about Churchill's son. And once again, the similarities between Winston and Randolph II seemed disconcertingly close. As Sam Hoare put it in 1934: 'I do not know which is the more offensive or mischievous, Winston or his son.'[45] In the years before his unexpected apotheosis in 1940, such unflattering comparisons did Churchill himself no good at all.

2

Churchill and Germany

GORDON A. CRAIG

IT is a curious fact that Winston Churchill, whose long career was so directly affected by events that occurred in Germany and whose place in history is impossible to define without reference to that country, knew very little about it in any formal sense. This is not said in derogation, for his relative ignorance served his people better than the prescriptions of those who pretended to be more knowledgeable in German affairs. It is nevertheless worth noting that he had small acquaintance with the Germans and their land and their culture. His visits to Germany were rare and short (two before 1914 and then no more until a brief visit in 1932); his knowledge of German was virtually non-existent ('I'll never learn the beastly language', he said on the eve of the First World War, 'until the Kaiser marches on London!');[1] and, unlike his colleague Haldane, he was unversed in German philosophy, literature, art, or—because his musical sense was not highly developed—music. Nothing that he ever said or wrote indicated that he had any real understanding of the nature of the political process either under the Empire or during the tragic days of the Weimar Republic. Even his knowledge of Germany's history was partial and selective. In the social, economic, and intellectual history of the German states he showed little interest. It was—and this was, for the most part, true of his attitude towards other countries as well—only Germany's role in foreign affairs, its role as a Great Power, and its relations with its neighbours and rivals that held his attention.

In a brilliant essay, Isaiah Berlin once pointed out that it would be idle to criticize Churchill for not possessing the gifts of the professional historian. His vision was always romantic, and in a real sense he saw history as a great Renaissance pageant, with the nations of the world standing out as strikingly differentiated images.

The units out of which his world is constructed are simpler and larger than life, the patterns vivid and repetitive like those of an epic poet, or at times like those of a dramatist who sees persons and situations as timeless symbols and embodiments of eternal shining principles. The whole is a series of symmetrically formed and somewhat stylized compositions, either suffused with bright light or cast in darkest shadow, like a legend of Carpaccio . . .[2]

The painterly figure may be reinforced by a political-philosophical one. Without ever having read Leopold von Ranke, Churchill was a Rankean in his world-view. Born into a world in which Europe was still the political centre, he regarded the continent, as Ranke had, as an agglomeration of Latin and Germanic nations that had been brought together by a common historical heritage and spiritual development and now formed an interrelated community in which whatever happened in one nation affected all of the others, for good or for ill. He believed, as Ranke had, that in Europe national individuality and the aspiration towards unity would always be uncomfortable allies and that rivalry and contention was inevitable. It was for that reason that, over the centuries, history and statecraft had devised two instruments for controlling the tendency towards international violence: the distinction between Great Powers and lesser ones, the former of which, few in number and rarely changing, were capable of restraining the passions of the latter; and the principle of balance of power, which was intended to keep the ambitions of each of the Great Powers within limits acceptable to all.[3] Ranke had seen the Great Powers as individuals with their own lives, 'progressing amid all the turmoil of the world . . . each in its own way . . . celestial bodies, in their cycles, their mutual gravitation, their systems'.[4] Churchill's view was not essentially different, and for this reason his attention was always drawn less to the domestic fortunes, the social tensions, the internal political rivalries, and the intellectual movements of Germany, France, Austria, and Russia than to their international behaviour, their mutual relations, and combinations, and how these influenced the always fragile balance of power and the security of his own country.

The fact that he was, by temperament and inclination, a soldier not only encouraged this but gave authority to his judgements. Thinking naturally, as he did, in terms of relative military force, and weapons systems, and military productive capacity, and the time needed to repair deficits in different categories of arms, he was more sensitive than others to changes in the international balance of forces and quicker to detect potential threats to his own country. Nor was he easily persuaded that to warn of potential military dangers undermined the general public desire for peace by poisoning relations with other powers. He knew that dangers were not overcome by ignoring them, and that an effective balance of power could not survive lack of readiness on the part of peace-loving states to defend it, if necessary with sword in hand. Great Powers, after all, were supposed to act like Great Powers. Such views made Churchill an unpopular figure with many of his colleagues during what he himself called 'the locust years' after 1931,[5] but they were vindicated in the end, although at great cost.

Because Churchill's world-view resembled that of Ranke, he was protected from the kind of hatred of the enemy that affected so much of public opinion during the two world wars of the twentieth century. History taught him that Great Powers are prone to fits of lack of perspective and miscalculation in which they resort to force and are subdued only by the concerted effort of their neighbours. For such transgressions, Churchill believed that they should be punished but not destroyed. For the sake of the international order, the Great Powers, who are its guarantors, however frail, must abide. Thus, if, both before 1914 and before 1939, Churchill was tireless in his efforts to show that Germany's actions threatened the balance of power and the security of his own country, he was also, after 1918 and again after 1945, among the first to call for its re-admission to the European society of nations. The failure of his countrymen to follow his advice in 1918 was, he remained convinced, one of the principal causes of the Second World War, and his eloquent address in Zurich in 1946—the first clear call for a new European Community—was a warning that that mistake must not be made again.

Winston Churchill was thirty-six years old and well advanced on his political career before he showed any great interest in Germany or concern about the state of Anglo-German relations. During the years of his active military service with the Malakand Field Force on India's northwestern frontier in 1896, and during the Sudan campaign of 1898, his thoughts were remote from European politics, and if he shared the common British irritation over Kaiser Wilhelm II's threatened intervention in South Africa during the Boer War, this does not seem to have made a lasting impression upon him.[6] As a young politician in the first years of the new century, he was too concerned with defining his own political position to have much time to think about foreign affairs, and once he had shifted from the Conservative to the Liberal Party he became involved with problems remote from them. When he thought about Germany at all it was favourably, for once he had become President of the Board of Trade and deeply involved in the social question, he became interested, thanks to Lloyd George's suggestion, in German social insurance legislation and particularly in German success with labour exchanges, which served as clearing houses for information about job opportunities for the unemployed. In 1909, when Churchill visited Germany and attended the annual army manœuvres, he took the occasion to visit labour bureaux in Strasburg and Frankfurt am Main. After his return to England, he told his constituents in Dundee about this experience and about the social insurance benefits of German workers, and said: 'My heart was filled with admiration of the patient genius which had added these social bulwarks to the many glories of the German race.'[7] This was at a time when worry over the apparent deterioration of the international system had led the British government to abandon its tradition of splendid isolation and to conclude an alliance with Japan and an entente with France, and when many Englishmen were saying that war with Germany, given the adventurism of its foreign policy, was inevitable. Yet Churchill seemed unmoved by this, and a recent historian has written that he was 'among the last of the Edwardians to appreciate the menace of the Kaiser'.[8] Within a few weeks of joining the Cabinet, he launched an attack upon the army estimates and then, in collaboration with Lloyd George, opposed the Admiralty's plan for laying down six new battleships in 1909–10. To the annoyance of the Foreign Secretary, Sir Edward Grey, he ridiculed the idea of an Anglo-German conflict in a speech at Swansea in August 1908, in which he said: 'Although there may be snapping and snarling in the newspapers and in the London press, these two great peoples have nothing to fight about, have no prize to fight for, and have no place to fight in.'[9] He followed this up with a letter to the chairman of the Dundee Liberal Association, in which he criticized the proponents of naval building and pronounced that, 'in spite of the evil forces that we see at work in every land, the foundations of European peace are laid more broadly and more deeply every year'.[10]

But he was not as confident as these partisan comments made him appear. Despite his preoccupation with social questions and his resistance to the diversion to military expansion of funds that might alleviate them, he had continued his own connection with the Oxfordshire Yeomanry, in which he held a major's commission. He performed his annual reserve duties and confessed to his wife his wish to command larger formations than his own squadron: 'On nothing', he wrote, 'do I seem to feel the truth more than in tactical combinations.' He was an avid observer of army manœuvres, in 1908 and in 1910 those on Salisbury Plain and, thanks to invitations from Kaiser Wilhelm II, the exercises of the Prussian army in 1906 and 1909. He thus acquired a basis for comparative judgements, and, after watching German manœuvres in 1909, seems to have revised his earlier view that the Kaiser's forces were inferior to those of his own country. He wrote to his wife from Würzburg:

This army is a terrible engine. It marches sometimes 35 miles in a day. It is in numbers as the sands of the sea—& with all the modern conveniences. There is a complete divorce between the two sides of German life—the Imperialists & the Socialists. Nothing unites them. They are two different nations. . . . Much as war attracts me & fascinates my mind with its tremendous situations—I feel more deeply every year—& can measure the feeling here in the midst of arms—what a vile & wicked folly & barbarism it all is.[11]

These somewhat disjointed sentences suggest that their author's interest in German socialist reforms was already balanced by concern over the growing military power of the German state, and there is an intimation also that Churchill was beginning reluctantly to admit to himself that war with Germany was not as completely unlikely as he had thought.

However that may be, the folly of the 'Imperialists' soon disabused him of his confidence in European stability. In 1907, in a secret Foreign Office memorandum, Sir Eyre Crowe had analysed the latent dangers of the international system and had warned that Great Britain must prepare itself to intervene in order to protect the balance of power against German domination. The German ultimatum to the Russian government in March 1909, at the height of the Bosnian crisis, had underlined his warning, and in July 1911 European chancelleries were given new reasons for concern over German intentions by the dispatch of the cruiser *Panther* to the port of Agadir. This action was as maladroit as it was threatening; whether the Germans were attempting to subvert the recent Algeciras agreement on Morocco or merely to blackmail France into making territorial concessions was never clear.[12] But the British government had not been consulted, and this was enough to persuade the Liberal Cabinet to warn Germany, in a speech by Lloyd George at the Mansion House on 21 July, that the country would not tolerate an attempt to treat Britain, 'where her interests were plainly affected, as if she were of no account in the Cabinet of Nations'. The Germans backed down, but the crisis greatly heightened tension between Britain and Germany, accelerated the armaments race, and encouraged in the governing class the feeling that the chances of preventing war were weakening.[13]

Certainly this was true in Churchill's case. On 5 July he wrote to his wife, 'If [Germany] thinks Morocco can be divided up without John Bull, she is jolly well mistaken'; and a few days later, in a memorandum presumably written to clarify his own thoughts, he expressed the view that Britain should support France in any negotiations over Morocco, and, in the event that Germany attacked it in the course of the discussions, '(unless F[rance] has meanwhile after full warning from us taken unjustifiable ground) we shd join with France. Germany should be told this now.'[14] This was a good deal farther than the Foreign Office or most of Churchill's Cabinet colleagues were prepared at this time to go, but from now on Churchill was convinced that, if war came, Britain must intervene on France's side. Indeed, in the middle of August 1911, he circulated a long memorandum in which, with what can only be described as extraordinary prescience, he described the opening phases of a war between the Triple Alliance and the Triple Entente, predicting the course of a German offensive that would roll through Belgium and break through the line of the Meuse but begin to lose momentum as it approached Paris on the fortieth day, and outlining the measures that Britain must take, including the dispatch of 107,000 troops at the outset of the war to support the left of the French army.[15]

Three months after the Moroccan crisis Asquith asked Churchill to take over the Admiralty, an offer that he accepted with alacrity and with a determination to put the fleet into a condition of war readiness. His appointment seems to have impressed the German Kaiser, for early in 1912, using Sir Ernest Cassel as intermediary, he took the extraordinary step of sending Churchill the details of the new Navy Bill that he proposed to lay before the Reichstag in May 1912. Cassel then followed this up by suggesting that Churchill go to Germany for exploratory talks with the Kaiser, designed presumably to moderate the pace of the naval race. In a letter to Cassel in January 1912, the new First Lord explained the constitutional circumstances that made this impossible, writing that in any case talks would do little good unless Germany were prepared to drop its challenge to Britain's naval power. He added:

I deeply deplore the situation for as you know I have never had any but friendly feelings toward that great nation & her illustrious Sovereign & I regard the antagonism wh has developed insensate. Anything in my power to terminate it I wd gladly do. But the only one I see open is one which I fear Germany will be reluctant to take.[16]

In the event, it was the War Minister, Haldane, who went to Germany to try to negotiate a naval agreement, and, although his mission may have been doomed to failure, it must be said that Churchill did not make things easy for him by delivering a speech at Glasgow in which he said that, while a fleet was a necessity for Great Britain, for Germany it was 'from some points of view . . . more in the nature of a luxury', a remark that was deeply resented in Germany. The salient point, however, was that Tirpitz's dominance in German counsels made agreement impossible unless the members of the British government were prepared to pledge neutrality in the case of a Franco-German war, which they were not. In April, when Churchill himself tested German willingness to treat by proposing a naval holiday, the Kaiser answered that such an arrangement would be possible only between allies, and Churchill's subsequent efforts, through the good offices of Cassel and Albert Ballin, to make the Kaiser 'appreciate the sentiments with which an island state like Britain views the steady and remorseless development of a rival naval power of the very highest efficiency' also came to nothing.[17]

After that, Churchill had no doubt that the development of the Germany navy was 'intended for a great trial of strength with . . . the greatest naval power'. In a memorandum to the Committee on Imperial Defence in July 1912, he wrote, in language that reflected a belief in standards of civility between Great Powers that were soon to be belied by the brutalities of war:

I do not pretend to make any suggestion that the Germans would deliver any surprise or sudden attack upon us. It is not for us to assume that another great nation will fall markedly below the standard of civilisation which we ourselves should be bound by; but we at The Admiralty have got to see, not that they will not do it, but that they cannot do it.[18]

For the rest, as Europe moved as if doom-stricken towards war, he did not waver in his belief that if the Germans attacked France Britain must stand at her side.

About Churchill's duties during the First World War and how he fulfilled them, this is not the place to speak. His attitude towards the foe, however, must be investigated, and here, as has already been intimated, his views were remarkably untouched by the 'hatred of the

Hun' that the war's intensity and duration aroused in others, although sometimes he felt it expedient to make verbal concessions to it.

He never wavered in the belief that Germany, having embarked upon the war voluntarily, must be utterly defeated and must pay the price for its subversion of the European order. In the course of the long and grinding conflict, there were moments when others faltered: defeatism was strong in France after the failure of the Nivelle offensive in 1917 and in Italy after Caporetto, and in his own country there were people who felt that the continuation of war would make victory mean-ingless. As Minister of Munitions after 1917, Churchill was well aware of the extent of war-weariness and its reflection in work stoppages and protests against rising prices, and he combated this by alleviating com-plaints and improving working conditions as far as he could and by preaching constantly to working-class audiences that 'if ever there was a time in the history of this island when Britain should be a rock, it is now'.[19] The thought of compromise with the enemy he resisted implacably. When the former Foreign Secretary Lord Lansdowne, in a letter to the *Daily Telegraph* in November 1917, urged that a negotiated peace be arranged while there was still something of European civiliza-tion to save, he argued vigorously against the proposal, although with-out subscribing to the campaign of abuse and invective against Lansdowne that was launched by the Northcliffe and the Rothermere press.[20] Lansdowne's argument, however, seems to have left him not unmoved, and in the great crisis of 1918 he appears to have feared that its logic might appeal to his countrymen. His own public speeches became shriller and more insistent. The war had become a conflict between 'Christian civilisation and scientific barbarism', between 'right and wrong'. 'Germany must be beaten; Germany must know she is beaten; Germany must feel she is beaten. Her defeat must be expressed in terms and facts which will, for all time, deter others from emulating her crimes, and will safeguard us against their repetition.'[21] Again, in August 1918, in a letter to his constituents, he felt it necessary to refer to Lansdowne and belittle his proposal.

To set out to redress an intolerable wrong, to grapple with a cruel butcher, & then after a bit to find him so warlike that upon the whole it is better to treat him as a good hearted fellow & sit down & see if we can't be friends after all, may conceivably be a form of prudence but that is the best that can be said of it.[22]

But although he wanted no 'pact with unrepentant wrong',[23] Churchill desired Germany's return to the society of nations as a peaceful and collaborative member, and he knew that this would be possible only if the punishment inflicted upon the beaten foe was, if stern, also just. His definition of what this might mean tended to broaden as the conflict endured. At a meeting of the War Council in March 1915, while he was still at the Admiralty, he did not object to the feeling expressed by Kitchener and Grey that it would be a mistake to deprive Germany of colonies, since this, in Kitchener's words, would 'interfere with the future establishment of goodwill between Germany and ourselves after the war'. In this first discussion of war aims since the beginning of the conflict, Churchill limited himself to insisting upon the importance of destroying the German fleet and removing the Kiel Canal from German control.[24] By November 1918, however, he was claiming that 'practically the whole of the German nation was guilty of the crime of aggressive war conducted by brutal and bestial means' and that the penalty for this should be punishment of individuals guilty of definite breaches of the laws of war, and the loss of Alsace-Lorraine, the Polish provinces, and all of Germany's colonies. This bill of particulars was, to be sure, laid out in an election speech, and it should be noted that, despite the temper of the crowd, Churchill sought to disabuse of it of the notion that Germany could pay all of the expenses of the war, and that he pointed out that German punishment had already begun with the collapse of the imperial regime and the outbreak of revolution in Berlin.[25] His true sentiments were probably accurately expressed on Armistice night, when he dined at 10 Downing Street with Lloyd George, F. E. Smith, and Sir Henry Wilson. The conversation ran, he wrote later, 'on the great qualities of the German people, on the tremendous fight that they had made against three-quarters of the world, on the impossibility of re-building Europe without their help'. When the near-starvation of the Germans was mentioned, he proposed sending 'a dozen great ships crammed with provisions' into Hamburg at once.[26]

Churchill had no part in the deliberations of the Paris Peace Conference, except for a brief and unsuccessful mission to encourage a common allied front on action in Russia. As far as the German question was concerned, he privately urged a generous, speedy, and humane peace settlement, and he was distressed that what emerged was in every respect the opposite of that. He deplored the fact that the Germans were given no opportunity to respond to the terms set and to negotiate modifications, arguing at the time that it was only by giving careful attention to German counter-proposals that the allies would 'get a genuine German acceptance of a defeated peace and not be drawn into new dangers measureless in their character'.[27] The economic terms of the Versailles Treaty, were, he wrote later, 'malignant and silly to an extent that made them obviously futile';[28] and the intransigence of the French, he felt, was not only self-defeating but bound, in the long run, to drive a wedge between the allies. He was aware that France, having abandoned its claims on the Rhine frontier in return for an Anglo-American guarantee of its security, which in fact it never got, was in an aggrieved and truculent mood, but actions like the occupation of the towns of Darmstadt, Hanau, Frankfurt, and Hamburg by Senegalese troops during the troubles that followed the Kapp *Putsch* in 1920 struck him as pointless and provocative. He told the Imperial Conference in July 1921 that Anglo-German friendship was in Britain's best interest ('I am anxious to see trade relations develop with Germany naturally and harmoniously. I am anxious to see Britain getting all the help and use she can out of Germany in the difficult years that lie before us') but that this would be resented by France unless Britain gave it some assurance of support in the event of a German attack. He urged that such a guarantee be given, a pledge 'not connected with the militaristic triumph of one set of nations over another' but one that 'aims entirely . . . at the appeasement and consolidation of the European family'.[29] His advice was not followed.

In the days of classical diplomacy, there was a feeling that it was normal and right that there should be five Great Powers, and that the disappearance of one of them would have ruinous results, similar to those—it was Ranke who first used the simile—that would be caused by the death of the first violinist of a quintet that had played together for a long time.[30] After the Peace Conference, the normal international system had suffered the disappearance of two traditional Great Powers, Austria-Hungary and Russia (for Churchill did not recognize that Soviet Union as a legitimate successor), and the serious crippling of a third, Germany, and its exclusion from the new League of Nations. In Churchill's view, every effort must be made to repair these grievous blows to the European order. In 1919, he wrote that there would be 'no peace in Europe until Russia is restored', and there were rumours in 1920 that he would not be averse to the use of German troops to effect this result.[31] If this were true, it was one of his less brilliant ideas, and nothing came of it. Sadly, this was true also of his efforts to solve the Franco-German problem and 'get an appeasement of the fearful hatreds and antagonisms which exist in Europe and to enable the world to settle down'.[32]

In September 1924 Churchill wrote an article in *Nash's Pall Mall* magazine, entitled 'Shall We All Commit Suicide?', in which he talked about the horrors of a future war and warned of the unsolved problems that might encourage one. The article included a passage of almost prophetic weight.

From one end of Germany to another an intense hatred of France unites the whole population. This passion is fanned continuously by the action of the French government. The enormous contingents of German youth growing to military mankind year by year are inspired by the fiercest sentiments, and the soul of Germany smoulders with dreams of a War of Liberation or Revenge. These ideas are restrained at the present moment only by physical impotence. . . . But physical force alone, unsustained by world opinion, affords no durable foundation for security. Germany is a far stronger entity than France, and cannot be kept in permanent subjugation.[33]

It is likely that few people in public life were disturbed by these words, for 1924 seemed to mark a turning-point in international relations, with the German government being invited to participate in the London conference on reparations, with the subsequent negotiation of the Dawes Plan, and at the end of 1925 with the conclusion of the Locarno Pact, which appeared to guarantee security in western Europe and to signal a *détente* between France and Germany. These hopeful developments, which were crowned by Germany's admission to the League of Nations in 1926, were less substantial than they appeared. The Dawes Plan was accepted by the German Reichstag only after a debate that showed how irreconcilable the forces of the right were, and French reluctance to make further concessions on reparations or occupation of German soil in the years that followed fuelled resentment across the border. Finally, the coming of the world depression created a situation favourable to the rise of political extremism: Communism grew in strength and, in the elections of September 1930, Hitler's National Socialist Party won six and a half million votes and 107 Reichstag seats.

Outside Germany this portentous event was largely unnoticed in a world preoccupied by the problems caused by the Great Depression. Churchill, however, seems to have regarded it as a confirmation of his earlier fears. A month after the German elections, he had a meeting with Prince Otto von Bismarck, counsellor in the German embassy in London, and expressed the liveliest alarm over their results. Bismarck reported to Berlin that he had said that the Nazis had contributed towards a considerable deterioration of Germany's external position, particularly with respect to France, whose apprehension he found completely understandable. The counsellor quoted Churchill as saying further that 'Hitler had admittedly declared that he had no intention of waging a war of aggression; he, Churchill, however, was convinced that Hitler or his followers would seize the first available opportunity to resort to armed force.'[34]

This was a puzzling remark, which would have been difficult to justify if challenged. Churchill seems at one time to have read an early translation of *Mein Kampf*, but he certainly did not have more than a newspaper reader's knowledge of the nature of Hitler's party or its current views on foreign policy. His remarks were probably designed not to be taken at their face value but as a warning that any attempt by the German government to undercut the Nazi movement by taking an extreme nationalist line would make France even more resistant to concessions of any kind and would probably destroy British goodwill as well.

This was advice that the government of Heinrich Brüning could hardly afford to take. The temptation to solve his domestic problems by diplomatic means was too strong for the German Chancellor to resist, the more so because he had no other means of increasing support for his government, committed as he was to a deflationary economic policy at a time when there were 4,380,000 unemployed. Brüning therefore set his hopes upon a scaling down of the Young Plan schedule of reparations payments and the regaining of German parity with respect to armaments. He knew that these goals could be attained only with Western agreement, but for domestic purposes he found it expedient to announce them in forthright if not demanding accents. This alarmed the British Foreign Office, especially when officials in the Brüning government began to talk publicly about other sensitive matters, such as the state of the Saarland and the eastern frontiers. In July 1930, the Permanent Under-Secretary of Foreign Affairs, Sir Robert Vansittart, said darkly that they would be talking about *Anschluss* next, and in October a Foreign Office official noted the sudden emergence of a demand for the abolition of the demilitarization restrictions in the Rhineland.[35] Finally, as if to confirm Vansittart's apprehensions, came the sudden announcement in the press in March 1931 that the German and Austrian governments intended to establish a customs union between their two countries.

Churchill was by this time out of public office and in the political wilderness in which he would dwell for the next nine years. This did not prevent him from reacting to Brüning's action, complaining in an article in the Hearst newspapers about the lack of consultation with other powers before the announcement and pointing out that France and Czechoslovakia could only suspect that this was the first step towards political union, which would threaten them. He added, however, that if the union could be strictly limited to economic matters, it might strengthen Brüning's hand against the forces of extremism in Germany.[36] The European powers were not disposed to give much weight to that consideration. The plan was submitted to the World Court and declared to be in violation of treaty law, a blow to Brüning's prestige that naturally made him doubly desirous of achieving a breakthrough at the Conference for the Reduction and Limitation of Armaments that opened in Geneva in February 1932.

Since Brüning was by this time fighting for his political life, his demands were far from modest; they included not only a proposal for general reduction of armed forces but provisions for a shortening of the German term of service, which would facilitate the raising of a large trained reserve, and the right to raise a militia in addition to the regular army.[37] The refusal of France to show any inclination to grant these demands led the German army to bring pressure upon Brüning to raise the ante and, in case of further French intransigence, to sabotage the conference.[38] When the Chancellor showed no disposition to do this, General Kurt von Schleicher began the intrigues that led to Brüning's fall in May 1932.

Churchill knew nothing of the struggle behind the scenes, but he was well aware of Brüning's predicament and of the rising tide of German nationalism, and until the situation was clear he was not in favour of making any concessions to Germany. He said as much in the House of Commons in May, when he declared, 'I should very much regret any approximation in military strength between Germany and France. Those who speak of that as if it were right, or even a question of fair dealing, altogether underrate the gravity of the European situation.'[39] He was confirmed in his view by the swift disintegration of what was left of the Weimar Republic and the coming of Hitler to power in January 1933. Two months after that event, he spoke sombrely to the House of Commons.

I dare say that during this anxious month there are a good many people who have said to themselves, as I have been saying for several years, 'Thank God for the French army!' When we read about Germany, when we watch with surprise and distress the tumultuous insurgence of ferocity and war spirit, the pitiless ill-treatment of minorities, the denial of the normal protections of civilised society, the persecution of large numbers of individuals solely on the ground of race—when we see all that occurring in one of the most gifted, learned, and scientific and formidable nations in the world, one cannot help feeling glad that the fierce passions that are raging in Germany have not yet found any other outlet but upon themselves.[40]

The speech was more important than its occasion, a consideration of MacDonald's proposal for limiting the calibre of mobile artillery. In a real sense, it marked the beginning of Churchill's long campaign to awaken Parliament and people to the dangers of war and to persuade them to hasten the pace of British rearmament, to engage in joint deterrent action against any German threats to European treaties, and to reject appeasement of Hitler as self-defeating.

These are matters that are discussed elsewhere in this book and need not be rehearsed in any detail here. But some general questions may be raised. In recent scholarship in Germany on the background of the Second World War, there is a strong undercurrent of criticism of Churchill, who is accused among other things of contributing, by his persuasive rhetoric and his exaggerated estimates of German strength, to Britain's failure to take advantage of Hitler's genuine desire for friendship with Britain. He is also accused of being obsessively opposed to Germany's regaining the Great Power status that it had before the First World War. In a variation of the charges, one historian has accused him of being incapable of drawing any distinction between Hitler and the German people, whom he regarded with 'the same feeling of secret dread that he once felt when he took the field with the Malakand Field Force against the wild mountain tribes on the Northwest Frontier'.[41]

It is difficult to regard these views as being anything but obtuse. It is, of course, well known that, when he was writing *Mein Kampf*, Hitler expressed the view that the most valuable of allies for Germany would be Great Britain, 'as long as its leaders and the spirit of its masses permit us to expect that brutality and toughness' that had characterized Britain's policy in the past. This was written in a chapter that posited the expansion of Germany into Russia as the objective of future policy, and it is not too far-fetched to assume that Britain's role as an ally was conceived of as being to prevent France from interfering with that design. Hitler was always willing to be friendly with powers that were willing to help him achieve his desires, but his offers of friendship and alliance to Britain never got beyond the idea that, if Britain would not object to his controlling Europe, he would not interfere with the affairs of its Empire.

It was Hitler's designs on non-German areas of Europe that made it impossible for Churchill to recognize Germany as a Great Power in the old sense of the word. After the First World War he had hoped that Germany could return to the society of nations on terms of equality with the other Great Powers. That hope had been defeated by the absence of the United States from Western councils and the failure of Britain and France to co-ordinate their policies on the German question,[42] and, in the end, by the rise of extreme nationalism in Germany. Within a year of Hitler's coming to power, he had given evidence, with the Austrian *Putsch* of 1934, of aggressive tendencies, and the pace of his armaments programme after 1935 underlined these. Churchill's position was simply that one should not make territorial or other concessions to a power that did not promise to be a peaceful member of the international order and an upholder of the balance of power. To argue that this represented a desire to deny Germany Great Power status is simply to play with words. In actuality, it was, as Churchill once pointed out to a critic of his 'obsession with Germany', an expression of Great Britain's traditional balance of power policy, practised since Elizabeth's time and that of Cromwell.[43]

Churchill had always admired the courage and cultural achievements of the German people, but he can be pardoned if, after 1933, he found it difficult to draw a line of political differentiation between them and their leader. Hitler's popular support grew steadily stronger from year to year after 1933, and there was reason for this, since his achievements were undeniable. A German writer has said that, if Hitler had died in 1938, he would have been universally regarded as one of the greatest figures in German history.[44] But, even after 1938, as he entered the dangerous phase of his policy, there was no conspicuous falling off in his popularity. A thoughtful German observer wrote in his diary in September 1939, 'the fanfares of victory are now drowning out every word of criticism and any thought of concern over the future'.[45]

The time is long past when it was possible to see the protracted debate over British foreign policy in the 1930s as a struggle between Churchill, an angel of light, fighting against the velleities of uncomprehending and feeble men in high places. It is reasonably well known today that Churchill was often ill-informed, that his claims about German strength were exaggerated and his prescriptions impractical, that his emphasis on airpower was misplaced, and that his belief that bombing would produce an army revolt against Hitler was just one more instance of his lack of knowledge about Germany's internal affairs. We are also readier than was an earlier generation to admit that the policy of Chamberlain and Halifax had an element of consistency about it, based as it was on the belief that, if war could be avoided until British armed strength was built up, Hitler would be bound to moderate his ambitions and become a good neighbour. But the fact remains that Churchill's exaggerations were more accurate than Chamberlain's realism (a word, incidentally, used so often by Chamberlain and his associates to distinguish their policy from the ideas of Churchill and Eden that the French became anxious about 'the dreaded realism of the British' and Axis diplomats made certain that they used it a lot in communication with the British).[46] His judgement of Hitler and his intentions was always sounder than that of the dozens of European statesmen who made the pilgrimage to Berlin or Berchtesgaden and came away reassured, sounder than the bizarre notions of Franklin Delano Roosevelt, which in retrospect do little credit to his ambassadors,[47] and certainly sounder than those of the Prime Minister, who wrote plaintively on 10 September 1939:

With such an extraordinary creature one can only speculate. But I believe he did seriously contemplate an agreement with us and that he worked seriously at proposals (subsequently broadcast) which to his one-track mind seemed fabulously generous. But at the last moment some brainstorm took possession of him—maybe Ribbentrop stirred it up—and once he had set his machine in motion he could not stop it. That, as I have always recognised, is the frightful danger of such terrific weapons being in the hands of a paranoiac.[48]

Why Churchill understood Hitler so well is not quite clear. It may have had something to do with the similarities between their early lives and the circumstances in which their characters were formed, a theme elaborated on by John Lukacs.[49] But it certainly was connected also with his study of history and the evidence that it provided to show that the cyclical movements of the Great Powers are not directed by moral considerations, and that great leaders intent on the aggrandizement of state interest can be restrained only by force in default of an effective international order.

During the Second World War, Churchill was too busy fighting Germany to think much about what was to become of it when the war was over, and his occasional remarks on the subject were apt to be ill-informed and inconsistent. At the Atlantic Conference in Placentia Bay in August 1941, he told President Roosevelt, in words that reflected the history of Europe after 1918, that

We must disarm the Germans and their accomplices but give no undertaking, which they can afterwards exploit, that we shall give them within any measurable time any sort of equality as regards arms. On the contrary, we must take care to see that we are sufficiently strongly armed to prevent any repetition, in Europe or the world, of these catastrophes. On the other hand, we now take the view that impoverished neighbours are bound to be bad neighbours, and we wish to see everyone prosperous, including the Germans. In short, our intention is to make Germany 'fat but impotent'.[50]

This left aside all such difficult questions as punishment, partition, and reparations, on all of which Churchill was ambivalent. He could flare up in anger over Stalin's perhaps not entirely joking suggestion at Tehran that 50,000 German officers be killed, spluttering that he would not condone 'the cold blooded murder of soldiers who had fought for their country';[51] but on other occasions, in an effort to dispel Stalin's suspicion that the West was prepared to be soft on the Germans, he was apt to be less chivalrous in his demeanour and to hint at dire punishment to come.[52] In private, however, he always insisted that he saw 'no alternative to the acceptance of Germany as part of the family of Europe' after the war.[53]

What Germany's shape would be in the post-war world and what economic disabilities it might suffer were by no means clear in his mind. It is significant that there was never a full-scale Cabinet discussion of the German question during the war. Churchill left post-war planning to the German experts and technicians, but when planning began in the Foreign Office in 1942, he neither attended to it closely nor considered himself bound by it.[54] There were, in any case, strong differences of perspective between Churchill and the Foreign Office. Churchill was a European and interested in restoring the old European system, in ways that struck Eden's aides as antiquated and unrealistic. He was, for example, fascinated with Prussia, with which he had a love–hate relationship, regarding it as the centre of militarism and National Socialism but also as a necessary bulwark against Russia, and as early as 1940 he was sketching a future Europe in which there would be 'five great nations, England, France, Italy, Spain and Prussia' and four great federations: the northern with its capital at The Hague; Mitteleuropa, with its capital at Warsaw or Prague; the Danubian, consisting of Bavaria, Württemberg, Austria, and Hungary, with its capital at Vienna; and the Balkan, with Turkey at its head and the capital at Constantinople. Elements of this plan, which showed that there was great confusion in Churchill's mind about the incidence of National

Socialism in Prussia (which was to be punished by the loss of its industrial areas in the Ruhr) and Austria (which was to be rewarded by
union with Southern Germany) remained in his thoughts for the rest of
the war.[55] The Foreign Office, fresh from its successful negotiation of
the Anglo–Soviet Treaty of 1942, which Churchill privately thought
was dangerously generous to the Soviet Union,[56] was anxious to build
upon the treaty by means of a Four Power Agreement (Great Britain,
the United States, the Soviet Union, and—in deference to Roosevelt's
wishes—China) that would regulate the peace-making process and the
future of Germany. The irritation in the Foreign Office over its failure
to engage and hold Churchill's attention is shown by an entry in the
diary of Eden's private secretary in October 1942:

P. M. has sent another foolish minute about our post-war plan. He wishes to
put the clock back to the Congress of Vienna. With Roosevelt straining to put
the British Empire into liquidation and Winston pulling in the opposite direction to put it back to pre-Boer War, we are in danger of losing both the Old
and the New World.[57]

Instinctively, Churchill opposed plans that would tie his hands and
make concessions to the Soviet Union that would not be justified by
the military situation at the end of the fighting. He greatly overestimated the strength and freedom of political action that Britain would
have at that time and continued till very late in the conflict to believe
that it would be able to determine the nature of the new balance of
power in Europe virtually by itself.[58] Because of this, he did not feel
bound by arrangements made by his diplomats, and he was apt to make
impulsive decisions that were disruptive and self-defeating because he
had not studied his brief. Thus, at the Quebec Conference in
September 1944, he allowed himself to be talked into accepting the
Morgenthau Plan, a proposal for turning Germany into a pastoral state.
He had reacted originally to this notion with revulsion, protesting,
according to his doctor, that one could not indict a whole nation and
that the English people would not stand for the idea. But within two
days, he had been persuaded, largely by his intimate adviser Lord
Cherwell, that the Germans deserved the treatment proposed by
Secretary Morgenthau and that the destruction of Germany's industrial
capacity would save Britain from bankruptcy by eliminating a competi-
tor.[59] This argument astonished economists, who knew that it was nonsense, and Churchill's action infuriated the Foreign Secretary, Anthony
Eden, who could hardly speak coherently about it. Nothing came of the

Morgenthau Plan because the spirited opposition of Secretaries Hull and Stimson convinced President Roosevelt that he had made a mistake in initialling it; but even so Churchill seemed unrepentant about his signature, despite the fact that it flew in the face of his long record of opposing excessive punishment of a beaten foe, and later, in his history of the war, he refused to admit that the plan was a mistake.[60]

It was certainly, however, a sign of his failure to comprehend how far his own government, through its planning and that of the European Advisory Committee that had been authorized by the Big Three conferences at Moscow and Tehran, had already committed itself. Lothar Kettenacker has written that, even at the Yalta Conference in February 1945, Churchill assumed that as far as Germany was concerned nothing had really been so definitively settled that it would have to become part of the traditional peace treaty that he expected to be negotiated, neither the question of the partition of the Reich, nor the drawing of the definitive border in the east, nor the amount and division of reparations. But in fact, he adds, what was really to happen had

long been pre-programmed, and in part for several years: the casual, provisional state of affairs at the war's end simply froze as a result of the fall of the temperature caused by the Cold War. It was not by accident that Churchill— despite all of his failures a historical personality of great format—departed from the stage in order to make place for an upright bureaucrat like Clement Attlee.[61]

As he passed once more, not for the last time, from public to private life, Churchill retained his belief in the idea of a European system of which Germany would be a full member, working not for domination, but for peaceful collaboration. Even in the divided world that was emerging, that, he believed, was still an ideal to be followed. On 19 September 1946, in Zurich, he appealed, therefore, for the establishment of 'a kind of United States of Europe', created this time not by the divided Great Powers but by the united resolve of 'hundreds of millions of men and women to do right instead of wrong, and gain as their reward blessing instead of cursing'. As for where to begin, he said, he had a proposal 'that will astonish you'. 'The first step in the re-creation of the European family must be a partnership between France and Germany. In this way only can France recover the moral leadership of Europe. There can be no revival of Europe without a spiritually great France and a spiritually great Germany.' France and Germany must undertake together the urgent task of creating the new union, while Britain and the Commonwealth and 'mighty America, and I trust Soviet Russia, for then all would be well; all would be friends and sponsors of the new Europe and champion its right to live and shine'.[62]

Coming at a time when people were beginning to worry about the atomic bomb and the dissolution of the Grand Alliance, this proposal had a startling effect. One great European, who lived in the past as much as Churchill did, found it offensive. Charles de Gaulle, to whom Churchill wrote about his idea, told Duncan Sandys, who carried the letter to Colombey, that the speech had been badly received in France.

All Frenchmen were violently opposed to re-creating any kind of unified, centralised Reich, and were gravely suspicious of the policy of the American and British Governments. Unless steps were taken to prevent the resuscitation of German power, there was the danger that a United Europe would become nothing else than an enlarged Germany.

He went on to say that he made his support of the idea of European union conditional upon the designation of France and Britain as founding members, a precise understanding between them on how Germany was to be treated, and, among other things, a permanent allocation of coal from the Ruhr, consent to long-term occupation of Germany by French forces, possibly the incorporation of the North Rhineland in the French Zone, and the establishment of a regime of international control of the Ruhr industries satisfactory to France. 'Voilà mes conditions!'[63]

Churchill's ideas had often been known to produce violent reactions. He was probably not concerned about this one. If so, he was right not to be. Seventeen years later de Gaulle signed a Franco–German Friendship Treaty with Konrad Adenauer, and even before he did so the two countries were collaborating in laying the foundations of the European Community that Churchill had had in mind.

3

Churchill and France

DOUGLAS JOHNSON

O N 11 November 1944 Winston Churchill made a speech in
Paris. He included these words:

It is difficult for me to speak on a day such as this, which fills us with emotion. For more than thirty years I have defended the cause of friendship, of
comradeship and of alliance between France and Great Britain. I have never
deviated from that policy throughout the whole of my life. For so many years
past have these two nations shared the glories of Western Europe, that they
have become indispensable to each other. It is a fundamental principle of
British policy that the alliance with France should be unshakeable, constant
and effective. This morning I was able to see that the French people wanted to
march hand in hand with the British people.[1]

It was a moving speech and an emotional occasion: the commemoration of the armistice of the First World War whilst the Second World
War continued. There was a procession down the Champs Élysées led
by Churchill (who was dressed in RAF uniform) and de Gaulle. A
wreath had been laid beneath the statue of Clemenceau and the band
had played 'Le Père la Victoire'. Churchill had paid homage to Foch
and had contemplated the tomb of Napoleon in the Invalides. In the
War Ministry, rue Saint Dominique, where the reception had been
held and where Churchill made his speech, a bust of the Duke of
Marlborough had been tactfully (or miraculously) discovered and was
on display, so that Churchill was greeted there by his famous ancestor.
Everything was successful, and some half a million Parisians were present and enthusiastic.

But, perhaps significant in Churchill's relations with France throughout his long career, whilst the sentiments expressed and the emotions
felt were real enough, behind them lay many complexities. In 1944
much bitterness was still present. Without recalling all the quarrels
between Churchill and de Gaulle (although we might remember that in

June 1944 Churchill had threatened to denounce de Gaulle as 'the mortal foe of England'), the failure of the British government to recognize de Gaulle's administration as the official government of France until 23 October 1944 and the exclusion of France from a number of international conferences had made relations difficult. The fact that in August Churchill had gone to Algiers and that de Gaulle had pointedly chosen not to see him had wounded Churchill. That, in the same month, Churchill had visited Corsica without giving any advance notice to the French government had incensed de Gaulle. There was thus a personal element of considerable importance in Franco–British relations at this time. It threatened to become even greater when Churchill let it be known that he wished to visit Paris in November 1944, although he had not been invited. De Gaulle told the Quai d'Orsay, the War Ministry, the General Staff, the Préfet de la Seine and the Préfet de Police, that if Churchill came to Paris there was to be no recognition of his presence without his personal approval. He added that he attached to this matter 'une importance absolument capitale'. Churchill, learning of this reluctance, stated that he was prepared to go to France and to visit General Eisenhower without paying any attention to the French government. De Gaulle also objected to 11 November as the date for the visit, since he claimed that this was a date that was 'exclusivement français'. However, as shown, the efforts of diplomats were successful and the visit was a huge success (although reports that are difficult to verify suggest that at a certain moment de Gaulle asked why the Parisian crowds were cheering 'the old bandit'). The fact remains that behind the personal difficulties that existed between two exceptionally strong personalities, there were important differences with regard to policy. Appreciation of these differences, which were highlighted on 11 November 1944, when the speeches were finished and the cheering had been stilled and negotiations took place, is essential to an understanding of the subject, Churchill and France.[2]

Churchill frequently recalled his long association with France. When de Gaulle left England on 16 June 1944 he wrote an unusually friendly and generous letter to Churchill. The reply was somewhat ungracious ('I'm sorry but that's the best I can do', Churchill said to Duff Cooper who was present when he dictated the letter), but it contains the lines: 'Ever since 1907, I have in good times and bad times been a sincere friend of France, as my words and actions show, and it is to me an intense pain that barriers have been raised to an association which to me was very dear.'[3]

In the summer of 1946 Churchill wanted to visit Metz and he was anxious to clear this with the Prime Minister, Clement Attlee. He explained that the invitation from the municipality of Metz would enable him to fulfil an 'engagement' that he made with General Giraud in North Africa in 1942, when he had said 'I give you *rendez-vous* at Metz' (although the date was almost certainly 1943). But he added that his motives were entirely 'public' and that pleasure formed no part of them, since it was a great 'exertion' to travel all that way. He hoped that he would be able to say a few words of friendship and encouragement to the French, which would reach many homes in France and which would therefore further the general interest.

When he spoke in Metz, the main purpose of his speech was to urge the French nation to unite and to play its part in bringing Europe back to broader and better days, since without a strong France there could be no revival of Europe with its culture, its charm, its tradition, and its mighty power. But he also spoke of his personal memories of France. Sixty-three years earlier, when he was aged eight, his father had taken him to Paris. This was the summer of 1883:

We drove along together through the Place de la Concorde. Being an observant child I noticed that one of the monuments was covered with wreaths and crepe and I at once asked him why. He replied, 'These are monuments of the Provinces of France. Two of them, Alsace and Lorraine, have been taken from France by the Germans in the last war. The French are very unhappy about it and hope some day to get them back!' I remember quite distinctly thinking to myself, 'I hope they will get them back'.

He then recalled a visit to France in 1907, three years after the *Entente Cordiale* had been established, when he was Parliamentary Under-Secretary of State at the Colonial Office, in the government presided over by Sir Henry Campbell-Bannerman. He was the guest of the French army at its annual manœuvres, where he watched the French troops in their blue tunics and red trousers and listened to the bands playing the *Marseillaise*. He reflected that it was by 'those valiant bayonets' that the rights of man had been gained and that they would also guard the rights and the liberties of Europe.[4]

There can be no doubt: Churchill saw himself as France's 'old and faithful friend'. This is not surprising. France was the foreign country that he had visited more than any other, and by a wide margin. When Churchill went, as First Lord of the Admiralty, to France in November 1939, Martin Gilbert believes that he had already crossed the channel more than a hundred times. This journey, like those that had preceded it during the First World War, and like many that were to follow, was because Churchill wanted to be where the action was—he wanted to find out what was happening, or, particularly in peace-time, he sought to get information from his French contacts about what was happening in other countries. He made friends with many politicians and officials. On this journey to France, in November 1939, before visiting the head-quarters of the British Expeditionary Force in the north, he gave a din-ner at the Ritz in Paris. Naturally, his guests included those who were in charge of the French Navy, Campinchi (the Minister for the Marine) and Admiral Darlan, but also particular friends. There was the former Prime Minister, Léon Blum, the future Prime Minister, Paul Reynaud, and Clemenceau's former right-hand man, Georges Mandel. There was also present Alexis Léger, a very important official in the Quai d'Orsay (and future winner of the Nobel Prize for Literature). Possibly no other British statesman could have brought together so many people of importance in France, representing so many different opinions, who were his personal acquaintances (and there were others upon whom he could have called such as another former Prime Minister, Édouard Herriot).

But Churchill also visited France for pleasure. Staying with British or French friends or in hotels where he was well known, it was in France that he rested, recuperated, wrote his books and his articles, gambled in casinos, occasionally hunted, and, of course, painted. It should not be forgotten that his American mother's family, the Jeromes, had made their second home in Paris. His mother was brought up there and she gave him many introductions to friends in Paris. His letters to her contained many French idioms.

No-one can write about Churchill and France without addressing the problem of Churchill's spoken French. It has become a legend out of all proportion to its importance, one which has been in existence for a very long time. It was in 1915 that Asquith wrote to Venetia Stanley that he had taken part in a meeting with Delcassé and Cambon when Churchill's French had caused him much amusement. 'S'ils savent', he quoted Churchill as saying, 'que nous sommes gens qu'ils peuvent con-ter sur.' Some twenty-five years later, there are all the legendary stories of Churchill's conversations with de Gaulle, including such phrases as 'si vous continuez m'obstructer, je vous liquidaterai', or de Gaulle's alleged remark that since Churchill had been speaking to him in French, his English had greatly improved. Churchill has contributed to this legend by a number of humorous or self-deprecating remarks. Englishmen, he claimed, did not exist in order to speak foreign tongues, but foreign tongues existed in order to be spoken by Englishmen. In France, in 1946, he explained that he would not speak French, 'That', he said, 'was a sacrifice that had to be accepted in war-time.'

However, the evidence is that Churchill's spoken French had its very real qualities (which could, in comparison, put many other British Prime Ministers to shame). Although, at the age of 17, he had objected to being sent to France in order to learn the language ('I beg and pray that you will not send me to a vile, nasty, fusty, beastly French family'), once he was there (in Versailles) he enjoyed the experience and he was complimented on his French.[5] He was always fluent, and whilst manipulating the language in an obstinate manner, he succeeded in expressing himself, sometimes forcibly. His famous wartime broadcast to France in 1942 lost none of its force because of his accent. Many observers (Duff Cooper for example) commented upon the ease with which he spoke French, whilst noting his difficulty in understanding what was said to him. His capacious memory extended to French matters: General de Gaulle recalled that on one occasion Churchill sang him 'Le Père la Victoire' without forgetting anything and without a mistake. His knowledge of French history was considerable and was spread over a wide period. He yielded to no-one in his admiration for Joan of Arc, whom he described as 'the winner' (and he was always insistent that it was not the English who had burned her, but the Burgundians). His sense of humour sometimes misled others into thinking that he was ignorant of French history, as when he urged his compatriots to drink Veuve-Clicquot champagne, since it would support a worthy French woman who had been widowed in the First World War.

But mention of Churchill and the French language is particularly relevant to the subject of Churchill and France in another way. Just as it has for long been fashionable to mock him for his spoken French, so his contemporaries criticized his friend and colleague, Austen Chamberlain, for his excellent spoken French. It was widely claimed, after Chamberlain had become Foreign Secretary in 1924, that it was Britain's misfortune that he spoke such good French and that he enjoyed speaking French, because British policy had become dominated by France. In fact Chamberlain had a clearly determined policy with regard to France. This was not because of his attachment to the country, although he expressed this in words that were more fulsome than those used by Churchill, but because he believed that there could be no satisfactory settlement in the post-1918 world until France had been given a real sense of security. He worked efficiently to provide this security, an objective that took precedence over obligations to the League of Nations and other principles. One can cite French statesmen who felt the same about relations with Britain, such as Guizot in the nineteenth century, or those in the 1930s who felt obliged to turn, almost exclusively, to what has been termed 'the English governess'.

The question, therefore, remains: did Churchill, who is particularly known for his conception of the 'Special Relationship' between Britain and America, have some principle, other than sentiment and affection, that determined his attitude towards Britain's relations with France? We may find the answer by turning to certain specific moments in Anglo-French relations.

The first is obviously the crisis of 1914. As is well known, Churchill's first real concern with foreign affairs occurred in 1911, with the Agadir crisis, when he was Home Secretary. He had, with the habit that never left him of ranging beyond his ministerial briefs, written a memorandum on the possible course of a war between France and Germany, a memorandum that he was to circulate again when he was First Lord of the Admiralty in September 1914. This memorandum envisaged an initial German success in any invasion, both militarily and politically. It would be some weeks before this situation could be relieved by pressure from the Russian armies, and the arrival of British forces, together with the strain that constant advances would necessarily place upon the Germans. Whether the French would be able to with-stand invasion, the cutting off of provinces, the investment of Paris, and the reduction of their army 'to retrograde or defensive operations' would depend, he believed, on the amount of aid that Britain could furnish. However, whilst this memorandum had envisaged a triple alliance between Britain, France, and Russia as a means of preventing hostilities, it more particularly envisaged an outbreak of chaotic European conditions. Churchill did not believe in any direct obligation to France, nor was he a partisan of an Anglo-French alliance. He recognized (as did Sir Arthur Nicolson of the Foreign Office, when approached by the French ambassador, Paul Cambon, in search of such an alliance) that there was a strong pro-German element in the Cabinet. Churchill was not part of this group, as events were to prove, but he had always been in favour of improving Anglo-German relations.

The key to French diplomacy during 1912 was the attainment of an Anglo-French naval convention. What France wanted was for Britain to look after the Channel and the northern coasts of France, whilst the French would take on responsibility for the Mediterranean. This fitted in with naval policy as outlined in 1907 and 1908, when British planners had envisaged the possibility of gaining French aid in the Mediterranean. The bulk of the French fleet was already concentrated there, whilst the main force of the Royal Navy was usually stationed in home waters. However, whilst Churchill was worried by the dispersal of the British fleet over too wide an area, he was reluctant to be rushed by the French. The transfer of ships from Malta to Gibraltar was a more pressing matter for consideration. Still, on 4 July 1912, Churchill proposed to the Committee of Imperial Defence that a greater concentration of the fleet in home waters should take place at the expense of the Mediterranean. This was defeated, but by a complicated arrangement it was agreed that, subject to certain provisos, Britain would maintain a battle fleet in the Mediterranean only equal to a one-power Mediterranean standard (excluding France). Thus, in a sense, Cambon got something of what he had wanted and Churchill's defeat was, as has been said, 'more apparent than real'. But whilst the French believed that the positioning of the bulk of their fleet in the Mediterranean meant that Britain had an obligation to help France in the event of war with Germany, even if it were only a moral obligation, the position of the British government was that Britain had not made, and would not make, a commitment to assist France in the event of war.

Churchill understood this situation. As he put it to Asquith on 23 August: 'Everyone must feel, who knows the facts, that we have all the obligations of an alliance without its advantages and above all without its precise definitions.' There is no suggestion that he wanted such an alliance, but as the crisis developed in the course of 1914 his determination that the fleet should be ready included helping the French navy in every way possible and in arranging for troops to cross the Channel. Although Britain's only treaty obligation was to Belgium, as he told Kitchener on 27 July 1914, he believed that it would be a German invasion of France, rather than of Belgium, which would either split the Cabinet or determine the British entry into war. When the crisis reached its climax, although Churchill warned that Britain should wait without recklessly wasting her strength, he was also one of the principal forces in the government eager to take action and to put Anglo-French arrangements into force. He played a critical part in persuading Lloyd George, who was the only man who could have led a strong neutralist party, to join him, and to abandon his negative position.[6]

As the war proceeded, apart from his eight official journeys to France, which led to some criticism that he was not present at the Admiralty when needed, Churchill's attitude towards France is reflected in his very active participation in two attempts to relieve the stalemate on the Western Front from an alternative theatre. The one was the Dardanelles campaign, the attempt to use amphibious power to strike at Turkey and open a route to Russia. The other was the Salonika expedition, especially promoted by France, a plan to strike at the Central Powers by driving through the Balkans into Austria-Hungary. Churchill has always been identified with the former and had some contact with the latter, even as he has been associated with various proposed diversions in the Baltic and elsewhere.

The problem was whether or not such actions would weaken the defence of France. Churchill had earlier suggested that he believed that the front in France was the decisive theatre and had deprecated any temptation 'to win cheaper laurels in easier fields' (but this letter, 11 January 1915, was to Sir John French and was presumably meant to be reassuring). Subsequently, however, Churchill stressed the weakness both of France and of Russia and the futility of renewed offensives on the Western Front. It was necessary for one of the powers to speak with the unmistakable prestige of victory, and that Britain, by its wealth and sea-power, could do. The dilemma was always that the fear of French defeatism caused the British to participate in frontal attacks against the enemy, whilst at the same time seeking success in another sphere.

The Salonika expedition created a further dilemma. Whilst at times Churchill supported the idea, he was aghast at certain of the plans proposed. In October 1915 he expressed the view that to send allied forces northwards into Serbia without the support of Greece would be 'sheer madness', for 'the communications of our force would run through and be at the mercy of Greece, which had a pro-German King, a pro-German Queen, and was about to have a pro-German government'. Little more than a week after Churchill had made this statement (to the Dardanelles Committee on 6 October 1915) Alexandre Millerand, the French Minister for War, came to London, and later General Joffre himself arrived. Both claimed that if the British did not support the French in Salonika, then this would be the end of the *Entente Cordiale*, and possibly of Anglo-French co-operation in the war.

The complicated politics that lay behind the French determination to organize this expedition to Salonika thoroughly escaped Churchill, as it did most British soldiers and statesmen. Although out of office, he soon became a determined partisan of withdrawal from Salonika. One can clearly see from these episodes that he did not visualize the British role in the war as being the same as the French role. The British had power which the French did not possess. Churchill was well aware of both the political and the military weakness of France.[7]

Another occasion when one can examine Churchill's attitude towards France, this time in peace, came after the formation of Stanley Baldwin's second government on 5 November 1924. The two appointments that then aroused most interest were those of Winston Churchill as Chancellor of the Exchequer and Austen Chamberlain as Secretary of State for Foreign Affairs. Chamberlain's coming into government was important politically, because it brought to an end the split in the Conservative Party which had occurred with the break-up of the Coalition. But it was also significant in diplomatic terms because Chamberlain had earlier made a number of very pro-French statements, especially in July 1924. He had suggested that the Conservative government would make the maintenance of the *Entente* with France 'the cardinal object of our policy', and once in office he determined to demonstrate to the retiring French ambassador in London, Saintc-Aulaire, how he had always, in the past, been particularly loyal to French interests. Not all Conservatives thought like this. Some were more conscious of the difficulties and dangers that came from France, whilst others were in favour of Great Britain withdrawing from Europe, and concentrating on her Imperial connections; some were more insistent upon the importance of the League, others were disturbed that a policy of 'benevolent neutralism ad infinitum' was reducing British influence.

Austen Chamberlain was astonished that Churchill had become Chancellor of the Exchequer. Although Chamberlain always stressed his pleasure at their being friends and frequently recalled the friendship which had existed between their fathers, he had advised Baldwin, when the new Prime Minister was forming his government, that Churchill would be more dangerous outside than inside. 'If you leave him out he will be leading a Tory rump within six months time.' But Chamberlain had thought that Churchill should be at the Colonial Office or at the Ministry of Health, and his surprise at Churchill's new position at the Exchequer was mingled with some apprehension.

This apprehension seemed confirmed when Churchill not only showed himself to be ready to give advice (that the recognition of Soviet Russia should be revoked, for example), but also asked that copies of Foreign Office intercepts should be sent to him since, he claimed, a general knowledge of foreign affairs was essential to his position as Chancellor. He also warned Chamberlain that the financial policy that he intended to follow would be 'a heavy burden on your diplomacy' and that his insistence upon repayments of loans from France, amongst other countries, would mean 'sulky instead of smiling ambassadors'. On the whole Chamberlain felt less worried about Churchill than he was about Robert Cecil, who behaved with regard to the League of Nations as if he were the Foreign Secretary. Churchill was, Chamberlain thought, changeable in his ideas on foreign policy and he hoped that Churchill would concentrate on making a success of his new office. In a carefully worded letter to Churchill, Chamberlain predicted that he would 'greatly enhance your reputation in this post, which will give you an opportunity of showing to the country your possession of just those powers which perhaps hitherto have been recognised only by your personal friends' (15 December 1924).

The Foreign Office felt some alarm at Churchill travelling abroad, and the Paris embassy in particular was worried that he might go beyond 'the rather arid region' of financial affairs. There was some concern over his friendship with Louis Loucheur, a French politician with an industrial background who had been Minister for Munitions at the same time as Churchill had occupied that post in England. Loucheur worked closely with Briand and was thought to be influential. It was to Loucheur that Churchill had, in December 1921, expressed his alarm at the extent of French rearmament. 'Everyone realised', he had said, 'that France must have the finest army in Europe and be strong enough to keep Germany in order, but you could have too much of a good thing.' He had also pointed out that the French Air Force had an overwhelming superiority over the British 'for the time being', and certain French air officers had been talking indiscreetly and using foolish language as to what it was possible for France to do, which had offended some of the British air staff. But above all, Churchill was concerned at the reported French intention to build a submarine fleet, since he assumed that this could only be directed against Great Britain, and he held that such a vital menace would bring about a complete change of front on the part of the British. 'I said that not living on an island dependent on its food from outside, M. Loucheur could not appreciate how we felt about these things.'

Doubtless, Churchill's vaguely pessimistic view of what was happening in France was confirmed by Sir Edward Spears, his personal representative in France. Spears reported from Paris that there was a great deal of bitter feeling against Britain, in spite of the good intentions and, at times courageous, attitudes adopted by politicians such as Paul Painlevé and Aristide Briand.

This would help to explain the differences that appeared between Churchill and Austen Chamberlain. Whilst they were in agreement with regard to the ambitious scheme known as the Geneva Protocol, which was proposed in 1924 to enforce international obligations by common action, they did not agree on procedure. Once the Geneva Protocol had been rejected, Chamberlain thought it essential to reassure France. Fortified by a conversation with Gaston Doumerge, the President of the Republic, Churchill opposed the idea of an Anglo-French alliance, which Chamberlain put to the Committee of Imperial Defence, on 13 February 1925. Churchill had many supporters. Cecil had pointed out that although the British had heard a great deal about French security, the necessity for security for other nations was no less important for peace in Europe. The Treasury experts had reported that France was strong in economic terms and that her financial problems arose from under-taxation.

Churchill was forthright as usual. He wrote rather contemptuously of 'a pack of small nations in leash to France'; he insisted that Britain could always stand alone and declined to accept as an axiom that her fate was involved with France; he did not think that the British should bind themselves to going to war on the side of France as they should reserve for themselves full freedom to judge the circumstances and the occasion of the quarrel; he believed that it was only by standing aloof that Britain would be able to test her value to France and to exercise any real influence on that country. 'France will come to us if we do not offer ourselves to her', he insisted.

When his proposal for an Anglo-French pact had failed, Chamberlain was anxious to make some positive suggestion that would reassure the French, and he decided to follow up the proposal that Viscount d'Abernon had conveyed from the German Foreign Minister, Gustav Stresemann, in January 1925, for a mutual security pact. During Chamberlain's absence in Geneva, an informal Cabinet meeting was held in London, in March, at which Churchill joined with others in rejecting this proposition. According to Sir Eyre Crowe, in a private letter to Chamberlain, Churchill was all for letting France 'stew in her

own juice' (a frequent Churchillian phrase) and saw no reason why
Great Britain should take any action or decision.

Whilst Chamberlain for a time considered resignation and felt bitter
about the attitude of Churchill, the problem was resolved by a suddenly decisive Baldwin who directed the negotiations that eventually
led to the Locarno Agreement. But it is important to note that the disagreements between Churchill and Chamberlain, whilst magnified by
Churchillian language, often concerned procedure rather than principle.
Chamberlain had always believed that the reason for giving France
security was to encourage her to come to an understanding with
Germany. He had told the French ambassador in London, Fleuriau,
that Anglo-French negotiations always had the objective of bringing
about Franco-German negotiations, and that France could not suppose
that a combination of powers could hold Germany in a position of
abject inferiority and subjection for all time. This was on 20 January
1925. Ten days earlier Churchill had explained to the French President
that what was required was a complete agreement between England,
France, and Germany. And on 23 February he sent a memorandum to
Chamberlain in which he stated that when France had made a real
peace with Germany, Britain should seal the bond with all her strength.
This was the principle of Locarno, and Churchill warmly congratulated
Chamberlain once he had got Cabinet approval for his policy.

But Churchill never fully accepted 'the sunshine of Locarno' and the
view that it represented 'the real dividing line between the years of war
and the years of peace' (Chamberlain's words). He believed that the
Treaty of Versailles should be amended to revise Germany's eastern
frontiers, and he remained vigilant with regard to France's activities in
eastern Europe. He also was always aware of how, in France, 'the political kaleidoscope revolves'.[8]

Churchill's attitude towards France in the years preceding the
Second World War was, in many respects, a continuation of his attitude in 1925. In March 1933, after Hitler had come to power, he reiterated his conviction that Britain should not extend her obligations to
Europe or elsewhere. He hoped that the French would be able to look
after their own safety and that the British would again be permitted to
'live our life in our island without being again drawn into the perils of
the continent of Europe. But if we wish to detach ourselves and lead a
life of independence from European entanglements, we have to be
strong enough to defend our heredity'.

It was this question of armed strength which dominated Churchill's

thought in the 1930s. He did everything that he could to bring together
British and French thinking and mutual understanding: by newspaper
articles in Britain in which he sought to explain the position of a
France which, though still strong, was as in times past confronted by a
powerful and dangerous neighbour; by a lecture in Paris that was a call
for the closest possible Anglo-French co-operation and a rejection of
any subjection to either Nazi or Communist rule; and by frequent visits
to France in which he met military leaders ('the strength of the nation
resides in its army') and politicians (who could give him information
about German military strength). He even intervened in French politics
by persuading those who were not in favour of the Munich agreement
to stay in Daladier's government nevertheless.

Once he had joined the government in 1939, he pressed ahead with
making a working partnership with France real. He insisted that the
British contribution in terms of armed forces should be considerable
and he used his personal contacts, in particular that with General
Georges, to ensure that there were technical arrangements that would
ensure full co-operation.

At what point did Churchill begin to have doubts as to the efficiency
of the French army? In his memoirs he suggests that throughout the
winter of 1939–40 there was much lacking in French training and supplementary activity, and that the French army would have fought better in the autumn of 1939 than in the spring of 1940.[9] He certainly was
ready to believe as early as 18 May 1940 that there was a possibility
that the French would be ready to accept peace terms if they received
an advantageous offer, and he was positive about not committing too
much in the way of forces (especially aircraft) to France, since he foresaw the need for Britain to defend herself against invasion. Whilst concentrating on the need for American intervention in the war, he did
everything he could to sustain France, by frequent personal visits and
messages, by dispatching reinforcements, by giving the French a sense
of the fairness in the British attitude (he did this, for example, with his
expressions of sympathy, as well as by ensuring that French forces
were evacuated from Dunkirk as well as British), and finally by accepting the idea of a union between Britain and France.

It seems likely that the request for an armistice from the French did
not come as a complete surprise to Churchill, although subsequently he
expressed surprise that men whom he had known behaved as they did.
At all events, he did not waste time in recriminations, and he greeted
the arrival of de Gaulle in London and gave him every support.

However, as is always the case with Churchill's attitude towards France, there are certain elements to be borne in mind. One was his impression that de Gaulle was more important than in fact he was, an assumption based upon purely personal assessment and not on any information, official or unofficial. Another was his fear, which became almost obsessive, and which could not be alleviated, that the French fleet would be taken over and the French Empire invaded by the Germans. But equally important was his desire to show the world, particularly the United States, that Britain was determined to continue in the war. Therefore he attacked the French fleet and he recognized de Gaulle.[10]

But the recognition of de Gaulle was of a personal nature. He was not recognized as the head of a government in exile, but as the leader of a group that called themselves Free Frenchmen. Much has been written about this, and about the personal relations between Churchill and de Gaulle. It has been said, and rightly so, that Churchill's refusal to recognize de Gaulle as the leader of a government was simple prudence. No-one could see what would emerge from the chaos of France. As time went by, after de Gaulle's broadcast of 18 June 1940, which was the first statement of the foundation of Free France, his isolation became increasingly evident, and Churchill was sensitive to American reservations about him. Furthermore, de Gaulle's initiatives were directed towards the French Empire, whether in Africa, the Middle East, or the Pacific, which aroused memories of Anglo–French colonial rivalry in Churchill's mind. But essentially we can see the continuity of Churchill's thought. To have recognized de Gaulle as the head of a French government in exile would have been to commit Britain to a particular France. Churchill never wanted such a commitment. Even had his old friend Édouard Herriot emerged as the victor from the confusions of 1944, Churchill would have been reluctant to commit Britain to this alliance. To Herriot, or to any French leader, he would have given the same answer as he gave to de Gaulle after the sentimentalities of 11 November 1944. There was not to be an exclusive alliance between Britain and France. De Gaulle's biographer, Jean Lacouture, has pointed out that, as has every French leader from Francis I to Raymond Poincaré, the General turned to the East.[11] It is almost certainly not true that Churchill ever said, as de Gaulle has recorded in his memoirs, that if he had to choose between France and the ocean, then he would always choose the ocean. But although Britain recognized that France had to play a vital role in Europe, and Churchill insisted that France should be a permament member of the Security Council of the United Nations and one of the occupying powers in Germany, there was no mention by Churchill of Britain being tied to France and French policy (in Indo-China, for example).

After the war, in Churchill's final period as Prime Minister, one finds a revival of old Churchillian ideas. When the subject was Europe, when the issue was the organization of European defiance against the menace of the Soviet Union, then France had to come to an agreement with Germany: if not, with certain French ministers Churchill posed threats (Georges Bidault and Laniel); with others Churchill reasoned (Pierre Mendès France).[12] But France had to fit in to a vision of British policy, an idea of Europe, and an acceptance of British pre-eminence. The pro-French sentiment was genuine and real. But so was the *realpolitik*.

4

Churchill and Social Reform

PAUL ADDISON

AMONG his other claims to fame, Winston Churchill ranks as one of the founders of the welfare state. With Asquith and Lloyd George, he was the principal driving force behind the Liberal welfare reforms of 1908–11. At the Board of Trade he pioneered measures to reduce poverty and unemployment through state intervention in the labour market. In 1909 he toured the country campaigning for the 'People's Budget' and its radical proposals for the taxation of wealth. At the Home Office his penal reforms, and his measures to improve working conditions in shops and coal-mines, were reflections of a continuing drive for social reform that was cut short by his transfer, in 1911, to the Admiralty. The Board of Trade and Home Office years stand out from the rest of Churchill's career as the only period in which his energics were concentrated in the social field. But in the course of a lifetime in party politics he often touched on social questions, and there were other phases of his career in which he bore some responsibility for the development of social policy. As Chancellor of the Exchequer from 1924 to 1929 he encountered once more the problems of poverty and unemployment. As Prime Minister from 1940 to 1945 he presided over the post-war plans of the Coalition government, and returned to power in 1951 at the head of a Conservative administration in charge of the new welfare state.

How important was social policy to Churchill? On a sceptical reading it was never of great significance. His true 'destiny' lay in military and imperial affairs. Opportunism and ambition led him to play, for a while, the role of radical reformer, but the performance was mainly rhetorical. His Tory and aristocratic background divorced him from a true understanding of social conditions, and he lacked the commitment of the principled social reformer. His belligerence during the General Strike betrayed his lack of sympathy for the working class, and his patent lack of interest in social reform contributed heavily to his electoral defeat in 1945.

An alternative reading, which may best be described as romantic, identifies in Churchill a lifelong strand of interest in the improvement of social conditions. In his earliest speeches, we learn, he spoke of the need for old age pensions and other reforms. In later life he consistently supported the improvement of the social services. But for his defeat at the polls in 1945, he would have carried through the Beveridge plan and introduced a National Health Service. As Martin Gilbert writes: 'Both in his Liberal and his Conservative years, Churchill was a radical: a believer in the need for the State to take an active part, both by legislation and finance, in ensuring minimum standards of life, labour and social well-being for its citizens.'[1]

The aim of this chapter, in setting out the record, is to see how far it corresponds with either of these readings of Churchill's connections with social policy.

Winston Churchill entered politics as the political heir of his father, Lord Randolph Churchill. From Lord Randolph he took the cry of 'Tory Democracy' and a rhetoric of concern for the condition of the working class. He first stood for Parliament, in 1899, as the candidate for Oldham, a predominantly working-class constituency which returned two MPs. Both seats were vacant, and Churchill stood in alliance with a rare Tory trade unionist, James Mawdsley. The Conservative government of Lord Salisbury was notable for its negative approach to social policy, but Churchill did his best to identify the party with social reform: 'To keep our Empire we must have a free people and an educated and a well-fed people. That is why we are in favour of social reform.'[2] Mere rhetoric, perhaps, but a subaltern who only the previous year had fought at Omdurman was more entitled than most to make the connection between imperial power and the 'condition of England'.

In 1901, on the recommendation of John Morley, Churchill read Seebohm Rowntree's study of poverty in York. In an unpublished review of the book, intended no doubt for an army periodical, he described Rowntree's findings in great detail and concluded that poverty was a threat to the health and fitness of army recruits. 'And thus, strange as it may seem, eccentric, almost incredible to write—our Imperial reputation is actually involved in their condition.'[3]

Contrary to Churchill's opinion, the view that poverty was a threat to the Empire was almost a commonplace of the period. The disappointing performance of British forces in the South African war gave rise to the gospel of 'national efficiency' proclaimed by Churchill's friend and mentor Lord Rosebery. Churchill, however, was inhibited on questions of social reform by an overriding commitment to the retrenchment of public expenditure. He was a disciple and ally of the Treasury in its campaign to reduce government spending in the aftermath of the South African war. The need for economy was one of the principal themes of his attack upon the army reforms of the Secretary of State for War, St John Brodrick.

Churchill, therefore, did not draw collectivist conclusions from Rowntree. Speaking in the House of Commons in May 1902 he argued that reductions in public expenditure offered the best hope for the poor:

The only chance the struggling millions of whom we read in Mr Rowntree's book . . . ever have of enjoying the bounties of nature and science, lies not in any socialistic scheme of taxation, but, solely and simply, in an effective and scientific commercial development. I apprehend very grievously that there will one day come a government in England which will put upon its programme a great Navy and a great Army; £20,000,000 for old age pensions and the housing of the poor; £25,000,000 for an elaborate system of education.[4]

When Joseph Chamberlain raised the banner of tariff reform in 1903 Churchill opposed him and soon afterwards crossed the floor of the House to join the Liberals. For the time being this made no difference to his negative view of state intervention. On the contrary, free trade was another Treasury orthodoxy which harmonized with the cause of economy. When the Webbs sounded him out on social reform in June 1904, Beatrice recorded waspishly in her diary: 'I tried the "national minimum" on him but he was evidently unaware of the most elementary objections to unrestricted competition, and was still in the stage of "infant-school economics."'[5]

When the Liberals took office in December 1905, Campbell-Bannerman appointed Churchill to the Colonial Office as Under-Secretary. It was during his period at the Colonial Office that Churchill first declared his support for the establishment by the state of a 'national minimum'. In a speech in Glasgow in October 1906 he declared:

It is not possible to draw a hard-and-fast line between individualism and collectivism . . . Man is at once a unique being and a gregarious animal. For some purposes he must be a collectivist, for others he is and will for all time remain an individualist . . . The whole tendency of civilisation is, however, towards the multiplication of the collective functions of society . . . I should

like to see the state embark on various novel and adventurous experiments . . .
I look forward to the universal establishment of minimum standards of life and
labour.[6]

He returned to the theme with greater force in the New Year of
1908 in an article for the *Nation* entitled 'The Untrodden Field in
Politics'. What can account for this development in Churchill's thinking? His conversion to collectivism was the result of his change of
party. The Liberal party was a broad coalition of forces in which the
initiative was beginning to pass from the Gladstonian Liberals, whose
doctrine was *laissez-faire*, to the 'New' Liberals whose doctrine was
state intervention. Churchill was captured by the New Liberals, whose
aim was to reconstruct the party on the basis of a 'progressive alliance'
with Labour.

Churchill was in touch with so many radicals and reformers at this
juncture that it would be hard to say which, if any, had the greatest
influence. Lancashire, his political base, was a stronghold of Lib–Lab
politics and the New Liberalism. C. P. Scott, the editor of the
Manchester Guardian, acted as mentor and publicist.[7] But Churchill was
also in contact with such leading propagandists of reform as H. W.
Massingham, the editor of the *Nation*, Sidney and Beatrice Webb, and
Charles Masterman. Somewhere in the picture we also catch a glimpse
of Lloyd George: but his relations with Churchill between 1906 and
1908 have left only a faint blur.

The electoral dimension of social policy was well to the fore in
Churchill's thinking. His declaration in favour of collectivism, already
quoted, was intended to consolidate the electoral alliance between the
Labour and Liberal Parties by minimizing the policy differences
between them. As he explained to the Scottish Liberal Whip, his purpose was 'to isolate the wreckers who vilify the Liberal party and hand
over its seats to the Tories'.[8] Churchill put the electoral point more
broadly in a letter to J. A. Spender, the editor of the *Westminster
Gazette*, in December 1907:

No legislation at present in view interests the democracy. All their minds are
turning more and more to the social and economic issue . . . Minimum standards of wages & comfort, insurance in some effective form or other against
sickness, unemployment, old age, these are the questions and the only questions by which parties are going to live in the future. Woe to Liberalism if
they slip through its fingers.[9]

When Asquith succeeded to the premiership in February 1908,

Churchill at first accepted his offer of the Local Government Board, the department which supervised the Poor Law. But at the last minute Asquith switched him to the Board of Trade. This was fortunate for Churchill. The Local Government Board had a well-deserved reputation as a bastion of administrative inertia. The Board of Trade, on the other hand, was under the direction of two leading officials who favoured a measure of state intervention in the labour market, and possessed the necessary information and expertise: the Permanent Secretary, Sir Hubert Llewellyn Smith, and the Director of the Labour Department, Wilson Fox.

The principal measures which Churchill sponsored at the Board of Trade were unemployment insurance, labour exchanges, and statutory minimum wages in the 'sweated trades'. None of these proposals originated with Churchill. Unemployment and labour exchanges had been under discussion inside the Department in connection with the proceedings of the Royal Commission on the Poor Law. Intervention in the 'sweated trades' had long been advocated by Sir Charles Dilke and others. Nor is there any doubt that in the preparation of legislation, Churchill relied heavily upon his officials.[10]

While Churchill's impact ought not to be exaggerated, in certain respects it was decisive. He was a dynamic force who arrived at the Board of Trade with a strong commitment to reform. As he confided to Charles Masterman shortly before his appointment, he believed that he was called upon by providence to do something for the poor: 'Why have I always been kept safe within a hair's breadth of death', he asked, 'except to do something like this?'[11] It was Churchill who gave the instructions for legislation to be drawn up in advance of the findings of the Royal Commission on the Poor Law, and persuaded Asquith and the Cabinet to support him. It was Churchill, acting on the advice of the Webbs, who appointed William Beveridge to the Board of Trade with instructions to draw up a scheme of labour exchanges. Beveridge proposed two alternative types of scheme: one run by local authorities, and the other by central government. It was Churchill who decided that labour exchanges should form a single organization run from the centre. He also insisted that they should be staffed by trade unionists, social reformers, and others appointed directly by the President of the Board, instead of by civil servants—an extension of ministerial patronage that was later reversed.[12] Finally it was Churchill who first introduced unemployment insurance into the realm of practical politics. Subsequently, the plans for unemployment insurance were taken over by Lloyd George, and amalgamated with health insurance in the National Insurance Act of 1911.

The social reforms of the Liberal government have often been described as 'laying the foundations of the welfare state'. But in the Edwardian period the very phrase 'welfare state' was unknown. Churchill, Asquith, and Lloyd George conceived of their reforms as creating a strictly limited safety net. It was not intended to provide social security for all, but to assist families in the struggle to avoid the worst extremes of poverty, or dependence upon the much hated Poor Law. Unemployment insurance applied only to selected trades and benefits were only payable for fifteen weeks. It was assumed that interference in the labour market was to be kept to a minimum. Churchill regarded the Board of Trade reforms as an alternative to socialism. Like so many of his contemporaries, he was impressed by the example of Germany, where labour exchanges and health insurance had been introduced by Bismarck with the aim of integrating the working class into the nation. Comparing Germany with Britain he wrote to Asquith in December 1908: 'She is organised not only for war but for peace. We are organised only for party politics. The Minister who will apply to this country the successful experience of Germany in social policy may or may not be supported at the polls, but he will at least have a memorial which time will not deface of his administration.'[13] In an interview with a reporter from the *Daily Mail* in August 1909 Churchill said: 'The idea is to increase the stability of our institutions by giving the mass of industrial workers a direct interest in maintaining them. With a "stake in the country" in the form of insurance against evil days these workers will pay no attention to the vague promises of revolutionary socialism . . .'[14]

Churchill's contention that his Board of Trade reforms were conservative in character was confirmed by the welcome they received from the Conservative front bench. But his Bismarckian language was accompanied by a lively compassion for the underdog. When the rules governing entitlement to unemployment benefit were under discussion at the Board of Trade, Churchill objected strongly to Beveridge's proposal that workers dismissed for drunkeness or dishonesty should be disqualified from benefit. He wrote:

I do not feel we are entitled to refuse benefit to a qualified man who loses his judgment through drunkeness. He has paid his contributions; he has insured himself against the fact of unemployment, and I think it arguable that his foresight should be rewarded irrespective of the cause of his own dismissal, whether he lost his situation through his own habits of intemperance or through his employer's habits of intemperance. I do not like mixing up moralities and mathematics.[15]

Churchill, however, lost this particular argument. The safeguards Beveridge recommended were incorporated in the subsequent legislation.

In January 1910 Asquith promoted Churchill to the Home Office. In his new office Churchill proposed to carry through a comprehensive reform of penal policy in which the lightening of sentences was accompanied by the exclusion of various categories of offender from prison, and the improvement of prison conditions. Owing to the fact that he was at the Home Office for only a short time, he left with much of his agenda unfulfilled. But it was a dazzling performance while it lasted, and exemplified the kind of Liberalism that was most in harmony with his personality: the extension of mercy to the weak and powerless.

Though Churchill paid close attention to individual cases, his main concern was to reduce the blatant social bias of the courts against the poor and the working class. The overwhelming majority of crimes in Edwardian Britain consisted of petty offences committed by poor people. These offences were often punished by imprisonment, and offenders with three or more convictions were liable to be sentenced under 'preventive detention', a regime of imprisonment for up to ten years which had been introduced by Churchill's predecessor, Herbert Gladstone.

As Home Secretary, Churchill had the right to vary the sentences imposed by the courts. He decided to pursue a systematic policy of reducing sentences wherever it seemed to him that the punishment was disproportionate to the crime. Unlike his predecessor, he did not wait for pleas of mercy, but searched the criminal calendars for relevant cases. He was particularly active in reviewing sentences of preventive detention and threatened at one point to abolish the act which authorized it. He would liked to have gone much further and imposed on the judges a new scale of penalties, but left the Home Office before he could pursue the idea.[16]

Churchill's compassion for the underdog ought not to be confused with the permissive liberalism of the later twentieth century. His policies fully reflected the authoritarian strand in Edwardian social thought. He was eager to introduce compulsory labour colonies for vagrants, a favourite conception of the Webbs. For young offenders he proposed, as an alternative to imprisonment, 'defaulters' drill' to be performed at police stations. This was a wholly Churchillian idea, inspired no doubt by his experience in the army.[17] In the event, neither labour colonies nor defaulters' drill was introduced. It was the duty of the Home Secretary to review all death sentences and recommend clemency wherever he felt it was justified. Churchill recommended a reprieve in 21 cases out of 43. But the rate of reprieve was already running at 40 per cent in the first decade of the century.[18] Like his Board of Trade reforms, Churchill's penal policies were broadly in line with long-term trends in opinion and practice. But in penal policy he was more independent of the experts; the regulation of the labour market involved technical problems in which he lacked expertise, but he was confident that he understood the basic issues of crime and punishment. He took the initiative in policy-making and pressed ideas on his officials. Sir Edward Troup, the Permanent Secretary of the Home Office, later recalled: 'Once a week or oftener Churchill came to the office bringing with him some adventurous or impossible projects; but after half an hour's discussion something was evolved which was still adventurous but not impossible.'[19]

The Home Office was the department responsible for the regulation of working conditions in mines, factories, and shops. This enabled Churchill to consolidate his record on welfare legislation through the passage, in 1911, of the Coal Mines Act and the Shops Act. The Coal Mines Bill, a measure to improve health and safety in the mines, arose mainly from the recommendations of a Royal Commission, but was enthusiastically promoted by Churchill in the hope of improving his relations with the miners after the Tonypandy affair. The main provision of the Shops Bill, a proposal to limit the hours of shop assistants to 60 hours per week, was wrecked by the opposition of large retailers, who feared that it would benefit the self-employed shopkeeper at their expense. The Shops Act of 1911 was a feeble measure, though it did ensure, subject to Home Office arbitration, a weekly half-holiday for shop assistants.[20]

The reforms Churchill sponsored at the Board of Trade and the Home Office were, broadly speaking, bipartisan. Hence he was able to recommend them in 'Bismarckian' terms as contributions to the strength and unity of the nation. But in wider party politics Churchill was a radical who consistently attacked the Conservatives as a party of wealthy vested interests conspiring to exploit the poor. In the budget of 1909 Lloyd George proposed a range of new taxes on wealth and landed property. The Conservatives attacked them as socialist, and the rejection of the budget by the House of Lords precipitated a constitutional crisis. Churchill campaigned for the budget, and against the House of Lords, with all the pugnacity of which he was capable. He believed, no doubt, what he said at the time. But as a radical demagogue he was not wholly plausible. As Lady Violet Bonham Carter pointed out, Churchill picked up the language of radicalism from Lloyd George, but 'the words that rang true in his mouth rang false in Winston's. For the first time in my experience of him I felt that he was—quite unconsciously—wearing fancy-dress.'[21]

Churchill's *paternalism* was never to disappear from his politics. But his *radicalism* faded between 1911 and 1914. In October 1910 Lloyd George canvassed his secret proposal for a Coalition government; Churchill expressed great enthusiasm, but the plan fell through. After this Churchill and Lloyd George began to diverge. Churchill continued to hanker after a *rapprochement* with the Conservatives. After his appointment to the Admiralty in October 1911 he began to see himself as an increasingly 'national' figure and to champion naval rather than social expenditure. Lloyd George reverted to his radical roots and began to prepare the great land campaign of 1913–14. Churchill displayed very little enthusiasm. In the end, he agreed to support the campaign, but only as part of a deal whereby Lloyd George promised to finance naval expansion.[22] The deal broke down in January 1914, when Lloyd George openly attacked the naval estimates and Churchill was almost forced to resign. Lloyd George and Churchill were both highly pragmatic politicians, but they were playing from different strengths and backgrounds. Lloyd George understood the class consciousness of the radical dissenter, who viewed the landlord class from below. Churchill was the paternal aristocrat who believed in the improvement of the social order from above.

From 1911 to 1918 Churchill was absorbed in naval and military affairs. But an underlying paternalism was sometimes visible. At the Admiralty he improved the pay and conditions of the lower deck. As officer in command of the sixth battalion of the Royal Scottish Fusiliers, in the trenches in 1916, he was solicitous for the welfare of his men, who were mainly miners from Ayrshire.[23] From the backbenches, in August 1916, he argued in favour of rationing to protect the poor from the effects of rising prices. After the Coalition victory in the general election of 1918 Churchill wrote to Lloyd George to say that in his view the main task of the new government would be to 'rescue the weak and the poor'.[24] In the Lloyd George Coalition of

1918–22 Churchill was Secretary for War and Colonial Secretary. It was during this period that Churchill, who had already lost his reputation as a radical, came to be widely regarded as a reactionary. His anti-Bolshevik crusade in Russia, and strident hostility to the Labour Party at home, produced a transformation of rhetoric. He abandoned the language of social progress in favour of a language of negative anti-socialism. Former Liberal allies like H. W. Massingham, or MacCallum Scott, his first biographer, turned sharply against him.

Churchill's shift to the right was a consequence of the polarization of British politics. The disintegration of the Liberal Party, the rise of Labour, the syndicalist challenge, and the fear of Bolshevik subversion brought out in him the latent conservatism of the Edwardian era. But it is also true to say that Churchill exploited the polarization of politics in his own interest. As a Coalition Liberal, dependent on the patronage of Lloyd George and the goodwill of the Conservative party, he was insecure. In calling for the creation of a permanent anti-socialist bloc, he was trying to resolve the problem of his own political identity.

This helps to explain why Churchill banged the anti-socialist drum so loudly after 1918. But as the records of the Lloyd George Coalition show, he was more favourable to a policy of social appeasement in the Cabinet room than on the public platform. In April 1919, for example, against a background of severe industrial unrest, he urged the Cabinet to adopt a recommendation of the National Industrial Conference in favour of a minimum wage: 'The Secretary of State for War strongly approved recognition of the principle of wage minima. In his opinion the real answer of ordered society to Bolshevism was the frank recognition of minimum standards and open access to the highest posts in industry.'[25] Of all the members of the Lloyd George Cabinet it was Churchill who most strongly favoured a levy on war wealth, an issue on which he eventually found himself in a minority of one.[26] In July 1921 he strongly opposed a cut in the housing programme but was overruled.[27] As Colonial Secretary he urged the adoption of two imperial schemes to reduce unemployment at home: assisted emigration to the Dominions, and loans for the promotion of capital projects in the colonies.[28] Churchill evidently feared that the Coalition was losing working-class support to Labour, and probably realized that class politics were undermining his majority in Dundee. When he lost the seat in the general election of 1922, he wrote in a private letter: 'When one thinks of the kind of lives the poor of Dundee have to live, one cannot be indignant at the way they voted.'[29]

In 1923 Baldwin fought and lost a general election on a protectionist platform. With protectionism out of the way, Churchill could hoist once more the anti-socialist 'flag. In March 1924 he stood as an Independent at the Abbey by-election. But while he still emphasized the primacy of anti-socialism, Churchill now adopted a more positive tone on social reform. He was eager to attune himself to the Baldwinite mood of social reconciliation, and began to play on his Edwardian past. He reminded the electorate of the Abbey division of his progressive credentials:

Although my war record is frequently referred to, I have a large number of measures of social reform to my credit. These seem to have been forgotten. My interest in social reform is very real, and it is only because I feel that I will be able to assist in remedial legislation dealing with housing, and the extension of National Insurance, so as to give real security against the common hazards of life, that I am willing to stand before you.'[30]

Churchill's reference to housing deserves elaboration. In 1923 the Glaswegian industrialist Lord Weir unveiled a plan for the mass production of prefabricated houses by unskilled labour. Since it was likely to set the government on a collision course with the building trades, the Weir plan was problematical, and cautiously received by Baldwin and Chamberlain. But Churchill adopted it with enthusiasm as a means of tackling simultaneously the problems of housing and unemployment. Another point in its favour, he believed, was the potential appeal of an ambitious housing programme to women voters.[31]

When the Conservatives won the general election of 1924, Baldwin rewarded Churchill for his return to the party by appointing him to the Treasury. Generally speaking, Churchill was an orthodox Chancellor. Though he sometimes practised a little sleight of hand with the figures, he believed in the balanced budget and the other principles of orthodox finance. But in another sense, he was less orthodox. He inherited from his father, Lord Randolph, a conception of the Treasury as a platform for popular politics. He had also, no doubt, learned much from Lloyd George and the 'People's Budget'—but as a Conservative Chancellor he had no wish to imitate the radicalism of 1909. His aim was to convert the Treasury into the headquarters of a Tory Democracy. In the words of his Private Secretary, P. J. Grigg, Churchill intended to make the Treasury 'an active instrument of Government social policy instead of a passive concomitant or even, as it sometimes was, an active opponent'.[32]

One of Churchill's first decisions as Chancellor was to lend his support to the proposals of Neville Chamberlain, the Minister of Health, for the extension of social insurance. The Widows, Orphans and Old Age Pensions Bill was of great personal significance to Churchill as a continuation of the system of social security which he and Lloyd George had founded. Lloyd George had, indeed, intended to include pensions for widows and orphans in his National Insurance Bill of 1911, but had been forced to abandon the idea because of opposition from the friendly societies. By adopting the Bill as Treasury policy, Churchill was able both to identify himself with Baldwin's Conservatism, and to emphasize the continuity of his own commitment to social reform. As Churchill saw it, the case for social insurance was exactly the same as it had been in 1908, and he fortified himself by dipping into the phrases and arguments he had used in the past. When a delegation of employers warned of the damaging effects for industry of an extension of social insurance, Churchill replied:

Personally, I feel that the system of insurance, whatever may be the effects on the self-reliance of the individual, is going to be an absolutely inseparable element in our social life and eventually must have the effect of attaching the minds of the people, although in many cases their language and mood may not seem to indicate it—it must lead to the stability and order of the general structure.[33]

Whatever Churchill may have wished, his achievement in social policy at the Treasury was strictly limited. This was partly for the obvious reason that it was the role of Treasury to control and contain public expenditure. In addition Churchill was under strong pressure, as a Conservative Chancellor, to reduce taxation for the benefit of employers and the middle classes in general. He deliberately coupled the announcement of the social insurance scheme with a reduction of sixpence in the income tax—the tax on profits, fees, and salaries. At the same time he announced that Britain would return to the Gold Standard. This, too, restricted his room for manœuvre. By depressing trade, and precipitating a long and costly dispute in the coal industry, the Gold Standard also restricted the revenue at Churchill's disposal.

The social policy of the Baldwin government was largely the work of Neville Chamberlain, the Minister of Health. Shortly after his arrival at the Treasury, Churchill proposed to Chamberlain that they should co-operate politically in framing the government's programme. No doubt he had in mind the relationship between himself and Lloyd George in the Asquith Cabinet. But Churchill and Chamberlain seldom worked easily together and their conceptions of politics were different. Churchill wanted a few bold strokes that would lend themselves to electoral propaganda, Chamberlain a more efficient administrative structure for the social services. Housing policy was a case in point. Churchill would have liked to see a bold experiment in mass housing along the lines of the Weir plan. But Chamberlain preferred a modest pilot scheme.[34]

A notable feature of Churchill's period at the Treasury was his persistent concern over the high levels of unemployment which had prevailed since the onset of the depression in 1920. It is well known that fear of the consequences for employment lay at the root of his apprehensions over the return to Gold. Though he defended the decision stoutly in public, in private he blamed both Montagu Norman, the Governor of the Bank of England, and Sir Otto Niemeyer, the Controller of Finance at the Treasury, for leading him up the garden path of deflation. This had produced, wrote Churchill in a blazing letter to Niemeyer, 'bad trade, hard times, an immense increase in unemployment involving costly and unwise remedial measures, attempts to reduce wages in conformity with the cost of living and so increase the competitive power, fierce labour disputes arising therefrom, with expense to the State and community measured by hundreds of millions'.[35]

As this letter makes clear, Churchill did not believe that public works ('costly and unwise remedial measures') offered an effective solution. If he had not been overborne by the Bank and the Treasury, his own preference would have been for a more reflationary fiscal and monetary policy, with less emphasis upon the strict Treasury principles of a balanced budget, provision for the Sinking Fund, and high interest rates. But in all these respects Churchill was boxed in.

Churchill was not an incipient Keynesian. In his view the consequence of the strict deflationary policies of the Bank and the Treasury had been to overburden industry with taxation: one of the keys to industrial revival was therefore to cut taxes. But as this was an extremely difficult goal to achieve, Churchill hit on the alternative of redistributing the tax burden by derating industry and transferring the cost to the consumer. His derating scheme, announced with a great fanfare in the budget of April 1928, was undoubtedly an employment policy, though not intended as a panacea or quick solution to the problem. Churchill regarded Lloyd George's campaign for loan-financed public works as unsound and unconvincing.

To sum up Churchill's period at the Treasury, we can say that he carried into the age of Baldwin a residue of the politics of pre-war social reform. But he was far less successful in translating his ideas into practice than he had been from 1908 to 1911. A Conservative Chancellor of the Exchequer was not the same thing as a Liberal Home Secretary. But in any event Churchill's room for manœuvre was strictly limited after the major decisions announced in his first budget.

After the Conservative defeat of 1929, Churchill continued for a time as an Opposition spokesman on economic affairs. He attacked the Labour government for liberal and extravagant expenditure on the 'dole'. But in January 1931 he resigned from the Shadow Cabinet in order to lead the Tory diehards in their revolt against Baldwin over India. After this he seldom intervened in domestic affairs. In 1932–3 he was strongly critical of the National government for its failure to pursue a more energetic attack on unemployment, which had risen to three million in the slump. In March 1936 he suddenly rose one evening in the House of Commons to attack the government for imposing a Household Means Test on the unemployed:

When we were introducing the legislation in regard to Old Age Pensions the whole trend of it . . . was to consolidate the home, and give the old man and the old woman who sit by the ingle nook something to pay their way in the cottage home, something to give them the right to sit there and make it possible for their dependants and children to support them. It was a matter of weaving together the ties of the family. Now this household means test, which is so much considered at the present time and which has much to be said for it plausibly at first sight, is found to work a splitting function in regard to this home life, and to invite people in the same family, under the same roof, to ask, 'What are you doing, what are you bringing in?' and to assess in a meticulous and invidious fashion each other's relative contribution to the maintenance of the family circle.[36]

Apart from such rare interventions, Churchill had nothing to say of social policy after 1931. India, rearmament, and foreign policy occupied him to the exclusion of all else. The social surveys of the 1930s, and the evidence they supplied of poverty, malnutrition, and ill-health, passed him by. His view of social policy was increasingly retrospective. He regarded it, like the Empire, as a great British achievement in which he was proud to have played a part. Addressing social workers at the Edinburgh University Settlement in 1931 he declared that he had been 'directly concerned and mainly responsible for more social legislation than anybody else':

If he looked back on his early days at the Board of Trade, when they established the Labour Exchanges and the outline and foundation of unemployment insurance . . . and the legislation affecting coal mines, the regulation of trade disputes and the more humane treatment of the convict population in prisons—in all these matters he was thrown closely into touch with social workers, and learned to have a respect for those who made it part of their life and duty to champion the cause of the weak and the poor.'[37]

In later years Churchill was often to reiterate his claims to a prominent place in history as a social reformer. Churchill also maintained that social reform had fulfilled its Edwardian promise by strengthening and uniting the nation. In March 1936 Hitler marched his troops into the Rhineland. Six weeks later, Churchill spoke in the debate on Neville Chamberlain's budget. After complimenting Chamberlain on the success of his economic policy, he turned to the subject of the social services:

The Chancellor of the Exchequer spoke with pride the day before yesterday about the increasing growth of our social services. I share in that feeling. I will only say about our social services, with the creation and development of which I have been connected on and off for many years, that they must not be considered as a weakening of the strength of the nation. On the contrary, I believe they have greatly added to our strength; I believe they have given us that foundation which is essential to national unity, and without which it would be hopeless for us to make headway against the many perils which are moving towards us.[38]

In June 1939, shortly after the introduction of conscription, Churchill spoke with pride of the greatly improved physique of the new recruits by comparison with the soldiers of 1914: 'What a vindication all this has been for our social services and those who have worked for them! There is no more far-seeing investment for a nation than to put milk, food and education into young children.'[39]

To Churchill, social policy was less a problem for the future than a record of progress accomplished. This is one reason why, as Prime Minister from 1940 to 1945, he took for so long a negative view of the clamour for social reform. In August 1940 the War Cabinet set up a committee to discuss war aims. Churchill felt that there was little need for a declaration on domestic reform. The Tory party, he reflected, was 'the strength of the country: few things needed to be changed quickly and drastically; what conservatism, as envisaged by Disraeli, stood for was the gradual increase of amenities for an even larger number of people, who should enjoy the benefits previously reserved for the very few.'[40]

Churchill was also opposed to the discussion of post-war reforms in wartime for a more substantial reason, as he explained to the editor of the *Manchester Guardian* in March 1941:

The necessary thing was to win the war, and any statement on peace aims would either be a collection of platitudes or would be dangerous to the present unity. We did not want a statement that dealt with any of the hotly disputed things in domestic affairs, and it was going to be difficult at the end of the war not to have a breach on questions like property and socialism.[41]

Churchill tried hard to prevent the raising of peacetime issues in wartime. He rejected the proposals of the War Cabinet's Committee on War Aims. He forbade R. A. Butler to proceed with an Education Bill in wartime. He sacked Reith, the Minister of Works and Planning, for going too far to the left in his proposals for a central planning authority to control land use. But Churchill's negative approach produced a result that was entirely unexpected. In creating a policy vacuum he also created the opportunity for William Beveridge.

In his report of December 1942 Beveridge proposed a comprehensive system of social insurance supported by family allowances, a national health service, and policy to maintain employment. Both Churchill, a former Chancellor of the Exchequer, and Kingsley Wood, the current Chancellor, feared that the Beveridge proposals would cost too much and impose too heavy a burden on post-war industry. But so great was the groundswell of popular support for Beveridge that it would have been dangerous to reject it out of hand. More pressing, for Churchill, was the need to maintain the unity of the Coalition government. The Labour Party was profoundly pro-Beveridge and some compromise was essential if the leaders of the party were to remain in office. The War Cabinet accepted Churchill's ruling that there was to be no legislation in wartime. But the government accepted many of Beveridge's recommendations in principle, and undertook to prepare the plans for post-war legislation. In February 1943 Churchill complained to his Parliamentary Private Secretary, George Harvie-Watt, that the government had gone further towards accepting the Report than he would have done himself. Beveridge, he grumbled, was 'an awful windbag and a dreamer'. But Churchill quickly realized that if the Report could not be resisted the best course was to appropriate it. In March he went on the radio to announce that his government would prepare a 'Four-Year Plan' of post-war social reform. On the specific topic of social insurance he declared: 'You must rank me and my colleagues as strong partisans of national compulsory insurance for all classes for all purposes from the cradle to the grave.'[42]

Attlee was once asked why action on the Beveridge Report was postponed. He replied: 'I think the real reason was that Winston planned to come in as the first post-war Prime Minister and he thought it would be a nice thing to have the Beveridge Report to put through as an act of his Government.'[43] There is much evidence to support Attlee's contention. By the spring of 1945 the Coalition government had prepared draft bills for comprehensive social insurance, family allowances, and a national health service. This is not to say that a Churchill government after 1945 would have introduced a welfare state identical to that which Labour introduced. The health service would certainly have been organized differently. On the eve of the general election Churchill's 'Caretaker Government' made concessions to the doctors that would greatly have weakened the government's control over the administration of the scheme. Churchill forbade an announcement of the changes proposed.[44]

In the general election campaign Churchill again spoke of his 'Four-Year Plan', and much of his second broadcast was devoted to the subject of health. But his references to social policy were almost entirely eclipsed by anti-socialist scare tactics, of which the most preposterous was his warning that a Labour government would inevitably introduce 'some form of Gestapo' into Britain. Churchill plainly failed to appreciate the importance attached by the electorate to such issues as housing and employment policy: but he was, of course, physically and mentally exhausted—and under the illusion that he was going to win.

As Leader of the Opposition between 1945 and 1951 Churchill confined himself mainly to opportunist attacks on the economic record of the Attlee governments. But in social policy he invariably contested the Labour Party's claim to a monopoly of social concern, and insisted that the credit for devising the post-war welfare state should be given to the wartime Coalition, and not to the Attlee governments. In a House of Commons debate of 1949, he declared:

It really is remarkable that the accusation of being callous about unemployment or the welfare of the people should be launched against me, the author of the labour exchanges and the first Unemployment Insurance Act, and, as Conservative Chancellor of the Exchequer, of the Old Age Pensions Act being lowered from 70 to 65 and the institution of the Widows and Orphans Act. When the right hon. and learned Gentleman or anybody on those benches can show services to the working classes equal to those I have mentioned they will be more free to throw stones at others. All the benevolent and beneficial aspects of this Parliament were actually planned . . . by the National Coalition government of which I was the head and which rested on an overall Conservative majority in the House of 150.[45]

Churchill no doubt judged that a strong declaration of support for the welfare state was a necessary precondition of a Conservative return to power. But he did not envisage another round of expansion in the social services. Talking to R. A. Butler in 1950 he remarked that the politics of social policy were wearing thin, owing to the fact that the worker now had to pay: 'There will, in future, be much less politics in social reform though much perhaps in economic breakdown.'[46]

When Churchill returned to office in October 1951, the Conservative strategy was to retain the welfare state and full employment, while dismantling as fast as possible the Labour government's apparatus of economic controls. The case for continuity in welfare and employment policy was reinforced by the narrow margin of the Conservative victory. With an overall majority of 17 the government was secure enough in the House of Commons. But more votes had been cast for Labour than for the Conservatives: the party, it seemed, was still on trial.

Churchill's outlook in 1951 has been well described by .Kenneth Morgan: 'He was above all anxious to demonstrate his capacity for ordered, peaceful statesmanship, carrying the working class with him in patriotic endeavour, and to refute early accusations that he was an unreconciled class warrior.'[47] His first ministerial appointments appeared to signal a government of social conciliation. R. A. Butler was to be Chancellor of the Exchequer, Walter Monckton Minister of Labour, and Harold Macmillan Minister of Housing. But the position was complicated by the balance of payments crisis inherited from the previous government. This led the Treasury to press on the new government two radical courses of action that would have been deeply unpopular if implemented.

First the Treasury demanded swingeing economies in the health service. The Minister of Health, H. F. C. Crookshank, and the Secretary of State for Scotland, James Stuart, were eager to oblige with a long list of cuts and charges. Crookshank, for instance, wanted to charge patients a guinea a week for hospital maintenance, with graduated charges for hospital appliances. Fortunately for the government, these proposals never became public knowledge. They were whittled away in ministerial discussions and Crookshank was left with only minor economies to announce.[48] But even these aroused strong Conservative hostility, and Crookshank was plainly losing his grip on the House of Commons. In March 1952 Churchill was present in the House when Aneurin Bevan denounced the government for dismantling the National Health Service. He was answered, in a fine attacking speech, by the Conservative MP Iain Macleod. Two months later Churchill appointed Macleod as Minister of Health. It is not clear what Churchill's own view of the health service controversy was. He may have appointed Macleod for his debating powers rather than his commitment to the health service. But the consequence was that the NHS was now in the hands of a politician who believed in it, and entered a phase of comparative tranquillity.

In February 1952 the Bank of England and the Treasury tried to bounce the Cabinet into 'Operation Robot', a plan to make sterling convertible and float the pound. The Chancellor, R. A. Butler, was converted, and put the proposal to the Cabinet. The Robot plan was a radical attempt to cure the balance of payments problem by abandoning the managed economy and the Conservative commitment to full employment. As Butler explained to Churchill:

It will be seen that this new course in our external policy requires a complete rethinking of the whole of our economic policies which have been in operation, fundamentally with the support of all parties, during the past few years . . . the basic idea of internal stability of prices and employment, which has dominated economic policy for so long, will not be attainable.[49]

At the end of February the Cabinet was divided over the plan and Churchill was unable to make up his mind. A few days later Cherwell, a strong opponent of 'Robot', overheard Churchill musing on the attractions of 'setting the pound free'. He wrote to the Prime Minister:

I hope you will be under no misapprehension as to what all this means. It means that whenever our exports fail to pay for our imports, the value of the pound will fall until imports diminish . . . If this fails to close the gap the Bank Rate will have to be raised until more firms close down and dismiss their workers, leading to a further fall in demand for imported materials and food. If a 6% Bank Rate, 1 million unemployed and a 2s loaf are not enough, then there will have to be an 8% Bank Rate and a 3s loaf . . .

To rely frankly on high prices and unemployment to reduce imports would certainly put the Conservative Party out for a generation.[50]

After some hestitation, Churchill postponed a decision on 'Robot'. The plan faded away, and full employment was preserved.

After this, Churchill was free to pursue his policy of outflanking the

Labour Party by conciliating the trade unions and the working class. In July 1952 a delegation from the General Council of the Trades Union Congress went to Downing Street to put the case for a million workers covered by wages councils in the distributive and allied trades. According to the report in *The Times*:

Mr Churchill listened attentively to all that the TUC representatives had to say. In promising to give full consideration to their arguments he recalled that when he was President of the Board of Trade, over forty years ago, he was responsible for the legislation which established trade boards to protect conditions of employment for the lowest paid workers, and added that he had always taken a close personal interest in the subject.[51]

In June 1952 Churchill was alarmed when the unemployment total threatened to rise above half a million. This would have made the government vulnerable to a Labour accusation of abandoning full employment. Churchill therefore appointed a committee to propose the creation of more jobs through public works. As unemployment figures then fell without government intervention, no action was required and the committee lapsed.[52] But the episode demonstrates Churchill's sensitivity to the politics of employment.

His other main concern was the housing programme. As Leader of the Opposition, Churchill had strongly attacked the Labour government's record on housing, and promised that a Conservative government would improve on it. Then, in October 1950, the party conference had carried a resolution from the floor which pledged a future Conservative government to build a minimum of 300,000 houses a year. Churchill had promised that such a programme would be 'our first priority in time of peace'. During the summer of 1952 there was a prolonged dispute between the Treasury and Harold Macmillan over the scale of capital investment in the housing programme. Determined that the party must redeem its pledge of 300,000 houses a year, Churchill summed up in favour of Macmillan.[53]

Churchill lived too long, and played too many roles, to rank as a consistent figure in the history of social policy. From a review of his record some conclusions may be drawn. Firstly, the Edwardian period was plainly the most important, and demonstrates the significance of political leadership in translating ideas into policies. Without Asquith, Lloyd George, and Churchill, the welfare reforms of the period might never have been enacted. Secondly, the Edwardian period was not an isolated episode. Churchill's interest in social policy owed something to the rhetoric of Tory Democracy. To some extent, also, he carried forward his ideas of social reform into the 1920s. Thirdly, the social problems of the 1930s were a blank page in his mind. He was a negative influence in the Second World War and a reluctant convert to social reconstruction. The welfare state of 1911 had, in a sense, been his; but the welfare state of 1951 was thrust upon him.

Churchill was a great believer in historical continuity, and managed to invest his own career with a consistency it seldom possessed. But he was consistent in his general view of society. He formed early in life a strong sense of the value of social reform. It was the constructive alternative to socialism, and a source of unity and strength for Britain as a Great Power. Over a period of more than half a century his language on the subject was remarkably consistent, and we should not dismiss it as mere rhetoric. It was an outlook firmly grounded in Churchill's personality and social background. Contemporaries recognized in Churchill, at widely different periods, a paternal view of society. Charles Masterman, who saw him in action at the Board of Trade and the Home Office, wrote of him: 'He desired in England a state of things where a benign upper class dispensed benefits to an industrious, *bien pensant*, and grateful working class.' The press proprietor, Lord Riddell, whose diary records many conversations with Churchill, wrote in 1919: 'His conception of the State consists in a well-paid, well-nurtured people, managed and controlled by a Winston or Winstons.' Finally Herbert Morrison, Home Secretary in the wartime Coalition, remarked of him in 1942: 'He's full of sympathy you know, for the ordinary British man and woman, and doesn't like inflicting hardship on them. He's the old benevolent Tory squire, who does all he can for the people—provided always that they are good obedient people and loyally recognise his position, and theirs.'[54]

Where did this paternal disposition come from? It can hardly have come from Lord Randolph, whose Tory Democracy was nothing but cold calculation. It is unlikely to have come from Rosebery or Lloyd George or the other father figures of his youth. One explanation may be that it stemmed from his childhood relationship with his nanny, Mrs Anne Everest. The one person who loved and cared for him when he was a child, she brought out in him a chivalrous attitude towards his social inferiors. At the age of 19 he was outraged when she was dismissed from the employment of the Churchill family, and did his best to ensure that she was provided for in old age. Churchill was, of course, an aristocrat in his conviction that he was born to rule. But he saw it as the duty of his class, and hence of the state, to protect the weak and the poor. The strong and rebellious were an altogether different matter.

5

Churchill's Economic Ideas, 1900–1930

PETER CLARKE

A T the general election of 1922 Churchill stood as a Liberal, albeit one who had been closely enmeshed with the Conservative Party during the Coalition period. He was defeated and did not enter Parliament for two years. During this time he was clearly moving towards the right. The prospect of a Labour government clarified his attitude: 'The enthronement in office of a Socialist Government', he proclaimed, 'will be a serious national misfortune such as has usually befallen great states only on the morrow of defeat in war.'[1] He urged the Liberals to join hands with the Conservatives in opposing it. This was his own course during the MacDonald government's short term of office in 1924; and by the time another general election came that October Churchill had been adopted as a candidate by the local Conservatives for the safe seat of Epping. When the Conservatives swept to power under Baldwin, it was widely expected that Churchill would be asked to take office. In the course of an interview with the new Prime Minister, he was offered no less a position than that of Chancellor of the Exchequer. Afterwards he professed himself astonished: 'I should have liked to have answered, "Will the bloody duck swim?" but as it was a formal and important conversation I replied, "This fulfils my ambition."'[2]

Churchill threw himself into his work at the Treasury with characteristic energy. His father had, briefly and notoriously, served as Chancellor, and Lady Randolph had kept the robes 'in tissue paper and camphor' for forty years.[3] But there was more to it than sentiment. Although Churchill is often remembered in a highly selective way, and seldom for his economic views, his Chancellorship was no anomaly in his career. He came to it better prepared than predecessors like Lloyd George, Baldwin, or even Neville Chamberlain. His tenure of the Treasury was for the length of a full Parliament—more than twice as long as any other Chancellor since 1914. Nor was this period uneventful,

still less uncontroversial. It was under Churchill that 'the authorities'—
the Treasury and the Bank of England—made their last stand in
defence of a conception of sound finance which had been canonical
since Gladstone's day.

Churchill used his Romanes Lecture at Oxford in June 1930 to
explain what was at stake:

> The classical doctrines of economics have for nearly a century found their
> citadels in the Treasury and the Bank of England. In their pristine vigour
> these doctrines comprise among others the following tenets: Free imports, irre-
> spective of what other countries may do and heedless of the consequences to
> any particular native industry or interest. Ruthless direct taxation for the
> repayment of debt without regard to the effects of such taxation upon individ-
> uals or their enterprise or initiative. Rigorous economy in all forms of expendi-
> ture whether social or military. Stern assertion of the rights of the creditor,
> national or private, and full and effectual discharge of all liabilities. Profound
> distrust of State-stimulated industry in all its forms, or of State borrowing for
> the purpose of creating employment. Absolute reliance upon private enterprise,
> unfettered and unfavoured by the State.

Churchill justifiably identified these principles as 'part of one general
economic conception, amplified and expounded in all the Victorian
textbooks'. In 1930 he simply commented: 'we can clearly see that they
do not correspond to what is going on now.'[4] Yet his own work at the
Treasury, so recently concluded, had been bounded and constrained by
exactly these assumptions and conventions, precepts and postulates.

Even when Churchill had bucked against these stern rules, he had
never challenged their validity. Thus he had piously upheld in public
'those sound principles that you have to pay your debts, you have to
balance your Budget', even if in practice he had often been ready to
exploit dodges like raiding the Road Fund to help him paper over the
cracks which regularly opened up between his buoyant forecasts of revenue and his scanty provision for future expenditure.[5] In his determination to uphold Victorian values, he talked like Mr Gladstone but
behaved like Mr Micawber. Human nature, in short, kept breaking in.
The Treasury mandarins, with their abiding belief that the Treasury
'exists in order to curtail the natural consequences of human nature',[6]
knew that they had to be vigilant. Hence the concern of Sir Otto
Niemeyer, as Controller of Finance, that he 'did not want to have
elasticity' over the provision for the sinking fund: 'It is putting temptation in the way of the Treasury to which they had much better not be
subjected.'[7]

As Chancellor, then, Churchill's fervent prayer was to be delivered from temptation. James Grigg, his private secretary during this period, caught just the right note in saying that 'his financial administration as a whole displays a great hankering to be considered orthodox'.[8] This should be borne in mind when considering the two episodes where Churchill could, with some plausibility, be represented as an unwilling dupe of the authorities: the decision to return to the Gold Standard in 1925 and the promulgation of the Treasury view on loan-financed public works in 1929. In both cases Churchill became the mouthpiece for an unflinching reassertion of the established orthodoxy, in the face of provocative challenges from John Maynard Keynes. Indeed Keynesian economics could be seen as a vast elaboration of the fallacy embodied in the Treasury view of 1929 and as a triumphal monument erected on its dishonoured grave. On the Gold Standard, likewise, Keynes's line was apparently vindicated by events in such a way as to enshrine his lambent polemical tract, *The Economic Consequences of Mr Churchill*, as the received wisdom of the next generation about the folly of the decision taken in 1925.

'Why did he do such a silly thing?' was Keynes's manifestly tendentious way of framing the question, to which he gave the answer: 'Partly perhaps, because he has no instinctive judgement to prevent him from making mistakes; partly because, lacking this instinctive judgement, he was deafened by the clamorous voices of conventional finance; and, most of all, because he was gravely misled by his experts.'[9] Keynes thus helped fuel speculation as to whether the authorities had used their technical expertise to foist their own opinions upon an untutored Chancellor, whose acquiescence was nominal, reluctant, and rueful. There is, moreover, some fragmentary evidence which can be read as supporting such an interpretation of the return to Gold, and which certainly indicates the distaste which Churchill came to feel for the leading advocate of that policy, the Governor of the Bank of England, Montagu Norman.

'You and the Governor have managed this affair', Churchill told Niemeyer in 1925. 'Taken together I expect you know more about it than anyone else in the world.'[10] There is an unmistakable undercurrent in such remarks by Churchill, suggesting that he chafed against their superior wisdom. It was a mood which he echoed three years later, looking at the already unpromising results of the policy, in a comment to Grigg about 'the complacency of the Treasury and the Bank': 'They have caused an immense amount of misery and impoverishment by their rough and pedantic handling of the problem.'[11] As the 1931 crisis subsequently brewed, throwing doubt upon Britain's ability to remain on the Gold Standard, Churchill became alarmed that 'something terrible is going to happen financially', and added: 'I hope we shall hang Mantagu Norman if it does. I will certainly turn King's evidence against him.'[12] By 1948 Grigg could write in his memoirs: 'The legend has grown up and has obtained such currency that Winston himself has almost come to believe it, that the decision to go back to gold was the greatest mistake of his life, and that he was bounced into it in his green and early days by an unholy conspiracy between the officials of the Treasury and the Bank of England.'[13] No doubt Grigg was aware of the sort of table talk which was apt to surface in the 1940s. 'The biggest blunder in his life had been the return to the gold standard', was how Lord Moran recorded Churchill in 1945. 'Montagu Norman had spread his blandishments before him till it was done, and had then left him severely alone.'[14]

If the bitterness of Churchill's subsequent disillusionment should not be ignored, however, nor should the possibility that it stemmed from the fervour with which he had embraced the illusion in the first place. Churchill could hardly plead ignorance of the fact that the Gold Standard and free trade interlocked as the international dimension of the system of sound finance to which he had always been committed. If he spoke of it as an orthodoxy, it was an orthodoxy which he had upheld with a peculiar degree of conviction. Indeed, if one is looking for consistency in his political career in the period up to 1930, it is to be found more clearly in his economic ideas than almost anywhere else.

The big issue in British politics in these years was tariffs. From the moment Joseph Chamberlain launched his tariff reform campaign in 1903, this became the main line of division between the Conservative and Liberal parties. The general elections of 1906 and 1923 were fought chiefly on this issue, giving the Conservatives their two biggest defeats, and in each case unifying and reviving the Liberal Party on the great sacrosanct principle of free trade. Whatever the other temperamental attractions of the Liberal Party for the young Churchill, it was in fact on the issue of free trade that he joined it in 1904; and it was only when tariff reform was effectively eliminated from the Conservative programme in 1924 that Churchill returned to the fold. 'I am still a free-trader and opposed to the protective taxation of food and to a general tariff', he declared in his campaign at Epping. 'The leader of the Conservative Party has declared that there is now no general tariff in the party programme, and that, in no circumstances, will they propose any protective taxation upon food.'[15] Churchill's prompt appointment to the Treasury signalled the party's betrayal (yet again) of its ostensible Chamberlainite commitment. Churchill's free trade principles, in short, amid the shifting sands of his other vicissitudes, formed a rock to which he clung.

Free trade was a noisy political slogan which rested on a frequently unspoken premise: the axiom of a perfectly flexible and self-righting free market. Hence the deep affinity between free trade and Treasury orthodoxy. Since the Treasury did not conceive its role in terms of general economic responsibilities but rather of particular tasks in the field of public finance, the way the economy worked was not seen as its problem. Instead the role of 'the authorities' was seen as that of servicing a self-acting system. As long as the principles of sound finance were upheld, there was no need for the Treasury to become involved in a task of economic management for which it was unsuited. It maintained a self-denying ordinance against assuming the functions of an economic ministry.

In the self-acting system, the Gold Standard underpinned free trade, by regulating the level of prices through the instrument of bank rate. The Bank of England was left with only the barest margin of room for manœuvre in operating a domestic credit policy dictated by its defence of sterling. Well might Lord Bradbury, with the authority of a former Permanent Secretary to the Treasury, commend this system on the ground that it was 'knave-proof'. The merit of a knave-proof system was precisely that it was self-acting and that government was insulated from its economic consequences. One result was that, except when the politically sensitive nerve of free trade was exposed, the way the system worked was usually taken for granted. These were mysteries discussed, if at all, only by a select group of initiates.[16]

When the Macmillan Committee on Finance and Industry was sitting in 1930, however, it had the temerity to ask the Governor of the Bank of England for an account of how the Gold Standard actually worked. In his evidence Norman stressed the international aspect: the way that a depletion of the Bank's gold reserves would prompt it to take remedial action by raising the discount rate and thereby attracting funds to London to defend the parity of the pound sterling. But the unanswered question concerned the impact of dear money on the real economy at home. As a member of the committee, Keynes had already given it an exposition of 'what I believed to be the orthodox theory of the Bank Rate, the theory that I thought all authorities would accept'.[17] Yet Norman's insistence that the domestic impact of dear money was 'much more psychological than real'[18] blandly evaded the issue. A fascinating passage in the Committee's published evidence therefore consists of Keynes articulating the orthodox theory for the benefit of a far from articulate Governor of the Bank of England.

What I thought was the more or less accepted theory of Bank Rate was that it works in two ways. It has the effect on the international situation that has been described to-day, and its virtue really is in its having an important effect on the internal situation. The method of its operation on the internal situation is that the higher Bank Rate would mean curtailment of credit, that the curtailment of credit would diminish enterprise and cause unemployment, and that the unemployment would tend to bring down wages and costs of production generally. We should then be able to increase our exports, with the result that the high Bank Rate which was put on to check foreign lending would no longer be necessary . . . The virtue of Bank Rate is that, while it would have a quick effect on the international situation, it would also have a slow effect on the internal position, by setting up tendencies to bring about a new level of money costs of production, so as to enable us to have more nearly that level of exports which the international position requires of us.

Challenged by Keynes as to whether he accepted this, Norman replied: 'I should imagine that, as you have stated it, that is the orthodox theory, taking a long view, and as such I should subscribe to it—I could not dispute it with you.'[19] Now this was an unimpressive display on the part of one of the leading experts, whose advice the Chancellor had naturally treated with considerable respect. The fact that Norman was almost dumb when asked to justify the time-honoured orthodoxy may suggest that Churchill was completely blind in taking it on trust.

How seriously, then, can we take Churchill's commitment to free trade? Did he, as a mere working politician whose fame lies elsewhere, show any appreciation of the way that bank rate and the Gold Standard integrated free trade into the self-acting 'knave-proof' model of the economy? Is there any evidence that he knew what he was talking about?

One place to look is in Churchill's pre-First World War speeches. The basic case for free trade, which he frequently developed, was that an open economy enforced cheapness, and thereby efficiency, through competition. This was obviously to the advantage of those capitalists who were free to shift their capital around the world, looking for the best return. But free trade, so Liberals tirelessly reiterated, was also to the advantage of the working class in so far as they were all consumers. Tariffs, on the other hand, made an appeal to them in so far as they were producers for markets threatened by foreign competition. Thus the Liberal cliché, 'Hands off the people's food', was countered by the Conservative cliché, 'Tariff Reform means work for all'.

These were familiar arguments which Churchill knew backwards. He knew that there were two answers to the protectionists' case for the producer. One was simple—'The greatest producer is the greatest consumer'—and could be applied particularly to a great export trade like cotton.[20] The other was more complex and rested on assumptions which were seldom articulated. It was, however, seen as the knockdown argument in favour of the play of market forces because it contended that free trade too meant work for all—and in better jobs, with cheap bread thrown in. Employment could not, of course, be guaranteed within a particular fossilized industrial structure; instead, sunrise industries were set free to respond to the signals and incentives of the market. Tariffs, Churchill proclaimed in 1909, 'have warped and restricted the growth of the industries of the nations who have adopted them'.[21] The efficient, competitive, dynamic enterprises which thrived under free trade were thus a better source of employment than the sclerotic industries which depended on protection.

Such contentions had been present in Churchill's speeches since the early days of the tariff reform controversy, when he was first brought to consider his position as a Conservative MP. It is worth quoting at some length the digression he made in a speech in the House of Commons on the Sugar Convention Bill in 1903.

Old countries in which there are no new discoveries—of mines, mineral oil, or water power—must look not so much to their basic industries for the development and expansion of their trade as to the more complicated and secondary processes of manufacture. As the primary industries are brought more and more into competition with the resources of new countries, possessing perhaps greater natural facilities, it will undoubtedly be necessary for the older countries gradually to move on to the more complicated and secondary processes of manufacture, and in the higher grades of manufacture to obtain the expansion of their trade which they need . . . So far as it is effective, I think we ought to contemplate that evolution and the transference of our people from being, as it were, hewers of wood and drawers of water to the more elaborate processes of manufacture with unmixed satisfaction.

It is not the sophistication of this speech which is significant so much as its unsophistication. For Churchill had prefaced his little essay on the division of labour, broaching insights which a less original mind might have gleaned second-hand from Adam Smith, with the remark: 'I have a theory which I should very much like to have examined by competent persons.'[22] But if he was innocently re-inventing the wheel, it is revealing that he insisted not only on making the basic reasoning his own but also on taking a routine matter of party controversy back to first principles. In subsequently developing his case, moreover, Churchilll became more practised in seizing on the essential point in a way that was perfectly in tune with the conventional wisdom of the economists of his day.

The thinking is certainly similar to that of Alfred Marshall, whose argument it was that Britain's industrial leadership was reinforced by free trade. Marshall maintained that foreign trade gave an opportunity 'for measuring the skill with which each nation applies her industry to producing great results with small manual effort; or, in other words, in making commodities cheap relatively to effort, and effort dear relatively to commodities'. The moral for England was obvious: as a means of 'increasing the alertness of her industrial population in general, and her manufacturers in particular', there was 'no device to be compared in efficiency with the plan of keeping her markets open to the new products of other nations'.[23] Likewise, Churchill maintained, it was under free trade, 'where readjustment of labour and redistribution of capital are more easy, where enterprise is more varied and elastic', that the best results could be expected.[24] Thus, whatever might be true for individuals, the 'dumping' of imported goods did not cause unemployment for the nation as a whole but applied the spur of competition. 'At every step our industries move forward into those higher grades where labour is more skilled, more varied, more generously rewarded, and by proficiency in which an old country can alone maintain that "leadership" in respect to quality vital to her industrial strength.'[25]

In his attachment to free trade throughout this period, Churchill betrayed his characteristic mind-set in generalizing his position into a number of axioms, lucidly restated in a simple and sonorous form. He held that free trade 'enshrines certain central truths, economic truths, and, I think, moral truths'.[26] The belief that it preserved the state from corruption consorted happily with the belief that it preserved the economy from monopoly. British industries stood 'upon the solid ground of merit and efficiency', and the intervention of government—'particularly party Government'—was to be deplored.[27] Not only 'taught by well-established theory' but also 'confirmed by long and mature experience',[28] free trade was a cosmopolitan doctrine fortfiied by the object lesson of British economic predominance. Churchill had swallowed the free trade bolus whole.

The truths of free trade, which Churchill had assimilated, thus took on a universal and timeless quality. When he returned, at a by-election in 1908, to defend the Manchester seat that he had held since the 1906 general election, he staked out his claims with confidence.

Have the essential truths of economics undergone any modification in the interval? Trade is still exchange. Imports are still paid for by exports. There can be no exportation without a corresponding importation. There can be no increased imports without a corresponding increase in exports. In the transactions of States scarcely any money passes. The goods which are bought and sold between great Powers are not paid for in money. They are exchanged one with the other. And if England buys from America or Germany more than she has intended to buy, having regard to our own productions, instantly there is a cause for the shipments of bullion, and bullion is shipped to supply the deficiency. Then the Bank rate is put up in order to prevent the movements of bullion, and the rise of the Bank rate immediately corrects and arrests the very trade which has given rise to the disparity.—(Hear, Hear).

That is the known established theory of international trade, and everyone knows, every single business man knows, it works delicately, automatically, universally, and instantaneously. It is the same now as in January, 1906, and it will be the same as it is in 1908 when the year 2000 has dawned upon the world. As long as men trade from one nation to another and are grouped in national communities you will find the differences of free trading are adjusted almost instantaneously by shipments of bullion corrected by an alteration in the Bank rate.[29]

This account is embalmed in the prelapsarian assumptions of a world that ended in 1914. The young President of the Board of Trade did not have to face the awkward question which baffled the Governor of the Bank of England in 1930, about *how* 'the rise of the Bank rate immediately corrects and arrests the very trade which has given rise to the disparity'. True, Churchill did not anticipate the explication of the *modus operandi* of bank rate which Keynes was to specify, to universal applause at his brilliance, some twenty years later. But, judged by the standards of his own time, Churchill surely manifested an impressive ability to grasp the issues at stake. No wonder that, having mastered the essential workings of this system, he remained enraptured by the 'beautiful precision' with which free trade and the Gold Standard complemented each other—or had done, as he put it subsequently, 'not in this disastrous century but in the last'.[30]

As Chancellor, Churchill was pressed at an early stage to put Britain back on the Gold Standard, which had been effectively suspended since 1914. If Norman and Niemeyer were the most resolute advocates of this step, Keynes emerged as, in Churchill's words, 'the most distinguished and able exponent of the opposition to the return to gold'.[31] Not only were his published articles, notably in the Liberal weekly paper, the *Nation*, studied by the Chancellor, but as an ex-Treasury man Keynes was also brought into the private discussions that took place. The Chancellor would, Norman acknowledged, meet criticism whatever he did. If he decided to return to Gold, he would be abused 'by the ignorant, the gamblers and the antiquated Industrialists', but if he refused he would be abused 'by the instructed and by posterity'.[32] In fact, what happened was almost the opposite. When Churchill announced the return to Gold in 1925 he met with little immediate criticism; the judgement of posterity, on the whole, has been that it was an error.

For going back to Gold at the pre-war parity of $4.86 meant that sterling was revalued upwards; British exports consequently cost more in foreign markets; and the difficulties of industry were increased accordingly. It became necessary to reduce domestic costs, most obviously by reducing wages; and it was a proposal to cut wages in the coal industry which led to the miners' strike in 1926. Moreover, since there was in practice no significant decrease in money wages in the late 1920s, costs were stuck at a high level; with high prices, exports were relatively low; with low output, unemployment remained high. A perverse logic spelt out this anomaly. Admittedly, the difficulties which ensued cannot simply be attributed to the Gold Standard, but this undoubtedly introduced an unhelpful new constraint into an existing problem.

Though Churchill identified himself strongly in public with the return to Gold, in private he frankly recognized the difficulties which ensued. Paul Addison has brought this out nicely in his chapter in this volume (Chapter 4), quoting Churchill's reproach to Niemeyer and Norman in 1927 over 'bad trade, hard times, an immense increase in unemployment'—problems which must have been especially galling for the Chancellor since he could claim to have anticipated such hazards in

1925. Indeed he had interrogated his official advisers with considerable acumen along such lines before taking the fateful decision. In the conditions of the 1920s, with the collapse of Britain's export staples, Churchill saw that the interests of industry and finance did not axiomatically coincide. He accused the authorities of, as he put it, not facing 'the profound significance of what Mr Keynes called "the paradox of unemployment amidst dearth." The Governor shows himself perfectly happy in the spectacle of Britain possessing the finest credit in the world simultaneously with a million and a quarter unemployed.'[33] Churchill's difficulty was that the system he had taken on trust for twenty years now seemed incapable of delivering the goods, putting all the old controversies in a different light. In his pre-1914 public speeches on the free trade platform, Churchill had always been able to raise a laugh with a reference to '60 years of living ruined'.[34] By 1925, in private at any rate, he adopted a less triumphalist and more rueful register in his rhetoric: 'I would rather see Finance less proud and Industry more content.'[35]

There is a puzzle in reconciling the private musings of the old freetrader with the public stance of the new Chancellor. Fresh in office, only recently restored to the Conservative fold, not anxious to go on his travels again, and lacking any formal expertise in economics, perhaps Churchill could hardly be expected to override the formidably marshalled advice of his best officials. To do so, moreover, would have challenged not only 'the authorities' but his own deeply internalized convictions. For he and his advisers were steeped in the same moral and intellectual presumptions, which reinforced their propensity to believe that the orthodox arguments were still right—and no less right for being inconvenient or unpalatable or unpopular. The politics of blood, toil, tears, and sweat were never temperamentally alien to Churchill, and in 1925 a first draft was made upon toil and sweat.

The Gold Standard was therefore imbued with the rectitude of hairshirt economics. The gist of Keynes's criticism of Gold was that it was a rigid link between the City and Wall Street. When Churchill had to defend his decision in the Commons, he seized on this as a virtue, claiming that the Gold Standard would not shackle Britain to the United States; the Government, he declared, had simply decided 'to shackle themselves to reality'.[36] Not only were these still economic truths, they were also still moral truths. Churchill contrasted his policy with that of using currency depreciation 'to reduce the wages of the working classes, almost without their being aware of it, to what is considered the requisite point by the currency manipulator'. This was likened to a grocer taking an ounce off the pound. As an economic analogy, with its implication of a sort of cheese standard, this was imprecise; but as an imputation of sharp practice it hit home. Such methods were 'altogether out of harmony with the sound and rugged principles on which British financial policy has been built up'. Advocates of the Gold Standard, by contrast, held that 'whatever our troubles may be, it is much better that all classes should face them with open eyes, that they should know the truth about what is taking place'.[37]

Churchill's fitfully iconoclastic interlocution of his advisers needs to be read in context rather than taken innocently at face value. 'Mr Churchill's Exercise' of 25 January 1925 is a substantial document which bears the unmistakable imprint of the Chancellor's own style.[38] When he said that 'we should be prepared to answer any criticisms which may be subsequently made upon our policy', he was manifesting his usual inveterate wish to thrash out all the difficulties, by provoking debate and discussion and argument. 'In setting down these ideas and questionings,' he concluded, 'I do not wish it to be inferred that I have arrived at any conclusions adverse to the re-establishment of the Gold Standard.' He was after 'good and effective answers to the kind of case which I have, largely as an exercise, indicated in this note'. Churchill thus sought to broaden the ambit of the debate, with a series of sceptical remarks. 'Why then should we not continue on the basis of a "managed" finance?' he asked. 'What risks shall we run? What evils shall we encounter?'

What is clear is that the tone of this paper lacks reverence. Norman's reply approached these awesome matters in an altogether different spirit, captured in his apophthegm: 'The Gold Standard is the best "Governor" that can be devised for a world that is still human, rather than divine.'[39] Of course, Churchill's disclaimer that 'I am ready and anxious to be convinced as far as my limited comprehension of these extremely technical matters will permit', is barbed with irony. There was a playfulness in the Chancellor's approach which the Governor found quite unbefitting. The contrast between them was one of style, and this was quite enough to provoke mutual suspicion. Norman cultivated an air of mystery, typified by his habit of booking his frequent transatlantic passages under the name of his secretary, Skinner. His reiterated assertions about the 'necessity' of the Gold Standard concealed everything except how much he took for granted. Churchill spoke feelingly when he said in the Commons that Keynes 'is a master of every aspect of this question, and discusses it with the utmost fluency and effectiveness upon all occasions, seasonable and unseasonable alike'.[40] If only the taciturn Governor had weighed in like this! Churchill always rebelled at being told by the experts; instead he needed to be persuaded by them. In Chapter 20 of this volume, Lord Carver makes a similar point about Churchill's attitude to Wavell during the Second World War. Like Wavell, Norman disdained to enter the rough-and-tumble style of diabolical advocacy which Churchill relished as both a competitive game and a dialectical approach to the truth. Churchill vented his frustration, first with mockery and later with suspicion of 'that man Skinner'. It was a temperamental aversion rather than a doctrinal disagreement which set them apart—an incompatibility over how policy should be made as much as over the policy itself.

Such personal complications did not arise over the formulation of the Treasury view in 1929. By the Niemeyer had moved to the Bank of England, and Churchill relied on an inner circle of advisers who were well versed in his habits. Sir Richard Hopkins, as Niemeyer's successor, was emollient and pragmatic; but the two civil servants with whom Churchill worked most directly—James Grigg and Frederick Leith-Ross—were cut from the same cloth, as rather testy and tough-minded defenders of Gladstonian Liberalism. This ideological heritage naturally gave them some common ground with Churchill, and both of them were ready to stand up to him in face-to-face discussions, with a confidence that they shared many basic premises. The nearest thing to a professional economist in the Treasury was R. G. Hawtrey, who was customarily regarded as rather a joke. While it is easy to see that the herbivorous Hawtrey was no match for fully-fledged carnivores like Niemeyer and Leith-Ross, he discovered an unexpected patron, as Grigg's cameo acknowledges.

Mr Churchill, when he became Chancellor, used to accuse us of giving Hawtrey too little scope. I remember his demanding from time to time that the learned man should be released from the dungeon in which we were said to have immured him, have the chains struck off and the straw brushed from his hair and clothes and be admitted to the light and warmth of an argument in the Treasury board room with the greatest living master of argument.[41]

The restless autodidact was as determined as ever to get to the bottom of the argument when, as the 1929 general election approached, the issue of loan-financed public works came to the top of the political agenda. When Keynes had broached such proposals in Beaverbrook's *Evening Standard*—the same paper in which Keynes had publicized his opposition to the return to Gold—he again tried to drive a wedge between Churchill and his advisers. 'I do not believe that the Chancellor of the Exchequer is naturally unsympathetic to this outlook', he wrote. 'But he has succumbed, just as Mr Snowden did before him, to the timidities and mental confusions of the so-called "sound finance" which established as an end to be worshipped what should only be pursued so long as it is successful as a means to the creation of wealth and the useful employment of men and things.'[42] The response among the Chancellor's guardians also had a familiar ring to it. 'I am sorry to see that Keynes is renewing the Press propaganda which has done him little credit as a politican and considerable harm as an economist', Leith-Ross commented. If Churchill had the benefit of forthright and hard-headed advice from this quarter, he also had the views of Hawtrey to guide him. What the unworldly Hawtrey did was to enclose a copy of an article which he had published in the academic journal *Economica* in 1925, arguing on highly theoretical grounds that, unless there were an inflationary expansion of credit, government borrowing was incapable of expanding aggregate employment.[43]

The whole argument came to a head at the beginning of 1929, culminating in the statement of the Treasury view. This was not, however, as has usually been supposed, a riposte to the pledge to reduce unemployment which Lloyd George gave in March 1929, but a response initially to an abortive ploy with the Conservative government in the previous month. A scheme for public works was put forward to the Cabinet by the unlikely figure of the Home Secretary, Sir William Joynson Hicks. He enlisted the heavyweight support of the Minister of Labour, Sir Arthur Steel Maitland, who asked whether 'after 8 years of financial orthodoxy and 8 years of unabating unemployment, ought we not to ask for a reasoned proof for some foundations of belief that the financial policy by which we guide our steps is right?'[44] But such backsliding was swiftly rebutted by the Chancellor. 'That policy has been pursued by all British Governments,' he told the Cabinet; 'and it seems to me very unlikely that a Conservative Government would be well advised in abandoning it or throwing doubts upon it.'[45] With Baldwin's backing, this was a sufficiently cogent party-political response to scotch the dissenters. 'We should not try to compete with L.G.,' was how Churchill put it in private, 'but take our stand on sound finance.'[46]

More remarkably, the intellectual conviction which Churchill could still summon for this task is shown by the way he personally took charge of how the Treasury case was mounted. Assisted by Grigg, Leith-Ross, and Hopkins, he put 'the orthodox argument against a policy of large Government loan expenditure to give increased employment' through draft after draft, until it was couched in terms with which he was happy. Though Hawtrey himself was away on a sabbatical at Harvard, Grigg was at Churchill's elbow to remind him that 'Hawtrey (in 1925) wrote an article (of extreme obscurity) proving that relief works were an absolute delusion unless they were accompanied by an expansion of banking credit, which would relieve unemployment without any intervening schemes'. So back numbers of *Economica* had to be ferreted out to appease the Chancellor's ingenuous thirst for wisdom in his refresher course in current economic theory. This was Churchill's finest hour in his self-education in economics; and, though a little learning may be a dangerous thing, it was enough to convince him that he had an irrefutable case. Just as he later became the amateur *par excellence* in dealing with the interpretation of decrypts during the Second World War (as Sir Harry Hinsley shows in this volume, Chapter 23), so Churchill put his own stamp upon the canons of sound finance in 1929. 'First set out the orthodox view as already drafted by me', he instructed Grigg, in a note on how the structure of the argument should be expounded for publication.[47]

The surviving evidence in the Treasury papers establishes Churchill's personal role in this controversy, which dominated the final weeks of the Baldwin government. It was Churchill's own strategy to take the high ground against public works and loan expenditure. Hence the use of his last budget speech for a pre-emptive declaration against their efficacy:[48]

. . . for the purpose of curing unemployment the results have certainly been disappointing. They are, in fact, so meagre as to lend considerable colour to the orthodox Treasury doctrine which has steadfastly held that, whatever might be the political or social advantages, very little additional employment and no permanent additional employment can in fact and as a general rule be created by State borrowing and State expenditure.

Like the defence of the Gold Standard, the Treasury view was thus thoroughly Churchillian: saturated with his own values, reasoning, and rhetoric. If it was explicitly identified as an orthodoxy, this was not with any undeclared iconoclastic intent of subverting its authority. It represented an orthodoxy of sound finance to which Churchill had been committed for more than a quarter of a century and of which he had opted to make himself the most prominent spokesman. It would be a mistake to underestimate the appeal of *system* to a mind which Professor F. A. Lindemann perceptively characterized as pre-eminently synthetic (a remark recorded by Professor R. V. Jones in this volume, Chapter 24). Churchill was thus susceptible to the allure of financial orthodoxy through intellectual conviction and moral commitment, reinforced by long habit and a craving for consistency.

Moreover, this orthodoxy underpinned the Victorian notion of Britain's greatness. For Britain's peculiarity as a Great Power, as Paul Kennedy's impressive analysis has put it, lay in the conjunction of three factors: her naval strength, her imperial possessions, and her financial hegemony.[49] Through two stints as First Lord of the Admiralty, and through two World Wars, Churchill devoted the lion's share of his time and energies to upholding these interlocking causes, making it conspicuously clear in the process that he had no intention of presiding over the liquidation of the British Empire. What is seldom recognized is that he was fighting the same unrepentant, unreconstructed, unrelenting rearguard action as Chancellor, in an ultimately unavailing assertion of these atavistic conceptions.

Churchill was no doctrinaire, and in the end he had to concede that his cherished economic principles had been worsted by brute facts. His Chancellorship was the final trial of the self-acting system, restored to full working order. Free trade was kept alive; the Gold Standard was resurrected; and the authorities maintained a hands-off, arm's length conception of their role. If the resolute application of *laissez-faire* principles had been all that was needed, this surely should have done the trick. The Chancellor fought down his doubts over whether the grand strategy as working—in 1928 he had let slip some angry remarks about the Gold Standard in the course of a Cabinet meeting[50]—only to reaffirm the Treasury view in double-or-quit style in 1929. But having loyally defended this policy while he remained in office, Churchill reluctantly surrendered to the evidence of his own eyes as the British economy went from bad to worse. By 1931 Britain not only suffered from massive unemployment but was forced off the Gold Standard in a way that could not solely be attributed to the incompetence of the second Labour government.

During the crisis, Churchill signed off as a free-trader. A year previously, in the 1930 Romanes Lecture, he had publicly voiced his recognition that in the post-war period his own long-standing precepts were no longer tenable and that party politics were entering a new era. 'It is no longer a case of one party fighting another, nor of one set of politicians scoring off another', he stated. 'It is the case of successive governments facing economic problems, and being judged by their success or failure in the duel.' He rightly identified the problem, as one to which his whole training in pre-war party politics was fundamentally irrelevant. 'The compass has been damaged', he said. 'The charts are out of date.'[51] By the 1930s, as the faithful Grigg put it, 'we could see that the two great stabilizing forces of the nineteenth century had lost their influence—the British Navy and the International Gold Standard worked by and through the Bank of England and the City of London'.[52] In this context two further implications about Churchill's subsequent career seem pertinent: first, that he thereafter became a disillusioned agnostic in his economic ideas, dealing with issues of economic policy in a purely pragmatic way; finally, that his wild attempt to save the British Raj, which almost sank his career for good, was symptomatic of his disorientation in a world where the pillars were tumbling—not least that of orthodox sound finance, which had for so long squared moral and economic truths with internationalism and British imperial hegemony.

6

Churchill and Lloyd George

JOHN GRIGG

FEW would deny that Winston Churchill and David Lloyd George were the two outstanding British politicians of the first half of the twentieth century. Each led the nation to victory in a world war, and each was manifestly endowed with genius (a term of art impossible to define but generally understood). Each had a mind of extraordinary quickness and scope, and each was possessed of phenomenal vitality. Both men, while making abundant use of other people's ideas, had fertile imaginations and original perceptions of their own; and both habitually expressed themselves in language that was sparklingly memorable. Both had such self-confidence and such a strong sense of their own historic uniqueness, combined with such an exalted view of the national interest, that they tended to be impatient of the restraints of party. Both therefore were regarded with suspicion by conventional politicians, and had to endure frustrating periods of isolation.

It would be interesting enough to compare two such men if they had had little or nothing to do with each other. But in fact their careers overlapped and interacted to a large degree. During the early years of the twentieth century they formed a partnership as radical reformers which decisively affected the course of British history at home. During the First World War and its immediate aftermath they were, for most of the time, colleagues whose relations with each other, whether they were agreeing or disagreeing, were always of special importance. Even in the Second World War, though Lloyd George was then an old man with waning powers, there were moments when they seemed once again to be joint, or alternative, men of destiny.

On the face of it their backgrounds could hardly have been more different, and all too much has been made of the contrast between Churchill, the child of privilege born in Blenheim Palace, and Lloyd George, the 'cottage-bred boy' from obscure origins in North Wales. In many ways this contrast is more apparent than real. True, Churchill inherited a famous name whereas Lloyd George had to make his famous; true, Churchill's formal education lasted several years longer than Lloyd George's. But it does not follow that Churchill had overwhelming advantages that Lloyd George lacked. If Churchill belonged from birth to a political élite, so also did Lloyd George. Churchill's, of course, was the traditional, hereditary ruling class of the country, but Lloyd George's was no less auspicious for a child of political talent: it was the cultured, Welsh-speaking Nonconformist élite of Wales, whose new-found dominance in the Principality, and consequent potential as a force in UK politics, more or less coincided with his arrival in the world.

As for education, Lloyd George entered manhood no less well trained intellectually than Churchill: probably better. His time at the village school at Llanystumdwy, followed by his training as a lawyer, both theoretical and practical, did at least as much for him as Churchill's experience at his preparatory school and at Harrow. In particular, Lloyd George was certainly the better read of the two, having read as a child works of history which Churchill did not read until he was a young officer in India, and having become familiar with classics of English literature, notably the works of Dickens, which Churchill read only much later, if at all.

In one respect Lloyd George was definitely the more privileged. Though his father died when he was an infant, he found a supremely effective father-substitute in his maternal uncle, Richard Lloyd, the philosophical, Hans Sachs-like master-cobbler of Llanystumdwy. 'Uncle Lloyd' recognized the boy's prodigious talent and devoted himself to cherishing it, while at the same time Lloyd George's widowed mother looked after him with loving care. Churchill, on the other hand, was a neglected child, whose father was remote and unsympathetic even before a terrible illness warped his mind (while bringing him to a premature death), and whose mother was feckless and self-centred. In truth Churchill was almost the equivalent of an orphan, whereas Lloyd George in his early years had the benefit of an exceptionally good home, with all the human warmth and encouragement he needed, and stimulus for his mind as well.

In any case, whatever their differences of background, they had one all-important characteristic in common. This was a driving, unlimited ambition to rule, which was just as strong in the cottage-bred as in the palace-born boy. Lloyd George's ambition was never (as some still appear to believe) confined to Wales. His first newspaper article, written at the age of 17, was not on any provincial theme but on Lord Salisbury's foreign policy,[1] and when he first saw the House of Commons the following year he dreamt of becoming its master.[2] He became a household name in Wales as a champion of Welsh national causes while he was still a young attorney, more especially through his spectacular legal triumph in asserting the posthumous rights of a Nonconformist quarryman against a bigoted Anglican parson. This helped to secure his election to Parliament in 1890 at the early age of 27. As a back-bencher he continued to exploit Nonconformist issues such as disestablishment and temperance, as well as other Welsh issues, with the utmost vigour, partly because he genuinely believed in them, but above all because they gave him the leverage he needed in British politics. Before long he was leader of the Welsh group of Liberal MPs in fact if not (by his own choice) in name, while he was also becoming accepted as a nation-wide political leader of Nonconformity and of the movement for more radical social reform. In 1899–1902 he became a household name throughout the whole country, and even further afield, as a result of his courageous and principled stand against the Boer War. As the long period of Conservative rule neared its end in the early years of the new century, it was clear that he would have to be included in the next Liberal government, and many rightly assumed that he would be appointed straight to the Cabinet.

Meanwhile Churchill, nearly twelve years his junior, had entered Parliament in 1900 as a Conservative, at much the same age that Lloyd George had first been elected. Churchill, too, had been made a national figure by the war in South Africa, as the hero of a story-book escape from Boer captivity. In 1901 the two men met for the first time, after Churchill's maiden speech in the House of Commons on 18 February, which followed one by Lloyd George. Churchill himself describes the encounter: 'After compliments he [Lloyd George] said "Judging from your sentiments, you are standing against the Light". I replied "You take a singularly detached view of the British Empire". Thus began an association which has persisted through many vicissitudes.'[3]

The association began in earnest three years later, when Churchill left the Conservative Party and joined the Liberals, ostensibly on the issue of free trade (Joseph Chamberlain having split the Conservatives by launching his campaign for tariffs with Imperial preference). In the way Churchill chose to execute his change of sides in Parliament he emphasized a specific intention to ally himself with Lloyd George:

. . . he entered the Chamber [on 31 May 1904] . . . stood for a moment at the Bar, looked briefly at both the Government and Opposition benches and strode swiftly up the aisle. He bowed to the Speaker and turned sharply to the right to the Liberal benches. He sat down next to Lloyd George . . .[4]

Within a week the two men were together addressing a mass meeting of Liberals at Alexandra Palace, and the following October Churchill visited Lloyd George's constituency, where he described his host as 'the best fighting general in the Liberal army'.[5]

When the Liberals returned to power at the end of 1905 Lloyd George was in the Cabinet as President of the Board of Trade, and Churchill, though the junior minister at the Colonial Office, was the department's spokesman in the Commons because the Secretary of State (Lord Elgin) was a peer. In 1908, when H. H. Asquith succeeded Sir Henry Campbell-Bannerman as Prime Minister, Lloyd George became Chancellor of the Exchequer and Churchill took his place at the Board of Trade, so joining the Cabinet. The same year Churchill married Clementine Hozier, and their wedding at St Margaret's, Westminster, was carefully choreographed with a view to politics. The Tory free-trader, Lord Hugh Cecil, was best man; Lloyd George's friend, Bishop Edwards of St Asaph, conducted the service; and Lloyd George himself signed the register—reporting afterwards that Churchill had talked politics to him in the vestry.[6] His present to the couple was a silver fruit basket, for which Churchill thanked him in fulsome terms, saying: 'It will always be preserved in my family as the gift of a remarkable man & as the symbol of a memorable political association.'[7] (In fact, it seems to have been lost.[8])

During the prolonged fight with the Lords over Lloyd George's 1909 budget Churchill was the Chancellor's most active and vocal ally, assuming the presidency of the Budget League and vying with him in colourful rhetoric at the Lords' expense. In 1911 Churchill was responsible for Part II of Lloyd George's National Insurance Act, which dealt with unemployment, while the Chancellor himself conducted all the negotiations and Parliamentary business relating to Part I, which established a system of health insurance. This marked the culmination of their partnership as social reformers, and it is a suitable moment to pause and consider how close their 'association' really was.

That they admired each other is beyond question, and for a time at any rate the balance of admiration was very much on Churchill's side. When he joined the Liberals he regarded Lloyd George as his mentor, because of the Welshman's greater experience, his virtuosity as a

Parliamentary and platform orator, and his proved political flair. But even then Churchill regarded Lloyd George more, perhaps, as an elder brother than as a father-figure. The age difference between them was not all that wide, and the analogy is apt for another reason: both men were influenced and inspired by the political example of Churchill's actual father, Lord Randolph Churchill. Lloyd George responded to Lord Randolph's cheeky, iconoclastic style no less eagerly than the young Churchill worshipped, as Violet Bonham Carter has written, 'at the altar of his Unknown Father'.[9] In 1884, when Lloyd George was 21, he listened from the gallery to a debate in which Lord Randolph stood up to Gladstone in the manner that he made his own. The amendment before the House would, Lloyd George later wrote, have been negatived at Gladstone's request

had it not been for the interposition of a lithe young man, who got up on the floor of the House below the gangway, and, in a merry and audacious utterance, completely restored his party to animation. This was Lord Randolph Churchill. He soon had many members on both sides of the House laughing gaily over his daring quips and cranks [sic] about the Prime Minister who had 'tried to terrify the House'. All enjoyed it save Mr. Gladstone.[10]

How often was Lloyd George to be the challenger in just such a scene, with Gladstone and other leading Parliamentarians as the targets for his cheerful impudence. Indeed, his maiden speech included jaunty attacks on Joseph Chamberlain and, suitably, Lord Randolph himself.

Lloyd George and Winston Churchill were both, therefore, in a sense Lord Randolph's political progeny, and this reinforced their alliance. Were they also friends? Up to a point, yes. Both were witty and high-spirited, with a shared adventurousness and agnosticism. They enjoyed each other's company, regardless of politics. But politics was, nevertheless, the dominating passion of both, and in politics—as Lloyd George often said, quoting Lord Rendel—there are no friendships at the top. When their association began, an old Welsh friend of Lloyd George's, D. R. Daniel, considered that they would 'meet face to face one day on the narrow path which leads to the highest pinnacle of honour'.[11] Things did not work out quite as he predicted, but essentially his judgement was correct. Their conflicting ambitions did make them rivals as well as companions, and Asquith, who was a shrewd manager of men, was able to take advantage of this to weaken their radical partnership. By appointing Churchill Home Secretary in 1910 Asquith gave him a position in the Cabinet that was on a par with

Lloyd George's, and so made it less likely that he would ever resign with Lloyd George on a radical issue.

When Churchill was moved to the Admiralty the following year the potential for conflict was increased, and there was indeed a major row between him and Lloyd George over the naval estimates for 1914. On New Year's Day 1914 the *Daily Chronicle* published an interview with the Chancellor in which he deprecated Churchill's 'feverish efforts' to add to Britain's naval power, which might 'provoke other nations'. Asquith supported Churchill and Lloyd George had to climb down. But it should not be thought that the dispute reflected pacifism on Lloyd George's part or, for that matter, excessive militarism on Churchill's. It was natural for Churchill, as First Lord of the Admiralty, to press for higher expenditure on the navy, and equally natural for Lloyd George, as Chancellor, to oppose it, more especially when he was planning another big reforming budget and was in a mood of false optimism about the international situation. If their ministerial roles had been reversed, so might have been their arguments. (In 1909 Lloyd George had had a similar row with the Admiralty over its estimates, and Churchill had then been on his side.)

Neither in the specific instance of the 1914 row, nor in their pre-war relations generally, was there any ideological rift between the two men on the issue of British power. Lloyd George had never been a pacifist, and had always regarded the Royal Navy as the most vital ingredient in the country's strength. Moreover, he had never been a Little Englander, and Churchill's complaint at their first meeting, that he had a 'detached view of the British Empire', was wide of the mark. He had no desire at all to see the dissolution of the Empire, though he wanted as much local self-government as possible for, at any rate, the white communities within it. His opposition to the Boer War was prompted neither by pacifism nor by anti-imperialism, but by a conviction that the war was a terrible mistake, not least because it was harmful to the Empire's own best interests. His attitude was much misunderstood at the time, and the misunderstanding still persists in some quarters, though the truth is obvious to anyone who cares to look at the evidence.

There was, therefore, no contradiction between Lloyd George's attitude to the Chamberlain–Milner policy in South Africa and his opposition to German pretensions in the 1911 Agadir crisis or, more momentously, his recognition of the necessity for war with Germany in August 1914. Nor is there much justification for the view that this conversion was due to Churchill. His doubts about intervention in support of France at the beginning of the 1914 crisis were doubts concerning expediency rather than principle. Churchill may have helped to resolve them, but Lloyd George was already strongly pro-French and well aware that Britain could not allow France to be knocked out by Germany. In all probability he would have decided as he did even if Churchill had not been a colleague. For him, as for many others, Belgium was crucial in providing a moral pretext for intervention, and in consolidating British public opinion in support of war.

Before long Lloyd George was accepted as the most dynamic of the country's civilian war leaders, though for a time Churchill had the edge in two respects. As First Lord of the Admiralty, Churchill was the only civilian in charge of a service department (the War Office having been entrusted to the famous soldier, Lord Kitchener), and he was also the only civilian member of the Cabinet who had taken part in military operations and heard shots fired in anger. On the other hand, precisely because he had direct responsibility for the war at sea, he was liable to be blamed indiscriminately for any naval failures; and he was particularly open to vindictive criticism from Conservatives, who had never forgiven him for deserting them and then vilifying them. Lloyd George's reputation with Conservatives was, meanwhile, transformed by his patriotic stand and the growing evidence of his effectiveness as a war leader.

Churchill's career suffered its first traumatic interruption as a result of the Dardanelles campaign and of Asquith's need, in May 1915, to form a coalition with the Conservatives who, as one price for their participation, insisted on Churchill's removal from the Admiralty, where he was replaced by the former Conservative Prime Minister, A. J. Balfour. He stayed in the Cabinet in a sinecure post until November, when he left the government altogether to serve on the Western Front, returning to office only when Lloyd George brought him back in 1917. In the crisis of May 1915 he was indignant with Lloyd George for not defending his supposed right to remain at the Admiralty: 'You don't care what becomes of me . . . You don't care for my personal reputation.'[12] He seems to have felt that his support for Lloyd George during the Marconi affair in 1912–13 entitled him to such unqualified backing in the very different circumstances of 1915. (The purchase of American Marconi shares by Lloyd George and two other ministers, soon after the British government had entered into a contract with the English Marconi company, was a gross impropriety, to say the least. But the reputation of the whole government, and not just that of the individual ministers, was at stake in the affair, because some of the shares had been bought by the Chief Whip for the Liberal party. Churchill's active support for Lloyd George was not, therefore, purely generous, but in a sense also self-interested.) In any case, in 1915, he was less bitter against Lloyd George than against Asquith, recalling no doubt that the ,Chancellor had openly opposed the use of troops at Gallipoli unless and until the navy succeeded in clearing the straits. Moreover, he could see that his future was likely to depend upon Lloyd George, whose claims to lead the country at war were enhanced by his achievement as creator of the Ministry of Munitions in the Coalition government.

When Clementine Churchill, after giving Lloyd George lunch one day at the end of 1915, wrote to her husband in France describing her guest as 'the direct descendant of Judas Iscariot', Churchill replied: 'I am very glad you had L.G. to lunch. Do this again: & keep in touch. It really is most important, a situation may develop at any time, wh will throw us inevitably together. Our relations are now good—& should be kept so.' A few days later he wrote again: 'Keep in touch with L.G. His necessities will keep him straight if a split occurs. Asquith on the other hand will never have need of me again.'[13] In fact, Lloyd George's 'necessities' made it quite impossible for him to offer Churchill a post when, after the fall of Asquith, he first formed a government in December 1916. Since the Conservative Party was the largest element in his coalition, the Asquithian Liberals having refused to participate, he could not at the outset bring in the Conservatives' *bête noire*. But by July of the following year he felt just strong enough to appoint Churchill Minister of Munitions outside the War Cabinet. Even so, Conservative wrath was extreme and the appointment was one of Lloyd George's most perilous gambles.

In the final stages of the war the two men were once again on excellent terms. Churchill fought the 1918 election as a Coalition (Lloyd George) Liberal, and, in the peacetime Cabinet that Lloyd George then formed, Churchill first held the post of War Minister combined with that of Air Minister. In 1919 he clashed with the Prime Minister over intervention in the civil war between Bolsheviks and anti-Bolsheviks in Russia. Lloyd George's attitude to Communism as a creed and as a system of government was no less hostile than Churchill's, but he was convinced that any attempt by foreigners to overthrow the revolutionary regime would fail ignominiously, and at vast cost. He therefore remonstrated with Churchill:

The reconquest of Russia would cost hundreds of millions. It would cost hundreds of millions more to maintain the new Government until it had established itself. You are prepared to spend all that money, and I know perfectly well that is what you really desire. But as you know that you won't find another responsible person in the whole land who will take your view, why waste your energy and your usefulness on this vain fretting which completely paralyses you for other work?[14]

The argument on the intervention issue runs to thousands of words on both sides, and was pursued over a period of months. Lloyd George is generally agreed to have had the better of it, and Churchill was forced to abandon his policy without, however, changing his mind.

At the end of 1920 Churchill was moved to the Colonial Office (the post which, incidentally, Lloyd George had advised Asquith to offer him in May 1915), and he remained there until the Lloyd George government fell in September 1922. The most important piece of business in which he and Lloyd George were closely involved together during this period was the 1921 Irish Treaty. Churchill's role in the negotiations leading to it, and in the events that followed it in Ireland, was valuable chiefly because of the working relations he established with the leading Irish rebel, or freedom-fighter, Michael Collins. In the 1922 Chanak crisis, which brought Britain close to war with Turkey, and which precipitated Lloyd George's fall, Churchill was at first inclined to caution; but once he had decided to support the Prime Minister's tough stand against the Turks he called upon the Dominions to send help, evoking rebuffs which showed that the days of Imperial tutelage were over. (Chanak is just across the straits from Gallipoli, and it is piquant to note that Lloyd George's ministerial career was in a sense brought to an end in essentially the same place that so nearly destroyed Churchill's.)

After seventeen continuous years in high office Lloyd George lost power for ever in 1922. But at the time, and for about the next ten years, it was scarcely possible for anyone to believe he would never return. He was still the dominant personality in British politics, viewed with apprehension by the Conservative and Labour leaders, Stanley Baldwin and Ramsay MacDonald. As leader of a reunited Liberal Party it seemed that he might stage a comeback in the 1929 election, but the electoral system—which he had failed to reform in 1917, when he had the chance—defeated him. He won a large popular vote, but his strength in Parliament was not remotely commensurate. In the 1931 crisis when, conveniently for his enemies, he was laid low with prostate trouble, he was excluded from the National government; and in the ensuing general election his following in Parliament was reduced to a handful.

Churchill meanwhile had worked his passage back to the Conservative Party, and had been given, much to his surprise, the office of Chancellor of the Exchequer in Baldwin's 1924 government. He still quite often saw Lloyd George, and one meeting in particular was the occasion for a much-quoted remark. As Chancellor he was still writing the last volume of his *World Crisis*, and he wanted to see Lloyd George to ask him questions that only he could answer about the war. They met for an hour in Churchill's room, and ten minutes after Lloyd George had left, Robert Boothby, Churchill's Parliamentary Private Secretary, went in 'to find the Chancellor sitting in an armchair, gazing into the fire, in a kind of brown study'. Boothby asked him how it had gone:

He looked up and replied: 'You will be glad to hear that it could not have gone better. He answered all my questions'. Then a hard look came into his face and he went on: 'Within five minutes the old relationship between us was completely re-established. The relationship between Master and Servant. And I was the Servant.'[15]

Churchill's words may have been exactly as reported, and it was indeed true that Lloyd George was the older man who had also, so far, been in the stronger position politically during most of their association. Yet the remark should on no account be taken as proof that Churchill had a pronounced feeling of inferiority towards Lloyd George. Certainly there was no politician for whose talents and achievements he had greater respect, and he tended to copy Lloyd George even in some matters that were not political. For instance, when he acquired Chartwell in the early 1920s, and wanted to make big structural changes to the house, he engaged the same architect, Philip Tilden, who had recently designed Lloyd George's house at Churt. He also embarked on farming ventures at Chartwell, which were markedly less successful in quality of output than Lloyd George's fruit-growing at Churt (though neither project was successful financially). But the spirit of emulation worked the other way as well, in that Lloyd George was undoubtedly spurred to write his *War Memoirs* by the example of Churchill's *World Crisis*. In any case, there was little enough to suggest an underdog psychology in either man; Churchill was no more capable than Lloyd George of being anybody's 'servant', and what he is alleged to have said to Boothby should not be taken too seriously.

When the Conservatives were in opposition again after 1929 Churchill quarrelled with Baldwin—over India—and left the Shadow Cabinet. Thus began his longest period in the wilderness, which lasted until the outbreak of war in 1939. Meanwhile the main target for his criticism of the Tory leadership, now the dominant force in the so-called National government, had changed from Indian constitutional reform to the policy of appeasing Hitler: a change wholly beneficial to his historic reputation. During this period of nearly ten years, when he and Lloyd George were both isolated, they saw each other quite often and their relations were never, perhaps, more mellow. In January 1938 the Churchills gave a lunch at the Carlton Hotel, Cannes, to celebrate the Lloyd Georges' golden wedding, at which Churchill in his speech proposing their health said that Lloyd George would figure greatly in the history of the world. Yet in politics the two men were on separate tracks which only occasionally converged. Though they shared an utter contempt for the government and its many abject surrenders, they seldom stood together on specific policy.

In September 1936 Lloyd George visited Hitler at Berchtesgaden and on his return wrote, disastrously, that the Führer was arming for defence not attack. Though he had no sympathy whatever with Nazism or any form of dictatorship, he was impressed by Hitler's conquest of unemployment and convinced that he was ultimately a man of reason. During the Munich crisis two years later Lloyd George did not speak out as Churchill did, partly because he hated and despised the Czech president, Beneš. All the same he voted against the Munich agreement, whereas Churchill as a Conservative merely abstained. When Hitler tore up the agreement the following March, and Neville Chamberlain felt obliged to offer a guarantee to Poland, Lloyd George argued that such a guarantee would be worthless unless there were also an understanding with the Soviet Union. On this point he and Churchill were at one, despite Churchill's militant anti-Bolshevism; but Lloyd George was still doubtful about backing the Poles. When at the time he and Churchill met the Soviet Ambassador, Ivan Maisky, he dwelt so much upon the deficiencies of the Polish army that Churchill rebuked him: 'You must not do this sort of thing, my dear. You are putting spokes in the wheel of history.' Harold Nicolson, who was present and recorded the meeting, felt that Lloyd George was 'not really in favour of the new policy'.[16]

Nevertheless when Hitler invaded Poland later in the year, and Britain declared war as a result of the guarantee, Lloyd George supported the decision to fight. He continued, however, to favour peace by negotiation, while even former appeasers were arguing that Hitler was not a man with whom it was possible to negotiate. When the House of Commons debated the Norwegian campaign he was at first reluctant to intervene, seeing that Churchill was apparently so vulnerable; but he was persuaded to do so, and his speech was most helpful to Churchill, since it was an attack of deadly effectiveness on Chamberlain. Churchill then came to power, but did not immediately ask Lloyd George to join his government because, like Lloyd George himself at the end of 1916, he felt he could not risk the loss of Conservative goodwill. In particular, he felt he could not invite Lloyd George without Chamberlain's agreement, and this both hurt and angered Lloyd George, whose dislike of Chamberlain was as intense as Chamberlain's of him. Before long Churchill did offer him a place in the War Cabinet, but Lloyd George then decided, after some hesitation, not to join, whatever he might have done earlier. At the end of the year, he was approached about succeeding Lord Lothian as Ambassador in Washington, but again refused.

His reasons for staying aloof were complex, but one of them, no doubt, was a belief that he might be needed to lead the country in negotiating peace if and when Churchill's policy of all-out defiance and intransigence were seen to have failed. In a debate in May 1941 Churchill hinted that Lloyd George's position was similar to that of Marshal Pétain, but this was unfair. Lloyd George's insistence that there would have to be a negotiated peace was based on realism, not defeatism. He wanted to negotiate, but only from strength; before there could be any worthwhile negotiation it had to be manifest, in his view, that Britain neither was, nor could be, defeated. Yet he could not see how Britain could hope to defeat Germany without the assistance of Russia or America, or both; and he could visualize no circumstances in which those countries would become involved in the war. His thinking was entirely rational, but the flaw in it lay in assuming that Hitler's was rational as well. In the event Churchill's irrational policy was vindicated when Hitler attacked the Soviet Union and then compounded his folly by declaring war on the United States.

Despite the 'Pétain' gibe, there was no personal breach between the two men. In September 1941 they had a lunch together at Downing Street which lasted from 1.30 to 4.30 p.m. When Lloyd George died at the end of March 1945 Churchill's tribute in the House of Commons was, perhaps, the warmest he ever paid; certainly much warmer and more eloquent than his tribute, soon afterwards, to Franklin D. Roosevelt. On Lloyd George his final verdict could hardly have been more glowing:

He faced undismayed the storms of criticism and hostility. In spite of all obstacles, including those he raised himself, he achieved his main purposes. As a man of action, resource and creative energy he stood, when at his zenith, without a rival. His name is a household word . . . He was the greatest Welshman which that unconquerable race has produced since the age of the Tudors. Much of his work abides, some of it will grow greatly in the future, and those who come after us will find the pillars of his life's toil upstanding, massive and indestructible.[17]

Any appraisal of the relative merits of Lloyd George and Churchill has to take as its premise the fact that Lloyd George, in most respects, was the pioneer. In peace and war he faced tasks and challenges that were without precedent. Churchill was able to profit from his example, and this included learning from his mistakes. In 1922 Lloyd George had been destroyed because the party that provided the bulk of his Parliamentary support was not his own party. In 1940, despite the much larger preoccupations of the hour, Churchill was careful to accept the leadership of the Conservative Party when Chamberlain died (though his wife did her best to dissuade him); he was determined not to be left high and dry after the war.

Both men were marvellous orators, and both took immense trouble over their speeches, though Lloyd George was more accomplished at making his seem natural and spontaneous. Churchill may command more space in the anthologies, but Lloyd George was on the whole better at commanding live audiences, whether in Parliament or from platforms. He also tended to be more persuasive than Churchill with individuals and small groups, mainly because he was as good a listener as talker, whereas Churchill was too much given to monologue. Though essentially Lloyd George was just as self-centred, his egotism was not of the sort to insulate him from the rest of humanity. He had the saving grace of being genuinely interested in every kind of person, the ordinary as well as the extraordinary. 'I am always interested in people', he once wrote to Frances Stevenson, 'wondering who they are—what they are thinking about—what their lives are like—whether they are enjoying life or finding it a bore.'[18] Churchill lacked this capacity to project himself imaginatively into the thoughts and feelings of others, which may explain why he did not respond as Lloyd George did to novels. (Had Lloyd George's creative talent been for literature rather than politics, he might have excelled as a novelist.)

Though nothing in Lloyd George's career quite matches the heroic splendour of Churchill's leadership in 1940, in other ways his performance as war leader, both before and after he became Prime Minister, compares well with Churchill's. In 1917 and 1918 he was, moreover, a more powerful player on the world stage than Churchill from 1942 to 1945, because Britain's contribution to victory was more substantial in the earlier war. Despite Churchill's personal stature, the so-called Big Three at Yalta and Potsdam have fairly been described as 'the Big Two-and-a-Half', because Britain's material weight was that much less than America's and Russia's; whereas, if the Big Four at the Paris Peace Conference in 1919 had been described as the Big Three-and-a-Half, the half would certainly not have been Britain, but rather Italy.

In his method of running the war, Churchill was above all concerned to establish civilian control over the military, since he had witnessed Lloyd George's failure to control Haig. To this end he made himself Minister of Defence as well as Prime Minister, and the frequency with which he wore uniforms of one kind or another enhanced the impression he gave of being a super-warlord. But did he really succeed in dominating his professional advisers, and did he avoid having any general whom he could not remove? As Minister of Defence he had no ministry to back him up; the three service departments remained separate and unintegrated. Churchill was, therefore, at a disadvantage when dealing with the three Chiefs of Staff, who had all the departmental backing that he lacked. Alan Brooke and Charles Portal, in particular, nearly always got their way on strategic issues, if at the cost of endless midnight palavers and debilitating loss of sleep. Moreover, Churchill created in Bernard Montgomery (originally Brooke's choice rather than his) a field commander whose hyped-up reputation and hold over the media made him scarcely more removable than Haig, though there was surely a strong case for removing him after Arnhem.

Churchill also deviated from Lloyd George's mode of war leadership in having a War Cabinet most of whose members also had heavy departmental responsibilities. He did this deliberately, because he thought it would strengthen his own position to have colleagues who were too busy to compete with him in overall contemplation of war policy and grand strategy. In fact, it tended to leave him isolated and weakened his position *vis-à-vis* the Chiefs of Staff, thus diminishing civilian control. Churchill had no War Cabinet colleague as valuable as Lord Milner, for instance, had been to Lloyd George.

Lloyd George's literary output, though far from negligible, is less voluminous and impressive than Churchill's, and since most of Churchill's is devoted to himself, either directly or (as in his *Marlborough* and the life of his father) indirectly, it has helped to aggrandize his posthumous image. Solid political legacy is another matter, however, and there the balance seems to favour Lloyd George. Apart from his acknowledged primacy in founding the welfare state, he also has to be regarded as the chief modernizer of the British system of government, through his introduction of a Cabinet secretariat and his creation of new ministries such as Health, Labour, Housing, and Transport. In the fiscal sphere his innovation of the supertax established the principle of progressive taxation which, though carried for a time to gross excess by later Chancellors, is still recognized as equitable. Under his premiership, and with his active encouragement, women were enfranchized for national politics in Britain, a constitutional change more significant than any resulting from the period of Churchill's leadership (and one for which Churchill, unlike Lloyd George, had little enthusiasm).

In the outside world Churchill's legacy may seem larger, and so in a sense it is. Through his Fulton and Zurich speeches, above all, he clearly made a big contribution to the Western stand against Soviet expansion, and to the movement towards unification in western Europe. Yet he did not, of course, actually create NATO or the European Economic Community, nor did he ever intend Britain to be an organic part of the united Europe for which he called. More definite and measurable is his contribution to the revival of France as a Great Power. But for his persistent advocacy, against the combined hostility of Roosevelt and Stalin, France would have been denied her rightful status in the post-war world. Lloyd George's personal impact on Europe is perhaps rather less marked; though he helped to dismember the Habsburg empire, and to assert the principle of self-determination, his efforts to achieve a permanent European settlement were frustrated. On the other hand, his impact on the Middle East has proved all too lasting.

Beyond a certain point it is idle, as well as invidious, to try to decide between Churchill and Lloyd George, which was the greater. Both were outstanding in their day, and even as they recede in time they are not diminished. It was most fortunate for Britain, and perhaps also rather fortunate for the world, that they lived when they did and were willing, for some years, to deploy their talents and energies in concert.

7

Churchill and the Labour Movement

HENRY PELLING

W INSTON CHURCHILL'S long career in politics coincided almost precisely with the first sixty-five years of the existence of the Labour Party, from its founding in 1900 to its emergence under Harold Wilson's leadership as the reputed 'natural' party of government. His supposed role in the Tonypandy riots in 1910, when he was said to have sent in the troops, his vigorous assault upon the General Strike of 1926, and his warning in 1945 that the Labour leadership might 'have to fall back on some form of Gestapo' all contribute to an impression that Churchill was hardly friendly towards Labour. But his true attitude can be established only by removing the patina of myth and partisanship.

In July 1899 Churchill fought his first Parliamentary election in a double-member seat at Oldham. Quite exceptionally, it was a double by-election, for both seats had been vacated. His running-mate in the Conservative cause was the secretary of the Cotton Spinners' Union, James Mawdsley, who had been prominent on the Parliamentary Committee of the Trades Union Congress. Mawdsley declared himself delighted at what he called 'a compliment to the freedom of British institutions in the standing together on the same platform of a son of the old and well-famed British aristocracy and a spinner from the jinny-gate'.[1] Churchill, for his part, proclaimed his support not only for an imperial policy, but also for social reform. Although both seats had been held by the Conservative Party before the contest, the party's national unpopularity spelled narrow defeat for both Churchill and Mawdsley. The Oldham Conservatives were keen to keep Churchill as a candidate, however, and in 1899–1900 he shot to national fame as a result of his exploits in South Africa, where he escaped from a Boer prison camp and made his way back to the Cape by way of Mozambique. It was to this personal popularity that he attributed his victory in the 1900 general election, for his running-mate this time, a London stockbroker, was not elected and Churchill shared the representation with a Liberal called Alfred Emmott. As Churchill put it: 'It appeared that about 200 Liberals who had voted for Emmott had given their second votes to me out of personal goodwill and war feeling.'[2]

When in 1903 Joseph Chamberlain expounded his policy of protective tariffs, which deeply divided the Conservative Party, Churchill declared for free trade, and told the Oldham Conservatives that he was willing to resign and fight a by-election on the issue. His offer was refused; but in May 1904 he crossed the floor of the House. He had already been invited by the Liberals to contest the next election as a free trade candidate for Manchester North-West, the heart of the commercial district of the city. But while a member for Oldham, Churchill took up the interests of his constituents, including the trade unionists. He accepted the case, put to him by J. R. Clynes, secretary of the Oldham Trades Council and later Labour Cabinet Minister, for the restoration of trade union immunity from being sued in tort, which had been removed by an important judicial decision in 1901 in the celebrated case of the Taff Vale Railway Company against the Amalgamated Society of Railway Servants—a source of bitter grievance to trade unions throughout the country. In 1903 he voted in favour of a resolution put forward by David Shackleton, a Labour MP and member of the TUC Parliamentary Committee, to this end.[3] In 1904 he actually spoke in favour of a similar motion, arguing: 'It cannot, I think, be said that labour bulks too largely in English politics at the present time.'[4] This was the speech delivered without notes which he had to cut short because he lost his thread. He was obliged to sit down in embarrassment—an episode that led his friends to fear and his enemies to hope that he was suffering the same mental collapse that his father had suffered in the 1890s. Thereafter, he never made a major speech without full notes of what he intended to say, although he envied the fluency of his father and, years later, his son in this respect.

Churchill entered Campbell-Bannerman's Liberal Ministry as Under-Secretary for the Colonies, and in this post he had little contact with the labour movement, although the Labour Party was an ally of the government, and the Liberal Party also contained a number of so-called 'Lib–Labs'—trade unionists, mostly miners, elected on a broadly Liberal platform. But when Asquith succeeded Campbell-Bannerman in 1908, Churchill was promoted to the post of President of the Board of Trade, and thus entered the Cabinet at the age of 34. Because of the law which at that time obliged newly appointed ministers in the Commons to seek re-election he had to fight a by-election for his seat at Manchester North-West, and in the prevailing political climate he was defeated. But he was at once offered a candidacy at a by-election at Dundee, a double-member constituency where the other sitting member was a member of the Labour Party, Alexander Wilkie—a shipwright who was not a socialist. Churchill had to face three other candidates—a rival Labour candidate who was a socialist, also a Conservative and a prohibitionist; and a feature of his campaign was the vigour of his assault upon socialism. 'Socialism', he said,

seeks to pull down wealth; Liberalism seeks to raise up poverty. Socialism would destroy private interests; Liberalism would preserve private interests in the only way they can be safely and justly preserved, by reconciling them with public right. Socialism would kill enterprise; Liberalism would rescue enterprise from the trammels of privilege and preference.[5]

He won easily.

At the Board of Trade Churchill had to cope with issues that now lie within the compass of the Secretary of Employment. He took over, after a Commons Select Committee Report, legislation to establish trade boards, later known as wages councils, to fix wages in the so-called 'sweated trades' in which it had proved impossible to establish trade unions. In conjunction with Lloyd George, who was now Chancellor of the Exchequer, he planned to establish on the Bismarckian model a system of compulsory insurance against both sickness and unemployment. These measures, it should be emphasized, did not endear either Churchill or Lloyd George to the Labour Party, as the trade unions were afraid of encroachment by the state upon their own insurance schemes. The socialists had their own distinct plans worked out by Sidney and Beatrice Webb.

In late 1909, when the Lords rejected Lloyd George's budget, Asquith decided on a general election on the constitutional issue—the powers of the House of Lords. Labour backed him fully. Churchill and Wilkie fought what was virtually a joint campaign in Dundee in January 1910, but Churchill was much in demand as a speaker elsewhere, particularly in Lancashire. The election restored the Conservatives to almost equal strength with the Liberals, but Asquith continued in office with the backing of Irish Nationalists and the Labour Party. He promoted Churchill to Home Secretary, a post which he held until October 1911, winning a third election contest at Dundee in late 1910.

As Home Secretary Churchill promoted a Mines Act, which increased inspection in the mines and raised the minimum age of employment underground from 13 to 14. He was also responsible for a Shops Act, which limited the hours of shop assistants. But his main task was the enactment of Part II of the National Insurance Act, relating to unemployment. Some members of the Labour Party were very discontented to find that their attempt to establish themselves as a distinct Parliamentary entity was in danger of being submerged by the effective social policy of the Liberal government.

An opportunity to make clear Labour's distinct position came in November 1910, when there was a strike in the South Wales coalfield and rioting ensued at Tonypandy and elsewhere. Troops were dispatched to the scene, but not by Churchill, who decided to hold them in reserve and sent some mounted Metropolitan policemen to restore order. Of course the English police were unpopular; and Keir Hardie, the socialist MP and former chairman of the Parliamentary Labour Party, denounced their conduct. 'The colliers of South Wales', he said, 'have no intention of being bludgeoned in order to make a Liberal holiday.' He demanded an enquiry, which Churchill refused, saying of Keir Hardie: 'I know perfectly well, from every act and speech of his, his life is directed to injuring and assailing the party to which I belong. As he justly says, there is no love lost between us, though I entirely respect the consistency of his career.' And turning to the facts of the case, he added: 'I am quite prepared to do my best to see this matter through with the police, and if I succeed in using the police, and the police alone, though blood may be shed, most of it will be from the nose, which can be subsequently replaced.'[6]

Events turned out in South Wales as Churchill had hoped, and there were no serious casualties; but his own reputation as a soldier was against him, especially when a few weeks later, in January 1911, a gang of armed anarchists, who had already killed three policemen, were trapped in a house in Sidney Street in East London, and troops had to be ordered to the scene. It was not the intervention of the soldiers that impressed the public, but the fact that the Home Secretary was photographed surveying the scene in person. Worse still, he authorized the dispatch of troops to help quell disturbances during a transport strike in Liverpool in which two rioters were shot and killed. And when there was a threat of a national rail strike—at that time an unheard-of occurrence—Churchill sent troops to occupy various key installations around the country, thereby upsetting not just the left wing of the Labour

Party, but also its official leader, Ramsay MacDonald, who told the Commons:

If the Home Secretary had just a little bit more knowledge of how to handle the masses of men in these critical times, if he had a somewhat better instinct of what civil liberty does mean, and if he had a somewhat better capacity to use the powers which he has got as Home Secretary, we should have had much less difficulty during the last four or five days in facing and finally settling the very difficult problem we have had before us.[7]

Although MacDonald was posing as a conciliator, it was, in fact, Lloyd George who managed to make peace in the railway industry, partly by appealing to the men's patriotism at a moment when there was a danger of war owing to the Agadir incident. But before the men were all back at work an unfortunate incident took place at Llanelli, in South Wales, when rioters held up a train and soldiers on the spot opened fire, killing two men.

It was Churchill's obligation as Home Secretary to send the King a daily account of proceedings in the Commons; and the Labour members would have been very surprised had they seen his comments on their own Right to Work Bill, discussed in February 1911. Churchill wrote to the King:

The subject is a very great one and cuts down to the foundation of things. Mr Churchill has always felt that it ought to be possible with our present science and civilisation to mitigate the violent fluctuation of trade by some recourse to public works of a reproductive kind which could be carried on placidly in good times and actively in bad. As for tramps and wastrels there ought to be proper Labour Colonies where they could be sent for considerable periods and made to realise their duty to the State. Such institutions are now being considered at the Home Office. It must not however be forgotten that there are idlers and wastrels at both ends of the social scale.

This drew the Royal anger. Lord Knollys, George V's secretary, sent the letter to Asquith, the Prime Minister, with the comment that

The King thinks that Mr. Churchill's views, as contained in the enclosed, are very socialistic. What he advocates is nothing more than the workshops which have been tried in France & have turned out a complete failure. . . . H.M. considers it quite superfluous for Churchill in a letter of the description he was writing to him, to bring in about 'idlers and wastrels at both ends of the social ladder.'[8]

Churchill was not, of course, a socialist; but he was a member of a government that was allied to the Labour Party and the trade unions, and he spoke in favour of a bill designed to restore to them the power to finance Parliamentary candidates that they had lost by the Osborne Judgement of 1909. This made illegal the political levy on trade union funds which had been used to support Labour MPs. In the course of his speech on this topic, he said bluntly:

It is not good for trade unions that they should be brought in contact with the courts, and it is not good for the courts . . . Where class issues are involved, and where party issues are involved, it is impossible to pretend that the courts command . . . confidence. On the contrary, they do not, and a very large number of our population have been led to the opinion that they are, unconsciously no doubt, biassed.[9]

This observation from the Home Secretary much annoyed the Conservative Opposition, and a few weeks later, in June, an attempt was made to censure him by a motion for the reduction of his salary by £500. According to Churchill writing to the King, it was owing to the large number of government supporters already on holiday that 'this flagitious proposal was rejected only by a majority of 32'.[10]

In October 1911 Asquith offered Churchill the Admiralty, a post he accepted at once, although it was junior to the Home Office in the order of precedence of Cabinet offices. Churchill could foresee that there was much work to be done in preparing the navy for war, and especially in creating a naval war staff. From then until the end of the First World War Churchill was absorbed in the task of war preparation and then in the conduct of the war itself. He became steadily more bipartisan, as between the Liberals and the Conservatives; and in 1911 he founded, with his Conservative friend F. E. Smith, a dining club, known as 'The Other Club', to which members of all parties could be elected, it being accepted in its constitution that 'Nothing in the Rules or Intercourse of the Club shall interfere with the rancour or asperity of party politics'.[11] In fact, no member of the Labour Party ever became a member of this institution, which eventually became little more than a Churchill admiration society.

In the long succession of roles that Churchill performed during the First World War—First Lord of the Admiralty until the failure of Gallipoli, then Lieutenant-Colonel on the Western Front, and (from 1917) Minister of Munitions—he had little contact with the political labour movement, although as Minister of Munitions he had to negotiate with a Trade Union Advisory Committee. W. C. Anderson, a

Labour MP who was no friend of the Coalition, told the Commons in late 1917 that he thought Churchill had brought 'courage and a certain quality of imagination to the task of dealing with labour questions';[12] and Churchill's wife Clementine became absorbed in problems of factory welfare and canteens. In the immediate post-war general election, he accepted the Coalition platform headed by Lloyd George, with a programme of social reconstruction including the establishment of a League of Nations, improved housing, and the nationalization of the railways. Actually, he was misled about railway nationalization, because Bonar Law, leader of the Conservative Party which was the major component of the Coalition, refused to accept it. As before, Churchill fought the two-member seat of Dundee in an informal alliance with the Labour MP Alexander Wilkie who, like the majority of the Labour Party, had backed the Coalition during the war. The two men urged their supporters to vote for Churchill and Wilkie, and Wilkie was annoyed that another Labour candidate was put into the contest. All the same, in this overwhelmingly working-class constituency the 'old gang', as Churchill described Wilkie and himself, were returned with huge majorities.[13]

Nevertheless, the old pattern of politics was changing. The old Liberal Party had been split into the two rival factions of Asquithians and Coalitionists, and the Labour Party had emerged as a national force with a socialist constitution and a foreign policy critical of that of Lloyd George. Of course Labour's increase in Parliamentary strength from 42 in 1910 to 57 eight years later hardly seemed significant at the time, partly because several of the senior leaders—MacDonald, Snowden, and Henderson—had lost their seats in the 1918 election. But the party made great gains in local elections in the following years, and after the onset of a slump in 1921 posed an increasing challenge to the old party system.

It was Churchill's misfortune to find himself increasingly at odds with the labour movement in these years. One major reason was his support, as War Minister, for the anti-Bolsheviks in the Russian Civil War, and his attempt to persuade the Supreme Allied Council in Paris to make a combined intervention to help the White Russian cause. His efforts came to naught, partly because of war-weariness on the part of the Allies, partly because even Lloyd George was opposed to continued intervention on Russian soil. Publicly, Churchill denounced the Bolshevik regime as 'baboonery', and thwarted Lloyd George's attempts to recognize the Soviet regime. But at this time the Labour Party and the trade unions had high hopes for the first 'workers' state', as they saw it, and in 1922 the London dockers organized a Council of Action to prevent the shipment of munitions to Poland on a ship called the *Jolly George*. The armaments were intended for the Polish government, which was defending itself against invasion by the Red Army. The episode, in which Ernest Bevin was prominent, became, as Dr K. O. Morgan has written, 'hallowed in legend'. But as far as Lloyd George was concerned the trade unions were 'pushing at an open door'.[14]

In 1920 Lloyd George was already sufficiently worried by the weakness of the Coalition Liberals at by-elections and by the growth of Labour to float the idea of 'fusion' between his followers and the Conservatives. Churchill took up the idea as a means of resisting Bolshevism, at home and abroad, and in February in a speech at Dundee he described Labour as 'unfit to govern'. It was this, allied with, according to Morgan, 'crude and intemperate rhetoric' about the Bolsheviks, which 'underlined the gulf that had existed between Churchill and the working-class mind since the unrest in the Welsh valleys in 1910'.[15]

But the remainder of the Liberals did not favour the 'fusion' idea, and the Conservatives felt they had nothing to lose by regaining their independence. When the Coalition broke up in 1922 Churchill was in a weak position, fighting a working-class constituency against two candidates of the Labour left—E. D. Morel, a critic of the Versailles Treaty, and E. Scrymgeour, a Prohibitionist, who had fought the seat several times before. Churchill's former colleague, Wilkie, had now retired, and Morel and Scrymgeour inherited the Labour and socialist vote and won the election.

So Churchill was out of Parliament, but not for long. Bonar Law's premiership, owing to his illness, lasted only a few months, and his successor, Stanley Baldwin, decided to fight an early general election on the issue of tariff reform. This challenge reunited the old Liberal Party; and Churchill chose to fight a seat at Leicester, where he thought there would be no Conservative opposition. This was a mistake, and he was defeated in a three-cornered fight. The Labour Party had won more seats than the reunited Liberals, but with only 191 seats it could not form a government by itself. Churchill, fearing that Asquith, once again his leader, would put Labour in power, issued a statement saying: 'The enthronement in office of a Socialist Government will be a serious national misfortune such as has usually befallen great states only on the morrow of defeat in war.'[16] Nevertheless, this was what Asquith did;

and Churchill thereupon left the Liberal Party and declared himself an anti-socialist.

Thereafter Churchill's Parliamentary career depended on Conservative support. His path was greatly eased when Baldwin, accepting the verdict of the electorate, decided to abandon tariff reform. Churchill, as a free-trader, was regarded as a good catch for Conservative Associations which wished to make some appeal to the residual Liberal vote. In September 1924 he was offered, and readily accepted, the nomination for the relatively safe seat of Epping. He fought the seat under the title of 'Constitutionalist', and to his surprise and gratification was offered by Baldwin the Chancellorship of the Exchequer—a post that Neville Chamberlain had refused because, in view of Baldwin's pledge, he would not have been able to introduce tariff reform.

It has been suggested that, with his old friend F. E. Smith (now Lord Birkenhead), Churchill formed a 'war party' inside the Cabinet to fight the Miners' Federation, which was resisting wage cuts, and thereby precipitated the General Strike of 1926. In fact, there is no evidence to support this view, although it is true that both Churchill's acceptance of a return to the Gold Standard in 1925 and the vigour of his actions during the General Strike itself, particularly in running the *British Gazette* as a short-lived government newspaper, gave him the appearance of leading the anti-union campaign. But once the General Strike was over, Churchill turned his efforts to securing a compromise settlement to bring the miners back to work. Indeed, as Tom Jones, the Assistant Secretary of the Cabinet, has shown in his diaries, Churchill was on the point of securing agreement in September only to be thwarted by the mineowners.[17]

That Churchill was in no sense anti-union was demonstrated in late 1928, when, because of his well-known hobby of brick-laying, the Kent local secretary of the Amalgamated Union of Building Trade Workers invited him to become a member. Churchill replied 'I should be very pleased to join the union if you are of the opinion that it would not be unwelcome to your members', sent off a cheque in payment of the subscription, and was formally admitted a member at the Treasury: but the union's Executive Council ruled him ineligible, although he already had his certificate of membership.[18]

When Labour took office again after the 1929 general election, it was Churchill's task at first to 'shadow' the Labour Chancellor, Philip

Snowden. But he soon fell out with Baldwin over the latter's support for Indian self-government; and this issue ruled him out of the national government formed in 1931. Churchill fought bitterly inside the Conservative Party against what became the Government of India Act, 1935; and when he took up the cause of rearmament thereafter he must have appeared to many Conservatives as a perpetual political rebel, more interested in personal advancement than in the practical possibilities of government. It was only in 1936 that he began to make some progress in shaping an informal opposition to the Baldwin government on the need for rearmament. A body came into existence under the title of 'Arms and the Covenant', the 'Covenant' being the Covenant of the League of Nations. This drew in Liberal and some Labour support, as the Trades Union Congress led by Walter Citrine and Ernest Bevin had been shocked by Hitler's suppression of German trade unionism and were ahead of the Labour Party in supporting rearmament. Churchill spoke in the Albert Hall at a demonstration chaired by Walter Citrine. But the movement lost some of its impact because the meeting coincided with the crisis over the abdication of Edward VIII, from which Baldwin emerged with renewed popular support.

In 1937 Churchill welcomed Neville Chamberlain's succession to the premiership, rightly regarding him as a more efficient minister than Baldwin. He also respected the young Foreign Secretary, Anthony Eden, but he was shocked when the latter early in 1938 clashed with Chamberlain and resigned. Churchill was now advocating a 'Grand Alliance' of Britain, France, and Russia to keep the peace in Europe; and in March 1938 Kingsley Martin, editor of the left-wing *New Statesman*, went so far as to advocate 'a broadly based government which includes Mr Eden, Mr Churchill and the Labour and Liberal leaders'.[19] In the Commons, however, there was not even any sign of a 'cave' of Conservative supporters for Churchill in his opposition to Chamberlain's policy of appeasement of the dictators. Churchill's disappointment was acute when Chamberlain signed the Munich Agreement and left Czechoslovakia in the lurch. He had tried to get the Opposition leaders, Attlee for Labour and Archibald Sinclair for the Liberals, to sign a telegram warning Chamberlain of opposition in the House if he made more concessions at the expense of the Czechs; but Attlee would not sign without the consent of his colleagues, and Sinclair followed the Labour lead.

After Hitler occupied the rump of Czechoslovakia in March 1939, public opinion gradually moved against Chamberlain and in favour of

Churchill. It was therefore by popular demand that he was restored to the Cabinet on the outbreak of war, as First Lord of the Admiralty. It was ironical that in this post he had, along with the Prime Minister, responsibility for the unsuccessful Norway campaign in 1940, and that although he defended the government as best he could in the vote of censure in Parliament moved by Labour, it was Chamberlain who had to yield the premiership and Churchill who was able to succeed him. This was because the Labour leaders refused to serve under Chamberlain, and because Halifax, the other serious contender, 'felt a pain in his stomach' at the idea of taking over and refused to serve. In the small War Cabinet that Churchill at once formed, he was joined by the two Labour leaders, Attlee and his deputy Arthur Greenwood, and by Chamberlain and Halifax.

In the Coalition government, the Labour contribution was essential. Apart from recruiting other Labour MPs for important posts, Churchill brought in Ernest Bevin, the most powerful of the trade union leaders, as his Minister of Labour. In the crisis of the French collapse the little War Cabinet of five were at first divided on whether to try to buy off Italy; but Chamberlain and Halifax were voted down on this by Churchill and the two Labour leaders.[20] On 3 July Churchill personally ordered the destruction of the French fleet at Oran; and it was only after this stern measure that he really won the support of the Commons as a whole. As he put it in his memoirs: 'Up till this moment the Conservative Party had treated me with some reserve, and it was from the Labour benches that I received the warmest welcome when I entered the House or rose on serious occasions. But now all joined in solemn stentorian accord.'[21]

Early in October, Chamberlain having resigned owing to a fatal illness, Churchill increased the size of the War Cabinet to eight, including Ernest Bevin in its number. This remarkable promotion of the Labour Minister of Labour, who had been in the Commons for only three months, can only have been because Churchill had formed a warm respect for his abilities. The Prime Minister was invited to become Leader of the Conservative Party in Chamberlain's place, and he accepted, realizing that the only alternative would be Halifax, who was still Foreign Secretary but whom he regarded as partly responsible for the Munich Agreement of 1938.

Churchill had sent Sir Stafford Cripps, a former Solicitor-General, to Moscow as Ambassador, hoping that his socialist views would endear him to the Russian dictator. This did not prove to be the case; and when in April 1941 Churchill wanted to warn Stalin of an impending attack upon his country by Hitler, it took Cripps a long time to obtain an interview and his message was not effective, for the Russians were taken by surprise by Hitler's June offensive. But when the invasion took place, Churchill at once undertook to assist the Soviet Union in its resistance, and arranged for supplies of scarce munitions to go to the Russian front. For what it was worth, this drew to the Coalition government the warm support of the Communist Party. In fact, this extra aid was not worth much, considering that the party's strength was primarily in the trade unions, and if anything the number of strikes and days lost thereby actually increased, though not seriously.[22]

Churchill's control of offices in the Coalition government had to be tempered constantly by regard for the balance of parties. In July 1941 one of Churchill's best friends, Harold Nicolson, was replaced as Parliamentary Secretary to the Ministry of Information by a Labour MP, Ernest Thurtle, whose sole distinction was that he was the son-in-law of the former Labour leader, George Lansbury.[23] This move came about simply because the Labour Party had demanded representation at the Ministry of Information, and not because Thurtle was in any way qualified for the post.

Later in February 1942, at a time when the government was under heavy criticism because of setbacks on land and at sea, Churchill managed to remove Greenwood from office—he was an alcoholic and clearly incompetent—and replace him with Cripps, who had returned from Moscow and commended himself to the public as the man who, it seemed, had brought Russia into the war.[24] Cripps did not fit into Churchill's mode of government at all well; and in a few months' time he was asking to be given a departmental post. It was only in November, after the tide of arms had turned for the Western Allies at El Alamein, that Churchill decided to remove him and replace him in the War Cabinet with Labour's Herbert Morrison, who had proved a successful Home Secretary and Minister of Home Security. From this time onwards there were few alterations in the government before the final victory over Germany in May 1945.

It had been agreed that, once Germany was defeated, there should be a general election for a new Parliament. But Churchill, primed by his Conservative advisers, offered the Labour and Liberal Parties the choice of carrying on the Coalition until after the end of the war against Japan, which was not expected within the year, or an immediate break-up of the

Coalition followed by an early election. Attlee and Bevin, on being consulted privately by Churchill, both opted for the later date; but they were overridden by the Labour National Executive, and by the Party Conference, which met immediately afterwards. Thus after a brief caretaker government consisting of Churchill and his Conservative or non-party supporters, a general election took place early in July.

In his first election broadcast Churchill was anxious to establish his credentials with his Conservative supporters and to draw attention to the way in which the Labour National Executive could overrule Attlee and his senior colleagues. These factors accounted for his extraordinary statement that a socialist government 'would have to fall back on some form of Gestapo, no doubt very humanely directed in the first instance'. When Professor Harold Laski, then serving as the Chairman of the Labour Executive, suggested that Attlee, whom Churchill had invited to accompany him to the Potsdam Conference, could not commit a future Labour government, Churchill said in a later broadcast: 'Professor Laski, Chairman of the Socialist Party Executive . . . has reminded all of us including Mr Attlee that the final determination of all questions of foreign policy rests, so far as the Socialist Party is concerned, with this dominating Socialist Executive.'[25] Although Attlee replied firmly to these attacks, and Labour candidates naturally supported him, Churchill had put his finger on a weakness of the Labour Party constitution, which did not properly establish the relative importance of the Cabinet or Shadow Cabinet on the one hand and the National Executive on the other. The issue became a real one only when the party was out of office, notably in 1959–60 when the leadership of Gaitskell was challenged and in 1979 when Callaghan was forced to resign.

Churchill remained Leader of the Opposition after his defeat in 1945, but for some time he was distinctly lukewarm in attacking his former Labour colleagues. He approved of Bevin's role at the Foreign Office, and had no quibble with the nationalization of the Bank of England. He was away from Parliament for long periods, writing his history of the Second World War, painting in the Mediterranean sunshine, and receiving the plaudits of various European countries for his wartime leadership. His most powerful speeches were on the subject of what he called the 'Iron Curtain'—delivered in the United States—and on the need for European unity, at Zurich. As James Stuart, then Conservative Chief Whip, recounted in his memoirs, in 1947 Churchill was 'invited' to resign the party leadership, but he refused.[26] But by 1949 the prospects for a Conservative victory appeared far brighter. With the publication of *The Right Road for Britain*, drafted by R. A. Butler, Churchill placed a moderate Conservative policy before the electors, accepting most of Labour's nationalization except for road haulage and iron and steel, and acknowledging the importance of co-operation with the trade unions. When the 1950 general election took place, its principal novelty was a call by Churchill for a 'parley at the summit', that is to say, a fresh meeting with Truman and Stalin. The election was narrowly won by Labour, but it did not look as if the new Parliament could last for very long.

Partly because of the outbreak of the Korean War, Attlee held no new general election in 1950, but in the autumn of 1951 he again went to the polls. This election was almost a re-run of that of the previous year; but Churchill resented bitterly a suggestion by the *Daily Mirror* that he was a 'warmonger' and later won a libel action against the newspaper. Although the Labour Party gained the largest popular vote that any party has ever obtained in an election even to this day, the vagaries of the electoral system gave the Conservatives an overall majority of seventeen. Churchill was back in power.

Churchill's peacetime government began with an attempt on the part of the Prime Minister to recreate the atmosphere of the Coalition. He invited Clement Davies, the leader of the Liberal Party, to serve as Minister of Education; and Davies would have taken the post if his colleagues had allowed him to. He also sought to placate the trade unions by appointing as Minister of Labour Sir Walter Monckton, a man who had hardly served in politics before, and who was known only as a legal luminary with expert diplomatic skills. The General Council of the Trades Union Congress responded by declaring that they hoped that their practice of consultation with the government would continue, and that 'On our part we shall continue to examine every question solely in the light of its industrial and economic implications.'[27]

Churchill had rejected the idea of attempting to re-enact the Trade Disputes Act of 1927, which prevented civil servants from joining unions and introduced contracting-in for the Labour party political levy, instead of contracting-out. This act had been repealed by Labour in 1946. The question at issue was whether the political levy would be automatically paid by members unless they signified dissent or whether positive assent was needed. Although Churchill thought the political levy in its existing form was unjust, he argued that 'a wider spirit of tolerance has grown up and the question may well be left to common sense and the British way of settling things'.[28] Indeed there was only one occasion when the General Council came into serious conflict with the government, and that was as early as the summer of 1952, when Monckton, in his zeal to help the Chancellor of the Exchequer to hold back inflation, failed to confirm automatically some pay awards proposed by Wages Councils—the former Trade Boards that Churchill had helped to establish before the First World War. The TUC demanded and obtained a special meeting with the Prime Minister, and expressed their concern; and the upshot was that Monckton gave way and confirmed the awards without alteration.[29]

In 1953 Churchill invited the General Council to nominate a member to the post of full-time vice-chairman of the Iron and Steel Board, which was to supervise the industry when denationalized. The General Council agreed, and Sir Lincoln Evans, the General Secretary of the British Iron and Steel Trades Confederation, was duly appointed. Then in the same year, when national strikes were threatened on the railways and in engineering and shipbuilding, Monckton stepped in, to secure compromise settlements involving pay increases without compensating guarantees of increased productivity. Only in 1954 did the number of days lost in industry exceed the two million mark, for the first time since 1948.

Churchill's relations with the Labour Party also improved in these years, partly because of his evident enthusiasm for a 'summit' meeting and *détente* with the Soviet Union. The 'summit' idea was delayed, however, first of all by the death of Stalin in March 1953 and then by Churchill's own stroke in the following June. The reluctance of President Eisenhower and the need to complete the western security structure either by creating a European Defence Community or, in its absence, by bringing Germany into the North Atlantic Treaty also caused the loss of the opportunity in the year 1954. By this time Churchill had passed his eightieth birthday, and his retirement, already much discussed, could not long be postponed. But the enthusiasm for 'summitry' remained, and came to fruition a few months after his retirement.

On 25 January 1955 Churchill was the guest of honour at a trade union dinner—that of the National Federation of Building Trade Operatives, the union to a section of which he had been recruited in 1928. He said that 'trade unionism in Great Britain had worked well for the people', and added:

Much of the influence of the trade union leaders, which was perhaps greater here than in any other country, undoubtedly came from the long time they held office and the difficulty of getting them out. (Laughter.) Of course they were in that position able to serve causes irrespective of the feeling of popularity at the moment and did not have to compete with the latest bidder for leadership who came along under the difficulties of trade union disputes.[30]

Churchill finally retired on 5 April 1955. In the course of his peregrinations through the British party system he had retained a number of clear principles for his political conduct. One was opposition to socialism, which he regarded as an enemy of good government. As he said in 1908: 'Translated into concrete terms, Socialist society is a set of disagreeable individuals who obtained a majority for their caucus at some recent elections, and whose officials would now look upon humanity through innumerable grills and pigeon holes and over innumerable counters, and say to them "Tickets please." '[31] But another principle was sympathy for working people and for their representative leaders, that is to say, trade unionists, whom he regarded as an estate of the realm quite as much as any other. Of course he regretted their 'capture' in Britain by the socialist 'intellectuals', as he saw it. Having spent much of his political career sharing the representation of a double-member seat with a Labour MP in Labour's pre-socialist days, he was bound to regret the transformation of the Labour Party into a party at least nominally socialist. But he also remained proud of his own achievements as a social reformer in the years of his collaboration with Lloyd George before the First World War, and also of the contribution of the Coalition of the Second World War to the social reforms effected after 1945. These reforms were maintained almost in their entirety in his peacetime administration of 1951–5, which ended consequently in an atmosphere of as much consensus and goodwill as could be expected at a time of fierce political controversy.

At various times, but above all during the Second World War, Churchill depended on Labour leaders to further his own aims. The converse was also true after 1945 when Churchill, despite his rhetoric about the Labour 'Gestapo', accepted important Labour legislation after he returned to power in 1951. Thereafter he demonstrated that there was a much greater consensus in domestic as well as foreign affairs than one might be led to believe from the legend of Churchill as a reactionary. There was thus an overall symmetry to Churchill's career in regard to Labour issues.

8

Churchill and the First World War

MICHAEL HOWARD

MONG all the young Englishmen who in August 1914 thanked
God for matching them with His hour, none can have greeted
war more ecstatically than did Winston Churchill. 'Radiant, his
his face bright, his manner keen . . .' Lloyd George describes him; 'You
could see that he was a really happy man.'[1] He was at the height of his
powers, if not yet of his power, and he knew it. As First Lord of the
Admiralty, a post which he had held for three years, he was already a
key figure in the Cabinet. Still only 39, he was able by his sheer energy
to dominate his colleagues. He was eleven years younger than his closest
associate, David Lloyd George, the Chancellor of the Exchequer; eleven
years younger than the Foreign Secretary, Sir Edward Grey; twenty-four
than the Prime Minister, Herbert Asquith; and twenty-six years younger
than his colleague at the War Office Herbert Horatio Lord Kitchener,
under whose command he had served as a subaltern in the Sudan
Campaign sixteen years earlier. As for the venerable Lord Fisher, whom
Churchill perhaps unwisely recalled from retirement to resume his former post as First Sea Lord, his handicap was no less than thirty-five
years, and this told from the very beginning.

The enjoyment that he gained from his task alarmed even Churchill
himself. 'I am interested, geared up and happy', he wrote to his wife
on 28 July 1914: 'Is it not horrible to be built like that? I pray to God
to forgive me for such fearful moods of levity.'[2] Seven months later he
felt equally happy and equally guilty. 'I think a curse should rest on me
because I am so happy', he told Asquith's daughter Violet, on 22
February 1915. 'I know this war is smashing and shattering the lives of
thousands every moment—and yet—I cannot help it—I love every second I live.'[3]

This passionate interest in and commitment to war was by no means
exceptional in 1914. Churchill and Rupert Brooke were typical of their
generation, not only in Europe but in the America of Teddy Roosevelt.

After long years of enervating peace, they welcomed the war as a challenge to their manhood. But in Churchill's case there was more to it than that. Unlike his political colleagues and adversaries, he had trained as a professional soldier, and had abandoned that career largely because it was too constricting for his adventurous spirit. As a journalist he had been able to cover campaigns in Asia, Africa, and the New World in a way that uniquely broadened his military experience. He was not one of those who expected the forthcoming conflict to be brief and glorious; on the contrary he warned the British people, in one of his earliest speeches, that it would be 'long and sombre'.[4] None the less, he saw the war as a fulfilment rather than a frustration of his destiny, and he did not pretend otherwise.

Churchill's contemporaries observed this with mixed feelings. A not unsympathetic observer, the journalist A. G. Gardiner, wrote of him later that autumn: 'He sees himself moving through the smoke of battle, triumphant, terrible, his brow clothed in thunder, his legions looking to him for victory and not looking in vain.'[5] All was well so long as they did not look in vain; but as month succeeded disappointing month and Churchill's heroic ventures one after another collapsed, the feeling became general, not only among his colleagues but among the public as a whole, that he was an anachronism in twentieth-century warfare, and a dangerous one at that.

We must remember how very little political credit Churchill had to draw on anyway, when war broke out in 1914. For the Conservative Opposition, in spite of his robust attitude towards Germany, he was the blackest beast in the Liberal menagerie. In the first place, he was a political turncoat. In the second, he was seen as a dangerous radical. In the third, his provocative attitude during the Home Rule crisis had infuriated the Unionist politicians, notably their leader in the House of Commons, Andrew Bonar Law. The naval reforms that he had pushed through at the Admiralty, and the abrasive fashion in which he did so, had antagonized many retired and serving officers of the Royal Navy, who found ready sympathizers on the Conservative back-benches even when they did not sit there themselves. Among his Liberal colleagues, he was widely regarded as an adventurous and unpredictable maverick; while the Radicals, who had welcomed him as an ally when he had attacked the naval estimates five years earlier, now also saw him as a turncoat and detested him almost more than did the Conservatives. In the words of Lord Beaverbrook, who was in a good position to observe, 'he was now hated, he was mistrusted, and he was feared'.[6]

In spite of this political weakness, Churchill acted from the beginning of the war as if he had plenary powers, not only over the navy, but over everything else as well. His Cabinet colleagues, out of their depth in the new element of war, did little to check him. On 1 August, on learning of the German declaration of war against Russia and entirely on his own responsibility, Churchill ordered the mobilization of the fleet; a measure ratified by the Cabinet only the following day. It was indeed thanks largely to his own preparations, according to Arthur Marder, that 'every detail of the wartime disposition of the Navy had been so meticulously worked out that, within twelve hours of the issue of the mobilization instructions . . . every one of HM ships, including the ships in reserve, was already at her war station or had her war orders, ready for all contingencies'.[7]

On 3 August, when the news came through of the German ultimatum to Belgium, he ordered the implementation of the contingency plans made with the French navy to protect the English Channel, consulting only with the Prime Minister and the Foreign Secretary; a decision that converted what had hitherto been merely an unofficial understanding into a working military alliance. On 19 August, without even consulting Lord Kitchener at the War Office or his own naval staff, he proposed to the Russian High Command that the British should provide troop transports to land Russian forces on the German coast. Further, he created what was virtually a private army based on surplus naval reserve manpower, the Royal Naval Division: an army whose uniform he designed and into which he commissioned his personal friends.[8] And on 24 August, learning of the fall of the fortress of Namur, he ordered troops of that division to occupy Ostend; a measure which the Cabinet had, again retrospectively, to approve the following day.[9]

Churchill, indeed, found it impossible simply to remain at the Admiralty and watch the plans for war at sea over which he had brooded for the past three years gradually unfold: the assembly of the Grand Fleet at Scapa Flow, the hunting down of German commerce raiders, the imposition of the blockade, the patient wait for the German High Seas Fleet to sail out and give battle. Temperamentally, he was ill-suited to a role that demanded calm, patience, and faith in Britain's capacity through her command of the seas to bring Germany to her knees. 'From the very beginning of hostilities', as Arthur Marder has put it,

Churchill was bitten with the idea that the Fleet should 'do something'. Although he had been a prime originator of the distant blockade policy, he failed to appreciate the real power the Grand Fleet was exercising and the fact that it might go through the war without fighting a battle and yet might have been the dominating factor all the time.[10]

On 8 October we thus find Churchill declaring that 'it was to secure the eventual command of the Baltic that British naval operations must tend'.[11] For a decade past the navy had been revolving projects (it would be an abuse of the term to call them plans) for seizing offshore islands such as Borkum or Heligoland, either to compel the German fleet to come out and fight, or as a preliminary to landing forces on the German coast. Now Churchill bombarded his staff with proposals for capturing ports in neutral Holland, Denmark, Norway, or Sweden; seizing Heligoland or Sylt; landing in Schleswig-Holstein; and—a project that particularly took his fancy—a descent on the North Sea island of Borkum. 'Borkum is the key to all northern possibilities', he told Fisher on 4 January 1915; '. . . Ask that a regular division of infantry be assigned to the capture of Borkum and that plans be made on that basis for action at the earliest moment.'[12] The proposal struck his Assistant Director of Operations, Captain Herbert Richmond, as 'quite mad. The reasons for capturing it are NIL, the possibilities about the same. I have never read such an idiotic, amateur piece of work as this outline in my life.'[13] But within a few days, as we shall see, this project was also to be forgotten. Churchill became seized of the greater possibilities offered by the enemy's southern flank.

Naval operations alone could not satisfy Churchill's appetite for action. On 26 August 1914, when his brother Jack was posted to France, Churchill wrote to him enviously: 'As soon as the decisive battle has been fought at sea I shall try to come out too, if there is any use for me.'[14] The Marine Brigade did not stay in Ostend for long enough to enable Churchill to join them, but within a few weeks the scope of their operations was extended. First, Kitchener, fearing for the safety of the Channel Ports, asked Churchill to send the brigade to garrison Dunkirk. There they were supplemented with a regiment of yeomanry, the Oxford Hussars, in which Churchill himself had served for several years. To this Churchill added on his own account a massive component of Admiralty motor transport, including a squadron of armoured cars and, as we shall see, a detachment of scouting aircraft.

This quasi-autonomous force was beginning to harass the flanks of the advancing Germans when it was given a second and more ambitious task. On 2 October the Belgian government let it be known that the fortress of Antwerp would have to be abandoned, a decision that would release further German forces to sweep down the coast and outflank the British Expeditionary Force in its race to the sea. When the news reached London the Prime Minister was out of town, and Grey summoned a meeting of available members of the Cabinet. 'Until Churchill's arrival at about midnight', reported Hankey, 'nothing seems to have been evolved. On his arrival and initiative it was decided to urge the Belgian government to hold the fortress until the issue of the main battle had been decided in France, if only for a few days; also that Churchill should proceed at once to Antwerp.' On his return next day Asquith found himself presented with a *fait accompli*, but suspected that Churchill's mission had been undertaken only with Grey's 'rather reluctant consent'.[15] But Churchill had already gone. On his arrival he summoned the rest of the Naval Division, two of whose brigades had been recruited only in the past few weeks, to join the garrison. 'His proposal was sanctioned,' commented Hankey drily, 'but by whom it was not clear.'[16]

At Antwerp Churchill found himself in his element. In the distance, the mutter of guns; in the foreground, anxious figures working to strengthen the fortifications; the flaccid Belgian ministers to be exhorted and encouraged; the cheerfully imperturbable British soldiers and sailors to be allotted to their battle stations; this was the kind of war that he enjoyed. 'So great was his influence', wrote one of those who saw him, 'that I am convinced that with 20,000 British troops he could have held Antwerp against almost any onslaught.'[17]

This was exactly what Churchill wanted to do. Next day, 5 October, he sent Asquith what must surely rank as one of the most extraordinary communications ever made by a British Cabinet Minister to his leader. 'I am willing', he declared, 'to resign my office and undertake command of relieving and defensive forces assigned to Antwerp in conjunction with Belgian Army, provided that I am given necessary military rank and authority, and full powers of a commander of a detached force in the field.'[18]

The offer did nothing to enhance Churchill's reputation with his colleagues. It was greeted, so Asquith told Venetia Stanley, with 'a Homeric laugh';[19] although Kitchener did promise, perhaps ironically, to promote Churchill to Lieutenant General if Asquith made the appointment. Nor did the outcome of the expedition enhance his reputation with the country. Most of the troops sent to Antwerp were untrained, and barely knew how to use such few weapons as they had. Within a few days they were forced into retreat. Out of some eight thousand men, about two hundred were killed or wounded, nearly a thousand taken prisoner, and fifteen hundred took refuge in neutral Holland where they were interned for the rest of the war.

Churchill was unabashed by this outcome. On his return to England he badgered Asquith to give him a land command. 'I told him', Asquith later recorded,

that he could not be spared from the Admiralty, but he scoffs at that. . . . His mouth waters at the sight and thought of Kitchener's new armies. Are these 'glittering commands' to be entrusted to 'dug-out trash' bred on the obsolete tactics of twenty five years ago, 'mediocrities who have led a sheltered life mouldering in military routine' etc. etc.? For about a quarter of an hour he poured forth a ceaseless cataract of invective and appeal, and I much regretted that there was no shorthand writer within hearing, as some of his unpremeditated phrases were quite priceless.[20]

As for the campaign itself, Churchill always maintained that it had served its purpose. Had Antwerp not been defended, he argued in *The World Crisis*, the Germans would have found nothing to stop them penetrating to Ypres and beyond, thus outflanking the Allied armies. 'Ten days were wanted,' he declared, 'and ten days were won.'[21]

A good case for the operation can be made along these lines, but it did not appear so at the time. The opposition press was merciless. The retreat from Mons a few weeks earlier could be depicted, if not as a victory, then certainly as a glorious feat of arms. Antwerp appeared to be simply a muddle and an unmitigated disaster, for which Churchill was clearly responsible. His initiative in mobilizing the fleet at the outbreak of war had temporarily silenced the voices of his critics, but not for long. After that, his record at the Admiralty appeared lamentable. There had been the escape of the *Goeben* and the *Breslau* in the Mediterranean. There had been the torpedoing of the *Aboukir*, the *Cressy*, and the *Hogue* in the Channel, with the loss of 1,400 men. There had been the destruction of Cradock's squadron at Coronel, rapidly though this had been avenged by Sturdee at the Battle of the Falkland Islands. There had been the German shelling of Hartlepool, Whitby, and Scarborough. Against this there seemed nothing to show except the inconclusive forays of the Heligoland Bight and the Dogger Bank. By the end of the year, Churchill was beginning to look like a major liability to the government rather than its premier asset.

The press was unfair to focus on Churchill as a scapegoat for Antwerp. He had been sent there by his colleagues virtually with plenary powers. His measures had been supported throughout both by the Prime Minister and by Kitchener. The fault lay with the system, or rather the lack of one, that made necessary this kind of war by improvisation. Given the lack of any directing body where political authority

and military advice could come together; given an army whose commanders had effectively emigrated to France with their staffs to conduct
a war limited, so they believed, in duration and scope; and given a navy
obstinately following its own agenda, it was inevitable that the conduct
of British strategy should initially be chaotic, and at the mercy of anyone with the will and the authority to take the initiative. Kitchener,
believed by the public to be a veritable God of War, was submerged at
the War Office by the task of converting the most unmilitary society in
Europe into a Nation in Arms, whose armies might be effective in
about two years. Who else was there who could rise to the occasion and
take necessary, bold decisions?

Hankey, who from his humble position as secretary to the War
Council did his best to sort out the confusion, was later to pay tribute
to Churchill's powers of initiative. 'We owed a good deal in those early
days', he wrote in his memoirs,

to the courage and inspiration of Winston Churchill who, undaunted by
difficulties and losses, set an infectious example to those of his colleagues who
had given less thought than he, if indeed any thought at all, to war problems.
He may have been rash at times but he was a tower of strength, and I hope
his fellow-countrymen will never forget it.[22]

And Fisher, who as First Sea Lord had literally been driven mad by
Churchill's conduct at the Admiralty, maintained in retrospect: 'I
backed him up till I resigned, I would do the same again! He had
courage and imagination. He was a *war man!*'[23] He was indeed, but his
contemporaries were justified in wondering whether it was the right
kind of war.

Meanwhile, Churchill had been exercising his initiative in another
and less controversial direction. In addition to conducting the war at
sea and waging his campaign in the Low Countries, he was virtually
inventing both air and armoured warfare.

At the beginning of September 1914 the overburdened Kitchener
had asked Churchill to assume responsibility for the air defence of the
British Isles. On examining the problem Churchill came to the conclusion, several years before Douhet, Trenchard, Billy Mitchell or any of
the other Founding Fathers of Air Power, that the best if not the only
form of defence in the air lay in pre-emptive attack. He decided therefore to establish air bases, not just in the United Kingdom, but across
the Channel in France and Belgium, from which he could establish
command of the air within a hundred miles of the English coast. This

provided an additional rationale for the presence of the Marine Brigade at Dunkirk; also for the fleet of armoured cars he provided to patrol inland both to protect the British airfields and to prevent the Germans from establishing any of their own. Although land operations came rapidly to an end, British aircraft based on Dunkirk carried out perhaps the first strategic 'counterforce' air-strike in history, dropping bombs on a Zeppelin base in Düsseldorf as well as on the railway station at Cologne.

Furthermore, this early experience with armoured cars was not to be wasted. Within a few weeks of the beginning of the campaign, Churchill had initiated studies into the means of getting these vehicles over obstacles and trenches. By the end of the year, once the Western Front had become bogged down into trench warfare, he extended his vision to the possibility of devising armoured vehicles that could carry both men and machine-guns, moving on caterpillar tracks that could cross or crush all obstacles in their path. The same idea occurred simultaneously to Hankey and other observers, but Churchill was in a position to do something about it. On 5 January 1915 he wrote a memorandum to the Prime Minister urging action on the matter. Asquith passed it on to Kitchener, but Churchill, impatient with the dilatory approach of the War Office, set up his own 'Landships Committee' at the Admiralty. By April 1915 the production of prototype 'tanks' was well under way. The tank may have had many parents, but Churchill was without any question its prime *accoucheur*.[24]

Still, the effects of tanks and aircraft could only be felt in the long term. What was to be done in the meantime? By the end of 1914, Churchill had despaired of reaching a decision on the Western Front. 'I think it quite possible', he wrote on 29 December,

that neither side will have the strength to penetrate the other's lines in the Western theatre . . . although no doubt several hundred thousand men will be spent to satisfy the military mind on the point . . . On the assumption that these views are correct, the question arises, how ought we to apply our military power? Are there not other alternatives than sending our armies to chew barbed wire on Flanders? Further, cannot the power of the Navy be brought more directly to bear upon the enemy? If it is impossible or unduly costly to pierce the German lines on existing fronts, ought we not, as new forces come to hand, to engage him on new frontiers and enable the Russians to do so too?[25]

When he wrote this memorandum Churchill clearly had in mind an operation in the Baltic or North Sea; but within a few more days his attention was to be drawn to a far more attractive proposal.

The Dardanelles expedition, like the tank, had many parents, but as with the tank Churchill was to be the principal *accoucheur*. He had already been the prime mover in opening up the war in the Eastern Mediterranean. It had been on his initiative that the two warships being constructed for the Turkish Navy in British yards were impounded at the beginning of the war. He had been active in the Cabinet in urging war against Turkey. As soon as it was declared, on 31 October 1914, he ordered the bombardment of the outer Dardanelles forts. In November he had proposed an attack on the Dardanelles as 'the ideal method of defending Egypt'.[26] On 2 January 1915 he supported Kitchener in promising the Russians a naval demonstration to distract the Turks from their offensive in the Caucasus; and the following day he asked the naval commander on the spot, Admiral Carden, 'Do you think it is a practicable operation to force the Dardanelles by the use of ships alone? . . . The importance of the result would justify severe losses.'[27]

It will be remembered that at this time Churchill was still urging Fisher to make plans for an attack on Borkum. Indeed, as late as 4 January he tried to dissuade the old Admiral from his new interest in the Dardanelles. 'Germany is the foe', he reminded him, 'and it is bad war to seek cheaper victories and easier antagonists.'[28]

But Carden's positive if cautious reply to Churchill's query, and Fisher's offer of the *Queen Elizabeth* with her 15 inch guns to support the enterprise, put an end to his hesitations. On 13 January he took the initiative in formally proposing such an attack to the War Council, 'unfolding his plans', according to Hankey, 'with the skill that might be expected of him but without exaggerated optimism.' The idea caught on at once. 'The whole atmosphere changed. Fatigue was forgotten. The War Council turned eagerly from the dreary vistas of a "slogging match" on the Western Front to brighter prospects as they seemed, in the Mediterranean.'[29] The project was approved and Asquith drafted the ill-formulated instruction 'That the Admiralty should . . . prepare for a naval expedition in February to bombard and take the Gallipoli pensinsula, with Constantinople as its objective'.[30] As for Churchill, Borkum was forgotten. All his energies were focused, laser-like, on this new enterprise, with all the opportunities it seemed to offer for breaking the deadlock of the war.

This is not the place to rehearse once again the sad story of the Dardanelles.[31] In any case, the period during which Churchill was personally responsible for operations was brief. Once the naval attack was abandoned after the losses of 18 March and the decision taken to capture the Gallipoli peninsula by land assault, control passed out of his hands. It was now for Kitchener to decide what forces to send to the theatre, and for the commanders on the spot to decide how to deploy them. But Churchill continued to regard the campaign as his own enterprise. Apart from any other considerations, he had committed to it his own private army, the Royal Naval Division, in whose ranks were numbered some of his closest friends: Rupert Brooke, Patrick Shaw-Stewart, Charles Lister, Arthur Asquith; the brightest social and intellectual stars of their age. It was anyhow generally believed by the public at large (and not without reason) that had it not been for Churchill the campaign would not have taken place at all. So when the land assaults failed in April, and Fisher precipitately resigned in May, public opinion turned decisively against him. With Kitchener still regarded as being above criticism, responsibility for the whole endeavour was seen to be his alone.

By now Churchill had made himself almost as unpopular with his own colleagues as he was with the Opposition. Asquith told his wife on 7 March that Churchill was 'far the most disliked man in my cabinet by his colleagues', and indicated that his own patience was becoming overstretched: 'He is intolerable! Noisy, long-winded and full of perorations. We don't want suggestions—we want wisdom!'[32] Senior officers at the Admiralty made it clear that they would be glad to see the back of him. Most important, the leaders of the Conservative Party, when Asquith approached them to form a coalition cabinet, refused all cooperation so long as Churchill remained in any effective position of authority. On 4 May Asquith told him that he would have to leave the Admiralty. Churchill acquiesced with the worst possible grace. 'I am finished,' he lamented, 'finished in respect of all I care for; the waging of war.'[33]

Churchill was, of course, far from finished, but by the end of 1915, as the Dardanelles campaign fizzled out in humiliation redeemed only by the skill of the evacuation, most people would have agreed with his own verdict. For the next two years he was to remain in the wilderness. For the first six months of them he was still a member of the Cabinet; but without executive responsibilities he could only contribute advice that was increasingly unheeded and resented by his colleagues. In 13 November, when the abandonment of the Dardanelles had become a foregone conclusion, he resigned from the government. His request, bizarre even by his own standards, to be made Governor-General and Commander-in-Chief in East Africa in order to take charge of the campaign against the German guerrilla commander General von Lettow-Vorbeck, was predictably refused. Instead he was found a battalion command on the Western Front. There, at the age of 41, he was to serve for six months in the front line.

It is hard to think of any other statesman of Churchill's age and seniority who could have even considered the possibility of making such a transition, let alone doing so successfully. But he was, it must be remembered, a professional soldier by training and intermittently by inclination. He approached his new task with all his usual energy, rapidly overcame the understandable reservations with which he was regarded by his new colleagues, and thoroughly enjoyed the dangers and comradeship of the trenches. His front-line service was to give him an insight into the problems of contemporary warfare that was denied to other political leaders—and, it must be said, to many military leaders as well. Nevertheless he chafed at exile from what he felt to be his true environment. His occasional return to take part in Parliamentary debates only whetted his appetite. His command gave little scope for his talents, and political pressures (apart from the understandable scepticism of his superior officers) made it unlikely that he would be promoted to the higher military responsibilities to which he aspired. So at the beginning of May 1916 he took the opportunity offered by the dissolution and amalgamation of his battalion to resign his command and return to battle-stations at Westminster.

After six months' absence, Churchill now felt no inhibitions about attacking his former colleagues and their conduct of the war. He criticized the conduct of affairs at the Admiralty, and continued to argue against the concentration on the Western Front. He was now able to point, not only to the failure of Allied offensives over the past fifteen months, but to the example of the German attack at Verdun in February and March of 1916. 'Do you think', he wrote to his wife from France on 14 April, 'we should ever succeed in an offensive if the Germans cannot do it at Verdun, with all their skill and science? Our army is not the same as theirs; and of course their staff is quite intact and taught by successful experiment . . . We are children in the game compared to them.' For all these reasons he hoped that the Allies would harbour their strength in the West and focus on destroying Turkey. 'That is all we have the strength to do this year', he concluded. 'Next year victory may be won.'[34]

But that was precisely what the British government had decided not to do. Six weeks after Churchill's return to England the Allies opened their offensive on the Somme, and the battle dragged on for the rest of the year. At the same time the German U-boat campaign was taking a mounting toll of British shipping. The long-expected clash of battlefleets at Jutland on 1 June had been inconclusive and disappointing, and Churchill's journalistic skills had to be pressed into service to depict it as anything else. Asquith's conduct of the war was an easy target, and Churchill attacked it in Parliament and press with persistence and passion.

But these attacks did not make him any more popular. His most formidable philippics could always be countered by the ribald cry 'What about the Dardanelles?' However incompetent might be the government's conduct of the war, there was no inclination, either in Parliament or in the country as a whole, to entrust it to the hands of a man who had shown himself, when in office, to be so unpredictable and erratic. By the end of the year he was probably even more unpopular than the ministers he attacked; and when in December Lloyd George succeeded Asquith and created his new Ministry of All the Talents, the unyielding opposition of the Conservative Party prevented him from offering even the most menial job to Churchill.

So for another seven months Churchill remained in the wilderness, a Cassandra watching all his worst fears come true. In April 1917 the Allies launched yet another disastrous offensive on the Western Front, and U-boat attacks brought them within measurable distance of defeat. The Russians were on the point of collapse; and although President Wilson had decided that he was not, after all, too proud to fight, American help would not be forthcoming for another year. Churchill knew what should be done—or rather, what should not be done. On 10 May, in a Commons debate, he begged Lloyd George

to use . . . all his personal weight to prevent the French and British High Commands from dragging one another into fresh and disastrous adventures. Master the U-boat attack. Bring over the American millions. And meanwhile, maintain an active defence on the Western Front, so as to economise French and British lives, and so as to train and perfect our armies and our methods for a decisive effort later in the year.[35]

Even Churchill had now learned his lesson. The war was no longer to be won by strategic ploys or heroic adventures. Nothing would serve but skilfully applied attrition—but attrition applied with machines rather than with men.

Perhaps nobody except Lloyd George could or would have brought Churchill back into the government. Lloyd George could and did. As one of Churchill's oldest and closest associates he knew how much the country was missing so long as Churchill's talents were running to waste in Opposition. As an experienced politician he did not underrate Churchill's capacity for making trouble so long as he was left out in the cold. According to Beaverbrook it was the speech quoted above that brought matters to at head. 'Churchill could not be left out of the government. He must be fenced in, and that forthwith. What could not be squashed must be squared, and what could not be squared must be squashed.'[36] Furthermore Lloyd George knew where Churchill could now be employed to greatest effect: not in one of the Service Ministries where he was likely to do more harm than good, but in the Ministry of Munitions—that unromantic department which Lloyd George himself had created, and was perhaps more vital than any other to the waging of war in the industrial age.

Lloyd George did what he could to 'square' the opposition. Lord Northcliffe in particular, whose newspapers could make major trouble, was sent to comfortable exile on a mission to the United States. Even so (again according to Beaverbrook), 'never before in history has the selection of a Minister of the Crown given rise to such a vehement opposition. A stick had been thrust into the political beehive, and the rage of the drones and workers was terrible to behold.'[37] It was not only the drones and workers who protested. Lord Curzon, Lloyd George's senior Conservative colleague, warned that though Churchill was 'a potential danger in opposition . . . he will as a member of the Government be an active danger in our midst'.[38] The outcry indeed was so great that it shocked Churchill himself. He sadly confessed to Hankey that 'he had no idea of the depth of public feeling against his return to public life until his appointment was made'.[39] Lloyd George did his best to limit the damage by refusing to bring Churchill into the War Cabinet or to extend his responsibilities beyond the scope of his own Ministry, a refusal that Churchill found deeply humiliating. 'Not being allowed to make plans', he later wrote rather sulkily in *The World Crisis*, 'I was set to make the weapons.'[40]

At first, indeed, Churchill found it impossible to stick to his last. Within a few weeks he was intervening in the affairs of both the Admiralty and the War Office, and stubbornly argued his right to do so. It was not for him, he agreed, to formulate strategy. But if the Minister of Munitions did not have the right to adjudicate between the competing claims of the armed forces for scarce resources—resources on which the air arm now also had a claim—who did? 'It should be open to the Minister to draw attention to the relative merits of the competing services', he claimed, 'and use all such arguments as may prove necessary in that connection.'[41] This claim to what was effectively a *droit de regard* over the whole field of war-making was exactly what Churchill's colleagues had feared, and Lloyd George prudently ignored it.

Within his own department, however, Churchill found plenty to keep him occupied. His new responsibilities for procurement deepened his belief that the war was now one of *materiel*; not only of guns, but of the new weapons he had done so much to pioneer, aircraft and tanks. Having discerned so far ahead of his contemporaries the effect that these new arms would have on the conduct of warfare, he was now in a position to supervise their manufacture on a massive scale. 'There are only two ways left of winning the war', he announced on 4 September 1917, as the Passchendaele offensive was dragging out its sombre length, 'and they both begin with an A. One is aeroplanes and the other is America.'[42] The following spring he was urging that production of aircraft be increased by half, of tanks by four, and gas-shells (a weapon to which Churchill, like many of his contemporaries, was addicted) by five. The results would be decisive, he wrote, if either side 'possessed the power to drop not five tons but five hundred tons of bombs each night on the cities and manufacturing establishments of its opponents. . . . The resources are available, the time is available, the result is certain, nothing is lacking but the will.'[43]

As for tanks, Churchill was able to observe at first hand the impact of the forces he had created when the British Army took the offensive in August 1918. What he saw delighted him. The British Army was transformed. 'The moral', he told Lloyd George on 10 September,

appears to be training and Tanks, short advances on enormous fronts properly organised and repeated at very short intervals . . . It is the power of being able to advance a reasonable distance remorselessly day after day rather than making a very big advance in a single day that we should seek to develop. This power can only be imparted by Tanks and cross country vehicles on the largest scale.[44]

Churchill thus ended the war as he had begun it, a happy and fulfilled man. 'Coming over here', he wrote home from France on 15 September 1918, 'makes me thoroughly content with my office. I do not chafe at adverse political combinations, or at not being able to direct general policy. I am content to be associated with the splendid machines of the British Army and feel how many ways there are open to me to serve them.'[45] But like that army, and like his country as a whole, he had come a long way since 1914. He still hankered after brilliant coups, heroic adventures on a small but decisive scale, in accordance with what the British Army believed to be its historical traditions. He was to continue to hanker after them, even during the Second World War. But he had learned that against an adversary so formidable as the Germans there was no substitute for the massive organization and skilful application of force on the largest possible scale, backed by all the devices that science and technology could provide.

We may well wonder, as Churchill did so often himself, what he might have achieved had he continued in office during the crucial months between December 1915 and May 1917; especially during the winter of 1915–16 when the vital decision was taken to launch the series of offensives later to be known as the Battle of the Somme. It is perhaps unfortunate that, largely through his own later self-justifications, Churchill has become primarily associated with the concept of an alternative 'Eastern' strategy, based on a successful exploitation of the Dardanelles campaign. That is shaky ground on which to build a reputation. In the first place, neither he nor any other political leader could have done much to repair the operational inadequacies that brought that campaign to disaster. In the second, few historians would now claim that any help reaching Russia as a result of defeating Turkey could have turned the scale on the Eastern Front: the problems of the Russian Army, and the Russian Imperial regime, were too deep-rooted to be solved by short-term material or financial help. Finally, there is no reason to assume that the German Army could have been more easily defeated somewhere in Central Europe than it could be in France, where it had to be fought in any case. The military logic of the British High Command was, unfortunately, unanswerable.

Yet Churchill might, had he been given the opportunity, have engaged that High Command in savage and continuous dialogue about the nature, timing, and methods of their offensives in the West, as he was able to do with his military advisers during the Second World War. Subjected to his ferocious and well-informed questioning, it is at least conceivable that Haig might have been prevailed upon to intro-

duce very much earlier the reforms in his staff and procedures that
were to come about during the winter of 1917–18, and from which the
victories of 1918 were to follow. Further, the navy might have been
jolted out of its routine attitudes and introduced convoys long before
Lloyd George compelled them to do so in April 1917. But Churchill
could have taken on the armed forces only from a totally secure political base, and that, as we have seen, he never possessed. Even if he had
not been destroyed by the Dardanelles fiasco, it is unlikely that he
would have prevailed for long against the hostile forces building up
against him in press and Parliament, much less impose his will on the
conduct of operations. When he did return to office it was as a dependant on that masterly if unreliable policitian, Lloyd George; and a
dependant he remained until the end of the war.

Beaverbrook put his finger on one of Churchill's major weaknesses.
'He cared for the success of British arms', he wrote, 'and he cared for
nothing else. His passion for this aim was pure, self-devoted and all
devouring. He failed to remember that he was a politician and as such
treading a slippery path; he forgot his political tactics.'[46] And Robert
Rhodes James, in magisterial prose that owes something to Churchill's
own, describes some of his other drawbacks:

Even if Churchill was right over Antwerp and the Dardanelles, it would still
not meet the question of why Churchill's major enterprises had ended in vir-
tual disaster. . . . These points may be fairly made; he overestimated his own
knowledge and capacities; once enamoured by an idea or a plan, his total concentration on it and his devotion to it hindered him from a cooler appreciation
of the facilities available for its execution, and the probable hazards it would
face; he made insufficient use of the professional advice and experience that
was available to him and too often beat down criticism by argument rather
than heeding and utilising it . . . his approach was too personalised, too dramatic and too imperious . . . It is not necessary, when great measures are in
balance, to clothe every episode and fact with drama; nor is it necessary to
take personal charge of operations in order to ensure that they are being conducted with vigour.[47]

Such a verdict seems altogether fair.

By 1940, when he became Prime Minister and undertook responsibility
for leading his nation in a Second World War, Churchill had mellowed
and he had learned much. He no longer ignored his political base:
indeed he devoted a remarkable amount of his time to wooing and conciliating the House of Commons. He now knew from his First World

War experience that strategy could not be determined by an Aulic Council of politicians. Having appointed his nominees to the Cabinet, he left them to their departmental duties and ran the war himself. As for his military advisers, he regarded them as just that. The experience of 1914–18 had destroyed the majestic aura surrounding the reputation of the High Command, and Churchill made or broke generals as he saw fit. But the generals themselves now brought to their task a professionalism and a grasp of strategic realities that provided a necessary brake on the impulsive enthusiasm to which, even after half a century, Churchill was still prone. Both they and Churchill himself had learned enough from the experience of 1914–18 to make their co-operation in 1940–5 a   model of its kind. It was only after the chastening experiences of the First World War that Churchill could truly be said to be matched with his hour.

9

Churchill and Zionism

NORMAN ROSE

S OME people like Jews and some do not', Churchill observed. 'But no thoughtful man', he went on, 'can deny the fact that they are beyond question the most formidable and the most remarkable race which has ever appeared in the world.' After all, 'This wandering tribe . . . [had] grasped and proclaimed an idea of which all the genius of Greece and all the power of Rome were incapable', the idea of 'a universal God, a God of nations'.[1] This was the most precious of inheritances, and, for a historical mind like Churchill's, it should be preserved and nurtured for the generations to come.

But did Churchill actually 'like' Jews? By any reckoning, he must be counted amongst those who did. Not all, of course; as in the same way he did not like all Englishmen or Americans. But he never spoke of the Jews in the same disrespectful terms that he sometimes applied to Negroes, to whom he would refer scornfully as 'blackamoors' or 'niggers', or to Arabs and Indians and others whom he would just as scornfully call 'baboos' or 'Hottentots'.[2] Not too much should be read into these terms: they indicate merely that he was an all too typical son of his class, generation, and background. Although naturally subject to the anti-Jewish strains that permeated western Christian civilization, there is no evidence that he related to Jews on terms other than of tolerance and equality. Terms like 'Hebrew' or 'Israelite' were commonplace among members of his class and background, and should not be regarded too ominously—or should be taken as seriously as the expression 'goy', applied by many Jews to Gentiles. Other Gentile Zionists were more forthright, their ambivalence very much on display. John Buchan, whose works are peppered with 'Jewy' types holding court at Mayfair dinner parties, was a prominent supporter of Zionism. As was Harold Nicolson, who seemed to believe, in 1945, that the *Daily Mirror* was dominated by Jews who were corrupting solid English virtues: 'The Jewish capacity for destruction is really illimitable', he wrote, adding, in a revealing choice of words: 'Although I loathe anti-semi-tism, I do dislike Jews.' Many Gentile Zionists saw Zionism also as an antidote to those Jewish traits they most disliked. It would, so to speak, stiffen the Jewish back, and return to the Jews their 'national self-confidence' and 'corporate self-respect'.[3] Churchill may have been party to these widespread beliefs; but if so, he was sensible, or careful, enough not to air them in public.[4]

Perhaps something of Lord Randolph's attitude rubbed off on Churchill. He idolized his father. Churchill saw himself as Lord Randolph's heir, imitating his postures, his dress, his politics. Shocked at the anti-Semitic excesses in Russia in 1881, Lord Randolph called for 'formal enquiries' into the 'massacre and plunder' of Russian Jews. A rogue elephant in politics, Lord Randolph with his extravagant social style and 'exotic' friends also raised many well-bred eyebrows. His most intimate Jewish crony was Nathaniel ('Natty') Lord Rothschild, his financial adviser, whom he had known since his schoolboy days. Lord Randolph was a frequent visitor to Tring, Rothschild's estate in the vale of Aylesbury, and occasionally, as a special treat, he brought Winston along with him. There the impressionable young man would sit at the superbly appointed dinner table, uncharacteristically 'very silent', imbibing the excellent food and wine and absorbing the sophis-ticated, wordly conversation.[5] Winston's Rothschild was Sir Ernest Cassel, another of Lord Randolph's friends. Cassel invested Churchill's money earned from lectures and journalism—so necessary to further his political career. Later, this honourable friendship was exploited to hurt Churchill. Accused of plotting with Cassel to rig a panic on the London and New York stock exchanges, by issuing a false communiqué at the time of the Battle of Jutland, thus enabling Cassel to buy in a falling market and scoop enormous gains, he was portrayed as being willingly manipulated by an international Jewish banking conspiracy.[6] Lord Alfred Douglas, a notorious anti-Semite and the author of this scurrilous accusation, insinuated that Churchill had received a sweet-ener of £40,000 for his part in the ring. When the action for libel was heard, in December 1923, Churchill was cleared and Douglas was dis-patched to jail for six months.[7]

It was the Dreyfus case that first caused Churchill to take a definite stand. 'Bravo Zola!' he wrote to Lady Randolph from Omdurman.[8] Britain was relatively free of the anti-Semitic demonstrations that were disgracing France. But similar sentiments were voiced by his cousin 'Sunny', the 9th Duke of Marlborough, who protested vigorously when the *Daily Telegraph* published an unfavourable notice of Churchill's biography of his father. 'Sunny' accused the manager of the newspaper, Harry Levy-Lawson, of 'un-English' conduct, referring to him as 'that dirty Hebrew', and rejoiced at having rubbed his head 'in shit'. 'Sunny's' anti-Semitic outburst was quite foreign to Churchill's style and was met with a studied silence.[9] If 'Sunny' remained ignorant of his cousin's true feelings, Lady Randolph knew her son better. 'I see with the advent of Mr Montagu to the Cabinet,' she wrote in January 1916, 'that we shall soon have a Jewish Govt! They are undoubtedly clever—but have really no nationality. Probably you won't agree.'[10] He did not. In fact, the problem escaped him. For him, they were simply 'National Jews . . . Englishmen practising the Jewish faith'. On occasion, he would calm the Jewish conscience, so often in turmoil when faced with the spectre of 'dual loyalty'. 'Remember,' he told his Manchester Jewish constituents, 'the better Jews you become the better opportunity you will have to take your share in the service of the British Empire . . . no Jew who is not a good Jew can ever really be a good Englishman.'[11]

In April 1904 Churchill was adopted as Liberal candidate for the North-West division of Manchester. Seven hundred and forty Jews resided in the constituency and he served their interests until he moved on to Dundee in 1908. It is doubtful whether the Jewish vote was of much consequence to the election results. But industrious, ambitious politicians will apply themselves to raising support from every ethnic and sectarian quarter, conscious that in a tight fight it could swing the balance in their favour. Churchill was no exception. This is not to imply that he did not believe in the causes he upheld. There are occasions, even in a politician's career, when personal interest merges with high principle. He fought hard to smother the Aliens Bill of 1904 and amend its successor the following year, not only because the Manchester Jewish community opposed both bills, but also because he believed that the measures were wrong in principle. His energy was phenomenal. A member of the Standing Committee, he was criticized for 'speaking too often'. He took the credit for having 'wrecked the Bill'. Nathan Laski praised his 'splendid victory . . . for freedom & religious tolerance', while the Board of Deputies of British Jews applauded him for his 'eloquent championship' of their 'persecuted co-religionists'.[12]

Later, he wished to tighten up the regulations of the Bill, an aim that received widespread public sanction in the panic against 'aliens' and 'criminals' following the Sidney Street siege. Did this denote a basic change in his attitude? Hardly. Churchill was no longer the free agent of 1904–5. While it is possible to emphasize, for dramatic effect, his willingness to exclude certain categories of aliens (not only Jews) in 1910–11, which went without comment in the Jewish community, it would be just as worthwhile to pay attention to his firm actions to safeguard Jewish property and life in the South Wales riots of August 1911, which was greatly praised, or his defence of his Jewish colleagues during the Marconi scandal. In any case, owing to a crowded Parliamentary schedule no revisions in the Bill were made, an outcome that suggests he was not moved by any great sense of urgency in the matter.[13]

Only on one occasion was he accused of 'Jew-baiting'. It occurred in June 1914 during the debate on the acquisition of the Anglo-Persian Oil Company.[14] Churchill put the case for buying a majority share in the Company. A great imperial power needed to escape from the clutches of the giant oil monopolies and not be made 'a forced purchaser at artificial prices'. He singled out Sir Marcus Samuel, head of the Shell conglomerate, for special treatment: 'All the criticisms, so far, have flowed from one fountain.' But he also made plain that 'We have no quarrel with the "Shell".' The company was always ready, even anxious, 'to promote the interests of the British Navy and the British Empire', adding pointedly, 'at a price', as he beamed amiably across the benches at Sam Samuel, Marcus's brother.

Reading the speech today, it is difficult to decipher any 'Jew-baiting'. Certainly, Churchill's arguments were at time strained, playing up the hazards of monopolies and attributing strictly mercenary motives to Shell and its owners. Sir Marcus Samuel had due cause to feel that he and his firm had been unfairly used. But this would be stretching the term 'Jew-baiting' to breaking point.

Perhaps a more convincing case could be made for the period he served as Secretary of State for War. In 1920, at the height of his anti-Bolshevik crusade, he turned on 'the international Jews', a 'world-wide conspiracy' dedicated to 'the overthrow of civilization and the reconstruction of society'. The role played by these 'international and for the most atheistical Jews' in the Bolshevik revolution was certainly 'a very great one', and 'probably outweighs all others'. Churchill told Lloyd George that the Jews were 'the main instigators of the ruin of the Empire', and have certainly played 'a leading part in Bolshevik atrocities'. In Sunderland, he warned of the 'international Soviet of the Russian and Polish Jew'. He even unearthed evidence of a 'very powerful' Jewish lobby in Britain. His obsession with Bolshevism fuelled his most violent expressions aginst the Jews. To balance the scales, he saluted the Zionists. They would provide the antidote to this 'sinister conspiracy' and bestow stability instead of chaos on the Western world.[15] His high praise of Zionism, no less than his condemnation of 'international Jews', is significant here in the context of his tenacious, often bullheaded, battle against Bolshevism. At no time in his career had he employed such brutal language against Jews; nor would he do so again in the future.

Still, Churchill's speeches and writings do represent a general problem. Churchill was a rhetorician in the classical sense of the word: he used language, often extravagant and artificial, to persuade and impress and produce effect. In many ways, this is the key to his character and political career. He was intoxicated with words, particularly his own. As he developed his debating points, his imagination would catch fire. The potency of his richly expressive language would overwhelm him no less than it mesmerized his audiences. Churchill was quite aware of this problem.'I vy often yield', he confessed to Lady Randolph, 'to the temptation of adapting my facts to my phrases.'[16]

This is not to suggest that his public statements should be conveniently shelved—though, like all politicians' declarations, they should be treated with caution. In his own phrase, he erected a 'Scaffolding of Rhetoric', but it was a scaffolding supporting a set of beliefs and values firmly and genuinely held. His aversion to anti-Semitism was one of them. 'What are you doing to my Jews?' he repeatedly pestered Lord Lloyd, one of his Colonial Secretaries during the Second World War. There is no reason to question his assertion in 1946 that 'I have the strongest abhorrence of the idea of anti-Semitic lines of prejudice.'[17]

Churchill had no difficulty with his 'National Jews'. Things became more complicated when he applied himself to Zionism, a creed that set out its own national solution to the Jewish problem. Nor should this be surprising. Zionism saw itself, in modern parlance, as the national liberation movement of the Jewish people. Its interests were not necessarily those of Britain. At times, they coincided, most notably in late 1917 when they merged happily to bring forth the Balfour Declaration. On other occasions, they clashed, in particular when Britain felt itself under threat in the international arena, an almost permanent complaint for British policy-makers from the 1920s. In this clash between two conflicting national interests, it could not be expected that Churchill would choose the Zionist. In the end, it proved impossible to bridge the gap between Zionist expectations and the political reality as perceived by British statesmen. It was a dilemma that baffled not only Churchill. Also, the Zionists did not always smooth their friends' path. Often hopelessly divided over policy, they sent out muddled signals to their supporters: on partition, for example, the most crucial of all issues. 'Anthony [Eden] can argue that the whole policy was founded on consent, and that neither side has given it', cried 'Baffy' Dugdale.[18] If the Zionists were unable to agree, they could hardly hope that their sympathizers would form a united front.

Nor should one be too pedantic about looking for absolute consistency in a working politician's life—especially in a long life like Churchill's, one that encompassed many offices held in vastly different circumstances. Churchill was not blind to this in-built disability that plagued all but the most doctrinaire of politicians, and wrote an entertaining essay, 'Consistency in Politics', explaining away his own falls from grace.[19]

Apart from these general constraints, Churchill had learned from bitter experience that there are limits beyond which no minister, however talented, energetic, or masterful, dare ignore his officials' advice. The trauma of the abortive Dardanelles operation gave him no rest. If, finally, he attained his greatest ambition, the premiership, it was only because he had benefited from a set of unique circumstances, a fluke political constellation. 'My one fatal mistake', he wrote to his brother of the Dardanelles fiasco, 'was trying to achieve a gt enterprise without having the plenary authority wh cd so easily have carried it to success.'[20] But even during the Second World War, when his reputation stood high and he held 'plenary authority', he calculated his moves carefully. Until the winter of 1942–3, Churchill knew more crushing defeats than resounding victories. Nor did his position at home go unchallenged. He would not wilfully defy the opinions of his experts, particularly if to do so would undermine his authority and threaten his administration.

What attracted Churchill to Zionism? One looks in vain for the same kind of intellectual curiosity that moved, for example, Balfour. It is doubtful whether Churchill thought deeply or systematically about Zionism or the perennial Jewish question; and certainly not about the intricacies of Zionist politics or Jewish communal affairs.[21] Why should he have done so? Until very recently, few Jews have applied themselves to these bewildering questions. 'He was very moved by the information I gave him about Palestine, and also by the ideas about what should be done,' wrote Chaim Weizmann to his wife, 'but he has no notion about the complexities of the problem.'[22] Nor is there any evidence that he was motivated by any grand imperial design—at least not at the early stages of his career. Zionism confronted him at various moments in his career—as a young MP in Manchester, as a minister at the Colonial Office, as Prime Minister during the Second World War—and his immediate response reflected the spirit of the period.

Still, Churchill's basic sympathy for Zionism can hardly be disputed, though he was not above criticizing aspects of Zionist policy. Zionism—the vision of 'The Return', the restoration of an ancient people to its historic homeland—appealed to his regard for justice as well as to his abiding sense of history. He was fond of repeating Disraeli's dictum: 'The Lord deals with nations as the nations deal with the Jews.' 'We, the British,' he told Eliahu Eilath, the senior Israeli diplomat in London in 1950, were 'romantic idealists', a theme he had developed to a hostile Arab delegation in March 1921, in Jerusalem. Some months after the establishment of the state of Israel, he reminded the House that 'a Jewish state in Palestine is an event in world history to be viewed in the perspective of a thousand, two thousand or even three thousand years'.[23]

Churchill first spoke on a Jewish platform on 10 December 1905, at the Palace Theatre, Manchester. He moved the principal resolution protesting anti-Semitic outrages in Russia. On the platform beside him was Chaim Weizmann, then a lowly assistant lecturer in chemistry at Manchester University. That evening they met again at a dinner party. Two days later, Churchill's agent appealed for Weizmann's help 'to exert' influence among the Jewish voters of Cheetham Hill. Weizmann declined, claiming that he was 'a stranger in this land'—he had arrived in England in July 1904—and it would be unseemly for him to intervene in British domestic politics. During these brief moments they had 'hardly exchanged more than a few words'.[24] But here began a relationship that grew and developed throughout their lives, even blossoming at times despite the harsh climate.

Churchill and Weizmann were exact contemporaries. However, their backgrounds, their interests, their amusements could not have been more disparate. Yet Weizmann was important for Churchill's Zionist education. As for so many Gentiles, he personified the essence, the spirit of 'The Return'.[25]

Weizmann was the only major Zionist figure whom Churchill knew well and admired, and with whom he met regularly, if sporadically

Weizmann played on his conscience no less than testing him remorselessly with doses of Zionist logic. On the whole, his approach paid off. Whenever Churchill saw Weizmann, it gave him 'a twist in his heart'. What was the point of long conversations, he asked the Zionist leader, as in any case 'our thoughts were 99 per cent the same'. '[Weizmann] is so fascinating,' Churchill later revealed to his Cabinet, '2 hrs. go by in a flash and then I have a sleepless night.'[26] Pricking Churchill's conscience, however, was not always sufficient to remind him where his Zionist duty lay, as Weizmann discovered.

It was as a member of Lloyd George's post-war coalition that Churchill was first exposed to the Zionist problem, a quite different experience from his platform endorsements of Zionism. It was a stormy period for the Zionists. In the Balfour Declaration they had been promised that Britain 'would view with favour the establishment in Palestine of a national home for the Jewish people', though without prejudicing the 'civil and religious rights of the existing non-Jewish communities'. What did this cloudy formula mean? What was a 'Jewish National Home'? And, most important, how could they persuade the British government to translate these generous and well-intentioned, but loose, phrases into concrete political gains, namely a British mandate for Palestine under conditions that would enable the Yishuv (the Jewish community in Palestine) to thrive and prosper?

British policy during this period has been characterized as that of 'defensive imperialism'.[27] With resources spread thin, Persia, Iraq, and Egypt, linchpins of its Middle East policy, took first priority. In this context, Palestine appeared either as an appendage to Egypt, or as an excuse to keep the French at arm's length; in both instances a military and financial burden could be eased by turning the mandate over to a friendly power, perhaps the United States. This was a commonplace among British politicians at the time, with the notable exception of Lloyd George, who displayed little enthusiasm to relinquish anything. Balfour, the most distinguished of Gentile Zionists, upheld this view in a typically oblique manner: 'he himself was not in favour of a British mandate over Palestine, but . . . he would not oppose it'.

Churchill took a similar line. In March 1915 he had suggested that Palestine might be given to 'Christian, liberal, noble' Belgium. Now, in October 1919, as Secretary of State for War and conscious of the extreme urgency for cutting expenditure, he considered whether the European Powers should not resurrect the Turkish Empire, its integrity to be preserved by subjecting it to 'a strict form of international control'. This implied abandoning Palestine, potentially an enormous commitment. He returned to this theme in June 1920. Should not Britain 'clear out' of Palestine, which was already costing the British taxpayer £6 million a year? he asked Lloyd George. 'The Zionist movement will cause continued friction with the Arabs', he asserted, insinuating that in consequence British policy throughout the area would be placed in jeopardy, though admitting that 'the Palestine venture is the most difficult to withdraw from'.[28]

Churchill was not pursuing an anti-Zionist policy. It was quite possible to be a Zionist without committing oneself to administering Palestine. The Balfour Declaration, however it be read, contains no British obligation to do so. Churchill's questions to Lloyd George were entirely legitimate and, in the circumstances, perfectly understandable. Nor did he exclude other possibilities. Only months before his questionnaire to Lloyd George, in February 1920, he had envisaged 'by the banks of the Jordan' a state of three or four million Jews 'under the protection of the British Crown'.[29] Like any seasoned conductor, he could give different interpretations to the same symphonic work.

When Churchill entered the Colonial Office he was under tremendous pressure to cut expenditure and to revise Britain's Zionist commitment, which was still anchored in the vague phrases of the Balfour Declaration. He succeeded in both aims. During these years an anti-Zionist, anti-Semitic campaign was under way in the press, Parliament, and government. Churchill himself admitted to Weizmann that ninetenths of the British officials in Palestine were anti-Zionist.[30] As a working politician, Churchill could not remain indifferent to these currents of opinion, however distasteful he found them.

The press lords, Northcliffe and Beaverbrook, fostered this offensive. In May 1920 *The Times* gave credence to that notorious forgery, *The Protocols of the Elders of Zion*. A year later, the newspaper bravely retracted, but some poison had already seeped through. A *Daily Express* front-page lead article unearthed 'The Mystery of the Great Chaim [Weizmann]', 'the genius' who lured Britain 'into the morass of Palestine'. In London, in early 1922, a Palestinian Arab delegation lobbied the government to reverse its pro-Zionist policy. At the same time, an articulate and energetic pro-Arab lobby was active in Westminster. And as if to personify this mood, the House of Lords carried—by 60 votes to 29—a symbolic, but damaging, motion that questioned the validity of a British mandate for Palestine, despite a courageous maiden speech by Balfour, newly created an earl.[31]

Churchill had to tread a very thin line in this charged atmosphere. He certainly annoyed the Zionists. He rejected, on imperial grounds, Weizmann's plea to include Transjordan in the Jewish National Home. In Jerusalem, he advised the Jews to 'use prudence and patience' to allay Arab fears of being dispossessed and put under the rule of a minority. Back in Westminster, Churchill considered that the unrest in Palestine arose from 'the Zionist Movement, and our pledges in regard to it'. Weizmann was resentful of Churchill's attitude. They had 'a long argument'. Weizmann wrote, 'It is no use discussing academic declarations of sympathy' with him. At Balfour's house, Churchill defended his officials' restrictive policies, in particular immigration, while he professed to be 'greatly astonished' at the Lloyd George–Balfour chorus that 'by the Declaration they always meant an eventual Jewish State'. Weizmann summed up Churchill's performance: 'we were able to get little truth' out of him.[32]

For the Zionists all this was most unsatisfactory. But in fact Churchill came a long way to giving them what they wanted. True, he recommended reviewing in Cabinet 'the whole situation', and suggested 'proceeding cautiously' in Palestine to assuage the Arabs. But he upheld the essence of the government's Zionist policy. 'The problem . . . now is one of tactics, not strategy, the general strategic idea being the gradual immigration of Jews into Palestine to the extent to which they can be absorbed into the economic life of the country.' Despite Weizmann's unfavourable impression, Churchill was not indifferent to Zionist grievances. He argued for the maintenance of public security, for the punishment of Arab rioters, for the inclusion of Jewish colonists 'in an official reserve', for the sacking of officials and army officers who opposed government policy, and for closer co-operation with the Jewish Agency over immigration quotas and the development of Jewish economic enterprises. Not a bad haul, had the Zionists known of it.[33]

But if the Zionists complained of Churchill's hostility, the Palestinian Arabs suffered far worse. Churchill defended staunchly the British commitment to Zionism, on moral and political grounds. We 'cannot abandon to Arab fanaticism Jewish efforts', he told the House. He wished to take up a midway position. 'Our task', he continued, invoking, in vain, Lord Salisbury's aphorism, 'will be to persuade one side to concede and the other to forbear.'[34] In the face of Arab demands for a total reversal of policy, this symmetry proved beyond him. If for the Zionists he did not quite deliver the goods, to the Arabs he appeared as little more than a Zionist tool.

Given the level of anti-Zionist agitation, these months witnessed Zionist achievements no less considerable than the Balfour Declaration itself: the so-called Churchill White Paper and the mandate for Palestine, ratified by the League of Nations. At the same time, Churchill guided the controversial Rutenberg concession—a scheme that provided for the electrification of Palestine—through Parliament, a major triumph for the Zionists. However the clauses of the mandate are juggled, it reads as a Zionist document. Churchill's White Paper was more contentious, for it redefined the Declaration, not in the enthusiastic, positive terms previously employed by Lloyd George and Balfour, but in more limiting phrases. Although it recognized that the Jews were in Palestine 'as of right and not on sufferance', it viewed as 'impracticable' the proposition, expressed by Weizmann at the Paris Peace Conference, that Palestine would become 'as Jewish as England is English'. The Yishuv, with its distinct political, economic, and social organizations, and with the renaissance of the Hebrew language, had already acquired 'national characteristics'. What, then, was meant by a Jewish National Home?

It may be answered . . . [as] the further development of the existing Jewish community, with the assistance of Jews in other parts of the world, in order that it may become a centre in which the Jewish people as a whole may take, on grounds of religion and race, an interest and a pride.

Palestine as a whole would not be converted into a Jewish National Home. As for the explosive issue of immigration, that would now be regulated according to the principle of 'economic absorptive capacity'.[35]

However much the Zionists railed against the 1922 White Paper, they accepted it, extremists and moderates alike.[36] It enabled the Zionists to pursue their goals. Its phraseology was sufficiently flexible to satisfy both sides, after a hard argument. For Weizmann, it did not brazenly contradict his 'tree by tree, dunam by dunam' formula for creating the National Home. And this was precisely how the Yishuv developed, painstakingly building the economic, social, and political foundations that would eventually lead to the Jewish state. If Churchill is to be held responsible for Zionist disappointments—the lopping off of Transjordan, for example—he must also be credited with its successes, less dramatic but more lasting.

As the White Paper was inevitably referred to as Churchill's, he—having played no part in the Balfour Declaration negotiations—came to regard it as the epitome of his commitment to Zionism. When

Churchill later told Lord Moyne that he remained 'wedded to the Balfour Declaration as implemented by me',[37] he was referring to his paper of 1922. His fierce opposition to the May 1939 White Paper derived not only from its glaring injustices from the Zionist perspective, but also because it was, plainly, a flagrant breach of his word*. A British government, of which he was not a member and with whom he was in a state of permanent strife, had dared to break pledges that he had given.[38]

Churchill never recognized the validity of the 1939 White Paper. Reinstated as First Lord of the Admiralty, he argued against changes in policy that would 'prejudice the final form' the Palestine dispute would take. This formula proved to be the basis for Churchill's wartime policy. He fought hard, but in vain, to prevent the crippling land regulations of the White Paper from being brought into force, even absenting himself from the debate in order not to vote for the motion. All this was far from being the wartime 'truce' in Palestinian affairs that Weizmann wanted. The comparative ease with which Churchill's challenge had been mastered was an ominous portent of things to come. But in the circumstances, it was as far as Churchill could go. As Prime Minister, Churchill made clear his intention to annul the hated 1939 White Paper. 'It runs until it is superseded', he told the Cabinet.[39] But if not the White Paper, what then? Churchill was already toying with the idea of a Jewish state as part of an Arab Federation.[40]

When considering the Second World War, in particular the Holocaust, one feels, instinctively, that Western statesmen should not have accepted so readily the advice of their officials, should not have allowed themselves to be stifled by bureaucratic red tape, should have acted more decisively in order to save Jews. To have done so would certainly have been in keeping with Churchill's generous spirit. 'The terrible "Ifs" accumulate', Churchill wrote, reflecting on his period at the Admiralty during the First World War;[41] they accumulated again, dogging him, as they did all those who held political responsibility in the war against Hitler. At the same time, it is worth recalling Frederic

---

* The May 1939 White Paper formalized minority status for the Yishuv. It restricted Jewish immigration to a maximum of 75,000 for the coming five years, to be renewed only with Arab consent. In this way, the demographic balance of the country would be secured, about one-third Jewish, two-thirds Arab. Land sales to Jews were prohibited, or severely curtailed, in 95% of the area of Palestine. Finally, a Palestinian state, in treaty relations with Britain, was to be established after a transition period of ten years. There were additional flourishes: the possibility of a federal solution, or that independence would be withheld until the British government was entirely satisfied that Arabs and Jews could work together. This statement was viewed by the Zionists as an unmitigated disaster.

Maitland's cautionary words to every working historian: 'It is hard to remember that events now long in the past were once in the future.' The pressures on Churchill were tremendous: the problems he dealt with were many and complex: his overriding goal, to win the war as expeditiously as possible. In October 1943, defending his national coalition government's domestic policies, he said: 'Everything for the war, whether controversial or not, and nothing controversial that is not bone fide needed for the war.'[42] His maxim applies equally well to the broad range of his foreign policies.

In Britain, Jewish topics were not usually dealt with at Churchill's level. Considered within the general context of overall British wartime strategy, they were allotted a low priority. When Jewish representatives and members of the government did meet to discuss ways to rescue Jews, they inevitably terminated their parleys on the same depressing note: the most effective way of saving Jews was to bring the war to a rapid end. But when Churchill's attention was roused, when he did intervene, he did so with his pro-Zionist disposition and his sympathy for the plight of the Jews very much on display. The Moscow Declaration of November 1943 (indistinguishable from Churchill's original draft) promised retribution for the Nazis' 'abominable deeds'.[43]

Over Jewish immigration to Palestine, pared to the bone by the 1939 White Paper, and the creation of an independent Jewish fighting force, not established until the autumn of 1944, Churchill took a far more favourable attitude than most of his advisers. But he would not overrule them to the point of a break. He upheld the right of the Jews 'to go down fighting', as Weizmann put it. He also questioned the use of the navy against the so-called 'illegals' (those Jews who were not included in the official government immigration quotas and who entered Palestine defying the ban of the British authorities), and argued continually and consistently for a more humane policy, pressing for the release of internees in Palestine, or the entry into Palestine of those Jews fortunate enough to have reached its shores, having successfully run the British blockade.[44]

These were the most disquieting features of Britain's Palestine policy. Official justifications—that to do otherwise would inflame the Arab world against Britain, that Palestine would be 'flooded' with Jewish refugees, some of whom might be Nazi agents, or that the 'illegals' did not constitute 'a genuine refugee movement' but 'a political [Zionist] conspiracy' designed to 'fill Palestine with Jews and secure [military] domination over the country'—cut little ice with Churchill. Such fantasies were impossible to rationalize except by the most convoluted mental gymnastics, or by minds paralysed by prejudice. Both of these ailments were apparent in some government circles. Eden's mind was clouded by 'the Arab myth . . . He loves Arabs and hates Jews', wrote his private secretary, Oliver Harvey. 'They [the Jews] hate us,' one senior official reckoned, 'they hate all Gentiles.' Churchill's mind, fortunately, was not subject to these extreme disorders.[45]

It was the decimation of Hungarian Jewry in the summer of 1944 that triggered off two of the more controversial bids to rescue European Jews. The 'blood for goods' deal that Joel Brandt brought to the West was, on the face of it, a fantastic offer: a million Jews in return for ten thousand trucks—to be used on the Eastern Front—and considerable quantities of essential foodstuffs. The Zionists were divided in their estimation of this macabre proposal. The British, however, had serious and weighty reservations and were suspicious of Brandt's credentials, suspecting a German ploy to split the Allies at a critical juncture both on the Eastern Front and France after the recent Normandy landings. The scheme also flatly contradicted the principle of 'unconditional surrender', of not bargaining with the Nazi enemy. Giving expression to these anxieties, Churchill commented to Eden on 'the greatest and most horrible crime ever committed', but ruled that there should be 'no negotiations of any kind on this subject'. As for the Brandt project, he though it 'to be of the most nondescript character. I would not take it seriously.'[46]

At the same time as the Brandt affair hung fire, the Zionists were exploring another possibility for aiding European Jewry: the bombing of Birkenau, that part of the great complex at Auschwitz where the gas chambers and crematoria were located, and the railway lines leading to it. Churchill was favourable to the idea. He instructed Eden to bypass the Cabinet and to 'Get anything out of Air Force you can and invoke me if necessary.'[47] Once the problem was delegated to the operational level, it was buried under the weight of technical and logistical data, most of which was highly specious. In mid-July 1944, news reached the Foreign Office of the stoppage of the Hungarian deportations, another reason to let the matter slide, overlooking the fact that the killings were still going on. The Americans, with whom the British consulted, had already rejected the proposal, and it petered out at the end of August.

It is abundantly clear that had the Allies wished, they possessed the capacity to carry out the bombings.[48] Churchill did not follow up his minute to Eden, not out of ill-will or lack of sympathy or blunted sensibilities, but because other urgent business occupied his limited time:

the liberation of France; Greece; above all, the Warsaw uprising and relations with the Soviet Union. In fact, during the latter half of August, when these adverse decisions were being taken, Churchill was in Italy settling Mediterranean and Balkan affairs.[49] Naturally, none of this placated the Zionists. They too realized that bombing the camps would have little practical value, but they considered that it would have 'a far-reaching moral effect'.[50] Even this slight, but meaningful, gesture proved unobtainable. And it typified the Zionists' position. Unable to bring effective relief to the Jews of Europe, their frustration and anger grew. It was directed mainly against the petty bureaucrats who sabotaged their every effort. Churchill escaped this form of criticism. Despite all the setbacks and disappointments, Churchill remained for Weizmann 'our one great friend in England' who saw himself as Balfour's heir.[51] But how would Churchill deal with Balfour's inheritance? The decisive question was still the nature of the political solution, yet to be worked out. Would the Balfour Declaration lead to a Jewish state, as Balfour intended, or not? Churchill's government would have to decide.

Churchill first spoke of a Jewish state in 1908. The context was the great Zionist debate on a Jewish settlement in East Africa. Churchill, initially, had dallied with the 'territorialists' (Jews who sought a territorial solution to the Jewish problem, not necessarily in Palestine), who were particularly strong in his Manchester constituency. But opposition within the Colonial Office and among the British settlers, buttressed by mainstream Zionist opinion, had cooled his ardour. He wrote to Jacob Moser, a leading Manchester Zionist, that 'the only ultimate goal' was Jersualem, and went on: 'The establishment of a strong, free Jewish state . . . would not only be an immense advantage to the British Empire but a notable step towards the harmonious disposition of the world among its peoples.'[52]

It is unlikely that Churchill had a concrete political programme in mind. Rather, he gave free rhetorical rein to the 'romantic idealist' in him, a strain in his character that continually floated to the surface. In February 1920 he fired off another public salvo in favour of a Jewish state.[53] But as Colonial Secretary he was more circumspect, professing great 'astonishment' when Lloyd George and Balfour intimated that by 'the [Balfour] Declaration they always meant a Jewish State'. He took his 'astonishment' a step further, to outright opposition, when the Peel Commission recommended a partition of Palestine in July 1937. He did so by invoking Britain's greater imperial and strategic interests. At constant odds with Neville Chamberlain's government, he advised the Zionists to 'Persevere, persevere, persevere [in the mandate and his White Paper]'. His concern to preserve the mandate was so great that he threw in his own ten-year plan, limiting Jewish immigration to 20,000–25,000 a year, an influx that he hoped would maintain the demographic balance between Jew and Arab.[54] In the face of the Arab revolt in Palestine and a resurgent anti-Semitism in Europe, these suggestions were unlikely to pacify the Zionists.

Although the two leading Zionists, Weizmann and Ben-Gurion, favoured partition, many hotly refuted the idea. And this pattern was repeated among Gentile Zionists. 'Baffy' Dugdale and Leo Amery were notable exceptions. 'Baffy' is *sui generis*; but Amery's position is worthy of note. Whereas Churchill's Zionism was wholly British-oriented, Amery was able to grasp the complexities of the Jewish question also from a Jewish perspective, and somehow to reconcile what he saw with his wider imperial outlook. Like Weizmann, Amery realized that the old mandate was dead and could no longer be resuscitated, and that partition into a Jewish state offered the only way out. Churchill was unable to take this broader view. Britain was now very much under siege: in Europe, in the Mediterranean, in the Far East. Any surrender to violence, any capitulation to political blackmail, any deviation from this straight path would deal a mortal blow to the Empire and its ideals that Churchill held so dear. It was a valiant, but rigid, stand, relevant to some situations but not to all. On the eve of war, the mainstream Zionists expected a more flexible stand on partition.

Once the war had begun, Churchill registered support for a Jewish state, making plain his intent to Weizmann. In October 1941 he minuted: 'If Britain and the United States emerge victorious from the war, the creation of a great Jewish state inhabited by millions of Jews will be one of the leading features of the Peace Conference.'[55] Churchill swung round to partition in the spring of 1943. Prompted by a letter from Weizmann, Churchill—enclosing Weizmann's plea to Lord Moyne—made clear in a covering note that only 'the exigencies of war' have prevented a reconsideration of the policy of 'our predecessors'. Churchill told a bewildered General Edward Spears, no Zionist sympathizer, that 'he had formed an opinion which nothing could change. He intended to see to it that there was a Jewish state.' 'There is no arguing with him on this subject', complained Spears.[56]

In this manner there began an internal debate about future Palestine policy. Much of this comment, particularly from the military authorities, was highly, even pathologically, anti-Zionist.[57] None of this had much effect on Churchill. In reply, he circulated his speech against the 1939 White Paper. Weizmann had raised a point that was impossible to refute, and it weighed heavily upon Churchill. 'The slaughter of European Jews', he claimed, 'can only be redeemed by establishing Palestine as a Jewish country.' What, indeed, could be more just? As for the Arabs, Churchill always turned to the Rashid Ali rebellion as 'proof' of their 'worthlessness'.[58] When the Cabinet discussed Palestine on 2 July 1943 Churchill delighted Amery, for a change. 'On the whole a great day for the Jews if they had known of it—perhaps some day they may include Winston with Balfour (and to some extent myself too) as one of their real friends.'[59] The Cabinet committee on Palestine that Churchill set up was dominated by Zionist supporters, and remained so despite persistent murmurs of discontent from the Foreign Office. By January 1944 the Cabinet accepted in principle its recommendation in favour of partition. Once committed, Churchill became a firm partitionist.[60]

Churchill's conversion sprang from his expectations of the Anglo-American relationship, and in particular from his intimacy with Roosevelt. The 'first step was to get America in with us', he told the Cabinet. For some time he had been dazzling Weizmann with the prospect of an overall Middle East settlement, sponsored by Roosevelt and himself, that would raise up Ibn Saud as the 'Boss of the Bosses', and that would include an autonomous Jewish state in Palestine.[61] The priority Churchill now gave to the American connection was a tacit admission of British weakness. Britain, alone, was unable to carry the Palestine burden. As the war progressed, and well into the post-war years, this feeling took root, and it figured as the main theme of Churchill's pronouncements on the Palestine question. Either joint responsibility with the United States, or else Britain should return its mandate to the United Nations. Churchill's commitment to a Jewish state was in line with his Zionist principles. But the timing of his change of view also stemmed from his deepening conviction that Britain no longer had the power to fulfil its mandatory obligations, a reflection of her changed status as a world power.

On 4 November 1944 Weizmann met Churchill at Chequers. It was 'a long and friendly conversation'.[62] The usual ground was covered: partition; massive Jewish immigration; American co-operation; and the demise of the 1939 White Paper. But there could be no definite statement until the end of hostilities, a period Churchill envisaged as about six months off. Twenty-four hours later, Lord Moyne, the senior British official in the Middle East, was gunned down by Jewish terrorists outside his home in Cairo. Moyne (Walter Guinness) was a long-standing and intimate friend of Churchill's, and his senseless murder affected him profoundly. One of his private secretaries, John Martin, remarked that it was impossible to talk to him of Palestine for months after Moyne's death.[63] Typically, Churchill's revulsion first found expression in the flavour of his rhetoric; he bracketed 'Zionism' and 'a set of new gangsters worthy of Nazi Germany', and threatened to reconsider his own position.[64] But Churchill was not panicked into taking punitive measures against the Yishuv, as he was being pressed to do. Weizmann assured Churchill that the Jewish Agency would co-operate with the British authorities to stamp out the terrorist organizations, a pledge he kept.

For all that, the Moyne assassination was a real turning-point.[65] Something snapped in Churchill's relations with the Zionists. Despite his genuine affection for Weizmann, they never met again. In an age of mass politics this might appear to be of small consequence. But in fact the quality of the relationship between these two eminent leaders, who both set, for obvious reasons, the highest premium on their ability to dominate events, was of crucial significance. Politically, partition, while not officially discarded, was set aside. In this way, Churchill enabled the anti-partitionist, anti-Zionist forces in the government to gather momentum and kill partition—as they had done in 1937–8.[66] A British-inspired partition, guided by Churchill, was no longer practicable politics.

By the time the European war came to an end, the 1939 White Paper was still in force. The Zionists' one substantial achievement, a Jewish fighting force, despite Churchill's support, had been allowed only grudgingly and tardily. For all their diplomatic efforts and manœuvring, the Zionists had been driven back to square one. On 22 May 1945 Weizmann appealed to Churchill: 'This is the hour to eliminate the White Paper, to open the doors of Palestine, and to proclaim the Jewish State.' Churchill's concise and unambiguous reply, putting off any arrangement until 'the victorious Allies are definitely seated at the Peace table', shattered Weizmann. He wrote back, renewing his appeal, but Churchill declined to answer.[67] Understandably bitter at Churchill's 'do-nothing policy', Weizmann considered resignation. 'If Mr Churchill had wanted to settle things, he could have done so', he told a Zionist meeting. Other Zionists were more outspoken, while in

Palestine Jewish extremists intensified their terrorist campaign. 'I stand before young Jews today', Weizmann protested a year later, 'as a leader who failed to achieve anything by peaceful means.'[68] In a very real sense, Churchill's reluctance to meet him half-way during these crucial weeks contributed to Weizmann's downfall at the Zionist Congress in December 1946.

Soundly beaten at the elections in July, Churchill went into Opposition. It proved most difficult to draw him back into active Zionist work. As Leader of the Opposition he had little to offer except the enormous prestige attached to his name. Yet to the Zionists, virtually on their knees, this would have been a considerable bonus. He avoided meeting Weizmann, 'his conscience', claiming that, in the circumstances, he was sure Weizmann 'would understand'. 'Well, as a matter of fact, I don't understand at all!' Weizmann snapped testily. 'I know, of course, that he is none too well. Neither am I if it comes to that.' When Weizmann appealed to him, 'in extremis—as to an old friend', he was treated to another disappointment. Churchill passed Weizmann's message on to Attlee, replying 'there is nothing that I personally can do in the matter', while still insisting that the Palestine question 'continues to be of profound interest to me'.[69]

At the most critical juncture in Zionist fortunes, Moyne's brutal murder had caused Churchill to stumble, to lose direction. Weizmann offered an explanation for his lapse. He has 'more or less withdrawn from Zionist work because he is disgusted by the terrorists and terrorism'. To Boothby, Churchill fulminated against 'the Irgun terrorists': 'I will never forgive [them] . . . they are the vilest gangsters.' He told the House of Commons that terrorism would 'destroy the inclination to make further efforts in British hearts'. As Britain's Palestine policy disintegrated into anarchy, giving way to a vicious bloody spiral of punitive measures and terrorist reprisals, Churchill's reluctance to become involved hardened. In July 1948, through Walter Elliot, he sent Weizmann his warmest personal regards, but added: 'The Palestine position now, as concerns Great Britain, is simply such a hell-disaster that I cannot take it up again or renew my efforts of twenty years. It is a situation which I cannot help in, and must, as far as I can, put out of my mind.'[70]

This was, however, only partially true. Churchill was unable to resist putting to use the most effective weapon in his armoury, his oratory. In August 1946 he praised Weizmann highly to the House, and counselled the Zionists to respect his authority 'in this dark hour'. He continued to advocate partition, though he did not believe that the Palestine problem could be solved 'by a vast dumping' of the Jews of Europe into Palestine, an idea 'too silly to consume our time'. In the winter of 1948–9 he delivered a series of telling speeches calling for the recognition of Israel and castigating Ernest Bevin's policy, riddled with 'bias and prejudice'.[71]

After Britain recognized Israel, Churchill renewed contact with Weizmann: 'I look back with pleasure on our long association', adding, in his own hand; 'The light grows'.[72] His relationship with Zionism moved into its 'golden age'. Nostalgia tended to blur ancient disagreements and highlight bygone achievements, a situation that suited both parties. For the remainder of his active life, he cultivated his Zionist, now Israeli, interests.[73] When James de Rothschild suggested, in February 1955, that perhaps Israel should be admitted to the Commonwealth—the hoariest of chestnuts—Churchill did not rule out the idea. 'This is a big question', he advised Eden. 'Israel is a force in the world & a link w the USA.'[74]

One reliable guide to Churchill's attitude to Zionism must surely be how the Zionists themselves—whose memory was notoriously long in such matters—came to regard him. Of course, they often differed, at times they quarrelled, on occasion harsh words were used. In a relationship that extended over fifty years, and was focused on such a complicated and controversial issue, it could hardly be otherwise. But the overall impression is one of mutual regard and affection: certainly for Weizmann, who, despite Churchill's inconsistencies, always regarded him as 'a friend of the Jews and the Zionists', in fact their 'one great friend' in England during the war.[75] But no less for Ben-Gurion, a far more prickly character: 'I am full of admiration for him', he told Lord Lloyd at the height of their wartime quarrels.[76]

The Balfour Declaration, and the British mandate for Palestine that sprang from it, were among the most extraordinary acts in the history of British foreign policy. They raised problems that proved beyond the wit of any British statesman to solve satisfactorily, Churchill included. Yet few Englishmen have a better record on behalf of Zionism, and few can equal Churchill's high reputation among Zionists. If Balfour was more intellectually in tune with Zionism and Amery more aware of its needs, if Lloyd George was more decisive and 'Baffy' Dugdale more committed, Churchill has still earned the right to stand in the front rank of the Gentile Zionists of his day.

10

Churchill and the British Empire

RONALD HYAM

How can one best approach the subject of Churchill and the British Empire generally, and more specifically in the aftermath of the First World War during his period as Secretary of State for the Colonies, February 1921 to October 1922? Although the Middle East should be included, as a central part of Britain's 'informal empire', the Irish Treaty (to which Churchill contributed so much) must be ruled out, since Ireland was not really a colonial problem. The Imperial Conference of 1921 (which he master-minded) yields nothing distinctively Churchillian. Despite his fertile engagement with the colonies as Parliamentary Under-Secretary of State, 1905–8, was Churchill thereafter even interested in the colonial Empire? Was it not the case that 'His interest in the empire never absorbed him entirely at the Colonial Office, and it may indeed have been very nearly exhausted by it'?[1] He never set foot again in India after leaving it in 1897, or in South Africa after 1900. Although he made many trips across the Atlantic and several to North Africa and the Middle East, he never visited Nigeria and the Gold Coast, let alone Australia and New Zealand or Malaya and Hong Kong. His last sight of a British African colony was in 1907–8. He meant to revisit Kenya and Uganda as Secretary of State but never made it. India excepted, on no aspect of Churchill studies has so little been written by so few as 'Churchill and the Empire'.

The coruscating minutes in red ink, the elegantly polished memoranda, and the long reflective letters to colleagues which characterized the earlier period 1905–8 are simply not there for the years 1921–2. It may not be strictly true that 'he who drafts the document wins the day', but it is certainly the case that ministers who write the best papers most readily ensure the attention of historians: something Churchill understood perfectly well. So what was he trying to tell us, both archivally and autobiographically, *ex silentio*? On investigation, it rapidly becomes clear, in fact, that the astonishing Churchillian written output on colonial issues for the earlier period was the product of a very particular combination of circumstances. The Liberal government was faced with the aftermath of African partition as well as of South African war. It had one major constructive job to do: to settle the future of southern Africa. And at the same time it was earnestly trying to introduce a new tone into colonial administration. Put crudely, this involved cutting down proconsular pretensions and reasserting trustee-ship. Churchill himself was seeking to make his name. A post which enabled him to combine helping forward a South African settlement with exposing abuses of power and bureaucratic incompetence was ideal for his purpose. Also, he was long enough in office, almost two-and-a-half years, to have some real impact.

In 1921 everything was different. He was Secretary of State for little over eighteen months—and whatever the case in politics that is not a very long time in administration. By this date he had developed a habit of concentrating on one problem at a time; this led to a backlog of files, and then insufficient time for reflective comment. (L. S. Amery in fact believed that, Iraq and Ireland apart, Churchill neglected the work of the Colonial Office.)[2] There was no government mission to purify colonial rule in 1921, and without this political imperative Churchill found it hard to reactivate an interest in colonies. Moreover, Churchill was now an experienced Cabinet minister, no longer needing to impress his seniors. Nor did the Colonial Office occupy a central position in post-war government policy as it had done briefly in 1905–6. When Curzon as Foreign Secretary complained that Churchill was constantly interfer-ing in foreign policy (and how would Churchill have liked it if Curzon had made unauthorized interventions in colonial policy?), Churchill shoved a note across the Cabinet table, insisting on his right to an opinion, because 'there is no comparison between those vital matters which affect the whole future of the world, and the mere departmental topics with which the Colonial Office is concerned'.

Some allowance has to be made for self-defensiveness as well as per-haps for self-deprecation, but of the sincerity of Churchill's anxiety about the vulnerability of Britain's post-war position in the world there can be no doubt. 'The whole accumulated greatness of Britain is under challenge', he wrote in 1922. Every separate foreign or nationalist embarrassment, created by the 'rascals and rapscallions of mankind', he saw as a threat to her crumbling global position. A humiliation by the Turks at Chanak would above all else be a disastrous blow to imperial prestige. Straitened economic circumstances meant that 'the British Empire cannot become the policeman of the world'. Yet there was trouble everywhere, and so 'we may well be within measurable distance of universal collapse and anarchy throughout Europe and Asia'. All over the world, countries were 'relapsing in hideous succession into bankruptcy, barbarism or anarchy', not least within the ambit of the Pax Britannica. Ireland was suffering an 'enormous retrogression of civilisation and Christianity'. Egypt and India were in revolt, on the edge of a blind and heedless plunge back into 'primordial chaos'. At Camberley in December 1921 he talked on 'The passing of the British Empire'.[3] His predecessor Lord Milner had complained that 'the whole world was rocking', and in this situation colonial business got pushed aside.[4] It was the same for Churchill. Russia and Turkey, America and Japan—these were the issues that he felt should preoccupy him. Nor were his domestic British causes forgotten either. He was a notably disputatious member of the Cabinet. Nevertheless, during Churchill's time as Secretary of State, important decisions were taken for the future of Palestine and Iraq, Kenya and Southern Rhodesia, and it is these problems that should mainly be considered.

We may start by stating the legacy of his earlier years as an Under-Secretary. There was a negative impact, as has been seen. Was there anything more positive? Perhaps the most significant point is the substantial contribution the colonial experience had made to his perceptions of domestic and international policy: the potential value of state intervention to protect the welfare of the poor at home, and international intervention to protect the democratic rights of small states abroad. More specifically, the main conclusions he had come to were that the Empire should be a 'family not a syndicate', and that justice should be done to all individuals within it, not least its own servants. An especially incandescent example had been his defence of the Batawana chief Sekgoma in Bechuanaland.[5] In addition he had acquired an incisively opinionated world-view. South Africa was 'a country of conflicting dualities and vicious contradictions, where everything is twisted, disturbed and abnormal'. Natal had by its treatment of the Zulu people shown itself to be the tyrannical 'hooligan of the British Empire'. Sir Frederick Lugard's Northern Nigeria was a nuisance and Churchill could see no reason why 'these savage tribes should not be allowed to eat each other up without restraint'. Somaliland was 'just a wilderness of stone and scrub', and there was little point in trying to hold the interior. Kenya's 'first few ruffians' among the settlers should not be allowed 'to steal [it] from us, upon some shabby pretence of being a responsibly governed Colony'. The Kikuyu were 'light-hearted, tractable, if brutish children . . . capable of being instructed and raised from their present degradation'. (Mau Mau later took him greatly by surprise.) Uganda was an African pearl, highly suitable for a 'practical experiment in state socialism'. His views were not immutable; some of his opinions were subject to subsequent modification, as we shall see. It simply is not true that Churchill's world-view was stuck in the attitudes of the 1890s subaltern, nor even in those of the Edwardian junior minister.

Perhaps the two early interests which induced the closest involvement both developed directly out of his being in those days MP for Manchester North-West, a constituency with a community of notable Jewish businessmen and Lancashire cotton manufacturers. As well as embracing Zionism, he became an enthusiast for developing the Empire's 'great estates', taking a close interest in the work of the British Cotton Growing Association. At one of its meetings in Manchester in 1907 he said he looked forward to the emergence of 'a second India' in British West Africa, based on railways and cotton, with 'the two Nigerias, the Gold Coast and Sierra Leone woven together as one vast dependency of the Crown'. 'Cotton', he was fond of saying, 'is the thread which unites the material interests of British industrial democracy' with the development of the tropical possessions of the Empire. When Milner was about to be appointed Secretary of State for the Colonies in January 1919, Churchill told Lloyd George he ought to be given £50 million a year to develop Africa. (The amount of the first Colonial Development and Welfare allocation in 1929 was £1 million a year, while even after 1945 it was only £12 million p.a.) As Secretary of State himself, Churchill was quick to reassure the Manchester cotton entrepreneurs that he remained keen to promote their interests. He hoped to do this by diverting government expenditure away from its unproductive new responsibilities in the Middle East: 'In Africa the population is docile and the country fertile. In the Middle East the country is arid and the population is ferocious. A little money goes a long way in Africa, and a lot of money goes very little way in Arabia.'[6] Already in May 1921 he was protesting to the Prime Minister that it was 'a most improvident policy to starve and neglect the whole development of our tropical colonies'. The comparatively small sums he needed to 'foster an active productivity' in the 'very valuable estates' of East and Central Africa were being denied him by the Treasury. They had slashed more than £600,000 from his estimates of £1.5 million for Tanganyika alone, so that it was 'rapidly relaxing' from the level of development it had attained under German rule, and its great railway was falling into serious disrepair. Since colonial development would also create a demand for British manufactures and open up supplies of raw materials for British industry, he warned Lloyd George that he would unrepentently continue to press for a switch of expenditure to Africa away from their sterile obligations in the Middle East.[7] This was a major part of the theme of his first public survey of colonial problems, made during the Supply debate in July 1921, when he reiterated the comparison between 'tractable and promising' African colonies and Middle Eastern regions 'unduly stocked with peppery, pugnacious, proud politicians and theologians, who happen to be at the same time extremely well armed and extremely hard up'.[8] The trouble was, however, that Churchill was never able to persuade his colleagues to make this diversion of expenditure, and, being himself an incurably parsimonious minister, he was not prepared to campaign for *additional* financial resources.

Ironically, therefore, the Middle East proved to be an easier place than Africa for the fulfilment of expectations held of him. Churchill had some success in laying down a position which held the line for Zionists through to the White Paper of 1939—which he never accepted, but could not dislodge, as government policy in wartime. Three characteristically Churchillian concerns underpinned his attraction to Zionism: his interest in strategy and geopolitics, his interest in the development of 'great estates', and his interest in visionary schemes of social engineering. As early as 1908 he had declared: 'The establishment of a strong, free Jewish state astride the bridge between Europe and Africa, flanking the land roads to the East, would not only be an immense advantage to the British Empire, but a notable step towards the harmonious disposition of the world among its peoples.'

As prophecy this proved to be tragically naive. As geopolitics it is a good example of what one general called his imprecise 'cigar-butt strategy', making a sweeping gesture over a map. But it is not essentially different from Amery's conception of Palestine as the keystone of the geopolitical arch which would enable the 'Southern British world', running from Cape Town through Cairo and Baghdad and Calcutta to Sydney and Wellington, to go quietly about its business. The mobilization of Jewish support for the Allied war effort through the Balfour

Declaration of 1917 was something Churchill regarded as a 'definite, palpable' political and strategic advantage to Britain. But he also believed that here was the chance to remove an 'inefficient and out-of-date' Turkish control which had 'long misruled one of the most fertile countries in the world'.

Merely maintaining an economic status quo was, of course, anathema to any good Victorian, and Churchill wanted to let the Jews come in and develop this 'great estate':

Left to themselves, the Arabs of Palestine would not in a thousand years have taken effective steps towards the irrigation and electrification of Palestine. They would have been quite content to dwell—a handful of philosophic people—in the wasted sun-scorched plains, letting the waters of the Jordan continue to flow unbridled and unharnessed into the Dead Sea.

(The *rallentando* effect in this final cadence must have been worth hearing.[9]) Finally, Zionism appealed to him because 'such a plan contains a soul'. He once told a hostess that her distinctly floppy-looking pudding required a theme. If even puddings needed a theme in the Churchillian scheme of things, how much the more did politics. So he liked strong, romantic, even audacious schemes in government: the reconciliation of Briton and Boer in a South African Union, the Salvation Army settlement proposal which through 'super-economic influence' might transform Southern Rhodesia, the 'big slice of Bismarckianism' thrust over 'the whole underside of our industrial system', the strategic push through the 'soft underbelly of Europe', the quixotic wartime offer of an Anglo-French political union, and so forth. His support for these, and for Zionism, is all of a piece. For Zionism, as he declaimed in 1905, 'enlists in its support energies, enthusiasms and a driving power which no scheme of individual colonisation can ever demand'. And so in 1921 he would not go back either officially or personally on a British pledge, which he regarded as a commitment to 'a great experiment which deserves a fair chance', even if this meant maintaining a considerable garrison, encouraging an armed Jewish gendarmerie, and holding in suspense for the time being the representative institutions which would curtail Jewish immigration.[10]

Churchill, however, had no desire to sully his hands with the perplexing realities of administering Palestine, and he was content to rely—and rely heavily—on John Shuckburgh (Assistant Under-Secretary of State) for the working out of the government's Palestine policy which was eventually enshrined in the White Paper of June

1922. (Churchill was reluctant to rush into a public declaration.) Its purpose was to gloss or modify the Balfour Declaration by a careful balancing of the allegedly incompatible earlier promises. Starting from Churchill's premise that 'we have a double duty to discharge', the White Paper argued that the Balfour Declaration did *not* mean 'that Palestine as a whole should be converted into a Jewish National Home, but that such a Home should be founded *in* Palestine'. There was to be a Jewish 'centre' in Palestine, 'internationally guaranteed and formally recognised to rest upon ancient historic connection'. (The Jews must know they were there as of right and not on sufferance.) On the other hand, the future development of the existing Jewish community must not lead to the imposition of a Jewish nationality on the inhabitants of Palestine as a whole; and Jewish immigration should not be so great as to go beyond the economic capacity of the country to absorb it. There must be no subordination of the Arab population, or its language or its culture. Churchill thus rejected both an Arab national state and a Jewish national state; instead there ought to be a shared bi-national state. This was the first clear attempt to articulate properly the essential duality of British policy, promoting collaboration within a common territory. But neither Jews nor Arabs were really interested in such an outcome. The British delusion was that Arabs and Jews were ultimately reconcilable.

In Churchill's view they would be reconciled through economic development—in the shape of hydro-electric schemes, hill terracing, irrigation, and agricultural improvements. This would divert Zionist attention away from politics, and demonstrate to Arabs the practical advantages of the Jewish influx. A new Palestine would be created by the Jews performing an archetypal European settler function, bringing the 'good gifts' of prosperity, and a 'higher economic and social life to all'. Accordingly the Arabs should see them 'as their friends and helpers, not expellers and expropriators', and could not be allowed to prevent continuing Jewish immigration. It was not perhaps entirely tactful to accuse the Arabs of being 'guilty of a breach of hospitality'. He also appealed to them not to deny history, for 'all history shows the relationship of these two races' to be closely intertwined. Hence his rather exasperated cry: 'Why can't you live together in amity and develop the country peacefully?'[11]

At the War Office in 1920, Churchill had already attacked the waste of money in the newly acquired Mandate of Iraq, or Mesopotamia as it was then known. As Secretary of State for the Colonies, his role in this

turbulent land was to set up a system of 'informal control', gradually
reducing British military responsibilities without a 'policy of scuttle'.
(He could not, however, do much about prospecting for oil because of
complications with the Americans.) His intention was that Iraq should
become 'an independent Native State friendly to Great Britain,
favourable to her commercial interests, and casting hardly any burden
upon the Exchequer'—a native state, that is, analogous to princely
states in India (which, incidentally, he thought would be a good model
for India as a whole). The costs of the enormous post-war garrison
would be run down, and a treaty relationship would be substituted for
the remainder of the mandatory period. Not to cut costs in this way
would be 'politically indefensible and from an imperial viewpoint would
misapply our limited and over-strained resources'. The Cabinet
approved the terms of the proposed treaty in 1922 as satisfactory.[12] All
this was the classic mid-Victorian policy of 'informal empire'. The
difference was that instead of gunboats in the background there would
be aircraft overhead; only the reliance on nascent but 'proven aerial
power' would make it possible for Iraq to be held with such a small
military force as he now envisaged. Churchill, as ever, was quick to
take up the latest technological tools for the task in hand. This use of
aircraft, he claimed, 'may ultimately lead to a form of control over
semi-civilised countries which will be found very effective and infinitely
cheaper'. He argued that air power could be used as an instrument of
imperial control in India and Afghanistan as well; and in years to come
he would also urge its value in intimidating the Mau Mau rebels.[13]

Out of the frustrations of the Middle East—which occupied too
much of his time (he was the first but not the last Secretary of State
for whom this was true)—came a few authentic Churchillian flashes. In
Iraq, he said, the British were paying huge sums for the privilege of
living on 'an ungrateful volcano'. It was 'a poor, starving, backward,
bankrupt country', a 'wild land filled with a proud and impecunious
chief and extremely peppery well-armed politicians'. King Feisal (the
government's chosen imperial collaborator) was getting into 'a perpetual
ferment' and becoming tiresome—'has he not got some wives to keep
him quiet?' When the re-employment of 'Philby of Arabia' in
Transjordan (after dismissal from Iraq) was urged upon him by officials
he riposted: 'I cannot take a Philby in a poke', but would like to see
him first. When Shuckburgh decided, somewhat prematurely, that King
Abdullah in Transjordan was 'a complete failure', Churchill was not to
be seduced: 'I do not mean to throw him over easily. He has an impos-

1 Blenheim Palace—where Churchill said he took the two most important decisions of his life, 'to be born, and to marry, and I never regretted either'

2 Lord Randolph Churchill, 1849–95

CHURCHILL COLLEGE

3 Lady Randolph Churchill with her two sons, Jack and Winston, 1889

HULTON

4 2nd Lt. Winston Churchill, 4th Hussars, *c*.1895

5 Drawing by 'Spy' in *Vanity Fair*, 10 July 1900

6 During the Boer War, 1900

7 'Mr. Churchill and the Rhinoceros at Simba'
PHOTOGRAPH AND CAPTION IN *MY AFRICAN JOURNEY* BY WINSTON CHURCHILL, 1908

8 Campaigning in Manchester, April 1908

9 Sidney Street Siege 1911. Churchill is top-hatted at the left of group in centre of picture

10 Giving evidence at the Sidney Street inquest, 18 January 1911

11 Shaking hands with the Kaiser during pre-war manoeuvres in Germany

BRAVO WINSTON!

The Rapid Naval Mobilisation and Purchase of the Two Foreign Dreadnoughts Spoke Volumes for your Work and Wisdom.

MR. WINSTON CHURCHILL, FIRST LORD OF THE ADMIRALTY

AND (INSET) HIS CHARMING AND BEAUTIFUL WIFE

If you listen to the opinion of the navy in general upon Mr. Churchill you will be thankful that such a man has been in control of our navy in the immediate past. Mrs. Churchill must be a proud woman. Mr. Churchill has fought and overcome the Little Navyites in the past so that our fleet may fight and overcome our foes in the future

12 On the eve of war, 1914. Photograph in the *Tatler* with inset of Clementine Churchill.

CHURCHILL COLLEGE

13 Drawing of Admiral Fisher and Churchill at the Admiralty, December 1914
ILLUSTRATED LONDON NEWS PICTURE LIBRARY

14 With A. J. Balfour, May 1915
HULTON

15 With Lloyd George in Whitehall, October 1915

16 In Egypt, March 1921, with his wife (left), and Gertrude Bell, T. E. Lawrence (right)

17 Churchill as Chancellor of the Exchequer, April 1925, in the *Illustrated London News*

18 After being hit by a truck in New York City, December 1931

19 With Lord Halifax, 1938

20 As a co-pilot visiting an Auxiliary Air Force Squadron, 16 April 1939

21 With Anthony Eden on the way to the House of Commons, 29 August
1939

FROM THE *TATLER*, 6 SEPTEMBER 1939

22 Making his first wartime broadcast, 1 October 1939

23 Portrayed as Commandant of Concentration Camp during the Boer War in
'Ohm Krüger', 1941

24 Cartoon in the *Evening Standard*, 13 November 1939

"Himmel! It's That Man Again"

sible task.' When the Opposition complained that a major concession in Palestine was being made to Rutenberg, who was a Jew, Churchill replied that of course he was a Jew, but they could hardly inscribe over the portals of the new Zion 'No Israelite need apply'. The House of Commons rocked with laughter, apparently.[14]

As far as Kenya is concerned, we find Churchill pursuing the same kind of balancing act between conflicting interests as he was attempting in Palestine. In the early 1920s, the Kenya debate was dominated by a crisis over the Indian problem. Indian colonizing pretensions tended to grow as their existing overseas communities felt more and more excluded politically; there was vague talk of turning East Africa into the 'America of the Hindu'. Unsurprisingly Churchill had some hard words for the Indian delegation in August 1921. They must accept as 'an agreed fact' the reservation of the Kenya highlands for white settlement, since the Europeans had gone there on the basis of the Elgin Pledge of 1908. It was 'no good expecting that could be set aside as if it were nothing', for this would be a breach of British good faith. He was not prepared to tell the white settlers they were going to be put unfairly into a minority position under an Indian majority government; such a system would actually 'make the path of the Indians far harder and would cause every kind of disaster', since Europeans simply would not stand for being subordinated in this way. Of course he would apply Rhodes's maxim of 'equal rights for [all] civilised men'—*except* in the highlands. Nevertheless he thought it a valuable principle, because 'it would be absurd to give equal electoral rights to the naked savages of Kikuyu and Kavirondo', even though they were human beings: 'there has to be a line'. He dismissed with an equally patronizing sneer the Indian claim to have developed Kenya: they had helped, but 'you would not have invented the railway let alone constructed it'. In conclusion, he said his aim was to find 'an interdependent general settlement', or at least 'a general proposition', which would reassure the settlers, protect the 'aboriginal native' (who had the first claim), and give Indians the benefits of applying 'equal rights'.[15] However grudgingly, he was committed to doing something to improve the lot of the Kenyan Indians, and, although it is noticeable that he took a more favourable view of the possibilities of European rule in Africa than he had done fifteen years before, he had a much less indulgent attitude towards settler shortcomings than Milner or Amery.

Instructions to construct a package deal along these lines were discussed in the Colonial Office with the Governor, Sir Edward Northey, and presented to him in a memorandum dated 26 August 1921. This memorandum set out nicely balanced concessions to each side, but it did not represent a Cabinet decision on policy: rather, the matter would not go to the Cabinet until the Governor had held full local consultations and reached an agreement. The memorandum shifted significantly beyond both previous policy and local advice, in the direction of greater partnership with Indians, by ruling against commercial segregation in towns, and by declaring in favour of a common electoral roll in elections to the Legislative Council. Officials were careful to note that by supporting a common roll embracing all races Churchill was insisting on an essential change on behalf of the Indians. At the same time, Kenya must not become predominantly Indian, since fear of this was general among the settlers. The contrary pressures on Churchill were complex indeed. At the end of November, Northey reported that even his compromise proposals had completely failed. He had not been able to persuade the Europeans to entertain in any shape or form the idea of a common roll franchise with Indians. This was the rock on which the talks foundered, the settlers arguing that it would 'cut away the very foundation on which we feel our future is fixed'. They also began to dig their heels in over residential segregation as a supposedly pledged principle. In his telegram reporting all this, the Governor stressed 'the very serious position which I am satisfied will occur if the demands of Indians are accepted *in toto*. Europeans have organisation complete for resistance as last resource.' This was neither the first nor the last of such warnings about settler revolt. The Colonial Office was not unduly alarmed by them, although they certainly indicated the desirability of not taking as decision in a hurry and not refusing to make some concession. Meanwhile the settlers announced their intention of sending a deputation under Lord Delamere to the Secretary of State. Since his own proposals had already been leaked, Churchill was convinced he had no option but to see them, despite E. S. Montagu's protest (as Secretary of State for India) against the further delay it would involve.

At his meetings with Churchill in February 1922, Delamere indicated willingness to be flexible over some Indian demands, provided urban residential segregation was 'definitely laid down', and provided some sort of immigration control board was set up, on which Europeans would have an 'effective' voice. Churchill reported to Montagu: 'I feel bound to tell you that my mind is working very much on the same lines.' Montagu was furious: 'I cannot possibly agree . . . I cannot consent to any permanent disability on Indians *qua* Indians.' For Montagu this was the last straw in his fraught relations with Churchill on this and other questions. In October 1921 he had been angered and bewildered by Churchill's description, in a personal letter, of the Indians in East Africa as 'mainly of a very low class of coolies and the idea that they should be put on an equality with the Europeans is revolting to every white man throughout British Africa'. This sentence Montagu thought 'might have been written by a European settler of a most fanatical type'; in any case nobody had suggested giving political rights to a low class of coolies. Then on 27 January 1922 came the bombshell of Churchill's unexpected (but not off-the-cuff) remarks at the annual East African Dinner. There should, he said, be no invidious legislative distinctions or colour bar to advancement, and a broad imperial view should be taken of the position of Indians in Kenya and Uganda. Nevertheless—and here came the balancing announcements— European settlers could be relieved of their anxiety: the pledged exclusive reservation of the white highlands had been 'definitely settled'. A federal amalgamation of East African colonies was also to be studied. Moreover, there was a grandiloquent peroration:

We do not contemplate any settlement or system which will prevent . . . Kenya . . . from becoming a characteristically and distinctively British colony, looking forward in the full fruition of time to responsible self-government.[16]

This statement—though welcomed by Delamere as a 'charter' courageously laying 'the foundations of a future self-governing colony, in the face of very great opposition'—did not mean much in practice. (It was heavily qualified.) But in combination with the other remarks it put Montagu into a cool rage of amazement. He took 'the strongest exception' to Churchill's 'unjustifiable and indefensible' way of proceeding, which had gravely breached Cabinet conventions and anticipated a Cabinet decision on the highlands. Churchill had also made a further pledge to the Europeans, which brushed aside all the suggestions Montagu had made. Why was Churchill apparently dissociating himself from 'our policy as a government'? Churchill defended himself before a Cabinet committee by warning against any attempt to force a withdrawal of his remarks:

The demands of Indians as regards their treatment in East Africa were unreasonable, and if they were conceded they would throw the whole of British East Africa into confusion. We had no force there to coerce the white population, who felt strongly on this question, and any repudiation of the statement he

had made might lead to them ejecting the Indians from East Africa . . .
[Indians] claimed that they must be treated as ordinary voters. This was quite
impossible in Africa.

At the full Cabinet on 13 March Montagu formally charged
Churchill with having acted without Cabinet authority. Churchill simply rejected this out of hand: he had initiated no new unapproved policy, created no precedent, and had not even exceeded his departmental
discretion. Montagu, he alleged, had agreed with the proposals now
being made, although he did not like them.[17] No other minister is
recorded as having expressed any view, but it is impossible to suppose
that Churchill would have found much support. The truth is that he
could not on occasion resist doling out some sensational journalistic
copy, regardless of the consequences.

In the wake of this nasty ministerial quarrel, it was decided that the
two Under-Secretaries of State should be left to thrash out an agreed
interdepartmental formula: Edward Wood (later Lord Halifax) for the
Colonial Office, and Lord Winterton for the India Office. The
Wood–Winterton scheme was announced in September 1922 and provisionally accepted by the two Secretaries of State for reference to the
government of Kenya and the government of India. (On the merits
Churchill did not specifically endorse it.) Since the proposals stuck to a
common electoral roll and envisaged neither urban segregation nor
immigration restriction or control, they caused a storm of protest in
Nairobi, and the threat of settler resistance hotted up. Churchill
shocked the settlers by recalling Northey, and, according to Sir Ralph
Furse's memoirs, Churchill let it be known he would send a cruiser to
Mombasa and blockade them.[18] However, it fell to his successor the
Duke of Devonshire actually to defuse the crisis. As is well known, he
did this by abandoning the common roll, sugaring the pill for Indians
by rediscovery of the principle that African interests must be para-
mount if they conflicted with those of immigrants, whether Indian or
European. Churchill's attempt to balance the interests of all three was
thus summarily and dramatically dropped. He had tried to give the
Indians something of substance and make a declaration on behalf of the
settlers, while preserving the status quo for Africans, whereas
Devonshire denied the Indians the substance and made a declaration on
behalf of Africans, merely preserving the status quo for the settlers.

Concurrently Churchill was also juggling with conflicting claims
upon the future of Southern Rhodesia, where Smuts and the dream of
a 'Greater South Africa' pulled in one direction, and Sir Charles
Coghlan and the desire for settler autonomy in another. Within ten
days of taking office in February 1921, Churchill asked Lord Buxton

(the recently retired High Commissioner) to head a committee to make an urgent investigation of constitutional prospects after the end of British South Africa Company rule. Buxton reported in mid-May 1921, suggesting a referendum on the possibility of responsible government (internal self-government). Churchill accepted this proposal, despite Smuts's protest that it would prejudice Rhodesia's future possible entry into the Union, under the procedure provided for in the Act of Union. Churchill did not think it need do so, but Smuts kept up the pressure, and on 21 September 1921 Churchill decided to let Smuts declare the terms on which Southern Rhodesia would be admitted as a province of the Union. It was, he said, his 'personal wish' to proceed in this way. The referendum would now offer a choice between the two alternative solutions for Rhodesia's future. The Cabinet agreed Churchill should continue to hold discussions with all the parties, putting 'the bias a little in favour of joining the Union'. Stronger pressure would be counter-productive. In the event, 59.43 per cent of the white Rhodesians voted against the Union.

Both sides disapproved of Churchill's stance and tactics, which suggests a certain even-handedness. Coghlan complained that Churchill was 'out to get us into the Union if he could', while Smuts blamed Churchill for the adverse result from the Union point of view. Undoubtedly Churchill preferred the Union solution as a way of strengthening geopolitically the British position in southern Africa. (As early as 1906 he had recognized the potential of Southern Rhodesia as 'the weight which swings the balance in South Africa decisively on the side of the British Crown'.) With all the Empire's other problems, he would gladly have dispatched the Rhodesians into the care of the local imperial collaborator, who happened also to be a statesman of international standing. Financial constraints made it in any case impossible to match the generous inducements Smuts had offered. Churchill did not think a Union government would ill-treat the Africans, and pointed to the recent Native Affairs Act (1920)—certainly quite liberal by South African standards—as evidence. At the same time, he was throughout extremely careful to avoid dictating a solution to the settlers. It is surely not without significance that he refused to give Smuts the unequivocal pro-Union lead for which the latter had urgently appealed as necessary to ensure the outcome. Churchill's advisers were in genuine doubt as to how to respond to this. Churchill himself did nothing. And this was in sharp contrast to his unorthodox rush barely a year earlier to break official precedent by congratulating Smuts on winning the South African election of February 1921.[19]

Before we come to a conclusion, a brief look at Churchill's subsequent encounters with the Empire is necessary. His pessimism about an impending 'wreck of our great estates' persisted for the rest of his career. As is notorious, he opposed the Government of India Act, 1935 ('a monstrous monument of sham built by the pygmies'), and he had no intention of helping a constitutional solution forward in India in the 1940s. On the other hand, the Viceroy Lord Wavell and Secretary of State Amery felt that Britain owed a great deal to Churchill for his firm line against emerging forms of international trusteeship and accountability, which might allow 'America to push us off the map'. Churchill himself thought it was 'pretty good cheek' for the Americans 'now coming to school-marm us into proper behaviour' in the Empire. And he was not going to 'preside over the liquidation of the British Empire' in Hong Kong or anywhere else at their behest.[20]

It was not only Americans he was wary of in the higher direction of imperial affairs. Colonials such as Australia's Prime Minister John Curtin, who wanted all Australian and New Zealand forces to be concentrated in the Pacific, got scant consideration. With his mind on the total strategic picture, and the Empire as the buttress of British power, Churchill took the simple view that Dominion troops should be available for general deployment as seemed best as judged from the 'effective centre of gravity' in London.[21] Clearly, however, he was becoming increasingly out of touch with feelings and developments in Commonwealth countries. This was true even in respect of South Africa, with which he was comparatively familiar. A notable illustration of this was his accusation in 1941 that the High Commissioner, Lord Harlech, was 'unconscious' of some of the 'basic realities' of South Africa. Harlech had diagnosed the British South African community as too introverted, refusing to take an interest in public life, and he pointed to Natal as the worst offender. The situation there was 'lamentable', he thought, because it played into the hands of the Afrikaners, who were thus outstripping the British intellectually and beginning to monopolize political leadership. This was an important attempt to sound a warning about the future fundamental weakness of the Union within the Commonwealth; Churchill could not see this, and dismissed Harlech's judgements as 'supercilious and superficial' (though he relented to the extent of excising these words from the circulated version of his memorandum). Instead, he offered the following decidedly fanciful analysis: 'Natal is one of the very few spots in the British Empire where the people are really devoted to the Old Country. They have the New Zealand touch.' The maintenance of a distinctive British standpoint and loyalist community—'the Ulster of South Africa', which the 'predominant Dutch find it most necessary to woo'—was of positive value in reducing the risk of civil war. Moreover:

There ought to be room for many different kinds of people and many different kinds of culture in the British Commonwealth and Empire. Totalitarianism has great attractions to some minds; but he would be a poor artist who tried to paint a picture by mixing up all the colours in the paint-box.

Churchill added that if South Africa had declared herself neutral in 1939, 'there was always Natal, which would instantly have seceded from the Union and placed the fine port of Durban at our disposal'. There was no real evidence for this assertion.[22]

In the last phase, as Prime Minister in the 1950s, South Africa remained one of the few parts of the Empire he kept an eye on. He was against the transfer of the High Commission Territories to be administered by South Africa 'in accordance with very old-fashioned ideas'. He was determined to maintain British interests in the Simonstown naval base as an effective link in the imperial line of communications to Australasia. Negotiations over its future had begun under the Labour government but ran into stalemate. Determined that South Africa's strategic ports—'more important to the British Commonwealth of Nations than Gibraltar or Malta'—should not 'go down the drain like Southern Ireland', Churchill held out for the best possible terms, despite the need for economies in the defence estimates. In this respect he maintained continuity of policy with the tough bargaining stance of Attlee and Shinwell, and expressly rejected the advice of Secretary of State Lord Ismay and the attempt of the Commonwealth Relations Office not only to re-open negotiations but to do so on a more conciliatory footing. Following Churchill's lead, the Defence Committee accordingly agreed in March 1952 not to take any fresh initiative. By the summer of 1954, however, the South African government was again pressing, and pressing hard, for the transfer of Simonstown. Why, asked Churchill? Was it because Dr Malan as Prime Minister was working towards the final severance of South Africa from Britain? If so, the surrender of Simonstown would be taken as a symbol of British decline and fall. In his last extended minute on South Africa, written nearly fifty years after the first, he returned again to his Natal fantasy. If South Africa declared itself a republic and quit the Commonwealth—which might not happen, though anti-British sentiment and the division between Britain and white South Africans on the colour question was growing—Natal might 'remain faithful to the Crown', in which case Britain would need to be in a strategic position 'to defend her rights to an independent choice, by force of arms if necessary'. In the Cabinet, although admitting that the significance of Simonstown was becoming largely symbolic, Churchill was 'reluctant to contemplate any transaction which would be presented as yet another surrender of the political rights and responsibilities of the United Kingdom'. Nor did he want to do anything which might discourage the 'loyalist elements in South Africa'. So the hard bargaining continued. It was strongly kept up, too, by Eden, who had no love for South Africa. As a result in 1955 Britain obtained agreements on Simonstown which were astonishingly favourable. Whilst not actually congratulating him, Churchill assured Eden he did not see what else he could have done: 'we live in days when neither South Africa nor Naval defence stand on their foundations of a few years ago'.[23]

One reason for his vigilance over Simonstown was his realization that the Suez Canal was no longer of much value as a Commonwealth link, nor the Egyptian base of such strategic importance. Negotiations over the future of the Canal Zone were far more difficult than those with South Africa, and Churchill was more consistently attentive to the Egyptian files than to any others from overseas. His approach was fundamentally pragmatic. We must not be misled by his anxiety about the domestic political reaction and his private growling about evacuation. Officially, Churchill recognized that there was much to be said for a fresh start on a new basis of 'vigorous and effective' troop redeployment throughout the Middle East.

The same pragmatic if rather reluctant good sense was displayed in Africa. He 'noted' (rather than personally approved) the declaration made on behalf of his government that continuity in the goals of colonial policy would be maintained (November 1951). He grumbled that they were forced to make constitutional concessions to Nkrumah's Gold Coast as the 'consequences of what was done before we became responsible'. But there was no obstruction—and no atavistic reassertions of imperiousness. During the anti-Mau Mau operations, Michael Blundell found him keen to promote a conciliatory settlement. There must be nothing like mass executions by courts, Churchill warned the Cabinet, because British public opinion would criticize anything resembling that. And there was also a nice Churchillian intervention on behalf of cattle seized from the Kikuyu:

Is it true that they are dying for want of attention? They must be fed, watered and milked; who is doing this? Remember they belong to the innocent as well as to the guilty. I hope that this point is being well-looked after by the Government on the spot.

Finally, it is by no means unfitting that Churchill's last recorded utterance in the Cabinet on colonial problems showed him in his states-manlike mode. Concern had been expressed about the tensions caused throughout the Commonwealth by Indian communities, and by Indian government encouragement of opposition to colonial rule in multiracial societies. Churchill, however, advised against any drastic action which might offend India, because they needed India's moderating influence and help with major international problems in Asia. Nor, he suggested, should it be assumed that Indian immigrant communities would prove an embarrassment: they might in some cases be 'a balancing factor'. Thus he steered the Cabinet to the conclusion that they should watch the problems carefully but avoid any precipitate action. Precisely the same policy was adopted with respect to West Indian immigration into Britain.[24]

There have been some extraordinary academic judgements upon Churchill's attitude to empire, as crude as they are emotive: for example, it is alleged that he was 'a profound and reactionary imperialist' and a 'malignant racist'.[25] The conclusion to a brief essay like this is not the place to start a semantic analysis, but perhaps it may be asserted: *racism* is the institutionalized form of racial prejudice, manifesting itself in social and economic domination, while *imperialism* is the structured form of pride in empire, manifesting itself in territorial and international domination. If these definitions—or perhaps any others—are valid, then Churchill was neither a racist nor an imperialist. That he believed in British superiority over non-Europeans and thought the Empire was a good thing is not denied. But he loathed racial exploitation, and he never had an imperial programme. He expressly rejected 'imperial federation' and Joseph Chamberlain's creed that the future lay with great empires rather than small states; and in practice he was mainly interested in the colonial Empire only when he had to be by virtue of office. Adverse judgement of his attitudes has focused too much on what Churchill *said*, mostly when relaxing in private, rather than on what he *did*.[26] Of course he had his personal preferences—pro-Zionist in Palestine, pro-settler in Kenya, pro-Union in Southern Rhodesia, and so forth, but in no case were his private prejudices allowed to distort his ministerial actions or official decisions, which were invariably geared towards compromise, reconciliation and even-handed justice, however paternalistic the presentation might be.

The Churchill who emerges from this investigation is a pragmatist and a conciliator, a man who believed the Empire should be useful to Britain, but also bring benefits and harmony to the populations it ruled. He may never have referred to the 'dual mandate', but in many ways it reflected his ideas. He saw nothing reprehensible in using the Empire to advance British national interests and power, because 'the mutually advantageous exchange of goods and services between communities is the foundation alike of the prosperity and peace of the world'; but if Britain was never to have any advantage from the colonies except the satisfaction of behaving in a purely philanthropic way, then 'a good many people would argue that we had better spend our money on improving the health and social services of our workers at home'.[27] If bits of the Empire were not useful, or cost too much to maintain, then there was no point in holding on to them, at least formally. This prag-matic outlook was a consistent thread in his policy from Northern Nigeria in 1906 and Somaliland in 1907, through to Egypt in 1954, by way of Iraq in 1922. Even so, the duties of a trustee, when deliberately entered into, as in Palestine, must be upheld; while as far as India was concerned, he found it hard to believe that the Raj was as yet expend-able (in terms of his own far from incoherent criteria) without danger to both sides.

This quintessential pragmatist always asked what was feasible, even if some of his answers were adventurous. Churchill was opposed to send-ing gunboats to Nanking in 1927, because 'punishing China is like flogging a jellyfish'. No latter-day Palmerston he. (After 1945 the neo-Palmerstonians were all on the Labour side.) Indeed, he yielded noth-ing to Cobden and Bright, or to J. A. Hobson and E. D. Morel for that matter, in his hatred of imperial exploitation. In 1899 he published an account of the reconquest of the Sudan, in which he compared Kitchener's campaign of vilification of the Mahdi with 'the habit of the boa constrictor to besmear the body of his victim with a foul slime before he devours it'. Bold stuff. It bothered him that the inevitable gap between conquest and dominion in the Sudan might become filled with 'the greedy trader, the inopportune missionary, the ambitious sol-dier and the lying speculator'.[28] As an Under-Secretary, he denounced Milner's Chinese Labour scheme in the Rand mines as 'a horrible experiment', and he accused the government of using Cyprus as 'a milch-cow' (though he was probably mistaken about this): 'There is scarcely any spectacle more detestable than the oppression of a small community by a Great Power for the purpose of pecuniary profit.' That was a courageous thing for a junior minister to write in an official memorandum in 1907, and it remains one of the fiercer critiques of British policy still on the Cyprus files, which is saying quite a lot. Churchill paid dearly within the establishment for such opinions. If similar protests cannot be quoted from a later period it is not because he became less radical, but because administration was largely purged of earlier abuses—a process in which Churchill himself had played no small part. In the context of his reputation as a stereotypical 'diehard' on India, it is worth recalling the sensitivity and insight into the fundamental flaw of British rule which he showed in his reflection of 1953: 'If we had made friends with them and taken them into our lives instead of restricting our intercourse to the political field things might have been very different.'[29] His efforts as Secretary of State to reconcile Jews and Arabs in Palestine, and Europeans and Indians in Kenya, may not have met with much success, but he surely deserves credit for trying: nothing could have been further from the easy options of 'divide and rule'. If in India the last word for him remained with Lord Morley rather than Lord Macaulay, in other respects his vision was entirely in the liberal cultural tradition of Macaulay's 'imperishable empire' and of Sir Charles Dilke's 'Greater Britain'. This is nicely illustrated by his minute on promoting the world-wide use of the C. K. Ogden–I. A. Richards system of 'Basic' English. This, he wrote, 'would be a gain to us far more durable and fruitful than the annexation of great provinces'; it would also help to promote his policy of closer union with the United States, by making it even more worthwhile for her to 'belong to the English-speaking club'. Unfortunately for 'Basic', the support of Churchill proved to be the kiss of death.[30]

11

Churchill and the Monarchy

PHILIP ZIEGLER

CLEMENTINE CHURCHILL wrote to reproach her husband when he had failed to do his duty as Lord Warden of the Cinque Ports by meeting Queen Juliana on her arrival at Dover. 'It was just a slip,' she added, 'because you are Monarchial No. 1 and value tradition, form and ceremony.'[1] 'Fealty to the monarch was a religion with the Prime Minister', the Canadian historian Brian Villa has more recently concluded.[2] 'His respect for the monarchy amounted almost to idolatry', affirmed his private secretary, Sir John Colville.[3] If the general public were asked for its impression of Churchill and the Crown, the image that would most probably come to mind would be that of the bare-headed old statesman standing before a slim, young Queen, his attitude a nice blend of the deferential and the avuncular, his expression radiant with affection. Like most popular images it is substantially correct; like most popular images it conceals a multitude of qualifications and tells only part of the truth. The family into which Churchill was born was far from one in which loyalty to the blood royal transcended every other consideration. Dukes tended to believe that they were as good as any monarch. His father, Lord Randolph, had quarrelled so ferociously with the Prince of Wales that there had been talk of a duel and he became for some years a pariah in London society. That was far in the past by the time Winston Churchill began to come into contact with the royal family; his father had long been forgiven and his mother was high in the royal favour. But though he was brought up to regard the monarchy as a powerful institution deserving of respect, there was no suggestion that the occupant of the throne should be treated with undue deference. 'Will it entirely revolutionise his way of life?' Churchill asked his mother when Edward VII succeeded to the throne. 'Will he sell his horses and scatter his Jews . . .? Will he become desperately serious? Will he continue to be friendly to you? Will the Keppel [Mrs Keppel, the Prince's mistress] be appointed 1st

Lady of the Bedchamber?'[4] These may not have been the questions of a young republican, but they do not suggest that Churchill viewed his monarch with the awe that the King-Emperor might have felt his due.

This disrespect did not imply any serious reservations about the institution itself. He did indeed, as his wife said, value 'tradition, form and ceremony'. In 1897, commenting in retrospect on Queen Victoria being made Empress of India, he admitted: 'I must array myself with those who "love high-sounding titles", since no title that is not high-sounding is worth having.'[5] But even the most high-sounding of titles did not excuse weakness or stupidity on the part of the holder. The office of King-Emperor was to be revered; King Edward VII received less deferential treatment.

The relationship began with considerable goodwill on both sides. 'It is quite true that we have known your parents for many years . . . and you and your brother since your childhood', wrote the King. 'Knowing the great abilities which you possess—I am watching your political career with great interest. My one wish is that the great qualities you possess may be turned to good account and that your service to the State may be appreciated.'[6] The wish was sincerely held, but the King had his fingers crossed. By the time he expressed it he had already had cause to protest over Churchill's description of the army leaders as 'gorgeous and gilded functionaries with brass hats and ornamental duties' and to dismiss his opinions of Lord Milner as 'simply scandalous'.[7] When Churchill, then at the Board of Trade, argued in favour of large cuts in military expenditure, the King, with the schoolboy ribaldry so characteristic of his house, remarked 'the latter's initials—WC—are well named'.[8] But Churchill's attack on the peers in 1909—'a miserable minority of titled persons'—so outraged the King that his private secretary, Lord Knollys, wrote to *The Times* in protest. 'He and the King must really have gone mad', expostulated Churchill. 'The Royal Prerogative is always exercised on the advice of ministers, and ministers and not the Crown are responsible . . . This looks to me like a rather remarkable Royal intervention and shows the bitterness which is felt in those circles. I shall take no notice of it.'[9] The bitterness was indeed deeply felt, but it never obliterated Edward VII's affection for his turbulent young minister. When Knollys told him that Churchill was a dishonest intriguer and that the very idea of his ever acting from conviction or principle was enough to make anyone laugh, the King answered mildly that he was still young, he would grow up and 'change very much'.[10]

With King George V there was less disposition to hope for the best or to look for redeeming features. Edward VII had appreciated Churchill's eloquence and shared some at least of his more hedonistic traits; the bluff, no-nonsense naval officer who succeeded him distrusted verbal trickeries and found merely vulgar what had entertained his father. The relationship got off to a bad start when, at his first audience with the King, Churchill characteristically allowed his preoccupation with the need for sweeping constitutional change so to possess him that he failed to express more than the most cursory regret at the death of the late King.[11] George V was hurt and offended. Edward VII had once told his son that Churchill was 'almost more of a cad in office than he was in opposition';[12] George V heartily agreed and found the epithet more damning than it would have seemed to his father. In an unguarded moment he described Asquith to Churchill as 'not quite a gentleman'. 'It was a damned stupid thing to say', he remarked ruefully afterwards, 'but Winston repeated it to Asquith, which was a monstrous thing to do.'[13]

Churchill's attitude towards his monarch was vividly illustrated by the celebrated controversy over the name to be given to a new battleship. He wanted HMS *Oliver Cromwell*: the King refused to call one of his ships after a regicide. Churchill revived the idea the following year, claiming that Asquith agreed with him that the Lord Protector had rendered unequalled service to the Royal Navy. The King was unimpressed. Churchill returned to the charge: 'His Majesty is the heir of all the glories of the nation, and there is no chapter of English history from which he should feel himself divided.' He would have continued the battle indefinitely if Louis of Battenberg had not persuaded him to drop it.[14]

George V's doubts about his minister's good judgement were reinforced when, in a letter reporting the day's debate in the House of Commons, Churchill said that there should be proper labour colonies for 'tramps and wastrels', adding for good measure: 'It must not however be forgotten that there are idlers and wastrels at both ends of the social scale.' The King, through Lord Knollys and Asquith's private secretary, denounced these 'socialistic' ideas and complained that the reference to upper-class wastrels was gratuitous and provocative. Churchill was hurt and proposed to discontinue sending Parliamentary reports to the King; no-one, he complained, had given him any guidance on the form such letters should take. That was because he had never asked for any, retorted Knollys drily. In the event a reconciliation was patched up, but it did not go deep.[15] Churchill's reply was meant to be conciliatory, Knollys supposed, 'but he is rather like a Bull in a China Shop'. Churchill for his part had no higher opinion of George V's abilities than George did of his. 'The King talked more stupidly about the Navy than I have ever heard him before', he complained to his wife. 'Really it is disheartening to hear this cheap and silly drivel with which he lets himself be filled up.'[16]

It would be wrong to suggest that Churchill's irritation at what he saw as George V's obstinate folly seriously affected his loyalty towards the institution of monarchy. It only took a crisis like the Mylius case, in which George V found himself accused of having married and fathered a child while serving with the fleet in Malta, for all Churchill's chivalrous instincts to be revived and his support of the King to prove as doughty as could have been expected from the most ardent royalist. Nor did George V wholly despair of his errant minister. When the naval estimates were presented in 1914 he wrote to the First Lord in his own hand, assuring him: 'Since you have been at the Admiralty you have by your zeal and ability done great work for the Navy and I sympathize with you in your present position.'[17] But the two men did not greatly like or respect each other. As war approached Churchill wrote to his wife: 'I wondered whether those stupid Kings and Emperors cd not assemble together and revivify kingship by saving the nations from hell, but we all drift on in a kind of dull cataleptic trance.'[18] He did not specifically include his own King-Emperor among the 'stupid Kings and Emperors', but it is hard to imagine that he did not feel it was a category into which George V neatly fitted.

The war did nothing to soften this mutual antagonism. When the 73-year-old Admiral Fisher was resurrected to replace Prince Louis of Battenberg as First Sea Lord, the King strongly opposed the appointment; Churchill, with Asquith's support, overruled him. A few months later George V was rejoicing at the creation of a national government: 'Only by that means can we get rid of Churchill from the Admiralty. He is intriguing also with French against Kitchener, he is the real danger.'[19] The rest of the royal family seem to have felt the same. The Prince of Wales had before the war held Churchill in high esteem—'He is a wonderful man and has a great power of work'[20]—but by 1915 he had absorbed the distrust of the First Lord which was shared by almost every officer of the British Expeditionary Force in France. 'It is a great relief to know that Winston is leaving the Admiralty . . .' he wrote to his father. 'Sir Charles always described him as "the public danger", perhaps this is rather too strong, but one does feel that he launches the country on mad ventures which are fearfully expensive both as regards men and munitions and which don't attain their object.' When Churchill was readmitted to the government, the Prince professed disgust, though he grudgingly admitted: 'I expect he'll run the Munitions ministry well and perhaps it's safer to give him a job than to have him hanging around unemployed, which gives him more time to work out and push his intriguing schemes.'[21]

With the passing of time George V grew less irascible, Churchill perhaps more circumspect, and the occasions on which the one had cause to cross the other more rare. In 1922 Churchill observed the Shah of Persia losing large sums of money at the gambling tables at Deauville. 'Really, we are well out of it with our own gracious Monarch!' he observed.[22] It was hardly a resounding affirmation of loyalty towards the Crown, but it was warmer than it would have been a few years before. George V for his part thought Churchill unnecessarily provocative in his talk about the use of the armed forces at the time of the General Strike, but he admired the 'skill, patience and tact'[23] which the minister had shown in the negotiations for an Irish settlement, and though he was surprised at Churchill's appointment as Chancellor of the Exchequer at the end of 1924, the King does not seem to have felt that there was anything in it which called for a royal remonstrance. When Churchill visited Balmoral in 1927 he told his wife that he had had 'a particularly pleasant luncheon with the King . . . and a very good talk about all sorts of things'. He was very glad, he went on, that George V 'did not disapprove of my using the Ministerial room as a studio, and I took particular care to leave no spots on the Victorian tartans'.[24]

The animosity which George V's successor, Edward VIII, felt towards the First Sea Lord in 1915 had long faded and he was one of the group of friends who had subscribed to the gift of a motor car when Churchill was convalescing after his accident in New York in 1932.[25] Edward thought that Churchill was dangerously wrong-headed about international politics, but he felt the same about Duff Cooper too, and that did not stop him ranking both men among his closest friends in public life. Churchill for his part knew enough about the new King's private life as Prince of Wales to have some reservations about his future as a monarch. But on the whole he subscribed to the 'Prince Hal' view of the new reign and believed that Mrs Simpson would now be dropped with the same suddenness as Henry V had despatched Falstaff and Pistol some five hundred years before. When nothing of the sort occurred in the early months of the reign, Churchill persisted in his belief that it was a matter of time. 'Women play only a transient part in his life', he told Mrs Belloc Lowndes; 'He falls constantly in and out of love. His present attachment will follow the course of all the others.'[26] Alan Lascelles, the Prince's secretary, used to complain that Churchill was convinced he knew the Duke of Windsor well and thoroughly understood him, while in fact this had never been the case.[27] Certainly, his views about the King's tenacity over Mrs Simpson suggest a fundamental misjudgement of Edward's character.

This conviction that, as he put it to Colville, the King's love for Mrs Simpson was 'a temporary passion' and given time would softly and silently vanish away, was certainly one of the elements which explained Churchill's conduct at the time of the abdication. He barely conceived the possibility that Mrs Simpson might become Queen, he played with the idea that she might be morganatically married and reappear as Duchess of Inverness or Edinburgh, he thought it most likely of all that in the course of 1937 or 1938 she would lose the King's favour and retire to enjoy her rewards elsewhere. To play the question long was the best way to solve it to everyone's satisfaction except, presumably, that of Mrs Simpson herself. But this was only one of a complex of motives which induced Churchill to take on the role of royal champion. One certainly was a romantic appreciation of the power of love. When the marriage was first mooted between Princess Margaret and Group Captain Townsend in 1953, Churchill's first instinct was that the course of true love should be allowed to run smooth. His wife remarked that, if he advocated this, he would be making the same mistake as he had made at the time of the abdication. On reflection, Churchill admitted that this might be so. But it had not seemed like a mistake at the time.[28] All he wanted for the King, he told Duff Cooper, was that he be given the right accorded to 'the meanest of his subjects'—to marry the woman he loved.[29] Churchill did not find Mrs Simpson intrinsically as unappealing as did most other members of the establishment, and his heart was touched by the spectacle of this lonely and unhappy man who had at last found love and emotional security. This feeling was strongly reinforced by his belief in the inviolability of the principle of the hereditary monarchy. 'The hereditary principle must not be left to the mercy of politicians trimming their doctrines "to the varying hour"', he argued. The King was King, and could only be unmade if he gravely offended against the state. 'What crime has the

King committed?' he asked Duff Cooper. 'Have we not sworn allegiance to him? Are we not bound by that oath?'[30] He might not have felt quite so squeamish about that oath, or have defended the hereditary principle with such vigour, if it had not been assailed by his political adversaries of the moment headed by Baldwin and Chamberlain. His friend, Lord Beaverbrook, when asked by Randolph Churchill why he had taken so royalist a line over the abdication, replied succinctly: 'To bugger Baldwin!'[31] This was by no means the whole story even in the case of Beaverbrook, and would have been still less so in the case of Churchill, but the fact that by his championship of the King he was causing alarm and distress to the Prime Minister must certainly have added piquancy to the battle. And yet as important as anything must have been the instinct of chivalry, which impelled him to take up arms in defence of the beleaguered King. Edward VIII was not just his monarch to whose defence he was by oath bound to rally, he was his friend in need who had appealed for help. Churchill could be ruthless in the shrugging off of unwanted responsibilities, but he was capable of great, even quixotic generosity, and he was deeply moved by the plight of the man who, as Prince of Wales, he had regarded as a protégé for many years. No doubt he calculated the possible profits and losses before he took his stand, but when he acted it must have been in the knowledge that he stood to lose much and gain little.

Certainly, if self-interest had been one of the factors that led him on, he miscalculated badly. To the more nervous members of the government it seemed evident that he planned to lead a King's Party and form a ministry if Baldwin resigned because the King would not take his advice over Mrs Simpson. That Baldwin envisioned the possibility is shown by his efforts to associate Churchill with the Labour and Liberal leaders, Clement Attlee and Archibald Sinclair, in an undertaking that they would not form alternative governments if the King's obduracy forced him to resign. In the clubs people amused themselves with constructing 'Cavalier' ministries that Churchill might lead; Alfred Duff Cooper, Sir Samuel Hoare, Leslie Hore-Belisha, Philip Sassoon, and W. S. Morrison were all tipped as future office-holders.[32] If either the King or Churchill flirted with such fantasies, no trace of it remains. But the feeling that Churchill was exploiting the crisis for his own ends was strong in both the House of Commons and in the country. It is hard to understand today quite why the Commons which had heard him sympathetically only the week before, should have turned on him with such ferocity when in the debate of 7 December he urged further delay before any final decision was taken, but whatever the causes his intervention proved disastrous. 'You have delivered a blow to the King . . . far harder than any that Baldwin ever conceived of', Boothby accused him bitterly. 'You have reduced the number of potential supporters to the minimum possible—I should think about seven in all.'[33] As with most such brief storms, it was forgotten far more quickly than at first seemed possible. No lasting damage was done to Churchill's career and, whatever Boothby may have believed, the King's position was hardly affected by the proceedings in Parliament. But the new King had not failed to notice Churchill's turbulent championship of his brother, and although nothing had been said to which he could overtly take exception, the feeling was strengthened in his mind that Churchill was erratic, dangerous, and unsound.

Churchill himself lost no time in coming to terms with the new regime. 'The stronger an advocate of monarchical principle a man may be,' he pronounced in the House of Commons when the abdication had become a *fait accompli*, 'the more zealously must he now endeavour to fortify the Throne and to give to his Majesty's successor that strength which can only come from the love of a united Nation and Empire.'[34] He was undoubtedly sincere, but what George VI must have noticed still more acutely was that Churchill was one of the most persistent in trying to ensure that the Duke of Windsor was generously treated in financial terms, and that he did not hesitate to hint that there would be public scandal if it seemed that agreements entered into in good faith by the Duke when he was King were not honoured now that he was in exile. 'You were right', Churchill said to his wife at the Coronation. 'I see now the "other one" wouldn't have done.' To George VI, though, Churchill remained his brother's champion. As the relationship between the royal brothers became more acrimonious, so it became harder for Churchill to dissociate himself in the King's mind from this inconvenient encumbrance. But for the war it seems likely that George VI would have continued to view Churchill with some unease as a man to be, if not kept at arms' length, then at least not embraced as a trusted confidant.

Sir John Wheeler-Bennett, biographer of George VI, told Harold Nicolson that the King had been 'bitterly opposed' to Churchill's appointment as Prime Minister after Chamberlain's resignation.[35] The King's own diary is more temperate. 'I, of course, suggested Halifax . . .', he wrote, 'as I thought H. was the obvious man, and that his peerage could be placed in abeyance for the time being.' Once it was clear that

Halifax did not wish to be in the running, however, 'then I knew that there was only one person whom I could send for to form a Government who had the confidence of the country.'[36] From the moment of Churchill's appointment, the King gave him the most complete and committed support. To all outward appearances the relationship between the two men could not have been more trusting or harmonious. The reality was not so very far from the appearance, but there were nuances of difference all the same.

'He was funny about Winston,' wrote Halifax about the King in his diary for June 1940, 'and told me he did not find him very easy to talk to. Nor was Winston willing to give him as much time, or information, as he would like.'[37] George VI was soon finding his Prime Minister exceptionally easy to talk to, but the time available for doing so remained a constant problem. Churchill had far more to do than the King, and though he gave his royal audiences a high priority, other things were more important still. The King and Queen, noted Colville, were 'a little ruffled by the offhand way he treats them—says he will come at six, puts it off until 6.30 by telephone, then comes at seven.'[38] Sometimes he would forget to consult or even inform the King on matters in which George VI clearly had a constitutional interest and a right to be heard. When he worked on the draft Declaration of Union with France in 1940, he gave a copy to de Gaulle before the King was given any inkling as to what was in the wind. 'Meanwhile the King does not know what is being done to his Empire', commented Colville.[39] In the end Chamberlain was sent off to the Palace to break it to him.

When the King did have an opportunity to express his views he sometimes found himself ignored or overruled. When George VI tried to stop Beaverbrook's appointment as Minister of Supply, Churchill paid little if any attention to the royal objections. Churchill wanted Brendan Bracken to be created a Privy Councillor. The King protested that this was an honour intended for those who had attained high office or served the state for a long time; Churchill's reply, though deferentially expressed, really said little more than that he relied on Bracken and wanted him to be a Councillor whatever the King might think. The King gave way. The last thing George VI wanted to do, wrote his private secretary Hardinge, was 'to create difficulties for you when you are bearing such an overwhelming burden'.[40]

It was notable too how, consciously or unconsciously, Churchill usurped the King's place as the focal point of the nation's fervour. It was bound to happen. The people needed a heroic figure who would excite and inspire them; temperamentally and physically George VI was unable to fill this need, while Churchill did so to perfection. But though the King could understand why it happened and might even accept rationally that it was necessary, it still sometimes rankled. 'The K[ing] and Q[ueen] feel Winston puts them in [the] shade', recorded Edward VII's friend and frequent hostess, Mrs Ronald Greville. 'He is always sending messages for Nation that King ought to send.'[41]

None of this is of great significance. The two men were of enormous importance to each other and both realized it; deep trust and affection grew between them. 'He tells me, more than people imagine, of his future plans and ideas,' wrote George VI proudly, 'and only airs them when the time is ripe to his colleagues and his Chiefs of Staff.'[42] 'Your welfare means a great deal not only to the United Nations, but to me personally', he wrote to his Prime Minister.[43] Churchill responded whole-heartedly and grew to attach real value to the King's experience and common sense. When George VI wrote him a congratulatory letter after the Battle of El Alamein, Churchill in his reply said that he would always treasure it

as a record of the support and encouragement given by the Sovereign to his First Minister in good and dark days alike. No Minister in modern times, and I dare say in long past days, has received more help and comfort from the King . . . It is needless for me to assure Your Majesty of my devotion to Yourself and Family and to our ancient cherished Monarchy—the true bulwark of British freedom against tyrannies of every kind, but I trust I may have the pleasure of feeling a sense of personal friendship which is very keen and lively in my heart and has grown strong in these hard times of war.[44]

The fact that it was not so much the monarchical principle as the British monarchy that Churchill espoused was made clear in those last few months before he left office. 'I have had many kings on my hands', he mused to Pierson Dixon. 'I have fought hard for George and Peter. The King of Italy slipped through my fingers. President Roosevelt supports me: he likes to keep kings on their thrones.'[45] Other things being equal, Churchill too liked to keep kings on their thrones, but far from being the most important figures on the chessboard, they were never more than pawns in the political game. Far from fighting hard for Peter of Yugoslavia, he made it clear to that luckless monarch that, if he did not accept the dispensation that confirmed Tito in power, he would be in effect abandoned. King George of Greece was of value as a potential rallying point against the Communists, but if it seemed easier to keep them at bay by installing a republican government, then the King would have to go. 'The peoples of these countries should have a free and fair chance of choosing', Churchill told Stalin.[46] If Churchill had been returned to power in 1945 it would have made no appreciable difference to the chances of survival of such client monarchs.

When Churchill lost power in the general election of 1945, the King was shocked and dismayed. 'I thought it was most ungrateful to you personally after all your hard work for the people', he wrote, with most unusual indiscretion for so impeccable a constitutional monarch. Later the same day he wrote again in his own hand to emphasize his personal regrets. But his letter indicated also his acceptance of the will of the people and his recognition of what that entailed. 'I shall miss your counsel to me more than I can say', he concluded. 'But please remember that as a friend I hope we shall be able to meet at intervals.'[47]

Observing Princess Elizabeth at the age of two Churchill remarked that she was a character: 'She has an air of authority and reflectiveness astonishing in an infant.'[48] It may reasonably be felt that that sort of comment is conventionally made about princes or princesses who may one day inherit the throne. Nevertheless, what evidence there is suggests that Churchill did feel that Princess Elizabeth was exceptionally well equipped to take over as Queen. All his romantic instincts too were stirred when she acceded to the throne at the age of 25: 'A fair and youthful figure, princess, wife and mother, is the heir to all our glories and traditions.'[49] 'He was madly in love with the Queen,' wrote Colville, 'and this was clear from the fact that his audiences had been dragged out longer and longer as the months went by and very often took an hour and a half.'[50] She, for her part, though in every way preternaturally discreet over her relationship with her various prime ministers, has never concealed the fact that she got more fun out of her audiences with Churchill than with any of his successors. When he resigned, she wrote to assure him that, though she had total confidence in Eden, neither he nor any of those who would in time replace him would 'be able to hold the place of my first Prime Minister, to whom both my husband and I owe so much and for whose wise guidance during the early years of my reign I shall always be profoundly grateful'.[51] Having been assured by Colville that it would certainly be refused, the Queen offered Churchill a dukedom. There was an alarming moment when it seemed as if, in a rush of sentimental fervour, the old man might accept, but he remembered his resolve to remain the Great Commoner and in the end declined the honour—'and do you know, the Queen seemed rather relieved', he remarked afterwards, no doubt in affected puzzlement.[52] Avuncular affection, the romantic excitement of one who saw in the young Queen a dramatic symbol of national regeneration, was there more to it than that? That Churchill saw himself as Lord Melbourne to Queen Elizabeth's Victoria seems more than probable, but if he did so he deliberately averted his eyes from the fact that the role of the monarchy had altered radically in the 115 years or so since Victoria's accession. Victoria was still the repository of an extraordinary amount of constitutional power, and for Melbourne—though he saw the facts through a rosy haze of loyal deference—the Queen was a means by which he could hold on to a power that was otherwise escaping him. Churchill knew more about power than any man alive, how to acquire it and how to use it, and he knew that no power of use to him was to be derived from his relationship with the Palace.

Probably it never had been. With the solitary exception of the abdication, it is hard to think of a single instance in which Churchill changed his views or his course of action on any important question in accordance with his perception of the wishes of the monarch of the time. He did not just pay lip-service to the idea of a hereditary monarchy. All his historical romantic instincts ensured that he would view it with profound respect or even reverence, but that was something distinct from the business of governing the country. He would have died for the cause of the King if this had seemed necessary, but it would not have occurred to him to alter a detail of his budget or to shuffle the members of a ministry because he believed that to be the King's desire. He was indeed, in his wife's phrase, 'Monarchial No. 1', but if the circumstances had been different or the provocation had arisen he could have made a splendidly robust republican.

12

Churchill and Appeasement

DONALD CAMERON WATT

WHAT might loosely be called the Churchillian critique of appeasement has played a major role in the deliberations of governments in moments of international crisis ever since 1945. It involves a series of assumptions about patterns of behaviour in these crises to which appeal has frequently been made both in Britain and in the United States. Indeed, the actual course of some of these crises could be regarded as material on which these 'Churchillian' assumptions could be tested. The reactions of the British government to the North Korean attack on South Korea, and the rhetoric of appeal to the 'lessons of the 1930s' played a major part in the debate in the purlieus of the United Nations, the British Cabinet, and in the Truman administration. Sir Anthony Eden regarded the action of the Egyptian government in nationalizing the Suez Canal in 1956 as a re-run of the crisis of March 1936, twenty years previously, which arose from the German remilitarization of the Rhineland. The belief that economic sanctions, if properly applied, would have brought Mussolini to withdraw from his attack on Ethiopia in 1935–6 has been appealed to repeatedly, as when they were applied to Ian Smith's Rhodesia after the Unilateral Declaration of Independence, and most recently against Saddam Hussein's Iraq. In America, the notion that appeasement does not pay and that its advocacy as a policy is a symptom of imperial decline, if not a yardstick by which it can be measured, has passed into the folklore of politics.

There are, of course, elements in this critique which are not particularly Churchillian. As we shall see, Churchill's support for the application of sanctions against Mussolini was somewhat less than whole-hearted. The critique has, in fact, taken on a whole series of accretions from the idealistic and internationalist rather than the imperial strain in British political debate. What is characteristic of this critique is that while purporting to be an argument about political realism, it is in fact one which is about morality. The term 'appeasement' itself has lost its original meaning of the defusing of conflict and taken on the meaning of purchasing peace for one's own interests by sacrificing the interests of others. It is only where such a policy is unsuccessful, where it has fired the appetite of the acquisitive and encouraged the bully to believe he lacks serious opposition, that it is called 'appeasement'. Where such a policy succeeds, as, for example, with President Kennedy's intervention in 1963 to secure the Indonesian occupation of the formerly Dutch occupied west of New Guinea at the expense of sacrificing the native independence movement, then it is defended as *realpolitik*. Appeasement, like treason, has to be unsuccessful to be both immoral and unrealistic.

The debate over appeasement has thrived on the ambiguity of the term. Is it an aim, or merely a method? The appeasement of Europe, the proclaimed theme of British policy in Europe from 1920 onwards, was certainly seen as a desirable aim in itself, linked with those other two uncriticizable desiderata, peace and disarmament. But to many of those in the Cabinet, in the government, in the administration of Britain under the governments of Ramsay MacDonald, Stanley Baldwin, and Neville Chamberlain, it was part of the machinery of conflict avoidance and crisis management deemed necessary until Britain's rearmament policy had produced a position where further unilateral action on the part of Hitler and his imitators would no longer seem worth while risking. A state of affairs would be reached where, in the jargon of the 1950s, Britain could 'negotiate from strength'. There is increasing evidence to show that for Chamberlain 'appeasement' was a means, not an end, though the avoidance of war had a very high priority with him; though perhaps not so high a priority as that of reducing the number of Britain's potential enemies, an end he certainly shared with Churchill. But Chamberlain saw appeasement as the only possible form of accommodation between the opposed and mutually conflicting and contradictory sets of convictions about the nature of relations between states that obtained in Europe before 1939 as, for that matter, in the world after 1945.

In its extreme form the Churchillian critique of appeasement can be summed up in the phrase 'the unnecessary war', to which he first gave circulation in a speech delivered in Brussels in November 1945.[1] 'If the allies had resisted Hitler strongly in his early stages . . . the chance would have been given to the sane elements in German life, which were very powerful—especially in the High Command—to save

Germany from the maniacal system into the grip of which she was falling.' This claim was, in fact, one he had advanced earlier, in the aftermath of the Munich crisis, when in a broadcast to America he had said: 'If the risks of war which were run by France and Britain at the last moment had been boldly faced in good time and plain declarations made and meant, how different would our prospects have been today . . .' If Hitler, he continued, had faced 'a formidable array of peace-defending powers . . . this would have been an opportunity for all peace-loving and moderate forces in Germany, together with the chiefs of the German army, to make a great effort to re-establish something like sane and civilized conditions in their country'.[2]

These two speeches provide part of the elements in the post-war Churchillian critique of appeasement—a firm attitude by France and Britain which would lead to a military coup in Germany against Hitler. To this other elements in the post-war version of the Churchillian fight against Hitler can be added: more rapid armament in the air and a grand alliance in 1938, if not earlier, with the Soviet Union. All of this would have had the result of an internal eruption in Germany which would have overthrown Hitler and restored a government with which some form of accommodation was possible. It is incidentally worth making the point that those admirers of Churchill among the professional historians who did most to propagate his views, such as Sir Lewis Namier and Sir John Wheeler-Bennett, stopped a long way short of endorsing Churchill's hypothesis of a coup in Germany. Namier had always loathed establishment German nationalism, and dealt very firmly in his post-war works with the memoirs of survivors of the internal conservative 'opposition' in Germany. Wheeler-Bennett devoted his largest and most tendentious post-war work, *The Nemesis of Power*, to a comprehensive denunciation of the German army leadership and the military conspiracy. It is possible that they feared the creation of a new *Dolchstosslegend*, by which the responsibility for the outbreak of the Second World War would be laid on British shoulders for Britain's failure to take the conspirators at their own value, to afford them the promises that they required as a preliminary to any action against Hitler, and to show herself prepared to allow a post-Hitlerian Germany to enjoy the fruits of Hitler's piracies. In the absence of any spelling out of how a different policy on the part of the British government would have made the outbreak of the Second World War more 'evitable', Namier and his supporters laid themselves open to the accusation that they would have avoided war in 1939 by fighting it in 1938,

1937, or even 1936. 'Croque-mitaine se dégonflera' as Paul Claudel wrote, satirizing this view in retrospect in *Figaro* in July 1939.[3]

The Churchillian critique has been set out so often in the form of a purely English tragedy, as a dialogue of the few who were right but not listened to and the all-powerful but pig-ignorant Chamberlain (dismissed as a good Lord Mayor of Birmingham in a bad year), that it seems extraordinary to have to point out that it can only really be validated by comparison not with Chamberlain's policy but with what we know about conditions in Germany. The Churchillian critique can be reduced to three propositions: that a greater rate of British rearmament would have deterred Hitler; that a more aggressive style would have deterred him at crucial moments in his advance; and that a grand coalition would have deterred him or led to his overthrow.

It is worthwhile, therefore, to consider Churchill's contemporary record on these issues and to match it against what we know of Hitler. On armaments, the British government was confronted in 1934 by the report of its official committee on Britain's defence requirements.[4] This report saw Nazi Germany as the single greatest threat to British security, rewriting in the process of its deliberation the terms of reference that had made Japan the most probable enemy. The shopping lists of the three services, however, envisaged different wars against different enemies, and together involved public expenditure greatly in excess of the surplus predicted by the Treasury. In Cabinet this conflict was resolved by a deliberate strategic choice which put naval rearmament second to rearmament in the air and eliminated any major commitment to army intervention on the European mainland, nullifying Britain's Locarno commitment in the process. The Royal Air Force, although beneficiaries of the final allocation of funds, were infuriated to find the bulk of their allocation allotted to building up the air defence of Great Britain instead of giving them the strategic bombing force they demanded.

There ensued a period of guerrilla warfare between the Service Chiefs, the Treasury, and the Cabinet in which Churchill in effect became one of the weapons on which the dissidents in the Admiralty and the Air Ministry relied. He found himself provided with a flow of information, which he turned to such effective use that he became the principal Parliamentary critic of the speed and scale of the British rearmament programme. It is interesting, therefore, to find that in his criticism of that programme he concentrated almost exclusively on the issue of rearmament in the air. He paid no attention to the issues of a military commitment, as in 1914, to the Continent. For him the French army was enough. 'The peace of Europe dwells under the shield of the French army', he wrote to Lord Linlithgow, then Viceroy of India, in November 1937,[5] at a time when the French army was riven by the discovery of the *Cagoulards* conspiracy, and its military thinking was fixed firmly on the refighting of the battle of Verdun.

One looks in vain for any appreciation by him of the revolution in tank warfare pioneered by Wavell's experimental tank force in the early 1930s, or any realization of the extent to which British tank production was falling in both volume and prototypes behind that of Germany. The backward state of British artillery and anti-tank weapons escaped him; where France was concerned, he was ignorance personified.

Nor, although the First Sea Lord, Lord Chatfield, kept him fully informed as to naval matters, was he any more concerned with rearmament at sea. The passing of twelve of the fifteen British capital ships into obsoleteness (all but the *Hood*, *Rodney*, and *Nelson* were over 26 years old by 1936), the failure to catch up with the revolution in naval air warfare, the lack of an adequate British escort vessel programme to match the German submarine programme, the weakness of Singapore, the impossibility of meeting Britain's naval commitments to the Far East and Australia when Italy was an enemy and the Middle East at risk, seem to have remained outside his area of concern. China would provide 'the exemplary discomfiture of a brutal aggressor—cheer the democracies of the western world and teach them to stand up for themselves while time remains', he wrote in May 1938;[6] the following March, writing to Chamberlain, Halifax, Hore-Belisha, and to Chatfield, now Minister for the Co-ordination of Defence, he advised concentration on the Mediterranean and Germany, trotting out his obsession with a break into and domination of the Baltic, something Britain had only achieved in 1811–12 against Napoleon, and in 1918–19, after the German collapse, against Leningrad. 'Singapore', he wrote, 'will hold out with naval aid in the event of war with Japan', which he thought unlikely unless 'England has been decisively beaten'.[7] As he revealed early in August 1939 to Chamberlain, he shared the Prime Minister's view that if Britain had to go to war in Europe it would not be possible to make commitments in the Far East.[8] For Winston, the Pacific was a faraway country of which he knew nothing.

Where air matters were concerned, he echoed the Air Ministry line. Parity with Germany in the air was the yardstick for British influence in time of peace. A hidden minor assumption in this was the view that

British parity in the air with Germany would operate as a deterrent. Over British armament in the air, he found himself at odds with an Air Ministry that showed itself both doctrinaire and complacent. He became a thorn in the side of successive Air Ministers, most notably Londonderry and Swinton, and certainly played a part in forcing their resignations. He was kept accurately supplied with information by the disaffected in the Air Ministry and the RAF. But he seems to have been little aware as to the bitter battle that was being fought between the dominant bomber-oriented establishment in the Air Staff and the advocates of Fighter Command and the Air Defence of Great Britain, although he knew of the backwardness of Britain's fixed air defences from young officers in the Territorial Army. Nor was he made aware of the hopes pinned by the Air Staff on the four-engined heavy bomber programme that was initiated in 1935.

He was, however, kept more than adequately supplied by the misinformation as to German air production put out by Erhard Milch and other members of Goering's air staff. He shared in the British conviction that the major threat to Britain was in the air. And no more than his informants did he realize that the capacities of the aircraft in production in Germany and Britain up to 1939 made it impossible for either country to launch a serious bombing attack against the other from bases on their own territory.

Where he was uncharacteristically uninformed and blind to the major issue was the question as to whether there was any evidence to suggest that German official opinion took the 'threat from the air' seriously in the way British opinion did. British opinion had been fed on prophecies that a new war would begin with an all-out air attack on London in which both bombs and gas could well produce a quarter of a million casualties and a total breakdown of public order in the first few days.[9] True, it would have been difficult to cull such evidence from the Nazi press; but German opinion in the upper levels of the state was still much more open to British visitors in the first years of the Hitler regime than after Munich. In fact, the Luftwaffe failed to develop either a doctrine or a bomber capable of exercising the kind of strategic attack from the air that the Air Ministry had been preaching (rather than practising) since the early 1920s.[10] The hard truth must be that Churchill's campaign for British rearmament never focused on the issues that might have made an impact on German military opinion—military arms production, conscription, a Continental commitment. Romantic memories of Joffre, Gallieni, and Foch were no substitute for political realism, the discovery of accurate intelligence, or an appreciation of the authentic quality of French thinking on defence. Had Churchill rather than Inskip become Minister for the Co-ordination of Defence in 1936, there is no evidence to suggest that British rearmament would have been such as to exercise any more of a deterrent effect on Hitler than in fact it did.

The second issue is that of deterrence through alliance. Churchill seems to have turned to this idea initially in the aftermath of the Rhineland crisis. It was at this time too that he fell into the clutches of Ivan Maisky, the Soviet ambassador in London. In April 1936 we find him writing to Viscount Cecil of the need to 'organise a European mass and, perhaps, a world mass which will confront . . . overcome . . . and perhaps let their peoples loose upon the heavily armed unmoral dictatorships'[11]. Ten days later he is urging on Hankey the need to send part of the fleet to the Baltic. Much the same idea emerges in a letter to Lady Violet Bonham Carter in May. He hoped that Mussolini might participate in a Mediterrean pact 'for mutual protection against further aggression' and that this regional pact might, under the League, be linked with a front 'of all the countries including Soviet Russia from the Baltic southwards right round the Belgian coast all agreeing to stand by any victim of unprovoked aggression'. In the case of Mussolini refusing and leaving the League he would fall back on 'a strictly limited regional pact among the western states, Holland, Belgium, France, and Britain for mutual aid in the event of unprovoked attack, and for keeping in being a force great enough to deter Germany from making such an attack'.[12]

The purge of the Soviet High Command in June 1937 severely shook his belief in Soviet strength. But with the German annexation of Austria in March 1938 and the opening of the crisis over Czechoslovakia, Churchill returned to the theme. As Halifax told the Foreign Policy Committee of the Cabinet on 18 March 1938, Churchill advocated an Anglo-French alliance and a joint effort to persuade the states of central Europe and the Balkans to unite against Hitler. Halifax himself drew a distinction between 'Germany's racial efforts' (i.e. the support of the Sudeten Germans) 'which none could question' and a 'lust for conquest on a Napoleonic scale' with which presumably Churchill credited Hitler but which Halifax himself 'did not credit'.[13] Churchill visited France at the end of March 1938 and returned to press the need for Anglo-French staff talks on the Cabinet. He was not apparently aware of how little Britain had to offer, with the bulk of the regular army tied up in Palestine and the Middle East, and neither its forces nor those of the Territorial Army trained or equipped for a Continental war. That was left to the Daladier government to discover at the end of April.

Churchill's intelligence continued to be influenced by desire rather than knowledge. On 10 September, according to Sir Samuel Hoare, Churchill appeared at Downing Street to demand an immediate ultimatum to Germany, both France and the Soviet Union being ready for an offensive against Germany.[14] His information about French intentions was demonstrably untrue. In the absence of documentation on Soviet military planning no such certainty exists as to Soviet intentions. The problem of transit between Soviet territories and the German frontier, let alone the Czechoslovak front, is, however, sufficiently well known as to cast a certain doubt on the effectiveness of Soviet offensive intentions had they existed. Hoare's information, for what that was worth, was 'directly contrary'.

Churchill, like others in his position, was aware of the anxieties being expressed in German military circles. These were confirmed to him by Ewald von Kleist-Schmenzin during his visit to London on 19 August 1938.[15] If they 'received a little encouragement', said Kleist-Schmenzin, the army would refuse to march. Once the generals had decided for peace, Hitler would be overthrown within 48 hours and a new government 'probably of monarchist character' would end the fears of war forever. No-one can doubt his informant's courage or degree of commitment against Hitler. But overt opposition to Hitler's plans had collapsed among the German generals with the resignation of General Beck, the Army Chief of Staff, on 18 August. His successor, General Halder, was to plan a military conspiracy; but its organization and planning had not yet begun when Kleist-Schmenzin was seeing Churchill, and he was not privy to it.

Churchill was to return to the theme of deterrence through alliance in 1939; but with no more success. Stalin's decision to accept the German option rather than that offered by the western powers most probably arose from his realization that in a western alliance intended as a deterrent to Hitler the Soviet Union would be shouldering the burden of a war against Germany if it failed without any commensurate reward should it succeed; such pragmatic calculation does cast a little doubt on the sincerity of the Soviet desire to pursue an anti-Fascist front in 1938, or the scale or effectiveness of the Soviet military action which might have followed. But the conclusion of the Munich agreement without Soviet participation makes speculation as to how Stalin would have acted before so overt a humiliation, otiose.

Stalin's possible reactions have, however, little bearing on the real points at issue, which are in the effect of British policy on Hitler and whether or not he would have been deterred by a different policy. The evidence here fails to support the Churchillan analysis in three aspects. In the first place Hitler's decision, communicated in November 1937 to the audience of his so-called Hossbach speech,[16] to force the pace on his expansionist programme, was influenced by his conviction of British hostility to his aims, a desire to act before the British rearmament pro-gramme destroyed Germany's lead, and a conviction that the British Empire was far less monolithic a force than it appeared. In the second place, Hitler's final decision 'to smash Czechoslovakia at the first avail-able opportunity', issued on 31 May 1938,[17] was the direct result of the Anglo-French *démarche* in Berlin received over the weekend of 20–1 May warning him against a coup directed at Czechoslovakia; without this the evidence is that Hitler's failure to secure the signature of a German–Italian alliance on his visit to Rome on 5–8 May had decided him to put his plans against Czechoslovakia on to the backburner for the time being.[18]

In the third place, the news of Britain's decision to mobilize the fleet, and the warning conveyed by Sir Horace Wilson, when coupled with the failure of the military march in Berlin and the intervention of Mussolini, did deter Hitler from his planned attack on Czechoslovakia, to his very considerable fury. It is arguable that it was the combination of the diplomatic initiative and the last-minute nature of the British action which drove him to the conference table. A longer lead-time would have been utilized by him for diplomatic counter-moves designed to break up or disarm the coalition against him, perhaps with more effect than in 1939.

By contrast with this, one looks in vain through the voluminous German military or political records for the years before 1939 for any evidence that German military or political planners, let alone Hitler, took Soviet military strength at all seriously, let alone included it in their detailed military planning. Both Case Red and Case Green as drawn up in the summer of 1937 envisaged war with a Franco–Czechoslovak–Soviet alliance.[19] The only reference to military planning against the Soviet Union is an oblique reference to the trans-ference by Germany of Luftwaffe units to East Prussia 'for his own [unstated] operational purposes'. But the context here is of a war in which Poland has joined Germany's enemies; there is still no reference to operations against Soviet territory or Soviet forces. In 1939, as part of Case White, the Kriegsmarine considered operations in the Baltic against Soviet naval forces until ordered to desist.[20] But the German army and the Luftwaffe do not seem at any time to have taken Soviet military strength into their calculations. If the need to counter the use of Soviet forces against Germany was so absent from their thoughts, it was hardly likely that the Soviet contribution to an anti-German front would have played any part in discouraging the German generals from supporting Hitler's plans. The Soviet agreements concluded with France and Czechoslovakia in 1935 had already been accepted and discounted in German military thinking.

Contrary to Churchill's interpretation of the situation, it was the prospect of Britain joining the Franco–Czechoslovak–Soviet line-up ('Extended Red Green' in the 1937 military orders) which confronted the German military with the prospect of mutiny. The orders of June 1937 had expressed pessimism as to the prospect of victory for the German forces in such eventuality. If Germany went to war against a coalition of which Britain was a member, Germany would be defeated as she had been in 1918. On this, German military thinking was axiomatic.

Hitler knew this well: the vulnerability of Britain was a constant theme in his talks with his military from 1937 onwards. The thought of war with Britain did not deter him. From the Hossbach meeting onwards he had been quietly encouraging the aspirations of the Kriegsmarine: it had, after all, originally been summoned to decide on the allocation of armour-plate between the three services, a decision which had gone in favour of the Kriegsmarine. The events of the 'weekend crisis' drove him to order Admiral Raeder, the Commander-in-Chief of the Kriegsmarine, to produce a new naval construction plan, the Z Plan, which would enable Germany to challenge and defeat the Royal Navy at sea by 1944 at the latest.[21] And in January 1939 the Kriegsmarine was given priority in the allocation of armour-plate over the army and the Luftwaffe.[22] War came in September 1939, to Raeder's dismay, four years too early.[23] But the scale of Hitler's planning shows that for him or for the German military, the threat of British power loomed larger than that of the Soviet Union.

The question that must arise is whether a British initiative on Churchillian lines, as advocated by Ivan Maisky, would have caused Hitler to rethink his plans against Czechoslovakia. If such an initiative had been taken at the end of March it would have anticipated the military discussions from which we know of the hopes he pinned on his visit to Rome. Since his orders to the Sudeten leader, Konrad Henlein, always to demand more than the Czechs would concede were given in the last week of March 1938, Hitler had, it must be presumed, already begun planning in his own mind. Overt British action, especially if it took on the nature of a pre-emptive move (and the anti-Hitler press, which played so large a role in the outcome of the 'weekend crisis', would certainly have hailed any such move), could well have turned his mind to the kind of diplomatic preparations which occupied so large a part of 1939. It would seem unlikely that it would have actively deterred him, let alone have resulted in his overthrow.

Much of March and early April was, in fact, occupied in Berlin digesting the fruits not of the *Anschluss* but of the series of internal coups which had resulted in the resignation of the Minister of War, Field Marshal von Blomberg, the bringing of forged charges of homosexuality against General von Fritsch, the Commander-in-Chief of the Army, and his resignation, the metamorphosis of the War Ministry into the Supreme Command of the Armed Forces (OKW) under Hitler himself, and the selection and appointment of General von Brauchitsch, a man indebted to Hitler for the financial support which made possible his divorce and remarriage to a fanatical admirer of Hitler, as Fritsch's successor.[24] It was not until mid–April that the two staff officers who were to embody Hitler's control of the new OKW, General Keitel and General Jodl, had taken up the reins of office. Much of the Army Staff's time was taken up with the redeployment of units arising out of the occupation of Austria and the extension of the German military presence along the southern borders of Bohemia and Moravia. The sense of crisis over Czechoslovakia was much stronger in London and Paris during this period than in Berlin. A positive British initiative might have altered matters. It could even have brought the issue of the orders of 31 May forward by two months.

At this time the main efforts of General Beck, Chief of Army Staff, were directed towards attempting to stiffen Fritsch into confronting his SS accusers and winning back the ground lost to the army. Fritsch, however, was unstiffenable. (He was eventually to seek his death in the front of the offensive against Poland in September 1939.) It is unlikely under the circumstances that Beck, the most upright and honourable of men, would have contemplated conspiracy against Hitler at that time. The conspiracy only began in earnest at the end of August after his resignation. It is difficult to argue that the conditions for the realization of Churchill's hopes of deterrence were present in Germany in March–April 1938, or indeed at any time before the staff conferences in Berchtesgaden on 24–30 May, out of which the decisive orders of 31 May emerged.

The best conditions for the realization of Churchill's hopes arose in September 1938 when a military conspiracy was actually in preparation. According to the survivors and the very considerable literature their memoirs and claims have generated, this conspiracy turned on two eventualities being realized. The first was the actual outbreak of war with Czechoslovakia and its escalation into an Anglo-French war against Germany. The second was that the Commander-in-Chief of the Army, General von Brauchitsch, should order the coup to begin. Brauchitsch's subsequent record suggests that it might well have proved impossible to bring him to so decisive an act. But the summoning of the Munich conference destroyed any realization of the first eventuality; the conspiracy was, therefore, stood down. The conspirators shared the view of Churchill and the opponents to Hitler that the outcome of the crisis was a major victory for Hitler. In the views of the survivors the heart went out of their potential supporters. History seemed to be on Hitler's side.

Churchill's hopes for the conspiracy were based on the expectation that its members would act before war broke out; that the appearance of a Grand Alliance would not so much deter Hitler as drive the military leadership to overthrow him on the eve of war. Bound up in his hopes there lay his own confusion of mind on the subject of the Prussian aristocracy, Nazism, and the sources of German militarist expansionism, a confusion manifest in his attitude to the wartime conspirators, which the disappointment of his hopes of 1938 may have intensified. As was remarked earlier, Churchill's view of Germany in the 1930s was remarkably similar to that entertained by Sir Robert Vansittart and Sir Warren Fisher; that is to say, it arose from a combination of almost racialist antipathy and balance of power calculations. To apply the term 'social Darwinism' to his attitude would not be to misuse that somewhat elastic concept. It was tempered in Churchill's case by an equally Victorian respect for the German contribution to European culture, a potential source of conflict he was, after 1940, increasingly to resolve by identifying those 'national characteristics' he detested as 'Prussian' rather than 'German'. This confusion reinforced his proposed division of the Reich into separate states and the linkage of some parts of southern Germany and Austria into a Danubian confederation.

His obsession with Germany is the more striking when Churchill's attitude to the appeasement of Italy and Japan is examined. The anti-appeasers of the left had a simplistic outlook. They ranged from the Beaverbrook stable of 'Guilty Men' hunters to A. J. P. Taylor and his pupils, to the disciples of the Comintern propaganda manufactured by the Willi Muenzenberg *équipe*, and spread in Britain and America by the Left Book Club. To them the behaviour of the British government over the Italian conflict with Ethiopia and over non-intervention in Spain was all of a piece. Behind this attitude lay their belief in the existence of a combination of industrial and financial support for Fascism as a bulwark against Bolshevism, and the socialist radical attack on 'monopoly capitalism'. The same forces, 'the City', were alleged to dominate the Conservative Party, the bulk of the British press, the thinking of senior military figures, and the intellectual and religious establishment. Roosevelt, the radical wing of his New Dealers, as well as old-style American radical isolationists like Senator Borah, derived their picture of British motivation from the British end of the Muenzenberg empire, the more so once Muenzenberg himself broke with Moscow and the lead passed to publications like Claude Cockburn's *The Week*.[25]

The deification of Churchill during the war by the radical critics of appeasement in Britain required of them a certain selectivity of approach, a certain 'economy' with the truth when examining Churchill's record on the issue of Ethiopia and the Spanish Civil War. The facts are that Churchill, sharing Vansittart's obsession with the 'German threat', could see no sense in driving Italy, the one power prepared to move troops to secure the protection of Austria against a Nazi takeover in 1934, into the German camp. He had never been prepared to share the admiration for and dedication to the League of Nations preached by the centre and left of the Conservative, Liberal, and Labour Parties in the inter-war years. His record during the height of the Italo-Ethiopian crisis can only be stigmatized as one of equivocation and absenteeism. He took no part in the major Parliamentary debates of the winter of 1935–6, most of which he spent in the south of France. When he did speak finally, on 6 April 1936, it was to attack the maintenance of sanctions against Italy.[26] Nor was his record on the Spanish Civil War any more secure from criticism. None of this affected his romantic admiration for Anthony Eden, expressed in a

famous passage in the *Gathering Storm* on the impact of Eden's resignation upon him. But at this time it was an admiration without intimacy,
an admiration, too, which projected upon Eden a determination to
resist the appeasement of Hitler which it is difficult to discover in
Eden's contemporary records. It was for Mussolini that Eden's hatred
and detestation were reserved.

It is unfortunate for the credibility of the Churchillian critique of
appeasement that there is no evidence of serious dissidence among the
conservative opposition to Hitler, military or civilian, before 1938. At
the time of his earlier coups, the walk-out from the League of Nations
and the Disarmament Conference in November 1933, the failure of the
Austrian coup and the assassination of Dolfuss in June 1934, the
proclamation of German rearmament in March 1935, the reoccupation
of the Rhineland in March 1936, there may have been strained nerves
among his military and diplomatic advisers; but there is no whisper of
dissidence. The army leadership was bought off by the suppression of
the challenge from Roehm and the SA in the 'night of the long knives',
and hog-tied thereafter by its own traditions when the death of
President von Hindenberg was followed by the exaction of their oaths
of loyalty to Hitler himself. Hjalmar Schacht, who by his economic
skills made the German economy boom between 1933 and 1936, thus
eliminating the mass unemployment which had helped Hitler to power
but which could well have destroyed him in the early years of his rule,
was left to fight Goering and his Four Year Plan organization on his
own. The leaders of German heavy industry were divided, some
appeased, some flattered, some driven into exile. But without access to
the press, financial support for rival political parties, or control of their
own industrial organizations, they were deprived of whatever political
clout they had enjoyed under Weimar.

The autumn of 1937 saw Hitler in direct conflict with the Vatican.
Pius XI was a formidable enemy and the German Catholic Church
fought Hitler to a stand-off. But the strength of the Church lay in its
willingness to defend its own ground. Hitler had broken the Catholic
Centre Party in 1933, driven its leaders into exile, and negotiated a
Concordat with the Vatican. The conflict in 1937 arose because his
minions broke the Concordat in both letter and spirit. Its resolution
took place without reference to any external crisis; and the German
church as such observed the biblical adage to render unto Caesar the
things that are Caesar's very carefully. Matters of foreign policy were
clearly Caesar's business.

To recapitulate, the policy of appeasement began as a technique for conflict resolution. With the recognition in 1934 of the threat from a rearmed Germany it evolved through stages of conflict avoidance, conflict limitation (Ethiopia, Spanish Civil War), conflict management (1938), to deterrence (1939). From 1936 onwards Churchill seems to have accepted the views of the Germanophobes within the administration and seen Hitler as a new Napoleon of unrestricted ambitions and drive. Chamberlain and Halifax, wishing to avoid war, believing or hoping a stage would arrive when British rearmament would make the hazards of further expansion unacceptable to Hitler, were unwilling to accept so black and white, so pessimistic a view of Hitler, until events forced it upon them. For Churchill, further appeasement of Germany only increased the dangers the expansion of German power represented. His alternative was to create a coalition to restrain Hitler—in the hope of provoking the elements which had brought Hitler to power, to remove him from it.

There is, of course, the additional issue of 'leadership' versus 'public opinion'. The defenders of Chamberlain's policy point to the evidence of the fear of war and the will for peace and disarmament among the British people, and argue that after the marked success of the various anti-war and pro-disarmament movements *before* the 1935 general election, any stronger, more interventionist action on the part of the national government would have merely divided the country openly and made Hitler aware that his actions would not be opposed. The Churchillians argue that more outspoken leadership on the part of MacDonald, Baldwin, and Chamberlain would have changed opinion. More recently they have come to support such arguments with the newly available evidence of the degree to which Chamberlain sought by covert means to isolate his critics, to manipulate the media against them, and to keep all talk of war out of the press.[27] The debate on this is still far from settled. There were many other influences abroad in the British press at the time, and the proliferation of newsletters, pamplets of all kinds, the Left Book Club and Penguin special publications, shows that debate was far from stifled.

Thus stated, the contrast between the two approaches seems clear and easy to grasp. The problems arise firstly when the Churchillian analysis is applied to Germany, and secondly when his views are contrasted with the diplomatic, military, and financial advice at the disposal of the Cabinet. On the first it would be true to say that Churchill's conception of German military anxieties does not match the German realities. The Germans were not afraid of war in the air; they were not touched by the spectacle of Soviet military power. Fear of Soviet power among the other states of Europe was in fact the most powerful instrument available to German foreign policy in Europe. Regarding the possibility of these fears animating the military leadership to the execution of a *coup d'état* against Hitler, the only possible occasion was in September 1938. The Chamberlain government was not prepared to risk a war, the outcome of which was regarded with the utmost of pessimism by their military advisers, on the possibility of a conspiracy of whose reality they had no independent evidence, and whose emissaries, in a famous phrase, struck Chamberlain as resembling the Jacobite exiles in the Court of Louis XV.[28] They did not believe Hitler would be deterred. In the event he was deterred but not appeased. War was avoided. 'Appeasement' and 'Munich' acquired a pejorative association with the ignominious surrender of principle and the purchase of peace by the sacrifice of the interests of the weak and the defenceless, which they will never lose. Churchill's parliamentary attack on Munich made him the central figure in all eyes, including those of Hitler, in British opposition to Nazism and its leader.

His alternative to British policy lies, however, in the area of counterfactual history. The experience of those governments who have appealed since 1945 to the 'lessons of appeasement' is not entirely encouraging. Eden in 1956 did not find that British opinion rallied behind him. America in 1950, as in 1990, found, as did Britain in 1935, that taking the lead against an aggressor in the name of the world community risks many of its members seeing the resultant conflict as bilateral rather than collective in nature. Appeals to the experience of the 1930s won America little support in Britain in 1965–6 for its involvement in Vietnam. The dismissal of all policy options save conflict as 'appeasement', and the constant reiteration of the adage 'appeasement never pays', are together one of the legacies of the Churchillian legend. For the record, it is worth recalling that in the 1930s Churchill did not oppose the appeasement of either Italy or Japan. And that in so far as both Italy and Japan remained neutral in 1939, leaving Britain to face one enemy in Europe instead of three worldwide, the appeasement of Italy and Japan did, for a time, pay handsome dividends.

13

Churchill, Radio, and Cinema

D. J. WENDEN

I. RADIO

CHURCHILL was on his way to becoming a radio or, as he would have put it at the time, a wireless fan in September 1927. Brother Jack produced a portable set 'and we had a wonderful concert each night'. He contemplated buying a receiver for £30 instead of an electric piano for his daughter. Four months passed before a set arrived at home. It received fifteen to twenty stations and he listened to a splendid concert from Berlin.[1]

His acquaintance with radio began before 1914. After his unhappy experiences with Marconi and Lloyd George, he learnt as First Lord of the Admiralty the value of radio for naval communications. Regular public programmes from the British Broadcasting Company started in 1922. Churchill's first broadcast was made in June 1924. There is no comprehensive list of all his subsequent broadcasts: 148 from BBC stations have been identified. In addition in the 1930s, he made four American broadcasts and one French broadcast transmitted from foreign stations only. There may have been others, and more than the single post-war American occasion recorded in 1946. The 148 BBC performances divide up as in Table 1.

Churchill's first broadcast was of a speech delivered at the London School of Economics on 27 June 1924, the second from more familiar ground, the Savoy Hotel, on 23 October 1925, at the Engineers' Club dinner. Although he had promised to obey the BBC's injunction to avoid controversial political comments, complaints from listeners arrived. The Chairman of the BBC, Lord Gainford, commented:

There is always a great public demand to hear public men, and Churchill is perhaps a better draw than any other Minister or ex-Minister. The occasion on which he spoke at the Engineers' Club was a non-party one and I think our staff were well advised in not switching off Churchill in the middle of his speech when he was making an appeal for fair play to those who are at present in office.[2]

TABLE I. *Churchill's BBC broadcasts*

Period	Number	Average per year
June 1924 to 3 Sept. 1939 (None between April 1938 and Sept. 1939)	19	1.25
Sept 1939 to 10 May 1940	7	10.5
10 May 1940 to end 1940*	7	10.5
1941*	18	18.0
Jan. 1942 to 26 July 1945*	24	5.25
26 July 1945 to 26 Oct. 1951	37	6.0
26 Oct. 1951 to 5 April 1955*	23	6.5
April 1955 to end 1959	13	2.4
Total	148	4.2

*indicates in office as Prime Minister

In view of his later stormy relationship with the BBC it is surprising to find Winston so stoutly defended by the Chairman, but more surprising that the latter took for granted the right to throw the switch.

The General Strike demonstrated the power of radio to affect the course of events. Winston and Birkenhead's assertion that the government should commandeer the service in such an emergency was resisted by John Reith, the Managing Director and disregarded by their colleagues.[3] The introduction of the BBC's first Charter from 1 January 1926 converted the British Broadcasting Company into a Corporation, with greater status and more freedom to handle news and items of public, even political, interest.[4] As early as 1924 Reith had argued for an extension of the scope of broadcasting that would create a more educated and responsible electorate. He and many others were fearful of the consequences of the post-war expansion of the franchise. Radio could educate our masters and mistresses but not until it was allowed to air political issues. Lloyd George and Churchill were among those who spoke up for change. In a broadcast speech at the Civil Service dinner on 10 February 1928, Winston noted that he was still under instructions 'not to let anything of a politically controversial nature fall from his lips'. He suggested that radio should enable 'the leading political figures to impact exactly that guidance to the vast mass of intelligent listeners which they ought to receive, and which I confidently believe they wish to receive'.[5] One hour a day should be dedicated to political and party controversy, the speakers being chosen according to the strength of the parties in any given House of Commons. He skirted round the difficulty of settling the details of the fine print, that were to be argued between the BBC and all-party committees for the next ten years. There was, however, some relaxation of the ban in March, and Churchill, as Chancellor of the Exchequer, was invited to present his budget to listeners in April. The Labour Party was given no chance to reply. Ramsay MacDonald explained to a party supporter that the Chancellor had been asked to deliver a purely factual account and that 'You really cannot draw a line between a factual speech and a Party one, especially when Churchill delivers it'.[6] Reith established a Controversy Committee. There was no Churchill budget broadcast next year, his last as Chancellor. He did give one more pre-war broadcast as a minister, a party political speech before the general election of 1929.

With the coming of MacDonald's second administration Winston began his ten years of exile from political office, almost from political respectability. Just as radio entered more directly into the public arena, Winston, out of favour, found it difficult to gain access to a microphone. Radio now rivalled the press and touched parts of public opinion that the press did not reach. By 1932 five and a quarter million radio licences were issued, covering almost half the population; on the eve of war nearly nine million sets were licensed. During the 'wilderness years' the BBC rarely broadcast Churchill's voice from that wilderness; he spoke only eleven times to home wireless audiences between June 1929 and September 1939, two of those being appeals for charitable causes. On those occasions he displayed compassion and a mastery of the medium. Listeners were asked to give generously to the Wireless for the Blind Fund: 'We cannot say "let the blind see" but we can say—and it is the motto of this fund—"Let the blind hear." We cannot rescue them from darkness but we can rescue them from silence.'[7]

Baldwin and the Conservative leadership regarded him as an unreliable party spokesman. Reith, his Chairman of Governors, and their overlord the Postmaster General, rarely gave him time as a political *franc tireur*. After January 1935 he broadcast more from foreign stations than from the BBC. He was invited to contribute to the reopening of Radio Toulouse in 1938, and broadcast at least four times on American networks, receiving fees of around £300 compared with the £25, later raised to £50 or guineas, offered by Langham Place. Between April 1937 and the outbreak of war in 1939 his views on foreign affairs were heard on radio only by American audiences. Of course he was not silent: he addressed public meetings, wrote constantly for the press, and made major, if infrequent, speeches in what was for him throughout his career the most important forum, the House of Commons.

But his exclusion from the microphone angered him and intensified the feud with Reith. A clash of personalities was likely between an embittered, egotistical Churchill and Reith, a man who wrote in his diary at the time of Munich, 'I have so much more ability than all these Prime Ministers and Wilsons [Sir Horace] and such like. I suppose it is too late to get to any position such as I should have. I ought of course to be dictator.' (Later, during wartime service under Winston as Minister of Transport, he concluded, 'I positively hate that man'.[8]) Reith resented Winston as a member of the establishment who treated him as an administrator, and who challenged his power over radio in Britain. Churchill for his part was irritated by the Director-General, a tool of the political establishment from which he felt excluded. Britain's position in India was being squandered and he was denied the chance to put his view before the nation. BBC Talks' producers invited him to speak on 'Great Escapes' or 'Great Politicians', but what he wanted to do was to broadcast on the 'Great Issue', the future of India.

He was willing to pay for time to explain his concern. In December 1929 he offered £100 for thirty minutes of radio time: 'How ashamed you will all be in a few years for having muzzled the broadcast.' Reith pointed out that the same amount had been offered for one minute, but the BBC was not a commercial operator.[9] The argument raged for the next five years, prolonged partly by a decision not to have a radio debate on India before a bill appeared in the House. Churchill understood the power offered by the microphone; Reith and his political masters were reluctant to hand him the opportunity to use it. In desperation Winston considered transmitting a speech on the monetary question, another of his obsessions, from the Eiffel Tower. When warned that the script would have to be submitted to the British ambassador in Paris, he appealed to the Foreign Secretary:

I should have thought that unless the discourse was subversive, indecent, flagrantly insulting, or calculated to cause distress or disorder in England, no objection could be entertained by Her Majesty's Government. Surely such a government containing so many eminent statesmen and supported by such overwhelming majorities, has no need to fear independent expressions of opinion upon controversies of the day.[10]

He backed down on this occasion, but continued the fight until 1935 when he was given a place in a series of broadcasts on the India Bill. He criticized the modest time alloted to the opponents of retreat from Empire:

Sir Samuel Hoare boasts that he has a majority of three to one in the House of Commons, four to one in the House of Lords and three to one in the National Union of Conservative Associations. He has certainly got a majority of eleven to two in the share that has been given to us upon the broadcast. No doubt these are great odds. But if our forebears had been cowed by heavy odds, the British Empire would have stopped at Brighton beach.[11]

Overall Churchill refused more invitations than he accepted. His complaint was not that he was barred from the microphone. He was asked to speak on literary or historical topics, but denied a platform for the big issues that aroused him. Such a denial might have been justified in the case of the other eminent outcast, Lloyd George, a less effective broadcaster. Churchill's more robust voice and style carried well: 'the perfect broadcaster', noted the producer of his 1930 appeal for the blind. His four major performances in the 1930s were *Whither Britain* and *The Causes of War*, both 1934, *The India Bill*, 1935, and *The Responsibilities of Empire*, 1937.

Relations with the Corporation were never simple. He missed no opportunity to twist their tail. When offered a fee of £25 to talk on *Whither Britain* in January 1934 he wrote to the producer querying the request to submit a script in advance:

I had not contemplated that it would be required beforehand to be submitted for censorship. I understand you are paying Mr [H. G.] Wells a fee of £100 and that even so he has given no such undertaking. If I am wrong, perhaps you will let me know what the precedents are. For instance did the Prime Minister, Sir John Simon, Mr Baldwin and others who have recently spoken submit their proposed speeches in advance? And if so, how was the tribunal composed which judged them?[12]

Even a less controversial toast to the Royal Society of St George did not pass without qualms:

Think of the risk these eminent men are running. We can almost see them in our mind's eye, gathered together in that very expensive building with the questionable statutes on the front. We can picture Sir John Reith, with the perspiration mounting on his lofty brow, with his hand on the control switch, wondering as I utter every word, whether it will be his duty to protect his innocent subscribers from some irreverent thing I might say about Mr Gandhi, or about the Bolsheviks, or even about our peripatetic Prime

Minister. But let me reassure him. I have much more serious topics to discuss. I have to speak to you about St George and the Dragon.[13]

From those occasions he gained experience that would serve him well in 1940 when he was called upon for clarion calls rather than political sermons. The speeches of the 1930s did not establish him as a contender for a return from the wilderness. Robert Rhodes James suggests that 'the audience listened with appreciation and interest, much as young audiences must have listened to Caruso in his last months, and carried away an impression of having been present at a great fascinating historical occasion—but no more'.[14]

His reputation rose after March 1939. His warnings about the threat from Hitler were borne out and were taken up by the vast majority of the politicians and the people. Churchill now represented a policy of resistance combined with enthusiasm for an Anglo-Russian alliance, as an alternative to the half-hearted stiffening of Chamberlain and Co. Even so he was not invited to Broadcasting House. Not only Winston was excluded. On 20 April 1939 O. S. Cleverly (Chamberlain's private secretary) remarked to Horace Wilson: 'it is definitely undesirable that at times like the present issues of Foreign Policy should be discussed on the air'.[15] When Churchill became First Lord of the Admiralty in September, he was still a comparative stranger to the generation called upon to fight the war. 'Winston is back' signalled the Admiralty. But who was Winston? His journalism had appeared in the popular press, the *News of the World* as well as the *Daily Telegraph*; he seemed, however, an outdated figure from a different class and a different era, associated with lost causes, Gallipoli, anti-Bolshevism, India, and misjudgement over the abdication. Within nine months he would be called upon to lead the nation in a heroic bid for survival. He made this transformation and established a popular reputation to challenge Hitler largely by appearances on radio and in the cinema where he had been virtually unheard and unseen for a decade.

It was achieved almost single-handed. We have become so accustomed to the post-1960 phenomenon of packaged politicians on television, created by their 'minders', speech-writers, make-up artists, hairdressers even, that it is not easy to appreciate that Churchill was his own Frankenstein, the creator not the monster. His friends and advisers were that and no more. Some have left invaluable testimonies that serve to emphasize their secondary roles. Even the unwritten diaries or memoirs of Brendan Bracken would probably not alter the picture. Clementine restrained him occasionally, but like the others she was a sounding board, a critic not a source of ideas or an image maker. The Ministry of Information, his least satisfactory department, 1940–1, played no part comparable to that of Goebbels in building up the cult of the Führer from 1930 until 1942–3 when Hitler faded into the shadows of his bunker. Stalin's dominance was less personal, the product of a system more than a personality. Never has such a vast effort been generated under an almost invisible leader.

During the war Churchill gave fifty-six broadcasts, forty-nine of them as Prime Minister, to British audiences. They vary in length (excluding his contributions to transmissions featuring several speakers, for example the Lord Mayor's Luncheon) from eighty-four seconds for the first announcement of the Fall of France to forty-eight minutes for his address to the US Congress in May 1943. Eleven of the forty-nine lasted for less than five minutes. The most significant speeches were uttered in 1940 and 1941 when he had to inspire the British to fight on alone until great allies arrived to secure an otherwise improbable victory. Once the tide had turned in the autumn of 1942, the need for such impassioned broadcasts diminished. Good news carries its own inspiration.

The transformation begun on radio was supplemented and later dominated by film. After the 'gleam of victory' talk in November 1942 he broadcast less frequently. Film appearances could be more frequent and could catch him on the hoof with none of the agonizing preparation needed for a speech. The nation saw him doing his job, conferring with Allied leaders, visiting warriors at home and abroad, touring docks, dwellings, and factories. He could speak personally with only a limited number of men and women in the street. Newsreel and documentary footage enabled almost all to feel his personality, to believe that they knew him and he knew them. Churchill's premiership was a shared experience in a way that Lloyd George's equally vital role in 1917–18 had never been. That is a major reason why Churchill, unlike Lloyd George, was both respected and loved. Yet at the end of their wars, Lloyd George returned to Downing Street, Churchill was dismissed from office. These contrasts in fortune reflect verdicts on the parties rather than on the men themselves. Lloyd George split the Liberal Party, leading a minority into a continuing coalition with the Tories: Churchill, however, split, or was forced by the Labour Party to split, his wartime coalition. The gratitude and affection of the nation did not stop it from voting Winston and the discredited Conservative Party out of office.

As First Lord of the Admiralty Winston made seven policy broadcasts; he was more confident, colourful, and aggressive than Chamberlain, Halifax, and Simon. As an orator and broadcaster he was in a different class from the rest of the cabinet. The old guard were tired and discredited. The new guard after May 1940, Attlee, Bevin, Morrison, Eden, Sinclair, Beaverbrook, could not arouse the same enthusiasm. When for a brief period Sir Stafford Cripps was thought of by some as a replacement Prime Minister it was in spite, and not because, of his oratorical style. But Winston's opening broadcasts were not completely successful, sometimes displaying more boastful chauvinism than good sense. Within the BBC talks department his *First Ten Weeks of the War* on 12 November was considered to be 'deplorable but probably good propaganda in Canada and America'. A newly arrived young Canadian lawyer described its unfortunate effect: 'Propaganda of the complete confidence in the collapse of Germany was discouraging Canadians from making any sacrifice and Americans from bothering about the war at all.' Sir Richard Maconachie, Director of Talks, noted, 'this is interesting and makes one more doubtful than ever about the value of Mr. Churchill's broadcasts. In addition of course he has managed to offend both Italy and the U.S. in successive talks.'[16] The First Lord's next speech impinged on Foreign Office territory, and he was rebuked by Lord Halifax.[17]

After a warning of *Alarm and Menace* on 30 March 1940 the next time he spoke was as Prime Minister on 19 May. *Arm Yourselves* put the nation on guard for the crisis ahead, reinforced by a short statement on the French collapse on 17 June. His most memorable appeals, that established him as a radio orator, followed on 18 June, *Their Finest Hour*; 14 July, *We Are Fighting by Ourselves Alone, but We Are Not Fighting for Ourselves Alone*; and 11 September, *The Battle of Britain and Invasion*, exhorting his nation to resist an air offensive that they survived, and an invasion that was never launched. The impact was almost equally significant abroad, especially in America whose sympathy was indispensable. Winston's words were carried to the New World by radio, where Quentin Reynolds and Ed Murrow placed them in context for their compatriots. Murrow proclaimed that Winston 'mobilized the English language and sent it into battle to steady his fellow countrymen and hearten the Europeans upon whom the long dark night of tyranny had descended'.[18] In May 1940 Murrow had sensed another vital feature of the oratory: 'Mr Churchill can inspire confidence. And he can preach a doctrine of hate that is acceptable to the majority of this country.'

Winston's own verdict was that 'the people's will was resolute and remorseless. I only expressed it. They had the lion's heart. I had the luck to be called upon to give the roar.' Oratory that would before long seem flamboyant, and after the war outmoded, fitted the mood of heightened emotion and fear in 1940 and 1941. His next messages, delivered on 9 February 1941, *Give Us the Tools and We Will Finish the Job*, and 27 April, *But Westward, Look, the Land Is Bright*, indicated a change in emphasis. Churchill comforted his compatriots, but also switched to a wider, above all American, audience. Six key broadcasts between May 1940 and April 1941 were not many for the job that had to be done. This underlines the power of his words. Once he had struck the right chord and rallied confidence, he was reinforced, not outshone as some later commentators have argued, by the weekly special postscript broadcasts by different speakers, including J. B. Priestley.

His scripts, like his other speeches, were meticulously prepared by Winston. Colville testified that 'he never to my knowledge spoke words not his own in a political speech delivered as Prime Minister'.[19] (Towards the end of his career in the mid-1950s he did call on the services of Anthony Montague Browne to prepare drafts.) Grace Wyndham Goldie, for many years a BBC producer, admits, 'Churchill took broadcasting seriously. He shaped each of his radio broadcasts with infinite care.'[20] The time he took is one reason why there were so few. He was not a spontaneous performer. Delivery as well as composition was exhausting. On four separate occasions between April 1928 and January 1942, he asked that speeches made to what was always for him the supreme arena, the House of Commons, should either be broadcast from the House (1928) or recorded for later transmission over the air;[21] each request was rejected. A supporter, Leslie Boyce, considered that the objectors 'were hopelessly out of touch with the sentiments of the nation'. Few of his Parliamentary speeches were repeated as evening broadcasts. David Irving has suggested that on at least two occasions when Churchill could not, or would not, perform in the evening, an actor (Norman Shelley) mimicked 'the prime minister before the microphone, and nobody was any the wiser'. The evidence does not support Irving's hint of deception by the BBC or the Premier.[22]

Although records of many of those crucial addresses can still be heard, it is difficult to establish or measure their impact. Unfortunately the BBC's audience listening research bureau monitored only one performance. His appearances were set up at short notice, too short to organize the bureau's network of local correspondents and their panels of listeners. The exception was on 15 February 1942, his most difficult broadcast, made immediately after the fall of Singapore. On that evening the correspondents had been alerted to monitor the Postscript that was dropped to make way for the Premier. The majority stood down but forty-six did file their copy. The broadcast was heard by 65.4 per cent of the potential audience. (This compares with Winston's high point of 77 per cent in 1941, 71.3 per cent on VE day, and the highest figure for any wartime transmission, which was 81.3 per cent for the 9 o'clock news on D-Day.) The 65.4 per cent who listened to Churchill in February 1942 gave him only a 62 per cent approval rating, low for Winston. The thirty Postscripts monitored from May to December 1941 had scored an average approval rating of 64 per cent, ranging from 90 per cent for Quentin Reynolds to 36 per cent for Duff Cooper. Although the listeners appreciated Winston's plight, they were not easily won over by his attempts to rally them. A housewife in Bacup concluded 'what he said was good, but what he did not say more significant'; and a social worker in Leeds, 'To many devoted admirers of the Prime Minster this was his first Postscript [*sic*] that failed to convince and inspire'.[23]

As the burden became more complex, winning the war rather than withstanding the onslaught, as casualties and strategic setbacks multiplied, his speeches tended to become longer and his prose style more prolix. There were fewer broadcasts but hardly any fewer words. The average duration of the four major statements in 1940 was 17.25 minutes; six in 1941 averaged 25.12 minutes each. Two the following year were 28.5 minutes, two in 1943 also 28.5 minutes, and in 1944 the only one lasted 46.18 minutes. Sometimes the heroic message was drowned in words. Such a tendency had always existed. There was now more time to examine the text. One of his most verbose, if not longest, broadcasts had been the declaration of solidarity with the Soviet Union on 22 June 1941. He castigated the enemy, perhaps in order to dispel any reservations about the new ally.

In the last eighteen months of the war he made few radio appearances, apart from party speeches and addresses to mark VE Day. A speech to a Conservative Party Conference in March 1945 was broadcast. The war in the Far East had still to be won, but Churchill had never regarded that as his war in the same class as the struggle against Nazi Germany. He now felt the call to revive the Tory Party, and made four pre-election broadcasts in June. They were an embarrassment. The language that had won support against the dictators seemed overkill when directed at Attlee or even Professor Laski. Five years earlier he had used radio in a crusade against Nazism, becoming the first warrior to lead his nation on the air, as Baldwin in London, Huey Long in Louisiana, and Roosevelt with his fireside chats from the White House, had pioneered the peacetime political use of radio in the English-speaking world. Stalin did little war-time broadcasting. Hitler after the triumphs of 1940–1 left Goebbels to rally a besieged Germany. Mussolini blustered but at a lower level of attainment. There were, however, two occasions on which surprisingly the British bulldog did not bark. On D-Day BBC listeners heard the King, Roosevelt, and Eisenhower but not Winston Churchill, and on the death of F.D.R. he was again silent.

Churchill's post-war radio appearances tended to be more ceremonial than inspirational, or even political. He was in demand as a speaker and a world hero. In the first few years his energies were devoted to writing the *History of the Second World War* and to excursions to receive honorary degrees or the freedom of cities. These provided occasions for frequent broadcasts, but of a different character; *tours d'horizon* replaced calls to arms. He was not interested in prepared addresses from a studio, and declined invitations to speak on literary and historical themes. He neglected the political role of radio. He was happier addressing a live audience of hundreds than performing before a microphone. Although it might open the door to millions of listeners, he could see only a producer and engineers. Dislike of Reith was replaced by a suspicion that Langham Place was a hotbed of 'reds'. The appointment of two wartime colleagues, Sir Alexander Cadogan and General Sir Ian Jacob, as key figures in the Corporation did not eliminate this suspicion. Even though his Cabinet ended the BBC's monopoly of television, partly at his insistence, Winston was little interested in its operations and did not like to become mixed up in it himself.

Churchill was happy to broadcast from his favourite celebrations, the Royal Academy Dinner, the El Alamein reunions in London's Royal Albert Hall, the Lord Mayor's Banquet. He paid tribute on the deaths of King George VI and Queen Mary and welcomed Queen Elizabeth II. But until the Cold War intensified he had no great theme to nourish. When he was aroused by the need to come to terms with nuclear armed Bolsheviks, his power and appeal had diminished. Nine transmissions in 1954 shrank to five in 1955, and three in 1956, and thereafter one or two to the end of the decade. Almost the last correspondence in his BBC file concerns a young producer's suggestion in 1956 that Winston might contribute to a programme on Buffalo Bill, to whom he had been introduced as a boy of thirteen.[24] Sadly his superiors vetoed the idea. Churchill would have shown more sympathy with the showmanship of William Cody than with that of the party television agents of the 1960s.

II. CINEMA

Churchill was not born into the motion picture age. He was already 21 when the Lumière Brothers gave the first successful commercial demonstration of their films and projector on 27 December 1895, the date usually accepted as the birthday of cinema. He did not grow up as children of the twentieth century in the Western world have done, taking its wonders for granted and adjusting to rapid technical development. He is 35 in the first surviving motion pictures of him as a political figure, over 60 when he was drawn into the industry as an aspirant script writer, and 65 before he was a familiar figure on the screen. In 1940 he became a film star, a political Douglas Fairbanks, but he was not a statesperson made by the moving or television image, like Ronald Reagan or Margaret Thatcher. He considered movies a diversion, not an art form. He might have produced a list of his ten favourite films, hardly of his ten *best* films. *Citizen Kane* would not have been on either.[25] His favourite pastimes were more active reading, writing, painting, Chartwelling, above all talking, even occasionally listening. He respected theatre but eventually saw more films than plays. After he became Prime Minister films were brought to him and could be enjoyed privately with family, friends, and colleagues.[26]

His enthusiasm for movies began at the end of the silent era. But he was presumably aware of their existence when he recalled that his vision of the Battle of Omdurman 'flickered exactly like a cinematograph picture, and besides I remembered no sound. The event seemed to pass in absolute silence.' These sentences from *The River War* (1899) give a more convincing impression of early films than of a battle, where for most participants sounds are equally as, or more, overwhelming than sights.[27] When he planned his South African trip in October 1899 he hoped to take with him a movie camera and an operator to make a film of the war. Learning that an American company, better able to market the footage, already had the same idea, he reluctantly abandoned the idea. W. K. L. Dickson, cameraman for Thomas Edison's company, travelled on the same ship as Churchill, and General Buller and his staff took pictures of the latter but not of the young war correspondent. Until the late 1920s Winston, in common with most upper- and middle-class men, probably saw films as an occasional novelty, treating them as a working-class entertainment. This attitude began to change at the end of the decade. A 1932 report on the 'The Film in National Life' commented that 'A fellow of an Oxford College no longer feels an embarrassed explanation to be necessary when he is recognised leaving a cinema'.[28] Churchill changed with the times. When preparing his budget in March 1926 he had contemplated cancelling the 'invidious Snowden [tax] remissions to the cheap and trashy cinema entertainments' to help the live theatre. But on 5 April 1928 he wrote to Clemmie, 'I am becoming a Film fan and last week I went to see *The Last Command* and *Wings*'.[29] He preferred action films, especially those dealing with war or politics. Sound increased his interest; he had never appreciated the aesthetic merits of silent cinema. Sadly he passed up the chance of being the first British politician to speak on the screen. On 20 September 1928 Beaverbrook invited him to record a message to be included in an exhibition of talking pictures with Coolidge, Mussolini, and Poincaré. He refused, suggesting that he 'was in a far humbler class than the individuals you mention'. He wished 'to eschew Ambition and Advertisement for the future'.[30] The film opened on 11 October with Birkenhead in the speaking role. In the 1930s association with Alexander Korda stimulated his enthusiasm for cinema. During the war Churchill, Hitler, and Stalin had one thing in common: each found their main relaxation in watching movies around midnight.

But unlike Hitler and Stalin the figure of Churchill has rarely appeared in feature films. This is true, surprisingly, also of George Washington, but not of Lincoln, Napoleon, or Queen Victoria. Winston Churchill was, however, represented in an American wartime feature film *Mission to Moscow* (1943). Based on Joseph E. Davies's best-selling account of this period as Ambassador to Stalin, it was intended to foster American regard for their new Soviet ally. Davies visits Churchill in Britain in 1938 and is asked to encourage American resistance to Fascism.[31]

The only Churchill 'biopic' is *Young Winston*. He had sold the film rights of *My Early Life* for £7,500 in 1941 to Warner Brothers; they did not proceed and gave the rights back. After abortive negotiations in 1956 with MGM, they were bought for £100,000 by Carl Foreman in 1961, and made into a movie by Foreman and Sir Richard

Attenborough ten years later.[32] Foreman consulted Churchill before he began the script. *Young Winston* is a worthy, wordy story of his life up to 1901, with first-class costumes, decor, and cast.[33] Much is omitted, but there is a Freudian portrayal of his parents, especially his mother. Winston and Lady Randolph seem at times like Hamlet and Gertrude. One does not readily identify Churchill with the indecisive Dane; any Shakespearean comparison might rather be with Prince Hal in his youth, perhaps Falstaff in late middle age, and Lear at the end. His mother is played by Anne Bancroft, fresh from her role as Mrs Robinson seducing Dustin Hoffman in *The Graduate*. Such a mother might well have married a man only sixteen days older than her son, as Jennie did, and have cultivated a galaxy of lovers. Simon Ward plays Winston in a flatteringly romantic vein. The feature ends with a conversation between mother and son after the young MP has attacked the army estimates of Lord Salisbury's government, foreshadowing Churchill's move towards the Liberal Party. It speaks of this moment as an 'End and a Beginning', with a premature reference to Clementine Hozier. There are two ends and beginnings, one the end of his period as a militant young Tory with a shift to radical Liberalism, the other a change in his relations with women. He moves from dependence on his mother towards marriage with Clementine, embracing her support and mothering.

The film's respect for Churchill and the Empire seem out of tune with the spirit of the time in which it was made. *Young Winston* (1971), *Zulu* (1963), and *Khartoum* (1966) are among the last of the many imperial epics made in American and British studios before the war, and predominantly in Britain after 1945,[34] just as Winston was the last of the great Tory imperialists before Macmillan acknowledged the wind of change and Britain turned slowly towards Europe. The film reflects also the spirit of the 1970s in its frank treatment of the sexual split between his parents, the parental pressure on their son and the anti-establishment creed he inherits from Lord Randolph. The script portrays him as an idealist rather than the opportunist he was in 1900–6.

Churchill was the arch-villain in several Nazi and Fascist propaganda films[35] and was used as the model for the savage concentration camp commandant in *Ohm Krüger* (1941). This German feature on the Boer War pilloried Britain's cynical treatment of Paul Kruger and his people. Hitler's New Order would unite Europe and destroy the common enemy. Emil Jannings (the professor humiliated by Marlene Dietrich in *The Blue Angel*) played Kruger as a pioneer of the resistance and an example to encourage the Germans in their struggle against British imperialism. Queen Victoria pronounces on her death-bed the main threat to her nation: 'On the day when nations cease to hate one another Britain is lost.' Victoria, Chamberlain, Rhodes, even John Brown, are characters in the film. Winston, at that time comparatively obscure, is not directly represented, but the vicious commandant of the camp in which Boer women and children are herded together is clearly modelled on him. He tosses meat to his bulldog while the inmates starve, and shoots them down when they protest. In the closing moments Kruger predicts that although his *Volk* have been subdued, one day a greater race will crush Britain. This is the German message for 1941. Fifty years later the film is still a powerful propaganda vehicle, even though to our eyes the commandant looks and behaves more like Goering than Winston.[36]

Young Winston was the first film biography directed by Sir Richard Attenborough. Eleven later he created *Gandhi* (1982), not a subject that would have appealed to Churchill. But a subsequent venture, a life of Charlie Chaplin, celebrates the career of a film star who captivated Winston. Towards the end of his American tour in 1929 Churchill visited California, stayed at San Simeon with Randolph Hearst and Marion Davies, and lunched at the MGM studios with Louis B. Mayer and a cast of 200. He was attracted most of all by Chaplin, talked of writing a script on Napoleon for him, and returned his hospitality at Chartwell in 1931; Charlie was there over the mid-September weekend as Britain went off the Gold Standard. Chaplin contributed to the car presented to Winston on his return in 1932 from his street accident in New York.[37] In the home movie footage of their encounter at Chaplin's studio, Churchill is upstaged by a greater performer.[38]

Little pre-1914 film of Winston has survived; little of that is available for viewing, and even less can be copied on to video. Party political films did not exist. Newsreels were in their infancy, short and silent with an emphasis on movement and location. With no hand-held cameras, zoom lenses, and above all no sound, political figures, even political meetings, made poor cinema. Silent newsreels tell the historian little about *personality* that cannot be gleaned from still photographs. They can portray movement, settings, and the reaction of people to each other and to events, but not much more. The suffragette demonstrations and the Tonypandy disturbances were dramatic events but we have no film material involving Churchill. As Home Secretary his most spectacular appearance was in the Sidney Street siege in 1911, which

was photogenic and only a few miles from the offices of the early newsreel companies.[39]

The siege appealed to Winston the frustrated military leader, who
emerged disastrously from Antwerp and Gallipoli, and more happily,
for him at least, in the Second World War. The Sidney Street film is
poor quality, shot on a dank, smoky January day with primitive equipment, and it has not improved with age. One of the two surviving rem-
nants is from a print sold to Germany, indicative of the European
interest in the affair. Paris, with recent memories of the 37-day siege of
nationalists in 'Fort Chabrol', admired the success of the British
action.[40] Viennese papers divided on racial lines, the Jews fearing a
backlash against the Jewish immigrants, and the nationalist press condemning British tolerance of their lawlessness. St Petersburg warned
London against criminal elements from Russia. The Germans were
contemptuous of English military and police who had to deploy 130
soldiers and hundreds of police to subdue two anarchist gunmen, 'comparable to the shooting of sparrows with cannon'.[41] Happily the three
Royal Horse Artillery gun crews galloping from St Johns Wood arrived
too late to join the fusillade in which nearly 2,000 rounds were
expended between 7.30 a.m. and 1.30 p.m. However, the Home
Secretary later assured the House of Commons that the day's work had
cost the War Office only £6.[42]

What can the historian glean from the film? It clearly shows the
intense public interest in the event, as we see from the crowded streets.
Every day from 17 December to 21 January *The Times* published
accounts of developments and five leading articles on the anarchists,
overshadowing a Bolton mine disaster with 322 dead, Scottish and
Welsh train crashes that killed twenty passengers, an attempted assassination of M. Briand in the French Chamber of Deputies. All had to
compete with the hunt for and siege of small-time criminals who had
murdered three policemen on 16 December and were holed up in
Sidney Street, public opinion being inflamed by hostility to Jews and
angered by a weak Aliens Act weakly enforced by the Liberal government.[43] The film shows the crowds that at one stage pushed the police
cordon off their feet and out of control. The large police presence was
prompted more by the need to keep public order than by an overkill in
dealing with besieged criminals.

Winston makes only a fleeting appearance on the screen. We see,
however, the scene that awaited him at 11.50 a.m., the cohorts of
officials and police chiefs, the wild exchange of close-range fire across a

narrow street, nurses at the ready, volunteer Scots guardsmen, with standard service rifles, in a makeshift operation that included no attempt to parley with the besieged or to await their surrender. Churchill did not summon the troops to Sidney Street: as Home Secretary he approved a request made by officials on the spot. As he explained later, there was for them a financial incentive: 'When a local authority asks for police from other districts it has to pay, yet when it obtains soldiers it gets them for nothing.'[44] The siege touched the tense, partly anti-Semitic nerves of the time and was used to belabour the Liberal government and Winston's melodramatic forays into social reform. The siege and Tonypandy continued to haunt Churchill. He was taunted in the Commons by Balfour: 'He was, I understand, in military phrase, in what was known as the zone of fire—he and a photographer were both risking valuable lives. I understand what the photographer was doing, but what was the Home Secretary doing? That I never understood at the time, nor do I understand now.'[45] Examination of the film helps a historian to understand more clearly the episode and how Winston was dragged into it by the misjudgement of others as much as by his own. The modest British feature film *The Siege of Sidney Street* (see note 31), made nearly fifty years later, re-enacts the events in Houndsditch and weaves around them a fanciful tale of radical refugees driven to violent crime in support of their political ideals. It is of minimal interest to a political or film historian.

In the 1930s Churchill enjoyed, or endured, his closest and longest association with film-making. Alexander Korda, a flamboyant Hungarian Jewish movie mogul, came to England in 1931 via Vienna, Berlin, Los Angeles, and Paris, and attempted to create a British Hollywood in the Home Counties, financed by the Prudential Insurance Company.[46] Eager to gain prestige and social status he cultivated prominent people and through Bracken, at that time a perfect target for Korda's charm, met Churchill. Soon Randolph was on Korda's payroll, with the sons of two Prime Ministers, Anthony Asquith and Oliver Baldwin, and even Winston himself, as consultant and script writer. In April 1917, when D. W. Griffith was in London to make a propaganda film *Hearts of the World*, Lloyd George had encouraged the American director to urge Churchill to take up script writing, hoping that might keep him out of mischief.[47] But Winston was not to be distracted from his part in winning the war.

By the early 1930s Winston needed money; Korda could give, or promise, it on a generous scale. From initial social contacts sprang the suggestion that Churchill should co-operate with London Film Productions, Korda's company, to create a series of short factual films on topics of current interest. Had the Churchill–Korda scheme matured, a British production comparable to Henry Luce's *The March of Time*[48] might have reached London screens in the early summer. But like so many of Korda's plans it foundered; he was an impressario whose reach regularly exceeded his grasp, but not for want of trying on the part of his political adviser. A press release was made in London on 12 September 1934, announcing six films on subjects including *Will Monarchies Return?*, *The Rise of Japan, Gold, and Unemployment*. The next day Churchill submitted the first script to an astounded Korda.[49]

In less than two weeks this project was overtaken by a more ambitious, and for Winston a more lucrative, proposal. Winston would write the scenario for *The Reign of King George V* to celebrate the Silver Jubilee the following summer:[50] 25 per cent of the net profits should accrue to the author. He and his solicitors struggled to define net profits, always a contentious and, for those operating with Korda, a horrendous concept. A minimum of £10,000 was offered, beginning with £2,500 on 1 January 1935. A first outline script was promised in 7–10 days and was duly delivered. Seven thousand words, dealing with the years from 1910 to 1919, cover enough ground, including the Irish troubles, the suffragette outbursts, the origins and events of the First World War (but with no reference to Gallipoli), the Russian revolutions, and the Peace Settlement, to fill the screen for hours. Winston's passion for detail is revealed by his 'anxiety that the Suffragette girl's activities in the war should take place in a munitions factory rather than a hospital, as shells more impressive than bed pans'.[51] But the script quickly joined the pile of abandoned paper in Korda's offices, when it became clear that the film could not be finished and registered for release to coincide with the Jubilee. Churchill accepted £4,000 for his contribution, another £2,000 for the continuation of the political shorts, and £1,000 for material on a new theme, *Conquest of the Air*. This film, a patchwork of material, was eventually cobbled together and appeared in 1940, including a brief speech by Churchill. It was overshadowed by Hitler's conquest of France. Winston sold the George V material to the press for £2,500. As the dreams collapsed his assurances to Clemmie on a long ocean trip that 'Korda certainly gives me the feeling of a genius at this kind of thing' were met with a warning response from Clemmie in New Zealand: 'I hope Korda is worthy of your confidence? he seemed to me an honest man, but there is something tricky about all these film undertakings I'm told'. He, but not his wife, was for once out-buccaneered.[52]

Nevertheless he persevered with attempts to break into the film world. In 1937 he agreed to act as consultant for a film on T. E. Lawrence. Korda owned the film rights of *The Seven Pillars of Wisdom*. Winston subcontracted his task to Lord Winterton, who had ridden into Damascus with Lawrence. His comments were more detailed than those of T. E. himself, who had told a friend that the only treatment he favoured would be one by Walt Disney with 'me and my army jogging across the skyline on camels'.[53] The rights had been sold on the understanding that no film would be started in the author's lifetime. Korda's normal time-scale made that unlikely even had Lawrence not crashed a few months later. T. E. assessed the impresario shrewdly; he described the Hungarian as 'like an oil company that has drilled often and found two or three gushers and has providentially invested some of the proceeds in buying options on more sites. Some he may develop, some he may not.'[54] The rights were eventually sold on to Sam Spiegel who converted them into David Lean's *Lawrence of Arabia*.

Winston remained on friendly terms with Korda, even after the latter's financial crash in 1938 and retreat to America the following year. In 1941 he made Churchill's favourite film, *Lady Hamilton*, with Laurence Olivier and Vivien Leigh.[55] He also promoted the British cause in North America. His knighthood in 1942, on the premier's recommendation, was the first to be awarded for film-making. He returned to Britain in 1942, and four years later gave Churchill £50,000 for the film rights to *The History of the English-Speaking Peoples*. Their combined imaginations would have found it difficult to hack a scenario out of that wide-ranging work. They remained on friendly terms until Korda's death in 1956. Winston, however, fully occupied out of and in office, composing his version of the Second World War, never returned to script writing. Painting, a more restful and creative activity, suited him better. But Alex and the film world had aroused his interest and sustained his finances during the lowest ebb of his career.

For the harassed premier, watching films was a welcome diversion. He took an interest in patriotic documentary and feature films, but did not assume with Hitler and Stalin a right to vet and veto production. On a few occasions, though, he expressed concern about specific projects. *Ships with Wings*, made at Ealing studios by Michael Balcon in 1941, was an adventure film boosting the Fleet Air Arm with sequences shot on HMS *Ark Royal*. It ends with a leading character redeeming himself by flying a suicidal mission to wreck an Italian dam. After seeing an early print, around the time of the sinking of HMS *Ark Royal* in November 1941, Winston suggested that the film would be bad for morale and should be withdrawn. However, he left the matter to the First Sea Lord, Sir Dudley Pound, who passed it for general release in January 1942.[56] He expressed similar reservations about the heroic but depressing *San Demetrio London* (1943). A memo, 'Pray who is responsible for this dastardly film? It must be stopped', was also referred to Sir Dudley, who concluded, 'I think that the British Navy can take this and a great deal more'.[57] *Next of Kin* (1942), a feature film designed to emphasize the importance of security, told a story of a British raid on France betrayed by careless talk. When Winston saw an early print he objected to the harrowing pictures of army casualties. After thirty cuts amounting to a little over twenty seconds on the screen had been made, Winston retired from the fray.[58]

In spring 1942 he initiated a more prolonged objection to the proposal to make a film entitled *The Life and Death of Colonel Blimp*. It was not the happiest of times to call attention to David Low's cartoon figure, parodying pre-war reaction, snobbery, and appeasement. Singapore had fallen, the *Scharnhörst* and *Gneisenau* had slipped past the British navy in the Channel, and Rommel was rampaging in North Africa. The War Office queried the script. Churchill thought 'it a foolish production' and hoped it could be stopped. In the late summer *Pravda*, chafing at the absence of an Allied Western Front, used a cartoon of Blimp to illustrate the effete military leadership of Britain. However, despite Winston's misgivings the film went into production. By the time it was completed in May 1943 the enemy were on the run and the alliance with the USA stood firm. The Cabinet briefly noted that the film should be vetted by the Ministry of Information and the War Office. It aroused little or no concern. The film was held back from overseas distribution for a few months.[59] Accusations that Winston was eager to stifle the freedom of the screen fall flat. They do not justify a comment that 'Churchill's vigorous if unsuccessful efforts to suppress feature films he disliked . . . are notorious'.[60] He was too genuine a democrat, and unlike real tyrants, not obsessed by trivia, at least not this trivia. Roger Livesey as the Blimpish figure behaves more like James Hilton's Mr Chips. There can be no comparison between Winston's indignation at four films and the systematic censorship practised under Hitler and by Stalin. These, the only cases so far discovered, all peak in the crucial twelve months between autumn 1941 and

1942. Despite the entry into the war of the Soviet Union and America, the British suffered some of their most humiliating disasters at this time. Churchill was anxious to maintain morale at home and to gain the full confidence of the American Chiefs of Staff. It was vital that they should sustain the 'Europe first' strategy, and these four films promised to have exactly the opposite effect. He demurred, but did not suppress (as with his later objections to the BBC broadcasts to Greece in 1944). Sidney Bernstein, producer of *Next of Kin*, who made some minor changes, commented: 'I suppose the Prime Minister had no powers to stop the film but I would not have cared to put his authority to the test.' He also saw the force of the objections, especially after he had read the report, from David Selznick, the Hollywood producer of *Gone with the Wind*:

Release in this country of the film in anything like its present version would be a dreadful error from the standpoint of British–American relations . . . All the English officers are portrayed as stupid, careless and derelict . . . Calculated to increase the fears of Americans and mothers especially that the British are simply muddling along, and that their sons will die because of British incompetence. This is aggravated by contrast with portrayal of brilliance and complete efficiency of German intelligence . . . Perhaps even worse is the portrayal of so many British civilians as informers and spies, giving the impression that Britain is overrun by traitors.[61]

For the historian the major interest in Churchill and the cinema rests in the newsreel material of him as a wartime leader. Newsreels of the 1930s had contained only short political sequences. Sport, fashions, earthquakes, and floods were more prominent than political events, pictures of foreign dictators shown more often than those of home politicians. T. J. Hollins analysed the content of British newsreels from 1933 to 1937: he estimates that under 20 per cent of the material included some reference to home political affairs, and a substantially smaller percentage dealt with serious political questions. When such matter did appear, it normally showed ministers or government spokesmen. There was little room for Opposition Labour or Liberal leaders and even less for the 'private' statesmen, Lloyd George and Churchill. Surprisingly, Winston did make a brief appearance in March 1931 to comment on the Round Table conference on India: 'British Movietone News thus fulfils its aim of presenting all sides of the most vital problem of our day.'[62] Winston was not asked to follow this up and nearly four years passed before the BBC gave him a similar opportunity on the air.

However, after his entry into the Cabinet in September 1939 Churchill the war leader made regular appearances on the screen. In his finest hour as Prime Minister he rallied the nation and was photographed visiting bombed cities, army depots, and RAF stations. Film of him speaking into a microphone in a studio is uninspiring, but Churchill giving live speeches before live audiences makes compelling cinema. He prepared his Parliamentary and radio speeches meticulously, but made few preparations for formal, and many more informal, appearances before the cameras. Newsreels show how an Edwardian Parliamentary figure became, partly fortuitously, the hero of the British people. He appeared, undaunted, with a bulldog air, in a variety of costumes and hats, stomping around with a cigar and walking stick, raising the morale of cinema audiences. No such heart-warming populist appearances were made by Hitler, Stalin, not even Roosevelt. Newsreels projected this image to at least half the British people almost every week. Those newsreels survive as supplementary evidence for the historian.[63] Post-war footage illustrates his declining force, and popularity, until the final surge of nostalgic veneration.

In Churchill's relations with cinema there is one intriguing 'might have been'. Before his marriage to Clementine, Winston had considered a few other possible partners: one was the stage, and later screen, actress Ethel Barrymore. He met her *chez* the Sutherlands at Dunrobin, and she was later a guest at Blenheim. Around the turn of the century she spent several summers acting in London and being entertained by society hostesses. Winston is said to have proposed marriage in 1900, perhaps not too fervently. Ethel declined. She had already been engaged to Laurence Irving, and Gerald du Maurier, and was to have other fiancés before, as 'Ethel Barrymore the most engaged girl in America', she married Russell Colt, the son of Colonel Colt, the gunsmith.[64] How would Winston have fared with an American wife, in addition to an American mother, and a Catholic to boot?

APPENDIX: THE NORMAN SHELLEY SAGA

In *Churchill's War*, David Irving asserts that on the evening of Tuesday 4 June 1940 the BBC transmitted the Premier's speech after the news. 'The nation thrilled not knowing that Churchill had refused to repeat it before the microphone. A BBC actor—"Larry the Lamb" of the Children's Hour—had agreed to mimic the prime minister before the microphone.'[65] Irving's footnote refers to 'Author's interview of Norman Shelley, Dec. 1981'. Shelley died on 22 August 1980. He had been a member of the BBC repertory company and a regular performer in Children's Hour plays about 'Toytown', often supplying the voice for 'Dennis the Dachshund', but not for 'Larry the Lamb', a role reserved almost exclusively for 'Uncle Mac', Derek McCulloch. The names recall the sound of radio in the 1930s and 1940s.

Irving repeated his assertion commenting on a letter to the *Guardian* 22 April 1991. He suggested that Shelley was called upon to read Churchill's speeches [plural]—for instance on 4 June—and that 'several times in 1940 millions of radio listeners were tricked into believing that they were hearing Churchill's voice'. For this expansion of his suggestion no reference is given. Irving does not specify the audience that was tricked, but the text implies that he is writing of transmissions by the BBC to home listeners.

It is not easy to prove or disprove Irving's theory. Towards the end of his life Shelley claimed to have mimicked Churchill's voice for radio. In a book, *Those Vintage Years of Radio*, published in 1972, Shelley's claim to have recorded a Churchill speech in the House of Commons on 4 June 1940 to be used in overseas broadcasting seems to have surfaced for the first time.[66] This became part of Shelley's stock in trade in his final years. It was picked up in some newspapers, but with reference to only the one speech, the crucial 'we shall fight on the beaches' challenge. Sally Hine of the BBC Sound Archive states that Shelley did make a recording of the speech at the Transcription Service Studios near Regent's Park.[67] The transcripts of Home News Broadcasts in the BBC Written Archives report no broadcast by Churchill himself on that evening. They indicate that in the 6 p.m. and 9 p.m. news broadcasts, the *newsreader* quoted verbatim several passages from the Premier's oration in reported speech, but not direct speech as if Winston himself were broadcasting. The newsreader is unlikely to have been Shelley, since the BBC's policy was to establish a team of regular newsreaders whose voices could be readily identified by the public in case the Germans attempted to transmit false news at the time of an invasion. After hearing the news Vita Sackville-West wrote to her husband, Harold Nicolson, of the uplifting effect of Churchill's words: 'Even repeated by the announcer it sent shivers (not of fear) down my spine.'[68]

The story of Shelley's recording a Churchill speech for transmission later in America has, nearly fifty years later, prompted some authors, attacking the 'myth of 1940', to present another myth, that several of Winston's rallying calls to the nation were uttered by an actor mimicking the leader. Churchill was reluctant to, and had little time to, prepare and deliver a broadcast during that hectic summer. His first radio address as Prime Minister on 19 May was at the prompting of Neville Chamberlain. On 19 June, after hearing Churchill's broadcast the previous evening, Nicolson, working then at the MOI, wrote in his diary: 'How I wish Winston would not talk on the wireless unless he is feeling in good form. He hates the microphone, and *when we bullied him into speaking last night*, he just sulked and read his House of Commons speech over again. Now as delivered in the House of Commons that speech was magnificent, especially the concluding sentences. But it sounded ghastly on the wireless. All the great vigour he put into it seemed to evaporate.'[69] Clive Ponting, a former Civil Servant, favouring the idea that Shelley on several occasions (including that of 18 June 1940) became his master's voice, gives no convincing evidence and quotes the last three sentences of Nicolson, ignoring the first two, indicating that Churchill broadcast himself.[70] American speech researchers have analysed the voice patterns on twenty of Churchill's recorded speeches. They conclude that three speeches, first made in the House on 13 May, 4 June, and 18 June 1940, do not match with the print of Winston's delivery as established by five speeches recorded on public occasions with the accompanying introductions and background, and therefore, according to the Sensimetric research team, undoubtedly of Churchill's own voice. Twelve of the other recordings match the model sound patterns, but the remaining three are 'alien', and could be the voice of another speaker. Only one, that of 18 June, was broadcast by the BBC at the time. The recording is described as a speech delivered to the House of Commons on 18 June 1940, and is presumably a recreated version of the parliamentary, and not a wireless, version. The recordings were taken from the LPs issued by Decca in 1964, and include some of the remakes by Churchill in 1949. If the three are 'alien', they may have been made by Winston later, when his voice pattern had altered, or may have been imitations by another speaker. This evidence by itself does not establish that they were made by Shelley and broadcast in 1940 to mislead the British people in their finest hour.[71] Recordings of many Churchill speeches are held in the BBC Sound Archive and can be heard most readily in the National Sound Archive of the British Library in Kensington. Two collections on tape cassettes are currently available in Britain: Argo 1118, *Winston Churchill, A Selection of His Wartime Speeches*, and Argo 1232, *Winston Churchill: 25 Years of His Speeches 1918–1943*. Both contain a mixture of original material and post-war studio recreations. Several are of addresses that were never broadcast but were made to live audiences in Parliament and elsewhere.[72]

14

Churchill in 1940: The Worst and Finest Hour

DAVID REYNOLDS

6 'I_T was the best of times, it was the worst of times.' The opening words of *A Tale of Two Cities* might stand as a motto for Winston Churchill in 1940. Britain faced the greatest crisis in its history since Napoleon's armies massed on the French coast in 1804–5. Yet at the same moment Churchill at last attained his cherished ambition, becoming Prime Minister of Britain and, moreover, leading his country at a time when his peculiar talents could be given full rein and just appreciation. Although not a notably religious man, Churchill had a profound sense of providence (especially where he himself was concerned). To quote his later evocation of the night of 10 May 1940, when the King asked him to form a government: 'I felt as if I were walking with destiny, and that all my past life had been but a preparation for this hour and for this trial.'[1] One might add that his subsequent life, for all its distinction, always seemed something of an anti-climax by comparison. Britain's worst hour was also Churchill's finest.

So far, so conventional. But recognition of Churchill's remarkable role in 1940 must be balanced by acknowledgement that he was not always right in his decisions. The old Winston, renowned for his mercurial brilliance, was not banished by new responsibilities. It is a fundamental contention of this chapter that a sober examination of Churchill's performance as war leader in 1940 does not belittle his greatness. On the contrary, it makes him a more human and thereby a more impressive figure than the two-dimensional bulldog of national mythology. Churchill's greatness is that of a man, not an icon.

To take an example that serves also to introduce my subject. Churchill spent Christmas Day 1939 working at his desk in the Admiralty. Both his assiduity and his project were characteristic. He was engaged on one of those sweeping strategic surveys that he so relished, in this case on the prospects for the war in 1940. First Lord of the Admiralty since the outbreak of war in September 1939, Churchill naturally looked back to his previous tenure of the post in 1914–15. 'I feel we may compare the position now very favourably with that of

1914', he wrote. 'And also I have the feeling (which may be corrected at any moment) that the Kaiser's Germany was a much tougher character than Nazi Germany.'[2]

Despite the parenthetical caveat, those words seem absurd today. It is but one reminder that Churchill, for all his vision, was not uniquely foresighted. Like many of his contemporaries in that year of revolutions, 1940, he was often wrong-footed by events. In what follows I explore his role as war leader in three main areas: first, naval strategy during the Phoney War while he was at the Admiralty; then the realignment of British foreign policy following the French collapse; and finally defence policy and domestic leadership during the Battle of Britain.

'Winston is back.' The famous signal from the Admiralty on 3 September 1939 informed the fleet of Churchill's return as First Lord to what he called in his memoirs 'the room I had quitted in pain and sorrow almost exactly a quarter of a century before'.[3] His immediate, invigorating effect is celebrated. Replacing Lord Stanhope, a leisurely and thoroughly unnautical gentleman, Churchill stirred up a service to which he was deeply committed. Visits to dockyards and ships, memoranda to all and sundry, late nights and relentless pace—it was all totally Churchillian and thoroughly necessary as the country geared up creakily for war. Equally typical was his eye for publicity. The regular Wednesday radio broadcasts were calculated both to encourage the public and promote his Department. As the Director of Naval Intelligence recalled, 'good news was made to seem better; bad news was toned down, delayed or sometimes suppressed. Any particularly spicey bit of news might be held up for three or four days until it could be included in the First Lord's broadcast and no one was more conscious than Mr. Churchill of the popularity of the bringer of good tidings.'[4] Nor was he content to preside over the Navy. Colleagues and the Cabinet were bombarded with advice about how to conduct the war—shipping, supply, diplomacy, bombing. This was also the familiar Winston. As Sir Arthur Steel-Maitland, a Cabinet colleague back in 1926, had observed: 'He's jolly difficult when he's in a napoleonesque attitude, dictating instructions in military metaphors, and the spotlight full on him.'[5] It was this that had strengthened the desire of Chamberlain, as premier, to keep Churchill out of the Cabinet. Chamberlain and others began to feel during the autumn of 1939 that the stream of memoranda was also 'for the purpose of quotation in the

Book he will write hereafter'.[6] 'Another one for the book' became an in-joke in Whitehall.

The temperamental differences between Churchill's energetic individualism and the more deliberate, sometimes lethargic, habits of his political colleagues would have emerged in any government. In 1939–40 they took shape around a more substantive disagreement about the conduct of the war. Since Chamberlain's name has gone down to ignominy in national mythology, and the period 1939–40 has been similarly dismissed as a pathetic prelude to the real war, it is important to be clear on the policy debate between Churchill and his colleagues.

It was axiomatic in Whitehall in 1939 that Britain should prepare for a long war, perhaps of three or more years' duration, in which the economic resources of its Empire would be crucial for victory as the blockade tightened on the enemy. That, after all, was traditional British strategy, emphasizing the navy and minimizing the need for a large land army on the Continent. It entailed gradually mobilizing Britain's global resources for an extended struggle, meanwhile trying to avoid an early confrontation in France that would favour Hitler's better-prepared armed forces. The Treasury, mindful of the foreign exchange crisis of 1916–17, had warned in July 1939 that Britain's 'war chest' of gold and convertible currency was in worse state than in 1914 and that, without American loans or gifts, 'the prospects for a long war are exceedingly grim'.[7] But Chamberlain and his colleagues took comfort in September 1939 from the fact that the feared three-front war had not broken out: Italy and Japan were still neutral. And the Premier and his close associates entertained the hope that German economy and morale might be far less ready for a long war than Britain's. Their goal was to squeeze Germany so that the Nazi regime was overthrown: 'the only chance of peace is the disappearance of Hitler and that is what we are working for', Chamberlain observed in October. 'My policy remains the same. Hold on tight, keep up the economic pressure, push on with munitions production and military preparations with the utmost energy, take no offensive until Hitler begins it. I reckon that if we are allowed to carry on this policy we shall have won the war by the Spring.'[8]

Thus the policy of gradual build-up suited both the strategy of a long war and the hope of a quick peace. The Cabinet's key decisions in September 1939 were taken upon these underlying premises: no offensive in the West, an energetic pursuit of the war at sea, the cultivation of Italian neutrality. As David Dilks has observed: 'With all these decisions Churchill was in full agreement. All were based on arguments that time was working for the western allies and that Germany might collapse under internal stresses, or at least find her war effort weakened.'[9] To take but one instance, Churchill, despite his subsequent image as an inveterate foe of appeasement, was a keen supporter of the government's Italian policy. 'Everyone can see how necessary it is to have Italy friendly and how desirable to have her an Ally', he reminded the Cabinet in October 1939.[10] And the 'Note on the War in 1940', quoted earlier, shows that even he was not immune from hopes of an early end to hostilities.

While continuing to share the official consensus, however, Churchill gradually developed deep doubts about the government's conduct of the war. The main immediate issue was the Baltic; the underlying point became the whole strategy of 'cunctation'—of playing for time on the assumption that time was on the Allies' side.

The detailed story of the many plans for operations in the Baltic is beyond the scope of this essay and the outline can be summarized briefly. Churchill's basic idea for 'Operation Catherine' was to project a small, self-sustained battle-fleet, including two or three battleships and an aircraft carrier, into the Baltic. He hoped to have this ready in the early months of 1940. Among his aims were to cut off Germany from Scandinavian iron ore and encourage the Baltic neutrals to join the Allies. His ideas, advanced in the first days of the war, were gradually overwhelmed by opposition from within the Admiralty. As the First Sea Lord, Admiral Sir Dudley Pound, warned in December: 'Until the trade routes have been cleared of raiders, and the U-boat menace, whether from torpedoes or mines, has been destroyed, it will be quite impossible to spare the force which will be required . . .'[11] As a more limited alternative, Churchill spent much time in early 1940 arguing for an attempt to cut off the Narvik ore traffic, by mines or perhaps destroyer operations. This fell foul of Foreign Office concern not to antagonize Norway and Sweden. The project gained new life in January and February when linked with the idea of sending an Anglo-French force via Narvik to aid the Finns against Russia, Hitler's ally. When the Finns capitulated on 12 March the Cabinet finally resolved to mine the Norwegian waters, but by this time Hitler had also developed his own Baltic strategy. The mines were laid on 8 April, the German invasion of Norway and Denmark began on the 9th, and the subsequent shambolic Anglo-French campaign in Norway was largely responsible for the end of Chamberlain's government on 10 May.

In evaluating Churchill's role in these events, it is important to distinguish between the *operational*, the *strategic*, and the *grand strategical*. On the first two points Churchill's record was distinctly mixed; on the last he was fundamentally right. Churchill undoubtedly unsettled the operational conduct of the Norwegian campaign by changing plans (particularly between Narvik and Trondheim as the main target) and by offering frequent advice to commanders on the spot. He also underestimated the potency of airpower and the capacity of the Germans to invade Western Scandinavia. But in all this, as Arthur Marder has observed, his faults were also those of the Chiefs of Staff and the senior Admiralty officials, including Pound. The First Lord was 'a main contributor' to the fiasco and not its sole author.[12] As for the larger strategic conception, Churchill was surely misguided in his fixation with Scandinavia. This was to recur throughout the war, echoed in plans for operation 'Jupiter' in 1942, and it reflected his abiding predilection for a 'peripheral strategy' rather than a direct attack on the Continent (Gallipoli in 1915, Italy in 1943–4). Not only would 'Catherine' have jeopardized a large part of the battle-fleet, it would also have been a distraction from the main war effort at sea and by land. And the danger of war with Russia would have been considerable. The fact that the German navy suffered heavy losses that incapacitated it for invasion of Britain later that year does not upset the basic balance of this argument.

Where Churchill was fundamentally correct was in the need for action, even if he wanted to act in an inappropriate place. While at one with the basic policy of avoiding an early confrontation he became increasingly anxious by early 1940 about the apparent total passivity of policy. In the argument over mining Norwegian waters in January 1940, the Cabinet minutes record him as follows:

He was not impatient for action merely for action's sake, but ever since the beginning of the war we had let the initiative rest with Germany . . . If, however, we opened up a new theatre of operations in Scandinavia, we had a fine chance of forcing Germany into situations which she had not foreseen, and of seizing the initiative for ourselves.

In the same meeting he began to cast doubt on the benefits of delay. 'Up to the present he had felt that time was on our side, but he was not sure that this would continue to be so.'[13] In mid-March, after the Finnish armistice ended those plans for a Scandinavian campaign, he told the Foreign Secretary frankly:

I am very deeply concerned about the way the war is going . . . There is no sort of action in view except to wait on events. In spite of all their brutality the Germans are making more headway with the neutrals than we with all our scruples. The Air Force is not catching up. The Army causes me much anxiety. The money-drain is grievous. There is no effective intimacy with the French. Public opinion is far from trustful of the Government. We have never done anything but follow the line of least resistance. That leads only to perdition.[14]

Subsequent research confirms the burden of Churchill's argument. Chamberlain and British intelligence were right that the Nazi war economy was over-stretched, particularly in shortages of raw materials. But no attempt was made to increase the tension by mining the Norwegian waters, blockading Italy instead of wooing her, and probing into the Saar.[15] Instead the Germans used the six-month interval in 1939–40 to improve their position and mount the western offensive where and when they chose. Indeed it was during the winter that they dropped their Belgian strategy in favour of the push through the Ardennes, which proved so devastatingly successful. Churchill's operational and strategic thinking may have been characteristically erratic, but on the essential thrust of grand strategy he was right. Within days of his assuming the Premiership the road to perdition was clear for all to see.

The circumstances under which Churchill became Prime Minister on 10 May 1940 are described in Lord Blake's essay in this volume (Chapter 15). Suffice it here to note that these political events occurred independently of, though simultaneously with, the opening of the German offensive in France which began on the same day and ended so triumphantly with the armistice on 17 June. This section of my chapter will concentrate on three related themes—Churchill's policy towards the French collapse, his attitude to a negotiated peace, and his wooing of the only potential ally left, the United States.

Recriminations over the Fall of France in 1940 will rumble on for years to come. The nub of the French case against the British is that the British were willing to fight to the last Frenchman. On 10 May the RAF had only 450 aircraft in France, about a third of its serviceable total, whereas the French had 1,400. In the crucial weapon of modern fighters, the British had only six squadrons in France when the Germans attacked. By the 16th another fourteen had been dispatched, but then all except three squadrons were withdrawn to Britain following a Cabinet decision on 18 May to concentrate on home defence. The British response was, of course, that the battle was lost almost before it started, with the lethargic French High Command wrong-footed by the

German drive across the Meuse at Sedan. At 7.30 a.m. on 15 May Churchill was appalled to hear Pierre Reynaud, the French Premier, moaning over the phone: 'We are beaten; we have lost the battle.'[16] Under these circumstances the British would seem to have had little choice but to save themselves. But the issue is more complex than that. Despite having twice the manufacturing output of France, Britain had done little to translate that economic power into military might where it mattered in May 1940. Of the 144 Allied divisions on the Western Front, 104 were French, 22 Belgian, 10 British, and eight Dutch. Brian Bond has suggested that 'an earlier British commitment would have enabled the allies to check the German advance in 1940'.[17] But that would have required a greater concentration on the army, especially on mobile, armoured forces, than prevailed in the 1930s. Instead British defence policy had emphasized airpower—first the bomber deterrent and then, from 1938, fighter and radar defence. The latter helped ensure survival in the crisis of 1940; the interesting if imponderable question is whether a different defence policy earlier might have averted that crisis in the first place.

In a marginal and ironic sense Churchill contributed to the bias of British rearmament towards airpower. His warnings about the Luftwaffe's expansion helped arouse concern at Westminster but his exaggerated figures about German operational, front-line strength contributed to the panic about aerial bombardment that so skewed British defence policy and so enfeebled British diplomacy in the 1930s.[18] Churchill was out of office until 1939, however, and prime responsibility for the deficiencies of British policy lay on other shoulders. Churchill simply had to make do with what he had in 1940. And it is clear that, within tight limits, he did his best to aid the French, repeatedly challenging the Chiefs of Staff to do more, both in the middle of May and again when the battle of France was resumed after Dunkirk.[19] Similarly, he tried to head off a French surrender in the middle of June by agreeing to the proposal for an Anglo-French union hastily concocted by Jean Monnet and Charles de Gaulle.

From mid-May, however, British policymakers had been forced to consider their position 'in a certain eventuality'—the Chiefs of Staff's euphemism for the Fall of France. On 26–8 May, during the early days of the Dunkirk crisis, before it was clear that many troops could be evacuated, the five-man inner War Cabinet debated whether there might be grounds for a negotiated peace.[20] The prime mover here was Lord Halifax, the Foreign Secretary and, shortly before, the alternative candidate for the premiership, who argued that Mussolini (still neutral) could be used as an intermediary to see if terms might be secured from Hitler that guaranteed Britain's integrity and independence, even at the loss of parts of the Empire. Halifax was initially supported by Chamberlain, and the argument with Churchill became sufficiently heated at one point for the Foreign Secretary to consider resignation. Halifax confided in his diary that 'it does drive me to despair when he works himself up into a position of emotion when he ought to make his brain think and reason'.[21] Against Halifax, Churchill argued that no peace was even conceivable until Britain had shown Hitler that she was unconquerable. Even to inquire about German terms at this stage would be a sign of weakness and would 'ruin the integrity of our fighting position in this country'.[22] As the evacuation from Dunkirk gained pace, so this argument became more compelling. On the evening of 28 May Churchill told the outer circle of ministers that 'we must fight on' even if it meant that 'this long island story of ours' would end when 'each one of us lies choking in his blood upon the ground'. He was greeted with a spontaneous display of support which moved and fortified him.[23] When he learned in mid-June that Halifax and R. A. Butler, the Parliamentary Under-Secretary at the Foreign Office, had made noises via the Swedish ambassador that 'common sense and not bravado would dictate' British policy, Churchill was sharply critical of such 'odd language' and of the 'strong impression of defeatism' conveyed.[24]

All this fits grandly with the familiar image of Churchillian pugnacity, encapsulated in his rousing words to the Commons on his first appearance as Prime Minister: 'I have nothing to offer but blood, toil, tears, and sweat . . . You ask, What is our aim? I can answer in one word: Victory—victory at all costs, victory in spite of all terror; victory, however long and hard the road may be; for without victory there is no survival.'[25] We shall see in a moment how Churchill projected his bull-dog image to the country and the world during the Blitz, but it is worth noting here that his private position was more nuanced. Although we are talking here on the level of largely 'unspoken assumptions' it does seem that Churchill's conception in 1939 of how the war would be won corresponded broadly with that of Chamberlain, namely a sudden German collapse, akin to that of 1918, which would overthrow Hitler and bring to power a government with whom it would be possible to talk about lasting security. He was not thinking in terms of 'unconditional surrender'—a doctrine promulgated in 1943 from the strong point of a global alliance. Thus in October 1939 he drafted a possible answer to Hitler's peace-feelers, telling Chamberlain that, although its tone was negative, it 'does not close the door upon any genuine offer' from Germany.[26] During the fraught Cabinet debates of late May 1940 he took a similar line in principle, saying, for instance, that 'if Herr Hitler was prepared to make peace on the terms of the restoration of German colonies and the overlordship of Central Europe, that was one thing', but he felt that such an offer was 'quite unlikely'.[27] And he was despondent at times that summer about Britain's prospects. Returning from his penultimate meeting with the French on 12 June, Churchill was driven back to the airport with his military secretary, Hastings Ismay. At one point he turned and said 'that, it seems, "we fight alone". Ismay said he was glad of it, that "we'll win the Battle of Britain". Churchill gave him a look and remarked, "You and I will be dead in three months' time".'[28]

To some extent the debates about peace in May 1940 turned on gut instinct. Halifax and Butler abhorred the prospect of carnage inflicted from the air, imagining it, like most of that generation, as being on holocaust scale. Churchill, by contrast, was a fighter, a romantic militarist, for whom capitulation was unthinkable at least until battle had been tried. But if that was Churchill's underlying conviction, he still needed to express it in terms of a credible strategy. What Halifax called his 'rhodomontades' could not suffice and sustain for the long haul. And Churchill found himself hard pressed that summer to develop rationalizations for his gut instinct. For the prospects of survival, let alone victory, as he at times confessed, appeared slim indeed.

Prompted by Churchill, British strategy rested on two main pillars. The first was the continuing conviction that the German economy was close to breaking point and that further pressure might bring about an internal collapse. The problem was that the main instrument of pressure, the naval blockade, was now almost irrelevant. The Nazi–Soviet pact had already given Hitler access to Soviet manpower and resources; in the summer of 1940 most of Europe was within his orbit, from Scandinavia to Sicily, from the Bay of Biscay to the Black Sea. Instead, Churchill now insisted that the RAF constituted the decisive weapon. By protecting the British Isles, the

Fighters are our salvation, but the Bombers alone provide the means to victory. We must, therefore, develop the power to carry an ever-increasing volume of explosives to Germany, so as to pulverise the entire industry and scientific structure on which the war effort and economic life of the enemy depend, while holding him at arm's length from our Island. In no other way at present visible can we hope to overcome the immense military power of Germany . . .[29]

Just as British rearmament had been channelled into the air weapon in the 1930s, to buttress the diplomacy of appeasement, so it was from 1940 to constitute a strategy for victory. It remains an intriguing question whether, had Britain been a more formidable land power earlier in the war, either the disaster of 1940 or the delay in the second front, with all that this implied for eastern Europe, might have been averted.

The second pillar of Churchill's rationalization for fighting on was his hope that the United States would soon be in the war. Churchill was half-American and, although in the 1920s he had something of a reputation as an 'anti-American',[30] he had bent his energies in the late 1930s to forging closer Anglo-American ties. Chamberlain, by contrast, was habitually suspicious of the United States, convinced it was 'always best and safest to expect *nothing* from the Americans except words'[31] and reluctant to alter his own policy, in peace or war, to take much account of American sensibilities. While at the Admiralty in September 1939 Churchill had received an invitation from President Roosevelt to keep him personally informed on any matters of interest. A similar letter was sent to Chamberlain, but it was Churchill who seized on the proposal with alacrity and fed F.D.R. information about the naval war throughout the winter. Once at No. 10 he used this channel with increasing frequency. 'My relations with the President gradually became so close that the chief business between our two countries was virtually conducted by these personal interchanges between him and me.'[32]

Churchill's sensitivity to the American connection was of crucial importance in 1940 because, as the Chiefs of Staff observed in their paper on 'a certain eventuality', without 'full economic and financial support' from the USA '*we do not think we could continue the war with any chance of success*'.[33] Yet Churchill's conduct of policy towards America was more complex than the subsequent myth of the 'Special Relationship' would suggest. On the one hand he insisted to the Cabinet and Parliamentary doubters that it was only a matter of weeks or months before America would enter the war, at most after the November presidential election. In one of many instances, he told a secret session of the Commons of 20 June, according to his notes:

Attitude of United States.

Nothing will stir them like fighting in England . . .

All depends upon our resolute bearing and holding out until Election issues are settled there.

If we can do so, I cannot doubt whole English-speaking world will be in line together.[34]

The general line was that bombing and attempted invasion would so move the American public, many of them linked by ethnic bonds to Britain, that they would be pulled into the war. Although mistaken, or at least premature, this was an important rationalization to reinforce British official hopes for fighting on in 1940.

Yet this emotional Americanism in semi-public statements was complemented by hard-headed bargaining in transatlantic diplomacy. On 27 May 1940 Churchill observed bitterly in Cabinet that the United States 'had given us practically no help in the war, and now that they saw how great was the danger, their attitude was that they wanted to keep everything which would help us for their own defence'.[35] To those who favoured an open-handed offer to share military secrets, such as Radar and Asdic (an anti-submarine detection system), he responded in July: 'I am not in a hurry to give our secrets until the United States is much nearer war than she is now.'[36] In his efforts to obtain American destroyers for the Royal Navy during the summer, he was anxious, despite Britain's dire straits, to strike a bargain. Against Halifax and the Foreign Office he argued that the US proposal in August for a formal deal was unacceptable; this would have given the British fifty destroyers in explicit consideration for the right to build bases on eight British possessions in the Western Atlantic and for a public assurance that the British fleet would not be sunk or surrendered but would go to Empire ports. Conscious that the United States might very well be seen as getting the best of the bargain if these elements were directly linked, he preferred to represent the arrangement as 'measures of mutual assistance rendered to one another by two friendly nations'.[37] Materially, the fifty old US destroyers were of limited importance in 1940. Only nine were in service with the Royal Navy by the end of the year and only thirty by May 1941.[38] But the 'Destroyers Deal' of 2 September—however it was represented for domestic politics—was a portentous sign internationally, marking the first major step towards what became the wartime Anglo-American alliance. As Churchill told the Commons, it meant that

these two great organisations of the English-speaking democracies, the British Empire and the United States, will have to be somewhat mixed up together in some of their affairs for mutual and general advantage . . . I do not view the process with any misgivings. I could not stop it if I wished; no one can stop it. Like the Mississippi, it just keeps rolling along. Let it roll. Let it roll on—full flood, inexorable, irresistible, benignant, to broader lands and better days.[39]

Important though Anglo–American relations were for the long term, they were largely irrelevant to the vital matter of August 1940, namely the Battle of Britain. It was here, above all, that Churchill's reputation as war leader was made.

In the actual conduct of the Battle, Churchill took a secondary role. In contrast with his tendency to get involved in the operational details of the navy, he generally left the air war to the airmen, though often visiting the operations room of Number 11 Group, Fighter Command, at Uxbridge, in west London, the nerve centre of the battle. The detailed account in his memoirs of the atmosphere there on 15 September 1940, the decisive day of the battle over London, is justly famous, particularly the dramatic moment when Churchill broke silence to ask 'What other reserves have we?' and was told 'There are none'.[40] But a similar situation had apparently arisen during his visit a month before. As they left by car Churchill told Ismay: 'Don't speak to me; I have never been so moved.' Then, after brooding for a few minutes, he leaned forward: 'Never in the field of human conflict has so much been owed by so many to so few.' Four days later he used the phrase in the Commons and it passed into history.[41]

The role of Churchillian rhetoric will be discussed in a moment. Here I should mention two less public but important contributions he did make to preparing the British war machine in the summer of 1940. The first was the invigorating effect of his leadership on Whitehall, symbolized in the celebrated 'Action This Day' tabs stuck on priority documents. Sir John Colville served as private secretary to both Chamberlain and Churchill. He recalled later:

Seldom can a Prime Minister have taken office with 'the Establishment', as it would now be called, so dubious of the choice and so prepared to find its doubts justified. Within a fortnight all was changed. I doubt if there has ever been such a rapid transformation of opinion in Whitehall and of the tempo at which business was conducted.[42]

In the diary he kept at the time Colville noted on 13 June that Churchill had 'really galvanised the country and the Government departments'. He added a few days later that 'one of the great differences between Chamberlain and Churchill' was that 'the former, in reading Cabinet papers, seldom made any comments and only on questions of the highest policy' whereas 'Churchill scrutinises every document which has anything to do with the war and does not disdain to enquire into the most trivial point'.[43] The restless energy that had often seemed disruptive when tenuously confined within a single ministry was now able to flow freely over the whole war. Or as Sir Ian Jacob, then in the Cabinet Secretariat, observed, it was 'the difference between a human dynamo when humming on the periphery and when driving at the centre'.[44]

Churchill helped put the whole of Whitehall on its mettle that long, hot summer. Less evident but perhaps even more important was his interest in and use of secret military intelligence, a topic discussed by Sir Harry Hinsley in this volume (Chapter 23). It is surely right to say that 'no previous British statesman and no other war leader equalled his grasp of its importance'.[45] By happy coincidence he came to power just as British cryptanalysts were beginning to provide a regular supply of 'Enigma' decrypts of German signals traffic. Churchill took the keenest interest in these 'golden eggs', as he called them, demanding not merely summaries but also raw intercepts in his daily buff-coloured box, and chafing at the bit to put the material to operational use. Equally important, Churchill shook up the intelligence organizations. He had long believed in the need for a unified secret service, to maximize the co-ordination of information, and on 17 May 1940, a week after taking office, he gave the Cabinet's Joint Intelligence Committee (JIC) enhanced status as the central body for producing intelligence appreciations.[46] This was an early attempt to transcend the bureaucratic rivalry between the Foreign Office, MI5, MI6, and others. The full significance of these developments lies outside *annus mirabilis*, 1940. Though 'valuable', Enigma was only 'fragmentary' and 'incomplete' during the Battle of Britain,[47] while the JIC did not achieve real co-ordinating authority until May 1941 when supported by a proper back-up staff. But Churchill's immediate grasp of this secret weapon—the 'missing dimension . . . of most diplomatic history'[48]—would prove of profound importance in the future.

Enigma was one of the best-kept secrets of the war. As Churchill said, 'the geese who laid the golden eggs . . . never cackled'.[49] Much more public, and the heart of Churchill's reputation as leader in 1940 was his public persona. This was a compound of what he did and what he said.

That summer Churchill travelled widely, visiting invasion defences, fighter bases, and bombed-out streets. The response was generally enthusiastic. One famous incident occurred in the ruins of London docklands. 'Good old Winnie', people in the crowd shouted. 'We thought you'd come and see us. We can take it. Give it 'em back.' According to Ismay, who accompanied him, 'Churchill broke down, and as I was struggling to get him through the crowd, I heard an old woman say, "You see, he really cares; he's crying."'[50]

Churchill's other great contribution that summer, in the words of Edward R. Murrow, was that 'he mobilized the English language and sent it into battle'.[51] In the past his carefully wrought speeches had often seemed ponderous, even pompous, ill-timed for the national mood, as over India and the abdication in the 1930s. But in 1940, to borrow the metaphor of biographer Piers Brendon, 'the nation changed and Churchill stayed the same. For a short time, indeed, he created a new Britain in his own heroic image.'[52] Language that had previously sounded archaic now struck a chord. The writer Vita Sackville-West told her husband: 'I think that one of the reasons why one is stirred by his Elizabethan phrases is that one feels the whole massive backing of power and resolve behind them, like a great fortress.'[53]

Passages from Churchill's speeches have passed into the treasury of the English language. Several have been quoted already. Here is an excerpt from what is perhaps the best remembered, delivered on 18 June 1940, the day after the French capitulated, when he warned that the

whole fury of the enemy must very soon be turned on us. Hitler knows that he will have to break us in this Island or lose the war . . . Let us therefore brace ourselves to our duties, and so bear ourselves that, if the British Empire and its Commonwealth last for a thousand years, men will still say: 'This was their finest hour.'[54]

Churchill took the three final words as the title for the 1940 volume of war memoirs; equally aptly his official biographer used the last two for the tome on 1939–41.

Actions and words that summer brought Churchill to the pinnacle of his national reputation. A Gallup poll published in the press on 8 August indicated that 88 per cent approved of his leadership and only 7 per cent were definitely hostile. This rating was higher than anything Chamberlain achieved, even in the days of near-deification after Munich.[55] Churchill's place within the Tory Party was also transformed. Widely regarded as a maverick and outsider in the 1930s, he became Prime Minister without being party leader. Chamberlain retained that role and Churchill was keenly conscious in his early weeks as Premier that he did not have the full support of Conservative MPs. 'To a large extent I am in y[ou]r hands', he wrote to Chamberlain immediately after being asked by the King to form a government.[56] But the events of that summer transformed his position and, when Chamberlain died of cancer in November, there was no question that Churchill would succeed him as Conservative leader.

Yet one must, in fairness, note that the Churchillian image of 1940—man of the people, voice of the British bulldog—was somewhat incongruous. For one thing Churchill, the aristocrat, had lived most of his life remote from the bulk of the British population. All his daily needs were satisfied by a loyal valet. As Colville remarked: 'I doubt if he had ever travelled on a bus, and it must have been many years since he bought anything in a shop. When I knew him, he did not even carry money with him.'[57] The story behind the great speeches is also more complex than convention suggests. Some of the glittering phrases were reminted from previous, now forgotten occasions. David Cannadine notes that 'so much owed by so many to so few' had first been coined, in somewhat different form, as early as 1899.[58] And, contrary to the myth of Churchill inspiring the nation huddled around its crackling wireless sets, he spoke mostly to the House of Commons. As D. J. Wenden has pointed out in this book, in 1940 only five of Churchill's speeches as Prime Minister were broadcast to the British people (19 May, 17 June, 18 June, 14 July, and 11 September). The second of these was less than two minutes in length.[59]

Undoubtedly 1940 was Churchill's finest hour. But it is likely that the sharpness and the colour of our image of that year owes much to the fact that Churchill published his version of the story before virtually anyone else and because it could be encapsulated in such memorable one-liners. As he said in 1944, at the end of one row with the Americans about strategy, he would leave the controversy to history but would be one of the historians.[60] And there he succeeded triumphantly. Subsequent historians of 1939–45 have borrowed his phrases and adopted his phases. As J. H. Plumb noted: 'They move down the broad avenues which he drove through war's confusion and complexity.'[61] For many of the generation of 1940, in short, what happened was what Churchill said had happened. And woe betide those young whippersnappers who have the temerity to read the documents and then ask awkward questions![62] Nevertheless, the work of historical reappraisal goes on. What is certain is that the Churchill of 1940 is great enough to survive both the hagiographers and the historians.

15

How Churchill Became Prime Minister

ROBERT BLAKE

When the Conservatives narrowly lost the general election of June 1929 to a combination of Labour and Liberals, Churchill was 54. He had held all the principal offices of state except those of Prime Minister and Foreign Secretary. He had been successively President of the Board of Trade, Home Secretary, First Lord of the Admiralty, then, after a short interval, Minister of Munitions, Secretary for War and Air (the two posts were held in conjunction), Secretary for the Colonies, and, after another brief interval, Chancellor of the Exchequer in Baldwin's second Cabinet, 1924–9. No man had more experience in public life, and, though much of it had been conducted in a blaze of controversy, he had every reason to expect high office when Baldwin returned to power—an event expected soon in light of the fragile position of the second Labour Cabinet under Ramsay MacDonald, 1929–31.

Churchill threw away his chances by resigning on 27 January 1931 from the Conservative 'Business Committee', the equivalent of the modern Shadow Cabinet. The cause was India. Baldwin supported the tentative moves by Lord Irwin (later Viscount Halifax) towards Indian self-government. Irwin had been Baldwin's appointee as Viceroy in 1926. His approach to the Indian problem had the support of MacDonald and Labour, but it was a matter of high dispute among Conservatives. Churchill believed that the Irwin–MacDonald–Baldwin policy would be a disaster for Britain, India, and the Empire. He also believed that most Conservatives were on his side and that India would be at the top of the political agenda for many years to come. He was wrong on both counts. He never had more than minority Conservative support, and the economic crisis of August 1931 altered the whole configuration of British politics, blowing India into the background. It resulted in a 'national' coalition under Ramsay MacDonald of Conservatives, most Liberals, and a handful of Labour. Baldwin was 'the Mayor of the Palace'. MacDonald, once described by Churchill as 'the boneless wonder', had no cause to recruit him after the government's landslide victory in October. Nor was Baldwin going to push Churchill's claims after the bitter and provocative language that he used over India. The India Bill occupied many columns of *Hansard*, but it was a peripheral affair, and Churchill did himself little but harm by his verbose, bombastic, and intemperate personal charges.

The Bill became law in August 1935, but from early 1933 onwards Churchill had combined his India campaign with a more promising political theme—the threat of a resurgent rearming Germany under Hitler with Mussolini's Italy as a potential ally. Churchill's outlook on foreign policy and defence has been given a retrospective consistency that the facts hardly warrant. He referred in 1933 to Mussolini as 'the greatest law giver among living men' and as 'the Roman genius'.[1] In 1935 he wrote a piece on Hitler which gave him, if not the benefit of the doubt, at least the possibility.[2] As late as 1937 he thought that Hitler might yet do good for Germany.[3] He took no lead in the debates about Abyssinia or the Spanish Civil War. He was, however, a consistent supporter of rearmament, though whether he supported the right kind of rearmament is open to argument, and his public expression of his policy varied over the years, influenced by his political prospects.

Churchill deeply desired office. In Opposition, or even as a back-bench nominal government supporter, he was a fish out of water. But office eluded him till war broke out in September 1939. He had no chance while MacDonald was Prime Minister. He had high hopes after Baldwin took over in June 1935 and won a decisive victory in the election of October. Nothing happened. He had hopes again after the Rhineland crisis of March 1936. There was public demand for the creation of a special ministry to oversee the rearmament programme. Churchill seemed an obvious candidate, but Baldwin appointed as Minister for the Co-ordination of Defence the Attorney General, Sir Thomas Inskip, who had never been in the Cabinet or had any experience with the services. There was general astonishment. Churchill behaved with dignity and constructive restraint. But he then threw away whatever he had recently gained in terms of 'respectability' by espousing at the end of 1936 the dubious cause of Edward VIII and Mrs Simpson. He was shouted down in the House. His prestige reached its nadir. Office seemed further away than ever.

His prospects were not improved when Baldwin resigned in May 1937 in favour of Neville Chamberlain. There was no personal animosity, and Churchill was happy with the new Foreign Secretary, Anthony Eden, who had succeeded Sir Samuel Hoare at the end of 1935. Chamberlain could easily have brought Churchill into the Cabinet despite the misgivings of colleagues and supporters, if he had wanted. He did not. He told Leslie Hore-Belisha, the War Secretary who argued for Churchill's inclusion: 'If I take him into the Cabinet he will dominate it. He won't give others the chance of even talking.'[4] Loquacity may seem a trivial objection to the most experienced public figure in the field of defence, but one should not underestimate how tedious people can be who talk on and on at meetings of limited time and tight agenda.

Chamberlain had other reasons too for blocking Churchill. He was determined on a policy of 'appeasement', the merits of which are discussed elsewhere.[5] It is enough to say that the issue involved negotiation with Hitler and Mussolini to defuse conflict by discovering what their 'grievances' really were and whether peaceful compromise could be achieved. The first phase began with Halifax's visit to Germany in November 1937, when he talked to, and was taken in by, Hitler and Goering. It ended with Eden's resignation in February 1938, not on the German but on the Italian question—Mussolini's supply of arms to Franco in the Spanish Civil War. He was succeeded by Halifax, who was almost at once confronted by the *Anschluss*, the annexation of Austria. It was clear that Czechoslovakia, with its large German-speaking minority, would be the next state after Austria to be in peril. Churchill favoured a 'Grand Alliance' of as many as possible of Germany's neighbours or near-neighbours (such as Soviet Russia) against Nazi aggression. This was anathema to Chamberlain. Like most Britons who thought about the matter at all, he considered that the 'Big Four' at Versailles had committed a major injustice in drawing the map of Czechoslovakia. The second phase in the policy of appeasement, which had begun with Eden's resignation, ended in the Munich settlement.

This led to a complete breach between Churchill and the Conservative establishment, though he never renounced his membership of the party. In the debate on Munich he made one of the greatest speeches of his life.[6] Hitherto his words had fallen on deaf ears, often indeed on very few ears. Like Cato the Elder, who ended every speech in the Roman Senate with an injunction to destroy Carthage, Churchill was in danger of crying 'Wolf' too often. He may not quite have rivalled Edmund Burke's reputation as 'the dinner bell', but he seemed to many people a monologist and a bore, and he was liable to find himself addressing an almost empty chamber on a well-worn theme. The Munich speech on 5 October 1938 was a different matter. Circumstances made for a crowded House. He commanded attention—indignant attention among most Conservative members, but attention all the same. When he uttered the words 'we have sustained a total and unmitigated defeat', he had to pause for some moments in face of the angry storm of protest which followed. His peroration was heard in silence but it was to be remembered later: 'And do not suppose that this is the end. This is only the beginning of the reckoning. This is only the first sip, the first foretaste of a bitter cup which will be proffered to us year by year unless by a supreme recovery of moral health and martial vigour, we rise again and take our stand for freedom as in the olden time.'

Meeting Chamberlain on 2 October on his return from Munich and driving back with him from Heston airport to Downing Street, Halifax, according to his own account, had suggested the need for a government of national unity. He urged Chamberlain to invite Labour to join, also Churchill and Eden. Chamberlain was taken aback but said he would think about the idea.[7] If he ever considered it seriously, he would certainly have abandoned it after Churchill's speech three days later.

Yet Churchill's speech, by an irony of events, was to be one of his principal stepping stones to premiership. If Chamberlain's claim after Munich of 'peace in our time' had turned out to be true, if Hitler had been ready to restrict his aims to German irredentism and righting the wrongs of Versailles, it is safe to say that Churchill's exile in the political wilderness would have been permanent. But on 15 March 1939 an event occurred that totally transformed the situation. Hitler marched his forces into Prague and in effect annexed what remained of Czechoslovakia. After that no amount of wishful thinking could obscure the reality: the Western Powers were confronted not with a Bismarck, or even with a Kaiser Wilhelm, but with a Napoleon—moreover, a Napoleon with none of the redeeming features of the ruler of the First Empire.

Churchill's warnings seemed to be fully vindicated. There was immediate pressure in several organs of the press for him to be included in the Cabinet, now that war seemed, if not inevitable, at least highly probable. Chamberlain had been persuaded to give the guarantees to Poland that, of course, made war even more likely. But paradoxically he still clung to the belief that war could be avoided and that Churchill's presence in the Cabinet would be provocative. 'If there is any possibility of easing the tension and getting back to normal relations with the dictators', he wrote, 'I wouldn't risk it by what would certainly be regarded by them as a challenge.'[8] It was not till war actually broke out that he felt obliged to offer a seat in the War Cabinet to the man who had not only given such a striking warning of the future course of events but who had also had more experience of the problems of war than any other major public figure. Churchill accepted with alacrity as a Minister without Portfolio.

Chamberlain had originally intended to create a small War Cabinet excluding the service heads, as in 1916–19, and consisting mainly of non-departmental ministers. But he changed his mind. This enabled him to invite Churchill to return to his old post as First Lord of the Admiralty, but it made the War Cabinet larger and more cumbersome than its Great War analogue. Criticism on this score gave Chamberlain an excuse to exlude the other leading critic of his foreign policy: the most he was prepared to offer Anthony Eden was the Dominions Office, a backwater post without membership of the War Cabinet. By patriotically accepting this somewhat demeaning offer Eden effectively put himself out of the running for succession to the premiership. In April an opinion poll had given him 38 per cent support as the next Prime Minister if Chamberlain resigned, and only 7 per cent each to Churchill and Halifax.[9] Had Eden either insisted on War Cabinet membership or stayed wholly aloof, he might have been a serious contender in May 1940. In the event his name was not even considered.

Churchill's second spell at the Admiralty was by no means an unmitigated success. On the asset side was the destruction of the *Graf Spee*; on the debit, the sinking of *Royal Oak* and *Courageous* and, worst of all, the Norwegian campaign launched early in April 1940. Norway was a disaster from beginning to end. Chamberlain as Prime Minister had to take—and rightly—the major responsibility. His critics did not forget his ill-advised declaration two months earlier that Hitler had 'missed the bus'. Churchill as First Lord and recently appointed Chairman of the Military Co-ordination Committee had a responsibility second only to Chamberlain's. The campaign had sinister echoes of the Dardanelles. By the end of the first week in May, it was clear that the Anglo-French attempt to prevent Hitler conquering Norway had been a fiasco. On 7 and 8 May the subject was discussed with much passion in the House of Commons. On the first night, L. S. Amery, a Conservative back-bencher and ex-Cabinet minister, pointed at the government front bench and quoted in ringing tones Oliver Cromwell's famous adjuration to the Long Parliament: 'You have sat too long for any good you have been doing. Depart, I say, and let us have done with you. In the name of God, go!' The debate was technically on a motion that 'this House do now adjourn'—a procedural device to enable a general debate. It is not necessarily followed by a division. The Labour Party at the beginning did not intend to press for one. If the motion were to be defeated, the result would be tantamout to a vote of no confidence in the government, and the Labour leader, Clement Attlee, feared that party loyalty and the power of the Whips would merely confirm the government's majority. But he changed his mind on seeing the Conservatives in palpable disarray. It was Churchill's task to reply for the government at the end of the second day.

Before Churchill spoke, Lloyd George had made an attack scarcely less devastating than Amery's. Chamberlain, he said, 'has appealed for sacrifice . . . I say solemnly that the Prime Minister should give an example of sacrifice because there is nothing that can contribute more to victory in this war than that he should sacrifice the seals of office', and he urged Churchill not to let himself become 'an air-raid shelter to keep the splinters from hitting his colleagues'. He wondered whether the First Lord was 'entirely responsible for what has been done at the Admiralty'.

Churchill defended himself and his colleagues with combative vigour. He refused to accept Lloyd George's attempt to drive a wedge between himself and the Admiralty. He took full responsibility for the Norwegian campaign. He was so vigorous, even bellicose, that there was something of an uproar in the House with fierce exchanges between him and the Opposition. The vote was taken amidst great excitement. Chamberlain was not actually defeated: given his great majority that was hardly conceivable. But it fell from 213 to 81. No fewer than 33 Conservatives and another eight members who normally supported the government voted against it. Another 60 abstained.

Prime Ministers are not elected either by the people, like the President of France, or an electoral college, like the President of the USA. They are not even elected by the House of Commons. They are appointed by the monarch. The Prime Minister must, however, be able to command a majority in the House. Normally, there is only one person who can do this, the leader of the party that has won the last general election. Nine times out of ten the Crown has no choice. But it is important to remember that the two offices of majority party leader and Prime Minister are distinct. There can be occasions—and have been—when the Prime Minister has not been the party leader, though he or she obviously could not accept or carry on the premiership without the support of the majority party. Lloyd George was leader of no party when he was appointed Prime Minister in 1916, yet he carried on with Conservative support till 1922. Ramsay MacDonald was in a similar position from 1931 to 1935.

Prime Ministers remain in office till resignation or death. They may resign at any time and for a variety of reasons. The one event which *must* make them either resign or hold a general election is defeat in the House of Commons on a vote of confidence. They need not resign even after defeat in a general election, but Prime Ministers normally do because the new Parliament is certain to carry a vote of no confidence, and there is neither purpose nor dignity in waiting for it. Today, if a Prime Minister in possession of a Parliamentary majority resigns or dies, the party concerned would hold an election to choose a new leader who would automatically be invited by the monarch to become Prime Minister. In the case of the Conservative Party, the electors are the sitting Conservative MPs. But this system only dates from 1965. In 1940 the Conservatives had no electoral rules. The matter was held to be part of the royal prerogative, and the choice lay with George VI, if Neville Chamberlain decided to resign.

The precedents for what the King should do in such circumstances were by no means clear. He could in theory take any advice he saw fit to take—or none. Whatever advice he took, even from the outgoing Prime Minister if the latter was willing to give it, could not be 'binding' in the constitutional sense, as it would be when, for example, the King was 'advised' by the Prime Minister to appoint X as Archbishop of Canterbury or Y as a Field Marshal. An outgoing Prime Minister cannot give that sort of 'advice'. Otherwise one would have the *reductio ad absurdum* of a Prime Minister defeated in a general election 'advising' the King whom to choose from among his various opponents. The decision was the King's responsibility and his alone.

Neville Chamberlain could in theory take one of four courses. He could simply carry on; he could dissolve Parliament to seek a fresh mandate from the electorate; he could reconstruct his government on a coalition basis as had Asquith in 1915; or he could resign as Asquith did eighteen months later in favour of a new Prime Minister. To stay on as if nothing had happened was politically inconceivable. To hold an election was constitutionally possible but widely regarded as most undesirable in wartime, and the Quinquennial Act (which mandates general elections to be held at least every five years) had, as in 1915, been suspended for the duration of the war to avoid the necessity for a general election before it ended. This left the alternatives of a reconstructed government under Chamberlain or under a new Prime Minister. The real question was who the new man should be, for it was never a serious option that Chamberlain could carry on, though he sometimes deluded himself to the contrary.

In retrospect Churchill seems the obvious choice and the right choice. Right it certainly was, but by no means obvious at the time. Lord Halifax, the Foreign Secretary, was in many ways a stronger runner. He had been the least enthusiastic among Chamberlain's informal Inner Cabinet for the Munich settlement and had misgivings almost at once. Those in the know were aware that he had successfully urged Chamberlain not to cash in on post-Munich euphoria and hold a general election in the autumn of 1938. He was a quintessentially 'establishment' figure, friend of the royal family, great Yorkshire landowner, Fellow of All Souls College, Oxford, and devoted high churchman. Tall, distinguished, and sinuous, he was a man of intellectual power well capable, as he had shown in India, of administering an empire. Had he lived in another era, he might have been a Mazarin or a Richelieu. He was widely respected across the whole party political spectrum. No breath of scandal ever touched his name.

Churchill was very far from commanding united support among the Conservatives. The Dardanelles, India, and the abdication were remembered all too well. Despite his ducal connections—and anyway the Marlborough family had a dubious reputation—he was widely regarded as an adventurer and a buccaneer. He was distrusted in many quarters, and his acolytes such as Brendan Bracken, Robert Boothby, Duncan Sandys, and F. A. Lindemann (later Lord Cherwell) were unpopular figures. His son Randolph was another liability. Lord Beaverbrook, with whom he had a long-standing ambivalent relationship—half love, half hate—was anything but *persona grata* in the respectable Tory world. It is significant that the 'Eden Group', as they were called, who opposed Chamberlain's foreign policy, kept well clear of Churchill in 1938–9. By May 1940 there was a small minority of Conservative MPs who saw in Churchill the one hope of injecting purpose, energy, and originality into the war, but there can be little doubt that the party would have chosen Halifax had there been an election. But there was not; the question turned on advice to the Crown rather than counting of heads, and Chamberlain seems to have taken it for granted that the

King would ask his advice, as indeed proved to be the case.

If there was to be a coalition with Labour as the junior partner, further problems arose. It was unlikely that the party would agree to serve in a reconstructed government under Neville Chamberlain. There could be no repetition of Asquith's coalition in May 1915. The question of who should succeed as Prime Minister was another matter. Some favoured Churchill, but there were those who remembered Tonypandy and the General Strike, the India Bill, and the abdication. Labour was only united in their determination to oust Chamberlain. It was not for them to choose a successor, who must come from the top level of the Conservatives. Labour had a veto, not a choice. They were not prepared to veto Churchill, though he might not have been the man they would have chosen.

On the morning after the crucial division on 8 May, Chamberlain, who still half-hankered for survival as Prime Minister, asked Halifax to see him at No. 10. He told Halifax that a coalition was essential but agreed that his own chances of heading it were 'negligible', as Halifax records in his diary. Halifax goes on:

He thought that it was clearly Winston or myself, and appeared to suggest that if it were myself he might continue to serve in the Government. I put all the arguments I could think of against myself, laying considerable emphasis on the difficult position of a Prime Minister unable to make contact with the centre of gravity in the House of Commons. The PM did not think so much of this, arguing that, *ex hypothesi* in the new situation there would be comparatively little opposition in the House of Commons. The conversation and the evident drift of his mind left me with a bad stomach ache. I told him again as I had told him the day before that if the Labour people said they would only serve under me I should tell them that I was not prepared to do it, and see whether a definite attitude would make them budge. If it failed we should all, no doubt, have to boil our broth again. He said he would like to have a talk to Winston and me together in the afternoon.[10]

That talk was destined to be crucial, and it settled the succession. Meanwhile it is worth recording that Halifax had received messages through his Under-Secretary at the Foreign Office, R. A. Butler, both from Hugh Dalton and from Herbert Morrison that Labour would serve under him 'but not under the PM or in the company of Simon . . . Dalton said there was no other choice but you. Churchill must "stick to the war" and Anderson[11] had not been sufficiently "built up". He saw no objection in the Lords difficulty.'[12]

Dalton was right about the 'Lords difficulty'. It was true that no peer had been Prime Minister since the 3rd Marquess of Salisbury retired in 1902 and that Lord Curzon had been passed over in 1923, largely because he was a peer, in favour of Stanley Baldwin. But there was nothing to stop Parliament in the crisis of war from passing an *ad hominem* Act allowing Halifax to answer questions and speak, if not vote, in the House of Commons. There would have been no serious opposition to such a measure, if Halifax had wished to be Prime Minister. One can imagine how little Churchill would have worried about this 'obstacle', had the roles been reversed, he a peer and Halifax a commoner.

But Halifax did not want to be Prime Minister. The very thought of it made him feel sick. His biographer writes:

He had no illusions whatever as to his suitability for the role which a Prime Minister would have to play at this desperate moment in history. He was acutely conscious that his great gifts were in many ways the exact opposite of those required in the fighting leader of a forlorn cause and that he was lacking in the drive and ruthlessness which the situation demanded. He knew that Churchill was pre-eminent in both . . .[13]

At 4.30 that afternoon the three men met again at No. 10 Downing Street with the addition of David Margesson, the Conservative Chief Whip. Chamberlain said that he himself must resign and, in Halifax's words, 'it must be either Winston or me. He would serve under either.' Halifax in his diary goes on:

It would therefore be necessary to see the Labour people before they went to Bournemouth[14] and ask them whether they would, on principle, be prepared to join the Government (a) under the present Prime Minister or (b) under other leadership. David Margesson said that unity was essential and he thought it impossible to attain under the PM. He did not at the moment pronounce between Winston and myself, and my stomach ache continued.[15]

It is slightly surprising that Chamberlain still envisaged Labour ministers serving him under him, or at least still considered the question worth asking. Halifax in his account reiterated the arguments against himself which he had used that morning. 'Winston, with suitable expressions of regard and humility, said he could not but feel the force of what I had said, and the PM reluctantly, and Winston evidently with much less reluctance, finished by accepting my view.'[16] Churchill and Halifax had a cup of tea while Chamberlain fulfilled another engagement. At 6.15 Attlee and Arthur Greenwood, the Labour deputy leader, joined the group of four who had been discussing the crisis. 'They were a bit evasive', wrote Halifax, 'but eventually said that they did not think they could get their Party to serve under the PM.' It was finally left that they should consult their Executive and get an answer as to whether Labour would join a coalition under Chamberlain or under someone else. Thus ended a memorable day.

Churchill's account differs in some details from Halifax's and is more dramatic, dwelling on the long pause that followed Chamberlain's question 'whom should he advise the King to send for after his own resignation had been accepted?' Halifax says nothing about this, and Churchill's account need not be taken too literally, though it makes good reading.

I have had many important interviews in my public life and this was certainly the most important. Usually I talk a great deal but on this occasion I was silent . . . As I remained silent a very long pause ensued. It certainly seemed longer than the two minutes one observes at the commemoration of Armistice Day. Then at length Halifax spoke. He said that he felt that his position as a Peer out of the House of Commons would make it very difficult for him to discharge his duties as Prime Minister in a war like this . . . He spoke for some minutes in this sense and by the time he had finished it was clear that the duty would fall upon me—had in fact fallen upon me.[17]

Churchill was writing over six years after the event, whereas Halifax recorded his account on the actual day, 9 May. Churchill by a curious lapse of memory places the crucial meeting at 11 a.m. on 10 May. In general, therefore, Halifax's version must be regarded as more reliable, but Churchill may well be right about the pause, though it is inconceivable that the silence lasted for more than two minutes. The matter is not as trivial as it sounds, for there is at least some evidence that Churchill was at one stage ready to serve under Halifax. Lord Moran states in his diary for 7 December 1947, on the basis of a talk with Brendan Bracken, that Churchill had actually told this to Halifax himself.

Early on the evening of May 9th [clearly an error for 8 May] 1940 word reached Brendan that Winston had come to an agreement that he would act as his second-in-command if Halifax became Prime Minister . . . He went about London searching for Winston. At one o'clock in the morning he found him. 'You cannot agree to this,' Brendan spluttered, but Winston was obdurate; he said he could not go back on his word. 'Well,' Brendan persisted, 'at least you must promise you will not speak first when you get to No. 10. Promise?' At last Winston said he would promise.[18]

Bracken's biographer rightly points out that Moran's account was not contemporaneous but observes that it 'is corroborated by a note made by Lord Beaverbrook at the time, and also by several other versions probably deriving from Bracken'.[19] According to Anthony Eden, another source of advice to Churchill was Sir Kingsley Wood,[20] who lunched with him and Churchill on 9 May. In his diary Eden writes: 'Kingsley thought that W. should succeed, and urged that if asked he should make plain his willingness.' In retrospect, not in his diary, Eden wrote: 'I was surprised to find Kingsley Wood there giving a warning that Chamberlain would want Halifax to succeed him and would want Churchill to agree. Wood advised: "Don't agree and don't say anything".'[21] This may have been, as A. J. P. Taylor surmises, 'an unconscious transference of credit from Bracken to Wood'.[22]

It is reasonable to assume from these fragments of evidence that Churchill did express willingness to serve under Halifax—perhaps to Halifax himself, though there is apparently nothing in the papers of either to confirm it. One can also assume that Bracken—and possibly Wood—advised him to preserve silence at the crucial meeting and wait for Halifax to speak. Whether advised or not, he did exactly that.

On 10 May in the early hours of the morning, Hitler's forces invaded the Low Countries. The political situation in Britain was thrown again into the melting pot. Chamberlain's reaction was to postpone his resignation. Could a Prime Minister retire with propriety at the height of a major military crisis? The numerically small anti-Chamberlain Conservative group thought he could and should, but there was nothing they could do except utter indignant cries to each other. 'It's like trying to get a limpet off a corpse', Bracken furiously said to Macmillan. It seemed possible that Chamberlain might survive either because Labour agreed to serve under him or because their leaders refused to join a coalition of any sort under anyone. After all, he still had a big majority in the House even if the rebels persisted in their rebellion. But Kingsley Wood and others in the War Cabinet made it clear that he could not go on. There were three meetings of that body on 10 May, and during the third at 4.30 p.m. Chamberlain received official confirmation that Labour would join a coalition but not under him. The Labour leaders made no recommendation about who should be his successor, and there is some conflict of evidence as to whom they expected or preferred.

According to Amery, Attlee dining with Brendan Bracken on 7 May said that 'his people' would expect a coalition government to be headed by Halifax with Churchill as Minister of Defence. 'Bracken, entirely on his own responsibility, had insisted that Churchill could not and would not serve under Halifax . . . and had persuaded Attlee at any rate not to refuse to serve under Churchill if the occasion arose.' As a result, so Amery says, Churchill briefed by Bracken could afford to ignore the argument that he would have major difficulties with Labour.[23] There is some doubt whether this conversation ever occurred. Bracken was capable of inventing it to fortify Churchill,[24] and Attlee, according to his biographer, Kenneth Harris, had no recollection of ever dining alone with Bracken.[25] It is most unlikely that Attlee would have been dining with him of all people on the first night of the Norway debate. Harris states that Attlee preferred Churchill;[26] on the other hand, Dalton declares in his diary, Attlee 'agrees with my preference for Halifax over Churchill but we both think that either would be tolerable'.[27]

On receiving the news that he would not be acceptable to Labour, Chamberlain informed the War Cabinet that he would resign. He correctly did not tell them whom he would recommend as his successor. The appointment was by the King, who might or might not consult the outgoing Prime Minister and who was not bound to accept his advice. The King's diary records what followed.

I saw the Prime Minister after tea. He told me that Attlee had been to see him & had told him that the Labour Party would serve in the new administration of a new Prime Minister but not one with himself as PM. He then told me he wished to resign . . . I accepted his resignation, & told him how grossly unfairly I thought he had been treated & that I was terribly sorry that all this controversy had happened. We then had an informal talk over his successor. I, of course, suggested Halifax, but he told me that H. was not enthusiastic, as being in the Lords he could only act as a shadow or a ghost in the Commons where all the real work took place. I was disappointed over this statement, as I thought H. was the obvious man, & that his peerage could be placed in abeyance for the time being.

The King's official biography points out that the term 'abeyance' had nothing to do with the technical use of the word in peerage law. The King meant legislation to enable Halifax to speak in the Commons. Chamberlain must have made it clear that the peerage question was not the only issue, for the King goes on:

Then I knew that there was only one person I could send for to form a Government who had the confidence of the country, & that was Winston. I asked Chamberlain his advice & he told me Winston was the man to send for.

I said good-bye to Chamberlain & thanked him for all his help to me . . . I sent for Winston & asked him to form a Government.[28]

Churchill gives his own account of the interview which occurred at 6 p.m.

His Majesty received me most graciously and bade me sit down. He looked at me searchingly and quizzically for some moments and then said: 'I suppose you don't know why I have sent for you?' Adopting his mood I replied: 'Sir, I simply could not imagine why.' He laughed and said: 'I want to ask you to form a Government.' I said I would certainly do so.[29]

Churchill's appointment was by no means popular. He would probably not have commanded a majority among any of the political parties. He rose by default. Halifax could have had the job for the asking. Beaverbrook summed up the events pithily but erroneously: 'Chamberlain wanted Halifax. Labour wanted Halifax. Sinclair[30] wanted Halifax. The Lords wanted Halifax. The King wanted Halifax. And Halifax wanted Halifax.'[31] But the last of these brief sentences is simply wrong. Had it been true, Churchill would not have become Prime Minister—anyway not in May 1940.

Churchill at once formed his War Cabinet, and submitted the names to the King at 10 o'clock. It was a much slimmed down version of Chamberlain's, consisting of only five members. Anxious not to appear vindictive about Munich and well aware of his precarious Conservative support, he invited Chamberlain to be Lord President and Leader of the House, and Halifax to remain as Foreign Secretary. The other members were Attlee and Greenwood, Leader and Deputy Leader respectively of the Labour Party. Labour vetoed Chamberlain as Leader of the House, not surprisingly for Chamberlain had never concealed his contempt for them. He remained Lord President with a general responsibility for home affairs. A significant sign of the political situation was that he retained the leadership of the Conservative Party: Churchill did not press for it and would not have got it if he had. The Conservatives as a whole resented Churchill's appointment as Prime Minister, in which they had had no say and which they almost certainly would have blocked if they had been consulted. When Parliament met on 13 May Chamberlain, on entering, received vociferous applause from the Conservative benches. Churchill coming in a few minutes later was applauded by Labour and Liberals but only sporadically by the Conservatives. The announcement of his appointment as Prime Minister was received with dead silence in the House of Lords.

Churchill was very careful to be as conciliatory as possible towards the members of the late government. He made Sir John Simon Lord Chancellor, a post he had long coveted. He made Kingsley Wood Chancellor of the Exchequer—admittedly a last-minute convert to his cause but hitherto an arch Chamberlainite. Lord Reith as Minister for Information—'that Wuthering height' as Churchill called him—was removed to make way for Duff Cooper, the only member of the Cabinet who had resigned over Munich. Oliver Stanley, Secretary for War, resigned in a huff on being asked to change places with Eden at the Dominions Office. So Eden duly went to the War Office and a new Dominions Secretary was found in the person of Inskip (now Lord Caldecott), who relinquished the Lord Chancellorship in favour of Simon. Sir Samuel Hoare, Air Minister, was the only prominent member of Chamberlain's War Cabinet to be displaced, but he was almost at once appointed Ambassador in Madrid, an important post, given what then seemed the high likelihood of Spain intervening on the side of Hitler.

The most important innovation made by Churchill was to confer upon himself the office of Minister of Defence, as well as Prime Minister and Leader of the House of Commons. This was a new post unknown to the British constitution. Churchill did not seek any statutory authority for its creation and he was careful to avoid defining its scope and powers. But the mere fact of being called Minister of Defence gave him an authority in the conduct of war that no previous Prime Minister had possessed. The service ministers were kept out of the reduced War Cabinet and gradually dwindled into mere administrators. Churchill could deal directly with the Chiefs of Staff in somewhat the same way as an American President. This did not mean that he could override them or get his way when they were united against his proposals, but it did mean that he had a far greater say in the making of strategy than any previous holder of his office.

It was not only the majority of Conservatives who viewed Churchill's advent to power with apprehension. The civil servants and administrators were full of alarm. As Sir John (Jock) Colville, later to be one of Churchill's devotees, wrote, the thought of Churchill as Premier 'sent a cold chill down the spines of the staff at 10 Downing Street . . . Our feelings were widely shared in the Cabinet Offices, the Treasury and throughout Whitehall . . . Seldom can a Prime Minister have taken office with the Establishment . . . so dubious of the choice and so prepared to find its doubts justified.'[32]

That sector of opinion cannot have been reassured any more than the Conservative stalwarts were by the company kept at the outset by the new Prime Minister when forming his government. He depended much on the advice of Lord Beaverbrook, with whom he lunched and dined alone on 10 May and lunched again alone next day.[33] Despite the ups and downs of their relationship over thirty years, he could talk to Beaverbrook with an intimacy that he shared with no-one else in the political world—and it was a world that Beaverbrook in some respects knew better than Churchill himself. This intimacy was regarded with alarm by most members of the 'Establishment', which in general detested 'the Beaver'. The King himself strongly remonstrated when Churchill submitted the name of Beaverbrook for the newly created Ministry of Aircraft Production,[34] but Churchill insisted.

Nor were the fears of the 'respectable' allayed by Churchill's other choice of a confidant, Brendan Bracken, who acted as an informal Parliamentary private secretary. In June Churchill recommended him for a Privy Councillorship, overriding the King's objections, and a year later made him Minister of Information. Bracken was widely regarded as a conspiratorial adventurer. The *canard* was spread that he was Churchill's illegitimate son, which was totally untrue but, teasingly, not always denied by Bracken. In fact both Beaverbrook and Bracken were far less black than they were painted and they served Churchill well. In any case he did not rely only on their advice. He consulted the Chief Whip, David Margesson. Churchill did not worry that Margesson had done everything he could to block his plans and his promotion during and after Munich. 'Politicians', as Dryden observed, 'neither love nor hate', and the Chief Whip had no difficulty in serving a new master as efficiently as he had the old; the new master fully recognized the value of his expertise.

The major posts and nearly all the lesser offices were filled by the end of 14 May. Churchill was now in power and in control. But he knew that he was there on sufferance and by default, and he knew that the House of Commons, which he had never fully mastered, could do to him what it had done to Chamberlain. He had to succeed; nothing succeeds like success just as nothing fails like failure, and he was well aware of the ruthlessness with which the Conservative Party could get rid of a liability. 'The Tories don't trust Winston', wrote that supreme Tory *éminence grise*, Lord Davidson, to Baldwin on 11 May: '. . . After the first clash of war is over it may well be that a sounder Government will emerge.'[35] Colville noted in his diary: 'There seems to be some inclination to believe that Winston will be a complete failure and that Neville will return.'[36] Chamberlain himself appears to have believed for a time in such a possibility. Ex-Prime Ministers are liable to that illusion. Hence Chamberlain's readiness to retain the party leadership, till cancer removed him from active political life late in September, and Churchill succeeded him on 9 October.

By then the political scene was very different, but in May Churchill was still regarded with much misgiving. Davidson wrote: 'his appointments are heavily criticised in private . . . the crooks are on top, as they were in the last war—we must keep our powder dry!'[37] Halifax said to a friend, 'He's an odd creature', and told Rab Butler that he deplored some of his new colleagues. When Butler wondered why Halifax had not himself accepted the premiership he curtly replied: 'You know my reasons, it's no use discussing that—but the gangsters will shortly be in complete control.'[38]

These uncomplimentary remarks are not printed for endorsement by reader or writer. Churchill and his entourage were not crooks or gangsters any more than were Lloyd George and his friends in 1916, who were obviously in mind. The quotations are there to remind us of the difficulties under which the greatest British Prime Minister of the twentieth century laboured when he first took office. One should not forget his assets: a small but devoted group of supporters; galvanic energy; an unrivalled power of oratory when words really mattered; a simple British patriotism; a real sense of destiny, that he was the chosen man to save the nation; above all an extraordinary optimism and confidence against all the odds. Churchill became Prime Minister by default against the wishes of his own party and with only tepid acquiescence by the others. This did not prevent him from exploiting the powers of his office with masterly skill and guiding his country, in conjunction with more powerful allies, to victory over one of the most evil regimes that has ever existed.

16

Churchill, Japan, and British Security in the Pacific 1904–1942

ROBERT O'NEILL

THE challenge that Japan offered to Imperial Russia in 1904 was watched with keen and sympathetic interest by two observers whose paths were destined to cross. In Linz an der Donau the 14-year-old Adolf Hitler, already fascinated by the 'summer lightning' of the South African War, weighed into local discussion groups in support of the Japanese who showed so clearly by their performance in the field and at sea that they were a coming world power. Hitler was imbued with hatred of the Slavs and rejoiced when new champions, who had absorbed Aryan ideas and technology, emerged in the East to consign the inferior Slavic race to what he saw as their deserved place of ignominy and humiliation.[1] When he came to office Hitler continued to be guided by his early admiration for the Japanese and ultimately they became his allies in war.

In London the 19-year-old Member for Oldham also assiduously followed day-to-day developments in the Russo-Japanese War. For Winston Churchill this conflict was a watershed: looking back on the whole pre-First World War period when he was writing *The World Crisis*, he characterized Russia's defeat as a surprise to all the powers of Europe except one, the victor's ally, Britain. To Japan's defeat of Russia Churchill credited pronounced increases in Germany's self-assertion and France's anxieties regarding isolation and threatening danger. The result, he continued, was the Anglo-French *Entente*, by which Britain's 'ancient enemy [France] sought her friendship'. The Royal Navy had to face the rising German threat. But Churchill concluded with satisfaction that Britain at least could bring home its battleships from the China station, and be secure in the knowledge that Japanese naval power would protect British interests in the Pacific.[2]

Churchill had many other strategic issues to absorb his attention in the years before the outbreak of the First World War. Apart from his succinct appreciation of the worth of the alliance with Japan as revealed in his own retrospective writing of the period, Japan and events in the Far East in the years 1905-14 played little part in his thinking and virtually none in his contemporary speaking and writing. His interests were bound up in Europe. Although he had opportunities for travel, and had spent his early twenties in Egypt and India, he chose to focus on the Continent of Europe rather than the Far East. His fascination with Germany and the direct threat that its policies posed to Britain itself displaced wider concerns he might otherwise have had for the security of the Empire. But as soon as the First World War broke out, he hoped to employ the strength that Japan had now developed and sought to use it both to contain the Turks and to help the ailing Russians.

In the first week of hostilities Churchill was appalled by Sir Edward Grey's reluctance to accede to the Japanese proposal that they should become full belligerents, on the understanding that Japan should be free to take as many of the German territories in the Pacific as it could. He minuted to the Foreign Secretary as soon as he had seen the latter's cable to the Japanese government:

. . . I must say I think you are being chilling indeed to these people. I can't see any half way house myself between having them in and keeping them out. If they are to come in, they may as well be welcomed as comrades. This telegram is almost hostile. I am afraid I do not understand what is in yr mind on this aspect—tho' I followed it so clearly until today. . . .

This telegram gives me a shiver. We are all in this together & I only wish to give the fullest effect & support to your main policy. But I am altogether perplexed by the line opened up by these Japanese interchanges.

You may easily give mortal offence—wh will not be forgotten—we are not safe yet—by a long chalk. The storm has yet to burst . . .[3]

Churchill achieved his aim of forcing Grey to send a more conciliatory telegram to Tokyo, although not to the extent of promising the Japanese everything under the German flag in the Pacific. Stepping more fully into the domain of foreign policy, the First Lord of the Admiralty followed up with a much warmer message of his own to the Japanese Minister of Marine, Admiral Rokuro Yashiro. His personal sentiments were even more permissive to the Japanese than he told them. In the Pacific he could be generous at the expense of others. Reportedly in private conversation, Churchill said that he was ready to offer the Japanese China if they asked for any inducement to enter the war.[4] Even had Churchill been aware of the extreme alarm Japan's seizure of German New Guinea would have caused in Australia and New Zealand, it is most unlikely that he would have changed his belief in the overriding importance of giving the Japanese a substantial *quid pro quo*.

In late August 1914, already scheming to take the Dardanelles, Churchill sought a Japanese battle squadron for the Eastern Mediterranean. Failing in this attempt to exploit the strength of Britain's Pacific ally nearer to home, Churchill then suggested that the Japanese be asked to consent to a contingent of 50,000 Russian soldiers being sent via Port Arthur by sea to take Gallipoli.[5]

Churchill's departure from the Admiralty and his subsequent preoccupations at the front and at the Ministry of Munitions removed him from contact with distant theatres. It was not until 1919, when he was Secretary of State for War, that Japan reappears in his writings and speeches. The prime occasion was the abortive Allied attempt through Siberia to topple the Bolsheviks. Once again Japan figured as an important ally in a cause that Churchill felt to be of the utmost importance. His writings and speeches over the following three years demonstrate his continuing view of Japan as an asset to Britain in containing the evil influence of Communism, notwithstanding the dwindling away of support for the anti-Bolsheviks among his colleagues.[6]

Yet he also was aware that Japan had the strength to harm the British Empire. As Colonial Secretary he warned the assembled Imperial Conference on 4 July 1921 that Japan was 'the danger to be guarded against'. Churchill used the occasion of a debate on the possible renewal of the Anglo-Japanese Alliance to urge its abandonment for a British-United States treaty. Japan, in his view, was the only real danger to British interests in the Pacific: 'Getting Japan to protect you against Japan is like drinking salt water to slake thirst.'[7]

For other reasons, including American pressure, the Anglo-Japanese Alliance was set aside in December at the Washington Naval Conference. The non-binding Four Power Pact linking Britain, France, Japan, and the United States was no real compensation, either to Britain or to Japan. The latter, in fact, deeply resented the loss of status as Britain's preferred partner in the Pacific, the inferior position forced on her by the naval ratios established by the Five Power Treaty, and the limitations placed on her ambitions in China by the Nine Power Treaty.

Churchill's loss of his seat at the November 1922 general election severed his official connection with the world of foreign politics for two years. His return to the Conservative Party and appointment as Chancellor of the Exchequer under Stanley Baldwin in 1924 gave him a further five years in a high office that had direct impact on Britain's defence and foreign policy stances. By virtue of his control over the flow of the nation's resources, he had ample opportunity to make a deep impact on Britain's longer-term defence strength. During these years he chose to return to his more benign evaluation of Japan.

Opposing the Admiralty's case for a substantial increase in funds in his first few weeks in office, Churchill dismissed the notion of a Japanese threat to Imperial interests:

A war with Japan! But why should there be a war with Japan? I do not believe there is the slightest chance of it in our lifetime . . . Japan is at the other end of the world. She cannot menace our vital security in any way . . . The only war it would be worth our while to fight would be to prevent an invasion of Australia, and that I am certain will never happen in any period, even the most remote, which we or our children need foresee. I am therefore convinced that war with Japan is not a reasonable possibility any reasonable Government need take into account.[8]

In taking this line Churchill was aiming at the heart of the Admiralty's rationale for its modernization plans. Given the disarmed state of Germany, the Washington Naval Treaty, and the absence of serious friction in the Mediterranean, there was not much of a case to be made for substantial naval procurement in the European theatre. But given the Baldwin government's espousal of the concept of the Singapore base as the foundation of British security in the Pacific, the Admiralty had a new case for new ships, submarines, and extensive base facilities.

Churchill, as Chancellor of a straightened Exchequer, took it as his role to defend the nation's resources by demolishing arguments to which he might well, had he held a defence portfolio, have given credence. The Singapore base and the fleet, Britain's response to the dangers of Japanese aggression emphasized by Lord Jellicoe in reporting on his 1919 mission to the Pacific dominions, had been an object of controversy for three years before Churchill brought it under attack. The proposal, adopted by the Lloyd George government on 16 June 1921, had already been dropped by the MacDonald government in March 1924 as an unnecessary expense. The Labour government preferred to place its faith in stronger support for international co-operation through the League of Nations.[9]

Churchill's determined opposition to the project forced Baldwin to set up a Cabinet subcommittee under Curzon in early 1925 to consider the whole concept. Churchill was not successful in killing the idea, but his persistent and forceful criticism compelled the Admiralty to accept a one-third reduction in the proposed level of expenditure on the base. Churchill, in criticizing the Admiralty's case, expressed astonishment that 26-year-old Japanese warships could cause concern to the Royal Navy (although the Japanese had many of much more recent origin, and indeed were continuing a substantial naval construction pro-gramme). He declared that an expansion such as the navy desired would lead to an arms race in the Pacific, which the Japanese might well win, and called for the deferral of the stationing of a fleet at Singapore by ten years.

After Baldwin's fall, the MacDonald government reduced the rate of construction of the base in 1930. It was not until the collapse of the Disarmament Conference in 1933 that work was accelerated again. The Japanese, having initiated hostilities in Manchuria in 1931, were by now sliding fast down the road to rule by the military and the exacer-bation of serious tensions in relations with other Pacific powers that was to lead to war. Still Churchill chose to dismiss the idea of a Japanese threat to British interests. Speaking to the Anti-Socialist and Anti-Communist Union on 17 February 1933 he touched on the deteri-orating situation in China:

I must say something to you which is very unfashionable. I am going to say one word of sympathy for Japan . . . I hope we should try in England to understand a little the position of Japan, an ancient state with the highest sense of national honour and patriotism, and with a teeming population and a remarkable energy. On the one side they see the dark menace of Soviet Russia. On the other the chaos of China, four or five provinces of which are actually now being tortured under Communist rule.[10]

Churchill's natural sympathy for the Japanese as the guardians of East Asia against Communism did not survive long as the army gathered more and more political power. Following the breakdown of the London Naval Conference in January 1936, he wrote to his wife expressing serious concern about the growth of Japanese armaments and the extent of Japan's military ambitions in China. He doubted that the Baldwin government would take effective action against the twin menace of a Nazi Germany and a militaristic Japan.[11] He seemed, how-ever, to have no regrets over his own failure to perceive the speed with which the structure of Japanese politics and the wider international sit-uation in the Far East could be transformed. Nor did he show much realization of the predicament Britain and the Empire as a whole would face in trying to meet threats in Europe and the Pacific at the same time.

Apart from the Royal Navy, the chief losers as a result of Churchill's opposition to expenditure on the Singapore base were Australia and New Zealand. Despite the useful protection that the Imperial Japanese Navy had afforded Australia during the First World War through escorting troop convoys across the Indian Ocean and patrolling the east coast of Australia itself in the absence of the Royal Australian Navy, Australians and New Zealanders had long been apprehensive regarding the 'Yellow Peril' from the north.

Indeed, both the decision of the Balfour government in 1904 to withdraw most of the Royal Navy from the Pacific and the demise of Germany as a power in the Pacific as soon as hostilities had opened raised acute concerns in Australia that after the war there would be nothing but Japanese power to fill this vacuum. By 1918 many Australians believed that Japan would soon dominate the central and southern Pacific, virtually to Australia's northern shores. Japanese discontent with Australia's racially based immigration policies was well known, and this made Prime Minister William Hughes all the more determined to uphold them at Versailles.

Australian security specialists, civil and military, feared that the Japanese would be unable to resist the temptation to take a virtually defenceless and largely empty continent into their own orbit. The nature of Australian society would be then transformed from the tolerant, well recompensed European system that had been produced from the foundations up during the nineteenth century, to being a repressed, poor minority within a larger Japanese polity. The mandates over former German territories secured by Hughes at Versailles in 1919 did much to placate fears that the Japanese sphere of influence would stretch to Australia's shores, but there remained absent a countervailing naval presence to maintain a balance against Japanese power.

By the time of the 1921 Imperial Conference, Hughes believed that war with Japan was inevitable in the longer term.[12] He fought to extend the Anglo-Japanese Alliance as a means of gaining time for the development of countervailing naval and military power in the Pacific, and he was disappointed by the Four Power Treaty which succeeded it. The building of the Singapore base and the stationing of a substantial British fleet there was not the best form of security that Australia could have, but as Britain was unwilling to build the base in Australia itself, the Singapore concept had to suffice. As a second best means of defence, therefore, Australia (and New Zealand) sought all the more keenly to keep the British government up to the mark in the pace of construction.

The cancellation of the project by the MacDonald government in 1924 met with strong criticism from Australia and New Zealand, where many regarded Britain's action not only as rank ingratitude for the sacrifices borne by both dominions during the First World War but, worse, as a betrayal of one part of the British peoples by another. The Baldwin government's decision to resume construction went some way towards satisfying the Antipodeans, but they continued to be frustrated by Churchill's dogged and successful attempts to reduce the level of expenditure.

Controversy over the Singapore base extended well beyond the question of its cost. Once built, how was this expensive and vulnerable fixed asset to be defended in the face of strong Japanese naval and air attacks? The Royal Air Force naturally argued that aircraft were essential for defence at adequate range, both to keep a Japanese fleet at bay and to deter an overland attack via the Malay Peninsula. The Royal Navy argued for coastal artillery. There was, of course, a case for both but Churchill's stringency made such apparent redundancy impossible. Initially the Committee of Imperial Defence settled for coastal batteries (facing seawards and leaving the land approach from the north uncovered), and then in 1932 adopted a combination of guns, aircraft, and ships. Too little of any of these means was provided to make a credible protection.

Critics of the various defensive schemes abounded in Australia, where the overland approach, which the Japanese were indeed to use in 1941, was already a topic of discussion among military writers and planners. There were also many who pointed to the problems which Britain would face in sending a fleet to Singapore when under pressure in Europe. These insights did Australia and New Zealand little good in practical terms because Antipodean governments spent so little on defence until the mid-1930s. Even in naval terms, where Australia and New Zealand were weakest in terms of being able to deter Japanese aggression, per capita levels of expenditure in 1925 were two-thirds and one-quarter of the British figure respectively.[13]

The two episodes for which most Antipodeans knew Churchill best in military terms before the Second World War were the Dardanelles disaster and the slowing of the rate of construction of the Singapore base. These hardly made him a national hero in either country. Australians and New Zealanders also knew him, of course, for his economic policies, particularly his return to the Gold Standard. In view of the severity and length of the economic depression, there were many Antipodeans who were inclined to give Churchill more than his fair share of the blame for their misfortunes in the 1930s. The redeeming qualities that were evident in the context of British politics were far less obvious in the Antipodes.

There is very little direct evidence as to what Churchill thought of Australia, New Zealand, and Antipodeans generally. He mentioned them rarely in his speeches and writings and then only briefly. Australian and New Zealand servicemen had impressed him favourably at the Dardanelles and on the Western Front, and he had expressed the view that if Japan threatened Australia, however unlikely that contingency seemed to him, Britain should come to that Dominion's defence. But there was simply not enough knowledge in his head of what the Pacific dominions thought and offered for them to achieve even a small fraction of the attention that he paid to the state of affairs in Europe and to Anglo-American relations. One wonders how much the Antipodeans ever did to aid their own cause; did they consider inviting Churchill to visit during the inter-war years, or try to arouse his interest in other ways? If his only experience of contact with Australians had been to feel the weight of their censure of his Dardanelles policy or their protests against his financial stringency, it would hardly have been surprising had he regarded them as tiresome people with whom contact should be kept at a minimum. The fact that Churchill, for all his imperial sympathies, never visited Australia or New Zealand says a great deal.

Wherever the fault lies, there was little by way of rapport between Churchill and the Pacific dominions. Therefore it is not difficult to see how he justified to himself the acceptance of the risks to the security of Australia and New Zealand inherent in his Singapore policy. The central calculus of European security was vastly more important to Churchill, and his view towards Japan was shaped by the positive role he hoped it might continue to play initially as an informal ally in the 1920s and then in the 1930s as an ideological foe of Communism.

It was thus far from easy for Australia and New Zealand to accord with Churchillian strategy in the opening phase of the Second World War. There had also been important differences between Churchill and Australia's Prime Minister, R. G. Menzies, on the policy of appeasement in 1938 and 1939, which further complicated relations between them. But despite the dangers posed by Japan, the Australian government chose both to enter the war with Britain on 3 September and to send most of its forces to Europe and the Middle East. Menzies took the view that if Britain was at war then so was Australia. Despite the possibility of a Japanese drive southwards across the Pacific, Menzies accepted that the best way to security for Australia lay in first overcoming the threat presented to Britain. Churchill could not have been displeased with Menzies' ready response in the first six months of the war, although like most members of the Chamberlain government he probably wished that Australia had agreed to send more than a single division of its army to the Middle East in early 1940.

Once Churchill had taken over the leadership of the government in May 1940, Menzies became increasingly concerned that Australia's interests might be given very short shrift. Menzies was particularly concerned to obtain a firmer guarantee from Churchill that in the event of a Japanese attack Australia would be supported by a strong British naval force based on Singapore. Menzies' concern was amplified by Churchill's uses of an Australian cruiser in the abortive attack on Dakar in September 1940 without any discussion with the Australian government. An angry exchange between the two Prime Ministers ensued. It became increasingly clear to the Australian government that the only way to obtain satisfaction was to send Menzies to London to press Churchill directly.

When Menzies arrived on 20 February 1941 he made a strong and favourable impression on the press and in the nation at large. At a time of trouble and continuing tactical defeat, Menzies' cheer, ebullience, sharp wit, and physical bulk seemed very reassuring, and his impact was stronger than might have been expected of a dominion leader. But his relations with Churchill were of a less exciting and more hard-headed nature. It is clear from Menzies' diary entries, particularly those dealing with his weekends at Chequers when he had opportunities for extended discussion with his host, that substantial differences remained between them, particularly over Churchill's dominant style of leadership and his determination to pursue outright victory whatever the cost.

Virtually nothing remains to convey Churchill's impression of his guest. The fact that he made only the briefest of factual references to Menzies in his memoirs and official papers suggests that Churchill rarely gave the Australian Prime Minister a second thought. We know from Colville's memoirs that Churchill found Menzies to be an agreeable table companion on occasion.[14] Churchill as a politician must have had respect for Menzies' undoubted gifts in this quarter. But they were very different types of men in their basic attitudes towards war and diplomacy. The realities of power meant that Churchill had far less cause to let his mind dwell on Menzies than vice versa. Menzies lacked any countervailing personal connection to offset these realities of power; indeed, there were probably elements in Menzies' personality that had a negative effect on his tired and troubled host at Chequers.

Menzies soon found it hard to make progress on his two basic objectives: to compel Churchill to give the dominion leaders a much bigger voice in the determination of imperial policy; and to persuade the British government to devote a much larger share of its resources in naval, air, and military terms to the defence of the Far East. Churchill allowed Menzies to speak his mind in the War Cabinet and at other meetings, but gave little ground and continued to fob him off with vague and virtually meaningless promises over Singapore.

In the process of trying to win Churchill over, Menzies in turn was drawn by Churchill into the disastrous British commitment to Greece, in which some 2,800 Australians were lost on the mainland and a further 3,900 on Crete. New Zealand losses were of a similar magnitude. Menzies had given assent to Australia's participation in the campaign on the mistaken assumption that General Blamey, who was in overall command of the three Australian divisions then in the Middle East, agreed that the operation had a reasonable chance of success. This was what was implied to him by British authorities in London. Menzies' concerns over Churchill's capacities to direct the overall war strategy were further reinforced. Moreover, the part Menzies appeared to the Australian public and his ministerial colleagues in Canberra to have played in the débâcle caused him such serious embarrassment at home that he lost his grip on power.

Menzies' fall from office on 28 August 1941 further complicated relations between London and Canberra. He was succeeded for five weeks by his deputy, Arthur Fadden. Then the Conservative, imperialist Churchill had to face all the problems and sensitivities of working with a nationalistically inclined Australian Labor Party Government under the leadership of John Curtin. In his memoirs Churchill commented on the increased difficulty of working with each of these new partners.[15] While the Curtin government was determined to continue the fight, rather than to seek a negotiated settlement, its inclinations were much less imperially oriented than those of its two predecessors.

One immediate bone of contention was the way the three Australian infantry divisions in the Middle East had become separated. Fadden and then Curtin applied strong pressure for the Australian division which was immured in Tobruk to be relieved for necessary rest and to be reunited with the other two. Churchill resisted stoutly, but not to the point at which he would effectively have denied sovereignty to the Australian government. He had to recognize, as he admitted to Oliver Lyttelton, British Minister of State in Cairo, that shortage of British troops for the Middle East was 'leading the world and Australia to suppose that we are fighting our battles with Dominions troops only'.[16] Clearly, Anglo-Australian relations were heading into greater difficulties, just at a time when huge strains were about to be added by the materialization of the Japanese threat, which Churchill had chosen to discount for so long and to such powerful effect.

For most of 1941 Churchill had been preoccupied with finding ways to hold a firm position in the Middle East. Hitler's offensives into the Balkans and the Soviet Union in spring and summer and the countervailing improvement of relations with the still non-belligerent United States in the second half of the year had focused his thinking even more intently on the European theatre. The magnitude of what was at stake and the strength of the German and Italian challenges during this period compelled him to give Europe virtually the whole of his attention. His first priority was to preserve a strong forward position from which a series of Allied offensives against the European Axis could be launched once the United States was fully in the war. It was not until late 1941 that Churchill decided to send a naval force to Singapore to deter the Japanese from attacking, should they decide to exploit Britain's problems elsewhere.

Churchill's tardiness in reinforcing the Far East was less a product of his old attitudes towards Japan than of the resources crisis that he faced. But as late as mid-1939, before he had returned to any official position that might prevent him from speaking his mind fully, he opposed dividing the fleet between Europe and the Far East. Rather, he urged, in the event of hostilities with Japan, Britain would have to cut its losses in the Pacific and concentrate on defeating Germany. A settlement could then be reached with Japan after the war.[17] It was not surprising, therefore, that Churchill cut back an Admiralty plan to send a force of seven battleships and two or three aircraft carriers to Singapore in late 1941. All that went were one battleship and one battlecruiser: the one aircraft carrier that Churchill was willing to send was damaged on a training cruise and the tiny fleet had to sail without its own air-power. On 10 December, three days after the Japanese attack on Pearl Harbor, the much vaunted British Fleet that succeeding British governments of the inter-war years had promised would secure the Dominions had shared the fate of the US Pacific Fleet.

On re-reading the terse and dramatic interchange of cables that ensued between Curtin and Churchill in December 1941 and January 1942, one must be struck by Churchill's stubborn refusal to acknowledge the serious weaknesses of defences at Singapore and the likely fate of the fortress (and the Australian division and three air squadrons there). Curtin raised concerns that had been expressed by his predecessors over many years. But it is scarcely to Australia's credit that it had preferred to take British reassurances at face value and to do so little of its own volition to exploit the defensive worth of the long approaches to its own shores. Australian recriminations over the British government's tardiness in recognizing the seriousness of the Japanese threat would have carried greater weight had Australian governments placed a little more faith in the warnings of their military advisers.

By the middle of February 1942 Singapore had fallen, and the Japanese army, driving deeply into Burma, was already across the Salween. The Japanese navy was free to range without fear of challenge over the whole of the western and central sectors of the Pacific. Of the Australian army's four combat divisions, one had been captured at Singapore and the other three were either in the Middle East or moving in convoy across the Indian Ocean. The grave consequences of these Allied defeats for Australia and New Zealand were readily grasped by Churchill. In his war memoirs he wrote of this time:

In spite of the new burdens which fell upon us there was no addition to our dangers at home. Australia and New Zealand, on the other hand, felt suddenly plunged into the forefront of the battle. They saw themselves exposed to the possibility of direct invasion. No longer did the war mean sending aid across the oceans to the Mother Country in her distress and peril. The new foe could strike straight at Australian homes. The enormous coastlines of their continent could never be defended. All their great cities were on the seaboard. Their only four well-trained divisions of volunteers, the New Zealand Division, and all their best officers, were far away across the oceans. The naval command of the Pacific had passed in a flash and for an indefinite period to Japan. Australasian air-power hardly existed. Can we wonder that deep alarm swept Australia or that the thoughts of their Cabinet were centred on their own affairs?[18]

What Churchill did not go on to say, as he might have, is that this predicament was not a total surprise to well-informed Australians. Experts had been writing about this kind of contingency for years. Where there was surprise was over the totality of the Japanese naval triumph: nobody had expected that the United States Pacific Fleet would be crippled by the opening Japanese blow.

The ignominious end of the whole Singapore strategy formed a watershed in Australian strategic policy. For far too long Australians had placed value in the Imperial defence connection. The events of December 1941 had proven for once and for all the bankruptcy of the notion that Australia could achieve security by contributing the greater part of her forces in the form of infantrymen to the Imperial cause elsewhere while relying on British naval power to protect the approaches to Australia itself. Unable herself to become a major naval power, Australia had to seek another protector. Curtin named Australia's hoped-for saviour in a signed article in the Melbourne *Herald* on 27 December 1941. He wrote:

We refuse to accept the dictum that the Pacific struggle must be treated as a subordinate segment of the general conflict. By that it is not meant that any one of the other theatres of war is of less importance than the Pacific, but that Australia asks for a concerted plan evoking the greatest strength at the Democracies' disposal, determined upon hurling Japan back.

The Australian Government therefore regards the Pacific struggle as primarily one in which the United States and Australia must have the fullest say in the direction of the Democracies' fighting plan.

Without any inhibitions of any kind, I make it quite clear that Australia looks to America, free of any pangs as to our traditional links with the United Kingdom.

We know the problems that the United Kingdom faces . . . But we know too that Australia can go, and Britain can still hold on.

We are determined that Australia shall not go, and we shall exert all our energies towards the shaping of a plan, with the United States as its keystone, which will give to our country some confidence of being able to hold out until the tide of battle swings against the enemy.[19]

Churchill was appalled by Curtin's statement. On the basis of no quoted evidence, and, one suspects, only that of his own wishful thinking, he commented in his memoirs: 'This produced the worst impression both in high American circles and in Canada. I am sure that these outpourings of anxiety, however understandable, did not represent Australian feeling.'[20] Churchill was never more wrong than in that last statement. I was only five when Curtin made his statement, but all the memories I have of the war, its subsequent course, and its aftermath confirm my belief that the fall of Singapore was the final straw for Australians generally as far as reliance on partnership with Britain for security was concerned. From them on, it was the United States or nothing.

The loss of Singapore caused a profound shock to public and political opinion in many parts of the world. British public confidence in the capabilities of the government, the Royal Navy, and the Prime Minister himself was severely shaken. The British people perceived that if the war was to have a successful outcome it would have to be fought hard on several continents and oceans over a long period. President Roosevelt worried deeply at the extent to which the Japanese might be able to exploit their victory in south-east Asia. He feared even that the entire British position in India might be overthrown in a tide of external pressure and internal commotion. To Australians, coming after the Dardanelles tragedy with which Churchill was clearly identified in public thinking, the Singapore débâcle drove home the thought that no reliance could be placed in the future on British power and guarantees, despite the most fervent of promises that eloquent British Prime Ministers might make.

Churchill consoled himself that the loss of Singapore, while a grievous blow, was not sufficient to cancel out the strategic gains of having the United States as a full comrade in arms. The outcome of the Battle of Midway in mid-1942 showed that he was essentially correct in this view. None the less, what a huge set-back for the Allies the surrender of Singapore was: so much manpower, scarce equipment, shipping, and aircraft lost; such a huge capital investment in base facilities and fortifications brought to nought; such a tremendous blow to Allied morale and status in the Far East.

The question naturally arises as to how far Churchill himself was responsible for these losses. Taking the twenty-one months for which he was Prime Minister before the fall of Singapore it is clear that the pressures of Nazi Germany were so acute that, with the best will in the world, Churchill could have done little more to make the great base in the Far East impregnable against the type of force which the Japanese had developed to throw against it. But on looking further back in time and enquiring as to why the Singapore base was so weak when the Chamberlain government began to accelerate the pace of construction, one cannot escape the conclusion that Churchill's determined slashing of naval expenditure in the 1920s was very much at the root of the problem. Had Churchill been a consistent reformer of Britain's structure of global dependencies, cutting off those which posed a drain on resources rather than trying to cling to the full extent of empire, and had his Cabinet colleagues and their successors been better able to utilize the fiscal savings he made for the rebuilding of Britain's economic strength, the country would have been in a less vulnerable position when Hitler presented his challenge. Churchill's own reputation as a statesman and strategist would have been all the greater.

But this was not to be: instead the Far East revealed the basic inconsistencies in Churchill's position as an advocate of the Empire who was at the same time trying to put the country's finances into order. To those inconsistencies much of the Japanese victory of early 1942 is due.

Fortunately, the strategic insights of Churchill's arch-opponent Adolf Hitler were more seriously defective. He was able to achieve an alliance with the Japanese but then did remarkably little to exploit its latent strengths. There was no co-ordination of thrusts before the fall of Singapore and a striking failure to work together between the fall of Singapore and the surrender of the Germans at Stalingrad. The former schoolboy of Linz had little feeling for the power of his heroes in the Russo-Japanese war and the wars in which it could have been used to help him in his drive into the Soviet central and southern heartland. Churchill, with his wider view of the world, saw that allies were essential to Britain's survival, and concerted planning as soon as the Americans were willing to do so. The shock of defeat at Singapore was profound. By then, however, Churchill knew that through the alliance with the United States the foundations for victory had been well laid. Hitler, curiously, had made his own task impossible by gratuitously declaring war on the United States. The testing ground of the Far East not only revealed Churchill's limitations but also, and more to the point, demonstrated his strategic ascendancy over Hitler. Britain's ally in the Pacific was a wonderfully effective partner: Germany's fought an entirely separate war.

17

Wheel Within a Wheel: Churchill, Roosevelt, and the Special Relationship

WARREN F. KIMBALL

'THE war has breathed new life into the "special relationship" between the United States and Britain.'[1] That has the ring, though not the vigour, of a statement by Winston Churchill in 1940 or 1941. In fact, it was the opening paragraph of a *New York Times* analysis, written in late January 1991, about one side-effect of the Persian Gulf War. It illustrates the tenacity of the idea, and perhaps the reality, of the Special Relationship.

Over forty-five years after the end of the Second World War, American images of its closest wartime ally remain dominated by the Battle of Britain, the desert war, and Winston Churchill—all of which bombard American television audiences almost weekly in one documentary or another, usually in living black-and-white. Added to that is a constant stream of motion pictures and television docu-dramas set in wartime Britain. Nor is that all. Publishers, keenly aware that readers have not tired of the Second World War, remain committed to putting Winston Churchill, snarling at a swastika, on the cover of almost anything vaguely related to the war—irrespective of subject.

At the root of that hypnotic spell is a perception of the conflict as an unambiguous, just war against evident evil. That patriotic, idealized, romanticized image makes American students and the general public recoil, even half a century later, from evidence of selfish American war aims or even Anglo-American discord or competition for wartime glory and post-war advantage. An attack on the image of the Second World War as 'The Good War' brings immediate outrage, and books that depict tensions between British and American leaders get front page treatment, as if they were truly newsworthy.[2]

But even the Second World War pales next to what one observer called 'the Churchill Cult', perpetuated by an informal public relations machine that should be the envy of most governments. The International Churchill Society (which counts as members a number of American political leaders), Churchill dinners (black tie, of course), and an endless stream of quotations (columnist William Safire was found to have a reference to Churchill in one-fourth of his published articles): these are but part of the industry. Perhaps only the Temperance Union has failed to find a Churchill aphorism to fit the occasion. A statue of Winston and Clementine Churchill—'married love' is the title—gazes out over the Missouri River as it wends it way through the heart of Kansas City, a positioning that would surely have prompted a puckish remark punctuated by a stab of that ubiquitous cigar.[3] The post-war generation of American politicians has regularly exploited the public's veneration for the Churchill legend. His 1946 'Iron Curtain' speech became an unchallenged scripture that American leaders cited to justify their policies. Even historians took to blaming or praising Churchill for leading the United States into the Cold War.[4] Presidents from Kennedy to Bush have quoted him regularly, most often when their own actions forced them to look for some kind of historical imprimatur. Vice-President Dan Quayle, eager in 1990 to defend the 'Star Wars' missile defence system, expressed public elation at his discovery of a biography of Churchill, for it finally alerted him to the dangers of another Munich. Even one of those convicted in the Watergate affair during the Nixon years adopted as his public motto a Churchill admonition not to give way 'in things great or small, large or petty'.[5]

Part and parcel of that heroic depiction is the link between the two national leaders—Churchill, and President Franklin D. Roosevelt. Studies of the two men evoke strong images of a special personal partnership operating within the already special Anglo-American relationship. Titles of various reviews of books about Churchill and Roosevelt catch the tone—'The Big Two', 'The World Was Their Oyster', 'Tracing a Friendship that Helped Shape an Age', 'The Supreme Partnership', 'Allied Spirits', 'As One Titan to Another', 'Serenely in Agreement'.[6] One letter writer to the *New York Times*, upset at what he saw as over-emphasis by historians on friction between Churchill and Roosevelt, argued that 'what matters is that the two leaders continued to work together and to keep their countries working together'—a characterization that could, and perhaps should, apply to Stalin's relations with either Churchill or Roosevelt, since maintaining that relationship was a much more difficult task. In that same letter to the editor, the author mentioned having worked in the Lend-Lease programme and pointed out that the organization had tried to protect the interests of the United States, just as Churchill pursued British interests.[7] There was no mention of the obvious—that unless those interpretations of national interests coincided perfectly, disagreement and friction were inevitable.

Despite a growing array of solid analytical studies assessing and reassessing the Anglo-American relationship, the Churchill–Roosevelt association continues to appear as variations on a simple theme—as the late Joseph Lash labelled it: 'The Partnership that Saved the West'.[8] It was not an 'alliance declining' at war's end, argued one director of the Franklin D. Roosevelt Library, it was 'alliance victorious'. The conventional image is clear and forceful. Whatever the problems caused by America's growth and Britain's decline, whatever the tensions created by the clash of empire and anti-colonialism, whatever the differences between Churchill's 'realism' and F.D.R.'s 'idealism', whatever the conflict between Churchill's distrust of Bolshevism and Roosevelt's desire to co-operate with the Soviets—all that pales alongside the singular and personal relationship between the two men that made possible victory against Germany, Italy, and Japan.[9]

Is that a true and accurate picture? Was the pairing of Churchill and Roosevelt even necessary to the defeat of Hitler? That may not be mere ahistorical speculation, for historians do have the evidence needed to assess whether or not the two men, in tandem, made decisions and did things that could not or would not have been done without that wheel within a wheel—the personal Churchill–Roosevelt relationship that operated within the larger Anglo-American Special Relationship.

Churchill's memoir-history of the war should have made us cautious. For over two decades it set the parameters for histories of wartime politics and diplomacy, although what it said about the Churchill–Roosevelt relationship is ambiguous. As I have argued elsewhere, 'the Prime Minister drew a much-exaggerated portrait of himself as the wise and prescient leader who foresaw Soviet expansion, while Roosevelt comes off as a pleasant Pangloss, unwilling to accept the facts of geo-political power. The President's failure to support Churchill's position became an example of young "Jonathan's" admirable but foolish idealism.'[10] History, at least Churchill's history, has (in the words of Roosevelt speech-writer Robert Sherwood) created a sacred tradition, that 'when an American statesman and a British statesman meet, the former will be plain, blunt, down to earth, ingenuous to a fault, while the latter will be sly, subtle, devious and eventually triumphant'. Sherwood went on in a vain attempt to correct that impression: 'In the cases of Roosevelt and Churchill, this formula became somewhat confused. If either of them could be called a student of Machiavelli, it was Roosevelt; if either was a bull in a china shop, it was Churchill.'[11]

Sherwood's iconoclasm could not unseat the British and Continental depiction of Roosevelt and the Americans as short-sighted and 'unrealistic'—the ultimate insult. Anthony Eden warned a colleague not to 'regard R[oosevelt] as either "simple or naif"', but the belief persisted. Nor has that assumption been restricted to the east side of the Atlantic. One student of international affairs who, by 1990, had become a regular contributor to the 'OpEd' page of the *New York Times*, wrote in a 1988 dissertation, 'that Washington and London came into the post-war world as Tom Sawyer and Perfidious Albion. Tom was full of faith in reason, in the ability of man to solve things . . .' But Britain 'knew how games were played and knew what its interests were'. A. J. P. Taylor's barb—'Of the great men at the top, Roosevelt was the only one who knew what he was doing: he made the United States the greatest power in the world at virtually no cost'—like Sherwood's irreverence, had little effect.[12]

There had been early warnings. Churchill himself quipped that 'history will bear me out, particularly as I shall write that history myself', a promise backed up by his admission that he would 'often yield to the temptation of adapting my facts to my phrases'. Sir William Deakin, who helped with research for the wartime history, recalled that 'Winston's attitude to the war memoirs was, "this is not history—this is my case"', while John Colville recorded in his diary that Churchill had to cut material from the last volume lest he offend the newly elected president, Dwight Eisenhower. The reflections of historian William H. McNeill about Anglo-American disagreement amidst alliance were written before Churchill's memoirs made their pre-emptive strike. The same was true for Sherwood's perceptive and still unsurpassed *Roosevelt and Hopkins*, in which Anglo-American agreement and disagreement appear hand-in-hand.[13]

In 1970, McNeill reassessed his work of twenty years earlier, concluding that 'by 1952 almost all the important facts available from British and American sources had entered the public domain'. With a bit of self-satisfaction he commented that, after re-reading his book, he found 'much to be pleased with and nothing that seems clearly wrong'.[14] But within two years, in 1972, the British opened their Second World War archives, and the United States quickly followed suit. Without question, the broad parameters of Anglo-American, as well as Big Three, politics could be discerned from the evidence available before then. But good history is more than 'broad parameters'. The new archival materials provided a vast array of detail and nuance hitherto unavailable, stimulating a deluge of new monographs and syntheses that helped weaken, though not break, Churchill's stranglehold on our memory.[15] Even so, historians writing over half a century later still found it necessary to begin examinations of 'Roosevelt, Churchill, and the Wartime Anglo-American Alliance' with a warning about the 'roseate hue' given Anglo-American relations by Churchill, and here I am doing much the same thing.[16]

There are other cautions to consider before dealing with the Roosevelt–Churchill pairing. Should we look at the wartime experience from just the vantage of those two leaders? There is ample evidence that Great Power policies were often influenced by the localized and even domestic policies of less powerful nations. The Polish Government-in-Exile and Chinese internal disputes are but two obvious examples. Even more pressing is the need to incorporate Soviet and Stalin's perspectives into any study of the war, although that remains difficult in the absence of reliable evidence. The occasional and unsubstantiated revelations and exposés of *perestroika/glasnost* are tantalizing and useful, but remain suspect in the absence of systematic archival access for even Russia historians. As of autumn 1991, promises of such access remain just that—promises, although we have acquired enough bits and pieces to indicate that Soviet archives do contain a great deal of information.[17]

But historians cannot, and should not, await the opening of every archive before doing their work. To do so would be to make Leopold von Ranke the first and most extreme historical deconstructionist. By insisting on the recreation of history as it happened, critics can always argue that this or that event cannot be understood without adding this or that unattainable fact or perspective—in this case, the argument is that we run 'the risk of making it [the Second World War] appear like an Anglo-American film with occasional Russian subtitles'.[18]

In reality, both the Anglo-American relationship and the Churchill–Roosevelt link were quite different from the tripartite connection with the Soviet Union and Stalin. Part of that difference flowed from broad dissimilarities—those of language, history, and ideology. But those deep divergences were accentuated by more immediate, geopolitical influences. Perhaps foremost among these was Stalin's unwillingness to join in the war against Japan until the complete defeat of Germany. Beginning with his refusal to send a Soviet representative to a proposed four-party meeting in Chungking, China, shortly after the Pearl Harbor attack, Stalin stubbornly rejected any involvement in the war against Japan. That policy made sense early on when the Soviets had to avoid a two-front war in order to concentrate all their resources against Hitler's attack. But the Soviet stance did not change, even in 1944 when Germany's defeat had become certain. It was an opportunity lost, for it made the Soviets 'associates' rather than partners in the wartime coalition—making efforts to perpetuate the wartime alliance even more difficult.

Churchill and Roosevelt met eleven times without Stalin. On most of those occasions they held discussions of extraordinary candour—the exceptions being the short meetings they held preceding and following the 'Big Three' conferences at Tehran and Yalta.[19] Churchill did meet twice just with Stalin, and the second of those meetings, the so-called TOLSTOY conference, found the two bargaining with remarkable directness as they agreed to a crude geopolitical division of eastern Europe. Even so, that Stalin–Churchill relationship never threatened to become anything more than opportunism, either in reality or in myth.[20] Anglo-American strategy and intelligence were 'combined', whereas strategy between the Anglo-Americans and the Soviets merely intersected. Britain and America shared the atomic secret, while agreeing to exclude everyone else, including their Soviet associate. Roosevelt planned and worked for the tripartite wartime coalition to develop into a close post-war association, but, during the Second World War, the 'Grand Alliance' was largely an Anglo-American partnership that included the Soviet Union only so long as there was a common enemy.

What, then, of the 'partnership that saved the west'? Since 1985, three professional writers have drafted scripts for a docu-drama based on the personal relationship between Roosevelt and Churchill. Even I found two of them boring, and none of the three generated any interest from producers. Why not? Actor Richard Burton was able to recreate the Prime Minister brilliantly in a filmed adaptation of a portion of Churchill's *The Second World War*, although that barely rescued the production itself.[21] American actor Ralph Bellamy demonstrated that F.D.R. as a person could hold an audience. Why not the Churchill–Roosevelt relationship? Both were fascinating men who captivated their publics. A pairing should have been guaranteed box office. But that was not the case. Whatever the shortcomings of those scripts, the problem at first seemed that the events overpowered the individuals. The war simply stole every scene. But on closer examination all three authors—and this adviser—began to question the drama and depth of the personal relationship itself. Perhaps some vignettes of Churchill and Roosevelt interacting will illustrate the chemistry.

Their early contacts offer no hints of a special affinity for each other. In 1918, then Assistant Secretary of the Navy Franklin Roosevelt spoke at a dinner at Gray's Inn, one of London's traditional legal associations. Also in attendance was the former First Lord of the Admiralty, Winston Churchill. Roosevelt later accused the Englishman of having been rude, a 'stinker', and of 'lording it all over us'. To add insult to injury, when next they met, in August 1941 at the Atlantic Conference, Churchill did not recall having been introduced to the young Roosevelt, something F.D.R. complained about enough to make an impression on his cronies. That tells us a good deal about Roosevelt's ego, but also illustrates that no immediate sparks of friendship and admiration were struck when they first came face to face—whatever hyperbole Churchill later put in his memoirs about remembering Roosevelt's 'magnificent presence in all his youth and strength'.[22]

A decade after that London dinner, Roosevelt ignored attempts by Churchill, then an out-of-office politician and author, to arrange a meeting during a visit to New York in autumn 1929. Perhaps F.D.R. was too busy, having just been elected Governor of New York; but perhaps what he earlier perceived as rudeness had not been forgotten. With Roosevelt's election to the presidency, Churchill followed his routine practice of cultivating contacts with important people—an autographed copy of his biography of Marlborough, dated 1933, arrived via Roosevelt's son, James.[23] A few years later, Churchill used the same messenger to send the President a sketch of the 'currency of the future'—a bill with the dollar and pound signs woven together. But none of those politic courtesies could be confused with camaraderie or early signs of a 'special relationship'. Nor did Roosevelt respond . . . until the Second World War intervened.

Winston Churchill was not the only one to cultivate contacts. On 11 September 1939 Roosevelt initiated their remarkable correspondence with a letter suggesting that either Churchill, or Prime Minister Neville Chamberlain, might want to 'keep me in touch' by writing personal, sealed letters.[24] The President told Joseph Kennedy, his ambassador to Great Britain, the reason—to establish contact with one of the likely successors to Chamberlain. Almost simultaneously, F.D.R. expressed concern about Churchill's antiquated, 'Victorian', views and his excessive drinking—hardly expressions of confidence or closeness.[25] (To be fair, Churchill later expressed concern—horror might be a better word— about Roosevelt's drinking habits as well, though in this case it was the President's custom of concocting what he called martinis—a mixture of gin with both dry and sweet vermouth, stirred vigorously by F.D.R. himself.[26])

Churchill may have quipped that 'the Prime Minister of Great Britain has nothing to conceal from the President of the United States', when F.D.R. wheeled into the Englishman's room to find a naked and dripping wet Churchill finishing a dictation he had begun while in his bath.[27] But that image of total candour between Churchill and Roosevelt is belied by the visit of Harry Hopkins, the President's alter ego and primary adviser, at a meeting of the British Cabinet shortly after the German attack on the Soviet Union. It was a carefully orchestrated charade. Once the American heard what he was supposed to hear, he was told the meeting was over, then escorted out while the Cabinet took up' the touchy issue of the United States and Japan.[28] And more serious questions of candour remain. Doubts have not yet been laid to rest concerning still-closed British intelligence files about the Japanese attack on Pearl Harbor: information that Churchill may have chosen not to pass on to the Americans in the hope that such an attack would draw the United States into the war.[29]

Emotions and crises did often make for a special relationship, though calculation was always part of the equation. In June 1942, while Churchill was at the White House for his third meeting with Roosevelt, news came of the surrender of the British garrison in Tobruk to a German force half its size. The President's simple response was to ask: 'What can we do?' During staff discussions that followed, Churchill quickly endorsed the American military's favourite project, an invasion of France in 1943. He then left Washington with a sizeable commitment for tanks and artillery. Three years later, with Roosevelt refusing to respond to proposals that they take a hard line against Soviet policies in eastern Europe, Churchill plaintively recalled their friendship and the days when F.D.R. had provided comfort after the loss of Tobruk. But the plea was to no avail.[30]

They did establish a personal relationship, but the images of Harry Hopkins staggering back to his room after an evening with Churchill muttering 'Jesus Christ! What a man!', and Roosevelt telling the Prime Minister, 'it is great fun to be in the same decade with you', are offset a bit by the picture of Eleanor Roosevelt and Clementine Churchill struggling bravely but unsuccessfully to manufacture a personal relationship that would enhance that of their husbands.[31] More substantive were Roosevelt's concerns about Churchill's old-fashioned, nineteenth-century views. The Prime Minister ruefully admitted that 'in the White House, I'm taken for a Victorian Tory'. Fittingly, and perhaps not by accident, when Churchill stayed in the White House he slept in a room decorated with prints of the court of Queen Victoria. New Dealers, and Roosevelt himself, frequently expressed concern about Churchill's unsympathetic attitude towards the progressive reforms they felt were necessary in the United States—and throughout the world. Even though Roosevelt balanced that apprehension with the comment 'isn't he a wonderful old Tory to have on our side', the unmistakable conclusion was that Churchill posed a barrier to the kind of post-war world sought by F.D.R.[32]

Similarly, the fact that both men were proud that they represented democracies must be balanced against the remarkable ignorance each displayed about the political system in the other's country. Each was jealous of what they saw as the other's ability to wield political power. But Roosevelt had no appreciation for Churchill's difficulties with and responsibilities to both the Cabinet and domestic politics, while the Prime Minister mistakenly thought the Presidential system left F.D.R. free to do virtually as he pleased.[33]

However much they 'cussed each other out', or expressed affection and admiration for each other, the reality of differing views and goals kept creeping in.[34] The most obvious and somehow the saddest example is that of Roosevelt trying secretly in the summer of 1943 to arrange a meeting alone with Stalin—then lying to Churchill about having floated the proposal. That deception was followed by Roosevelt inventing a series of flimsy excuses to avoid a private meeting with Churchill before both the Tehran and Yalta conferences. F.D.R.'s agenda was changing as the Soviet Union and reform both grew more important than an alliance with old-fashioned, traditional Britain. Churchill's trip to Moscow in autumn 1944 for his own personal meeting with Stalin was by way of recognition that his dreams of an Anglo-American condominium had to be modified to include some sort of Anglo-Soviet settlement in eastern Europe.[35]

Perhaps the most telling of these images comes at the very end. On 13 April 1945, with Franklin Roosevelt dead for barely a day, Churchill cabled the new President, Harry Truman, to propose a continuation of the 'intimate comradeship'. How intimate could it have been if Churchill thought it could be continued with a man he had never met?[36]

All this is highly impressionistic and selective. Nevertheless, the collage suggests a superficiality and artificiality that does not fit within an 'intimate comradeship'. The Second World War forced the two together, but as that conflict wound down, so did the intensity of the Churchill–Roosevelt association. Their nearly 2,000 written exchanges comprise a unique and remarkable correspondence—but do not themselves make a unique and special relationship.

A major element of their relationship, and the alliance, was that Roosevelt and Churchill had little disagreement over immediate goals. Had the President been a prisoner of public opinion, as he is so often depicted, he would have followed the instincts and emotions of Congress, the press, and the public and turned westward, to respond to the Japanese attack. That would surely have ended any notion of a special Roosevelt–Churchill link. But the defeat of Germany and its allies, and the elimination of Hitler were givens from the outset—although both recognized that Soviet ground forces were needed to accomplish that task. Japan's defeat was likewise understood, though that part of the alliance rested firmly on F.D.R.'s agreement to the Europe-first strategy. Nor was it Churchill who persuaded the President to stick with the Hitler-first strategy proposed at the ABC-1 talks back in January–February 1941. Roosevelt avoided the Prime Minister's request to rush to Washington the day after the Pearl Harbor attack, and by the time the Englishman arrived, American military advisers and the President's own assessment and assumptions left the Europe-first strategy in place.[37]

Of course they had their differences about military strategy, although those arguments were sometimes related to, and even cover-ups for, disagreements about the post-war world. Their longest-running debate was over the proposal that Anglo-American planning should focus on a major invasion of western Europe—the Second Front. Whatever Churchill's reasons—fears of a repetition of a First World War-style stalemate and bloodletting, a desire to insert a British presence into the Mediterranean, concern about Soviet expansion (exaggerated in his wartime memoirs)—he and Roosevelt did differ substantially and consistently about the Second Front. The Prime Minister spoke supportively, but always in terms of such an invasion being only a part of an overall series of attacks on Hitler's Europe, thus preventing the

Germans from concentrating their forces. Roosevelt, however, maintained his support for the strategy recommended by his military chiefs—attack the Germans directly and in force. He suggested the North African campaign, to the dismay of General George Marshall, his Army Chief of Staff, not in response to Churchill's preference for a peripheral approach, but so as to 'bloody' American troops and thus forestall any shift in public sentiment towards a Pacific-first strategy, as well as to provide some small bona fide to the Soviets about Anglo-American intentions. As General Marshall had feared, Churchill tried to turn the Mediterranean campaign into a 'suction pump' that would devour the resources needed for the Second Front, but once the Italian campaign stalled before Naples, the Prime Minister's argument had no force.[38]

There is no small irony in Churchill's stubborn and obvious opposition to the American-style Second Front, for it helped push Roosevelt closer to the Soviets. Stalin had raised and used the issue as a lever in his relations with the Anglo-Americans, and Roosevelt reacted to that pressure. The President had accepted the recommendations of his military chiefs, and responded to their insistent prodding. Nevertheless, without Soviet support for the American view, even couched as it was in abrasive and demanding terms, the British might well have been able to ease away from such a strategy.

There were other military disagreements—the invasion of southern France, the 'race' for Berlin, strategy in south-east Asia, military aid to China—though most had political implications as well. And it was over post-war politics that the differences between Roosevelt and Churchill were most fundamental, both in their application of geopolitical considerations, and in their application of ideals—though for each leader geopolitical fire-fighting came first. Their concerns focused in Europe, although that does not do justice to lands like Australia where US influence seemed to be replacing that of Britain.[39] Roosevelt looked to create, or rather extend, the Great Power system that the Second World War had temporarily installed. Whatever his opportunism, self-deception, hedging, and political sail-trimming, he never lost faith in his, and America's, ability to seduce or persuade the Soviets. But Churchill's views were less consistent.

What the Prime Minister called the Grand Alliance (though he never put the USSR in the same category as the United States) had been forged in the cauldron of war, but he doubted that the experience had tempered the creation. Certainly the Soviets would have to prove their reliability first. Coupled with that distrust was the realization that, like it or not, the Soviet Union would be a major player in the post-war world. Lord Moran, Churchill's personal doctor, could not understand his patient's waffling regarding the Soviets. At the 1944 Moscow (TOL-STOY) meeting, after Churchill suggested that Stalin could be trusted, Moran wrote in his diary: 'The trouble is that when the P.M. gets an idea into his head he lets his imagination play round it and will not bother to fit it in with the facts. At any rate he still makes his plans in the faith that Stalin's word is his bond . . . It seems incredible, but for the moment the red light has gone out.' A few days later, the doctor, disdaining professional standards, offered a diagnosis that combined health and politics:

All this havering, these conflicting and contradictory policies, are, I am sure, due to Winston's exhaustion. He seems torn between two lines of action: he cannot decide whether to make one last attempt to enlist Roosevelt's sympathy for a firmer line with Stalin, in the hope that he has learnt from the course of events, or whether to make his peace with Stalin and save what he can from the wreck of Allied hopes. At one moment he will plead with the President for a common front against Communism and the next he will make a bid for Stalin's friendship. Sometimes the two alternate with bewildering rapidity.[40]

But it is too easy to say that Churchill was simply a geopolitician, even if his age and his dislike for economics and post-war planning made him appear that way. On the surface, Churchill wanted concrete geopolitical settlements with Stalin, whereas Roosevelt wanted 'to change the atmosphere of international relations'.[41] But that ignores the Prime Minister's ideological fears. Boundaries and spheres of influence were immediate, tangible problems that had to be solved, and solved quickly, lest the war end and British leverage disappear. That required co-operation with the 'Russians', as Churchill invariably referred to them when accommodation was afoot. But what about the 'Bolsheviks', as he called them when ideas reasserted themselves? Churchill never reconciled those elements of 'realism' and 'idealism', of force and fear. Even during his final tour as Prime Minister he remained ambivalent— wary of the 'iron curtain' he had made famous, yet counselling Eisenhower to reach an accommodation with the Russians. When Churchill's own party rejected that advice, he resigned.[42]

That ambivalence characterized the latter days of the Churchill–Roosevelt association. Shortly after the Yalta meetings, the Prime Minister launched a vigorous campaign aimed at persuading the President to get tough about Soviet policies in eastern Europe. But

Churchill seemed oblivious to the contradiction in his own plea. He had made a deal at the TOLSTOY talks—a deal that gave Britain a free hand in Greece. Now he looked for a way to have his cake and eat it too:

Since the October Anglo-Russian conversation in Moscow [TOLSTOY] Stalin has subscribed on paper to the principles of Yalta which are certainly being trampled down in Roumania. Nevertheless I am most anxious not to press this view to such an extent that Stalin will say 'I did not interfere with your action in Greece, why do you not give me the same latitude in Roumania?'

He then proposed that the President take the lead by sending a protest to Stalin about Soviet actions in eastern Europe.[43] A few days later Churchill reminded Eden to keep in mind 'that we, for considerations well known to you, accepted in a special degree the predominance of Russia in this theatre [Romania]'.[44] One of the elements in the Churchill–Roosevelt equation was that F.D.R. could, and did, assume British co-operation in the post-war world. Churchill could never make the parallel assumption, fearing instead either a resumption of what was misleadingly called 'isolationism', or a vigorous, unilateral assertion of American policies. Even as early as February 1942, only a few weeks after Pearl Harbor had brought the United States into the war, Churchill revealed his sensitivity to the dangers of too close an embrace from the Americans. In a draft of a message to F.D.R. about negotiations for a Master Lend-Lease agreement, the Prime Minister testily referred to Britain as 'no longer a client receiving help from a generous patron'. Practicality began to prevail in the next draft, as that wording became 'no longer a combatant receiving help from a generous sympathizer'. The phrase finally disappeared completely from the memorandum passed to the US Ambassador in London.[45]

That embrace became overpowering by war's end. A combination of tradition, economic aspirations, and an uneasy awareness (soon forgotten) of the strength of nationalism prompted Roosevelt to attack colonial empires. A pot-pourri of self-interest and belief found Roosevelt and his administration pushing for a multilateralist form of free trade as the solution to the world's economic and political tensions. The results were trusteeships under international supervision, civil aviation (dis)agreements, the Bretton Woods conference establishing a post-war monetary system based on the US dollar, a campaign to eliminate the British Imperial Preference System—and a string of hard words and hard feelings.[46]

The United States and Britain may have been, as Churchill told George VI in 1942, '"married" after many months of walking out',[47] but the marriage was characterized by more than occasional unfaithfulness. It held together largely because Britain, and particularly Churchill, saw no reasonable alternative. As in most marriages where a clear dominant/subordinate relationship exists, they spoke the same language, shared reminiscences, argued, loved, disagreed, and worked together. A 'special relationship', of sorts, exists so long as the subordinate partner plays the proper role. And at almost every critical juncture, Roosevelt—and the United States—had their way.

Churchill's decision not to attend Roosevelt's funeral was an attempt to bring the mountain to Mohammed—subtly to shift the focus of the Anglo-American relationship from Washington to London. 'I was tempted during the day to go over for the funeral and begin relations with the new man,' he wrote to the King, but 'I should be failing in my duty if I left the House of Commons without my close personal attention. . . . Moreover I think that it would be a good thing that President Truman should come over here at about the same time as was proposed by his predecessor.'[48] It is difficult to imagine Churchill letting political fence-mending at home interfere with his world-wide machinations, while the psychological advantage of having Truman trek to London was obvious.

Initially, Churchill, and even Roosevelt, could relax comfortably in anticipation of an Anglo-American condominium for the post-war world, giving them both time to work out the troublesome details of colonial empires, economic and political reconstruction, and how to ensure moderate not revolutionary change. Early in the war Churchill went so far as to predict that 'if Roosevelt and I come to the Conference Table, we can carry through all we want'.[49] But by the end of the Casablanca Conference in February 1943, such tranquil ruminations were no longer possible. By then the third party in the coalition had become a presence to be reckoned with—not just as an army capable of defeating the Germans, but as a force in the post-war world. Harold Macmillan acidly described Churchill and Roosevelt at Casablanca as the Emperors of the East and West, astutely noting that 'if we had had the Red Emperor as well, it would have made the thing perfect'.[50]

Their disagreement over how to treat the Soviet Union in the post-war world was only part of it. They also differed on who should deal with the Soviets. Churchill saw Britain as the logical, practical intermediary between a European (realistic) Stalin and a naive, well-meaning

Roosevelt. But the President rejected any notion of Britain as intermediary between Moscow and Washington, fearing that old arguments and ideological differences would push the Soviets in the wrong direction. The one-on-one meeting with Stalin that Roosevelt tried to arrange in 1943 had as one purpose to drive home to the Soviet leader that the United States and the Soviet Union did not need a 'friendly broker' in order to work together. Shortly after the TOLSTOY meeting, F.D.R. concluded that British efforts to recreate the *cordon sanitaire* gave Stalin the excuse to dominate eastern Europe.[51] James Forrestal recorded Roosevelt wisecracking that 'the British were perfectly willing for the United States to have a war with Russia . . . and that . . . to follow the British program would be to proceed toward that end'. In humour there is conviction.[52]

How then, to characterize the Churchill–Roosevelt relationship? Is it historically significant? If it is not 'the partnership that saved the west', what is it? The broad range of Anglo-American wartime relations followed a trajectory of an alliance developing, in place, and then declining. The Cold War alliance that emerged after Roosevelt's death had different goals and a much different structure. It was a new alliance for new purposes, even if it seemed to build on what had existed during the Second World War.[53]

The Churchill–Roosevelt relationship followed a trajectory much the same as that of Anglo-American relations during the Second World War, falling roughly into five stages. Prior to the French surrender in June 1940, the two men were at the 'get acquainted' stage, feeling each other out. Then, as Prime Minister, Churchill became a suitor, 'wooing' the President in hopes of gaining an active and open ally. The entry of the Soviet Union into the war against Germany did not change that pattern. Once Japan accomplished what Churchill sought, he and Roosevelt acted as equal partners throughout 1942 and into the following year. Although neither lost sight of post-war issues, the demands of military victory provided the grease that made the alliance, and the partnership, work. But sometime in 1943, that equality gave way to a junior–senior partnership. In part, the Soviet Union played the role of third party in the affair—and the eternal triangle seems as unstable in politics as it is in love. But the growth of American power and self-awareness also prompted Roosevelt to assert himself more forcefully. That pattern dominated the Churchill–Roosevelt relationship until the President returned from Yalta and fell ill, after which time he only occasionally set policy.[54]

But what of the significance of their personal link? The author and reporter John Gunther gave Roosevelt almost as much credit as Churchill for maintaining British morale early in the war, perhaps putting his finger on the one area where the two, individually and together, played a key role.[55] Leadership—the ability to motivate others —is intangible, but the testimony of contemporaries is near-unanimous about the inspirational effect each had on their own and the other's wartime society. It is hard to imagine Anthony Eden or Clement Attlee peering out pugnaciously from wartime recruiting posters, or Cordell Hull evoking spontaneous cheers when suddenly appearing among Allied troops. But Churchill and Roosevelt did those things effortlessly. In newspapers, radio broadcasts, pamphlets, posters, newsreels, and bar-room stories during the war, the two men came to symbolize their nations and the joint effort against a common and immoral enemy. Whatever the work of their propaganda machines to achieve that effect, their personalities and styles were an essential part of the process. Both had spent much of their public career making silk purses out of sows' ears. F.D.R. had turned the Great Depression into a hymn to the American way of life; Churchill had made Cassandra into a prophet. Those public relations skills were well-honed in each man by the time war came. Yet, perhaps Wendell Willkie could have risen to the occasion. Maybe a Lord Beaverbrook could have become an inspirational leader. Events make the man in the sense that the times present the opportunity—but one still has to grab the brass ring.

All this leaves the nagging suspicion that, had it been Neville Chamberlain and Wendell Willkie—a plausible prospect—wartime relations between the two nations would not have been fundamentally different. Churchill and Roosevelt did their job well, even magnificently at times, and they are great fun to study. After all, they are history, and we must probe their actions and personalities closely to understand what happened. But the basic relationship was that of Britain and the United States, allied in war in large part because of intersected histories, the forces of geography and economics, and a broad range of shared values. Those shared values found expression in the Churchill–Roosevelt relationship, with its massive correspondence, its personal touches, its role in smoothing over the rough edges. But it would have found expression, albeit in a different way, in a Willkie–Chamberlain, or Halifax–Hull relationship.[56] There would have been differences, particularly in the arena of post-war planning and relations with the Soviet Union, but Hitler's Germany and Japan would have been defeated, the Red Army would have liberated eastern and central Europe, the atomic bomb would have obliterated part of Japan, and the United States would have assembled its system of monetary, military, mercantile, and moral leadership in the post-war world.[57] Moreover, forces outside the grasp of Roosevelt and Churchill—forces of nationalism, revolution, change, and resistance to change—would have acted as much as they did to shape that post-war world.

18

Churchill and Stalin

ROBIN EDMONDS

NARROWLY defined, the personal relationship between Churchill and Stalin extended just over four years of their long careers, ending with Churchill's departure from Berlin, half-way through the Potsdam Conference in July 1945. By the time that Churchill returned to 10 Downing Street in October 1951, shortly before his seventy-seventh birthday, Stalin had not much more than a year to live.

Both Winston Churchill and Joseph Stalin, with just over five years' difference in age between them, grew up in the late nineteenth century. This apart, the protean English Parliamentarian, lineal (and in a way, spiritual) descendant of the great Duke of Marlborough, 'half American, but all British',[1] had little in common with the Georgian cobbler's son, a Marxist from early youth, who, having adopted Russia as his country, then ruled it for a quarter of a century in a manner that—in Russian history—can be compared only with the reign of Ivan the Terrible. The relationship established between these two national leaders in their late middle age was necessarily complex. Any attempt, therefore, to force it into the procrustean mould of a concept of the subsequent Cold War is likely to be misleading. But however the interplay between these two disparate men may be interpreted, its time-frame must be extended back to 1919. They then stood at opposite poles—Stalin as People's Commissar for Nationalities, a full member of Lenin's Politburo, and Churchill as Secretary of State for War in David Lloyd George's Coalition government: an antithesis that forms an extraordinary contrast to the ten-year period beginning in the mid-1930s. Soon after the October Revolution in Russia, Churchill may perhaps not yet have heard of Stalin (as opposed—say—to Lenin and Trotsky), but Stalin already had good reason to be aware of Churchill.

Churchill would gladly have strangled Bolshevism at birth. During the first year after the Russian Revolution, however, as Minister of Munitions at the climax of the First World War, he had no opportunity to share in the initial formation of British policy towards Soviet Russia, which was well described at the time by the Foreign Secretary as one of deliberate drift.[2] One of the consequences of this drifting was that, after an initial British attempt to establish a relationship of some kind with the Bolshevik regime had failed, in August 1918 small British forces landed at several strategic points in Russia, thousands of miles apart. The original purpose of these landings—to re-establish Russian resistance to the Central Powers—was by this time irrelevant, since the end of the First World War was fast approaching. Instead, these British forces became the initial focus of British entanglement in the Russian Civil War. One of the strategic points was Baku, where in the summer of 1918 the local Soviet came so close to inviting British troops to help them ward off the Turkish force advancing on the city that, on 21 July, Stalin (then in Tsaritsyn, the city which later took his name) categorically forbade the Baku Soviet to seek support from the 'Anglo-French imperialists'.[3] His order, endorsed by Lenin, was obeyed; Baku fell to the Turks; but by November 1918 it was under British occupation.[4]

This was the situation inherited by Churchill, when he was transferred to the War Office at the turn of the year 1918–19. Being Churchill, he threw 'the whole of his dynamic energy and genius into organising an armed intervention against Russia': a policy described by the Prime Minister at the time as 'a purely mad enterprise out of hatred of Bolshevik principles'.[5] It was Lloyd George who, by a devious route, in the end prevailed against Churchill. By the autumn of 1919 almost all British troops had been withdrawn from Russia; and when in March 1920 the post of British High Commissioner in Siberia was abolished, the Permanent Under-Secretary at the Foreign Office wrote: 'So ends a not very creditable enterprise'—a minute on which Lord Curzon, now Foreign Secretary, replaced the words 'not very' with 'highly dis'.[6] The Anglo-Soviet negotiations, which began at 10 Downing Street two months later, ended on 16 March 1921 with the conclusion of a formal agreement to resume Anglo-Soviet trade relations. This amounted to *de facto* British recognition of the Soviet government.

Nevertheless, the 1921 agreement was reached only after the British government, while maintaining its naval blockade of Russia, had sent military missions and substantial supplies, at a cost of about £100 million, to the anti-Bolshevik forces fighting in the four corners of the former Russian Empire. During this phase of British participation in the Russian Civil War in April 1919, Churchill publicly raised the possibility that Germany might find 'a way of atonement' through the fight against Bolshevism;[7] and in October of that year he even contemplated going to Moscow himself, if (the White Russian) General Denikin's offensive from the South succeeded, 'as a sort of Ambassador', in order to 'help Denikin mould the new Russian constitution'.[8]

What was remarkable about Churchill's advocacy of the anti-Bolshevik cause was not only its verbal vehemence. This was characteristically Churchillian. (In January 1920, for example, he wrote an article describing Communism as 'a pestilence more destructive of life than the Black Death or the Spotted Typhus'.[9]) Long after the final White Russian defeats by the Red Army, he remained committed to the cause within the Cabinet, where he was one of a small minority of ministers who opposed the Anglo-Soviet trade agreement—so much so that in November 1920 he contemplated resignation. He did not resign, but he came near enough to doing so for one of his closest friends, Lord Birkenhead, to write him a long letter before a critical Cabinet meeting, warning him 'very strongly' that, if he did resign, he would only find himself 'the hero of "Morning Post" and the leader of some thirty Tories in the House of Commons, who would disagree with you on 90 per cent of all the subjects about which you feel really deeply'.[10]

Churchill's reputation as the most eloquent and the most determined advocate of Allied intervention during the Russian Civil War lived on, until his view of the Soviet Union underwent a dramatic change nearly twenty years later. His own explanation of this change, given to the Soviet Ambassador in London, Ivan Maisky, during one of their lunchtime meetings in 1938, was this:

Twenty years ago I strove with all the energy in my power against Communism, because at that time I considered Communism, with its idea of world revolution, the greatest danger to the British Empire. Now Communism does not present such a danger to the Empire. On the contrary, nowadays German Nazism, with its idea of the world hegemony of Berlin, constitutes the greatest danger for the British Empire. Therefore, at the present time I strive against Hitler with all the energy in my power . . . we and you share the same path. This is the reason why I am in favour of close co-operation between England, France and the USSR.[11]

Whether Maxim Litvinov, then Soviet Foreign Minister, submitted this report to the Politburo, we do not know. But perhaps Stalin may later have recalled Maisky's prophecy, written about the same time:

Churchill is a major and forceful figure, whereas the other members of the cabinet are colourless mediocrities, fearful of letting the wolf into the sheepfold; Churchill can crush all of them especially in the event of some kind of crisis. Churchill will come to power when the critical moment in England's fortunes arrives.[12]

As well as his understanding of the Nazi threat in the 1930s, Churchill was one of the few men in the West at that time who had closely studied the Russian army's performance in the First World War. Thus he was aware of the fact that in 1916 the German and Austro-Hungarian forces deployed on the Eastern Front had outnumbered those on the Western Front. For Churchill, describing 'these terrible campaigns' in the *Eastern Front* volume of his *World Crisis*, they constituted 'a prodigy no less astounding than the magnitude of her [Russia's] collapse thereafter'.[13]

Against this background, it is paradoxical, but in no way surprising, to read the record of the House of Commons debate in May 1939 regarding the Soviet offer of a tripartite alliance (Britain, France, and the Soviet Union). Churchill then pleaded with Chamberlain and his colleagues to regard it as 'a fair offer, and a better offer . . . than the terms which the Government seek to get for themselves; a more simple, a more direct and a more effective offer. Let it not be cast aside and come to nothing.'[14] Even in his memoirs, written ten years after the conclusion of the Nazi–Soviet Pact in August 1939, Churchill could still describe Stalin's decision—and it certainly was his own decision—as 'realistic in a high degree'.[15] And in his first broadcast of the war, delivered just after the Fourth Partition of Poland, Churchill used these words:

Russia has pursued a cold policy of self-interest . . . that the Russian armies should stand on this line, was clearly necessary for the safety of Russia against the Nazi menace . . . I cannot forecast to you the action of Russia. It is a riddle wrapped in a mystery inside an enigma; but perhaps there is a key. That key is Russian national interest . . .[16]

As Prime Minister, Churchill's first significant direct overture to Stalin took the form of a skilfully worded personal letter in June 1940. The second, in April 1941, was his oblique warning of German intentions, based on an 'Ultra' decrypt about German forces in southern Poland, which illuminated the whole Eastern scene for Churchill 'in a lightning flash'.

Stalin rebuffed the first and ignored the second.[17] Thanks to the brilliant team of cryptographers at Bletchley Park, Churchill became aware in the next few weeks of the precise timing of Operation Barbarossa. Exactly a week before three million men crossed the Soviet frontiers, he telegraphed to Roosevelt: 'I do not expect any class reactions here and I trust a German–Russian conflict will not cause you any embarrassment.'[18] On the evening before the German invasion was launched, he remarked to his private secretary, John Colville, strolling on the lawn after dinner at Chequers, that if Hitler invaded Hell, he would at least make a favourable reference to the Devil in the House of Commons.[19] And twenty-four hours later he delivered a broadcast, which he had deliberately not cleared with his Cabinet colleagues:

No one has been a more consistent opponent of Communism than I have for the last twenty-five years. I will unsay no word that I have spoken about it. But all this fades away before the spectacle which is now unfolding. We shall give whatever help we can to Russia and the Russian people. . . . The Russian danger is therefore our danger, and the danger of the United States, just as the cause of any Russian fighting for his hearth and home is the cause of free men and free peoples in every quarter of the globe . . .[20]

Nevertheless, the new Anglo-Soviet relationship got off to a slow start, thanks both to Churchill's earlier reputation in the Soviet Union and to Stalin's obsession that Churchill's April warning—one among the mass of similar intelligence reports pouring into the Kremlin during the spring of 1941—was part of a gigantic act of provocation designed to embroil the Soviet Union with Germany. (The chilly tone of Vyacheslav Molotov's first telegram to Maisky, instructing him how to respond to Churchill's offer of help, speaks for itself.[21]) It was Churchill who broke the ice, with a personal message to Stalin, which the British Ambassador, Sir Stafford Cripps, delivered to Stalin himself, on 8 July. According to the Soviet record, Stalin (who had broadcast his famous 'Brothers and sisters, my friends' address to the Soviet people five days earlier) gave the ambassador a rough ride. Cripps resisted the conclusion of a formal Anglo-Soviet military assistance agreement together with a pledge not to conclude a separate peace with Germany; and he argued instead in favour of an exchange of notes. Stalin retorted that the British 'slowness and exaggerated caution' recalled the negotiations in 1939; there was, he said, 'danger' in delay. Churchill responded at once, on 10 July. Subject only to the agreement of the Dominion governments, the British government wholly approved of Stalin's proposal for an Anglo-Soviet Declaration. Forty-eight hours later the agreement, which embodied both the points discussed with Cripps, was signed in Moscow, by Cripps and Molotov.[22]

Stalin's next proposal fared less well. In a personal message to Churchill on 18 July, he suggested, although it was not yet described as such, the formation of a second front: 'a front against Hitler in the West (Northern France) and in the North (the Arctic)'. This request for 'active military aid to the Soviet Union' was repeated in a different form in Stalin's message of 13 September, when he even suggested that: 'England could without risk land 25–30 divisions at Archangel or transport them across Iran to the southern regions of the Soviet Union for military co-operation with Soviet troops on the territory of the Soviet Union.'[23] These Soviet proposals and Churchill's refusal marked the beginning of the long inter-Allied debate about the Second Front, which would not be resolved until the Big Three met at Tehran over two years later.

While the last German offensive against Moscow, Operation Typhoon, was still raging, Stalin sent a personal message to Churchill agreeing with him on the need to introduce 'clarity, which at present does not exist, in the mutual relations between the USSR and Great Britain'—the consequence, in Stalin's view, of the lack of 'definite agreement between our countries on war aims and plans for post-war organisation' and 'on mutual military assistance ·in Europe against Hitler'. Churchill, off to Washington for the Arcadia Conference himself, responded a ᐳ fortnight later, by offering to send his Foreign Secretary, Anthony Eden, to Moscow, accompanied by the Vice-Chief of the Imperial General Staff. His message making this offer gently suggested that the first task was to win the war, after which the three principal participants would meet at the table of the Peace Conference. He added that the fact that the Soviet Union was a Communist state, while Britain and the United States were not, was no obstacle whatsoever in reaching agreement on the three countries' 'mutual security and lawful interests'. In his reply welcoming Eden's visit, Stalin agreed.[24]

By this time Churchill and Stalin had reached the point of exchanging birthday greetings. Nevertheless, these December talks in Moscow ended only in a vapid communiqué, issued on the 29th.[25] They foundered on Stalin's insistence that it was 'absolutely essential' that the 'old frontiers, the frontiers of 1941' should be re-established. For Stalin, the frontiers meant the territories lost by the Soviet Union after the First World War. For Eden, they meant the new territories acquired by the Soviet Union as the fruit of the 1939 German–Soviet agreements. Eden took his stand on the Anglo-American declaration of common principles enshrined in the Atlantic Charter four months earlier and on the British government's need to consult with its other allies—above all the United States. Stalin ironically remarked that this gave the impression that the Atlantic Charter was 'directed not against those people who were trying to establish world domination, but against the USSR', the country which was engaging almost the entire German army in battle. Stiffened by telegrams from Churchill, Eden dug in. The Treaty of Alliance, which was to have been concluded in Moscow, was temporarily shelved.[26]

Early in the following year, Churchill himself veered towards the view that 'the Atlantic Charter ought not to be construed so as to deny Russia the frontiers she occupied when Germany attacked her'. He even asked Roosevelt for 'a free hand to sign the treaty which Stalin desires as soon as possible'. But in the end, in conformity with American opinion, the Anglo-Soviet Treaty of Alliance, finally signed in London on 26 May 1942 with a twenty-year duration, omitted all territorial commitments: a Soviet concession for which Churchill thanked Stalin warmly in a message sent on the following day. For his part, Stalin would describe the signature of this treaty, in a speech delivered on the anniversary of the Russian Revolution in November 1942, as 'an historic turning-point in relations between our country and Britain'.[27] By then Churchill and Stalin had met for the first time.

On 23 July 1942, five days before Stalin issued his *ni shagu nazad* ('not one step backwards') Order of the Day to the Red Army, he sent Churchill this message: 'I must declare in the most categorical manner that the Soviet Government cannot acquiesce in the postponement of the organisation of a Second Front until 1943.' A week later, Churchill proposed meeting Stalin himself in the southern Soviet Union, but he at once accepted Stalin's invitation to visit Moscow instead.[28] Together with Churchill's first meeting with Roosevelt a year earlier at Placentia Bay, this encounter in the Kremlin in August 1942 ranks as one of the most extraordinary of the Second World War. 'A somewhat raw job' was Churchill's own forecast before he left London.[29]

So it proved, for what Churchill had to try to explain to Stalin was that there could be no invasion of Europe in 1942, and to persuade him that the Anglo-American invasion of North Africa in November— Operation Torch—should be regarded as 'the very best form of second front in 1942'. With one exception, the British and Soviet records of these meetings—the two leaders met four times in as many days— reveal no major difference in their account of what each man said, with heavy pounding. The exception is the celebrated moment when, stung by Stalin's jibes about British unwillingness to fight Germans, Churchill launched into a philippic which left his own interpreter bereft of words. Stalin's response, according to both American and British witnesses of this exchange, but not included in the Soviet record, was that what Churchill was saying was not important—'what was vital was his spirit'.[30]

Although Stalin at once grasped the military advantages of Operation Torch, he also put his finger on its weakness, the political planning of the North African operation, which subsequent events were to prove up to the hilt. His personal approval of Torch—'May God bless its execution'—is common to both sets of records. But he did not accept it as the Second Front, and Churchill offered a hostage to fortune, leaving Stalin with the impression that, even if the invasion of France was ruled out in 1942, it was at least conceivable for 1943: a possibility to which Stalin would soon refer as a 'promise' on Churchill's part.[31]

The contemporary evidence regarding the moment at which Churchill, having intended to leave Moscow a day earlier, took the decision instead to ask Stalin for a final meeting, alone, is conflicting. According to one account, he had already made up his own mind by the time he breakfasted at his dacha on 15 August. According to the other, he was persuaded to 'swallow his pride' only after the British Ambassador—Sir Archibald Clark Kerr, who therefore claimed the principal credit—had taken him to task during a walk in the dacha grounds at noon. However that may be, on the evening of the 15th, armed with a new interpreter, Churchill began his final meeting with Stalin, which Stalin converted into a working dinner that lasted four hours.[32] At dawn on the 16th Churchill left Moscow believing—in the words of the telegram that he sent a Roosevelt—that he had established 'a personal relationship' with Stalin and that 'The disappointing news I brought could not have been imparted except by me personally without leading to really serious drifting apart. It was my duty to go. Now they know the worst . . . Stalin is entirely convinced of the great advantages of Torch . . .'

In Moscow, as at Placentia Bay, Churchill probably persuaded himself more effectively than he did his interlocutor. For his part, Stalin summed up their hammer and tongs argument with these words:

He and Churchill had got to know and understand each other, and if there were differences of opinion between them, that was in the nature of things . . . The fact that he and Churchill had met and got to know each other and had prepared the ground for future agreements had great significance. He was inclined to look at the matter more optimistically.[33]

It was not until amost the middle of February 1943 that Stalin was informed about the main strategic decision reached by Churchill and Roosevelt in January at the Casablanca Conference: namely, an Anglo-American invasion of Sicily once Tunis had been secured.[34] (Tunis was finally captured on 12 May.) Stalin's messages about the Second Front in the months that followed grew increasingly terse, culminating in one sent to Churchill on 11 June, by which time Churchill and Roosevelt had jointly decided to postpone the invasion of France for another year. Their decision, Stalin declared, created 'exceptional difficulties for the Soviet Union', whose government 'does not find it possible to associate itself with such a decision, taken moreover without its participation and without an attempt to consider jointly this important question, which may have grave consequences for the further course of the war'.[35]

Churchill and Roosevelt reacted differently to this 'castigation', as Churchill described it to Roosevelt at the time. Whereas Churchill suggested a summit meeting of the three leaders at Scapa Flow, Roosevelt, without telling Churchill, invited Stalin to meet him separately on either side of the Bering Straits. Stalin refused both; the biggest tank battle of the entire war—Kursk—was imminent. In the end, after prolonged triangular discussion, Churchill, Roosevelt, and Stalin (who detested flying) finally met at Tehran from 27 November to 1 December 1943: the seminal conference of the Second World War.[36] This was the last major meeting at which Churchill, once the hinge of the Grand Alliance, was able to speak as an equal partner. It was the first face-to-face meeting between Stalin and Roosevelt, who was able to test in practice his belief, first expressed with 'brutal' frankness in a message to Churchill in March 1942, that he could 'personally handle Stalin better than your Foreign Office or my State Department' and that Stalin 'thinks he likes me better, and I hope he will continue to do so'.[37]

Strategically, the three men agreed in Tehran on a more or less simultaneous invasion of both northern and southern France in 1944, timed to coincide with a major Soviet offensive; and Stalin undertook to enter the war against Japan once Germany had been defeated. With Roosevelt's help, Stalin had little difficulty in defeating Churchill's case for Aegean operations, which, as Churchill frankly admitted to his two colleagues, might delay the date of the invasion of France.[38] Stalin was also unimpressed by Churchill's forecast about the Italian campaign— that it would develop into 'a miniature Stalingrad'. In his bilateral meeting with Churchill at Tehran, he observed to Churchill:

If this operation [Overlord] does not take place, he [Stalin] must warn that this would provoke great disappointment and bad feelings. He feared that the absence of this operation could provoke a very bad feeling of isolation. Therefore he wanted to know whether operation Overlord would take place, or not. If it took place, that was good, but if not, he wished to know this in advance in order to be able to prevent the feelings which the absence of this operation might provoke. This was the most important question.[39]

It was also at Tehran that the three leaders together addressed for the first time the shape of the post-war political structure of the world, including Roosevelt's concept of the 'Four Policemen' (the USA, the Soviet Union, Britain, and China), and the critical question of the post-war frontiers of central Europe. In spite of Stalin's losing (in the words of the record prepared by Roosevelt's interpreter, Charles Bohlen) 'no opportunity to get a dig in at Mr. Churchill', of which Churchill was aware, and of Roosevelt's disparaging remarks about Churchill made in conversation with Stalin, of which he was not, it was Churchill who first suggested to Stalin that the Polish state might move westward after the war, like soldiers at drill 'taking two steps left close'. Although the debate on the exact location of the western frontier of Poland was not concluded until the Potsdam Conference, it was at Tehran that the fate of Polish territory east of the Curzon Line (and also of East Prussia) was decided for all practical purposes. (The Curzon Line was the line advocated by the British Foreign Secretary as the eastern frontier of Poland in 1920.)

The final words of the Declaration of the Three Powers, signed on 1 December 1943 and published a week later, record the three leaders as parting as 'friends in fact, in spirit and in purpose'.[40] During the fourteen-month interval between the Tehran and Yalta conferences Stalin replaced Churchill as Roosevelt's principal partner in the triumvirate directing the Grand Alliance. Yet at the same time Churchill's relationship with Stalin intensified. The main issue that brought this about was Poland. Churchill was Stalin's natural interlocutor on Poland, partly because the idea of leaving aside a difficult problem to sort itself out was temperamentally alien to Churchill. In any case Churchill had to attempt to mediate between Stalin and the Polish government, both because it was the Anglo-Polish Alliance that had obliged Britain to declare war on Germany in September 1939 and because the seat of the Polish government-in-exile was London. There was therefore no way in which the Polish problem could be ignored in London in 1944, especially after 10 January, when the Soviet government publicly proposed the Curzon Line as the eastern frontier of post-war Poland.

Hardly had Churchill returned to London at the end of January 1944 from convalescence in Morocco, after his pneumonia and heart attack, than he plunged straight into the confused conflict of ancient central European rivalries, advising the Polish Prime Minister, Stanislaw Mikolajczyk, to accept the Curzon Line as a basis for discussion, with territorial compensation for Poland in the west. Over the next six months the triangular argument about Poland went up and down. On 29 July Stalin sent Churchill a telegram about the Polish issue, which Churchill described to Roosevelt as 'the best ever received from UJ ['Uncle Joe' Stalin]'.[41] Three days later any hope of an agreed settlement was wrecked by one of the most traumatic events of the Second World War: the Warsaw Rising. The telegrams sent to Stalin by Churchill, urging him either to help the Polish Home Army (the Armja Krajowa) against the German army in Warsaw or to allow others to help, were flatly rejected by Stalin, who refused permission for aircraft of RAF Bomber Command to use Soviet airfields for dropping supplies to the AK.[42] After the AK's surrender in October 1944, however, Churchill was ready to accept absolutely Stalin's assurance that, after an advance of 400 miles to the Vistula, the Red Army needed a pause not of weeks, but of months;[43] and he overcame his initial revulsion quickly enough to spend ten days conferring with Stalin in Moscow during that month.

Once again the stumbling-block was the immediate recognition of the Curzon Line as Poland's eastern frontier, and in particular the future of the largely Polish city of Lvov. This time it was Churchill who lost his temper—with the Poles. In a report sent from Moscow to King George VI, he described 'our lot from London' as 'a decent but feeble lot of fools' and the Lublin Poles as 'the greatest villains imaginable'.[44] No agreement could be reached. Although the Polish government in London continued to be recognized by both the British and the US governments for another nine months, in effect it signed its own death warrant in Moscow in October 1944. Because Mikolajczyk and his colleagues remained rooted in their defence of a territorial claim which none of the Big Three would accept, in the end the Polish question inevitably reached the top of the agenda of the next conference between Churchill, Roosevelt, and Stalin: at Yalta, where only one of the three countries that went to war against Germany in 1939—Britain—was represented.

In spite of the amount of time taken up in Moscow by the Polish question, what history has above all recalled from Churchill's talks with Stalin on this occasion is what Churchill himself then called 'the naughty document', which he handed to Stalin at their first meeting, held in the Kremlin late on the evening of 9 October, and which, according to his memoirs, he suggested to Stalin that they should burn, because it 'might be thought rather cynical if it seemed we had disposed of these issues, so fateful to millions of people, in such an offhand manner'. Again according to Churchill's own account, Stalin's reply was 'No, you keep it.' The relevant passage in the notes of this celebrated exchange kept by Churchill's interpreter has been preserved; the Cabinet Office record was bowdlerized by the officials concerned.[45]

What Churchill's 'naughty' document (which he seems to have written out on the spur of the moment) proposed was a division of responsibility in the Balkans between Britain and the Soviet Union, expressed in percentage terms: a range that extended from a Soviet 90 per cent in Romania and a British 90 per cent in Greece to 50–50 for both countries in Yugoslavia and Hungary. Within forty-eight hours Churchill was himself doubtful enough about the wisdom of this document to write a letter of explanation to Stalin, which (on the recommendation of Averell Harriman, the US Ambassador in Moscow) was never sent.

As we now know, Stalin did not care for Resistance leaders, of whatever political complexion; the seeds of his great quarrel with Tito had already been sown; the leaders of the Greek Communist Party would soon learn that they were on their own; and Stalin's view of the Italian Communist leader, Palmiro Togliatti, unlike Churchill's, was based on many years of personal experience (a man who 'could tell Marshal Stalin to mind his own business'.) Nevertheless, Churchill's 'naughty' percentages were taken seriously enough in the Kremlin at the time for Molotov to engage Eden in a haggle about the exact proportions of the division of responsibility proposed. Greece, Romania, and Yugoslavia caused no dissent; but, after discussion, the Bulgarian and Hungarian percentages ended at 80–20 in the Soviet favour.[46]

The real failure of this, the last bilateral meeting between the two European members of the Big Three, was that they spent so little time during ten whole days—and that unprofitably—on the one question upon which the future of Europe above all depended: the future of Germany. On this, Churchill once again advanced his twin concept of a Germany divided into three and a confederation of Poland, Czechoslovakia, and Hungary. Both Stalin and Molotov were opposed, Molotov observing that 'after the last war many new small States had been formed. Many of them had failed. It would be dangerous to go to the other extreme after this war and to force States to form groups.'[47] So far as the future of Germany was concerned, at Quebec in September 1944 Churchill had agreed with Roosevelt on a solution which was nonsense—the short-lived Morgenthau Plan, for the 'pastoralization' of Germany. With Stalin in Moscow a month later he agreed on nothing at all.

Although an attack of fever kept Churchill in bed for one day during his stay in Moscow, and meetings at the Kremlin lasted almost until dawn, his report to the King leaves no doubt that in Moscow he enjoyed himself, in contrast to Tehran, where he had suffered from at least one wave of depression. His description, in his telegram of 11 October to Roosevelt, of an 'extraordinary atmosphere of goodwill' was not greatly exaggerated.[48] Not only did Stalin accompany Churchill to the Bolshoi Theatre; he came to lunch at the British Embassy (he rarely visited foreign missions); and he saw him off at the airport as well. Nevertheless, there was another more significant difference between this meeting of the two leaders and their first, just over two years earlier: this time it was Churchill who was in position of *demandeur*, although he disguised this in his farewell letter to Stalin on 19 October:

My hopes for the future alliance of our peoples never stood so high. I hope you may long be spared to repair the ravages of war and lead All The Russians out of the years of storm into glorious sunshine.

Your friend and war-time comrade,

Winston S. Churchill[49]

On 3 February 1945 Churchill and Roosevelt, with retinues totalling some seven hundred, flew into the Crimea, of which Churchill had remarked in January that 'if we had spent years on research, we could not have found a worse place in the world' for a meeting place.[50] In fact Churchill's own first suggestion—Invergordon, in Scotland—was little less improbable, as was his idea of King George VI entertaining Stalin at Balmoral.[51] His role at Yalta (unlike Stalin's) was essentially Eurocentric. Contrary to Churchill's suggestion, Roosevelt had excluded de Gaulle from the conference. Once the three leaders reached Yalta, Churchill argued strenuously—against opposition from both Roosevelt and Stalin—that France should be given both a zone of occupation in Germany and membership of the Allied Control Commission for Germany. At his first bilateral meeting with Stalin, Roosevelt told him that the British wanted 'to have their cake and eat it' over France; he himself thought that a French zone of occupation in Germany was 'not a bad idea . . . but . . . only out of kindness'. Nevertheless, on 10 February Roosevelt suddenly told his two colleagues that he had changed his mind, thus paving the way for agreement on this issue, with significant consequences for France and for European politics as a whole after the war ended.

At Yalta Churchill executed a similar 180-degree turn—over Germany. Whereas only four months earlier he had gone along with the American suggestion of the 'pastoralization' of Germany, at Yalta Churchill not only blocked the proposal for the dismemberment of Germany, but he also offered a red rag to the Soviet bull by contesting Stalin's proposal that the total amount of war reparations payable by Germany should be twenty billion dollars, half of which should go to the Soviet Union.

The eighteen thousand words exchanged about Poland at Yalta must be considered against the background not only of the discussion about Poland that had already taken place at Tehran, but also of two facts, of which all those who attended the Yalta Conference were well aware. The foremost western salient of Marshal Zhukov's advance from the Vistula line had now reached a point less than forty miles from Berlin. And on 1 January the Soviet government had formally recognized as the provisional government of Poland the so-called Lublin Committee, established with Soviet backing the previous autumn. At Yalta Stalin made no bones about Poland. 'The Polish question' was, he said, 'a matter of life and death for the Soviet Union'.[52] In these circumstances, the Big Three agreed that the Polish eastern frontier should follow the Curzon Line, with minor digressions, while in the north and west Poland 'must receive substantial accessions of territory'; and the 'final delimitation' of its western frontier (coded language for either the western or the eastern River Neisse) should await the peace conference. Meanwhile, Molotov and the British and US ambassadors in Moscow were to act as a consultative commission for the 'reorganization' of the Warsaw government.

This agreement papered over so many cracks between the American, British, and Soviet viewpoints—in particular the ambiguity of the words requiring the Commission to consult 'in the first instance in Moscow'—that it was bound to run into difficulties, as indeed it soon did. But a complicating factor was that, although not directly related to the Polish question as such at Yalta, the Joint Declaration on Liberated Europe issued there by the Big Three was in a sense superimposed upon the agreement over Poland; and subsequently the two became linked in the public mind. Although the Declaration had little or no legal force as a binding commitment upon the signatories and its implementation was made conditional—'where in their judgement conditions require'—none the less it awakened hopes of a post-war renaissance of democracy in countries such as Greece and Poland itself, which before the war had been governed by regimes that could not have been described as democratic in a Western sense.[53]

Churchill's immediate verdict on the Yalta agreements is a matter of record. On 27 February 1945 he said to the House of Commons:

The impression I brought back from the Crimea, and from all my other contacts, is that Marshal Stalin and the Soviet leaders wish to live in honourable friendship and equality with the Western democracies. I feel also that their word is their bond. I know of no Government which stands to its obligations, even in its own despite, more solidly than the Russian Soviet Government. I decline absolutely to embark here on a discussion about Russian good faith . . .[54]

A fortnight later, however, Churchill was seeking to convince Roosevelt that they were 'in the presence of a great failure and an utter breakdown of what was settled at Yalta'. Roosevelt's last word of advice to Churchill on the Polish question, which (unlike most of his messages sent during his final weeks) was drafted by the President himself, was to 'minimize the general Soviet problem as much as possible in Parliament'. In Stalin's perception, by contrast, during the spring of 1945 there was a Churchillian swing back to the *cordon sanitaire* policy of a quarter of a century earlier.[55]

Although the Grand Alliance continued after Roosevelt's death on 12 April 1945, the British position within it was accurately described by a shrewd British observer six months later as 'the position of Lepidus in the triumvirate with Mark Antony and Augustus'.[56] During the remainder of the Second World War, Churchill's influence within the Alliance visibly waned. By the time of the Potsdam Conference his performance was seen by all British participants as ineffective. Indeed, the Permanent Under-Secretary of the Foreign Office accurately described the meeting in his diary as that of 'The Big Two and a Half'.[57]

Even Churchill's skills could not indefinitely mask from public view the underlying trend: the British war effort had long since peaked. He himself was tired; distracted by the break-up of the coalition government in May and by the subsequent electoral campaign; and perhaps already affected by the 'subconscious conviction' that he had lost the general election, which hit him 'with a sharp stab of almost physical pain' early on the morning of 26 July.[58] In the triangular arguments that broke out at the beginning of March 1945 Churchill won only a single important round. This was on 31 May, when he insisted that the forthcoming meeting of the three leaders of the Alliance should be, like Tehran and Yalta, genuinely tripartite. (He categorically refused 'to attend a meeting which was a continuation of a conference between yourself [President Truman] and Marshal Stalin'.) Otherwise, he was obliged to accept a series of American—Soviet decisions. He was not even consulted about Harry Hopkins's mission to Moscow in May, during which the Yalta agreement about the Polish government was, in effect, renegotiated: a settlement that Churchill grudgingly accepted. Moreover, Churchill had wanted to schedule for mid-June the next summit meeting, which he intended as a 'showdown' with Stalin, where there would be the 'grave discussion on which the immediate future of the world depends'. Instead, he had to accept Truman's date (mid-July), apparently without realizing that the President had deliberately postponed the Potsdam meeting in order to ensure that the atomic test explosion at Los Alamos, New Mexico, should, if possible, precede it.[59]

In the run-up to Potsdam the greater part of Churchill's effort at persuasion was directed westwards, across the Atlantic. At the end of April 1945, however, he sent Stalin one last, long message about Poland, which ended with the prophetic sentence: 'But do not, I beg you, my friend Stalin, underrate the divergencies which are opening about matters which you may think are small to us, but which are symbolic of the way the English-speaking democracies look at life.' Stalin, who was kept well informed by his ambassador in London of Churchill's views at this time—and by no means only about the Polish issue—was unmoved by Churchill's appeal, which he rejected on 4 May. And by the end of that month Hopkins had arrived in Moscow.[60]

At Potsdam itself Churchill was outgunned. In his memoirs he wrote that, had he and Eden returned to Berlin, they would never have accepted the western River Neisse as Poland's western frontier.[61] But once the US–Soviet deal, linking this frontier with the reparations issue, had been clinched, what—had the Conservative Party won the British election—could Churchill have done about the Oder–Neisse line, on which (as we now know) Stalin's support had been promised to the Polish government even before the Yalta Conference?[62]

With hindsight, far more remarkable was Churchill's inattention to the great issues raised by the atomic bomb in the summer of 1945. The British official atomic historian, with justice, describes this as 'cursory'.[63] Moreover, even in his memoirs published ten years later, Churchill himself described his 'certainty' regarding the meaning of Stalin's enigmatic response to Truman's laconic mention on 26 July of a 'new weapon of unusual destructive force'. It was Churchill's conviction, formed when standing about five yards from 'these two potentates' during their brief exchange on that day, that Stalin had 'no special knowledge of the vast process' of Anglo-American research or of the 'heroic gamble' involved in the Manhattan Project (the American code-word for the development of the atomic bomb). This was indeed a profound miscalculation.[64] For, as we now know, as soon as he got back to his headquarters from the plenary session on the 26th, Stalin instructed Igor Kurchatov (the Soviet equivalent of J. Robert Oppenheimer) to hurry up.[65]

To illustrate the distinction that Stalin drew between his two partners in the Grand Alliance, his ironical quip is often quoted, to the effect that, although both needed careful watching, Roosevelt would take a rouble out of your pocket, whereas Churchill would even take a copeck. A more illuminating recollection is that of Mikolajczyk, who later recalled a remark made to him by Stalin, summing up Churchill late one evening at Potsdam: 'Churchill did not trust us and in consequence we could not fully trust him either.'[66] Like most remarks made very late at night, this one might have required some qualification in the cold light of morning. The earlier stage of the Churchill–Stalin relationship was different; but at any rate during the final months of the war, both parts of Stalin's observation were true.

Churchill himself remarked that he had wooed Stalin as a young man might woo a maid (although he also said—accurately—that no lover had ever studied every whim of his mistress as he had those of Roosevelt).[67] In reality, Churchill's attitude towards Stalin fluctuated. On the one hand, Churchill could not but be impressed by Stalin's qualities—a computer-like memory (he never took a note at a summit conference); lucidity in argument; and his ability suddenly to switch his mood and his negotiating technique from *grubost*' (Lenin's final description of Stalin) to charm.[68] He was also a good host, something that appealed to Churchill. Thus at the beginning of 1944 Churchill remarked of the Soviet–Polish dispute that if only he could dine with Stalin once a week, 'there would be no trouble at all'; and as late as Potsdam he could still repeatedly exclaim: 'I like that man.'[69] On the other hand, for an Englishman who had first held high office towards the close of the era of the Concert of Europe, the post-war balance of European continental power was a consideration of the first magnitude. And as the end of the Second World War drew near, the Anglo-Soviet Treaty of Alliance notwithstanding, the daunting prospect of Britain being alone with the Bear in Europe preyed increasingly on Churchill's mind. Something of the ambivalence between Churchill and Stalin may perhaps be reflected in Churchill's gesture at Potsdam, when in his own words: 'I filled a small-sized claret glass with brandy for him and another for myself. I looked at him significantly. We both drained our glasses at a stroke and gazed approvingly at one another.'[70] In the event this exchange proved to be virtually a personal farewell.

19

Churchill's Strategy

JOHN KEEGAN

'**H**E is an unwise man who thinks there is any *certain* method of winning this war . . . between equals in strength. The only plan is to persevere.'[1] This is Churchill the strategist at his best. The observation is judicious in itself, but it is also drawn from a document, written in October 1941, in which he rightly deprecates with absolutely sound strategic perception the belief of the Air Staff that victory might be won by strategic bombing alone: 'All things are always on the move simultaneously, and it is quite possible the Nazi war-making power in 1943 will be so widely spread throughout Europe as to be to a large extent independent' of the target system the air marshals sought to destroy. This shows remarkable strategic percipience: the German war machine was indeed stronger in 1943 than in 1941, and the efforts of the Allied air forces to weaken it had resulted in such dispersion of German war industry as to make their task not easier but more difficult.

Yet it is the moral rather than the intellectual content of his judgement that dominates. The Prime Minister, who was also Minister of Defence, confidently equates the power of his isolated island with that of the continental dictator whose armies at that time stood on the Channel narrows and menaced both Cairo and Moscow. In his heart of hearts he must have known how wide the disparity yawned; he refused nevertheless to be disheartened. 'The only plan is to persevere.' Willpower is a dangerous quality in warfare. 'A brave and stupid commander', the Chinese axiom has it, 'is a calamity.' Emphasis on will-power had led the French High Command calamitously astray in 1914, and by it Hitler was to drag the Germans down to disaster. There are times, nevertheless, when failure of will is the worst of strategic failings. For Britain, after the fall of France but before Pearl Harbor, it was Churchill's strength of will that made the difference between sustaining the fight and submitting to a dictated peace. There was, it must be remembered, the nucleus of a peace party; it would have found the voice of sweet reason had Churchill not shouted it down by his magnificent appeals to national greatness, to universal moral standards, to belief in ultimate victory.

There was, moreover, nothing feigned in these appeals, or in the courage that inspired them. '[Churchill] behaved in public just as he behaved in private. There were no two faces, no mask that would drop when the audience had retired. The sentiments he expressed abroad', recalled John Colville, one of his private secretaries, 'were familiar to those at home'—and by 'home' Colville meant Chartwell or Chequers.[2] Churchill was genuinely brave, physically and morally, and unflaggingly so. It is well known that he was a victim of occasional depressions, but they were short-lived, and he seemed to have the power to throw them off by conscious decision. Panic was absolutely foreign to his nature. He never gave way, even at what for him were the blackest moments of the war, the disaster in Malaya and the fall of Tobruk, to the mental paralysis that gripped Stalin in June 1941 and Hitler after Stalingrad. Churchill's will to victory, central to its final achievement and the deciding factor in Britain's survival as a combatant power in 1940, sprang from the very centre of his being.

The balancing factor, which ensured that his bravery would not lead to calamity, was the power and clarity of his intellect. Strategy is choice. Churchill had few choices in 1940 and later, when his scope widened, he made a number of bad choices and was talked out of more. Yet he never espoused any truly unwise strategic course, nor did he contemplate one. His commitment to a campaign in the Balkans was unsound, but such a campaign would not have risked losing the war, any more than would the Norwegian diversion he so much favoured. In large matters, the Churchill of the Second World War was a far more cautious strategist than the Churchill of the First: he had lost his belief in Gallipolis and urged prudence on the Americans throughout the discussions of a Second Front, not wholly because of his interest in 'the Mediterranean strategy'. The First World War had killed his youthful belief that war was an adventure—though not that there could be adventure in war—and he knew all too bitterly that great wars kill great numbers, waste the wealth of nations, and despoil the face of the earth. He hoped to win the Second World War at the least possible cost to Britain and her allies.

Hence his decision, almost as soon as he became Prime Minister, to put the higher direction of the war on a unified and rational footing.

'Churchill himself was no administrator', judged Colville.[3] Asquith's and Lloyd George's example, which had allowed politics to muddle strategy and generals to do as they chose, had convinced him, however, that the system of administering the war must be centralized and dispassionate. General Sir Hastings Ismay, his Chief Staff Officer throughout his premiership, saved him from a false step early on, when he successfully opposed the creation of an *ad hoc* staff, composed of his 'familiars—Oliver Lyttelton, Desmond Morton, Professor Lindemann and others'.[4] That was actually before Churchill's succession (as Prime Minister) to Chamberlain, who had appointed him Chairman of the Committee of Military Co-ordination in the last days of his administration. As soon as Churchill succeeded, he transformed that post by naming its holder Minister of Defence, which he became himself, without creating a ministry to support it. Instead Ismay, who was already a member of the Chiefs of Staff Committee, brought the Military Wing of the War Cabinet Secretariat, an already smoothly functioning staff of which he was head, to form a small Office of the Minister of Defence.

A regular officer much experienced in Whitehall ways, Ismay proved an excellent choice for the difficult role he had to fulfil. As Churchill's staff officer, he was a functionary; as a member of the Chiefs of Staff, he could influence executive decisions; he never confused the two positions. Sir Leslie Rowan, one of the wartime private secretaries, recalls Churchill asking Ismay what he thought of a COS opinion he had communicated. Ismay replied that, if the Prime Minister valued his services, he would never ask that question again. 'And he never did.'[5] The Chiefs of Staff Committee became, in time, the instrument through which Churchill fought Britain's war. Formally, the executive agency was the War Cabinet, to which reported two committees, the Defence Committee (Operations) and the Defence Committee (Supply). The latter, meant to free decision-makers from logistic involvements, did just that; the former, consisting of the Deputy Prime Minister (Attlee), the three service ministers and, later, the Foreign Secretary, was originally conceived as the War Cabinet's strategic arm; it was always attended by the Chiefs of Staff. In practice, and certainly before the end of 1940, the Defence Committee (Operations) had yielded its functions to the Chiefs of Staff Committee, with which Churchill worked on a day-to-day and sometimes hour-by-hour basis. It was served by a Joint Planning Staff and a Joint Intelligence Sub-Committee, whose functions are described by their titles.

General Sir Ian Jacob, Military Assistant Secretary to the War

Cabinet, 1939–45, has left a fascinating and important account of how Churchill actually worked.

The normal mode of operation would be something like this. About 9.30 a.m. Ismay would see the Prime Minister, usually in bed. He would often emerge with one or two Minutes that Churchill had dictated late at night or early that morning addressed to 'General Ismay for Chiefs of Staff Committee'. The Chiefs . . . met at 10.30 a.m. every day, the Agenda having been sent out by Jo Hollis, the Secretary, the afternoon before. There would be the C.I.G.S. in the chair [Brooke, in fact succeeded Pound as Chairman only in January 1942] . . . The meeting usually lasted until noon or later, and resulted in instructions to the Planning Staff, or to a Commander-in-Chief . . . It was the job of the secretariat to draft the necessary terms of reference for the Joint Planning Staff, or telegram to the Commander-in-Chief . . . Often the Chiefs would go on to a meeting with the Prime Minister at 12.30 p.m. or later in the day (or night), or there would be meetings of the Defence Committee or Cabinet. Often the Prime Minister would send for C.I.G.S. to have a discussion with him. A day rarely passed without some personal contact between him and one or all of the Chiefs, though Ismay had often to act as the intermediary, receiving, when there was any lack of harmony, the ill-humour of both parties.[6]

Churchill's timetable is significant because it demonstrates order, consistency, and devotion to all parts of government (including Parliament, of whose primacy Churchill was a passionate defender).[7] His routine was in marked contrast to that of Roosevelt, who gave time to people, great or small, according to no pattern discernible by his staff; Stalin, who terrorized subordinates and shifted responsibilities between the few he trusted apparently at whim; and even Hitler, who, though drearily predictable in his night-owl timetable, cut himself off completely from German domestic life after 22 June 1941 and dwelt with the outside world almost exclusively through his personal operations staff and the representatives, at his lonely headquarters, of a few key ministries. Churchill resisted the temptation both of Caesarism—elevating the conduct of war above that of government—and of Bonapartism, which may be taken to mean trying to do everything oneself. If there is any other war leader with whom a ready comparison suggests itself, it is Abraham Lincoln. Like Lincoln, Churchill remained throughout the war at the seat of government; like Lincoln, he embroiled himself throughout the conflict in the processes of representative democracy; like Lincoln, he never rested in his search for generals who could deliver victory, peremptorily discarding those who failed him; like Lincoln, he clung to no doctrinaire principles of strategy, preferring to trust in a few broad policies that he believed best served the long-term interests of the people and the alliance of states he represented.[8]

Hence the caveat to Jacob's generally encomiastic account of his working methods: 'The body that Churchill never understood or appreciated was the Joint Planning Staff . . . He found so often that they produced papers which proved conclusively that what he wanted to do was out of the question.'[9] Churchill enormously appreciated the Joint Intelligence Sub-Committee, and all the agencies that worked to it, particularly the Government Code and Cypher School at Bletchley, whose raw decrypts, 'Boniface' to him long after that cover name had been superseded by 'Ultra', he insisted on seeing for himself from the start. However, he was also interested by relevant information of all sorts – like Napoleon, a rare point of similarity, and unlike Hitler, who preferred to work from verbal briefs at his interminable situation conferences. He 'insisted on being informed constantly about details, and had a continuous flow of statistics and graphs prepared for him either by us [War Cabinet Secretariat] or by his private statistical office under Professor Lindemann'. The Joint Planning Staff (JPS), formed from middle-rank regular officers of the three services, differed from the other bodies with which he dealt. Working at a distance from him and, therefore, from his powers of direct persuasion, the JPS supplied not information he demanded but conclusions from which he all too often dissented. In so far as there was a doctrinaire strategic organization in Churchill's machine, the JPS was it. Its officers were the products of staff colleges, who had been schooled in the military orthodoxies. There were no military orthodoxies that applied, however, to Britain's predicament after June 1940, indeed until well after the United States had entered the war. On paper, in retrospect, Britain was doomed to defeat; it has even been argued that Churchill derived some of his determination to carry on the struggle from an underestimate of Germany's war productive capacity.[10] That may or may not be so. Whether misinformed or not, Churchill perceived that military orthodoxy offered no way out. As Ian Jacob observed, instead 'his pugnacious spirit demanded constant action. The enemy must be assailed continuously: the Germans must be made to "bleed and burn".'[11]

This was boldness incarnate. Britain's strategic predicament after June 1940 was not only extreme, but unprecedented in its extremity. It had no effective allies to speak of. Although the Dominions could supply men, they could provide little else. The willingness of the United States to deliver arms for cash required the liquidation of half Britain's overseas assets and threatened it with bankruptcy. The country was menaced by direct invasion. It was under direct physical attack by the German air force. It was fighting a battle for the sea lanes which, if lost, would starve the country in a few months. It had no effective means of striking back at its enemy, since Churchill, quite as much as the air marshals, grossly overestimated the power of strategic bombing in general and that of Bomber Command in particular. Its enemy was self-sufficient in both civilian and military resources, its economy offering no point of weakness at which British seapower might thrust. The German people were united by the elation of victory, while those of the countries they had overrun were – whatever Churchill's illusions to the contrary—cowed into passivity by the disaster they had suffered.

Military orthodoxy, in such circumstances, argued for a concentration on essentials—keeping the navy in home and North Atlantic waters, husbanding the strength of the air force, and deploying what was left of the army's mobile formations in reserve behind threatened invasion sites, unless and until allies could be found. Churchill, of course, never ceased for one day during the harrowing period of Britain's isolation from striving to induce the United States to enter the war, a personal contribution to grand strategy that requires ampler discussion. That overriding priority apart, what is most arresting about Churchillian strategy in the period before Pearl Harbor, and particularly in the year between the Fall of France and Hitler's invasion of Russia, is the extent to which the Prime Minister risked scarce resources far from home at points where he detected enemy weakness or suspected the enemy could be made to over-extend himself. That meant the northern and southern shores of the eastern Mediterranean.

Churchill's Mediterranean strategy forms, with the story of his American diplomacy, the most important element in the record of his higher direction of the war. It was rapidly to intertwine, however, with another strand to which Churchill deluded himself into attaching almost equal significance: the fomentation and support of anti-German uprisings in the occupied countries. 'Now set Europe ablaze' was Churchill's famous instruction to Hugh Dalton, Minister of Economic Warfare, on 16 July 1940, the order which led to the establishment of the Special Operations Executive.[12] Writing to Halifax next day, Dalton explained the objects SOE was intended to achieve: the organization of 'movements in enemy-occupied territories comparable to the Sinn Fein movement in Ireland, to the Chinese Guerrillas now operating against Japan, to the Spanish Irregulars who played a notable part in

Wellington's campaign'.[13] Disregarding the extent to which these words exaggerate the military importance of the movements cited, Dalton's—which was certainly also Churchill's—misappreciation was to prove unsound for another reason. It wholly underestimated both the skill and the ruthlessness with which the Germans were to implement occupation policy in the countries they already had or would soon conquer. A German historian, Werner Rings, has tabulated seven different and carefully calculated German approaches to imperial government, from toleration of a parliamentary regime in Denmark—where free elections were held as late as 1943—to indirect government by ministerial permanent secretaries in Holland, to limited autonomy in partitioned France, to sponsorship of puppet separatists in Slovakia. Almost everywhere the Germans preferred devolved administration, encouraged collaboration by apparently generous trade and labour recruitment policies, and turned to force only when softer policies failed. When they did so, as in Nedic's puppet Serbia, they behaved with a ferocity unknown in Europe since the Thirty Years' War.[14]

It was the variety of accommodations in German imperial policy for which Churchill failed to allow when he indulged in his vision of a continent throwing off the shackles in patriotic revulsion. 'Soft' German policies proved extremely successful, at least until the introduction of forced labour in 1942–3, largely because the middle classes did not want trouble, while the working classes at first were appeased by the inroads made by the demands of German war industry on unemployment in almost every occupied country. 'Hard' German policies were even more effective, except in Yugoslavia and Greece, where a tradition of inurement to massacre lingered from Ottoman days—though even there many Serbs chose to follow the puppet Nedic. Most European resistance movements preferred words to deeds, and with good reason: the premature maquis risings at Vercors and Glières were literally annihilated, the German assault forces killing everyone—prisoners, wounded, women—who fell into their hands. Churchill's belief in the powers of resistance movements had been formed above all by his experience in the Boer War, known not for nothing as 'the last of the gentleman's wars'. He forgot altogether the darker passages in Britain's long imperial history: the unrestrained suppression of Irish rebellion by Cromwell, the pitiless extermination of Indian mutineers. The Germans were building an empire in a hurry, and were ready to use every means to consolidate it, not least those which the British preferred to forget had once proved useful to them also.

The sponsorship of resistance movements would, therefore, serve Britain's direct military purposes very little. Only as the war drew to its close would Churchillian Mediterranean strategy be served by Britain's involvement with Tito and the Greek resistance movements very greatly indeed. This thought returns us to Churchill's Mediterranean strategy at the outset. What did he hope from it? Were his hopes realistic? This can certainly be stated: while Britain's historic and currently vital interests in the Mediterranean, the latter including the need to protect access to Middle Eastern oil and to deny it to the Germans, and to keep open communications between Egypt and India, required an effort to command its south-eastern waters, Churchill looked beyond mere necessity to perceive opportunity. He rightly saw that Mussolini was not only an Axis partner weak enough for Britain to humiliate, if the place and time of battle were chosen correctly; he also rightly guessed that the humiliation of Mussolini would provoke Hitler into gestures of support that might lead in turn to German humiliations as well. On 27 September 1940 he told Colville, 'I should like to wage war on a great scale ·in the Middle East. By next spring I hope we shall have sufficient forces there.'[15] Within the week, he was outlining to Robert Menzies, the Australian Prime Minister, the measures he was taking to see that such forces were in place:

We have had to face the threat of invasion here and the full strength of Germany's air bombing attack on our cities, factories and harbours. Nevertheless, we have steadfastly reinforced the Middle East, and in spite of all our perils at home and scanty resources have sent over 30,000 men, nearly half our best tanks, many anti-aircraft guns needed to protect our vital aircraft factories, two of the finest units in the Fleet, the Illustrious and Valiant, and a considerable number of Hurricane fighters and Wellington bombers.[16]

This commitment was extraordinarily bold. Its effect was to recreate a nucleus of the offensive army lost at Dunkirk, but to emplace it at a distance of 3,500 miles by sea (12,000 by the secure Cape route) from where danger most urgently threatened the home islands, whose defence, meanwhile, was to be entrusted to a collection of 'county' divisions which largely lacked artillery and even transport. Such boldness was only to be justified if Churchill's hunch about Mussolini's capacity to embarrass Hitler proved correct. It was so proved almost at once. On 28 October the Italian army invaded Greece from Albania; by mid-December the Greeks had driven it out and invaded Albania themselves. Hitler, who had not been forwarned, was infuriated, and all the more so because Mussolini had thereby provided Churchill with a pre-text to send air units to the Peloponnese and to occupy Crete. At a moment when he was reviewing a range of strategic initiatives, and completing an elaborate extension of the Tripartite Pact designed to bind all the South European states to Greater Germany, the British had suddenly narrowed his range of options. It was to be narrowed even further during December and January when British and Imperial forces in Egypt and East Africa peremptorily reversed the advances the Italians had made in the previous July–September. In East Africa, their success led on to the liberation of the whole of Ethiopia and the restoration of Haile Selassie to the imperial throne, while from Egypt Wavell's little mobile army drove forward to take the whole of Cyrenaica and 250,000 Italian prisoners.

Here was complete vindication of Churchill's risk strategy, more than cancelling out the bad odour left by the bombardment of the French fleet at Mers-el-Kebir in July and the failure to seize Dakar in September. Through Mussolini's ill-judged effort to emulate Hitler, the British were enabled to open an initiative of their own. It would inevitably distort the smooth development of Hitler's grand strategy. It was, however, only an initiative, not a consolidated victory. Churchill, unfortunately, mistook the achievement of the first for the second, with very mixed strategic consequences.

In the long run, Churchill's fixed belief that the northern shore of the Mediterranean was a theatre which offered wide strategic advantage was to be proved correct; without Britain's chivalrous intervention in Greece in 1941, it is unlikely that Churchill could have intervened decisively in the Greek Civil War in 1944; but for Churchill's prefer-ence for Tito over Mihailovic in 1943, it is unlikely that Yugoslavia would have detached itself from Stalin in 1948. To follow such judge-ments, however, is to take a longer view than a British Prime Minister ought perhaps to have been allowed at a moment when his country was fighting for its life. During 1941 Churchill's Mediterranean strategy moved from the dimension of risk-taking to that of suffering the conse-quences. Even allowing for his conviction that Turkey could be brought into the war—which the Turks, playing a skilful hand, were not unwilling to endorse—he unquestionably went too far in using small forces for large strategic ends.[17] 'Turkey, Yugoslavia, Russia, all perhaps favourably influenced by evidence of British support for Greece', Churchill suggested to Smuts in January 1941.[18] This was a total misappreciation. The volatility of Yugoslav politics, to say nothing of the fragility of its armed forces, made it a factor of quite marginal importance in the game Churchill was playing; Stalin, as we now know but Churchill ought to have been readier to perceive through the mist of his hopes, craved peace at all costs—except surrender to direct attack; the Turks, heirs to an ancient and subtle Ottoman tradition of diplomacy, would do nothing not to their advantage; the Greeks, by contrast, were a headstrong people who gambled for high stakes. Their attack on Turkey in 1920 ought to have warned Churchill that the Greeks were prone to ignore military realities when their blood was up; it was even more to the point that the Greek government had told Wavell in January 1941 that they did not want British military assistance.

Churchill determined to deliver it none the less. At a moment when Hitler, as part of a larger effort to reverse the British Mediterranean initiative—including intervention in Syria and Iraq—was beginning to deploy his own forces in support of Mussolini's in Libya, a Panzer corps commanded by Rommel, Churchill stripped Wavell of his best troops, notably the Australians and the New Zealanders, and sent them to Greece. In the face of a concentric German advance through pliant Bulgaria and a militarily inert Yugoslavia, British and Greek resistance collapsed simultaneously; the principal cause of the débâcle, however, was the predictable determination of the Greeks to defend their frontier with Bulgaria, for political reasons, rather than to agree a rational defence plan with the British.

Thereafter, for the next eighteen months, almost everything in Churchill's Mediterranean strategy went awry. The Royal Navy's maritime preponderance, which had yielded the victories of Taranto and Matapan over the Italian fleet, was cancelled out by the weight of German land-based airpower. German airpower in Crete plucked victory from the jaws of defeat; it also inflicted a major defeat on the Royal Navy in the operation covering the chaotic withdrawal from that island. When in consequence Malta became a key impediment to the resupply of the German–Italian offensives against the British army in the Western Desert, the Royal Navy actually found itself fighting on the defensive in what, for two hundred years, had been an extension of its home waters; forced to concentrate almost every ship not needed to wage the Battle of the Atlantic or hold in check the German 'fleet in being' in north Norway in order to convoy essential stores to Malta, it suffered heavy losses in every operation and was actually forced to turn back a convoy from Egypt in June 1942.

On land, meanwhile, the pendulum swung one way or the other; the determining factor was distance from main operating base, on lines of communication in the coastal strip between Alexandria and Tripoli, which could stretch to 1,500 miles. Churchill's worst set-back was the loss of the port of Tobruk in June 1942, news of which reached him, embarrassingly, in the White House; his great triumph was Alamein, four months later. Nothing should be said to diminish that victory. Churchill had worked for it, had chosen the right generals to fight it, notably the Cromwellian Bernard Montgomery, and had scrimped at home and beseeched abroad to find the means to win it. Nevertheless, it has to be recognized that Alamein coincided with the onset of Hitler's most crucial strategic crisis, brought about by his over-extension of force into the Caucasus in his drive for oil. Had Hitler had force to spare at that moment—such as the air reinforcement that he sent to Tunis the following spring—Rommel might well have been able to hold his line at Alamein.

Such speculation, however, carries us away from consideration of Churchill's original Mediterranean strategy and back to his other great post-Dunkirk preoccupation: how to bring the United States into the war against Hitler. Within the month after Alamein was won, a vast Anglo-American amphibious force had landed in French North Africa. This was concrete realization of Churchill's famous recollection, in *The Second World War*, of his emotions on hearing the news of Pearl Harbor:

So we had won after all! Yes, after Dunkirk; after the fall of France; after the horrible episode of Oran; after the threat of invasion . . . we had won the war . . . How long the war would last or in what fashion it would end, no man could tell, nor did I at this moment care . . . Hitler's fate was sealed. Mussolini's fate was sealed. As for the Japanese they would be ground to powder . . . Many disasters, immeasurable cost and tribulation lay ahead, but there was no more doubt about the end . . . Being saturated and satiated with emotion and sensation, I went to bed and slept the sleep of the saved and thankful.[19]

There is no reason to doubt that this is exactly what Churchill felt. He was entitled to his elation; he had worked for it. 'From the first', judges Eliot Cohen,

Churchill appreciated more fully than did any of his colleagues the import of American participation on Britain's side. Indeed, if Churchill had any grand strategy for victory in 1940 and 1941, it consisted chiefly in arranging the entrance of the United States into open hostilities with Germany in partnership with Great Britain. Of course, Churchill was not alone in thinking alliance with the United States highly desirable, even imperative. But he did surpass both civilian and military colleagues in the War Cabinet and military staffs in his unremitting concentration on this task, and in his appreciation of American military and industrial potential.[20]

To have worked towards an end and to have achieved it are, however, two quite different things; it is important to distinguish between them in assessing how realistic Churchill was in basing his hopes of salvation on eventual American intervention. His appreciation of America's war potential was, of course, absolutely correct. The American economy, already the largest in the world in 1939, retained enormous capacity for expansion. One statistic alone is sufficient demonstration: the United States aircraft industry was to produce as many military aircraft during the war as those of all other combatants put together, about 350,000, producing 96,000 in 1944 alone.[21] He was also correct, though one suspects a little *arrière pensée*, to discount British professional doubts of the combativeness of the American services, a judgement based, he said, on his study of the American Civil War. He had the advantage over his colleagues: not only was he half-American, he had visited the United States and cultivated friendships there, not least Franklin D. Roosevelt's. British soldiers, by contrast, were largely limited to an acquaintanceship with India; British civil servants, with fifth-century Athens.

Churchill, nevertheless, undoubtedly invested too large a hope in the likelihood of American entry. This is a ticklish subject, around which the establishment historians on both sides of the Atlantic continue to pussyfoot. Roosevelt's whole-hearted endorsement of the war against Hitler, once he was in, seems retrospectively to justify Churchill's faith that the President's commitment to United States entry matched his own in strength and date of conception. The destroyers-for-bases deal, Lend-Lease, the extension of the American neutrality zone in the Atlantic to the mid-ocean line, above all the proclamation of the Atlantic Charter and the agreement of the 'Germany-first' strategy at Placentia Bay in August 1941, lend credence to that view. It is, nevertheless, the credence of hindsight. Roosevelt, the supreme politician, had watched the polls of American public opinion creep from 70 per cent putting the avoidance of war above the need to help Britain in the spring of 1940, to 70 per cent for the contrary view a year later. That was not enough for him. 'All measures short of war' remained his position from Dunkirk to Pearl Harbor, despite all the intimacies of the

Former Naval Person exchanges. We may choose to believe—and any contrary belief would be almost impossible to support—that Roosevelt would have found the means to make Japan's attack of 7 December 1941 the pretext for a general declaration of war on the Axis. Constitutionally, however, the issue would have had to go to Congress, and it may be imagined that the China Lobby and the United States Navy, to name but two powerful voices, would have worked to protract the debate. The inescapable fact of the matter is that the issue was settled not by Roosevelt, not by Congress, not by the operation of some American moral identification with Britain's lonely stand, but by the arch-villain Hitler himself. It was his determination, against the dangers of which Ribbentrop issued a solemn warning, to deal the 'lout' Roosevelt a smack in the face that led to Germany's declaration of war on 11 December; in a bizarre mirror-imaging of Churchill's reaction to the news of Japan's attack on the American Pacific Fleet, Hitler had crowed, 'The turning point! . . . Now it is impossible for us to lose the war: we now have an ally who has never been vanquished in three thousand years.'[22]

Hitler was deluded in his estimate of the relative worth of Japan and the United States; Churchill was not. Nevertheless, the difficulties in Churchill's strategy date from after America's entry, not before. Strategy, it was said earlier, is choice. Before 7 December 1941, Churchill had made one supremely bold choice, which was to use the small surplus of force available to him to open a second front in the Mediterranean, with dramatic results. In other respects it was necessity that drove him down the roads he had taken. Before considering Churchill's contribution to 'coalition strategy', as the higher direction of the joint Anglo-American war effort is now commonly known, it is worth briefly reviewing his activities in the other strategic spheres during the period of isolation—at sea, in the strategic air offensive, in peripheral campaigns, and in the technological support of the war effort.

The Royal Navy was not, in 1939, the service Churchill had known as First Sea Lord at the outbreak of the First World War. Treasury parsimony, underpinned by the Ten Year Rule of 1919 and its extension, which affirmed that Britain would not face war with a major power for the next decade, had left the navy with a complement of over-age ships, or ships unsuitably designed or equipped for a world-wide war. There were too few aircraft carriers, the newer ones were too small, all embarked aircraft notably inferior to those they would have to meet in combat; there were too few escorts and those built hurriedly to meet the war emergency were too slow. These were not the navy's only material faults; but its human fault was a dearth of talent at the top. A century of supremacy had hardened the navy's arteries; Dudley Pound, its professional chief, was literally a victim of that condition. Pound was to suffer a stroke while in office, which forced on him the retirement even his most loyal subordinates thought overdue. Max Horton and Andrew Cunningham, commanders respectively of the escort and, during the crucial period, the Mediterranean fleet, were doughty fighters. Cunningham, when he became, against Churchill's preference, First Sea Lord, valiantly resisted the Prime Minister's worse ideas. The navy, however, produced no admirals to match the band of Americans who so brilliantly conducted the war in the Pacific. The American talents were, of course, illuminated by the wealth of resources they enjoyed and the quality of their ships and aircraft; there was, nevertheless, a spirit of flexibility and inventiveness in their approach to and execution of strategy and tactics that their British contemporaries did not display.

Even had it not been his inclination to do so, Churchill would have been obliged to take a direct hand in the command of naval operations. 'His concept of strategy was, from the beginning of both wars,' judged Stephen Roskill, ' "offensive" ';[23] it also imputed offensive intentions to the enemy that were not always present. Thus he seriously overestimated Hitler's will and capacity for maritime adventure, and his obsession with the danger of the German 'heavy' ships breaking out of Norwegian waters into the Atlantic caused him to deny force to the Mediterranean fleet at times when that fleet was most stretched. His decision to bombard the French fleet in June 1940, though an unavoidable pre-emption, was probably also based on an exaggerated estimate of its usefulness to Hitler, who had neither the crews to man it nor the means to motivate the French to fight.

By contrast, he gravely underestimated the aggressiveness and capabilities of the Japanese, a long-standing error in judgement that he did not modify even as the need to make a decision for 'Main Fleet to Singapore' approached. He appears to have believed right up to the last moment that the appearance of the *Prince of Wales* and *Repulse* would 'deter' the Japanese and that 'Fortress Singapore' was impregnable. His choice of Admiral Sir Tom Phillips to command the 'Main Fleet' was also an error in judgement; Phillips had no experience of handling ships under air attack, and he was known to minimize the danger.[24]

This was a fault Churchill shared; despite the evidence from the Norwegian campaign, he underestimated the deadliness of aircraft, particularly land-based aircraft, to large surface vessels. The débâcle off Crete and the *Prince of Wales* and *Repulse* disaster—which Roskill regarded as 'major strategic errors' by Churchill—might both have been avoided had he rid himself of the delusion that navies could act 'offensively' under hostile skies.[25]

Naval critics, Roskill foremost among them, also emphasize how Churchill, contrarily, declined to accept how deadly land-based aircraft were to the U-boat. No-one contests that he conceded a central importance to the Battle of the Atlantic, a term he himself coined in February 1941. It was he who arranged the 'destroyers for bases' deal; it was he who put the building of escorts at a higher priority than that of capital ships; it was he who sought by every means to involve the United States Navy in the defence of the convoys. Aircraft, however, he believed best committed to strategic bombing offensives against Germany itself. The naval critics claim that, in consequence, the U-boat bases went unattacked, while operational units were spared the risk of detection from the air while in great waters. These are, in fact two separate issues. The first is quickly disposed of: thanks to Hitler's remarkable prescience in building bomb-proof pens in the Atlantic ports, bombing submarine bases was futile; when Churchill sanctioned a major effort in 1943 (3,568 sorties, January–May), it destroyed no U-boats at all.[26] The second issue is more complex. The appearance of aircraft did force U-boats to dive, effectively robbing them of their attack speed. Until the end of 1942, however, there were so few Very Long Range (VLR) aircraft available that the question of whether the 'air gap' in mid-Atlantic might have been closed is academic. By mid-1943, when more VLR aircraft had been produced, the Battle of the Atlantic was already won by other means. Aircraft could, meanwhile, have been diverted from bombing to patrolling the Bay of Biscay, where the U-boats made surface passages to their patrol stations; the record of air successes in the Bay suggests, however, that bombers were no better employed there than in the German skies.

Were the bombers well employed against Germany? In his major memorandum of 3 September 1940, Churchill wrote:

The Navy can lose us the war, but only the Air Force can win it. Therefore, our supreme effort must be to gain overwhelming mastery in the air. The Fighters are our salvation, but the Bombers alone provide the means to victory. We must, therefore, develop the power to carry an ever-increasing volume of explosives to Germany, so as to pulverise the entire industry and scientific structure on which the war effort and economic life of the enemy depend, while holding him at arm's length from our Island.[27]

This is a statement of the theory of strategic bombing in its purest form. It was one Churchill sincerely embraced at the outset and, if computations of investment of war production resources are significant, to which he remained broadly true until the end. Although the official bomber historians put the investment at only 7 per cent, A. J. P. Taylor thought one-third nearer the mark.[28] Churchill's enthusiasm for bombing, a different matter, waxed and waned. For much of the period of isolation, he pinned high hopes on the bombers; there was, indeed, no other object for his optimism. Then, in October 1941, he was assailed by doubt; the quotation with which this essay begins—'he is an unwise man'—is taken from the paper in which he expressed his reservations. What led him to this feeling were the findings of his own statistical office, directed by Professor Lindemann, which demonstrated that, on moonless nights, only one-fifteenth of the bombs dropped by Bomber Command fell within five miles of the target; even with a moon, the figure rose to only two-fifths, at a time when the Command and could in any case carry only 200 tons of bombs to Germany at a time.[29]

Even the Air Staff, while it disputed Lindemann's figures, was forced to reconsider its theory. The man usually held responsible for the redirection of Bomber Command's strategy is Air Marshal Sir Arthur Harris, its chief from February 1942. There is no doubt, however, that Air Marshal Sir Charles Portal, whom he succeeded on the former's appointment as Chief of the Air Staff, had already been persuaded that precision bombing did not work and that 'area bombing' must be adopted instead. Portal is widely recognized as the most intelligent of the Chiefs of Staff; with Portal's hand on central policy and Harris mobilizing a thousand bombers at a time to raid German cities, Churchill's faith was partly restored. He was never again, however, to subscribe to the true faith. 'Harris could get much from Churchill, but he could not get the unconditional priority in production and allocation of scarce resources that he viewed as essential to securing the great strategic air victory of which he never ceased to dream.'[30] At Casablanca in January 1943, the Combined Chiefs of Staff agreed to a strategic concept that accorded a high place to strategic bombing. Even Portal was by then persuaded, none the less, that the decisive campaign would be fought on land; and as the priorities agreed at the conference were much to Churchill's taste, the bomber barons, British and Americans alike, were thereby diverted into organizing a Combined Bomber Offensive 'to weaken Germany's war-making capacity to the point to which invasion would become possible'. Airpower, in which Churchill had invested trust at a time when Britain had no other means to strike at the enemy, was thereby demoted to the role its professional advocates had always sought to evade, that of a supporting arm to the armies and navies.

This return to orthodoxy better represented Churchill's strategic instinct. A strand of the unorthodox was nevertheless deeply embedded in his military outlook. The Boer War had been a formative experience. Boer militancy had, persuaded him of the power of the armed citizens to defy an invader; Boer guerrilla tactics had reinforced his natural enthusiasm for the daring and unexpected stroke. The urge to do the surprising thing contributed to the Greek expedition, to Dakar, to the capture of Madagascar in 1942, perhaps to the campaigns in Lebanon, Syria, and Iraq, certainly to his—fortunately frustrated but persistent— urge to return to Norway. It unfortunately underlay his decision, so much disapproved of by the Americans that they would have no part of it, to seize the Dodecanese in the wake of the Italian surrender; refus- ing once again to heed warnings of the danger of enemy land-based air- power, he committed a force of high quality troops to defeat and capture, thereby restoring the confidence of Hitler and his armed forces in their ability to retain control of the Aegean and southern Balkans.[31]

No form of irregular operation more stimulated Churchill than Commando operations. The term was taken from the Boers. On 5 June 1940 he wrote to the Chiefs of Staff: 'Enterprises must be prepared with specially trained troops of the hunter class, who can develop a reign of terror first of all on the "butcher and bolt" policy. I look to the Chiefs of Staff to propose me measures for a vigorous, enterprising and ceaseless offensive against the whole German occupied coastline.'[32] The germ of the Commandos already existed in the form of several 'Independent Companies'. Under Churchill's goading, the Commandos became an élite, much to the disgruntlement of senior officers who lost their best junior leaders and soldiers to those units; and in the period of isolation they did much to hearten the British public by their raids on the French and Norwegian coasts. Cold analysis, however, estab- lishes that, although their raids infuriated Hitler, his strategy was dis- turbed by them scarcely at all. It was the vulnerability of Norway to a large amphibious operation, not any need to defend its coasts against

Commandos, that caused him to garrison it in disproportionate strength. Here his fears mirrored Churchill's ambitions in reverse. The one large amphibious thrust that Churchill actually essayed, at Dieppe in 1942, was repelled with humiliating ease and grievous loss of life.

The objective worth of the 'butcher and bolt' policy was therefore small, whatever its effect on national morale and Churchill's own spirits. His enthusiasm for what he called 'the Wizard War' was of altogether greater significance. For a man virtually without scientific education of any sort, Churchill had the keenest understanding of the importance of scientific innovation to the war he had to wage, a remarkably sure touch in choosing between good and bad advice, and an admirable readiness to put resources behind a promising line of research.

By far the most fruitful result of Churchill's concern to establish technical superiority over the enemy was the support he gave to the expansion of the Government Code and Cypher School at Bletchley and the effective use of its product. 'From the moment he became Prime Minister he showed that he had grasped, better than any other statesman of his time, the two main keys to an intelligence victory . . . the crucial importance of Sigint [Signal Intelligence] and the vital need to co-ordinate the still diffuse intelligence effort.' The solution to the second matter was organizational; to the first, however, it was one of investment, of both money and brains. In October 1941 the Bletchley cryptographers so feared that shortage of the two ingredients threatened to 'put them out of business' that they sent a delegate direct to 10 Downing Street. 'Almost from that day the rough ways began miraculously to be made smooth. The flow of bombes [electrical calculators] was speeded up, the staff bottlenecks relieved, and we were able to devote ourselves uninterruptedly to the business in hand.'[33]

A severe view is taken of Britain's comparative lag in most other scientific fields by historical critics such as Correlli Barnett. Barnett points out that by 1944 the only sector of research and development in which Britain remained ahead of competitors, allied or enemy, was jet propulsion. He also makes the excruciatingly embarrassing point that, even when British scientists achieved a clear breakthrough, as with the development of the cavity magnetron, heart of short-wave radar, British industry was unable to manufacture it in quantity and became dependent on re-imports from the United States to satisfy demand.[34] These were historical defects, however, which could not be corrected in wartime. Churchill cannot be blamed. Indeed, he ought to be praised for his decision—prompted in part, but only in part, by his desire to draw America into the war—to send the Air Ministry's Scientific Adviser, Sir Henry Tizard, to the United States in August 1940 with details and examples of all the military equipment under full-scale development in Britain at the time. Later, in an entirely justified but imaginative and generous transfer of material and talent, he would send the entire British atomic weapons programme ('Tube Alloys') to the United States to join the Manhattan Project, which produced the Hiroshima bomb.[35]

Though these were good decisions, since American industry thereby supplied the essential electronic equipment, British in origin, to British aircraft and ships which British industry could not produce in volume, Churchill is nevertheless accused of heeding much bad scientific advice. Such accusations should be treated with caution. Tizard, a wise and patriotic man, never caught the Prime Minister's ear. F. A. Lindemann, later Lord Cherwell, monopolized it. Lindemann was wrong on at least two major scores. He became an even more passionate advocate of 'area bombing' than Harris himself, and overcame both Tizard and the young P. M. S. Blackett on the issue, although the latter demonstrated that his estimates of damage were at least 600 per cent too large. More dangerously, he understimated the potentiality of Germany to develop rocket weapons. In May 1943 he gave as his considered opinion that he did 'not favour directing any considerable effort to coping with what seems to me a remote contingency'; only in July the following year was he prepared to concede that 'if the enemy has seen fit to divert so much of his resources to produce a long-range weapon, the threat cannot be altogether disregarded'.[36] Fortunately Lindemann's scepticism did not deter Churchill from approving a raid on Peenemünde in August 1943; it was an isolated attack, however, when persistence might have spared Britain much destruction and sorrow.

Criticism of Lindemann, nevertheless, is often personal. He was not a likeable man. Although John Colville found that 'it was impossible not to be fond of him', he also observed that Lindemann 'demonstrated an implacable, almost ludicrous dislike of anybody who had ever thwarted or opposed him', which comprised a large group.[37] Yet, if he aroused dislike in return, few denied that Lindemann had an eclectic scientific mind and a brilliant gift of exposition, precisely the qualities Churchill valued. Churchill was scientifically humble. Hitler, by contrast, as Albert Speer observed, was 'constantly endeavouring to show himself the equal or even the superior of the experts . . . he could grasp the essentials of complicated subjects [but] he arrived at the core of matters too easily and therefore could not understand them with real thoroughness'.[38] In those shortcomings lay the cause of many of Germany's failures in the wartime scientific field, notably the misapplication of jet propulsion to bombers and the extravagant dispersal of effort in nuclear research. If Churchill avoided comparable faults, it was because he trusted, and rightly trusted, Lindemann 'whose positive qualities outweighed the errors which, from time to time, vanity or miscalculation caused him to perpetrate'.[39]

This, then, is an audit of Churchill's strategic judgement at levels of importance immediately subordinate to the central issue of the war after America's entry.[40] That central issue was: how should the 'Germany-first' policy, agreed at Placentia Bay in August 1941, be implemented in practice? Much has been written on the subject, notably by Sir Michael Howard in his official history of Grand Strategy and in his digest of his conclusions, *The Mediterranean Strategy in the Second World War*.[41] The nub of the story may nevertheless be simply stated: it is one of the Americans' haste to open a second front by amphibious landing in north-west Europe, and of British, by which is meant largely Churchillian, efforts to slow, moderate, and even deflect the single-minded American dedication to that plan. Was Churchill right to pursue the policies that he did?

The question must be divided into three, chronologically: was he right in his policies between Pearl Harbor and the Anglo-American talks in London in July 1942; from then until the Trident conference in May 1943; and from then until the Tehran conference in the following November? The first period terminated with an agreement to abandon any thought of invasion that year, the second with an agreement to launch the Italian campaign, the third with a firm commitment to invade France in the summer of 1944.

Churchill's strategic judgement during the first period was correct without qualification. He was faced with an odd set of American attitudes. The United States Army's War Plans Division entered the war with a clear-cut plan, called the Victory Program, written by a graduate of the German Kriegsakademie, Lieutenant-Colonel Albert C. Wedemayer. It was based on 'Germany-first' but, unlike earlier and broader studies of that concept, Rainbow 5 and ABC-1, laid down precise targets for its achievement. The implementation of the Victory Program fell, however, not to Wedemayer, whose future lay in China, but to a new entrant to the War Plans Division, Dwight Eisenhower.

Eisenhower's initial reaction to the catastrophic news that flooded Washington in January 1942 was to discard the Victory Program and concentrate resources on stemming the Japanese tide. In mid-January he minuted: 'The whole Far East situation is crucial. My own plan is to drop everything else—Magnet [US troops to Britain], Gymnast [what would later be the Torch landing in North Africa], reserves to Ireland and make the British retire in Libya. Then scrape up everything, everybody, and get it into [the Netherlands East Indies] and Burma. We mustn't lose Netherlands East Indies–Singapore–Burma.'[42]

A week later, when it was obvious that MacArthur would have to abandon the Philippines, he swung to an exactly opposite position: 'We've got to get to Europe and fight—and we've got to quit wasting resources all over the world—and still worse—wasting time. If we're to keep Russia in, save the Middle East, India and Burma, we've got to begin slugging with air at Western Europe; to be followed with a land attack as soon as possible.'[43] Eisenhower very quickly converted General George Marshall, the US Army Chief of Staff, to his view, and Marshall believed that he had then converted Roosevelt. At any rate the plan was taken to London with presidential approval and presented to the British. Churchill and General Alan Brooke stonewalled but, anxious to avoid a breach at this early stage of the alliance, eventually acquiesced. They hoped, of course, to talk the Americans into postponing the early landing in Europe, 'Sledgehammer'. That was the main purpose of Churchill's visit to Washington in June. It had the opposite effect. When Marshall discovered that Churchill had indeed talked Roosevelt out of Sledgehammer but also into Torch—a North African expedition later in the year—the General joined forces with Admiral King to threaten that the United States should 'assume a defensive attitude against Germany, except for air operations, and use all available means in the Pacific'.

Marshall was playing politics: he remained true to 'Germany-first', but wanted to frighten the British out of what he saw as their procrastination and into a brisk timetable for action. In July he confronted the British Chiefs of Staff in London. Churchill mobilised the War Cabinet as well as the Chiefs of Staff to argue the American party down. There was unanimity among the British against an invasion in 1942, supported by detailed evidence to show that it would be premature. The Americans yielded to the argument and, to their surprise, found themselves drafting an alternative proposal that committed their forces to what would be Torch. On 25 July Churchill cabled Smuts that, after this Anglo-American meeting, there was 'complete unity between soldiers and statesman and our two countries'.[44]

So there was, for the time being. Sledgehammer had been an aberrant idea, and once the Americans' urge for precipitate action, fired by the outrage of Pearl Harbor, had cooled, they were ready to admit as much. That did not mean, however, that Roundup, the plan for an invasion in 1943, was to be abandoned also. Marshall expected that, after the successful conclusion of Torch, the American—and British— expeditionary forces would be transferred to the United Kingdom to prepare a cross-Channel invasion as soon as possible afterwards. It was in that expectation that Marshall arrived at the Casablanca conference in January 1943. Brooke, articulating both his own and Churchill's hesitations, argued that the Allies should persist with a strategy of 'overstretch', through attacks on Sicily and Sardinia and a threat towards Yugoslavia, thus forcing the Germans to divert force down the poor communications of the Italian peninsula and the Balkans. 'Diversion' to Marshall meant committing resources to 'a suction pump'; he found himself nevertheless agreeing to persisting with a strategy of attrition, against his better judgement.[45] At the Washington Conference in May his patience was tried even further. Churchill, through Brooke, demanded a commitment to the Sicily operation, and a prolonged strategic argument ensued. Marshall, for whom the Mediterranean had now become a 'vacuum', once again threatened to side with King and send forces out of the Mediterranean to the Pacific. Eventually the British and American staffs compromised by agreeing on Sicily but setting a date for Roundup, now codenamed Overlord, of 1 May 1944. Until November the British were to have a free hand in the Mediterranean; thereafter there was to be a major transfer of force to Britain. Churchill insisted on taking Marshall with him to North Africa to 'convince Eisenhower and others that nothing less than Rome could satisfy the requirements of this year's campaign'.[46]

If Churchill's position up to the London meetings of July 1942 had been correct, his manœuvring in the ten months between that time and the Washington Trident conference is much less justifiable. It is not only with hindsight that a German vulnerability can be perceived: the Wehrmacht could be seen to be grievously overstretched on the Russian front from Stalingrad onwards. Moreover, the Allies, after the Torch landings, had decisively seized the initiative in the Mediterranean. Even had they decided to reduce their commitment there as soon as Algeria and Morocco had been secured, there was no means open to Hitler to

retrieve the situation. It is therefore a nice question as to who was playing whose game in the Allies' widening of the Mediterranean campaign.
True, as Churchill foresaw, the invasion of Sicily led directly to the
overthrow of Mussolini and Italy's change of sides. It did not, however,
bring Turkey into the war. Nor did it compromise the German position in the Balkans. On the contrary, Hitler continued to hold down
Greece and Yugoslavia, without Italian assistance, at no great extra cost
to his resources, while the Allied offensive against Rome was to last six
months longer than Churchill had envisaged and commit some of the
best British and American divisions to the most gruelling of the land
fighting experienced in western Europe.

Since there is considerable doubt whether a cross-Channel invasion
could have been mounted once Algeria had been cleared, greater doubt
that it could have succeeded, and certainty only that Hitler would, at
whatever cost, have found the means to reinforce German forces in
France at the expense of the Eastern Front once he was alert to the
danger of an invasion in 1943, Churchill cannot be inculpated with an
unwillingness to win the war in 1943. He may, nevertheless, have been
guilty of hoping for more from indirect methods than such methods
could deliver, of underestimating the American armed forces' problem-
solving capabilities, and shunning too readily an equalization of sacrifice
with the Russians.

That was certainly Stalin's view, which surfaced starkly at the end of
the third period under consideration, culminating at the Tehran conference in November 1943. In the meantime Churchill had transferred
support from Mihailovic to Tito in Yugoslavia, a direct result of his
hopes that a Balkan strategy would pay dividends, and made his ill-
judged assault on the Dodecanese. At the Anglo-American Cairo conference, which preceded Tehran, he told those assembled that
' "Overlord" remained top of the bill, but this operation should not be
such a tyrant as to rule out every other activity in the Mediterranean';
at its end Ismay, his Personal Staff Officer, assured him that 'it looks as
if you can do all you want in the Mediterranean (including the Balkans
and Aegean) . . . provided that Overlord is postponed until the 15th
July'.[47]

The British in general, Churchill in particular, were deluding themselves. The Washington strategic powerhouse had had enough of 'suction pumps' and 'vacuums', while Roosevelt was determined that at
Tehran he would establish a personal relationship with Stalin, even if
that meant Churchill was left to argue his case with the Russians alone.

Churchill was so left. 'Do the British really believe in "Overlord"',
Stalin asked Churchill, 'or are they only saying so to reassure the
Soviet Union?'[48] As the conference wore on, Stalin increased the pressure. He demanded that Italy be recognized as a diversion, that a fixed
date be named for Overlord, and that a commander be nominated, if
not at the conference, then within a week of its closure. He got, with
Roosevelt's abandonment of Churchill, all he wanted. From that
moment onwards, Churchill's ability to deflect the course of Allied
strategy from anything but an all-out battle with the Wehrmacht in the
heartland of Europe withered away.

Yet it is on the story of Churchill's encounters with Stalin that a
review of his strategy ought finally to dwell, and by no means in negative
mood. There were wide areas of the world, beyond Britain's strategic out-
reach or at its very fringes, where Churchill had exerted minimal
influence or none at all. The best that can be said of the interest he had
taken in the Far Eastern war, acute though it had been at times, is that it
brought, late in the day, the recapture of Burma and an honourable place
for Britain at the Japanese surrender ceremony following the dispatch of
the Royal Navy to the Pacific, ill-adapted though British ships may have
been to fight with America's magnificent Task Forces. With the Russians
things were different. Britain, despite the agony of the Arctic convoys,
had contributed little to the Russian war effort in material terms; the
intangible aid it had furnished, through the provision of 'Ultra' intelligence, had not always been appreciated and often ignored.[49]

Nevertheless, if the longest view is taken, Churchill's strategic dealings with Stalin may be judged to have served Britain's interests very
well indeed. At Yalta, in February 1945, Churchill acquiesced in decisions about the future of several east European countries, notably
Poland, for which he has since been much reproached. Yalta, by any
rational analysis, was water under the bridge. The Red Army already
occupied the territories in hindsight alleged to have been 'given away',
and there was no means by which they could have been spared the
imposition of Soviet-sponsored governments. In Greece and Yugoslavia,
however, Churchill helped to achieve post-war outcomes very
favourable indeed both to his own country and to the Western alliance
at large.

It is conventional to ascribe these outcomes to the meeting he held
with Stalin in Moscow on 9 October 1944, where the Prime Minister,
apparently in levity, proposed to the dictator a set of 'percentages of
influence' that should operate in the Balkans.[50] In whatever spirit they

were offered, Stalin accepted them at face value. Thus armed with his acquiescence in Britain's 'ninety per cent of the say in Greece', Churchill in the following December sent British paratroops to intervene between Communists and monarchists in Athens, with decisive effect for the fortunes of the latter in the burgeoning civil war. Indeed, without Churchill's resolve to restore legitimate government in Greece, it is probable that the country would have fallen to the Soviet bloc.

The results of Churchill's agreement with Stalin to '50–50%' influence in Yugoslavia are more convoluted to trace. The single key element in ensuring Tito's freedom of action after the liberation of his country was the withdrawal of Marshal Tolbukhin's troops once they had captured Belgrade. That was agreed at Tito's unscheduled meeting with Stalin in Moscow in September 1944. It is difficult to judge which is the more surprising—Stalin's willingness to make the promise beforehand or his keeping it afterwards. It may be that he could not spare even a token Russian force to sustain a Soviet presence at that stage of the war; it seems more probable that he trusted Tito's loyalty to the Cominform. As things turned out, this was the single worst geopolitical judgement of Stalin's post-1941 career. By it he deprived himself of that secure position on the Mediterranean side of the Straits that it had been a Russian ambition to possess since the reign of Catherine the Great.

We cannot impute to Churchill the foresight of such an advantageous outcome from his switch of support from Mihailovic to Tito in September 1943; Tito's defection from the Soviet bloc lay five years in the future. Nevertheless—and here we work in the dark, since the politics of the episode are still hidden—Churchill may have calculated that, while there was a gamble to be taken on Tito, the future of Mihailovic, in an eastern Europe that Stalin was bound to dominate, was pregnant with doom. This was a harsh decision. Tito's determination to wage guerrilla warfare on the march brought atrocity and scorched earth in its wake. Mihailovic's policy—which we may now judge to have been more genuinely patriotic—of keeping his powder dry against the moment when he could forestall a liberation from outside by proclaiming the *ustanak*—national uprising—would certainly have condemned his followers to the fate suffered by the Polish Home Army when it instituted an identical plan in August 1944.[51] The Russians would have stood by, let the Germans exterminate the anti-Communist patriots, and then advanced to impose their own regime.

A concluding consideration of Churchill's strategy may, therefore, end where it began, in the eastern Mediterranean. His prevarication over a commitment to the cross-Channel invasion had only in part been motivated by belief in the opportunities that a Balkan strategy offered, much more by considerations of timetabling and fears of heavy casualties. His belief that the Middle East and southern Europe was a region both of immediate strategic opportunity and of long-term strategic importance was proved right from the start, and triumphantly vindicated at the end. By sending the best of Britain's army and navy to Egypt in 1940 he did indeed seriously distort the development of Axis strategy at a moment when it seemed that that alliance could not be deflected from triumph; and in 1944, by tweaking what appeared to be minor concessions from Stalin, by backing any group whose nationalism seemed to align it with British interests, and by doling out in penny-packets the armed force of which he had unilateral control, Churchill created conditions that were to deny the Soviet Union an effective military stance in the Mediterranean once the Cold War began. On 3 July 1940 Churchill was asked by Maisky, the Russian ambassador, about the nature of his general strategy. 'My general strategy at present', he answered, 'is to last out the next three months.'[52] In its cryptic concealment of a deeper purpose, it was an answer worthy of Maisky's master himself.

20

Churchill and the Defence Chiefs

MICHAEL CARVER

To understand the relations between Winston Churchill and the senior officers of the Royal Navy, the army, and the Royal Air Force in the Second World War, one must appreciate that he took a romantic view of war and how it should be conducted. His hero was John Churchill, first Duke of Marlborough, and, in his biography of his ancestor, he wrote the following passage, which is treasured by military men because it reveals Churchill's attitude towards war:

Accounts of battles and campaigns almost invariably describe the *qualitative* character of the manœuvres without reference to their *quantitative* side . . . Where, then, is the secret of victory?

The 'secret of victory' for Churchill had nothing to do with commonplace assumptions about the nature of war. He developed his own sophisticated interpretation:

It looks at first sight so simple to say 'turn the flank', 'pierce the centre' or 'cut the communications'. But apparently none of these processes work by themselves. All are liable to be countered by other equally obvious and desirable movements. Thus the text books on war too often merely show certain relations of the fronts and flanks of armies which have been as often favourable to one side as to the other. In truth, all these relations, though suggestive to a student, are meaningless apart from their *quantitative* data. Circumstances alone decide whether a correct conventional manœuvre is right or wrong. The circumstances include all the factors which are at work at the time; the numbers and quality of the troops and their morale, their weapons, their confidence in their leaders, the character of the country, the condition of the roads, time and the weather: and behind these the politics of their states, the special interests which each army has to guard, together with many other complications. And it is the true comprehension at any given moment of the dynamic sum of all these constantly shifting forces that constitutes military genius.

He goes on to establish the role of the individual:

The problem can seldom be calculated on paper alone, and never copied from examples of the past. Its highest solution must be evolved from the eye and brain and soul of a single man, which from hour to hour are making subconsciously all the unweighable adjustments, no doubt with many errors, but with an ultimate practical accuracy. Thus while nothing is more easy than to assign reasons for success and failure by describing the movements, it is between more or less equal opponents impossible to reveal the real secret of either. That is why the campaigns of the great commanders often seem so simple that one wonders why the other fellow did not do it as well. That is why critics write so cogently, and yet successful performers are so rare. Almost any intelligent scribe can draw up a lucid and logical treatise full of laboriously ascertained facts and technical phrases on a particular war situation. But the great captains of history, as has been said, seem to move their armies about 'as easily as they ride their horses from place to place'. Nothing but genius, the daemon in man, can answer the riddles of war, and genius, though it may be armed, cannot be acquired, either by reading or by experience. In default of genius nations have to make war as best they can, and since that quality is much rarer than the largest and purest diamonds, most wars are mainly tales of muddle. But when from time to time it flashes upon the scene, order and design with a sense almost of infallibility draw out from hazard and confusion.[1]

In Churchill's view few generals, admirals, or air marshals came up to that standard. Most of them, particularly the generals, seemed to him little more than the 'intelligent scribes' he scorned. He looked for debonair, swashbuckling heroes who would cast caution to the winds and dare all in one throw. Men like Roger Keyes, Carton de Wiart, and Orde Wingate met with his approval, as did the intrepid Bernard Freyberg, although at times he could be as cautious as at others he could be fearlessly bold; and Louis Mountbatten, whose verve, enthusiasm, and drive was matched by his charm. Churchill never ceased to favour Harold Alexander, although others, including Alan Brooke, saw through the courage and charm, which concealed a lack of firm grip over his subordinates and a failure to initiate action. In default of finding the qualities of leadership he sought in the senior officers of the armed forces, Churchill was determined to provide them himself, confident that he possessed them. Ironically, the general who at last brought him the victories he craved, Montgomery, exhibited all the characteristics that Churchill deplored. Montgomery's method was careful, cautious, and calculating, and he refused to move until he had all the resources he demanded. He openly proclaimed that he would not undertake an operation unless he was certain that it would succeed.

Churchill's experience in the First World War, especially of his brain-child, the ill-fated Gallipoli campaign, reinforced the determination he had always shown, in both peace and war, to direct everything himself and to prod and pester everyone else, whether subordinate or not, to exert themselves to the utmost both to find a solution to the problem and to execute it as rapidly as possible. From the start of the Second World War, his experience as First Lord of the Admiralty reinforced him in that resolution. He was appalled at the confusion and inefficiency with which the short campaign in Norway was conducted. The machinery for arriving at decisions of policy was, in theory, the Cabinet, a body too large for the purpose when decisions were needed at short notice and at frequent intervals. The organization for translating such decisions, if they had been clearly stated (which was seldom the case), into the higher direction of operations did not exist, until the Minister for the Co-ordination of Defence, the retired Admiral of the Fleet Lord Chatfield, established the Military Co-ordinating Committee, a ministerial committee, which the Chiefs of Staff attended. As the Prime Minister, Neville Chamberlain, did not preside, it lacked authority, and Churchill soon dominated it, his anomalous position being confirmed by Chamberlain appointing him Chairman of the Committee when Chatfield resigned on 3 April 1940. As the Chiefs of Staff Committee had no independent chairman and there was no joint service command, subordinate to them, to direct the operations of the navy, the army, and the air force in the campaign, Churchill characteristically seized the initiative in his thirst for action. He provided leadership, but he had no authority over the army and the air force, and the result was to make confusion worse confounded, although at times it produced action and resolution when they were sorely needed. At the heart of the matter lay the problem that the policy determining the aim of the campaign was never clear and kept on changing, with fatal consequences.

At least Churchill was able to introduce a leader after his own heart, Admiral of the Fleet The Earl of Cork and Orrery, a fiery, red-headed sailor who, at Narvik, pressed for resolute action in contrast to the cautious, methodical approach of Lieutenant General Pierse Mackesy, who was operating under totally different orders from the Admiral's. Churchill thoroughly approved of his replacement by General Sir Claude Auchinleck, who adopted a more positive attitude. Churchill's record over the confusion surrounding events at Trondheim, after the Germans had invaded Norway, does him little credit. One of the victims of events was his favoured Carton de Wiart, in command of the forces intended to attack Trondheim from the landward side, who was never told that Churchill had cancelled the naval assault.

Whatever responsibility Churchill must bear for the glaring errors of the campaign, there was no doubt in his mind that the organization for deciding policy and for translating decisions into military operations was far too cumbersome and inefficient. When, therefore, he succeeded Chamberlain as Prime Minister as the Germans invaded France and Belgium, he was determined both to simplify it and to guarantee its effectiveness by gathering all the reins into his own hands. With the King's approval, he appointed himself Minister of Defence and established a machinery, alien to British constitutional practice, which the French would have called his own 'cabinet militaire', known as the Defence Office, created out of the Secretariat of the Committee of Imperial Defence. The head of the Defence Office, an Indian Army major-general, Hastings ('Pug') Ismay, was to sit with the Chiefs of Staff as Churchill's personal representative, both telling them what Churchill wanted and relaying their views back to him. On occasions, Churchill would himself meet with the Chiefs of Staff or would summon them to a meeting either of the full Defence Committee of the Cabinet or of the War Cabinet; but, as the war progressed, meetings of the Defence Committee became a rarity and most business was conducted in what was called a 'Staff Conference', that is, a meeting of the Chiefs of Staff with Churchill. In this way he by-passed the First Lord of the Admiralty and the Secretaries of State for War and Air, who were generally relegated to routine matters, although they might intervene if their service was primarily involved.

Churchill was extremely fortunate in finding Ismay to head the Defence Office. Ismay proved ideal for his delicate task and remained in it throughout the war, enjoying the trust both of his imperious master and of all the successive Chiefs of Staff, as well as of the senior representatives of Britain's allies. Initially, with events in France and Belgium dominating every hour, Churchill made no changes among the Chiefs of Staff themselves, although he had tried to impose on them his old friend, the 68-year-old Admiral of the Fleet Sir Roger Keyes, the hero of Zeebrugge, as Chairman of the Committee. In face of their opposition, he had to fob Keyes off with the post of Director of Amphibious Warfare, and the Chiefs of Staff Committee remained without an independent chairman until 1956. Until then the Chief of Staff longest in post acted as chairman, this practice imposing on him a burden additional to that of acting as head of his own service. It is interesting to speculate whether or not the institution of an independent chairman would have worked satisfactorily, if at all, with Churchill. It should theoretically have prevented him from dealing directly with subordinate commanders, and should have acted as a buffer between him and both the Chiefs of Staff and subordinate commands; but one cannot imagine Churchill accepting such limitations, and the likelihood is that the chairman would have found his position intolerable, unless he acted, just as Ismay did, as a go-between, smoothing the waters, but not attempting to inject his own judgement or authority. Another attempt to insert an old favourite into the military hierarchy was defeated when the 67-year-old Marshal of the Royal Air Force Lord Trenchard refused the post offered to him by Churchill on 23 May 1940 of command of 'all land, sea and air forces at home in the event of invasion'. Trenchard's remark that the job could only be done properly by a Deputy Prime Minister is said to have infuriated Churchill.

In the aftermath of Dunkirk, Churchill had time to take stock of his senior officers. He had not been impressed by the performance of General Sir Edmund Ironside as Chief of the Imperial General Staff (CIGS), either in the Norwegian campaign or in the hectic fortnight between the German invasion of Belgium and the evacuation from Dunkirk. Churchill had given decisive support to Leslie Hore-Belisha, then Secretary of State for War, appointing Ironside as CIGS at the outbreak of war, when General The Viscount Gort was made Commander-in-Chief of the British Expeditionary Force (BEF) in France. 'Tiny' Ironside was the sort of general Churchill instinctively admired: large, energetic, and with a reputation for bravery and unorthodoxy; but he appeared to lack the agility of mind to be an effective operator in the War Office or on the Chiefs of Staff Committee. He spoke seven languages and his escapades as an intelligence officer in the Boer War were the model for Richard Hannay, the hero of John Buchan's novels. Ironside was moved to the newly created post of Commander-in-Chief Home Forces, his place being taken by General Sir John Dill, a different character. Dill allied a quick mind to a quiet manner, concealing a strong will. He had impressed everyone by his performance in command of 1st Corps in the BEF under Gort.

Churchill had no reason to wish to change the First Sea Lord, Admiral of the Fleet Sir Dudley Pound, who also acted as Chairman of the Chiefs of Staff, although it was generally known that his physical condition was not good. Pound had evolved a method for dealing with

Churchill when the latter had been at the Admiralty. Like Churchill a centralizer and workaholic, he would endure without complaint the former's demanding working habits and tolerate his interference in detail, unless it looked like leading to disaster. He was accused by some of not standing up to Churchill strongly enough and of allowing his subordinates to face the consequences. As a result, Churchill realized that, if Pound objected strongly to something, he must have gone too far, and drew back. Unfortunately his trust in Pound made him reluctant to replace him when he should have done so, when Pound's health had deteriorated to such a degree that he was no longer an effective head of his service or Chairman of the Chiefs of Staff. The burden this imposed on Pound must have contributed to his death in 1943.

Air Chief Marshal Sir Cyril Newall had been Chief of the Air Staff since 1937, and, at the age of 54, would in normal times have been due for retirement. Although he was highly respected in the Royal Air Force and outside it, he had not come well out of the arguments as to whether to accede to the French request to deploy more fighter aircraft to France, or those concerned with the strategy to be followed in the Battle of Britain. In both cases he appeared to have stood on the sidelines and let the Commander-in-Chief of Fighter Command, Sir Hugh ('Stuffy') Dowding, bear the burden alone. Churchill was glad to appoint the 47-year-old Air Chief Marshal Sir Charles Portal, then Commander-in-Chief of Bomber Command, to take Newall's place. He was, as Churchill wrote, 'the accepted star of the Air Force'. Like Newall a rather aloof character, Portal had a formidable intellect, capacity for work, and strength of will. He was to remain Chief of the Air Staff for the rest of the war, earning Churchill's deep respect, and was often the member of the Chiefs of Staff who proposed the solution all accepted to end a dispute between themselves or between them and Churchill.

Almost as soon as Portal had taken over, Dowding was retired. He had held his command for four years and was 58. He had been due for retirement in July, but had been asked by Newall to stay on until October, which he had 'stuffily', and fortunately for Britain, agreed to do. But his retirement seemed to him, and to others, notably in Fighter Command, to have been abruptly carried out and not accompanied by any signal honour. Churchill, who held a high opinion of him in spite of the taciturn stubbornness with which he had resisted pressure, was concerned and appointed him to head a mission to the USA, which did not prove a success. The fact that he was eleven years older than Portal may have influenced the latter to feel that the sooner Dowding left the better, his place being taken by Air Chief Marshal Sir Sholto Douglas, who did not have to face the same sort of concentrated test that Dowding had, although the Luftwaffe's night-time raids on cities meant that Fighter Command was never out of Churchill's mind. Sir Richard Peirse succeeded Portal at Bomber Command, where before long he was to disappoint Churchill's inflated expectations of what his operations could achieve.

By this time Churchill's attention was drawn to the only area in which the army was actively engaged, in the Middle East against Italy. After some sparring on the Libyan frontier, the Italian Tenth Army had cautiously advanced fifty miles into Egypt's Western Desert and halted there. Britain had no overall joint service commander to direct the operations of the services in the Middle East. Admiral Sir Andrew Cunningham commanded the Mediterranean Fleet whose base had been moved from Malta to Alexandria before the entry of Italy into the war. General Sir Archibald Wavell commanded the small, ill-equipped Middle East Army divided between Egypt, the Sudan, East Africa, Aden, and British Somalia—everywhere facing superior Italian forces. It also had to cope with Palestine bordering on Syria where the Vichy French were still in control. Air Chief Marshal Sir Arthur Longmore's Middle East Air Force had to deal not only with those countries but Iraq as well. Each man dealt with his own ministry and Chief of Staff in London, while together they formed the Middle East Commanders-in-Chief Committee. Wavell and Longmore both had their headquarters in Cairo, but Cunningham, when ashore, was in Alexandria, with a naval captain representing him in Cairo. The Commander-in-Chief East Indies, responsible for naval operations in the Red Sea and Indian Ocean, based at Trincomalee in Ceylon (as Sri Lanka was then called) was also officially a member of the Committee, although never attending in person.

Churchill now saw the Mediterranean and Middle East as the one possible area for offensive action, and he urged both Cunningham to attack the Italian fleet and Wavell and Longmore to deal with the Italian army, wherever it might be. For these purposes he took risks with the defence of Britain in sending reinforcements, although most of those to Wavell, other than tanks, came from India, Australia, New Zealand, and South Africa. Churchill dealt directly with Cunningham on naval matters and with Wavell on others, tending to treat the latter, as he did successive army Commanders-in-Chief Middle East, as if they were joint service commanders. Initially Churchill, disregarding the paucity of Cunningham's resources, thought him too defensively minded, and they clashed over the latter's unwillingness to take direct action against the ships of the French fleet in the harbour at Alexandria. The success of the Fleet Air Arm's attack on the Italian fleet at Taranto in November 1940 and other successful naval actions against ships in both the eastern and western Mediterranean led not only to a toning down of what Cunningham called Churchill's 'ceaseless prodding', but even to congratulations to Cunningham and to Admiral Somerville, commanding Force H in the western Mediterranean, about whom Churchill continued to harbour doubts. Those arose from Somerville's reluctance to attack the French navy at Oran and Mers-el-Kebir, and, although he could not in any way be held responsible for the escape of French cruisers from the Mediterranean to the Atlantic, which led to the dismissal of Admiral Dudley North (Flag Officer Commanding North Atlantic and also based at Gibraltar), Somerville's involvement in the abortive attack on Dakar did him no good in Churchill's eyes.

The dissatisfaction with what Churchill regarded as the timidity of the admirals in the Mediterranean surfaced again in April 1941, when, under pressure from Churchill, the Admiralty proposed to block Tripoli harbour by sinking the battleship *Barham* and an old light cruiser in it. Cunningham protested strongly and, after an exchange of signals, was allowed to restrict his action to a bombardment. This had followed the Battle of Matapan, in which Cunningham had inflicted a decisive defeat on the Italian navy, which did not prevent Churchill from sending over to the Admiralty a letter from Lord Salisbury, Secretary of State for the Dominions, recommending it as 'an important outside opinion': Salisbury had accused the Admiralty of not liking to risk their ships, citing the fact that at Matapan 'Our Fleet did not receive a scratch'.[2] The navy's participation in the short and disastrous campaign in Greece and Crete which followed shortly after these events was to confound such critics.

It was not only the admirals in that area who were to suffer from Churchill's 'ceaseless prodding'. Wavell had been at the receiving end of it ever since June 1940. In August he was summoned to London and did not make a good impression. He was not accustomed to the sharp, aggressive cross-examination which was Churchill's normal approach, and became even more taciturn than normal, if that was possible. This further prejudiced Churchill against him. Only strong pressure from

Dill persuaded Wavell to accept an invitation to Chequers for the weekend, where further talks merely served to prejudice the two against each other. Eden wrote in his diary:

More Wavell talks, when Winston told me he must stay another day. I was against this, for Wavell is doing no good here and should either return or be replaced. Winston asked me who was a possible alternative. I said Auchinleck, he agreed. But we both felt that he had not sufficient evidence to compel a change which at the moment might have a very bad effect on morale throughout Middle East. At a further meeting of the four of us in the afternoon, Winston suddenly agreed that Wavell should leave tonight.[3]

Churchill's feelings about Wavell were aggravated by his discovery, after Wavell had returned to Cairo, that British casualties in the evacuation from Somaliland (which had taken place while Wavell was in London) had been only 260, while the Italians had suffered 1,800. He demanded the dismissal of the commander, General Godwin-Austen, and that a general from Auchinleck's command in India should hold an inquiry. Wavell rejected both and ended his telegram with the words 'a big butcher's bill is not necessarily evidence of good tactics', which not unnaturally infuriated Churchill even more. His dissatisfaction with Wavell was not dispelled until Eden returned from a visit to the Middle East in November with details of Wavell's plan to attack the Italians in the Egyptian Western Desert, which led to Lieutenant-General Sir Richard O'Connor's brilliant campaign, ending in the total destruction of the Italian Tenth Army at Beda Fomm in February 1941. By that time Wavell's forces were on their way to victory in Ethiopia, and, without any undue pressure from London, he had committed other forces to the support of Greece, which was fighting the Italians, while the threat of German intervention loomed behind.

Churchill's attitude towards Wavell's campaign in Ethiopia was ambivalent. At one moment he was suggesting that the Italians there could be left to wither on the vine: at the next he would be urging Wavell to act more rapidly and making detailed suggestions as to how he should do so. Much the same happened over Greece. In both cases Wavell was consistently in favour of a forward policy, hesitating only, in the case of Greece, when General Metaxas, the Greek Prime Minister, in January 1941 rejected his offer of a British expeditionary force. A few days before, Churchill had told his colleagues that, from the political point of view, it was imperative to help the Greeks against the Germans; but, after the rejection of Wavell's offer by General Metaxas, and as Eden and Dill set off to the Middle East on 12

February (the day Rommel landed in Africa), Churchill took a realistic and generally pessimistic view of the chances of British intervention being successful. It was the advice of Wavell, backed by Eden and Dill and supported by Longmore, and more reluctantly by Cunningham, that persuaded a doubting Churchill and Chiefs of Staff that a British expedition to Greece, although a gamble, had a reasonable chance of success. On 20 February Churchill signalled to Eden: 'Do not consider yourself obligated to a Greek enterprise if in your hearts you feel it will be another Norwegian fiasco. If no good plan can be made please say so. But of course you know how valuable success would be.'[4] Having flown to Athens, Eden, Wavell, and Dill recommended that 'the maximum' British military and air support to Greece should be dispatched 'at the earliest moment'. This swayed Churchill 'in favour of going to the rescue of Greece'. As he put it to the War Cabinet: 'One of the results of it might be to bring in Turkey and Yugoslavia and to force the Germans to bring more troops from Germany', adding that the reaction of the United States 'would be favourable'. Each member of the War Cabinet was asked his individual view and all concurred.

That decision having been taken, Eden and Dill, visiting Athens again and finding the Greek Commander-in-Chief, General Papagos, pessimistic, signalled that the operation was likely to be 'more hazardous than it seemed a week ago' but 'still not by any means hopeless'. This prompted Churchill to make the unfair remark to John Colville, his private secretary: 'The poor Chiefs of Staff will get very much out of breath in their desire to run away.'[5]

From then on almost nothing went right for the unfortunate Wavell, starting with Rommel's riposte towards the end of March, which led to the collapse of the forces under Lieutenant-General Sir Philip Neame in Cyrenaica, the withdrawal to Tobruk and its encirclement, all within two weeks, eliciting a further comment by Churchill to Colville that he thought 'Wavell etc had been very silly in North Africa and should have been prepared to meet an attack there'.[6] This was immediately followed by the German attack on Yugoslavia and the disastrous campaign in Greece and Crete. Churchill was particularly critical of Wavell's failure to have provided adequate defences for Crete beforehand. While still attempting to recover from the evacuation from Greece, Wavell had been urged to provide forces, including some of de Gaulle's Free French, to invade Syria, held by French forces loyal to Vichy, and at the same time to send troops to Iraq to help the RAF at Habbaniya deal with Rashid Ali. He protested against both, saying:

'You must trust my judgement in this matter or relieve me of my command.'[7] This may have been the last straw which determined Churchill to do just that. He remarked to Colville, 'He sounds a tired and disheartened man'; and on the same evening, 21 May, Dill wrote to Auchinleck, who was due to meet Wavell at Basra to concert plans for Iraq: 'The PM has lost confidence in Wavell, if he ever had any. I maintain that in war you must either trust your general or sack him. That being so we *may* be faced with the withdrawal of Wavell from the Middle East—even before you get this letter. If that happens you must succeed him . . .'[8]

This was the day after the start of the German attack on Crete, and a week later the evacuation of Freyberg's defeated force began. Both Churchill and Wavell were under severe strain at this time, the sinking of HMS *Hood* by the *Bismarck* having added to the Prime Minister's woes and not being totally redeemed by the *Bismarck*'s own sinking a few days later. Churchill, at Wavell's request, had overruled the objections of the Admiralty to dispatching a convoy carrying tanks and aircraft through the Mediterranean, and he was greatly irritated when Wavell explained that he could not immediately employ them to satisfy Churchill's demand 'to fight a decisive battle in Libya and go on day after day facing all the necessary losses until you have beaten the life out of General Rommel's army'. When the attack was launched in the desert on 15 June and proved a dismal failure, Wavell saw as clearly as anybody that it was inevitable that he would be replaced, as he was, changing places with Auchinleck in India. Anxious lest his dismissal might be unpopular, Churchill meanly refused to allow him to return to England for a few days' leave.

Churchill placed high hopes on Auchinleck. He had been impressed by the positive attitude Auchinleck had shown in Norway and by the eagerness with which he had offered forces to deal with the situation in Iraq; but he was soon to be disappointed. Only two days after he had assumed command, Auchinleck prefaced a long signal with the words: 'No offensive Western Desert should be contemplated until base is secure.' Syria must be cleared up and Cyprus made secure, after which a methodical 'step-by-step' operation could be set in hand as the first step in the recapture of Cyrenaica. That would need strengthened armoured and mechanized formations, to which infantry divisions were only accessories.[9] Anxious to secure the airfields between Tobruk and Benghazi in order to succour Malta and attack the enemy's seaborne supplies, Churchill pressed for an early offensive, to be met by firm resistance from Auchinleck and his fellow Commanders-in-Chief, Sir Arthur Tedder having replaced Longmore whose realistic and therefore pessimistic reports about the air situation during the operations in Greece and Crete had annoyed Churchill. They maintained that no offensive could be considered at least until November, and that Auchinleck would need 'two, preferably three, armoured divisions to retake [the] whole [of] Cyrenaica' and would not even have the former until the new year. Churchill was already in a bad temper as a result of the refusal of the Chiefs of Staff to consider either an operation in northern Norway to link up with the Russians or a 'raid' into northern France to take the pressure off them. Both were favoured by Eden, whose private secretary, Oliver Harvey, wrote in his diary: 'It is worrying how little we apparently can do to help Russia . . . The slowness and lack of imagination of the Chiefs of Staff are enough to frighten one.'[10]

Auchinleck was summoned to London in July, where Churchill told him that 'the war could not be waged on the basis of waiting until everything was ready'.[11] Ismay, an old friend, anxious that relations between Churchill and Auchinleck should not go the way they had with Wavell, explained to Auchinleck Churchill's character and methods of work.

The idea that he was rude, arrogant and self-seeking was entirely wrong. He was certainly frank in speech and writing, but he expected others to be equally frank with him. A 'child of nature', he did not appreciate the changes that had taken place in modern armies with their heavy and complicated logistic needs . . . No commander who engaged the enemy need ever fear he would not be supported . . .

He begged Auchinleck not to be irritated by being bombarded 'with telegrams on every kind of topic, many of which might seem irrelevant or superfluous'. As Prime Minister he had a 'right to know' what use was being made of the resources he provided.[12] Auchinleck succeeded in getting reluctant agreement that the offensive should not be launched until mid-November.

Churchill could clearly not get rid of the Commander-in-Chief he had so recently appointed, but he remained dissatisfied and turned against Dill for supporting Auchinleck and for continuing, with the other Chiefs of Staff, to resist diversion of equipment to Russia. He accused the army of 'refusing to fight' and always wanting more divisions and equipment. When Tedder suggested that Auchinleck's offensive might have to be postponed because of German air reinforcements to the Mediterranean, Churchill sent the Vice-Chief of the Air Staff, Sir Wilfred Freeman, out to Cairo to challenge Tedder's figures, suggesting to Auchinleck that he might like Freeman to take Tedder's place. 'Do not let any thought of Tedder's personal feelings influence you', he signalled;[13] but Auchinleck was not one to betray his colleague.

In spite of all these misgivings, the hopes Churchill placed on Operation Crusader were high. He saw it as leading to the total defeat of German and Italian forces in North Africa, making it possible to invade Sicily and Sardinia and to base aircraft there, as well as in Malta. This would not only pose a direct threat to Italy, but also deter Franco from giving any help to Hitler. It would powerfully influence Vichy France, and especially French forces in North Africa loyal to it, to change sides, and even also Italy to do the same. Nevertheless he took a cynical view of the enthusiasm of his military chiefs. In a letter to his son Randolph, then in Cairo, at the end of October he wrote: 'The Admirals, Generals and Air Marshals chant their stately hymn of "Safety First" . . . In the midst of this I have to restrain my natural pugnacity by sitting on my own head. How Bloody!'[14]

The operation started well, but soon ran into difficulties. Auchinleck dismissed the commander of the Eighth Army, General Sir Alan Cunningham (brother of the admiral), whom he had appointed against the wishes of Churchill who, surprisingly, had preferred the ponderous 'Jumbo' Wilson, former commander of the expedition to Greece and favoured by Eden as a rifleman. Churchill urged Auchinleck to take the field and command the Eighth Army in person. That was what Marlborough did, and he could not conceive that a senior commander would not wish to do so; but Auchinleck installed instead his faithful lieutenant, Major-General Neil Ritchie, whom he had inherited from Wavell. (After the disasters of 1942, Auchinleck's judgement was criticized.) In his signal to Churchill reporting the appointment, he stated that it was temporary; but when, after several anxious vicissitudes, Ritchie succeeded in driving Rommel back to where he had started from in March, Auchinleck could hardly have removed him, even if he had wanted to.

By that time Churchill's anxieties had, in the short term, been increased, but in the longer term relieved by the Japanese attack on the US Pacific Fleet in Pearl Harbor, which coincided with those on Hong Kong, Malaya, and the Philippines. Another significant event had been his decision to relieve Dill as CIGS by General Sir Alan Brooke, although, astonishingly, he also considered General Gort, who, since Dunkirk, had been Governor of Gibraltar. He had consulted Lyttelton, who strongly favoured Gort. General Sir Frederick Pile, heading Anti-Aircraft Command, and the Vice-CIGS, Lieutenant-General Sir Archibald Nye, were also considered, Beaverbrook pressing for the latter on grounds of the political advantage of appointing a general who had risen from the ranks. But fortunately for Britain and the whole Allied cause, Churchill's judgement was sounder, and he plumped for Brooke. Their first contact had been by telephone when Brooke was commanding the force which was still in France after Dunkirk, most of it based on Cherbourg. Brooke had come to the conclusion that there was no point in attempting to give the French any more help and that his force should be withdrawn. Churchill opposed this, but Brooke's firmness and reasoning won the day. Churchill respected him for it, asked him to lunch after his return and kept in touch, often seeing him after he had replaced Ironside as Commander-in-Chief Home Forces in July 1940. Churchill knew that he was not choosing a yes-man, telling Nye: 'When I thump the table and push my face towards him, what does he do? Thumps the table harder and glares back at me—I know these Brookes—stiff-necked Ulstermen and there's no one worse to deal with than that.'[15]

The relations which developed between them are nowhere better described than in David Fraser's biography of General Sir Alan Brooke, later The Viscount Alanbrooke:

It was a stormy relationship. Alanbrooke profoundly admired Churchill yet found his ideas often unrealistic, his habits of mind irrational and infuriating, his method of work frustrating and exhausting, and his temper sometimes vile. He found some characteristics of Churchill intolerable—his unfairness, his pettiness, his fondness for unsound advice and advisers, his dislike of any but palatable facts when pursuing a favourite scheme. Yet he loved him. He loved his courage, his humour, his readiness to bear huge burdens for England. From all this stress Alanbrooke found relief in his diary. For his part, Churchill probably found Alanbrooke a trying subordinate. The latter's uncompromising negatives, his bleak resistance to cajolery, his practical approach, his reliance on facts alone were often tedious to Churchill. Yet Churchill loved Alanbrooke, and to others often said so. He had implicit trust in him. Where others would be tongue-tied or resentfully inarticulate beneath the bludgeoning of Churchillian invective or exhortation, Alanbrooke was eloquent, cogent and persuasive. Alanbrooke's was a dissective, Churchill's a romantic mind. To Churchill the war was a great drama, often terrible, generally exhilarating,

25 Churchill at the time he became Prime Minister, May 1940

26 Inspecting bomb damage in London, 8 September 1940

27 Followed by crowds, 10 September 1940

28 Leaving No. 10 Downing St. with the three Labour Members of the War
Cabinet, Ernest Bevin, Clement Attlee, and Arthur Greenwood, 4 October 1940
ASSOCIATED PRESS

29 Sunday Service on board the *Prince of Wales*, Placentia Bay, 10 August 1941
CHURCHILL COLLEGE

30 Addressing Congress, 26 December 1941

ASSOCIATED PRESS

31 In Cairo with Service Chiefs, 5 August 1942: Front Row: Field Marshal
J. C. Smuts, Winston Churchill, General Sir Claude Auchinleck, General Sir
Archibald Wavell. Back Row: Air Chief Marshal Sir Arthur Tedder, General
Sir Alan Brooke, Admiral Sir H. Harwood, the Rt. Hon. R. G. Casey.

32 In the Kremlin with Stalin, 16 August 1942.
Autographed by both.

33 With Roosevelt in the White House Rose Garden

34 With Roosevelt and Stalin in Tehran on Churchill's 69th birthday, 1943

LET US GO FORWARD TOGETHER

35 Wartime Poster

36 Inspecting the 101st Airborne Division with Eisenhower, 23 March 1944

37 Watching enemy planes in Normandy with (from right) Field Marshal Sir
Alan Brooke, General Montgomery, and Field Marshal Smuts, 12 June 1944
IMPERIAL WAR MUSEUM

38 In an observation post on the Italian
Front near Florence, 21 August 1944
IMPERIAL WAR MUSEUM

39 With Field Marshal Alexander in the Italian battle zone

40 Accompanying General de Gaulle at Besançon, 13 November 1944

41 The V.E. Day broadcast, 8 May 1945

42 With Nehru, whom he later called 'The Light of Asia', April 1949

43 Cabinet colleagues listen to Churchill's last Conservative Conference speech, October 1954

44 Portrait by Graham Sutherland, now destroyed

45 Winston with Lord Randolph as portrayed in the movie 'Young Winston'
COLUMBIA PICTURES

46 Churchill portrayed in the movie 'Young Winston'
COLUMBIA PICTURES

tragic and triumphant by turns, but never dull. He lived it to the full. To Alanbrooke, the soldier, it was a grim and distasteful business, a matter for exact calculations, hard logical thought, lonely constancy and iron will.[16]

One of Brooke's first acts, four days after Pearl Harbor, was to persuade a reluctant Churchill that Dill should go to Washington as a representative of the British Chiefs of Staff to keep in close touch with the American military hierarchy which, at that stage, had no joint machinery akin to that of the Chiefs of Staff Committee. Dill's straightforward and tactful manner, his clear mind and keen intelligence, and his experience impressed the Americans, particularly General Marshall; and he was to serve both countries exceptionally well until his death in November 1944 in Washington, where he was buried in Arlington National Cemetery. On many occasions he was able to find an agreed solution when deadlock between the British and American Chiefs of Staff appeared imminent and Marshall or his colleagues were liable to take offence at Brooke's abrupt and severe manner.

After the admirals and generals had been subjected to Churchill's pressure, the air marshals came under his scrutiny. On 7 November 1941 Air Marshal Sir Richard Peirse's Bomber Command sent 400 aircraft to bomb Berlin, the Ruhr, Cologne, and Boulogne, and 37 did not return, a degree of loss which could not be sustained. Peirse blamed the weather and deficiencies in the training of pilots in such conditions. An internal inquiry by the Air Staff showed that Peirse had failed to exercise effective command, and, when Churchill was shown the papers by Archibald Sinclair, the Secretary of State for Air, he agreed that Peirse should go (to the Far East as Air Commander-in-Chief at Singapore) and be succeeded by Sir Arthur Harris. This shake-up followed an inquiry, instigated by Churchill's personal scientific adviser Professor Lindemann (later Lord Cherwell), which had examined air photographs of Bomber Command's operations and come to disturbing conclusions, one of the most significant being that only about one-third of aircraft claiming to have reached the target area had actually done so. On 31 July 1941, before this (the Butt) report was available, the Chiefs of Staff had committed themselves to saying: 'After meeting the needs of our own security, we give to the heavy bomber first priority in production, for only the heavy bomber can produce the conditions under which other offensive force can be employed.' They had gone on to express their faith in 'a planned attack on civilian morale with the intensity and continuity which are essential if a final breakdown is to be produced', and concluded that: 'It may be that the methods described above will by themselves be enough to make Germany sue for peace and that the role of the British Army on the Continent will be limited to that of an army of occupation.'[17]

Alan Brooke would never have put his name to that. Churchill blew hot and cold on the subject. At times he appeared enthusiastic, particularly in revenge for German bombing attacks on Britain; but after the Butt report he became sceptical. In an exchange with Portal in September, he wrote: 'It is very disputable whether bombing by itself will be a decisive factor in the present war. On the contrary, all that we have learnt since the war began shows that its effects, both physical and moral, are greatly exaggerated . . . The most we can say is that it will be a heavy and I trust a seriously increasing annoyance.'[18] Portal argued strongly against this scepticism; but the furthest that Churchill was prepared to go was to write:

It may well be that German morale will crack and that our bombing will play a very important part in bringing the result about. But all things are always on the move simultaneously, and it is quite possible that the Nazi war-making power in 1943 will be so widely spread throughout Europe as to be to a large extent independent of the actual buildings in the homeland.

A different picture will be presented if the enemy's Air Force were so far reduced as to enable heavy accurate bombing of factories to take place. This however cannot be done outside the radius of fighter protection, according to what I am at present told. One has to do the best one can, but he is an unwise man who thinks there is any certain method of winning this war, or indeed any other war between equals in strength. The only plan is to persevere.[19]

One man certainly persevered. It was Air Marshal Sir Arthur 'Bomber' Harris. One of his early successes was to win the doubting 'Prof' (Lindemann) to his side; and, as his force of four-engined bombers was built up, as navigational and other electronic aids improved, and he was careful to concentrate on targets which were least well defended, his determination and pugnacity gained Churchill's approval, so that he was able to trade on the Prime Minister's support when the Air Staff or other air commands opposed him. Churchill's attitude to the strategic bombing campaign remained ambivalent and his support blew hot and cold; but he retained faith in Portal to the end and, with reservations, in Harris. His ambivalence and reservations became evident at the end of the war, when he failed publicly to pay tribute to Bomber Command or to Harris personally, perhaps because his humanity caused pangs of conscience about the civilian casualties the operations had inflicted.

When Churchill visited Washington with the Chiefs of Staff (taking Dill but leaving Brooke behind) at the end of December 1941, Roosevelt, at the instigation of General Marshall, proposed that an Allied command be established to cover south-east Asia and that Wavell should head it with an American general as his deputy. Neither Churchill nor the Chiefs of Staff liked the idea, feeling that Wavell would inevitably be the fall-guy, but decided that they could not refuse this first generous American offer.

Once more Wavell found himself burdened with an almost impossible task without the resources to deal with it. For Churchill one blow followed another: first the loss of the battleships *Prince of Wales* and *Repulse*, for the deployment of which to the Far East he had pressed against the wishes of Pound: then the débâcle in Malaya and Lieutenant-General Arthur Percival's surrender of Singapore. Receiving a stream of messages from Churchill urging resolution, Wavell did his best to instil some determination and energy into Percival and his forces; but, as he himself wrote after the surrender: 'The trouble goes a long way back, the atmosphere of the country (the whole of Malaya has been asleep for at least 200 years), lack of vigour in our peace-time training, the cumbrousness of our tactics and equipment, and the real difficulty of finding an answer to the very skilful and bold tactics of the Japanese in this jungle fighting.'[20] In spite of his disappointment, Churchill did not blame Wavell; but the surrender of Singapore reinforced his doubts about the fighting quality of the army and its generals. The subsequent loss of Burma did nothing to dispel that, although Sir Harold Alexander's decision to order a withdrawal almost as soon as he arrived did nothing to shake Churchill's faith in him: indeed he was admired for the conduct of the retreat back to India, where his forces, having lost all but what they could carry, arrived in May. Wavell returned to his post as Commander-in-Chief India.

During this period Churchill had frequently found himself at loggerheads with the Chiefs of Staff over the priority he attached to sending supplies to Russia by sea, urged on to do so by Roosevelt; and, in order to assist this, over his pet project of an expedition to occupy northern Norway. Behind this opposition lay that of the Commander-in-Chief Home Fleet, Admiral Sir John Tovey, never well thought of by Churchill, who now, somewhat surreptitiously, planned a shake-up of the admirals. In April 1942 Cunningham was suddenly recalled from the Mediterranean, ostensibly to replace Admiral Little as head of the naval mission in Washington; but actually because Churchill planned that he should take Tovey's place, which Cunningham refused to do. Pound confided in him that he believed himself to be out of favour and that Churchill planned to replace him by Mountbatten, then a mere post-captain, although granted the acting rank of vice-admiral as Director of Combined Operations. Pound suggested resigning and manœuvring Cunningham to succeed him; but the latter told him to 'glue himself to his chair', although he knew, as others did, that Pound's physical state was none too good. So Cunningham went off to Washington, returning in November to the Mediterranean to support Eisenhower in Operation Torch, while Tovey stayed on until replaced by Bruce Fraser in May 1943. Cunningham's place in the eastern Mediterranean was taken by Admiral Sir Henry Harwood, a favourite of Churchill's who proved a broken reed. Pound himself stayed on, Brooke having relieved him of the burden of also acting as Chairman of the Chiefs of Staff, until Pound's resignation in October 1943, following a stroke from which he died on Trafalgar Day. It would have been better for everyone if Churchill had hardened his heart and replaced his faithful servant earlier; but he probably sensed that none of the other admirals would have tolerated his interference and idiosyncracies as calmly as Pound had. Before then, Pound had made a significant contribution to the anti-submarine war in the Atlantic by selecting Admiral Sir Max Horton for command of the Western Approaches, rather than Percy Noble.

Churchill's relations with the admirals were always delicate. They knew the history of his personal intervention in naval operations as First Lord of the Admiralty in both World Wars and as Prime Minister thereafter, and they were on their guard against it. He was long accustomed to obstruction by admirals and determined to overcome it. The result was a permanent state of tension.

The gloom induced by events in the Far East was deepened by the reverse suffered by Auchinleck when Rommel, at the end of January 1942, repeated his performance of the previous year and drove Ritchie's Eighth Army back to Gazala, only twenty-five miles from the defences of Tobruk, depriving Tedder's aircraft of airfields from which they could give cover to ships attempting to reach beleaguered Malta from the east. It had the effect also of making it impossible to use Malta as a base for air or naval attacks on shipping supplying the German and Italian forces facing Ritchie. Churchill was deeply disappointed and pressed Auchinleck ceaselessly to take the offensive to regain the 'bulge' of Cyrenaica. Auchinleck, supported by his colleagues, maintained that he would not be able to do so until 1 June, and that to try before then, for the sake of Malta, could prejudice the security of the whole Middle East. Having had to provide forces for the Far East, he also had to face the potential threat from the north posed by the German forces in Russia which had reached the Caucasus. Churchill and the Chiefs of Staff thought that Auchinleck was exaggerating both the threat and his own difficulties, and was not making full use of all his resources. He was summoned to London, but refused to go. Instead Sir Stafford Cripps was sent with General Nye to Cairo. To Churchill's fury they backed Auchinleck, and the Defence Committee reluctantly accepted mid-May as the target date. Shortly before that, it became clear that Rommel himself was planning to attack, and Ritchie was allowed temporarily to assume the defensive.

In the confused battles which followed, Rommel gained the upper hand; Tobruk was lost and the Eighth Army driven back to El Alamein, only fifty miles from Alexandria. In an almost continuous exchange of signals, the tone became sharp when Churchill detected that Ritchie was withdrawing past Tobruk to the Egyptian frontier. Before that, on 14 June, he had signalled to Auchinleck: 'Your decision to fight it out to the end is most cordially endorsed. We shall sustain you whatever the result. Retreat would be fatal. This is a business not only of armour but of will-power. God bless you all.'[21] Later that same day, having realized that a withdrawal had been ordered, he signalled: 'To what position does Ritchie want to withdraw? Presume there is no question in any case of giving up Tobruk. As long as Tobruk is held no serious enemy advance into Egypt is possible. We went through all this in April 1941.'[22] This put Auchinleck and his colleagues on the spot. They had long agreed that the navy could not afford a repetition of the previous year's siege of Tobruk and that, if the Gazala position could not be held, the next step back should be to the frontier. As a result of Churchill's signal, Ritchie was given orders which evaded the issue and which he proved unable to execute, with the outcome that Tobruk was lost, surrendering after an incompetently conducted defence. The news reached Churchill when he was closeted with Roosevelt in the White House and was a bitter blow. He welcomed Auchinleck's decision to dismiss Ritchie and himself assume command of the Eighth Army in the field, bringing the exhausted Rommel to a halt at El Alamein, but failing, after several attempts, to drive him back. When Auchinleck reported, at the end of July, that it was 'unlikely that an opportunity will arise for resumption of offensive operations before mid-September' both Brooke and Churchill realized that new hands were needed at the helm in Cairo.[23]

The result is well known. The first problem was to find a new commander for the Eighth Army, and Churchill's first choice, on the advice of Eden, was Lieutenant-General William 'Strafer' Gott, a fellow-rifleman. Knowing that Gott was tired, Brooke demurred, whereupon Churchill offered him the command. Much tempted, Brooke refused, knowing where his real duty lay, and agreed with Auchinleck that Montgomery was the man. Churchill was annoyed, suspecting that it would mean delay; but shifted his ground by a proposal to split Middle East Command in two, moving Auchinleck to the eastern half and giving the western to Brooke with Montgomery to command the Eighth Army. Again Brooke resisted the temptation. After further discussion, in which Smuts took a prominent part, it was decided that Alexander, nominated to command the First Army under Eisenhower, in the planned landings in French North Africa, should replace Auchinleck as Commander-in-Chief and Gott take over the Eighth Army, Montgomery to replace Alexander in the First Army. When Gott, flying down to see Churchill, was killed, the final solution was that which Brooke had wanted all along. With Montgomery in command of the army, success was assured. Auchinleck returned to India, but was not employed again until June 1943, when he succeeded Wavell as Commander-in-Chief India.

That was as a result both of the dissatisfaction of Churchill and the Chiefs of Staff with what they regarded as Wavell's feeble attempts to take the offensive against the Japanese in Burma, and their difficulty in agreeing with each other and the Americans about what to do instead. No satisfactory conclusion had been reached when rival strategies were discussed in Washington in May 1943. After that, the idea of establishing an Allied Supreme Commander for the area was mooted. The problem was what to do with Wavell. Churchill thought of sending him to Australia as Governor-General, but that might look like breathing down the neck of MacArthur. Wavell assumed that he himself would become the Supreme Commander. The names of Sholto Douglas and Tedder and several others were canvassed, and Admiral Cunningham was strongly backed by Eden and Attlee; but Churchill had his own favourite, Mountbatten. He kept this to himself until he and the Chiefs of Staff set off to meet the Americans again at Quebec in August. Churchill took with him Orde Wingate, in whose Long Range Penetration Group, a godchild of Wavell's, he saw a cheap way of impressing the Americans and demonstrating to them that the British took seriously the need to open a land link to Stilwell with Chiang Kai-shek. The combination of Wingate and Mountbatten would, he rightly judged, impress the Americans. As Oliver Harvey recorded in his diary: 'People here are doubtful of Mountbatten being up to this but the P.M. and the Americans are het up on it. Mountbatten–Wingate is at least a refreshing contrast to Wavell–Auchinleck.'[24] The solution to Wavell's future was to make him Viceroy of India, dashing the hopes of a number of politicians. The post of Commander-in-Chief was transferred to Auchinleck, who was frustrated because the establishment of Mountbatten's South East Asia Command deprived him of all responsibility for operations.

Churchill now had all the teams in place which were to bring him the victories of which he had been deprived for so long, but to the foundations of which he had contributed so much. The principal change was that, as the American contribution in all theatres of war increased, he was no longer the supreme director of operations. That did not prevent him from continuing his habit of exchanging messages directly with British commanders, like Montgomery and Alexander, who were under Allied command. Although in most cases he and the Chiefs of Staff were united in the arguments with the Americans about Allied strategy, they were at times at loggerheads with each other: over the possibility of a cross-Channel operation in 1942 or 1943, or one in northern Norway as an alternative; and over Churchill's pet scheme for a landing in Sumatra. Over strategy in the Mediterranean neither Churchill nor the Chiefs of Staff were entirely consistent. Both got carried away by visions of the opportunities offered in the Balkans, even to the extent of favouring Alexander's dream of advancing through the Ljubljana Gap to reach Vienna before the Russians; but both were faithful to the commitment to a cross-Channel operation in 1944, provided that the conditions at the time did not make it too hazardous. Churchill, Brooke, and Cunningham always realized that, without it, Germany could not be defeated, although Portal remained faithful to his hope that the strategic bombing campaign, by the RAF at night and the USAAF by day, would make it unnecessary or just a walk-over. In their support for keeping up the pressure in Italy and opposition to diversion of forces from there to France, Churchill and Brooke were motivated by their desire to maintain Italy as an active theatre under primarily British command; Churchill also by a desire not to disappoint his favourite Alexander, and Brooke by genuine concern that removal of that pressure would let the Germans transfer forces to oppose Eisenhower in France.

Astonishingly, the Chiefs of Staff came near to resignation over the strategy to be pursued in the Far East once Burma had been cleared. Churchill, Eden, and Mountbatten gave priority to the liberation of British colonial territories, while the Chiefs of Staff, concerned to see that Britain should play a significant part in the largely naval operations required to achieve final victory over Japan, wished to build up a major amphibious force, based on Australia, to work with the Americans. Roosevelt's cold shoulder to the idea played into Churchill's hands; but the explosion of the atom bombs over Hiroshima and Nagasaki made the whole issue irrelevant.

Up to the end Churchill maintained his 'ceaseless prodding', inveighing against the caution of generals and their reliance on mountains of impedimenta; he was always looking for an easy way round, and any operation which appeared to offer something out of the ordinary. In this he met his match in Montgomery, impervious to rebuke, flattery, or cajolery, but on whom he relied most to produce those victories for which he craved both for his nation and for himself. At times, particularly in the months before the landings in Normandy, Churchill became jealous of Montgomery's popularity with the public. In the last years of the war, all the defence chiefs, not least Brooke, Alexander, Montgomery, and Mountbatten, had learned how to deal with Churchill: never to complain about the 'ceaseless prodding'; to stand firm, but to keep him sweet by a constant stream of information and an adroit balance of flattery, cajolery, and frankness. They knew that they could not do without him, and did not want to, and he knew that they were indispensable to him.

21

Churchill and the Navy

RICHARD OLLARD

'Not a man', wrote Cardinal Newman, 'that now writes against the Church but owes it to the Church that he can write at all.' To those like the present writer who grew up in the death-shadow of the Hitler period no criticism of Churchill can be more than a scholiast's note on the imperishable achievement of his having saved the country and, arguably, civilization itself in 1940.

But both Churchill and the navy are historical phenomena that reach back beyond the hideosities of Hitler and, mercifully, have outlived him. Perhaps no English institution, unless it be Parliament, sorted so profoundly with Churchill's genius or provided so grand a field for the display of his gifts and the exposure of his faults. Of all the dramatic resonances in which his career is so rich there is none more striking than the fact that the outbreak of war in 1914 and in 1939 should have found him occupying the First Lord's chair at the Board of Admiralty. 'My heart is in the Admiralty', he had said to Lloyd George in 1919 when the Prime Minister had offered him the choice between that and the War Office, to which in fact he was then appointed. Yet this emotional identification had not at once disclosed itself, for when eleven years earlier Asquith had brought him into the Cabinet he had declined this immensely prestigious appointment and accepted the Board of Trade. Various accounts of his reasons have been put forward. Lady Violet Bonham Carter's recollection[1] has him running almost immediately into Jacky Fisher,[2] who could scarcely credit his folly in turning down so glittering a prize and painted in characteristically vehement colours a view of how they might together astonish the world if Churchill were First Lord and he, as he then was, First Sea Lord. That Fisher, like Lloyd George, could fascinate Churchill would be clear from photographs, even if there were no other evidence (and there is a great deal). Churchill, according to Lady Violet's story, sped back to Asquith, only to find that the post had been offered to, and accepted by, Reginald McKenna.

When Churchill, some three years later, at Asquith's command, exchanged offices (he was by then Home Secretary) with McKenna, Fisher was no longer First Sea Lord, indeed was no longer in the country. The fearful broils with Admiral Lord Charles Beresford, the Commander-in-Chief of the Channel Fleet, had become a public scandal as well as a serious impediment to the well-being of the service. Beresford was relieved of his command in 1909 and Fisher resigned in January 1910, remaining, however, on the active list for a further year and certainly intending, if he could, to obtain his recall. From Italy, a base secure from observation, he conducted a voluminous and volcanic correspondence with those persons who might serve his great purpose.

It was therefore his successor, Sir Arthur Wilson, that Churchill found as First Sea Lord on his arrival at the Admiralty. Deeply loyal to Fisher though he was, Wilson personified the rigidity and uncommunicativeness of a service tradition against which Fisher's restless innovation and ceaseless flow of wit, irreverence, and malice beat like a storm tide. No doubt Wilson confirmed Churchill's view of the naval profession which Fisher, with his reckless contempt for brother officers who ventured to criticize or oppose, had helped to form. The old fossils who never read a book or entertained a fresh idea were the constant theme of Fisher's derision. How deeply that had sunk into Churchill's mind may be observed in many passages of his career and of his writings of which this, from *The World Crisis*, is an early example:

When I went to the Admiralty I found that there was no moment in the career and training of a naval officer, when he was obliged to read a single book about naval war, or pass even the most rudimentary examination in naval history. The Royal Navy had made no important contribution to naval literature; the standard work on Sea Power was written by an American Admiral. The best accounts of British sea fighting and naval strategy were compiled by an English civilian. 'The Silent Service' was not mute because it was absorbed in thought and study, but because it was weighted down by its daily routine and by its ever-complicating and diversifying technique.[3]

Both Captain Stephen Roskill in his *Churchill and the Admirals* (1977) and Admiral Sir Peter Gretton in his *Former Naval Person: Winston Churchill and the Royal Navy* (1968), two indispensable and scholarly studies, have pointed out that this is an overstatement, or perhaps a misstatement, of a case against the pre-1914 navy whose force must be at least partially admitted. The navy of that day was, by and large, hostile to criticism, suspicious of change and development, except for minor improvements within well-established technical enclaves, and prejudiced against intellectuals and general ideas. But is this an unusual condition for large and respected institutions or for the military profession in general? Churchill silently assumes a superior state of affairs in the army; but when war came in 1914 did he and Lloyd George find it to be so? The specific charges that he brings are at best half-truths. Naval history was taught, and well taught, by academic historians of distinction, at the Royal Naval Colleges of Osborne and Dartmouth. The first writers to address themselves to the study of naval strategy and the eliciting of its historical principles were two officers of the Royal Navy, the brothers Colomb. The Council of the Navy Records Society, which now has a thin sprinkling of naval officers among the academics and authors, was then stiff with the gold braid of flag rank. A number of brilliant young officers such as the future Admiral Sir Herbert Richmond were asking the most searching questions and enunciating new, or rather unfamiliar and unsettling, truths about the application of sea power. These men, and some of their seniors, were united in pressing for the creation of a proper naval staff.

'Staff Officer' in the poetry and prose of those who fought in the trenches has such powerful connotations of cowardice and stupidity that it may be necessary to define the requirement. A general staff or a naval staff is at once the memory, the filing system, and the think-tank of a fighting service. In almost every human activity, from gardening to morals, the rational reaction to the appearance of an unforeseen hazard or difficulty is to consult experience, first of all one's own and then the wider resource of the past. This last presupposes the existence of a body of records of what other people have thought and decided and done, together with a critical evaluation of their reasons and their actions. This is what R. B. Haldane, Churchill's colleague in the Cabinet and Asquith's closest political associate, had forced on a reluctant War Office by the instrument of a Committee of which Fisher had been a leading member. It was this that enabled General Sir Henry Wilson to outclass his naval namesake, Sir Arthur, at the crucial Committee for Imperial Defence Meeting on 23 August 1911. The young Maurice Hankey watched in silent dismay as the Admiralty was routed by the plausible and articulate soldier and the country was then and there committed to a continental as opposed to a maritime strategy. Churchill, also present though not yet First Lord, was most unfavourably impressed. 'I cannot help feeling uncomfortable about the Admiralty', he wrote to Lloyd George three weeks later. 'They are so cocksure, *insouciant* and apathetic . . . I cannot feel much confidence in

Wilson's sagacity after his performance the other day.'[4] What Wilson had in fact done was to assert in stumbling, almost schoolboyish, phraseology what Jacky would have enunciated with prophetic, seer-like, imagery: the necessity and the supreme advantage to Britain and her Empire of a strategy based on and determined to exploit her sea power. Of a reasoned, detailed prospectus of what this entailed, of what is called a war plan, there would have been none. Even as late as 1918 Fisher would boast that the War Plan for the Navy had existed only in his and Sir Arthur Wilson's heads. During his six years as First Sea Lord he had fought as fiercely as the most enraged Old Fossil would have done against the creation of a naval staff. Yet Churchill, whose reverence for Fisher's mastery of his profession resembles that of Dante's feelings towards Virgil, was determined to establish one and, against some powerful opposition, succeeded in doing so.

Why did two men who so often thought alike, whose temperaments and gifts were so strikingly similar, differ so diametrically on so cardinal a point? To think that one can explain either Fisher or Churchill is tantamount to thinking that one can draw out Leviathan with a hook. But there are certain suggestive indications to be found in the writings of both men. Fisher, as I have argued at greater length elsewhere,[5] prided himself on intuition as opposed to ratiocination. As he wrote in January 1910 to the woman whom he thought of as his possible biographer:

Impulse is all with me and I answer on the moment! (Out of the abundance of the heart the mouth speaketh!) Myself I hate a calculated letter or a prepared speech. You can go round the corner and get Buggins or Stiggins to do either for you . . . Whatever success I have had is more attributable to the action of the imagination than to the dictates of cold reason.[6]

Churchill, whose imagination and powers of rhetoric were certainly not inferior to Fisher's, prided himself on the exact opposite. His appeal is always to the written record and to reason. 'Nothing', he claims proudly in the opening pages of *The World Crisis*, 'Nothing of any consequence was done by me by word of mouth. A complete record therefore exists both of executive and administrative action.'[7] He was to use almost the self-same words in defending himself against the Motion of Censure moved against him by Sir John Wardlaw-Milne at the height of the Second World War. Churchill's place in history is that of a national leader, a greater master of the Parliamentary arts, and a statesman whose ideas continued to influence the course of events even after he had left office. But before he was any of these things he had proved himself a first-class departmental minister, working tirelessly through his papers, mastering his briefs, asking questions till he had sifted things to the bottom.

No-one gets anything in life for nothing. A minister who habitually insists on going down the mine may end with tunnel vision. Churchill's absorption in whatever he was doing at the moment remained a lifelong characteristic, sometimes remarked by colleagues as endearingly child-like, sometimes regarded as exasperating and obstructive. The departmental habit of mind certainly offers one explanation of the apparent gyrations of Churchill's attitude towards the financial needs of the navy: first of all Lloyd George's most vigorous and outspoken ally in the great Cabinet battles over the Dreadnought building programme, a position instantly abandoned on becoming the responsible Minister; then, as Minister for War and Air in Lloyd George's Coalition government, a strong supporter of Beatty's extravagant, not to say chimerical, programme of battleship building with the sole objective of maintaining parity with the Americans who, alone of the Great Powers, were never considered a possible enemy; next, as Chancellor of the Exchequer in Baldwin's administration only three years later, the ruthless reductionist of all service expenditure, driving Beatty, still First Sea Lord, to despair.

That extraordinary fellow Winston has gone mad. Economically mad and no sacrifice is too great to achieve what in his short-sightedness is the panacea for all evil—to take a shilling off the Income Tax. As we the Admiralty are the principle [*sic*] spending department he attacks us with virulence.

This Government . . . is actually behaving worse to us than the Labour Party. Of course it is all Winston as Chancellor. He has gone economy mad and the result is that the Government are not proposing to build any cruisers at all.[8]

'Of course it is all Winston as Chancellor.' Nowhere is the great man's passionate departmentalism, perhaps an extension of his passionate ego-centricity, more succinctly stated. If Winston were once again First Lord, as Beatty knew better than anyone else, it would have been a very different story. Beatty was one of the handful of Flag Officers with whom Churchill dealt as an equal rather than a servant. He had on his side the best of reasons for personal gratitude, for it was Churchill who had rescued a brilliant career rashly jeopardized by his refusal of the post of Second in Command of the Atlantic Fleet in July 1911. Their Lordships do not like the polite fiction of an invitation to be taken

literally any more than the Crown does when it sends a *congé d'élire* to
a Cathedral Chapter. Beatty would almost certainly have been left
unemployed and thus after a short time placed on the retired list had
not Churchill, the new First Lord, appointed him his Naval Secretary
in May 1912. His reasons for doing so disclose another important element in his relations with the Senior Service:

It became increasingly clear to me that he viewed questions of naval strategy
and tactics in a different light from the average naval officer: he approached
them, as it seemed to me, much more as a soldier would. His war experiences
on land [he had served with distinction in river gunboats in the Omdurman
campaign and had been severely wounded at Tientsin during the Boxer
Rebellion] had illuminated the facts he had acquired during his naval training.
He was no mere instrumentalist. He did not think of *matériel* as an end in
itself but only as a means. He thought of war problems in their unity by land,
sea and air. His mind had been rendered quick and supple by the situations of
polo and the hunting-field, and enriched by varied experiences against the
enemy on Nile gunboats and ashore.[9]

Beatty's chief recommendation as a naval officer was, in short, that he
was so unlike a naval officer, in fact much more like a cavalryman
whose eye and instinct had been schooled by polo and hunting. The
unselfaware egocentric simplicity is breathtaking. Can one imagine
Churchill's reaction if a Secretary of State for War had picked out a
future Field Marshal on the grounds that he had the unsleeping alertness of a submariner or a destroyer captain? Yet the same recommendations were to count again in the Second World War when Roger Keyes
was recalled from a harmless retirement to a dangerous eminence from
which he was able to prejudice the already precarious defence of Malta.
When thwarted by the soberer counsels of the Chiefs of Staff, he at
once invoked his and the Prime Minister's shared equestrian past.[10]
Was it prowess on the polo field that led to Mountbatten's appointment
to two of the most important inter-service commands, Combined
Operations and South-East Asia, and even, it was believed by Dudley
Pound, to his being considered for succession to his own office of First
Sea Lord? Certainly there was nothing in his unfortunate record as a
sea officer to justify so inexplicable a promotion.[11] Or was it, as perhaps
in Keyes's case, the shadow Churchill's past conduct in the First
World War cast on his direction of the second? Keyes, as Chief of Staff
to de Robeck, had been the one senior naval officer who had whole-
heartedly supported Churchill against all professional military and naval
advice in his belief that the navy alone, unsupported by a major land

assault, could carry the Dardanelles and maintain itself in the Sea of Marmara, thus dominating Constantinople and knocking Turkey out of the war.

Mountbatten was the son, the son bent on his father's vindication, of the Prince Louis of Battenberg who had been Churchill's First Sea Lord at the outbreak of war in 1914 and shared with him the credit for the fact that the fleet was at that moment fully mobilized. His dismissal at the end of October, partly as the result of a gutter press campaign against any connection with anything German, partly as a scapegoat for the failure to hold Antwerp and turn the German flank, may have left Churchill with a sense that he owed a debt of honour. But the opportunity offered to bring back Fisher, by then aged 73, had been irresistible. Plainly it was now or never, and a formidable body of official opinion, headed by the King, held that 'never' was the better option.

Fisher's relationship with Churchill is the key to Churchill's relation to the navy. Both, essentially, were, for all their dazzling gifts of communication and their power to entrance, men who were a cause unto themselves, to use the old medieval definition of freedom. Both were irreverent, witty, radical. Fisher's radicalism, amounting almost to republicanism, was entwined with his whole view of the service. 'Ever since Cromwell it has been the People's Navy' is his curious, idiosyncratic refrain, bearing little relation to the ascertainable facts of service history. The army, fossilized by the aristocratic and monarchical deposits of centuries, he regarded as no more than a projectile to be fired from the ever more powerful guns of the fleet. The second panel of this diptych would hardly have found favour with Churchill but the first was thoroughly congenial, as is evident from his tenacity in seeking against King George V's obduracy to name one of the new battleships *Oliver Cromwell*.[12] Fisher's radicalism had been at its most creative in its application to the material instruments of maritime war—scrapping obsolete types of vessel, closing superfluous bases, rationalizing, standardizing what remained, encouraging the development of new arms such as submarine and air warfare, as well as revolutionizing the concept of the capital ship. All this was carried on by Churchill, often in secret consultation with the Prince over the water. The greatest of his material innovations, the change from coal to oil, openly acknowledged its inspiration by the appointment of Fisher as Chairman of the Royal Commission on Oil Supply.[13]

Where Churchill's radicalism, cordially supported by Fisher, was at its most creative and attractive was in the improvement of conditions of service. Fisher had transformed the entry and training of officers by the institution of cadetships and of the Royal Naval Colleges at Osborne and Dartmouth. Churchill carried things a stage further by the introduction, against fierce opposition, of the so-called Special Entry Scheme by which a limited number of boys from the public schools could enter at the age of 18 (cadets entered at 13). He managed to achieve a slight improvement in officers' pay and argued strongly for a marriage allowance, not introduced until 1937. But it was for the improvement of the pay and conditions of the lower deck that he fought most manfully against Lloyd George at the Treasury. What a horrible, indeed barbarous, life it was on the overcrowded mess decks of the coal-burning, armour-plated warships of that day his own memorandum to the Cabinet of 17 October 1912 eloquently shows.[14] Barbarous except for the marvellous humanity and good nature of the sailors, whose exploitation Churchill and Fisher held to be a disgrace. The increase eventually obtained—the first for sixty years—disappointed the First Lord but was touchingly well received by its beneficiaries. 'Old Winston's got a nice old mug, like his Ma' remarked one of them on hearing the news, a singular characterization of the tigerish beauty of Jennie Jerome.

Churchill's other great redress of social injustice in the service was the reopening of the passage, regularly used in the seventeenth and eighteenth centuries, that led from the mess deck to the Ward Room. Here again Fisher was an enthusiastic supporter. The Napoleonic *carrière ouverte aux talents* was a principle dear to both men.

It was not in the articulation of maritime power but in its application in war that the two fell out, or rather that Fisher fell out with Churchill who seems never quite to have understood how he had offended. Churchill was every bit as keen on the all big-gun ship as his mentor. Both men shared an exuberant belief in the offensive. 'Hit first, hit hard and go on hitting.' Both despised as defensive the convoy-and-escort strategy which any serious study of naval history would have shown to be far the best method of bringing commerce raiders to action. Churchill's preference for what he called 'hunter-killer' groups, a heady term distilled from his love of rhetoric and belief in fox-hunting, was to survive, expensively, into the war of 1939–45. Even Beatty, whose cavalryman's approach to war had been so much appreciated by Churchill, had come to see the necessity of convoy by early 1917, the first Admiral afloat or ashore to do so.[15]

Fisher's vision of strategy overlapped Churchill's without being coterminous with it. He had infected Churchill with the idea of a Baltic offensive, followed up by a landing in North Germany, which seemed to his fellow naval officers and his military colleagues sheer lunacy. At least in 1914 it had the theoretical recommendation that Britain's Russian ally possessed valuable bases in that sea and that the Russian armies, transported by the Royal Navy, might take some of the weight off the Western Front. But even in 1914 to challenge the High Seas Fleet in its home waters, which would certainly be heavily mined, was a desperate undertaking. Yet so deeply had Churchill been influenced by Fisher that he raised the project with all seriousness in 1939 when German airbases would have made the venture little short of suicidal.

Churchill in 1914 was realist enough to admit the huge dangers of leaving the High Seas Fleet free to emerge from its bases on the Elbe, either to attack the lines of communication with the Baltic or to get up to mischief anywhere it chose. To prevent this he urged the capture of a strongly fortified island base in the Heligoland Bight, such as Borkum or Sylt, a prospect which Fisher, who had had experience of attacking fortifications from sea as a midshipman, was disinclined to face.[16] Besides its necessity in the event of a British incursion into the Baltic such a base would, Churchill argued, enable the Royal Navy to maintain a close blockade of the German coast.[17] The impracticability of such a scheme was demonstrated by one of the then very few thoroughly capable Naval Staff Officers, the future Admiral Sir Herbert Richmond. It is one of the many signs of an invincibly army approach to the use of sea power that Churchill never lost his hankering for capturing islands. His enthusiasm for Keyes's absurd scheme for adding Pantellaria to the already exhausting commitment to Malta at the most desperate moment of the war in the Mediterranean in 1941–2, the costly humiliation of the expedition against Cos and Leros in 1943,[18] and his scheme, unanimously rejected by the Chiefs of Staff, for taking an islet off Sabang in Northern Sumatra as a means of recapturing Singapore in 1944, are all of a piece.

It was this infusion of the Hussar into the ideas that he and Fisher so largely shared that caused the final explosion leaving, to all appearances, both their careers wrecked beyond repair. The story of Gallipoli is too well known to need any retelling. To disentangle a few strands of that tragedy that bear on our subject is not to project the blame for it on Churchill. But some characteristics of his conduct as First Lord are conspicuous. First, as has been emphasized in the preceding paragraph, was his inability or refusal to distinguish between the nature of land power and sea power, to recognize that there are things that ships can and should do that troops and artillery cannot, and vice versa. To a bred sailor like Fisher battleships are first, last, and all the time there to challenge and destroy enemy battleships or to threaten them into skulking in their bases. To a natural soldier like Churchill they are highly mobile floating batteries with exciting possibilities of engaging enemy fortifications, bombarding ports, and what have you. They are there to be *used*, to be constantly in action. For all his remarks about an American admiral having taught the Royal Navy its history, he seems never to have taken on board, as the sailors say, Mahan's splendid sentence about the far-distant, storm-beaten ships that stood between Napoleon and the dominion of the world. It was Churchill's readiness to risk the new *Queen Elizabeth* class battleships at the Dardanelles that drove Fisher to his decision to resign.

What precipitated Fisher to action was a second Churchillian trait, the itch to interfere in the actual conduct of operations, to draft and, worse still, to amend signals sent on the Admiralty's authority to the Commander-in-Chief on the spot. This was the obverse of one of Churchill's strengths as a minister already mentioned, his eagerness to master a matter, to get to the bottom of things, to know his onions so that he could not be baffled by what one of Charles I's ministers called 'a cloud of hard sea words'.[19] During his first year at the Admiralty he had been tireless in his application to technical questions of every kind and had spent more time at sea in the Admiralty yacht *Enchantress* visiting ships and shore establishments at home and abroad than any earlier or later First Lord. His energy even as an old man in the 1940s—if he ever was an old man: at any rate, technically, a senior citizen—was phenomenal. As a young one it was frightening. There is something about his arrival at the Admiralty not knowing the sharp end of a ship from the blunt, but confident of mastering a vast field of expert knowledge, that recalls the young Pepys suddenly finding himself Clerk to the Navy Board in 1660. Both men were demons for efficiency, both gluttons for work, both gifted with a rapidity and clarity of mind and a command of language that makes them a boon to the historian of their periods. But Pepys, as is well known, was also a glutton for pleasure. At the height of a war as dangerous to his country and to his own position as either of Churchill's two, he would blithely take the day off and have himself rowed up the Thames reading a treatise on hydrostatics the while. Such dereliction of duty was unthinkable to Churchill. The hotter the press of action the more he felt the compulsion to throw himself into it.

Nowhere is the evidence for all this better stated than in his own *The World Crisis*. In a not ungenerous and exceptionally well-informed review of that book, one of his predecessors at the Admiralty wrote:

'It was no part of my duty to deal with the routine movements of the Fleet and its squadrons, but only to exercise a general supervision.' These are Mr Churchill's own words, and yet his book is one long record of constant inter-ference in routine and consequent failure of supervision. The fundamental fault of his system is its restlessness. Great as his services were, they would have been greater if he could have refrained from trying to do his colleagues' and his subordinates' work as well as his own. The result was a diminution of his otherwise splendid driving power and a grievous injury to the value of his supervision. For what is the value of a man's criticism, when the order has been drafted by himself: or his supervision, when he himself is the author, approver and executor of the policy?[20]

The point is well taken. But Admiral Gretton, who quotes the passage, makes a fine defence of Churchill. Criticizing his own prejudices and assumptions he argues that the deeper he went into the records the more he was struck by the feebleness and complacency of the profes-sionals at the Admiralty in 1914–15. '*Someone* had to take action to pro-vide the imagination so lacking, to inculcate the spirit of the offensive and, above all, to build up an efficient machine for the direction of operations.' There is a magnanimity in this such as Churchill himself preached but did not always practise, notably towards Commanders-in-Chief during the 1939–45 war who warned or doubted or opposed.

Perhaps the unhappiest manifestation of this lack of confidence in the man on the spot was the habit of sending signals in which urgency of action obscured precision of instruction. Roskill quotes a series of confusing and unsettling directives sent to Rear-Admiral Hood who held the important Dover command in the opening months of the war.[21] In the most disgraceful episode of Churchill's time in office, the escape of the *Goeben* and the *Breslau*, it has generally been agreed that the weight of the blame lay on the shoulders of Admiral Sir Berkeley Milne, an officer whose appointment to the command of the Mediterranean Fleet in 1912 had led to one of Fisher's fiercest letters to Churchill: 'I consider you have betrayed the navy in these three appointments . . . I am going to transfer my body and my money to the United States . . . I can't remedy what has been done—and it's no d—d use squealing . . . Adieu.'[22] No one in high command emerges with credit from this miserable story. But two of the fatally ambiguous signals were drafted by Churchill himself in his own hand.[23]

If the Churchill–Fisher regime can take deserved credit for the success at the Falklands, Churchill has been held to a degree responsible for the antecedent disaster at Coronel and the earlier sinking, with heavy loss of life, of three elderly cruisers, pointlessly exposed and inadequately supported, off the Dutch coast. As Turenne remarked, 'He who has made no mistake has made little war': and the second of these two incidents may justly be ascribed to the inadequacies of the Naval War Staff which Churchill was doing his best to remedy. The great achievements of his years at the Admiralty are indisputable. No-one felt this more agonizingly than he. His dismissal from that office in 1915 was perhaps harder to bear than his dismissal by the electorate in 1945. By then he was a major figure in the history of his country and of his century, sure of a hearing far beyond the Cabinet Room, the Board of Admiralty, or the House of Commons. In 1915 he had fallen from the height of power to the depths of ineffectiveness. So shattering was the experience that his political sense of orientation deserted him and at his first opportunity to criticize and influence the conduct of the war at sea by his successor, he made himself a laughing-stock by urging the recall of Jacky Fisher, the author of his own ruin besides being a man whom neither King nor Prime Minister would ever again admit to their service.

As far as naval affairs went Churchill was out of it for the rest of the war. The inquiry of the Dardanelles Commission and his friendship with Hankey kept him in touch with what was going on and with some of the people. But when Lloyd George, greatly daring, brought him back into government in 1917 it was as Minister of Munitions. It was not until he held the offices of Secretary of State for War and Air in 1919 (which, as we have seen, was a near miss for a second spell at the Admiralty) and Colonial Secretary in 1920 that he was once again in a position to influence naval policy and appointments. Writing to Lloyd George from the War Office in May 1919 he showed all his habitual readiness to fight his departmental corner in suggesting that there was really, if President Wilson could be brought to abandon his big ship programme, 'no need for naval new construction, except of a minor character, for many years to come. The dockyards are choked with war vessels and I cannot conceive that any new construction is required.' Double-shotting his guns he concludes the letter:

Another point of the highest practical importance is this, and I am sure you will permit me to write frankly but in the greatest secrecy to you about it. Wemyss[24] is a very good First Sea Lord and I think, although I did not agree with it at the time, that your choice has been very largely justified. At the same time he is in a weak position in his own profession and far over-shadowed by Beatty. Beatty is very anxious to become First Sea Lord, and was, I believe, encouraged by Eric Geddes [First Lord 1917–19] to believe that his appointment was imminent. At any rate it seems to me that sooner or later Beatty will have to replace Wemyss, and in a reasonable time. I think this would be the right thing to do. On the other hand you must remember that once Beatty is enthroned he will be in a position to champion the particularist interest of the Admiralty to an extent it would be quite impossible for Wemyss to do. It is therefore extremely important that no change should take place at the present time, that the main finance of the three Services should be discussed and adjusted, and that any newcomer should be invited to come in on the basis that he accepts in principle the decisions arrived at.[25]

There is much in this very revealing passage that foreshadows Churchill's own preference and practice in such matters in the Second World War. Beatty, he says in effect, is professionally the most formidable candidate for the top job. For that reason a wise politician will take all the really important decisions before appointing him to it. It is this philosophy that kept Dudley Pound as First Sea Lord until he himself, crippled with arthritis and paralysed by a severe stroke, finally offered his own resignation. It was this that made Churchill fight hard against the appointment of Andrew Cunningham, who had shown on more than one occasion that he could stand up to the Prime Minister. It was this that kept Churchill from recalling Chatfield, Beatty's Flag Captain at Jutland and by far the most distinguished of his successors as First Sea Lord. His own experiences with Jacky Fisher and his observation of Lloyd George's difficulties with the Generals, notably Haig and Robertson, had made him want to bring his own authority as close as he could under a widely different constitution to that enjoyed by a President of the United States who is both head of the executive branch of government and Commander-in-Chief of the Armed Forces.

Beatty during his long tenure of the First Sea Lord's place experienced, as we have seen, the vicissitudes consequent on Churchill's exchanging the Colonial Office under Lloyd George for the Exchequer under Baldwin. As Correlli Barnett has pointed out, Churchill as Chancellor not only expostulated with the Prime Minister on the absurdity of considering the contingency of a war with Japan during their lifetime but was a party to the decisions that left Singapore undefended on the landward side, decisions of which in his memoirs he disclaims all knowledge.[26] On the all-important question of the Royal Naval Air Service, which as First Lord he had done much to foster, he found

himself not only with divided departmental loyalties—it was he who
brought Trenchard into the key position in the new Royal Air Force—
but faced by men and departments who were themselves determined
not to give an inch. Nevertheless it was he who, at last and too late,
threw the weight of his opinion, probably decisive although he was out
of office at the time, behind Chatfield's campaign to restore control of
the Fleet Air Arm to the Admiralty.[27] That was in 1937, on the very
eve of the Second World War.

Its outbreak, as we know, restored him to the Admiralty. 'Winston is
back.' The thrill conveyed by that signal to the fleet has not lost all its
voltage with the passage of half a century. And the personality that
inspired it had certainly lost none of its dynamism. There were other
things too that it had not lost: the memory of past humiliation, old
grudges, old loyalties, all centred on the still unhealed, perhaps incur-
able, trauma of the Dardanelles. Roger Keyes, who had not proved up
to the job of Commander-in-Chief Mediterranean, was still Churchill's
favourite, most valued naval counsellor while Chatfield, who had been
outstanding in that appointment and had gone on to be a great First
Sea Lord, was excluded from employment after his dismissal from the
Cabinet in March 1940.[28] Indeed the echoes of the First World War
sounded all too loudly with Churchill's immediate—and in the circumstances of 1939–40 even more grotesque—revival of Jacky Fisher's plan
for sending the fleet into the Baltic to mount an invasion of Germany.
So scathing was the reaction of an able young Captain in the Plans
Division that his career was blighted and another fire-eating veteran,
Admiral of the Fleet Lord Cork and Orrery, brought in to plan and
direct the operation.[29] No serving senior officer—certainly not the
Commander-in-Chief Home Fleet, whose ships would presumably provide the hecatomb to be offered on the altar of the Offensive Spirit—
could regard the scheme with anything but stupefied horror. Dudley
Pound skilfully concealed his own profound objections, wisely reckoning that enough difficulties would present themselves to sink the project
without his firing a shot. It was a technique in which he achieved a
mastery.

Unhappily it was not only the First World War that supplied
Churchill with ill-chosen advisers whom he consulted in preference to
those better qualified by professional experience and up-to-date knowledge. Professor Lindemann, later Lord Cherwell, had made himself a
friend of the family in the 1920s and 1930s, securing an apparently
unshakeable position as Churchill's scientific guru. At any rate it had

not been shaken by Lindemann's failure to back the development of radar by Sir Henry Tizard and his associates, which Churchill in 1940 had good reason to know was what enabled the Fighter Pilots to win the Battle of Britain. It also had enormous and obvious naval potentialities, both in locating enemy surface vessels, including of course surfaced submarines, and in warning the Royal Navy's own ships of impending air attack. How anyone could listen with anything but the deepest scepticism to an authority whose scientific opinion on a military matter of the first importance had proved so resoundingly wrong[30] is not intelligible to an ordinary man. But Churchill was not an ordinary man:

> Great wits are sure to madness near ally'd
> And thin partitions do their bounds divide.

Lindemann's advice continued to weigh with the Prime Minister on the purely military question of the best use to be made of Britain's bombing capability and, with the improved type of radar that became available from 1941, of long-range aircraft so equipped. How crucial this was to the war at sea Stephen Roskill's official history has long ago demonstrated. Lindemann was the passionate advocate of concentrating on the bombing of Germany at the expense both of the Mediterranean Fleet and of the unending battle that held the key to all the other battles, the Battle of the Atlantic.

More astonishing still is Churchill's failure to recognize the magnificent fighting spirit of the fine officers whom he was fortunate enough to find in the most important commands, and whose presence there was eloquent testimony to Chatfield's quality as a naval chief in the years leading up to the war. Cunningham, Somerville, Vian, Tovey, and Fraser exemplified the highest traditions of the service in their anxiety to get at the enemy and in their brilliant handling of forces usually much inferior to those pitted against them. The central figure was Cunningham. He had entered the navy in the same term as Somerville, his lifelong friend, and had done all he could to promote the careers of Tovey and Vian both of whom admired and loved him. Fraser he had not served with but it was Fraser who, offered the succession to Pound as First Sea Lord, declined in a phrase that ought not to be forgotten: 'that while he believed he had the confidence of his own Fleet [he was at that time C.-in-C. Home Fleet] Cunningham had the confidence of the whole Navy'.

Why was Churchill so set on preventing an officer who had proved his leadership in the most outstanding victories and in the worst adversities from occupying the chief position in the service? The reasons lie as deep in his own psychology as in the facts of history. He preferred to be first among inferiors rather than among equals. Above all he meant to have his own way. The high standing and great abilities of colleagues might prove formidable obstructions. This is the reasoning disclosed in his letter to Lloyd George already quoted. And when it came to the navy the ghost of Jacky Fisher and the nightmare of his own dismissal haunted his mind. Was he aware that Cunningham had served with great distinction and courage as a destroyer captain throughout that disastrous campaign and had, so far as can be gathered, no very high opinion of its strategical conception?[31] We do not know.

The clearest answer to the question is that given to me by the late Admiral Royer Dick, who served on Cunningham's staff through most of the war: 'Winston never forgave A.B.C. for Alexandria.' The story of that dramatic episode needs no retelling here.[32] Two aspects of it must be kept in mind: first, that Cunningham had steadily resisted the policy and, at the crux, refused to carry out a specific operational instruction clearly initiated on the personal authority of the Prime Minister; second, that his complete success had scored a bloodless military and moral victory, on which Churchill himself, grudgingly, had been obliged to send his congratulations. This was not the way to the Prime Minister's heart. On the contrary it set all the alarm bells ringing.

Somerville at the other end of the Mediterranean had protested against the same policy and had only with the deepest repugnance opened fire on the French fleet at Mers-el-Kebir. This was not forgotten: rather the Prime Minister's resentment expressed itself in unworthy and wholly unjustified doubts of the offensive spirit of the two Commanders-in-Chief. In November Somerville was ordered to take Force H to sea to cover a small, fast, and exceptionally important convoy to Malta. Off Sardinia he encountered a powerful Italian squadron to which he at once gave chase, breaking wireless silence to inform the Admiralty of his action. But as in nearly all these encounters the Italians with their faster, more modern ships quickly drew out of range. As Cunningham succinctly observed on another occasion, 'You can't catch ships that go five knots faster than you do'. Somerville therefore abandoned the pursuit and returned to the duty with which he had been charged, again reporting his action to the Admiralty. Returning to Gibraltar on the successful completion of this dangerous and important mission he was flabbergasted to find awaiting him a Court of Enquiry already convened with Admiral of the Fleet Lord Cork and Orrery as its President. Instead of receiving the congratulations of their Lordships he was to be accused of want of offensive spirit in abandoning the chase. Both Dudley Pound as First Sea Lord and A. V. Alexander as First Lord had shown deplorable weakness in agreeing to this procedure before the Admiral had even returned to harbour and made his report. A. V. Alexander had gone even further and had provisionally appointed Henry Harwood, the victor of the River Plate, to relieve Somerville before he had even been tried, a step which Churchill had personally approved. But Lord Cork was made of sterner stuff. Although recalled to active service entirely on Churchill's initiative, he was not his creature. The court wholly acquitted Somerville of any misconduct and approved his action in returning to protect the convoy. Cunningham at the other end of the Mediterranean was outraged by this scandalous treatment of a Commander-in-Chief made palpable by the verdict of the court. The public display of want of confidence in a Commander was prejudicial to the conduct of the war, contrary to the traditions of the service, and could only add to the difficulties, already serious enough, of such an officer. He expressed these views with some vigour in a letter to Pound which he must surely have expected to be shown to the Prime Minister.

He was to be in Churchill's line of fire soon enough himself. The passion for capturing islands of supposed strategic value, to which allusion has already been made, manifested itself in 1941–2 in Operation Workshop, a plan for seizing Pantellaria, in the narrows between the eastern and the western basins of the Mediterranean. Among its many disadvantages it had no harbour, no water supply, and no airfield capable of sustained military use. The Chiefs of Staff were unenthusiastic. But the Prime Minister remedied this by inviting the views of Roger Keyes and, on finding them, predictably, gung-ho, immediately offered him the command of the operation without any diminution of rank. Since Keyes was an Admiral of the Fleet of ten years seniority he would thus be superior to the Commander-in-Chief, to say nothing of the First Sea Lord who had once served as his Flag Captain. Cunningham did not disguise his opinion, which is summarized in his autobiography.

I considered it a wild-cat scheme. I had no doubt at all that the island could easily be captured, and held afterwards. But I was frankly aghast at the notion of adding to our already heavy commitments another island in a position more or less dominated by the enemy. We were having difficulty enough in maintaining Malta. To add to it Pantellaria with a garrison and its considerable civil population seemed to me to be the height of unwisdom. Nor could I see what possible use Pantellaria would be to us.

In reply to a personal signal from Churchill he stuck to his guns. As so often in war unforeseen developments suddenly transformed the situation. Workshop was postponed, and soon after abandoned. But there can be no doubt that in Churchill's mind Cunningham's criticism of a pet project had not passed unnoticed.

It was to be reinforced three or four months later by Cunningham's obdurate opposition to another scheme of Churchill's, that for sinking the battleship *Barham* as a blockship at the entrance to Tripoli harbour. Once again the First World War and Roger Keyes's exploits in it had returned to plague men hard enough pressed in the conduct of the Second. The attack on Zeebrugge in 1918 had been daring, imaginative, and well-publicized. Such recommendations had perhaps understandably obscured the fact that it had not obtained its object. The Tripoli proposal was tactically unfeasible and strategically valueless, quite apart from depriving an already overstretched fleet of one of its few battleships.[33] Cunningham's objection was even more profound, clearly as he stated these other points. It was not acceptable for a Commander-in-Chief to plan cold-bloodedly to send one of his ships with her company of close on a thousand officers and men to the bottom. If a ship were to be assigned to such a purpose she would have to be manned by volunteers with a clear understanding of what was intended and a chance, however slim, of not going down with her.

Can it be doubted that this occupation of a moral position inflamed the anger engendered by this repeated instance of independence of mind? Precisely because Churchill, unlike Hitler or Stalin, was a man of honour with an active moral sense he was particularly resentful of the criticism of proposals whose ruthlessness he had persuaded himself to be necessary. His wife's judgement, expressed to Asquith, that he had the deadliness to fight Germany was a penetrating observation, not anodyne compliment. Cunningham and Somerville had both touched this nerve over the business of the French fleet. Now Cunningham had pressed on it again. That the Prime Minister may in fact have felt some guilt or some shame is strongly suggested by the misrepresentation of the incident in the draft of his memoirs, against which Cunningham wrote to protest in October 1949.[34] Of the bombardment of the port that was substituted for the blockship scheme he then wrote:

After all these years my view remains as it was at the time; that is amazement at the ill advised and reckless irresponsibility of those who ordered the bombardment or its alternative.

The operation was successful but by good luck and the favour of Providence only. We might well have suffered complete disaster and lost the whole fleet.

It was the unseasonable, all but miraculous, presence of cloud cover for five continuous days at the sunniest time of year in the eastern Mediterranean that had saved the fleet. The Prime Minister's obstinate refusal to accept the fact, reported by every admiral who had flown his flag at sea, that capital ships without air cover were sitting ducks was to exact a terrible price in the loss of the *Prince of Wales* and the *Repulse* a few months later.[35]

It was in 1942 that the reverses suffered by the German army in Russia made the Arctic convoy route, hitherto relatively unmolested, a prime target for submarine and air attack and for the threat presented by the heavy ships now based in northern Norway. The defence of shipping in wind and weather generally agreed to be the worst in the world was daunting enough. With the nearest air cover hundreds of miles away and with enemy planes to be expected in constant attendance whenever flying was possible at all, the long Arctic nights offered welcome protection. But when these gave way to the long Arctic days in which the sun dipped below the horizon only to reappear almost instantly, the task became sisyphean. Sir John Tovey, who had been Cunningham's Rear-Admiral commanding destroyers in the Mediterranean, had been appointed to command the Home Fleet late in 1940. He crossed swords with Churchill over inadequate provision of air cover for Atlantic convoys and over the handling of the capital ships deployed in the pursuit of the *Bismarck*, a matter of operational detail in which the First Sea Lord should never have allowed the Prime Minister to interfere. When he raised doubts as to the wisdom of continuing the North Russian convoys during the continuous daylight of summer, Churchill took this as further evidence of his negative approach. The subsequent disaster to convoy PQ 17, which Pound ordered to scatter in a direct overruling of Tovey's instructions, only made Churchill more determined to get rid of him. On Cunningham's return the Prime Minister personally offered him the command only to be told that the only circumstances in which it would be accepted were if Tovey were to drop dead on his bridge. Tovey was therefore relieved by Sir Bruce Fraser.

Cunningham had, not unreasonably, expected to relieve Dudley Pound who had long been unfit and was by 1942 physically and mentally worn out. How Churchill, who had moved heaven and earth to prevent Cunningham's arrival at the Admiralty, was forced to accept it when the stricken Pound ultimately resigned the following year, the Admiral himself heard from A. V. Alexander after the end of the war:

Churchill was apparently frightened that my advent at the Admiralty would mean a very independent line and when finally consenting he said: 'You can have your Cunningham but if the Admiralty don't do as they are told I will bring down the Board in ruins even if it means my coming down with it.'[36]

This Samsonian termination of affairs was, as we know, happily avoided. But there were certainly times when exchanges were sharp and mutual exasperation evident. Cunningham came in time to develop his own method, less devious than Pound's, of deflecting the more dangerous impulses of his wilful master: 'I was quite firm with him but persuasive . . . As usual when one gets alongside him on a subject he knows little about I had my way. I was glad the First Lord was not there. He rather gets the PM's back up and he enjoys bullying him.'[37]

Cunningham continued to be amazed at how little this great war minister of unrivalled experience understood the nature or application of sea power. Churchill remained, as he had been in his youth, a cavalry officer, looking on naval men, however eminent, as narrow-minded experts, unfit to have a say in the larger use of their unsurpassed professional skill. Essentially it was the view of the pre-Pepysian navy when officers were generically classed as Gentlemen, whose function it was to lead men and fleets into battle, and Tarpaulins, who supplied the expert knowledge necessary to work the ships and fire the guns. In the twentieth century ministers such as himself and Lloyd George were the Gentlemen, the Admirals the Tarpaulins.

'The Prime Minister has gone all Army.' This cry of Cunningham's, whether provoked by the assignment of commands, the conduct of the war in north-west Europe, the distribution of honours and rewards, or a post-war speech at the El Alamein reunion in the Albert Hall, is a belated recognition of what had been true from the beginning. How little this brilliantly intelligent, supremely experienced man learned from experience when it came to naval affairs may be demonstrated from the one life or death naval issue of both wars: in one word, convoy. Hankey, who has probably the best claim of any individual to have saved the country from defeat in the First World War, always considered that the part he had played in the introduction of convoy was his chief contribution to victory. Churchill, in common with his naval advisers in 1914–15, had considered it a timid, defensive policy, preferring to employ forces available for the defence of trade in what he liked to call hunter-killer groups. Well, it may fairly be said, if he erred he erred in good, or at any rate numerous, company. But what do we find in the war of 1939–45? The naval officers, benefiting from the staff training that Churchill himself had championed, had learned this cardinal lesson. Not so their master. Indeed even after the war had been won (and how long the U-boats had been allowed to have things their own way), Churchill had still not accepted *in foro interno* what he had at length been forced to accept in practice. Admiral Sir Peter Gretton, the most generous of Churchill's naval judges and himself an escort group commander of long and distinguished service, tellingly quotes a passage written in 1948 which, he admits,

shows that he [Churchill] never understood the functions of the support groups . . . They were intended to strengthen the escort of convoys which were threatened or attacked, or, when *accurate* intelligence of a U-boat was known to seek it out and destroy it. Support groups never aimlessly swept the ocean; they were kept in positions from which they could best reinforce convoys and it was near convoys that they scored their greatest successes.[38]

In a personality of such force as Churchill's, prejudices are magnified to the strength of principles. If those of a young cavalry officer were not always conducive to the good of the navy there were others that certainly were. Churchill all his life preferred bounders to *bien-pensants*: his presence at the Admiralty was a refreshing and enlivening antidote to the stuffy and the sclerotic. His social and political prejudices were radical, again a valuable counterweight to the conservatism of the naval profession. Admiral Gretton cites a golden instance when Churchill as First Lord, suspecting prejudice against the social origins of three candidates rejected for cadetships, interviewed them himself and overrode the decision of the Selection Board:

I have seen the three candidates. Considering that these three boys were 5th, 8th and 17th in the educational competitive examination . . . I see no reason why they should have been described as unfit for the naval service. It is quite true that A . . . has a slight cockney accent and that the other two are the sons of a Chief Petty Officer and an engineer in the merchant service. But the whole intention of competitive examination is to open the career to ability, irrespective of class or fortune.[39]

Pepys no less than Jacky Fisher would have said Aye to that.

22

Churchill and Eisenhower in the Second World War

STEPHEN E. AMBROSE

THE rich, deep, difficult, and tumultuous but always amicable relationship between Churchill and Eisenhower had a major impact on how the Second World War was fought and won. The friendship stretched from the beginning of 1942 to Churchill's death in 1965. They came from different backgrounds, the Kansas boy born in a shack beside the railroad tracks in rural Texas and the British aristocrat born in Blenheim Palace. They disagreed, usually loudly and often violently, about issues of the most fundamental importance, from a proper strategy to implement against the Germans in 1942 to the question of taking Berlin in 1945. Yet they had unbounded affection and admiration for each other.

Each man took over a leadership role at a relatively advanced age, but Churchill was a world figure even as a young man, while Eisenhower was completely unknown until he was 52 years old. Churchill, for most of his life, was a professional politician, Eisenhower a professional soldier. The more important difference was in their view of themselves, their roles, and what might be called their world-view.

President Eisenhower summed up these differences best in a diary entry in June 1953, following a meeting with Prime Minister Churchill, who had flown to the United States to consult. After only a few minutes of conversation, in which Churchill tried to persuade Eisenhower to help Britain solve its problems in Iran, Egypt, and elsewhere, Eisenhower concluded that Churchill was 'unquestionably influenced by old prejudices or instinctive reaction'. He explained, 'Winston is trying to relive the days of World War II. In those days he had the enjoyable feeling that he and our president [Roosevelt] were sitting on some rather Olympian platform with respect to the rest of the world and directing world affairs from that point of vantage.'

The image of Churchill and Roosevelt sitting on their mountain tops, hurling thunderbolts at various places around the world, amused Eisenhower. He knew better, he insisted, because he was one of those 'in various corners of the world, [who] had to work out the solutions' in fixing and executing a strategy to win the war.[1] Indeed, in Eisenhower's view, Churchill and Roosevelt had frequently been more of a hindrance than a help, and what they had been able to accomplish was possible only because of the dedicated staff work of thousands of others. Churchill, for so long the loner in politics, was supremely confident of his own judgement, shown in so many ways but perhaps most of all in his famous 'action this day' memos. Eisenhower, for so long the staff officer, had no illusions about hurling thunderbolts, even from the White House. He believed above all in teamwork and wanted the views, opinions, and judgements of his staff before making up his mind.

Another difference: Churchill was a Victorian, a romantic, a colonialist, in some ways a man of the nineteenth century, while Eisenhower was more a realist, an anti-colonialist, a man of the twentieth century. Churchill led by inspiration, through exhortation and rhetoric; Eisenhower was more a manager who generally avoided exhortation and rhetoric.

From their first meeting, at the Arcadia Conference in Washington in January 1942, to the end of the war, Churchill and Eisenhower were on opposite sides on nearly every strategic decision, as well as on the larger issue of how best to utilize Allied resources to defeat Germany. Churchill's idea was to hit the Germans where they were not, on the periphery of their conquered empire, in Norway, North Africa, the Balkans. Eisenhower's idea (and of course here he was in full support of his boss, US Army Chief of Staff George C. Marshall) was to hit the Germans where they were, in northern France, then on to the Rhine and the Ruhr.

Churchill knew Eisenhower's views, but nevertheless was impressed by the man. In June 1942, when Marshall was making his selection of an American commander to take charge of the US build-up in the United Kingdom, Churchill told the Chief of Staff that he and the British High Command liked Eisenhower personally and were impressed by his dedication to the Alliance. They would be glad to have him come over to London to take command.

Of course there was a certain advantage in that arrangement for Churchill—with Eisenhower in London, the Prime Minister had ready access to him, could meet him regularly, exercise his considerable powers of persuasion, attempt simply to wear Eisenhower down until he gave in. Eisenhower became a frequent weekend guest at Chequers; on the evening of 5 July 1942 he recorded in his diary, 'We spent the early part of the evening on the lawn in front of the house and took a walk into the neighboring woods, discussing matters of general interest in connection with the war.' Churchill kept him up until 2.30 a.m.[2]

It was a pattern that persisted. In May 1943 Churchill flew to Algiers to persuade Eisenhower to follow up the impending invasion of Sicily with an invasion of Italy. 'The PM recited his story three different times in three different ways last night', Eisenhower complained in his diary on 30 May. That night, Churchill called after dinner to ask if he could come over. It was nearly 11 p.m. and Eisenhower wanted to sleep. He said he was tired of going over the same ground again and again. Churchill insisted: Eisenhower finally agreed. Churchill arrived fifteen minutes later, then talked non-stop for two hours, until Eisenhower's aide more or less pushed him out of the door. Field Marshal Alan Brooke saw the 'very sleepy Eisenhower' the next day and admitted, 'I smiled at his distress, having suffered from this type of treatment [from Churchill] repeatedly.'[3]

In 1942 Churchill got his way, as the Allies invaded North Africa instead of France, but he succeeded not by persuading Eisenhower but rather by convincing Roosevelt. Eisenhower (and Marshall) believed that Operation Torch (North Africa) was a sideshow, a waste of resources, an operation that could never have decisive results, and that it would be mounted at the expense of Operation Roundup (a 1943 invasion of France) towards which Marshall had been pointing the American army ever since it began to build up for a war with Germany. It made no sense to the Americans to go chasing hundreds of miles south of the UK, to North Africa, where the Germans were not, when the blow could be delivered across the Channel to France, where the Germans *were*. North Africa led nowhere, while Allied forces in France would threaten the German heartland, thus forcing Hitler to withdraw Wehrmacht units from Russia.

Churchill did not believe Roundup would work, but he was in the fortunate position of being able to argue not against it, but against Sledgehammer (a proposed 1942 invasion of France, in the nature of a suicide mission, designed to draw pressure off the Russians if it appeared they were about to surrender). In July 1942, when Marshall joined Eisenhower in London to argue out the strategy, the American generals had to hold out Sledgehammer as a feasible operation, even though Eisenhower gave it only one chance in five of working. One reason was, as Eisenhower put it, '*we should not forget that the prize we seek is to keep 8,000,000 Russians in the war*'.[4] A more important reason was that President Roosevelt wanted American troops in action against the Germans somewhere in 1942.

That gave Churchill the opportunity to sell Roosevelt on the idea that Torch was ideal for 1942—it would put American troops in action without risk of a humiliating defeat—and that it could be followed up by Roundup in 1943. Eisenhower and Marshall insisted that Churchill was wrong, that the drain on resources in North Africa would preclude Roundup. But the Americans could not mount Sledgehammer on their own, Churchill absolutely refused to participate, Roosevelt insisted on action, so Torch was it. Eisenhower thought the decision might well go down as the 'blackest day in history'.[5] What particularly upset him was the way Churchill meddled in military affairs about which he was uninformed or entirely ignorant. For example, one weekend at Chequers shortly before the North African invasion, Churchill was terribly upset when Eisenhower casually remarked that because of Torch it would be impossible to mount Roundup. Churchill said he was 'very much astonished' at this news, and kept coming back to the subject, jutting out his chin and declaring that it simply could not be so. He complained that 'this will be another tremendous blow for Stalin'. Eisenhower was astonished that Churchill could be astonished. All his arguments against Torch had revolved around its cost to Roundup, but evidently they had made no impression on the Prime Minister. Eisenhower told Marshall he was dismayed by Churchill's ignorance.[6]

Torch was a success, although the campaign was too long (November 1942 to May 1943) and too expensive for the gains. Eisenhower proved to be right about the cost: the huge Allied base in Algeria precluded mounting a force of sufficient strength to invade France in 1943. Roundup was off. This remains one of the great controversies of the war. Churchill and his supporters insisted that the Allies were in no way ready for a 1943 cross-Channel attack. They pointed out that landing craft were insufficient, that the Allies had not yet won mastery of the skies over France, that the American divisions still needed training, that the Wehrmacht was too strong. Eisenhower and the Americans insisted that a 1943 invasion could work and would lead to a quicker end to the war. They pointed out that there were sufficient landing craft for two major invasions in the Mediterranean, that German defences in France (the Atlantic Wall) would be twice as strong in 1944 as in 1943, that if the airpower used in North Africa, Sicily, and Italy were stationed in England in 1943 mastery of the air over France could be won, that German tank, aircraft, and artillery production was increasing and would peak in 1944, and so on. In other words, for every argument why a 1943 invasion of France could not work, there was a counter-argument. We will never know, as Roundup was never tried.

What did happen was exactly what Eisenhower feared. Once North Africa was cleared of the enemy, it was too late to go back to Roundup, which allowed Churchill to argue that it would be foolish to waste the great base built in the Mediterranean. He wanted action in 1943, and he got it, with the invasion of Sicily (July) and Italy (September). To Eisenhower and the Americans, this was continuing the sideshows and refusing to come to grips with the Wehrmacht in the only place it could be destroyed, north-west Europe. To Churchill, it was an application of his basic strategy of tightening the ring around Germany without taking undue risks.

Churchill got his way, but that was the last time he was able to do so. His hesitancy about the 1944 cross-Channel attack, Operation Overlord, and Eisenhower's enthusiasm for it are well known. It needs to be noted here that Churchill was a strong supporter of Eisenhower's appointment as Supreme Commander, Allied Expeditionary Force. Yet he did not make Eisenhower's task any easier as he shared his concerns with the general. Early in 1944, during the planning phase of Operation Overlord, Churchill told Eisenhower that he had nightmares in which 'the tides flow red with blood of American and British youths and the beaches are choked with their bodies',[7] which—one is bound to say— was hardly the appropriate thing to say to the commander of the impending operation.

They disagreed about tactics. Churchill was very much opposed to Eisenhower's Transportation Plan designed to limit German mobility in France by destroying railways. Churchill thought bombing the French railway system 'will smear the good name of the Royal Air Force across the world' and expressed his anxiety about 'these French slaughters'.[8] Eisenhower insisted on implementing it, and it was done. When Eisenhower asked the British Cabinet to impose a ban on privileged diplomatic correspondence leaving the United Kingdom, and when he requested that the Cabinet bar the entry of civilians into the southern coast areas, in each case on security grounds, Churchill was firm in his opposition—but finally gave way to Eisenhower's insistence. (Eisenhower's telling argument is worth quoting: 'It would go hard with our consciences if we were to feel, in later years, that by neglecting any security precaution we had compromised the success of these vital operations or needlessly squandered men's lives.'[9])

Slowly Churchill came around, even though he continued to lay his worries on the Supreme Commander, telling him again: 'When I think of the beaches of Normandy choked with the flower of American and British youth, I have my doubts. I have my doubts.'[10] Early in May 1944, after a lunch together, Churchill—with tears in his eyes—told Eisenhower, 'I am in this thing with you to the end, and if it fails we will go down together.'[11] But after the final review at St Paul's School, on 15 May, Churchill told Eisenhower, 'I am hardening toward this enterprise.'[12] One is again bound to comment that this was rather late in the day to get behind the plan.

They disagreed about the proper utilization of Allied strength in the Mediterranean. That argument began in June 1944, continued through July, and reached its climax in early August; it was carried on almost daily; it was, Eisenhower said, 'one of the longest-sustained arguments that I had with Prime Minister Churchill throughout the war'.[13] Eisenhower wanted to shut down the offensive in Italy in order to invade southern France (Operation Anvil) in mid-August. Churchill wanted further operations in Italy and an invasion in the Adriatic. Unable to persuade the Supreme Commander, on 4 August Churchill tried another tack—he wanted to shift Anvil (which he had renamed Dragoon, on the grounds that he had been 'dragooned' into it) from Marseilles to Brest.

To Eisenhower, this was amateur meddling in military affairs of the worst sort. D-Day for Dragoon was only eleven days away; Churchill was recommending transferring it some 1,600 miles from its base, beyond the reach of air cover, with no plan, no idea of how much shipping would be involved, and no assessment of its effect on current operations or the subsequent campaign. Eisenhower flatly refused. Churchill drove to his headquarters to make his case. He grandiloquently declared that history would show that Eisenhower had missed a great opportunity if he did not shift Dragoon to Brest. Eisenhower replied that it was too late to make a change, which was just the sort of argument that made Churchill most impatient. He believed that anything in war was possible if men just put their heads to it and their hearts in it. They argued for six hours; Eisenhower said 'no' all afternoon and 'ended saying no in every form of the English language' at his command.[14] By the end of the session, Eisenhower was limp, but Dragoon in its original form was still on. Still Eisenhower feared that the Prime Minister 'would return to the subject in two or three days and simply regard the issue as unsettled'.[15]

He was right. On 9 August, six days from D-Day, Eisenhower met Churchill at Churchill's insistence at 10 Downing Street. He later described the session that followed as one of the most difficult of the entire war. Churchill accused the Americans of acting as bullies and of being indifferent to British interests. It was painful for Eisenhower to see his friend so 'stirred, upset and even despondent', but he continued to say 'no' to Brest. Eisenhower reported to Marshall: 'So far as I can determine he attaches so much importance to the matter that failure in achieving this objective [Brest] would represent a practical failure of his whole administration.' At one point Churchill said that if he did not have his way, 'I might have to go to the King and lay down the mantle of my high office.'[16]

Thus did Churchill continue to add to Eisenhower's burdens. What stands out is Eisenhower's adroitness in handling Churchill. It was very much to Eisenhower's advantage to say that he was just a simple soldier with a clear-cut objective—to destroy the German army—and to charge that Churchill wanted to put political objectives ahead of military necessity (as if the destruction of the German army were not a political objective). Thus in the case of Dragoon, Eisenhower told Churchill to take his political points to Roosevelt. If he wanted to continue the offensive in Italy in order to get into the Balkans ahead of the Russians, he should say so—but to Roosevelt, not him.

Eisenhower said he well understood that military campaigns could be affected by political considerations, and if the heads of government should decide that getting into the Balkans was worth prolonging the war, then he would 'instantly and loyally adjust plans accordingly'.[17] But he insisted that so long as Churchill argued the matter on military grounds he was wrong. Churchill, knowing how much Americans disliked admitting to 'political' motives (which were somehow construed as tainted) and preferred making all decisions on 'military' grounds (which were thought to be straightforward), insisted that he had no political objectives. The correct military policy, he said, was to avoid the sterile campaign in the south of France, open Brest, and push on in Italy. Eisenhower said he was wrong and insisted that he would make no change so long as Churchill based the argument on military considerations.

The last great controversy between the two men came in the spring of 1945. Churchill wanted Eisenhower to direct the last offensive towards Berlin; Eisenhower insisted that the German army, not the German capital, was his proper objective. Eisenhower, therefore, stopped his advancing armies at the Elbe River and turned them south, towards the Alps, where he feared Hitler was building a redoubt to prolong the war. He left Berlin to the Russians. Churchill was aghast. On 31 March he wired Eisenhower, 'Why should we not cross the Elbe and advance as far eastward as possible? This has an important political bearing, as the Russian Army of the south seems certain to enter Vienna . . . If we deliberately leave Berlin to them, even if it should be in our grasp, the double event may strengthen their conviction, already apparent, that they have done everything.' In a later message, he told Eisenhower: 'I deem it highly important that we should shake hands with the Russians as far to the east as possible.'[18]

Eisenhower thought it more important to get a quick surrender. So did the American Joint Chiefs of Staff, who declared that such 'psychological and political advantages as would result from the possible capture of Berlin ahead of the Russians should not override the imperative military consideration, which in our opinion is the destruction and dismemberment of the German armed forces.'[19]

Eisenhower was keenly sensitive to his position. He was an agent of British and American policy, not a policy-maker. He told the Combined Chiefs of Staff (British and American Chiefs acting together) he would require a new directive from his superiors: 'if they should decide that the Allied effort to take Berlin outweighs purely military considerations in this theater, I would cheerfully readjust my plans and my thinking so as to carry out such an operation'.[20] The Chiefs made no change in his directive and Eisenhower did not change his plans. The Red Army took Berlin, at a cost of 100,000 casualties; on 8 May the war ended.

This brief survey of the Churchill–Eisenhower relationship during the Second World War has concentrated on their disagreements. What stands out is that until late 1943, Churchill got his way; from early 1944 to the end of the war, Eisenhower prevailed. This shift corresponds almost exactly with the change in the contribution to the whole force made by the UK and the USA. There were more British armed forces in the Mediterranean and European theatres than American until the end of 1943; after that, the Americans were the major partner.

It is necessary to point out here that their arguments were never personal. They had different responsibilities, and came from different nations with different interests. Inevitably the historian must concentrate on what they talked about, which was where they differed and why, rather than what they agreed upon, because they did not need to belabour or even discuss their agreements. As a consequence, any narrative of the Churchill–Eisenhower relationship necessarily leans towards a picture of irritation, harassment, bitterness, and disagreement.

But we should never forget that what they agreed on was far more important than their disagreements. Neither man ever wavered in the slightest degree from the conviction that the German war machine had to be crushed, the Nazi party destroyed. Neither man ever wavered in the slightest degree from the conviction that Anglo–American solidarity was the *sine qua non* for achieving the basic goal. Divorce was absolutely out of the question.

Both men were strong-willed. Both had immense responsibilities to their countries. Both fought long and hard for what they believed was in the best interest of their nations. But there always came a point at which one or the other gave in, and gave in without bitterness. For example, on 15 August 1944, Churchill watched the Dragoon forces go ashore. He wired Eisenhower to say that he had 'adopted' Dragoon and was delighted by the successful landings. After reading the message, Eisenhower said: 'I don't know whether to sit down and laugh or to cry.'[21]

One area in which they co-operated from beginning to end was in dealing with Charles de Gaulle. Without going into any details, it is fair to say that they entered into a conspiracy to undercut Roosevelt's anti-de Gaulle policy. Churchill's problems with de Gaulle are rightly famous; so too Eisenhower's. But the two men recognized that de Gaulle was a great man, and the right man, and that he simply had to be supported.

Churchill's tributes to Eisenhower's contributions to the victory were many and heartfelt. Eisenhower's tribute to Churchill's ability to forget the argument once a decision had been reached deserves to be quoted: 'In countless ways he could have made my task a harder one had he been anything less than big, and I shall always owe him an immeasurable debt of gratitude for his zealous support.'[22]

Churchill's eightieth birthday, in 1954, led Eisenhower to write a disquisition to a friend on the subject of greatness. He thought greatness depended on either achieving pre-eminence 'in some broad field of human thought or endeavor' or on assuming 'some position of great responsibility', and then so discharging his duties 'as to have left a marked and favorable imprint upon the future'. He insisted that one had to distinguish between a great man and a great specialist: for example, 'Martin Luther was a great man; Napoleon was a great general'. The qualities a great man should have were 'vision, integrity, courage, understanding, the power of articulation, and profundity of character'.

Under those definitions, Eisenhower said that Churchill 'came nearest to fulfilling the requirements of greatness in any individual that I have met in my lifetime. I have known finer and greater characters, wiser philosophers, more understanding personalities, but no greater man.'[23]

23

Churchill and the Use of Special Intelligence

F. H. HINSLEY

CHURCHILL was exceptional among British statesmen of his time for his familiarity with intelligence and his consuming interest in it. This familiarity began before the First World War. Having served as First Lord of the Admiralty from 1911 to 1915 and as Secretary of State for War and Air from 1918 to 1921, he, alone among the politicians who were prominent during the threat of a further war in the 1930s, had been involved in the creation of the British intelligence system in its modern form from 1909 and in its reorganization between 1919 and 1921. His interest in it was such that he contrived to receive copies of intelligence reports, sometimes with and sometimes without official permission, from 1931 until he returned to office.[1]

In the reorganization of 1919–21 the acquisition of special or clandestine intelligence was centralized in inter-departmental bodies, one for each of the major sources. The Government Code and Cypher School (GC & CS), undertaking or at least controlling all cryptanalysis, and the Secret Intelligence Service (SIS), directing all espionage, replaced the practice by which, despite earlier attempts at centralization since 1909, the Admiralty, the War Office, and the Foreign Office had continued to carry out these activities for themselves. This somewhat reduced the influence of the Directors of Intelligence in the Admiralty and the War Office. Hitherto, in controlling the assessment of intelligence and the use that was made of it as well as producing it for themselves, they had been powerful figures. Admiral Hall, the wartime Director of Naval Intelligence, had been only an extreme example of the general trend. But the reforms were incomplete in that they made no provision for placing on an inter-departmental basis the responsibility for bringing intelligence assessments to the attention of those who had to take decisions on them. After 1921 the Foreign Office came to assume that in peace it had the right to assess all intelligence, even on military matters, and to co-ordinate it with the political information received from the diplomatic missions. The views of the Foreign Office and of the service departments were co-ordinated and reconciled as far as possible by the Committee of Imperial Defence (CID), an infrequently meeting body composed of prominent ministers and the Chiefs of Staff supported by a permanent secretariat, which did little more than prepare agenda and follow up the CID's enquiries.

It was with the greatest difficulty that this weakness in the intelligence system was corrected when arrangements were rendered manifestly inadequate in the 1930s by the increasing gravity of the international situation and the growing complexity of intelligence assessment. The process began when the CID set up the Joint Intelligence Committee (JIC) of the Chiefs of Staff in 1936. On account of organizational resistance, of ministerial ignorance of intelligence work at its technical levels, and also, perhaps, of the dearth of reliable intelligence data, the process was not completed—the JIC was still only moderately efficient—before the summer of 1941. It was in these circumstances that Churchill made his greatest contribution to intelligence in the Second World War; but for his interest, the development of an effective system for co-ordinating the assessment of intelligence and giving general direction to its use would have taken even longer than it did. But it was the circumstances—the lack of such a system when he became Prime Minister—that account for his impact; it was not by his design, still less as a result of his experience, that the deficiency was rectified.

Churchill's contribution to intelligence has to be balanced by the contribution of intelligence to his place in history. No previous war leader had gained in stature as he did in the Second World War by benefiting from what became a magnificent intelligence machine. His appointment as Prime Minister coincided to the month with the first of many British successes against Axis cyphers—the initial breakthrough into the German 'Enigma' machine. This multi-purpose and endlessly variable cypher, used by the German armed forces for most of their radio communications, would have remained invulnerable but for the foresight of the British authorities, with some early help from the Poles, in concentrating against it an array of mathematical brilliance and non-mathematical ingenuity, which led to the invention of cryptanalytical machinery and methods of a sophistication hitherto undreamt of. The steady series of advances beginning in May 1940 gave Churchill opportunities to push for effective handling of special intelligence, or to turn himself into a one-man intelligence service. He seized on the second with enormous zest. The first he promoted only by inadvertence; but the efficient assessment system, which was in place from the summer of 1941 and which was in the last resort produced by the sheer volume of intelligence that became available, was perhaps the greatest among the assets he turned to the advantage of his reputation as an architect of the Allied victory.

One of Churchill's first actions on becoming Prime Minister was to order the Chiefs of Staff to review, in the light of its catastrophic failures before the invasion of Norway and the attack on France, the system by which intelligence was related to the government's procedure for taking operational and strategic decisions. The response of the Chiefs of Staff was to insist that the JIC must be solely responsible for assessing intelligence on operational and strategic developments for the central authorities and for ensuring that those authorities did not take action on information that had not been properly assessed. The Chiefs of Staff strengthened its secretariat and on 17 May 1940 instructed it to issue, at any time, assessments of any information received from the Foreign Office and the service departments that needed urgent attention, the implication being that these other departments must cease to report separately. As for the distribution of the JIC's assessments, their directive stated:

The distribution of these papers will be as follows:
   (I) The Prime Minister. Major-General Ismay in his capacity as Senior Staff Officer to the Minister of Defence, will be responsible for bringing the paper to the notice of the Prime Minister at any hour of the day or night and of taking his instructions as to action.
  (II) The other members of the War Cabinet.
 (III) The Chiefs of Staff.[2]

Although we may be sure that the provision relating to the Prime Minister was laid down at Churchill's express request, it was soon to emerge that the new arrangements did not satisfy him. One reason for this was that for at least another year the JIC failed to carry out the function assigned to it of rigorously analysing the evidence on new developments and reporting on it with a proper sense of priorities. The assessments that the JIC did make, moreover, continued to be supplemented by a flood of others, some from separate departments, some from other committees, some daily, some weekly, some purporting to be urgent and others merely up-dating in a routine fashion information on such peripheral matters as the state of opinion in the French Colonies.[3] In November 1940 Churchill objected forcefully in a minute to the War Cabinet Secretariat: 'Please look at this mass of stuff which reaches me in a single morning, most of it having already appeared in the Service and FO telegrams. More and more people must be banking up behind these different papers, the bulk of which defeats their purpose.'[4] Still, he had already made it plain by then that he was not willing to depend on the JIC to alert him to new developments, or to accept its assessment. The main reason for his dissatisfaction was that he wanted to be his own assessor.

In August 1940, in a minute to Ismay, he had disparaged assessments and summaries as 'a form of collective wisdom' and gone on to say:

I do not wish such reports as are received to be sifted and digested by the various Intelligence authorities. For the present Major [Desmond] Morton [his adviser on intelligence] will inspect them for me and submit what he considers of major importance. He is to be shown everything, and submit authentic documents to me in their original form.[5]

In October he had asked to see lists of those who were authorized to have access to 'the special material'—that is, the product of cryptanalysis—and had expressed indignation at 'this vast congregation who are invited to study these matters'. (His comment strikingly recalls the 'Charter' he had drawn up in his own hand for Room 40, the Admiralty's cryptanalytical bureau, in November 1914, which had restricted the circulation of decrypts to half a dozen most senior officers on the Naval Staff.) In September, on the other hand, he had directed the Chief of the Secret Service (C) to send him 'daily all Enigma messages'.[6] By temperament, as by experience, he belonged to the world in which an inner circle of prominent ministers had themselves determined the significance of intelligence data, guided, if guided at all, only by the colourful and autocratic Directors of Military and Naval Intelligence.

By September 1940, however, those days were long over. The special material had ceased to be circulated as translated decrypts even to senior ministers by 1927.[7] In March 1940, in a report on the Secret Service, Lord Hankey had insisted that it was imperative to maintain the practice by which, while the substance of special intelligence might be included in Cabinet minutes and documents circulated to ministers, its source was never referred to.[8] And had it been practicable to meet Churchill's unusual request for all Enigma decrypts, it would have been impossible for him or Morton accurately to assess their significance. Since May 1940 GC & CS had made the first decisive step in what was to be the greatest intelligence advance of the war by reading daily the messages encyphered in the general purpose Enigma key of the German Air Force. In the winter of 1940–1, when its success was confined to that key, the volume of decrypts was not overwhelming, rising from 50 to 250 daily as Germany expanded into the Balkans and North Africa, but their texts were indeed enigmatic. They abounded with so many code-names, technical terms, and intricate references to the names and numbers of enemy formations that to understand the significance of any one text commonly required the study of many. Throughout the war, and especially in those early days, their elucidation depended on sustained research by GC & CS and the Service Intelligence branches.

Churchill was evidently persuaded that his wishes could not be met in full. Though the surviving archive on this procedural matter is incomplete, it shows that from the summer of 1941 he was receiving at least once a day a special box containing, along with occasional reports from the SIS and memoranda on the progress of the cryptanalytical programme, a small selection of up to 20 German Air Force and Army Enigma decrypts, as elucidated at GC & CS, a short summary prepared by GC & CS of the more important naval Enigma decrypts, and occasional decrypts of outstanding messages in such other cyphers as those of the Abwehr Enigma or those used by the Axis diplomatic services.[9] But he placed immense value on whatever was sent to him, giving it the instant and avid attention that was to be expected from one who had written as long ago as 1924 that 'I attach more importance to them [decrypts] as a means of forming a true judgement of public policy . . . than to any other sources of knowledge at the disposal of the state'.[10] He insisted on receiving it when he was abroad, through the British Military Mission if in Moscow and the intelligence HQ in Cairo, and, after the Casablanca conference in January 1943, by a special radio link where no secure link already existed. From Casablanca he complained to C: 'Why have you not kept me properly supplied with news? Volume should be increased at least five-fold and important messages sent textually.'

This created problems for the Chiefs of Staff. Making no claim to competence in interpreting individual decrypts, but relying on the JIC

and the service branches to alert and advise them, the Chiefs of Staff
found that Churchill was liable to surprise them with questions
prompted by decrypts of which they had not heard, and with conclusions which, based on selected decrypts, did not accord with the wider
assessments of their intelligence advisers. Since they were already at a
disadvantage in their discussions with him—as a result of the enormous
influence he acquired from the critical circumstances in which he had
become Prime Minister; of the fact, attested to from time to time
throughout his life, that 'his judgement could be impaired by his love
of daring';[11] and of his impatience at being crossed—his initiatives
accentuated their difficulties when the Chiefs of Staff wished to restrain
or oppose him. But they were forced by his assertiveness to insist on an
improvement in the machinery for central assessment. From the
autumn of 1940 the Chiefs of Staff were constantly urging the JIC to
report to them in such a way that what was truly significant caught
their attention. In May 1941 the Chiefs of Staff at last gave the JIC an
adequate assessment staff. From July 1941 the Service Intelligence
branches provided the Chiefs of Staff with brief bulletins on the latest
special intelligence, as frequently as three or four times a day, to ensure
that they were properly briefed in their dealings with the Prime
Minister and to arm them against his proddings.[12]

This is not to say that Churchill's scorn for the machinery of central
assessment, as it functioned before his interventions had goaded it
towards efficiency, was unjustified. On the contrary, the outcome of
his first intervention of any note bore out his strictures on assessment
by summary and committee, and can only have increased his disrespect
for it.

   This was prompted in December 1940, not by special intelligence
but by statistical analysis of the German bomber effort during the Blitz
by Professor F. A. Lindemann, Churchill's adviser on technical matters, and it brought about the solution of a problem which had assumed
increasingly serious proportions—the growing divergence between the
estimates of the strength of the German Air Force produced by the Air
Ministry and by the Ministry of Economic Warfare. After failing to
resolve the discrepancy by calling for papers and holding meetings with
the Chief of the Air Staff—but not, noticeably, with representatives
from the Air Ministry's Intelligence branch—Churchill personally
drafted a memorandum which concluded that the Ministry of
Economic Warfare's estimates of aircraft production were compatible

with a German Air Force front-line strength of 3,000 aircraft, whereas the Air Ministry's estimate was nearly twice as high; and he then persuaded the parties concerned to submit evidence to an impartial referee. Neither Churchill, nor the Chief of the Air Staff or the referee—Mr Justice Singleton—found the explanation. Lindemann did this by establishing, on the evidence of the call-signs used by the German bombers, that the Air Ministry had been assuming that the fighting establishment of a German squadron was twelve when it was in fact nine. But it was largely due to the Prime Minister's involvement that the resolution of this problem, which had defeated the responsible assessment bodies, was accepted by the Air Ministry in February 1941.[13]

It was not the case, either, that his 'love of daring' required any stimulus from his access to special intelligence. Though he relished the excitement of putting his own stamp on the interpretation of decrypts, his predilection for the bold stroke, the instantaneous insight, had surfaced often enough before special intelligence was able to offer him this pleasure. At the end of June 1940, when the Chiefs of Staff were approving the attack on the French fleet at Mers-el-Kebir, he had pressed for a further operation—the landing of 25,000 troops in Morocco to seize Casablanca and set up a rallying point for Free French forces.[14] In July, thwarted by the refusal of the Chiefs of Staff to undertake that operation, as being militarily unsound and an unacceptable drain on scarce resources, and persuaded by de Gaulle that a landing at Dakar would be unopposed, he had obtained the reluctant acquiescence of the Cabinet and the Chiefs of Staff to that undertaking. They had regarded it as another unnecessary diversion of effort and an unwise further aggravation of the Vichy authorities.[15] In December 1940, undaunted by the fact that the Dakar project, launched in the absence of reliable intelligence as an ill-prepared attempt to make an opposed landing, had ended in disaster in September, he wanted to occupy the Cape Verdes and the Azores as a precaution and in the belief that Germany would enter Spain and try to take Gibraltar to counter Wavell's advance against the Italians in North Africa.

On this issue, as had not been the case with the earlier projects behind which he had been the restless driving force, intelligence had some influence on the outcome. There was no special intelligence—the German decrypts were silent about Spain—but it was known through Spanish contacts with the Madrid embassy that there was a real threat that Spain would join the Axis or be attacked by Germany; and troops and transports had been kept in readiness to occupy the islands if either of these eventualities materialized. By December, moreover, it was known from the same contacts that Germany's negotiations with Franco's government had reached a critical state. But the Chiefs of Staff, successfully opposing Churchill's wishes, took their stand on the knowledge, from photographic reconnaissance, that the Germans had as yet made no move to concentrate the shipping and the naval forces they would need for a descent on the islands. They were supported by the Foreign Office, which no doubt pointed out that a pre-emptive British occupation would have put an end to Franco's prevarication and thrown him into Hitler's arms.[16]

Special intelligence, for the first time throwing some light on Germany's intentions, had meanwhile established at the end of 1940 that she was extending her infiltration of the Balkans to Bulgaria, and the Cabinet had already authorized an attempt to bring Turkey into the war on the British side before the decrypts confirmed rumours from the embassies and the SIS that Hitler planned a considerable offensive through Bulgaria to Greece. Churchill's first reaction was to send, on 6 January 1941, a memorandum to the Chiefs of Staff: 'Nothing would suit our interest better than that any German advance in the Balkans should be delayed till the Spring. For this very reason one must apprehend that it will begin earlier.' And it was in this spirit that he applied his own assessment of the evidence from Enigma decrypts for the first time. On 5 January the War Office had concluded from a good number of decrypts that Germany was making thorough preparations and would not attack until the winter was over, in March. Churchill, however, jumped to the conclusion that the attack was imminent at the first mention in the decrypts of a date. A decrypt dated 7 January instructed rear detachments for intermediate landing grounds to be ready for their assigned tasks by 20 January, and on the strength of this he persuaded the Defence Committee on 8 and 9 January that the attack on Greece would begin on 20 January and that, as it was of first political importance to implement the guarantee given to Greece, the Commander-in-Chief Middle East should be instructed to fly to Athens and offer the fullest possible assistance.

General Sir Archibald Wavell, the Commander-in-Chief, whose forces were in hot pursuit of the Italians in North Africa, questioned the instruction—'it fills me with dismay'. In the belief that the German infiltration into the Balkans was designed only to upset Greek nerves and stop the British advance in Libya, he asked the Chiefs of Staff 'to re-consider whether the enemy's move is not bluff'. It was Churchill who answered him on 10 January: 'Our information contradicts the idea that the German concentration is merely a move in the war of nerves . . .' This was correct; though it is now known that until he learned that British forces were arriving, Hitler had intended to occupy Greece only down to Salonika, in an operation taking only a week, to guard his flank while he turned on Russia. The Prime Minister continued: 'We have a mass of detail showing that a large-scale movement, through Bulgaria towards the Greek frontier aimed presumably at Salonika will begin on or soon after 20 January.' This was incorrect. By 20 January the evidence from the decrypts, the SIS, and the embassies in the Balkans had confirmed that Germany would not be ready to open hostilities from Bulgaria for about two months.

Those two months were used not to reconsider the precipitate decision to offer help to Greece, but to increase the diplomatic pressure on Greece to accept it and on Turkey to participate in her defence, and to increase the help offered till it comprised the bulk of the Middle East land forces. What drove Churchill on was mainly the wish to preserve British credibility as an ally and, with an eye to the possible effects on Turkey and Yugoslavia, and perhaps even Russia and the United States, a potential ally. Uncharacteristically, however, he increasingly dreaded that the project would end in disaster, as is clear from his telegrams to Eden after Eden had been dispatched to the Middle East with the Chief of the Imperial General Staff (CIGS) and given plenipotentiary powers to cancel if discussions with Wavell and the Greeks made that seem wise. It would be a reasonable judgement from their correspondence that the project went forward only because, while Churchill wanted them to advise him to desist, the CIGS and Wavell put aside their misgivings because they felt Churchill had set his heart on it—as indeed he had up to the Cabinet meeting of 11 February that preceded their departure for Cairo. But there is one consideration that tells against this conclusion. Although he was, as he later conceded, 'sure that I could have stopped it all if I had been convinced', Churchill persisted in spite of the evidence of special intelligence, or at least of the interpretation put upon it by his advisers.

At the meeting of 11 February it was reported that, on the latest evidence, Germany would be ready to cross into Greece with five divisions by 12 March and, allowing for only Greek resistance, could be in Salonika a week later and in Athens, with ten divisions, from mid-April. Churchill was no longer attempting to stamp his own interpretation on the decrypts, but he accepted this schedule only after closely questioning the Director of Military Intelligence, who attended; and, arguing that it gave time for British forces to reach northern Greece, he overrode the arguments of the Chief of the Imperial General Staff against the decision to order Wavell to give priority to preparations for sending the bulk of his fighting force to Greece over pursuit of the Italians to Tripoli. Thereafter, the intelligence staff in Whitehall, as in Cairo, remained so convinced that the undertaking was strategically and militarily unsound that although the decrypts produced no firm grounds for modifying the appreciation made by 11 February, it became alarmist; and while stopping short of questioning the right of ministers to place political over military considerations the Chiefs of Staff did their utmost to persuade the Cabinet to heed its advice.

On 24 February, warned by the Director of Military Intelligence that the German attack might be more formidable than had been allowed for and that 'we must be prepared to face the loss of all forces sent to Greece', the Chiefs of Staff notified the Cabinet that in the absence of co-operation from Turkey and Yugoslavia support for Greece was 'unlikely to have a favourable effect on the war as a whole'. The Cabinet was undeterred, reaffirming its decision on 27 February. Between 2 and 5 March the JIC warned that a German attack with four divisions might be imminent, and on 5 March the Chiefs of Staff incorporated a less qualified version of the warning in an *aide-mémoire* drawing the Cabinet's attention to the increasingly unfavourable prospects for the undertaking: four divisions would be on the Greek frontier that day, and two might be approaching the Greek defence line by 15 March and five by 22 March. Churchill now seriously hesitated; but by 8 March, swayed, ironically, by the opinion of GHQ Middle East that the Germans could not reach the frontier before 11 March and that the Chiefs of Staff had underestimated the time the Germans would need to reach the defence line in force, the Cabinet had agreed to stand by its plans.[17]

By 27 February 1941, when the Cabinet reaffirmed the decision to go forward with the Greek expedition, Whitehall had learned that German armoured cars had been encountered in North Africa. Churchill refused to be pessimistic about the effect of this unexpected development on the plans for Greece, and no-one disagreed. No-one was pessimistic, either, about the consequences for Egypt's defence of the transfer of troops to Greece, until Rommel, to the complete surprise of the British, advanced to Benghazi by 4 April, two days before Germany invaded Greece, and, by-passing Tobruk, took up positions inside Egypt in the middle of the month. Rommel had moved against his instructions and against Italian protests, and the British had received no intelligence about his forces except that they were small.[18]

Churchill now resorted to a device that he was to use regularly for the rest of the war. On 2 April special intelligence provided the first of a number of indications that Rommel's advance was improvised, and probably unauthorized—a decrypt refusing his request for more air support on account of pressing demands in other theatres. Churchill sent Wavell a translation of the complete text, the gist of which had already been forwarded to Cairo, with the comment that it showed Rommel was not under orders to advance into Egypt. This was a perceptive assessment, endorsed by the JIC in the light of additional evidence a few days later. For Churchill to forward the assessment with the supporting text reflected an imaginative understanding both of Wavell's anxiety and of the risk that Cairo might not have effective arrangements for bringing the significance of decrypts to the Commander-in-Chief's notice. A signals link carrying the gist of decrypts direct from GC & CS had been opened as recently as 13 March, and before May the signals were circulated only to a small number of recipients in Cairo, not all of whom had been indoctrinated into their true source. But Churchill could not resist adding the further comment, gratuitous even after allowing for his own anxiety, that he trusted Wavell would make every effort to drive Rommel back.[19]

He repeated this procedure when General Paulus, sent to North Africa to curb Rommel's impetuousness, reported back to Berlin on 4 May that he had instructed Rommel, in view of the 'thoroughly exhausted' conditions of his troops, to make no further advance without permission before the whole of 15th Panzer Division had arrived. Churchill sent the text of this decrypt to Wavell on 5 May. On 7 May, in a commentary on it, he urged Wavell to take advantage of this respite to attack as soon as possible, and pointedly reminded him that the convoy of armoured reinforcements, recently routed through the Mediterranean at considerable risk, was on its way. It has been argued that the attacks Wavell made in mid-May and mid-June failed because they were made prematurely under the pressure which Churchill exerted with undue reliance on the hasty interpretation of a single decrypt. But Wavell had needed no prompting: he made the first attack (Operation Brevity) without waiting for the convoy to arrive and the second (Operation Battleaxe) before all the reinforcements could be ready for battle. Nothing in the Paulus decrypt, moreover, or in Churchill's commentary, had suggested that Rommel would be unable to hold his positions; and the pressure to act had come, rather, from the fact that special intelligence disclosed that 15th Panzer was arriving. The offensives failed because nothing had prepared Wavell or Whitehall for the shock of discovering the extent of Rommel's superiority in tanks, armoured cars, and anti-tank weapons.[20]

It had taken a great deal of prompting to persuade Wavell to dispatch a force to Iraq on the eve of Operation Brevity, following Rashid Ali's seizure of power there in April, and to invade Syria on the eve of Operation Battleaxe. He was all but forced to carry out these further diversions of his scant resources on the basis of intelligence that was anything but compelling. In the case of these undertakings, however, the Chiefs of Staff and their intelligence advisers generated the pressure and there are grounds for believing that Churchill was carried along by their alarmist conviction that, over and above the attack on Greece, Germany's strategic objective was a drive through Turkey, Syria, and Iraq to the Gulf or Egypt.

Against Rashid Ali the Chiefs of Staff first requested the dispatch of troops from India. Their arrival in Basra on 18 April completed his alienation, and when he had invested the RAF base at Habbaniya, and the advance of the Basra force was held up by flooding, Whitehall requested Wavell to send troops immediately to relieve the base, over-ruling on 4 May his preference for recognizing Rashid's government and relying on diplomatic pressure. He had still not complied by 8 May, by which date the RAF had broken the siege and Italian decrypts had disclosed that Rashid, his forces close to collapse under British air attacks, was entreating the Germans and the Italians to send him the air support he had first requested before the end of April; but Wavell was then urged to send a force to operate against Baghdad, there being 'an excellent chance to restore the situation by bold action'. Churchill intervened on 9 May when German decrypts indicated for the first time that the German Air Force was trying, with difficulty and on a small scale, to respond to Rashid's appeal. He pressed Wavell to meet the latest request: 'every day counts, for the Germans may not be long'.

On 13 May, by which time Wavell had complied, Churchill sent him the full text of a Japanese diplomatic signal from Baghdad; decrypted on 12 May, this stated that Rashid's resistance could continue only until 15 or 20 May but would collapse earlier if British forces advanced from Palestine. Exhilarated, no doubt, by what he took to be a vindication of the stand taken in London, he added only the comment: 'burn after reading'. Wavell might well have felt that it vindicated his reluctance to act. It is far from certain that Rashid would have survived, even with the small and ineffective air support which Germany provided, if the British had limited their intervention to the Basra force and a temporary reinforcement of their airpower.[21]

On 9 May, as well as pressing Wavell to move into Iraq, Churchill suggested to him that, in view of 'the danger of Syria being captured by a few thousand German troops transported by air', he should assist Free French forces in the Middle East to move into Syria. The Chiefs of Staff had asked Wavell at the end of April to consider what forces he could spare for this project. They were motivated by the argument that Germany would need to establish intermediate bases if she were to intervene effectively in Iraq, and also by the fear that this was indeed her intention. The argument was sound enough, but the fear was so unreasoning that the special intelligence was misinterpreted in an attempt to provide support for it. Decrypts had disclosed since mid-April that the Germans were planning a large airborne assault from Greek airfields; on 26 April they had referred explicitly to Crete, and on 1 May they unmistakably confirmed that Crete was the target of the assault. But the Chiefs of Staff maintained, irrationally and inexcusably, that the references to Crete might be part of a deception plan to cover a descent on Syria or Cyprus, on which the decrypts were significantly silent, and they were abetted by the intelligence bodies. These bodies did not question the authenticity of the decrypts; and they admitted that simultaneous assaults on Crete and another target were unlikely because Germany lacked sufficient transport aircraft. But they would not rule out the risk of a diversion against Syria if the British position in Iraq deteriorated.

Churchill fell in with this exercise in self-deception on 3 May when, despite the fact that he had correctly judged as early as 28 April that Crete was Germany's objective, he accepted that Germany might be 'only feinting at Crete'. But he still delayed until 9 May before joining the Chiefs of Staff in putting pressure on Wavell to act in Syria. One obvious reason for the delay has been mentioned: between 5 and 7 May he was himself pressing the Commander-in-Chief, who was already being pressed by the Chiefs of Staff to move a force to Baghdad, to take advantage of the Paulus decrypt by attacking Rommel as soon as possible. Another reason was that he was simultaneously preoccupied with another decrypt: on 6 May the Enigma provided the precise operational orders for the execution of each stage of the assault on Crete. It cannot be said that Churchill's contribution to so professional an exercise was strictly necessary, but he could not resist taking a full part in discussing the equally precise plans for countering the attack that were drawn up by the Air Staff in consultation with the Naval and the General Staffs and sent out to Wavell on 9 May. Nor could he refrain from adding, for Wavell's benefit, the comment that he had been presented with 'a heaven sent' opportunity to deal the enemy a mortal blow.

It is more to the point, however, that he did not add his weight to the pressure which the Chiefs of Staff continued to exert for action in Syria. On 19 May they instructed Wavell to improvise the largest possible force at the earliest possible moment. Next day, in instructions that crossed a telegram from Wavell reporting that the Free French were urging him to invade Syria with arguments that a German occupation was imminent and that the French in Syria were pro-British, the Chiefs of Staff directed the Commander-in-Chief to fall in with the Free French wishes. He offered to resign, but withdrew his offer when Churchill agreed to accept it on 21 May. He explained that, the Free French having conceded that the Vichy forces would resist an invasion, he had been objecting only to the immediate dispatch of a totally improvised force. Until 8 June, when Wavell finally moved, the decrypts not only continued to provide no evidence that Germany was preparing to intervene; they established that she was withdrawing the few aircraft that remained at Syrian bases after operating in Iraq. On 25 May Wavell pointed delicately to these negative indications, asking the Chiefs of Staff whether his advance should be made dependent on the arrival of a German force. They swept the evidence aside, their anxiety to forestall a German descent on Syria increasing as the fighting in Crete drew to a close.[22]

That Churchill did not comment during these exchanges, let alone agitate for action, may have been due to the fact that he sympathized with Wavell's interpretation of the intelligence, as also with his concern to give priority to the Western Desert. But it can be argued that, in view of the significance he had attached to another item of special intelligence of which Wavell remained unaware, he should have gone further and supported Wavell in his wish to defer or cancel the Syrian operation. Decrypts had revealed as early as 26 and 27 March that the movement of two German Army HQs and three armoured divisions from the Balkans to Cracow had been ordered soon after Yugoslavia had signed the Tripartite Pact, but had been cancelled within twelve hours of the coup in Belgrade. Unlike most of the intelligence authorities—the only exceptions were GC & CS and a few officers in the Air Ministry—and unlike the Chiefs of Staff, he immediately, and correctly, took this to be a powerful indication that Germany intended to invade Russia and that the invasion would be delayed only by her need to operate against Yugoslavia. He insisted on passing the information to Stalin, as having been received from 'a trusted agent', on 3 April: 'Your Excellency will readily appreciate the significance of these facts.' He was all the more ready to see their significance himself, because, long before any reliable intelligence had arisen, he had warned Stalin as early as June 1940 that Germany would turn east, and had told a meeting of senior commanders in October 1940 that she would inevitably attack Russia in 1941.[23]

It is unlikely that during all the subsequent turmoil in the Middle East Churchill forgot this first significant pointer to Germany's intentions which—as distinct from rumours that had long been coming in from embassies and agents—was central to an understanding of her strategic priorities. He kept an eye on the decrypts which, increasingly from the third week of April, confirmed that she was moving ground forces and preparing to move air forces to the Russian front: on 16 May he informed Smuts that 'it looks as if Hitler is massing against Russia. A ceaseless movement of troops, armoured forces and aircraft northwards from the Balkans and eastwards from France is in progress.' It does not appear, however, that he sought to dissuade the Chiefs of Staff from accepting the many intelligence appreciations which regarded the evidence as inconclusive and continued to dwell on the German threat to the Middle East—as the Chiefs of Staff did until, on 31 May, they at last advised the Commanders-in-Chief in the Middle East that Germany was concentrating her forces against Russia, was demanding concessions from her, and would march if her demands were refused.[24] Even at the end of May, on the other hand, it would not have been too late to cancel or defer the invasion of Syria, which turned out to be a costly move. Invading on 8 June, Wavell's barely adequate force met such fierce Vichy resistance that it had to be reinforced more than once before the end, on 12 July.

With the German invasion of Russia the process which Churchill called 'the widening war' took a huge lurch forward, and it was completed by the Japanese attack on Pearl Harbor, of which, despite subsequent claims to the contrary, Whitehall received no warning from intelligence for Churchill to pass to, or withhold from, Roosevelt. Pearl Harbor and its aftermath in no way reduced his appetite for and his immersion in the discussion of Allied strategy and operations. But there was a steady decline in the extent to which his influence on the decisions depended on his use of special intelligence to support his arguments.

This may seem odd in view of the fact that, far from seeing any decline in the amount of special intelligence, the months between the entry of Soviet Russia into the war and the entry of the United States exactly coincided with the period in which the Western Allies established the massive superiority over the Axis in signals intelligence which they were to retain till the end of the war. Quite apart from the Japanese decrypts that came on stream soon after Pearl Harbor, GC & CS extended its mastery of the general German Air Force Enigma key to the keys of the German navy from June 1941, to those of the army from September 1941, and to other Air Force keys by the end of the year; and from July 1941 it was regularly reading the Italian cypher that carried the bulk of the wireless traffic about Axis shipping in the Mediterranean. From the middle of 1942 it was producing between 3,000 and 4,000 German decrypts a day and a considerable, though smaller, volume of Italian and Japanese decrypts. But the proportion of this flood which Churchill could personally inspect inevitably declined and, on the other hand, the flood brought to an end the days in which, with only a limited supply of special intelligence and with a lack of experience in handling it, the machinery for the central assessment of it and the procedure for conveying it to the commands had been inadequate.

Churchill did not cease to pay close attention to such decrypts as he received. He continued to reveal the importance he attached to them by insisting from the end of June 1941 that a summary of them should be sent to the Soviet authorities; by arranging that General Sir Claude Auchinleck, who had succeeded Wavell as Commander-in-Chief Middle East, should receive the verbatim texts during the first battle of El Alamein; and by being always ready to lend his authority to efforts of the Sigint organization to uphold the strict security procedures that governed the use of special intelligence in the field.[25] But the outcome of these developments was that his response was increasingly confined to bringing decrypts to the notice of the Chiefs of Staff or a theatre commander. When he went beyond this, moreover, to make a complaint or give an order, he increasingly found that his initiative had either been anticipated or was resisted or went unheeded.

In the summer of 1941 he was much provoked by the fact that although Italian decrypts were now providing instructions for the movement of most of the convoys to North Africa, British forces were not preventing shipping from reaching Benghazi. He minuted the First Sea Lord: 'What action will C in C Med take on this information? Surely he cannot put up with this kind of thing . . . without making any effort by his surface forces to intercept . . . we are still at war.' But the Commander-in-Chief had already resolved to base cruisers and destroyers at Malta as soon as fuel supplies allowed—which was not until October. In November 1942 Churchill again prodded the Admiralty into alerting the Mediterranean authorities to decrypts relating to convoys bound for Tunis and Bizerta—convoys which were totally destroyed as a result of dispositions made before he intervened.[26] In March 1943 and again in January 1944, on the strength of decrypts disclosing German preparations for the resumption of bombing over the United Kingdom, he urged the Air Staff to take the counter-measures which, not surprisingly, they had already taken.[27]

After the middle of 1941, on the other hand, Churchill's attempts to intervene in the Western Desert met with a reception very different from that accorded to them in Wavell's time. During October 1941, the new Commander-in-Chief, Auchinleck, resisted pressure to take the offensive before 1 November. Churchill bombarded Cairo with appeals for action before Rommel could be ready to attack, singling out decrypts on 3, 22, and 25 October and having them repeated with the instruction that 'The Minister of Defence directs that General Auchinleck should see'. By 18 October, however, to Churchill's intense displeasure, Auchinleck had postponed his start to 11 November, and there were two further postponements before Operation Crusader was launched on 18 November. The fact is that the Commander-in-Chief and his staff were watching the decrypts no less closely than the Prime Minister and were discussing with Whitehall and with GC & CS how the evidence might enable them, as it did, both to strike before Rommel did and to take him by surprise.[28]

In a repeat of these exchanges from February 1942, after Rommel's counter-attack had taken him back to Gazala and Auchinleck, supported by the Middle East Defence Committee, was resisting pressure from Churchill and the Chiefs of Staff for an offensive in April on the grounds that he would not have the necessary numerical superiority in tanks before the beginning of June, Churchill entered into the intricate business of interpreting the detailed but incomplete evidence that the decrypts were providing about Rommel's tank strengths. On 15 March he pointed out to Cairo on the strength of a single decrypt that Rommel had 'barely half the number' of tanks that Cairo had credited him with at the beginning of the month; but he had failed to realize that the decrypt referred only to tanks in the forward area. On 26 April he incautiously repeated this exercise and made the different mistake of assuming that a decrypt referred to all tanks in the forward area when the figure it gave, which was again much lower than Cairo's estimate, referred to some smaller category. His signal to Auchinleck—'I should be glad to know how this important correction strikes you'—elicited an immediate and comprehensive correction. On 30 April, by which time a fuller decrypt had established that Cairo's estimates were essentially correct, he acknowledged his error: 'later most secret information . . . confirmed your [estimates] . . .'[29]

Although Auchinleck eventually submitted to a direct instruction to take the offensive no later than mid-June, Rommel attacked first, and in all the subsequent fighting—Rommel's victory in the battle of Gazala in June; Auchinleck's success in holding him in the first battle of El Alamein in July; General Bernard Montgomery's successes in holding him at Alam el Alfa in September and in defeating him in the second battle of El Alamein—Churchill made no attempt to insert himself into the enormously increased flow of decrypts to Cairo and the Western Desert. His next intervention came between the end of November 1942 and the beginning of January 1943, when he expressed his impatience and displeasure at the slow pace of Montgomery's pursuit of Rommel in a succession of signals to General Sir Harold Alexander, the new Commander-in-Chief Middle East. Each of them quoted the serial numbers of decrypts showing, as he said of one of them, 'a condition of weakness and counter-order among the enemy of a very remarkable character'.[30] His intervention was to no avail, and it was the last of any significance in which he used his extraordinary interest in special intelligence to increase his influence or support his arguments in operational decisions. With the decision to undertake Operation Torch, the Allied landings in north-west Africa in November 1942, his ability to do this was circumscribed not only by the sheer volume of decrypts and the increasing professionalism of the machinery for assessing and exploiting them, but also by the emergence of the Combined (Anglo-American) Chiefs of Staff Committee and the arrival of Dwight Eisenhower to take the supreme command, albeit at Anglo-American HQs, in the main operational theatres.

It was, perhaps, in part because Churchill chafed under these last restrictions that after Italy's collapse he sought opportunities for independent initiatives in the British-controlled Middle East theatre and tried to prevent the reduction, at the expense of other operations, of the Allied effort in the British-commanded Italian campaign. But he derived little satisfaction from his attempts to take advantage of 'the soft under-belly of the Axis', for which the decrypts provided little assistance.

He was thwarted in his wish to take Rhodes when special intelligence disclosed that Germany was sending heavy air reinforcements to the Aegean and, although garrisons were dispatched with his encouragement to Leros and the smaller islands, he appealed to decrypts in October 1943 in an attempt to persuade the Chiefs of Staff to arrange increased support for them, without success.[31] In the first half of 1944, during the prolonged debate with the US Chiefs of Staff, who wished to strip divisions from Italy for landings in the south of France, he used the evidence of the decrypts to argue, in personal appeals to General Marshall in April and to President Roosevelt in June, that Germany was so determined to delay the Allied advance in Italy that she would reinforce her armies there at the expense of the Western Front if forced to do so by an all-out Allied offensive against the Pisa–Rimini line. In this effort he had the support of the British Chiefs of Staff and all British commanders in the Mediterranean, but the appeals fell on deaf ears. The Americans felt that, as the JIC recognized, special intelligence, though providing excellent evidence on Germany's order of battle and present intentions in Italy, was necessarily inconclusive about what she would do in contingencies which had not yet arisen.[32]

Meanwhile, as Churchill scrutinized the decrypts from the main warfronts, he was distracted by an obsession with both the threat and the potential of chemical warfare. In October 1943 he ordered the Chiefs of Staff to consider the use of gas against the V-weapon sites and the advisability of warning the Germans that gas would be used in retaliation against any V-weapon attack. They firmly rejected the suggestions, as they also did, in the spring of 1944, his proposal that Germany should be warned of retaliation if she resorted to gas warfare in Normandy. But on 11 June 1944, at the first reference to gas equipment in a decrypt after the landings in Normandy—a reference which by no means implied that the enemy intended to use gas—he sent a copy to Eisenhower marked 'Action This Day' and asked him to discuss it with Montgomery; and on 6 July he requested the Chiefs of Staff to make 'a cold-blooded calculation' of the case for using gas in Normandy and against the V-weapon sites. On 18 July, impatient with their delay in reporting back and shaken by unexpected intelligence pointing to the imminence of the V2 rocket offensive, he stormed out of a meeting after declaring that he would consult the USA and the USSR about threatening Germany with gas warfare if the weapon was used. Not until 28 July, when the Chiefs of Staff finally insisted that the resort to gas would not be decisive, did he drop the matter.[33] He did so gracefully, not to say light-heartedly, with the comment: 'But clearly I cannot make headway against the parsons and the warriors at the same time.' And it is indeed difficult to be sure that his agitation had ever been wholly serious. To some extent at least, it may have been an outlet for the frustration he felt, as the war reached its climax, that, though in the thick of events, he was unable to use special intelligence to stamp his personal influence on them because the volume of decrypts was so great and the assessment machinery so efficient.

Much could be written on the theme that, in fact, the intelligence offered Churchill opportunities for asserting himself which he failed to take. When the Chief of the Air Staff advised him in June 1944 that the decrypt evidence dictated that first priority in the bombing of Germany should be given to oil targets he replied: 'Good.'[34] But he did not throw his weight behind the unsuccessful efforts by the Air Staff to direct the attention of Bomber Command to the intelligence which continued to justify this priority throughout the second half of the year. On 8 September 1944 he resisted the almost universal euphoric belief that Germany would collapse by the beginning of 1945, pointing out *inter alia* that the Allies still had no major port except Cherbourg and that the enemy was hanging on to the Scheldt. But he did not exert himself in the next few days to support the unsuccessful attempts of the Chiefs of Staff to persuade Eisenhower, and of Eisenhower to persuade Montgomery, that it was essential to neutralize Antwerp and the Scheldt before advancing to Arnhem and the Ruhr.[35] Many complex arguments would have to be weighed, however, and the mitigating circumstances would have to be considered, before Churchill could safely be accused of oversight in these and other missed opportunities.

24

Churchill and Science

R. V. JONES

HURCHILL'S attitude towards science and technology may be vividly traced through his words and actions at those stages of his life where they claimed his attention. As was the case with most public men of his day, natural science had but a minor part in his education at school: even so, on surveying his record at Harrow and preparing for the entrance examination to Sandhurst in 1893 he reckoned that chemistry was one of his only two good subjects, the other being English. He needed, though, to be strong in at least three subjects, and so he chose mathematics as his third: in this, with the aid of a crammer, he ultimately achieved sufficient competence to pass into Sandhurst on his third attempt, where he was cheered to find that:

There was a question in my third and last Examination about these Cosines and Tangents in a highly square-rooted condition which must have been decisive on the whole of my after life. It was a problem. But luckily I had seen its ugly face only a few days before and recognized it at first sight . . . if this aged, weary-souled Civil Service Commissioner had not asked this particular question . . . the whole of *my* life would have been altered, and that I suppose would have altered a great many other lives . . .[1]

A schoolboy enthusiasm for making bombs may perhaps have stimulated his interest in chemistry; and as regards other sciences he might well have developed a liking for natural history, to judge by his lasting memory of a lecture by a visiting biologist at Harrow:

There was a lecture about how butterflies protect themselves by their colouring. A nasty-tasting butterfly has got colouring to warn the bird not to eat it. A succulent, juicy-tasting butterfly protects himself by making himself exactly like his usual branch or leaf. But this takes them millions of years to do; and in the meanwhile the more backward ones get eaten and die out. That is why the survivors are marked and coloured as they are.[2]

As we shall see, his appreciation of natural history survived through

the intervening years, which took him as an army officer or war correspondent to India, Omdurman, Cuba, and South Africa, and as a politician to the Board of Trade, the Home Office, and the Admiralty. In
Parliament, one of his early speeches (12 November 1903) supported
free trade with the argument that 'The happiness of our people is to be
found in social reform rather than in fiscal malformations, by increasing
temperance rather than tariffs, through the schoolmaster, the scientist
and the physician rather than the tax gatherer and the Custom House
official . . .'[3] While Lady Violet Bonham Carter could drily comment
that 'These allusions to Temperance, schoolmasters and weekly bills
must in his mouth have had a strangely unfamiliar ring', his mention of
science suggests that he was early aware of its potential. Lady Violet
also remarked that, as First Lord of the Admiralty: 'He was enthralled
by the technology of naval warfare, and his sense of its results in
human terms was for the time being in abeyance.'[4]

After the Admiralty he went in 1916 to the trenches in Flanders
where he commanded the 6th Battalion of the Royal Scots Fusiliers,[5]
and his knowledge of natural history came again to the fore. One of his
officers, A. D. Gibb (later Regius Professor of Law at Glasgow),
recalled his first words of address to his officers: 'Gentlemen we are
now going to make war—on the lice!' Gibb further recorded:

With these words did the great scion of the House of Marlborough first
address his Scottish captains assembled in council. And with these words was
inaugurated such a discourse on *pulex europeaus*, its origin, growth, and nature,
its habitat and its importance as a factor in wars ancient and modern, as left
one agape with wonder at the erudition and force of its author . . . Thereafter
he created a committee of company commanders to concert measures for the
utter extermination of all the lice in the battalion.[6]

Gibb also noted from the enthusiasm with which Churchill would get
his medical officer to talk on his own subject that 'Winston had a flair
for a good man of science'.[7]

That same flair showed again when, in 1921, Mrs Churchill was
partnered in a tennis match for charity at Eaton Hall, home of the
Duke of Westminster, with the Wimbledon-playing and newly
appointed professor of experimental philosophy at Oxford, Frederick
Alexander Lindemann. At first sight it was remarkable that the two
men who now met were attracted by one another, for superficially they
were so different. Churchill, the older by a dozen years, ate, drank, and
smoked generously, and enjoyed a happy family life; Lindemann was a

non-smoker, an abstainer from alcohol, a vegetarian, and a life-long bachelor. Churchill had been in the midst of violent action in India, in the Sudan, in South Africa, and in the trenches of Flanders; Lindemann had led a life so socially sheltered that it was said that he had never been on a London omnibus or the London Underground. Churchill, though, as an outstanding polo player, would have recognized Lindemann's ability at tennis. They each had 'that saving sense of humour which is of high importance to all men and all nations but particularly to great men and great nations';[8] and they both enjoyed good English. I can recall a meeting in the Cabinet Room where they disagreed about the meaning of a particular word, and our discussion of progress in 'The Wizard War' was held up while the appropriate volume of the *Oxford English Dictionary* was sent for to settle the argument.

Moreover, Churchill would have heard of—and perhaps even envied—Lindemann's skill as a pilot, where he was famed as the first man to explain why an aircraft could go into a fatal spin, to work out the procedure whereby its pilot could recover it from the spin, and who then learned to fly and to demonstrate that his procedure worked. Churchill himself had tried hard to learn to fly while he was First Lord of the Admiralty and had made nearly 140 flights before the outbreak of war in 1914, despite the manifest dangers of flying in the primitive aircraft of the time. On 6 June 1914, though, he wrote to his wife telling her that for her sake, because she was so worried by the risks involved, he would give up flying:

This is a wrench, because I was on the verge of taking my pilot's certificate. It only needed a couple of calm mornings; & I am confident of my ability to achieve it vy respectably. I shd greatly have liked to reach this point wh wd have made a suitable moment for breaking off. But I must admit that the numerous fatalities of this year wd justify you in complaining if I continued to share the risks—as I am proud to do—of these good fellows. So I give it up decidedly for many months & perhaps for ever. This is a gift—so stupidly am I made—wh costs me more than anything wh cd be bought with money. So I am vy glad to lay it at your feet, because I know it will rejoice & relieve your heart.[9]

Churchill, a man of extraordinary courage himself, was bound to admire Lindemann's exploits in the air. Moreover, he soon discovered Lindemann's ability to answer questions about science in 'lucid, homely terms', and Lindemann quickly became a welcome guest at Churchill's home at Chartwell. Indeed, on an occasion in 1925 when Churchill had

not invited Lindemann to a party, he afterwards wrote to his wife: 'As
he [A. J. Balfour] was not coming, I did not invite Lindemann, and
now find Mary [Churchill's youngest daughter, aged 3] extremely disappointed at the non-arrival of the "Fesser".'[10] Later, Mary, then Lady
Soames, was to write that of all Churchill's friends and visitors 'By far
the most regular visitor outside the family was "The Prof". From 1925
until the outbreak of war, when his signature was transferred to the
Chequers Book, he signed the Visitors' Book at Chartwell 112 times.'[11]

Churchill's second daughter, Sarah, also had warm recollections of
Lindemann as a guest at Chartwell:

Prof had the gift of conveying a most complicated subject in simple form. One
day at lunch when coffee and brandy were being served my father decided to
have a slight 'go' at Prof who had just completed a treatise on the quantum
theory. 'Prof', he said, 'tell us in words of one syllable and in no longer than
five minutes what is the quantum theory.' My father then placed his large gold
watch, known as the 'turnip' on the table. When you consider that Prof must
have spent many years working on this subject, it was quite a tall order, however without any hesitation, like quicksilver, he explained the principle and
held us all spell-bound. When he had finished we all spontaneously burst into
applause.[12]

Churchill was soon drawing on Lindemann's wide knowledge of science. In 1924 he asked for comments on a report that 'a deadly ray'
had been invented, adding: 'It may all be a hoax but my experience has
been not to take "No" for an answer.'[13] In the same year he was telling
Lindemann of his intention to write an article on the 'future possibilities of war and how frightful it will be for the human race. On this
subject I have a good many ideas, but I should very much like to have
another talk with you.' The article appeared later in 1924 under the
title 'Shall We All Commit Suicide?' and was reprinted in *Thoughts and
Adventures* (1932). Among its prescient passages is the following:

'Are you sure,' I asked, 'that the wars of the future will be fought with Steel?'
A few weeks later I talked with a German.[14] 'What about Aluminium?' he
replied. 'Some think,' he said, 'that the next war will be fought with
Electricity.' And on this a vista opens out of electrical rays which could paralyse the engines of a motor-car, could claw down aeroplanes from the sky, and
conceivably be made destructive of human life or human vision. Then there
are Explosives. Have we reached the end? Has Science turned its last page on
them? May there not be methods of using explosive energy incomparably more
intense than anything heretofore discovered? Might not a bomb no bigger than
an orange be found to possess a secret power to destroy a whole block of

buildings—nay, to concentrate the force of a thousand tons of cordite and blast a township at a stroke? Could not explosives even of the existing type be guided automatically in flying machines by wireless or other rays, without a human pilot, in ceaseless procession upon a hostile city, arsenal, camp, or dockyard?

As for the Poison Gas and Chemical Warfare in all its forms, only the first chapter has been written of a terrible book . . . And why should it be supposed that these resources will be limited to Inorganic Chemistry? A study of Disease—of Pestilences methodically prepared and deliberately launched upon man and beast—is certainly being pursued in the laboratories of more than one great country. Blight to destroy crops, Anthrax to slay horses and cattle, Plague to poison not armies only but whole districts—such are the lines along which military science is remorselessly advancing.[15]

In 1926 Churchill was asking Lindemann: 'Have the relations between music and mathematics been examined in the same way as those between mathematics and physics? Is there any sort of correspondence? If so, there might be a correspondence between music and physics other than mere sound waves.'[16]

In 1927 he and Lindemann were corresponding with Sir Hugh Trenchard about the design of bomb sights for the Royal Air Force, and in 1928 their mutual correspondence took the lighter turn of designing the fountains at Chartwell. 'Theoretically,' wrote Churchill, 'I have always been told that water rises to its own level, so that presumably even an inch command would give a certain flow.' He asked Lindemann to work out the necessary diameter of pipe and head of water; and agreement between theory and practice was gratefully signalled in his subsequent telegram: 'Water flowing beautifully according to your calculations.'[17]

In 1931 another of Churchill's essays, 'Fifty Years Hence', showed further evidence of Lindemann's briefing:

There is no doubt that this evolution will continue at an increasing rate. We know enough to be sure that the scientific achievements of the next fifty years will be far greater, more rapid and more surprising, than those we have already experienced . . . High authorities tell us that new sources of power, vastly more important than any we yet know, will surely be discovered. Nuclear energy is incomparably greater than the molecular energy which we use today . . . If the hydrogen atoms in a pound of water could be prevailed upon to combine together and form helium, they would suffice to drive a thousand horse-power engine for a whole year. If the electrons—those tiny planets of the atomic systems—were induced to combine with the nuclei in the hydrogen the horse-power liberated would be 120 times greater still. There is no question among scientists that this gigantic source of energy exists. What is lacking is the match to set the bonfire alight, or it may be the detonator to cause the dynamite to explode. The Scientists are looking for this.

The discovery and control of such sources of power would cause changes in human affairs incomparably greater than those produced by the steam-engine four generations ago . . . The amount of rain falling yearly upon the Epsom race-course would be enough to thaw all the ice at the Arctic and Antarctic poles . . . Materials thirty times stronger than the best steel would create engines fit to bridle the new forms of power . . . With a greater knowledge of what are called hormones, i.e. the chemical messengers in our blood, it will be possible to control growth. We shall escape the absurdity of growing a whole chicken in order to eat the breast or wing, by growing these parts separately under a suitable medium . . .[18]

From the inspired prescience of this article and its predecessor of 1924 on 'Shall We All Commit Suicide?', it is clear that of all the politicians and statesmen involved in the Second World War Churchill had by far the widest and soundest briefings on matters of science. As for his personal attitude, I came across a pencilled note in Lindemann's papers of an assessment that he was to give in introducing Churchill at a public lecture; the note was undated, but is worth quoting none the less:

I have always looked upon Mr. W.S.C. as a scientist who has missed his vocation. All the qualities, or as the humaner elements might prefer to say the stigmata, of the scientist are manifested in him. The readiness to face realities, even though they contradict a favourite hypothesis; the recognition that theories are made to fit facts not facts to fit theories; the interest in phenomena and the desire to explore them; and above all the underlying conviction that the world is not just a jumble of events but there must be some higher unity, that facts fit together. He has pre-eminently the synthetic mind which makes every new piece of knowledge fall into place and interlock with previous knowledge; where the ordinary brain is content to add each new experience to the scrap-heap, he insists on fitting it into the structure of the cantilever jutting out from the abyss of ignorance.[19]

It is not easy, though, to fathom just how deeply Churchill's interest in science ran. With his profound sense of history we might have expected him to be alive to the part played by science in the history of our present millennium; but here he seems to have been hardly more sensitive than those 'arts men' who were subsequently rebuked by Lindemann in his 1954 Messel Lecture:

For some obscure reason it is considered in many influential circles that technological competence is not really on a par socially or intellectually with a knowledge of the older subjects. It would be really amusing (if it were not so tragic) to see how arts men, whose knowledge of the rudiments of technology is not even up to the standard of '1066 and all that', have the impudence to look down upon people who know far more about the arts subjects than the arts men do of technology. They seem to consider it quite natural and normal not to know how soda is made or how electricity is produced provided they once learnt something—which they have usually forgotten—about the mistresses of Charles II or the divagations of Alcibiades. Quite frankly I resent this attitude very much. I think it more important to know about the properties of chlorine than about the improprieties of Clodius; or about the behaviour of crystals than about the misbehaviour of Christina. Surely it is more important to know what a calorie is than what Caligula did; and anyhow what catalysts do is certainly more useful and less objectionable than what Catiline did.[20]

Certainly we might have hoped that, from his close friendship with Lindemann, the impact of science on history would have been given due weight in Churchill's *History of the English-Speaking Peoples*. But in the first three volumes, spanning from the earliest times up to Waterloo, the Royal Society is given but the merest mention; Francis Bacon, who blazed the trail for the scientific revolution, is dismissed simply as an 'ambitious lawyer'; and great figures like Gilbert, Harvey, and James Watt, and inventions such as the steam engine, despite its vital place in British history, are not mentioned at all. Churchill was, of course, using professional historians to provide him with drafts; these were mainly written in the years before 1939, and the overlooking of the parts played by science and technology may have been due to the neglect that then prevailed among historians generally.

The military and political aspects of history were, of course, Churchill's prime interests, and it was characteristic of him that when writing the biography of his great ancestor, the Duke of Marlborough, he wanted to see the Duke's battlefields for himself. In 1932 he visited the Blenheim battlefield accompanied by Lindemann, who could act as interpreter. 'As we wended our way through these beautiful regions from one ancient city to another', wrote Churchill, 'I naturally asked questions about the Hitler Movement and found it to be a prime topic in every German mind. I sensed a Hitler atmosphere.' The concern that this aroused in the minds of both Churchill and Lindemann cemented their relationship: 'We came much closer together from 1932 onwards, and he frequently motored over from Oxford to stay with me at Chartwell. Here we had many talks into the small hours of the morning about the dangers that seemed to be gathering on us.'[21]

As with so many of us, the prospect that dominated their minds was war with the Nazis, who would pose two main threats: the sinking of our shipping by U-boats and mines, and the bombing of our factories and cities. Means to find U-boats and to neutralize mines at sea, and of detecting the approach of bombers in the air, were thus immediate objectives for the application of science and technology; and it was natural for Churchill to press for these objectives to be tackled at the highest priority, with the observation that: 'My experience—and it is somewhat considerable—is that in these matters when the need is clearly explained by military and political authorities, science is always able to provide something.'[22]

The Royal Navy convinced him that its methods for detecting U-boats were developing satisfactorily, so much so that after witnessing a demonstration of 'Asdic' (Sonar) in June 1938 he wrote Lord Chatfield, who was co-ordinating the whole of the British defence effort: 'I am sure that the nation owes the Admiralty, and those who have guided it, an inestimable debt for the faithful effort sustained over so many years which has, as I feel convinced, relieved us of one of our great dangers.'[23] This, though, proved far too optimistic and ten years later he was regretfully to write that 'I had accepted too readily when out of office the Admiralty view of the extent to which the submarine had been mastered';[24] and also: 'In common with the prevailing Admiralty belief before the war, I did not sufficiently measure the danger to, and consequent deterrent upon, British warships from air attack.'[25]

Although Churchill's apprehension about the vulnerability of our warships to air attack was deflected by the confidence of the Admirals, it was otherwise regarding the vulnerability of our cities and factories. Briefed by Lindemann, he urged that the fullest resources of science and technology should be devoted to the problems of detecting and destroying incoming bombers. Providentially, the invention of radar in 1935 offered the prospect of a solution, and both Churchill and Lindemann henceforth involved themselves with the measures concerned with its development.

The ensuing acrimony between Lindemann and his erstwhile friend Henry Tizard is not part of our story, and accounts of it may be found elsewhere. What mattered was that through the efforts of many people Britain had a good enough radar system by 1940 to turn the tide in the Battle of Britain, and that Churchill, through his continuous interest and involvement, had a firm understanding of what radar could do. As always, he wanted to see its operation for himself, even to the extent of flying with an experimental airborne radar equipment on 20 June 1939. One of my colleagues, who flew with him to demonstrate the equipment, recalled the difficulty Churchill had in squeezing his bulky figure into the cramped space normally occupied by a slim operator in his twenties. Churchill was so impressed by the demonstration that he promptly wrote to the Air Minister, Kingsley Wood, of 'the marvellous progress' that radar had made in investing hunting aircraft with 'smelling power'.[26]

Within three months Britain was at war, and Churchill was back in government as First Lord of the Admiralty, just as he had been in 1914. And within a few further weeks he faced the first technological threat to British shipping, the magnetic mine. Fortunately its mechanism was quickly established, thanks to the bravery of naval officers who successfully dismantled a mine which had fallen on a foreshore in the Thames Estuary, enabling counter-measures to be urgently devised.

British reverses in Norway the following spring rapidly weakened public confidence in the Chamberlain government, and on 10 May the Cabinet was to meet in the expectation of being told of Chamberlain's intention to resign. It was likely that Churchill would be invited to succeed him; but that very morning the Germans invaded Holland and Belgium, and Chamberlain wondered whether he ought to stay in office. Churchill himself had to attend emergency meetings of the War Cabinet at 8 a.m., 11.30 a.m., and 4.30 p.m., as well as take the chair at meetings of the Military Co-ordination Committee at 7 a.m. and 1 p.m. With such a schedule, and with the momentous uncertainty of whether or not he was to become Prime Minister, as well as the direness of the military situation and all that it foreboded, it was hardly to be expected that Churchill could turn his mind to technical matters. But he actually held up the 11.30 a.m. meeting of the War Cabinet to show its members a model of an anti-aircraft homing rocket, anticipating in concept the modern surface-to-air missile, sponsored by Lindemann.[27] The fact that he could not only keep this in mind on one of the most hectic days of his life, but even hold up an emergency Cabinet Meeting in face of the expressed impatience of some of the other members, is telling evidence of Churchill's interest in promising technology. ('Do you think this is the time for showing off toys?', asked the Chief of the Imperial General Staff.)

Churchill's next acquaintance with new technology was to come from the German side, when he learned about the radio navigational beams that had been developed for the Luftwaffe, which would, therefore, be enabled to bomb British cities in cloud and at night when nightfighter and gun defences would be completely ineffective. Churchill described the episode in the second volume of his war memoirs in a chapter entitled 'The Wizard War', in which he explained how he relied on Lindemann:

I knew nothing about science, but I knew something of scientists, and had had much practice as a Minister in handling things I did not understand. I had, at any rate, an acute military perception of what would help and what would hurt, of what would cure and of what would kill. My four years' work upon the Air Defence Research Committee had made me familiar with the outlines of Radar problems. I therefore immersed myself so far as my faculties allowed in this Wizard War, and strove to make sure that all that counted came without obstruction or neglect at least to the threshold of action . . . Lindemann could decipher the signals from the experts on the far horizons and explain to me in lucid, homely terms what the issues were. There are only twenty-four hours in the day, of which at least seven must be spent in sleep and three in eating and relaxation. Anyone in my position would have been ruined if he had attempted to dive into depths which not even a lifetime of study could plumb. What I had to grasp were the practical results, and just as Lindemann gave me his view for all it was worth in this field, so I made sure by turning on my power-relay that some at least of these terrible and incomprehensible truths emerged in executive decisions.[28]

The facts that we had discovered the German beams just in time and that, backed by his authority, we were able to devise electronic countermeasures that reduced the effectiveness of the bombing, so impressed Churchill that he afterwards wrote:

Thus the three main attempts to conquer Britain after the fall of France were successively defeated or prevented. The first was the decisive defeat of the German Air Force in the Battle of Britain during July, August and September . . . Our second victory followed from our first. The German failure to gain command of the air prevented the cross Channel invasion . . .

The third ordeal was the indiscriminate night bombing of our cities in mass attacks. This was overcome and broken by the continued devotion and skill of our fighter pilots, and by the fortitude and endurance of the mass of the people, and notably the Londoners, who, together with the civil organizations which upheld them, bore the brunt. But these noble efforts in the high air and in the flaming streets would have been in vain if British science and British brains had not played the ever memorable and decisive part which this chapter records.[29]

Churchill was thus confirmed in the high value that he placed upon science by what he saw of the effect of radar in the Battle of Britain, and then by its impact in the Battle of the Atlantic. Moreover, this latter battle demonstrated the value not only of science as applied to the development of new weapons but also of the application of scientific method to the analysis of operations so as to improve their effectiveness. This had already become known as 'Operational Research' from its application to problems of air defence, and it was now applied effectively to such problems as the optimum setting for depth charges, the best search patterns for aircraft to follow when hunting for U-boats, and the number of aircraft required to patrol the Atlantic. When on one occasion the last calculation showed that aircraft would have to be diverted from Bomber Command, and its Commander-in-Chief, Sir Arthur Harris, remonstrated with Churchill 'Are we fighting this war with weapons or slide rules?', Churchill commented: 'That's a good idea; let's try the slide rule for a change.'[30]

Churchill took a vigorous interest in the technology of warfare, even to the extent of contributing ideas of his own from time to time, such as the tank and the mulberry harbour, and he appreciated science especially for its applications to new weaponry. Such decisions as to whether and when we should use the metal foil strips known as Window (Chaff) against German radar were taken by him personally, but only after he was satisfied that they were agreed by the Chiefs of Staff. If urgency demanded, however, he would take the decision himself, with minimal consultation. David Irving quotes a statement by Tizard that Churchill had said, in Marlborough fashion, 'I command that this be done!' on learning from me on 21 June 1940 that it should be possible to detect the German radio beams by sending up a search aircraft.[31]

There was an occasion in July 1944 when he was tempted to threaten the Germans with poison gas if they brought the V2 into operation against London; but after he found that the Chiefs of Staff and others were against his proposal he shelved it. In the course of the argument, though, the phrase 'or any other form of warfare which we have hitherto refrained from using' was added without Churchill's authority by an officer in the Joint Planning Staff to Churchill's request that the case for using 'gas', principally mustard gas, 'must be comprehensively examined'.[32] Wrongly attributing the addition to Churchill himself, some aspiring historians seized on the episode as indicating that Churchill intended 'to drench the Ruhr with anthrax'.[33] Churchill

certainly knew of the potential of anthrax as a weapon because he had
been so advised by Lindemann, and the necessary bombs had been
developed, but it did not enter into the 1944 argument. To judge by
the protracted discussion and trepidation that preceded his decision to
use such a relatively innocuous device as Window, there could have
been a deluge of debate before the threshold was crossed into biological
warfare.

A greater threat looming in 1944 was, of course, the atomic bomb.
Churchill had been alerted by Lindemann to the ultimate possibility of
releasing nuclear energy first in the 1920s, and again in 1939 following
the discovery of nuclear fission. Lindemann then advised that there was
no danger for several years and—in the light of the knowledge at the
time—even then the explosion would be only a mild one. But that conclusion was based on fission by slow neutrons, and by 1941 fission by
fast neutrons could be envisaged, and this could lead to an enormous
explosion. Lindemann then recommended that the development of a
bomb would be practicable within the expected duration of the war. In
referring the proposal to the Chiefs of Staff, Churchill recommended:
'Although personally I am quite content with the existing explosives, I
feel that we must not stand in the path of improvement, and I therefore think that action should be taken in the sense proposed by Lord
Cherwell, and that the Cabinet Minister responsible should be Sir John
Anderson. I should be glad to know what the Chiefs-of-Staff Committee think.'[34]

The subsequent history of Anglo-American co-operation in developing the bomb is outside the scope of this essay, beyond a personal
observation regarding Churchill's attitude in 1944 following the Quebec
Agreement, when it appeared to me that he would never have signed
away Britain's birthright in the post-war exploitation of atomic energy
had he fully appreciated the potential. I then persuaded Lindemann to
take Niels Bohr to see Churchill, in the hope that the obvious concern
of one of the world's greatest physicists would convince Churchill of
the power and imminence of the bomb; but the interview misfired and
Bohr afterwards told me that 'He scolded us like two schoolboys!' and
said: 'I cannot see what's worrying you. After all this new bomb is just
going to be bigger than our present bombs and it involves no difference
in the principles of war.'[35]

Churchill's last major speech on defence in Parliament, on 1 March
1955, reflected this attitude: 'The atomic bomb, with all its terrors, did
not carry us outside the scope of human control of manageable events

in thought or action, in peace or war.'[36] But he went on: 'When Mr. Sterling Cole, the Chairman of the United States Congressional Committee gave out a year ago—17 February 1954—the first comprehensive review of the hydrogen bomb, the entire foundation of human affairs was revolutionised and mankind placed in a situation both measureless and laden with doom.' He did, though, see a shaft of hope: 'It may well be that we shall by a process of sublime irony have reached a stage in this story where safety will be the sturdy child of terror, and survival the twin brother of annihilation.'[37]

When the atomic bombs were dropped on Japan in August 1945, Churchill was no longer Prime Minister; and the years before he returned to office in 1951 gave him time to reflect both on his wartime experiences and on the future of the world. Already, in Parliament in 1945 he was warning against turning government over to scientists:

There have been theocratic governments, military governments, and aristocratic governments. It is now suggested that we should have scientistic—not scientific—governments. It is the duty of scientists, like all other people, to serve the State and not to rule it because they are scientists. If they want to rule the State they must get elected to Parliament or win distinction in the Upper House and so gain access to some of the various administrations which are formed from time to time.[38]

Just as he seemed to distance himself from the more savage aspects of the bombing campaign against Germany, so he appeared now to lose some of his enchantment with science, at least to the extent of stressing that the humanities had at least as great a place in the field of intellectual endeavour, despite the repugnance for the Classics in his early years, which he had expressed regarding his attempt to go to Oxford: 'However, it appeared that this was impossible. I must pass examinations not only in Latin, even in Greek. I could not contemplate toiling at Greek irregular verbs after having commanded British regular troops . . .'[39] Now, in 1946 when accepting an Honorary Doctorate in Aberdeen, he expressed his regret.

But as my life has rolled out, I have regretted very much that I had no knowledge of the Classics, but have been compelled to read them only in translation. I have had to make my way through all the arguments and debates of forty or fifty years with just a handful of trusty, well-proved and frequently-exercised quotations, which have had to go out in all weathers to stand the battle and the breeze.

There would be a danger to education if it assumed in these formative years—the late 'teens and early twenties—a purely technical or specialized aspect. Without a knowledge of the humanities, without the great record and story of the past and of the ancients laid out before one, without having the lives of the noble Greeks and Romans and the writings of antiquity in one's mind, it is not possible to form those broad and inspiring views which should ever be the guide of men as they advance to serve in a country as great as ours.[40]

Again, on the same theme at the Massachusetts Institute of Technology in March 1949:

How right you are, Dr. Compton, in this great institution of technical study and achievement, to keep a Dean of Humanities in the gaining of which philosophy and history walk hand in hand. Our inheritance of well-founded, slowly conceived codes of honours, morals and manners, the passionate convictions which so many hundreds of millions share together of the principles of freedom and justice, are far more precious to us than anything which scientific discoveries could bestow.[41]

As I read these words, I wondered whether he was putting into practice the advice he gave me in 1946 on returning to university life: 'Praise up the humanities, my boy, that'll make them think you're broad-minded!'[42]

But Churchill was always concerned about how science could be mis-applied—in his 'Finest Hour' speech after Dunkirk he had warned that: 'If we fail, then the whole world, including the United States, including all we have known and cared for, will sink into the abyss of a new dark age made more sinister, and perhaps more protracted by the lights of perverted science.'[43] Again, in the 'Iron Curtain' speech at Fulton, Missouri, in 1946: 'The dark ages may return—the Stone Age may return on the gleaming wings of science.'[44]

In the MIT speech, though, he also pointed to a British weakness:

We have suffered in Great Britain by the lack of colleges of university rank in which engineering and allied subjects are taught. Industrial production depends on technology, and it is because the Americans, like the pre-war Germans, have realized this and created institutions for the advanced training of large numbers of high grade engineers to translate the advances of pure science into industrial technique, it is for that reason that their output per head and consequent standard of life are so high. It is surprising that England, which was the first country to be industrialized, has nothing of comparable stature.

Here, once again, the influence of Lindemann can be discerned in Churchill's words; and we hoped that these would be given practical effect when Churchill came back as Prime Minister in 1951. Little further happened, though, until he resigned in 1955. John Colville related what then happened:

After his resignation on April 5th, 1955, Sir Winston Churchill spent three weeks at Messina. Lord Cherwell and I (who had been his Principal Private Secretary since 1951) accompanied him. While in Sicily Sir Winston told me several times how much he regretted that owing to so many preoccupations he had not, while Prime Minister, devoted more of his energies to procuring an increase in facilities for giving the highest possible technological training. He was sure that for Great Britain, whose future depended on the brains of her inhabitants, this was a vital necessity. It appalled him to think that we, who had contributed more than any other nation by our inventiveness in the past, should now apparently be falling behind in the race . . . He would like to devote his remaining strength and his prestige to awakening the British people to the importance of these matters and to ensuring that steps were taken to remedy our deficiency.[45]

The upshot was that, after various possibilities had been considered, and with the support of Mr Carl Gilbert, Chairman of the Gillette Company in the United States and of the Ford Foundation, it was decided to found a new college in Cambridge 'heavily weighted towards science and technology'. (The phrase came from Dean Rusk, who was a prominent supporter.[46])

The foundation of Churchill College was marked by Winston Churchill himself in a tree-planting ceremony on 17 October 1959. His speech, one of the last he made, affirmed his belief in technology:

Let no one believe that the lunar rockets, of which we read in the Press, are merely ingenious bits of prestige. They are manifestations of a formidable advance in technology. As with many vehicles of pure research, their immediate uses may not be apparent. But I do not doubt that they will ultimately reap a rich harvest for those who have the imagination and power to develop them and to probe ever more deeply into the mysteries of the universe in which we live.[47]

Opened in 1964, the College is the firmest of testaments to Churchill's regard for science and technology and to his concern for their part in the future of mankind.

25

Churchill and Europe

MAX BELOFF

I N the period since Winston Churchill quit office for the last time
in 1955, the question of Britain's relations with the process of
European integration has been a recurrent one for successive
British governments, and a source of conflict between and within the
principal political parties. Despite the many changes on the world political scene, including above all the disappearance of the British Commonwealth as a serious factor in international affairs, both sides of the
argument have tried to enlist Churchill as a posthumous fighter in their
cause. In particular it has been claimed that he was an early convert to
the idea of a united Europe. This essay is an attempt to see what substance there is in that claim.

In dealing with the question, two facts need to be kept in mind. In
the first place, there is the extraordinary length of Churchill's political
career. He entered the House of Commons in 1900 and was elected for
the last time in 1959. Consistency of opinion in a career of that length
is hardly to be expected. Gladstone was first elected in 1832 and sat in
the Parliament elected in 1892; again, this sixty-year spell was not
marked by consistency of view. During most of Churchill's political
life, 'Europe'—in the sense we use it now—was not an issue much discussed by practical men. Yet in Churchill's mind, as in Gladstone's,
there was a certain idea of Europe which helped to colour his attitude
to events and policies.

This idea in Churchill's case sprang from the other important fact
about him, which is that he was not only a maker of history but himself a
historian.[1] His reactions to new problems were largely conditioned by the
international situation as he had seen it when first entering upon public
life and by his reading of the past. In his rather unsatisfactory schooling,
history was one subject in which he did well. Later he developed a taste
for serious historical reading and, as a young subaltern in India, wrote: 'a
good knowledge of history is a quiver full of arrows in debate'.[2]

For a late Victorian, modern British history had been marked by a series of combinations in which military and naval endeavour, and economic and financial strength as well as skilled diplomacy, had been used to prevent the threatening domination of the continent by a single power. Philip II, Louis XIV, and Napoleon had been thwarted. For most of the nineteenth century the European balance had been maintained with the minimum of direct British commitment, and this in turn had enabled overseas expansion to proceed unhindered. The ambitions of Russia which had threatened both the European balance and Britain's Indian Empire were checked in the Crimean War, and by Disraeli's diplomacy a generation later.

In the closing years of the Victorian era this situation was changing with the rise of a united Germany to a dominant position on the continent, and its bid to become a world power. Yet even the direct naval rivalry with Britain engendered by these ambitions might conceivably have been resolved had it not been for the irreconcilable nature of the Franco-German antagonism after the war of 1870. It was around this tension and the alignments to which it gave rise, combined with the rivalry between Slavs, Teutons, and Magyars in the Balkans, that European diplomacy revolved during Churchill's long period in office in the pre-1914 Liberal governments. The Asquith government failed to prevent the catastrophe of the Great War and the painful losses sustained by Britain as a result of its participation. After the war Britain was much preoccupied with explaining that failure and with possible methods of avoiding its recurrence.

Churchill's own account of the coming of the war appeared in the first volume of his *The World Crisis* which appeared in 1923. In it he referred to a theme which was to play a major part in his subsequent thinking about Europe: 'Could we in England, perhaps by some effort, by some compulsive gesture, at once of friendship and command have reconciled France and Germany in time and forced that grand association on which alone the peace and glory of Europe would be safe? I cannot tell.'[3]

In the fifth volume published six years later, Churchill wrote of the Treaty of Locarno as having at least provided such an opportunity for reconciliation. In bringing about the conclusion of this treaty a major role had been played by Sir Austen Chamberlain, Foreign Secretary in a government in which Churchill served as Chancellor of the Exchequer. But by the time this volume appeared, the clouds were thickening again and the challenge ultimately presented by Hitler did not appear capable of handling through British mediation. Nevertheless, hopes of a peaceful outcome were not easily abandoned, and gave rise to the policy of 'appeasement' of which Churchill became an increasingly vocal critic. But during these years, Churchill as a dissident member of the governing Conservative Party had no continuous political presence, and was largely engaged in preparing and writing his major historical work, *Marlborough: His Life and Times*.[4] In this work, the picture of Britain as the centre of a coalition against a power seeking to dominate Europe is central to the narrative.

When war came in 1939 and Churchill returned to office, historical musings gave way to the imperatives of action. In some quarters there was a good deal of discussion about some new European structure to deal with the situation after the Nazis had been defeated. Churchill's mind was on more immediate matters and this was equally the case when, as Prime Minister, he became responsible for the British war effort and British policy as a whole. All was subordinate to keeping the struggle going. And this determination rather than any wider perspective explains his embracing of the ill-starred project of Anglo-French Union.[5]

After the Fall of France, Churchill fended off proposals for exploring Germany's peace-feelers.[6] In this intransigent attitude he was obviously influenced by the feeling that any settlement which the Germans might offer would, as a minimum, lead to the acceptance of their claim to dominate the European continent. His espousal of de Gaulle's Free French movement, which contrasted with Roosevelt's wooing of Vichy, was based on the same fundamental perception of the future, although the stormy relations with de Gaulle himself precluded any return to the notion of a union between the two countries.[7] On the positive side, his attitude meant the acceptance of the Russians into the grand anti-Hitler alliance even though Churchill's long-standing antagonism to Bolshevism always lay near the surface. But the most important element in Churchill's thinking was that the United States should be brought into the war as the only hope for ultimate victory; and after Pearl Harbor he believed that no post-war settlement was possible which was not firmly based upon a partnership between the British Commonwealth and Empire and the United States.[8]

Such insights as we have to Churchill's musing on the future during the first part of the war already give some indication of the problems that he was later to grapple with in peacetime. Some form of European organization was postulated as part of measures for global security. But was Britain to be in or out of such an organization and how was the power of the United States to be associated with its defence? Indeed, he could contradict himself in the course of a single evening. He described in a conversation with intimates on 13 December 1940 a Europe of five Great Powers: England, France, Italy, Spain, and 'Prussia', together with four confederations: Northern, Middle European, Danubian, and Balkan: 'These nine powers would meet in a Council of Europe which would have a supreme judiciary and a Supreme Economic Council to settle currency questions etc.' The security functions of such a Council were spelled out; it would be unrestricted in its methods of dealing with a power condemned by the remainder in Council. But having said all this, Churchill then went on to say that 'the English-speaking world would be apart from this, but closely connected with it and it alone would control the seas as the reward of victory'.[9] It was the Foreign Office that needed to keep the question of the shape of post-war Europe on the agenda. On 3 November 1942, Anthony Eden's private secretary recorded one such Cabinet discussion:

Row in Cabinet today over post-war. There were two papers on the agenda, one about the Dutch and Norwegian proposals for establishing international bases in Europe, the other about relief in Europe after the war. These provoked the P.M. to the most obstreperous utterances. He said that the only way to run Europe after the war was for Great Britain and Russia to keep out and for Europe to be run by a Grand Council of 'the Great Powers including Prussia, Italy, Spain and the Scandinavian Confederacy'. He did not want America in Europe.

Here his instinct was that Britain should remain outside any European organization. Eden, who wanted both the Soviet Union and the United States involved in European security, was, as on other occasions, 'furious with Churchill's intervention'.[10]

Churchill's desire to see some form of European organization as a pillar of the post-war world and his hesitation about Britain's role do not seem to have abated. In a document headed 'morning thoughts' dated 1 January 1943, Churchill showed himself to be thinking of a post-war world dominated by Great Britain, the United States, and the USSR. As a part of the United Nations organization of which they would be the leaders, 'an instrument of European government' would be established embodying the spirit but not subject to the weaknesses of the League of Nations. Nothing is said as to whether Britain would be part of such a European instrument but the presumption must be that this was not Churchill's intention.[11]

An even more ambiguous version of his thinking was given to an important group of Americans with whom Churchill discussed post-war plans during a visit to Washington in May 1943. On this occasion he talked of the formation of a World Council to which should be subordinate three 'Regional Councils, one for Europe, one for the American hemisphere and one for the Pacific'. The European Council would consist of some twelve states or confederations of lesser powers. It would be essential that France should be recreated as a strong power since it was desirable to have on the map such a power between Britain and Russia. It seems fairly clear that Churchill did not see Britain as figuring among the twelve, since he referred to the difficulty for both Britain and the United States of maintaining 'large numbers of men indefinitely on guard in Europe'. What Churchill had in mind as an underpinning of the general security of the world was a 'fraternal association between the United States and the British Commonwealth' which might even take the form of common citizenship.[12]

Work within the Foreign Office on the whole problem of post-war organization took some account of the Prime Minister's views but gave greater prominence than he did to the role of the proposed world organization. The problem of Europe, which had as its main component preventing future German aggression, should be dealt with by a United Nations Commission for Europe representing the United Kingdom, the United States, and the Soviet Union, including France if circumstances allowed. The smaller European allies and Canada and South Africa might also be associated with its work if the Dominions were prepared to contribute to a policing system for the continent. In time this Commission might develop into a Council of Europe which should comprise all European states including the United Kingdom and the Soviet Union with, it was hoped, the addition of the United States. Germany could only be admitted by a unanimous decision of the World Council. 'A Council of Europe', warned the authors of this document, 'in which the United Kingdom, the United States of America and the USSR did not play an active part might become in the course of time an instrument through which Germany could recover peacefully that hegemony over Europe which she has momentarily established by force of arms during the present war.'[13]

It will be seen that the idea, dear to Churchill, of breaking up Germany and reviving Prussia as a separate power had been abandoned and, while the possibility of creating minor European confederations is retained, they no longer play the same role as in Churchill's earlier sketches. Most important of all, it is clear that no-one at this time seriously envisaged a 'united Europe' in which Britain might be included and the Soviet Union and the United States remain outside. There is no evidence of any impact of the movement in favour of 'federalism' which had a growing number of adherents among the European exiles and the members of the European resistance.

In the course of the subsequent inter-Allied negotiations which led up to the formation of the United Nations in 1945, the regional aspects of such a body were more or less abandoned in favour of the general powers of the proposed General Assembly and Security Council and of the five permanent members of the latter.

After the ending of the war the federal idea brought about the creation of a 'European' current of opinion which was represented in British politics but not with the same strength as in France, Italy, the Low Countries, and the reviving democratic Germany. When Churchill was asked to join the movement for a United States of Europe he had to balance his sympathy for its general aims against his unwillingness to join 'an organisation with such a markedly anti-Russian bent', since, while once more fully alive to the Soviet threat, he went on cherishing the belief that somehow the wartime partnership could be restored.[14]

Churchill's own views were expressed in his famous speech at Zurich on 19 September 1946, which is always cited by protagonists of the pro-European interpretation of Churchill's thinking. Yet while it is true that he urged the reconciliation of France and Germany, an old theme of his, as we have seen, and suggested their taking a lead in setting up 'a kind of United States of Europe', if this is to place him among the founding fathers of the European Community, it is equally clear that he saw no place for Britain in such an organization. He made it quite evident that Britain and the Commonwealth, like the United States and Soviet Russia, were to be merely the 'friends and sponsors' of the new Europe.[15]

At the time Churchill's appeal fell on stony ground. Writing to President de Gaulle on 26 November 1946, Churchill referred to his Zurich speech and to his contention that if France could take Germany by the hand and with full British co-operation rally her to the West and to European civilization, that would indeed be a glorious victory. De Gaulle's reply dashed any such hopes. For him the premiss of the Zurich speech was unacceptable since it treated Germany as a single unit whereas France was opposed to the recreation of the Reich. French support for any form of European union could only be obtained if France came in as a founder member alongside Britain, and this could not happen unless the two countries settled their outstanding differences outside as well as inside Europe.[16]

Churchill did not accept the finality of this rebuff and during the remainder of his period in opposition became more closely involved with the idea of a United Europe. Something of this involvement was undoubtedly due to the influence of his son-in-law Duncan Sandys.[17] He made an emphatic statement in favour of a United Europe in a speech at London's Royal Albert Hall on 18 April 1947 to a meeting of the Primrose League (the strongly European tone of the speech may have been the result of a last-minute insertion by Duncan Sandys).[18] But he took care to add that it must not be allowed to drive a wedge between Britain and the United States and the general unity of the English-speaking world. The importance of Churchill's contribution to what became the Marshall Plan for European recovery and the impetus which this gave to European economic integration was referred to by General Marshall himself in a press conference on 12 June 1947.[19]

This phase of Churchill's campaign culminated in his speech on 7 May 1948 at the Hague Conference of the United Europe movement. He noted that progress had been made towards realizing this idea owing to the need to co-operate in the measures flowing from the Marshall Plan and the reaction to the increasingly hostile pressure from the Soviet Union. Economic and military co-operation should be accompanied by 'a parallel policy of political unity'; nor did he shy away from the crucial issue of national sovereignty:

It is said with truth that this involves some sacrifice or merger of national sovereignty. But it is also possible and not less agreeable to regard it as the gradual assumption by all nations concerned of that larger sovereignty which can also protect their diverse and distinctive customs and characteristics all of which under totalitarian systems, whether Nazi, Fascist or Communist would certainly be blotted out for ever.[20]

The speech was followed by an exchange of letters with Attlee some three months later, in which Churchill supported a French proposal for a European Assembly which the Labour government was unwilling to countenance.[21] Such criticism should not blind one to the fact that there was no suggestion on Churchill's part that the process of coming together should culminate in a United States of Europe including Britain itself. Indeed, in a speech to the Conservative Party Conference on 4 October 1947, Churchill had called for a triple combination of the

British Commonwealth, a European Union, and the 'fraternal association' with the United States, with Britain as the vital link between them all.[22] Could Britain play this role as part of a federal union?

Progress in a less than federal mode was already taking place. The statute of the Council of Europe, an inter-governmental organization, was signed in London on 5 May 1948. Britain had already taken the lead in common military preparations by the Brussels Pact of 17 March 1948 and was playing a leading role in the Organization for European Economic Co-operation (OEEC), set up to administer the Marshall Plan.

At this time, Churchill's main preoccupations were with the common defence. He was busy with his war memoirs, *The Second World War*, of which the first volume, with its indictment of the failure of the democracies to unite in the 1930s, was published in 1948. To some extent, his anxieties were allayed by the conclusion on 4 April 1949 of the North Atlantic Treaty which embodied his central idea.

Meanwhile, however, an impetus to further progress on the European front was provided by a new movement on the continent. On the face of it, it was a renewal of Churchill's Zurich call for the reconciliation of France and Germany. But it was, in fact, both in its ultimate purposes and in its proposed method, far more the brain-child of Jean Monnet and embodied a 'Carolingian' vision of European history and Europe's destiny which was remote from Churchill's own Atlantic vision. The first outcome of the new initiative was the proposal for a European Coal and Steel Community (the Schuman Plan). And despite his ideological distance from the plan's progenitors, Churchill attacked the British government for refusing to take part in the conference at Paris called to discuss the plan, professing himself satisfied with the French assurances that taking part in the talks would not involve a commitment to accept any agreement that might arise from them.[23]

Churchill's own concern was with the defence of Europe rather than with moves towards economic integration. On 17 August 1949 he had urged the Council of Europe to invite German participation.[24] On 11 August 1950, after Germany had joined the Council of Europe, Churchill moved a resolution in favour of a European Army to which Germany had agreed to contribute forces. He regarded its passage as a triumph for his own belief in a *rapprochement* between France and Germany.[25] But this speech must be read in the context of his speech in the House of Commons on 26 June 1950 in which he had insisted that receiving Germany back into the European community was desirable only on condition that Britain and France should act together, since Germany was so much stronger than France alone. Once again, he had questioned whether in the contemporary world independent individual sovereignties were 'sacrosanct and inviolable'. Britain had accepted commitments to the defence of Europe and was itself financially dependent on the United States. The world as a whole was moving towards interdependence. Yet even at this high point of Churchill's European commitment, he distanced himself from the out-and-out European federalists. Britain was unique in the world because she had a part to play in all the three larger groupings of the democracies—Europe, the Commonwealth, and the Anglo-American association.[26]

When Churchill became Prime Minister again on 26 October 1951, his conduct of the nation's affairs seemed to some to belie his verbal commitments to European unity during the 1948–50 period. In particular he did not reverse the Labour government's decision to remain outside the Coal and Steel Community and refused to commit British forces to the proposed European Defence Community, which had clear federalist implications.

In deciding against further British involvement in the movement towards European integration, Churchill may have been in part influenced by his Foreign Secretary and heir presumptive, Anthony Eden, who was opposed to such commitments. And he was not swayed by the more European-minded members of his Cabinet quoting to him the speeches he had made in opposition.[27] A student of that administration endorses the view that Churchill was not being untrue to himself:

He disappointed enthusiasts for the European movement who expected great things of him when in office but it is most unlikely that he ever envisaged Britain becoming part of a federal Europe. His vision was conceived in abstract terms: by the time he became Prime Minister in October 1951 he was too old to undertake the translation of this general feeling into concrete policy.[28]

I do not myself think that age had much to do with it. Churchill showed abundant energy in pursuing two objectives to which he attached greater importance—the renewal of the Anglo-American 'Special Relationship', and bringing about a new dialogue with Russia's rulers to avert the danger of a new world war which the Korean War seemed to have brought closer. But another point made by this author demands more attention. In choosing Eden for the Foreign Office, Churchill not only chose someone opposed to closer ties with Europe, but also someone who in this respect was likely to be supported by his official advisers. The 'pro-European' attitude of the Foreign Office dates from at least a decade later. In the Cabinet as a whole, the only two strong 'Europeans', Macmillan and Maxwell Fyfe, were absorbed in their departmental duties. The question of closer economic ties with Europe was hardly discussed at Cabinet level during most of Churchill's last premiership. Nor was there much pro-Europeanism among the junior ministers except for Duncan Sandys, David Eccles, and John Foster, nor among back-benchers, nor indeed in the general public. Only at the very end of Churchill's tenure of office did Peter Thorneycroft produce a powerful paper in favour of closer economic integration; it was his department, the Board of Trade, which was the only exception to Whitehall's general indifference to Europe.

Pressure to modify this indifference came from the United States, and it was pressure that Churchill much resented.[29] During a visit to Paris in December 1951, Churchill declared himself in favour of the proposed European Defence Community, though arguing that Britain, while willing to co-operate with it, could not herself take part.[30] But in talks with the Americans in January 1952 he showed less enthusiasm for the whole concept of a European army, which he described as a 'sludgy amalgam'.[31] His growing determination to bring off a meeting with the Russians led him to brush aside Foreign Office fears that this might discourage the movement in western Europe towards closer integration.[32]

It cannot be said that Churchill had not given warning as to where his priorities in office would lie. In his speech to the European Movement on 28 November 1949 he had said that his view—that the European question should be on the agenda of the forthcoming meeting of Commonwealth ministers—did not imply that the Commonwealth would be directly involved in the continent's moves towards integration: and 'for Britain to enter a European union from which the Empire and Commonwealth would be excluded would not only be impossible but would enormously reduce the value of our participation'.[33] How indeed could he expect Commonwealth countries so sensitive about any encroachment on their sovereignty from Britain herself to accept subordination to a European authority?

Churchill had also to face the question of what role economic integration might play in Europe. His own instincts were those of a free-trader.[34] He had not been an enthusiast for imperial preference. But he had come to feel that it was necessary in order to help preserve the identity of the Empire-Commonwealth. He argued that this system was not incompatible with the aims of a United Europe, unless one was tied down 'to the alternatives of a choice between two rigid customs unions'; nor did he think Britain's imperial or its European economic policy need conflict with that of the United States.[35] In this respect at least his optimism now seems misplaced.

These occasional descents into the improbable, with their lack of clear-cut solutions to the problems that differences of outlook between the nations inevitably involved, does not oblige one to overlook what was consistent in Churchill's approach, of which the famous Zurich speech gives only one version. His thinking cannot be understood without reference to the speech he had made to the Red Cross at Geneva three days earlier:

In bygone ages, Europe was linked by many ties together: there were the Romans, there was the Empire of Charlemagne, there were the bonds of Christendom, there were aristocratic ties which were cosmopolitan, the great association of reigning houses which in the days of Queen Victoria gave something in common between countries. But all has disappeared this time. There was then chivalry in war which seemed in a way to disguise its guilt, and was still observed in the wars of the seventeenth and eighteenth centuries. But all has vanished in this terrible twentieth century. All relations have been shattered between opposing armies; between nations engaged in war there has been no point in common.[36]

Reconciliation was the guiding theme and the foundation for any true consolidation. Nor did he think the European idea could or should be limited to western Europe. The 'iron curtain' was not there for good. At the Hague Conference in 1948 he welcomed the presence of exiles from central and eastern Europe and declared that the aim must be 'the eventual participation of all European peoples whose security and way of life embodied human rights and democracy'.[37]

The movement for a United Europe was never, in Churchill's mind, something directed towards superseding the national states with which he was familiar. It was a matter of creating an atmosphere, a mood which would enable the governments of these separate states to reach agreements and avoid the horrible penalties of war: 'We do not aspire to compete with governments in the executive sphere. What we seek to do is to build up moral, cultural, sentimental and social affinities throughout all Europe or those parts of Europe where freedom still reigns.'[38] These European perceptions were not contradicted by Churchill's efforts in his last administration to reach an understanding with the Soviet government. No-one brought up in late Victorian Britain would have thought of Russia as being outside the European circle with which, at every level, political, economic, cultural, it had the closest connections. Churchill's timing might be injudicious but on fundamentals he was right here also.

Whatever ambiguities might be detected in Churchill's speeches in the post-war period, it must be clear that nothing could have been further from his thoughts than the emergence of a European super-state presenting exactly those pretensions to executive authority which Churchill regarded as the prerogative of the nation-state.

To this rejection of 'Europeanism' there is another and more positive side. General de Gaulle eventually came round to the idea of the European community as in part a bulwark against the increasing domination of western Europe by the United States, particularly in the cultural sphere. Such sentiments were not shared by Churchill. On the contrary it was in relation to the United States that his deepest feelings were evoked. It is all in keeping with his profoundest instincts that his last literary work should have been his *History of the English-Speaking Peoples*. And it is worth remembering that while the work was not completed and published until after Churchill's final retirement it had been planned and begun before the war and his partnership with Franklin Roosevelt.

'English-speaking' is itself a significant definition. Churchill was not only a master of the English language but also was not at home in any other, though his French, if idiosyncratic, was usable. Since he had no familiarity with the languages and literature of other European countries, his references to cultural ties were always somewhat abstract. One has only to compare him with Gladstone or Salisbury to appreciate his limitations. For a historical work like the *Marlborough*, which relied upon sources in German and Dutch, he had to depend upon a bevy of translators. Nor was this unfamiliarity with most of the continent made up for by foreign travel. When he went abroad it was to France, usually to paint or for less serious pursuits.

It is, of course, true that in the political sense France was an exception.[39] In the years leading up to the Second World War, Churchill cultivated and got to know a number of prominent Frenchmen, a fact which added to his disillusion when hardly any of them followed de

Gaulle into the Allied camp. His French associations also tended, especially when liberation was under way, to influence his attitudes to individuals; for instance, there was his attempt to create a role for General Georges, whom he had known before France's collapse, in the administration set up in North Africa after the demise of Darlan. The new Germany and its leaders meant little to him; nor did he foresee the extent to which Germany's economic recovery would weaken the prospect of France taking the lead in a new Europe. During his absence from the seats of power between 1945 and 1951, the essential components of a new Europe began to emerge; to Churchill, the Victorian, they were strange indeed. He was in no sense their prophet.

26

Churchill and India

SARVEPALLI GOPAL

ANYONE writing the article on India at a symposium on Winston Churchill is in the unenviable position of finding himself in a minority of perhaps one, for this is not an issue on which Churchill on the whole comes out well. It is symbolic that on the day he landed at Bombay in 1896 he suffered an injury which was to cause him pain throughout his life, for India has injured his reputation just as much. During the ten months he spent in India as a young army officer he saw little of the country except military barracks, polo grounds, and government houses; but the views he formed of India then remained the basis of his policies throughout his political career. Britain was doing great work in India and carrying out 'her high mission to rule these primitive but agreeable races for their welfare and our own'. The task was virtuous, the exercise invigorating, and the result profitable. But he did not care much for the British community in India; and as for the Indians, he did not come into contact with any except the servants, whom he found wholly subservient. 'For a humble wage, justice and a few kind words, there was nothing they would not do.'[1] That Britain had a duty to perform in India which was also to her advantage, and that the Empire could last for ever with the Indian people having no right to think of freedom while they had the good fortune of living under British administration—these ideas, rooted in Churchill's mind at this time, remained with him till the end of his days, unshaken by the many changes of the twentieth century.

He did, however, while leading a pleasant if boring life in the Indian army, recognize the strength of military influence in Anglo-Indian life and, in the controversy which surfaced in 1903 between the Viceroy, Lord Curzon, and the Commander-in-Chief, Lord Kitchener, as to civilian control of military policy, Churchill was whole-heartedly in Curzon's side.[2] The same principle inspired his initiative, as Secretary of State for War in 1920, in refusing further employment to General

Dyer, who had been condemned by an official commission for opening
fire in Amritsar on an unarmed crowd which had no means of escape
and killing a large number. Though, in his evidence before the commission, Dyer admitted that his action was not required to save the Raj
but was intended to strike terror not only in Amritsar but throughout
the Punjab, there was considerable sympathy for him in Britain; and
this was reflected in the ranks of the Conservative Party when the matter was debated in the House of Commons. So Churchill decided to
intervene. He told the House that he had informed the Army Council,
which had unanimously supported Dyer's dismissal, that he held himself perfectly free (whatever the Council's decision might be) and
would, if the Cabinet so decided, recommend Dyer's retirement from
the army. Whatever the provocation, the massacre at Amritsar was a
monstrous event without precedent or parallel in the recent history of
the British Empire, an event 'which stands in singular and sinister isolation'. Dyer had failed to ask himself the standard questions: was the
crowd attacking, was it armed with lethal weapons, and was he using
more force than was necessary to maintain law and order? Moreover,
Dyer had resorted to the doctrine of 'frightfulness', the inflicting of
great slaughter in order to terrorize not merely the rest of the crowd
but the whole district, even the whole country. 'Frightfulness is not a
remedy known to the British pharmacopoeia. This is not the British
way of doing business.' British rule in India did not stand on the basis
of physical force alone, and it would be fatal to try and make it so.
Close and effectual co-operation with the people of India was essential,
'that spirit of comradeship, that sense of unity and of progress in co-
operation, which must ever ally and bind together the British and
Indian peoples'.[3] Churchill's speech not only changed the tenor of the
debate. This was one of those rare occasions when he was in line with
nationalist sentiment in India, and his popularity in India was never
again to touch this peak.

    As a member of the Conservative government from 1924 to 1929,
Churchill seems to have taken little interest in Indian affairs; nor did he
need to, as for the most part the Secretary of State for India was his
friend Lord Birkenhead, whose views on India were the same as those
of Churchill, and there was no aspect of the government's India policy
with which Churchill disagreed. Nor was India an issue in the general
elections of 1929. It is said that, had the Conservatives returned to
office, Baldwin had intended to move Churchill from the Exchequer to
the India Office.[4] There would then, in the 1930s, have been not even a

semblance of change in India policy. But it was Labour that formed the government and in December 1929 the Viceroy, Lord Irwin (later Lord Halifax), appointed in 1926 by the Baldwin government, announced, with the backing of the Labour government, that Dominion Status was the objective of British policy in India. The statement in itself gave away nothing, and in fact Irwin believed that it would ensure that the essential mechanism of power would remain, as far as one could foresee, in British hands. But Churchill believed that Baldwin, in supporting the Viceroy's statement, was acting on the assumption that the times were too far gone for a robust assertion of British imperial greatness and was throwing away with both hands the British position in India.[5] He told Baldwin that he cared more about the Indian issue than anything else in public life; and Baldwin felt that Churchill, becoming 'once more the subaltern of hussars of '96', wished to go back on all British commitments and govern India with a strong hand.[6] An after-dinner joke of Churchill during these years was that Gandhi should be bound hand and foot at the gates of Delhi and trampled on by an enormous elephant ridden by the Viceroy.[7] The element of banter may have strengthened the general feeling that Churchill was only using the India issue to rally the right wing of the Conservative Party so as to replace Baldwin as leader.[8] It is indeed difficult to take seriously his speeches in 1930, picturing an India in which the Labour government had handed over complete control to the dictatorship of a Congress Brahmin oligarchy, which would hire an army of white janissaries with German officers to secure the armed ascendancy of the Hindus. But Churchill strongly believed that unless Gandhi and his movement were crushed, India would be lost and the downfall of the British Empire consummated, just as he was convinced that the national interests of Britain required the removal of Baldwin.

So, when, early the next year, the Viceroy released Gandhi and started negotiations with him—'drinking tea with treason', in the words of Churchill's supporter, George Lloyd—Churchill, in protest against Baldwin's support of Irwin's failure to assert 'the majesty of Britain', resigned from the Shadow Cabinet on 27 January 1931. But in his speeches he stressed not only the glory but also the necessity of empire; the loss of India would, in his view, mean famine in Britain and the final ruin of Lancashire. Better remembered in India than his denunciation of the doctrine of 'frightfulness' over ten years earlier was one of his perorations at this time, which considered it 'alarming and also nauseating to see Mr. Gandhi, a seditious Middle Temple lawyer, now

posing as a fakir of a type well-known in the East, striding half-naked
up the steps of the Viceregal Palace, while he is still organizing and
conducting a defiant campaign of civil disobedience, to parley on equal
terms with the representative of the King-Emperor'.[9] It has been esti-
mated that nearly half of the Conservative Party in Parliament shared
Churchill's conviction that the British must make clear their intention
to remain effective rulers of India for a very long and indeed indefinite
period, and were suspicious of Baldwin's seeming indifference in this
matter. On 1 March Baldwin decided to resign but reversed his position within twenty-four hours; soon after came news of Irwin's settlement with Gandhi and Baldwin's speech in the House justifying his
support of the Viceroy, which confirmed his leadership of the party.

Even so, Churchill believed that the Conservatives would be locked
in this controversy for several years, and it would become the dividing
line in England.[10] Therefore, though his hopes of ousting Baldwin
steadily receded, he did not give up the fight. He denounced Irwin's
settlement with Gandhi as 'such humiliation and defiance as has not
been known since the British first trod the soil of India',[11] and
described British policy in India as 'a hideous act of self-mutilation'
being performed to the astonishment of every other civilized nation.[12]
When Gandhi came to Britain that autumn he sought out Churchill but
Churchill declined to meet him.[13] But after the general elections in
October 1931 Churchill's sympathisers in the Conservative Party in the
House of Commons dropped from almost half to less than a quarter. In
two votes on India only 44 voted with him. So now Churchill, even as
he carried on a sustained campaign in Parliament against the
Government of India Bill, which was no revolutionary measure, took
the battle to the country and with greater success. At the annual Party
conference in 1933 he got a third of the votes, and in 1934 nearly half.
He could not stop the Bill being passed, but pledged to put an end to
this 'bogus Act' which had been forced on them. Meanwhile, with the
rise of the dictators in Europe, he claimed to find in Britain in the later
1930s a new climate of opinion, a sterner temper in the air; the 'lan-
guorous slothfulness' of the recent past had passed, and even in India,
'as if to strike a note of realism to Pandits, Mahatmas and those who
now claim to speak for the helpless Indian masses, the Frontier is astir;
and British officers and soldiers are giving their lives to hold back from
the cities and peace-time wealth of India the storm of Pathan inroad
and foray'.[14]

When, with the outbreak of war in September 1939, Churchill joined the Cabinet, he soon made his views on India felt. He insisted that no measures should be undertaken in India to associate Indian political parties with the war effort, which would weaken the supreme power of the Viceroy and Britain's freedom to deploy forces in India; nor should any constitutional legislation be initiated till the war was over or promises be made that would bind Parliament after the war. India had just to be kept quiet for the duration of the war. He also asserted in Cabinet that he did not share the anxiety to encourage and promote unity between the Hindu and Muslim communities for, if it were brought about, the immediate result would be that the united communities would join in showing Britain the door. The Hindu–Muslim feud was the bulwark of British rule in India.[15]

So, with Churchill becoming Prime Minister in May 1940 with no colleague able to influence his judgement on India, it could be taken for granted that any substantial change in policy in this regard was out of the question till the war was won. Halifax lamented that he found Churchill impossible to reason with on India; and Amery, whom Churchill appointed Secretary of State for India, though no radical himself and prepared to take only such steps as would confirm the British presence in India, was driven to protest that Churchill had no notion of the problem at all and 'is really not quite normal on the subject of India'.[16] While the Indian National Congress became more accommodating with every military reverse suffered by the British in the summer of 1940 and offered to assist in defence if a fully national government were established without any long-term commitment by the British government, Churchill would not allow the Viceroy, Lord Linlithgow, to go further than appoint a few 'representative Indians' to the Viceroy's Executive Council, set up a War Advisory Council, and declare that the future constitution of India should be framed by a body 'representative of the principal elements in India's national life' (including the princes and British commercial interests), and any decision of that body would be subject to the fulfilment of Britain's obligations in India (whatever these may be).

The Congress found this offer disappointing and, rejecting it, soon saw many of its leaders back in prison. This did not worry Churchill; and nationalist opinion in India, seeing no glimmers of hope from London, began to look for support from President Roosevelt in Washington. The pledge of Britain and the United States in the Atlantic Charter in August 1941, to respect the right of all peoples to choose their form of government, raised expectations; but within a month of signing the Charter, on 9 September 1941, Churchill informed Parliament that this clause applied only to European nations under Nazi rule; and it would seem that Roosevelt had agreed that no wider interpretation should be given.[17] Professor Reginald Coupland, visiting India at this time, thought that it was Churchill's categorical announcement which led to a spreading of a new and uncomfortable suspicion of British intent even beyond nationalist circles.[18]

In December 1941 the government of India favoured the release of all Congressmen in jail, and the War Cabinet, for once overruling the Prime Minister, supported this view, with Churchill deploring 'surrender at the moment of success' and muttering something to the effect 'when you lose India, don't blame me'.[19] But with Japan's entry into the war, pressure rose from public opinion in the United States, from Chiang Kai-shek, and in Britain from the Labour Party to win Indian support for the war. Churchill at first resisted this pressure; 'the rule of the Congress and Hindu priesthood machine' would paralyse defence and would not be tolerated by 'the martial races' of India who, in his opinion, were predominantly Muslim.[20] Then, for a fleeting moment, Churchill's romantic imagination prevailed over his fossilized prejudices, and he formulated a scheme for expanding the defence council in India, offered to broadcast to India recommending it, and even planned to fly out to Delhi. Amery and Linlithgow smothered this scheme as amateurish and weighted against the Muslim League in favour of the Congress; and Churchill without protest reverted to his usual attitude. But the idea of seeking a settlement with Indian political parties was accepted. Stafford Cripps was sent out to India with a set of proposals, whose main points were the convening after the war of a constituent assembly elected on a system of proportional representation by freshly elected provincial assemblies; the recognition of the possibility of Pakistan, by conceding the right of any province that was not prepared to accept the new Dominion constitution to retain its existing constitutional position; and the collaboration while the war lasted of Indian parties with the British government, who would continue to bear the full responsibility for India's defence.

Churchill assented to these proposals because they seemed to him 'essentially a pro-Moslem and reasonably Conservative policy'.[21] He was right, for all that the proposals offered were collaboration in defence and not control, which Churchill was determined to retain, and in the future a Dominion constitution with possibly a partition of the country as demanded by Jinnah and the Muslim League. But Nehru and the Congress were willing to set aside their objections to the long-term aspects of the proposals if they could collaborate in defence to meet the immediate crisis; and Cripps secured Churchill's approval for rewording the paragraph on defence arrangements. It was now affirmed that the task of organizing the defence of India must be the responsibility of the government of India with the co-operation of the peoples of India. But at this point the Viceroy stepped in and toned down the co-operation in the military effort, to mean merely the appointment of an Indian to some office connected with defence without in any way impinging upon the functions and duties of the Commander-in-Chief. Even this Cripps was optimistic enough to hope could in practice prove satisfactory to the Congress; but the Commander-in-Chief, Lord Wavell, refused to be responsive. Churchill, with the support of the War Cabinet, refused to back Cripps and informed Linlithgow and Wavell that he would not approve any steps taken by Cripps unless they were unqualifiedly endorsed in separate cables by the Viceroy and the Commander-in-Chief. Thus strengthened, Linlithgow and Wavell saw to it that all Cripps's efforts to reach an arrangement with the Congress came to nothing. The threat of Cripps to hand the matter over if he were not trusted was sharply repelled by Churchill, and Linlithgow was directly informed that there was no question of any convention, such as had been suggested by Cripps, limiting in any way his powers under the existing constitution.[22]

With the failure of the Cripps mission, the critics of Churchill's India policy in the United States and Britain were silenced, and Churchill was strengthened in his determination to take no further steps. Knowing that Roosevelt's personal representatives in India, Louis Johnson and then William Phillips, were dissatisfied with such a freeze, the Prime Minister enlisted the services of Harry Hopkins to ensure that Roosevelt did not raise the matter again. A national government in India, he told Hopkins, would certainly recall all Indian troops from the Middle East and make an armistice with Japan on the basis of free transit for Japanese forces and supplies across India, in return for which the Japanese would give the Hindus the military support necessary to impose the will of the Congress Party upon the Muslims, the princes, and the depressed classes.[23] Then, when the Congress, under Gandhi's leadership, in desperation planned a movement to force the British to quit India, Churchill and the War Cabinet supported the Viceroy in summarily arresting the leaders of the Congress and outlawing the party. Churchill was particularly allergic to Gandhi and would seem to have been convinced that he was following a pro-Japanese line. But his dislike of Gandhi and the Congress extended by now to cover the Indian people as a whole. 'I hate Indians. They are a beastly people with a beastly religion.'[24] For eighty years Britain had given India such peace and prosperity as she had never known in her history and it was thoroughly wrong to follow a policy of scuttle at the insistence of some mischief-makers. Though Britain gained nothing from India she would continue to do her duty there at any cost. For twenty-five years the Conservative Party had gone along the wrong tracks in India, but Churchill was not prepared for 'the humiliation of being kicked out of India by the beastliest people in the world next to the Germans'. If he were pushed much further he would drop everything else and go round the country rousing the Conservatives against this.[25] 'We mean to hold our own. I have not become the King's First Minister in order to preside over the liquidation of the British Empire.'[26]

In February 1943 Gandhi started a fast for twenty-one days. Churchill approved of the Viceroy's decision not to release Gandhi and prepared for Gandhi's possible death in detention. The British government was moving forward victoriously on the war fronts and this was 'not the time to crawl before a miserable little old man who had always been our enemy'.[27] Gandhi managed to survive the fast and the deadlock continued. That summer in Washington, when Phillips, Roosevelt's representative in India, saw Churchill with the President's encouragement and observed that Indians wanted power in the central government, Churchill exploded. 'My answer to you is: Take India if that is what you want! Take it by all means! But I warn you that if I open the door a crack there will be the greatest blood-bath in all history; yes, blood-bath in all history. Mark my words, I prophesied the present war, and prophesy the blood-bath.'[28] Wavell, meeting Churchill before taking up the Viceroyalty as Linlithgow's successor, felt that while Churchill knew nothing about the problem, he 'hates India and everything to do with it'.[29]

At the British government's farewell dinner to Wavell, Churchill expressed his 'subdued resentment' at the world's failure to appreciate Britain's great achievement in India. 'If the day should come, as I pray it may not, when we cast down for ever our responsibilities there and vanish from the scene, this episode in Indian history will surely become the Golden Age as time passes . . .'[30] Whatever the merits of British rule, the stated preference of the Prime Minister for its indefinite continuance ran so contrary to numerous political commitments that the

India Office ensured that Churchill's speech was not reported. But Churchill saw to it that at least while the war lasted the Indian problem was kept on ice. He agreed to Gandhi's release in the summer of 1944 because of the opinion of the doctors that Gandhi would not be fit again for active politics, and was annoyed that, far from dying, Gandhi succeeded in drawing Wavell into a correspondence. Gandhi even wrote to Churchill:

You are reported to have the desire to crush the 'naked faqir', as you are said to have described me. I have been long trying to be a faqir and that naked—a more difficult task. I therefore regard the expression as a compliment, though unintended. I approach you then as such and ask you to trust and use me for the sake of your people and mine and through them those of the world.[31]

This letter, which Gandhi signed 'your sincere friend', the government of India, through whom it was sent, claimed to have miscarried; so two months later Gandhi sent a copy. The officials at Delhi and Whitehall were for ignoring this letter; but Churchill, with better manners, had a formal acknowledgement sent.

Such formal correctness in personal dealings had nothing to do with policy, which remained as intractable as ever. Indeed, Wavell was courageous enough to complain to the Prime Minister that the British government were treating the vital problems of India 'with neglect, even sometimes with hostility and contempt'. Churchill might believe that in a mistaken view of Indian conditions and with an entirely misplaced sentimental liberalism Britain had taken the wrong turn with India twenty-five or thirty years earlier; but the clock could not be put back and the present attitude was aggravating the mischief.[32] But Churchill, who by now was regretting his appointment of Wavell as Viceroy, was not to be moved. He had no compunction in denuding India of food supplies because of the need for shipping in other theatres of war, for he believed that the starvation of Bengalis, who were anyhow under-fed, was less serious than that of sturdy Greeks.[33] He did, under pressure from Wavell, request Roosevelt for a special allocation of ships to move wheat from Australia to India; but when the United States replied that this could not be managed Churchill felt that nothing more could or need be done. Lord Mountbatten, in command in south-east Asia, on his own diverted 10 per cent of the shipping at his disposal for import of foodgrains into India, but Churchill, who seemed to regard famine relief as 'appeasement' of the Congress, vetoed this and reduced the shipping at Mountbatten's disposal by 10 per cent. But Mountbatten persisted and transferred 10 per cent of his reduced shipping to food imports for India.[34]

With the war drawing to an end, diverse and contrary thoughts floated through Churchill's mind as to the future of India. In resisting total withdrawal from that country at any time Churchill would seem to be reflecting the general mood of the Conservative Party. He told Amery that once the war had been won there was no obligation to honour promises made at a time of difficulty and not taken up by the Indians.[35] Contemptuous of Indian politicians at various times during the war, he sought to divert attention from problems of constitutional change to a vigorous policy of social reform[36] or the creation of large collectivized farms on the Soviet model to replace the existing system of fragmented land tenure. It would really pay the British to take up the cause of the poor peasant, to confiscate the lands of rich Congressmen and divide them up.[37] But Churchill did not follow up these ideas and probably did not take them seriously, knowing that, in spite of him, the British might well, in his own phrase, chatter themselves out of India.[38] At the time of the Cripps mission he cabled to Mackenzie King in Canada: 'We have resigned ourselves to fighting our utmost to defend India in order, if successful, to be turned out.'[39] Later, just before the detention of Gandhi, he amazed the King by informing him that his colleagues and both, or all three, parties in Parliament were quite prepared to give up India to Indians after the war. Cripps, the press, and American opinion had all contributed to reaching the conclusion that British rule in India was wrong and had always been wrong for India; and British political parties had already been talked into giving up India.[40] He normally had a regard for the Indian army which he believed (wrongly) was recruited mostly from among the Muslims, and he told Chiang Kai-shek that if the British withdrew their troops from India the Hindu parliamentarians would be rapidly dominated by the 'Muslim warriors'.[41] But he also some months later expressed to Amery his conviction that the Indian army was only waiting to shoot the British in the back.[42] Out of this effervescing, confused welter of comments and suggestions what emerges is that, while Churchill would have liked to maintain the Empire in India, or even hold on to a bit of the country, he was not hopeful of it. But he agreed with Jinnah that a united India was a British creation which could not survive under Indian rule. Pakistan was perhaps the only answer because Muslims and Hindus would never live together peacefully; and Churchill envisaged a situation where Britain could sit on top of a tripod—Pakistan, Princely India, and the Hindus.[43]

The general election of 1945 saved Churchill from taking decisions. His reactions to Attlee's policy were determined by his opposition to what he termed 'the handing over of India to Hindu caste rule'.[44] He stressed that the British should not be seen to be letting down the princes, the Muslims, and the scheduled classes, and kept in touch with Jinnah and with B. R. Ambedkar, the leader of the Harijans or 'untouchables'. He was in favour of making India a party issue, but Eden and Butler, while going along with Churchill in insisting that the British government should not take sides with any of the parties in India, declined to make India a partisan matter in British politics.[45] They could not, however, prevent Churchill from periodically airing his views in the House of Commons. By now Nehru had replaced Gandhi as the prime mover on the Congress side, and Churchill's attitude to him was mixed. In 1937 he had described Nehru as 'communist, revolutionary, most capable and most implacable of the enemies of the British connection with India'.[46] But Nehru's speeches and writings in Britain in 1938 advocating collective security and condemning the dictators and the Munich agreement seem to have won Churchill's approval, and in 1939, on the eve of Nehru's visit to China, Churchill sent him a message of goodwill through the Chinese ambassador in London.[47] Then in 1940, when Nehru was given a savage sentence of imprisonment for four years, Churchill instructed Amery to telegraph at once to the Viceroy expressing the hope that the actual rigour of the sentence would be moderated and Nehru not treated like a common criminal.[48] But events thereafter were such that Churchill thought Nehru had good reason to be Britain's bitterest enemy;[49] and Churchill, while claiming to have nothing personal against Nehru, and giving him credit for ordering the army to open fire on Hindu mobs,[50] denounced the British government for having brought the Congress into the Interim Indian government in September 1946 with Nehru as Vice-President of the Viceroy's Council. 'It was a cardinal mistake to entrust the government to Mr. Nehru . . . In handing over the Government of India to the so-called political classes, you are handing over to men of straw of whom in a few years no trace will remain.' Rather than utilize the services of Lord Mountbatten to carry through an Operation Scuttle, Churchill asserted that the government should consider inviting the aid of the United Nations.[51]

The hostility was toned down when Mountbatten succeeded in persuading the Congress to accept Dominion status if the date for the transfer of power were brought forward; and Churchill was willing to support the government if Pakistan would also agree to be a Dominion. As Jinnah was avoiding any commitment on this issue, Mountbatten sought Churchill's support in bringing Jinnah into line. 'By God,' Churchill is reported to have remarked, 'he is the one person who cannot do without British help.' He advised Mountbatten to threaten Jinnah by recalling all British officers from the units of the armed services transferred to Pakistan, thereby making it clear that it would be impossible to run Pakistan without British help. He also authorized Mountbatten to give Jinnah the message, 'This is a matter of life and death for Pakistan, if you do not accept this offer with both hands.'[52] It is not clear from the record whether Mountbattten passed on this message to Jinnah; but certainly Jinnah realized that with India becoming a Dominion, it would be hazardous for Pakistan to keep out, and on 15 August 1947 the establishment of the two Dominions received the support of all parties in Britain.

Churchill had encouraged Mountbatten to stay on as Governor-General of India even though he was not to have a similar position in Pakistan as well.[53] But Churchill's goodwill for India (which he insisted on calling Hindustan) was short-lived. He berated Mountbatten, with the conflict in Kashmir in mind, for having supported Britain's enemies against the Muslims, who were Britain's friends, and advised Mountbatten to get out quickly and not involve the King and his country in further backing traitors.[54] He was critical of India's police action in taking over the administration of Hyderabad and urged Eden to oppose as strongly as possible the Labour government's acquiescence in this, which was 'about the most odious of transactions as any in which a British Ministry has ever been implicated'.[55] But there was again a sharp shift in Churchill's attitude to independent India in the spring of 1949, when Nehru suggested that a way should be found for India, even after becoming a republic, to continue as a member of the Commonwealth. Drawing on his sense of history, Churchill found a precedent in Roman times for the presence of a republic in the Commonwealth and thought in terms of the King becoming the President of India.[56] After a formula was found in April 1949 for India's continuance in the Commonwealth Churchill expressed a desire to call on Nehru. The Indian Prime Minister went round himself and at their first meeting Churchill was emotional, saying something to the effect: 'Sir, I have done you great wrong. You are like the prodigal who has returned to the fold of the family.'[57] He advised the Conservative Party that it was absolutely necessary for it to have a policy which was not unfavourable to the new India,[58] and when Smuts cabled from South Africa deploring India's continuance as a republic in the Commonwealth, Churchill replied: 'When I asked myself the question, "Would I rather have them in, even on these terms, or let them go altogether", my heart gave the answer, "I want them in." Nehru has certainly shown magnanimity.'[59] Later that year, when Nehru was passing through London on his way to Washington, Churchill met him and said he would have liked to have had the opportunity to introduce Nehru to audiences in the United States. When Nehru was curious to know what he would have said, Churchill replied that he would have presented Nehru as the man who had 'conquered two great human infirmities: you have conquered fear and you have conquered hate.'

From this time, Churchill, whatever his attitude to Indian nationalism before 1947 and his continuing disappointment that the Indian Empire had become a part of history, developed a personal relationship with Nehru over which the shadow of the past did not fall. As Prime Minister from 1951 he was appreciative of Nehru's standing and significance in the world, paid attention to his views on Africa, and agreed with him on the anomaly of Portuguese imperial policy. Finding himself standing next to Nehru and his daughter while waiting for their cars after the coronation service at Westminster Abbey in 1953, he said to Indira Gandhi, 'You must have hated the British for the treatment meted out to your father. It is remarkable how he and you have overcome that bitterness and hatred.' When Mrs Gandhi replied, 'We never hated you', Churchill observed, 'I did, but I don't now.'[60]

That same year the British government sought Nehru's aid in recasting their relations with Egypt. At Cairo on his way back from London Nehru advised Nasser and his colleagues not to use harsh language against Britain even while standing firm on the issue of sovereignty. The tone of their speeches became milder thereafter, making discussion with Britain easier, and Churchill acknowledged Nehru's assistance. 'Thank you so much for your message and for the help you gave us over Egypt and Israel. Winston.'[61] He was, throughout his prime ministership in the 1950s, careful not to do anything which might give offence to the government of India, for India was in a position to exercise a moderating influence in Asia, and it was especially important for India and Britain to be in the closest possible association in the handling of all major international problems.

In 1955, Churchill retired, and his farewell exchanges with Nehru show that he realized the significance of India seeking to better herself by democratic means, and felt that India's Prime Minister could play a crucial role in world affairs.

I hope you will think of the phrase, 'The Light of Asia.' It seems to me that you might be able to do what no other human being could in giving India the lead, at least in the realm of thought, throughout Asia, with the freedom and dignity of the individual as the ideal rather than the Communist Party drill book.

And then again, a few months later:

One of the most agreeable memories of my last years in office is our association. At our conferences your contribution was a leading and constructive one, and I always admired your ardent wish for peace and the absence of bitterness in your consideration of the antagonisms that had in the past divided us. Yours is indeed a heavy burden and responsibility, shaping the destiny of your many millions of countrymen, and playing your outstanding part in world affairs. I wish you well in your task. Remember 'The Light of Asia!'[62]

It is difficult to say that Churchill was wholly serious about all this. One gathers from Lord Moran that Churchill was telling Nehru what he thought Nehru wished to hear.[63]

From start to finish Churchill was unshaken in his conviction that British rule in India was both good for India and advantageous to Britain. He could be just and generous, as in July 1920, imaginative, as momentarily in February 1942, or sentimental, as in April 1949; but basically he could not accept either that Indians genuinely wanted self-government or that Britain was no longer able to sustain an empire. He got to like Nehru personally and made the best of a bad job in maintaining good relations with a free India, even if this was contrary to his set views. As he once observed to de Gaulle: 'My conscience is a good girl. I can always come to terms with her.'[64] If Tom Paulin's interpretation of Larkin's lines in 'The March Past' is correct and the reference is to the loss of the British Empire,[65] they represent accurately Churchill's feelings, for the poet speaks of being overcome by a . . .

> . . .blind
> Astonishing remorse for things now ended
> That of themselves were also rich and splendid
> (But unsupported broke, and were not mended)

'History will record', Churchill told Eisenhower and Dulles at Bermuda in December 1953,

that Britain's desertion of her duty in India was the most serious political blunder of the past decade. I may personally not live to see all of the unfortunate results that will flow from that tragedy, but there are people around this table who will come to see that this act is certain eventually to bring grief and sorrow to the entire Western World.[66]

A few months later he reiterated to Dulles his bitterness at the 'give-away' of India. The Labour government had done it to the accompaniment of plaudits from the United States, but the result was something the Western powers would have to live with painfully for a long time.[67] His last words to his last Cabinet in April 1955 included the wish that his colleagues would weave 'still more closely the threads which bound together the countries of the Commonwealth or, as he still preferred to call it, the Empire'.[68] The refusal to part mentally and emotionally with empire made India Churchill's blind spot. The isolated instances of policy or improvements in personal relations with Nehru which bring him out in a better light deserve mention; but they cannot efface the shadow thrown on a glorious reputation.

27

Churchill and Eygpt 1946–1956

WM. ROGER LOUIS

6 '**W**HOSE finger on the trigger?' The question referred to the choice between Churchill and Attlee during the election campaign of 1951, but it has an eerie relevance to the Suez crisis of 1956. Shortly before he became Prime Minister for the last time, Churchill said: 'Least of all do we want a fumbling finger.'[1] He had very little to do with the Suez crisis itself, but earlier he had not flinched from pursuing a bellicose course. He believed that the Egyptians, like other 'Oriental' peoples, should be handled with firmness at all times and with force if necessary. If anything his attitude towards the Egyptians was even more contemptuous than his regard for Indians (as described in Chapter 26 above by Sarvapelli Gopal). 'Degraded savages', he commented characteristically in his Egyptian mood.[2] He wrote those words in anger at a time when British subjects had been murdered in Cairo in 1952, but the phrase represented views he had held since he first visited Egypt more than half a century earlier. He never wavered from his Victorian opinion that the Egyptians were an inferior and essentially cowardly people. He was persistently bullying and truculent in his attitude. Nevertheless he did, towards the end of his career as Prime Minister, decide in favour of evacuation of British troops from Egyptian soil and the peaceful resolution of the issue of the Canal Zone. As in the case of India, he ultimately took a magnanimous view which placed him on the side of disengagement and reconciliation.

That goodwill was no substitute for power was a theme running through his thought. On this point he differed fundamentally from the leaders in the Labour Party, above all Attlee and Bevin. Churchill believed—at least until 1953 or 1954—that the Canal Zone would continue to provide Britain with a commanding bastion in the East despite the irrevocable loss of India. Suez, in his view, remained the geographical keystone in the Middle East, and indeed one of the supreme geopolitical positions in the world. He never forgave the Labour government for proposing to withdraw British troops from Egypt in the spring of 1946. He also used the word 'scuttle' to describe the British evacuation from the Iranian oil fields and the refinery at Abadan in 1951. He occasionally made exceptions—notably on Palestine—but in general he denounced any suggestion of withdrawal from any British position in any part of the world as tantamount to treason. Why then did he change his mind in 1954 about Suez, which, to use his own phrase, he regarded as the 'lifeline of the Empire'?

This chapter will trace the evolution of Churchill's thought during the critical decade 1946–56, with emphasis on the time that he directly concerned himself with the issue while in office from 1951. It is useful at all times, whether he was in or out of office, to make the distinction between his public rhetoric, which was often dramatic, and his letters and minutes, which were no less dramatic but also pointed and insistent. Churchill worked by paper. He engaged in debate and argument, of course, but his minutes reveal most clearly the tactics as well as the aims, and the step-by-step method by which he accepted modifications of his position while rejecting others. In this chapter I shall use as a principal source his minutes in the Premier or PREM series at the Public Record Office, and—to provide perspective—two sets of diaries in which the Egyptian theme is prominent. One of the diarists was Sir Evelyn Shuckburgh, the Under-Secretary at the Foreign Office in charge of Middle Eastern affairs. Shuckburgh was critical of Churchill and believed his attitude towards Egypt to be one of Britain's sources of trouble in the Middle East. Another diarist who assiduously recorded the evolution of Churchill's Egyptian outlook was Leo Amery. Amery was Churchill's direct contemporary and had a parallel public career. In the 1920s he had served as Secretary of State for the Colonies and for the Dominions. He and Churchill had often clashed on colonial issues and later on India. Amery had also served as Secretary of State for India during the Second World War. He believed, rightly, that Churchill had been obstructive on the issue of national freedom for India. On Egypt, however, Amery after the war adopted a consistently hard-line attitude while Churchill gradually altered his views. They differed in assessing the part to be played in the Middle East by the United States. In the American dimension of the problem lies an important clue to the transformation of Churchill's attitude.

Churchill had a picture in his mind's eye of Egypt as he had known it at the turn of the century. He had been eight years old at the time of the British occupation of Egypt in 1882, eleven at the time of the death of Gordon, and he was present at the battle of Omdurman with Kitchener with 1898.[3] He made no secret of the influence of his past experience and indeed took unabashed pleasure in holding what he granted was an old-fashioned view. It was a view that seemed to others, then as now, more a caricature than a true picture. But, as he listened to military and political advice, and as he placed his ideas in a larger setting of Anglo-American relations and of technological change, he slowly and almost imperceptibly altered his outlook. In 1954, when he stated in the House of Commons that he now favoured British evacuation from the Canal Zone, Attlee was astonished. Churchill, the foremost critic of the Labour government's conciliatory policy, now seemed compelled, in Attlee's phrase, to reverse himself. What were the stages, to rephrase the question, at which Churchill adjusted his thought to the necessity of withdrawing troops from Egypt? Or, to pitch the question still higher, when did he reconcile himself, in the words he had employed previously in regard to India, to the sad spectacle of the British Empire in the Middle East 'clattering down . . . with all its glories, and all the services it has rendered to mankind'?[4]

The answer must begin with his preconceptions and, closer to hand, his policy towards Egypt during the Second World War. The picture in his mind from the beginning was one of unquestionable benefits brought by British rule and influence which had continued in one form or another since the British occupation in 1882. The modern landmark was the Treaty of 1936 whereby Britain acquired the right to station 10,000 troops in the Canal Zone. The Treaty would expire in 1956, a fact never far removed from Churchill's calculations. It was the legal basis of the British presence. As wartime Prime Minister, he had made it clear that the Canal Zone and indeed Egypt itself was vital to British security. In early 1942 he supported to the hilt the aggressive tactics of the Ambassador in Cairo, Sir Miles Lampson (Lord Killearn), who surrounded the Royal Palace with armoured cars to coerce King Farouk into forming a pro-British Egyptian government. Later in the same year Churchill made the famous statement that he had not become the King's First Minister to preside over the liquidation of the Empire in which, clearly, Egypt was one of the pillars. What might appear to others as British 'imperialism' was to Churchill an entirely natural and worthy enterprise. From the time of Lord Cromer the British had stood for economic progress and had imposed a peace that restrained the ruling class of 'Pashas' and landlords from exploiting the peasants, or fellahin. The belief that British influence was good for the Egyptians remained a constant ingredient of Churchill's basic assumption, which no Egyptian nationalist ever succeeded in altering.

'Egypt owes us a great debt', Churchill stated in the House of Commons in 1946. 'Since the days of Cromer we have done our best to shield her from the storms which beat about the world.' The Egyptians, or at least the great bulk of the people in Egypt, had cause for gratitude for internal reasons as well.

We have done a great deal, though not nearly as much as we ought to have done, to force forward the lot of the fellaheen and the masses of the people. We have been hampered by our respect for the authority of the Egyptian potentates and assemblies and by not wanting to interfere too much in the affairs of the country. But it is a shocking thing how little progress there has been among the great masses of Egyptian fellaheen.[5]

Churchill consistently demonstrated a concern for the welfare of the common people of Egypt. His attitude was paternalistic but none the less genuine. 'Unhappily', he concluded at another time, Egyptian prosperity was '. . . shared almost exclusively by the rich and well-to-do classes, while the peasantry seemed to remain in very much the condition in which I saw them when I first went to Egypt as a young officer towards the end of the last century.'[6] Again, his outlook never changed. 'It is most important', he wrote in 1952 in a minute that summed up his attitude towards social change in Egypt, 'that we should not appear to be defending the landlords and Pashas against the long overdue reforms for the fellaheen.'[7]

The British presence was, in Churchill's view, essentially benevolent but by no means supine. Ingratitude would be repaid in kind. Earlier in his career he had remarked that punishing China was like flogging a jellyfish. The same sense of frustration characterized his attitude towards Egypt after 1945, when he wished to teach Egyptian nationalists a lesson. His bellicose impulse was checked by the fear of being pulled into another full-scale occupation. Churchill's picture of Egypt was tinged with realism. But his sentiments remained constant. One of the first entries in Shuckburgh's diary relates a late-night meeting in December 1951 of Churchill, Anthony Eden (then Foreign Secretary), and various Foreign Office officials. They discussed Egyptian attacks on the British position in the Canal Zone. After heated exchanges—and a considerable amount to drink—Churchill concluded the meeting by giving strong advice on how to respond to the Egyptians. According to

Shuckburgh, he provided comic relief: 'Rising from his chair, the old man advanced on Anthony with clenched fists, saying with the inimitable Churchill growl, "Tell them that if we have any more of their cheek we will set the Jews on them and drive them into the gutter, from which they should never have emerged." '[8]

Before, during, and after the Egyptian revolution of July 1952, Churchill urged Eden not to be intimidated by threats of violence from the Egyptians. 'If . . . you make what looks like a surrender to violence and evacuation of forces by threats and atrocities', Churchill wrote in a minute that reveals his concern with the Iranian oil crisis as well as Suez, 'it may cause deep resentment in that element of British public life whose regard sustains you, and also mockery from the Party that scuttled from Abadan.'[9] In the summer of 1952 Farouk was deposed and Mustafa Nahas, the leader of the nationalist party, the Wafd, was thrown into disgrace. The champion of the new regime was Colonel Mohammed Neguib. Churchill was sceptical. Be it Farouk, Nahas, or Neguib, the Egyptian national character would not change. He again linked the question of the Canal Zone with the previous 'scuttle' in Iran a year earlier: 'I am quite sure that we could not agree to be kicked out of Egypt by Nahas, Farouk or Neguib and leave our base, worth £500 millions, to be despoiled or put in their care . . . How different would the position have been if the late [Labour] Government had not flinched . . . at Abadan.'[10] There was a powerful logic in this position. Had the Labour government held firm in Iran, there would be no crisis in Egypt. If Churchill did not draw the line in Egypt, the end would be in sight. Shuckburgh summed up Churchill's reasoning: 'If we go out of the Sudan and Egypt it will be another stage in the policy of scuttle which began in India and ended in Abadan. It will lead to the abandonment of our African colonies.'[11]

For well over his first year after returning to office, from October 1951 until sometime in 1953, Churchill's views remained essentially the same as in 1946, when he had protested against the attempt made by the Labour government to reach a settlement with the Egyptians whereby British troops would be withdrawn from the Canal Zone. In 1946 he had stated in the House of Commons: 'Things are built up with great labour and cast away with great shame and folly. . . . we know that there is no satisfactory method of keeping the Canal open, and making sure that it is kept open, except by keeping troops there.'[12] He now wrote in 1952: 'I do not think that we should in any case give up the Treaty rights which we possess and which we have the power to enforce. . . . We should stay where we are in the Canal Zone. . . .'[13] If anything, he became even more obdurate than before because of the indignation he experienced on 'Black Saturday' of January 1952 when mobs in Cairo burned down Shepheard's Hotel, a symbol of British and other foreign privilege, and murdered nine British subjects at the Turf Club. He wrote in response to these 'murders and massacres' that the Egyptians 'cannot be classed as a civilized power until they have purged themselves'.[14]

After the Egyptian revolution in July 1952, Churchill momentarily entertained the possibility that the military officers who had overthrown the old regime might now be able to lead Egypt back to the ranks of 'civilized powers' and might prove to be more accommodating over the issue of British troops in the Canal Zone. It was a fleeting moment but he thought, nevertheless, that the military men of the revolution might be impressed with British resolution to fire 'the decisive volley'. On the other hand, British willingness to deal with the revolutionary regime would depend on the capacity of the new Egyptian government to pursue economic reform. Here is Churchill's minute in which he took measure of the leader of the revolution:

I am not opposed to a policy of giving Neguib a good chance provided he shows himself to be a friend.

I hope he will do something for the fellaheen, but we must not be afraid of him or be driven by the threats of cowards and curs from discharging our duty of maintaining the freedom of the Suez Canal for all nations until we can hand it over to some larger, more powerful combination.[15]

It took only a few months for him to revert to form and to conclude that Neguib was 'a military dictator of about the feeblest nation alive'.[16] The 'Dictator Neguib' became the epithet that Churchill now used to imply that the situation in Egypt had taken another turn for the worse. He wrote in February 1953: 'This military Dictator is under the impression he has only to kick us to make us run. I would like him to kick us and show him that we did not run.'[17]

When Churchill referred to 'the freedom of the Suez Canal for all nations' and his desire to hand it over to a larger combination, he expressed the hope that a military defence pact comparable to NATO might be created in the Middle East. There would be a British rather than an American commander, but the United States would be a principal partner. The Canal Zone would be converted into a base occupied by American as well as British and Egyptian and other troops. The

formula of Britain *plus* the United States *plus* Egypt would allow a settling of the Canal Zone dispute in a manner that would, in Churchill's
view, benefit all parties. This solution never in fact had a chance of
success because, among other reasons, the Egyptians regarded the presence of British troops on Egyptian soil as a continuation of the occupation that had gone on some seventy years. British forces in new
camouflage would be unacceptable. Nevertheless, the new defence plan
was the key to Churchill's thought. After taking office in 1951, he had
proposed to state in the House of Commons that there should be a
'token' presence of American troops in the Canal Zone. Shuckburgh,
who helped to draft the speech, was sceptical. He suggested that the
reference to token American forces be omitted because the Americans
simply would not assent and would be irritated by being asked in public. 'No, you silly owl', Churchill shouted at him. 'That is the whole
point'—to put pressure on the Americans to deploy troops at Suez.[18]

In the spring of 1953, during Eden's prolonged illness, Churchill took
direct control over the problem of the Suez base. He read telegrams with
a sharp eye, determined not to be jockeyed or rushed by Foreign Office
officials pursuing a policy of reconciliation. He spoke of 'appeasement',
according to Shuckburgh, 'saying that he never knew before that Munich
was situated on the Nile'.[19] Churchill nevertheless accepted that in principle there must be a settlement. At best it would consist of the continued presence of British troops in the Canal Zone; at worst the British
would evacuate but would be allowed to return in the event of war. 'It
seems that the old man is now changing his ideas on Egypt', Shuckburgh
wrote in August 1953. 'He has come round to thinking that we must
have an agreement to evacuate the Canal Zone and seems to have
dropped his previous idea that we could not possibly go until a lot of
people had been killed.'[20] This was a turning-point. From the spring and
summer of 1953 Churchill fought a rearguard action to assure that the
withdrawal did not amount to 'dead-level scuttle'.

He sent his own chosen emissary, Robin Hankey of the Foreign
Office, to Egypt to ensure a robust outlook at the British Embassy in
Cairo. 'The Prime Minister asked me to dinner this evening', Hankey
wrote shortly before his departure, 'and over a period of well over an
hour explained his view about the policy we should pursue in Egypt.
He was most categorical. . . . At one point he said I should be a
"patient sulky pig".'[21] Hankey further stated that Churchill's bellicosity
had not diminished: 'The Prime Minister said he was not afraid of
physical trouble. Although we should not of course say so, he would in

some ways welcome it. It would do the Egyptians no end of good.'[22] Churchill trusted Hankey, in part because he too held right-wing views, in part because he was the son of Lord Hankey, the legendary Secretary of the Committee of Imperial Defence and now one of the directors of the Suez Canal Company. Lord Hankey had convictions about the British Empire that were as unyielding as Churchill's. The younger Hankey, however, began to see the Egyptian side of the case. He mistrusted the Egyptians as much as anyone else, but he believed they had their own reasons for wishing to reach a settlement over the Canal Zone and, moreover, that the leaders of the revolution possessed a 'standard of integrity . . . very much higher than anything that has been known in Egypt for years'.[23] It would do Churchill a disservice to believe that he was impervious to such views. If nothing else, they brought home the point that his leading advisers, including those appointed personally by himself, believed that the time had come to resolve the dispute over the Canal Zone.

The person responsible more than anyone else for wooing Churchill away from a diehard position was perhaps General Sir Brian Robertson. Robertson was Commander-in-Chief British Middle East Land Forces. He had served in that tour of duty since 1950. During the war, he had been a key figure in the logistical success of the Abyssinian campaign and later had won distinction as Field Marshal Alexander's chief administrative officer in Italy. After the war he became Military Governor and Commander-in-Chief of the British Zone in Germany. The son of the Field Marshal of the 1914–18 war, he had a clear intellect, a commanding presence, and considerable powers of persuasion. In April 1953 Churchill announced to the Cabinet that Robertson would be the principal military representative to discuss issues of the Canal Zone with the Egyptians. Churchill respected Robertson's points of view and listened to his arguments. Robertson believed among other things that the Suez base was becoming strategically obsolete and that British forces should be deployed elsewhere in the Middle East, notably in Libya and Jordan. In the spring of 1953, Churchill seemed, very slowly, to acknowledge the advantages of redeployment. Then in June he had a stroke.

During Churchill's convalescence, the political direction of the Suez problem was delegated to Lord Salisbury, who held the position of Lord President of the Council and commanded respect not merely as a leader of the Tory Party but as a person of considerable experience in foreign affairs. Salisbury was impressed with 'the immense strain, both military & economic, which the keeping of 70,000 men on the Canal imposes on us'.[24] He now began to work with Robertson. By the time that Churchill had recovered some months later, Salisbury and Robertson had established a basis for withdrawal; it included the British right to reactivate the base in the event of war. There would be a time limit for the evacuation of British troops, which in the event took place by mid-1956. Against this powerful combination of Salisbury and Robertson—and, above all, Eden, when he returned in October 1953—it might seem that Churchill had no alternative but to acquiesce. In fact his previous attitude sometimes reasserted itself. He continued to play a central part, which was marked by suspicion and obstruction. 'He starts confused and wrong on almost every issue', Shuckburgh wrote in December 1953. Even though evacuation might be necessary, Churchill still wished to teach the Egyptians a lesson. 'Always he has wished a war with Egypt', Shuckburgh concluded, 'after which we would march out and leave them.'[25]

Sometimes Churchill's written comments, not to mention his utterances, failed to do justice to his actual assessment, which was more flexible and far-seeing than some contemporary observers believed. He had gradually shifted in his outlook. By the end of 1953 his views were not far removed from those of Salisbury and Robertson, or, for that matter, Shuckburgh. 'He hates the policy of "scuttle" which the Foreign Office and Anthony have persuaded him to accept about the Suez Canal,' his doctor, Lord Moran, wrote in October, 'but tries to console himself with the fact that the eighty thousand troops can be used elsewhere, and that it will mean a substantial economy.'[26] His natural inclination was to take an emphatic stand against evacuation and his exclamations made it easy to caricature his true position. He also relinquished his original ideas only after prolonged resistance. The final blow came when he failed, utterly and unequivocally, to persuade President Eisenhower of the merits of holding on to the Canal Zone.

It is illuminating to review briefly the exchange of views of Eisenhower and Churchill because it reveals the latter's methods as well as his aims. From 1951, as has been shown, Churchill hoped to resolve the issue of the base's future by bringing in American help. The problem in part was one of expense, which was significant. The Chancellor of the Exchequer demanded prodigious cuts in defence expenditure, eventually of £180 million. The upkeep of the military installations in the Canal Zone alone was £56 million a year. Only with American financial assistance could the British hope to continue over a long period. Churchill was well aware of this dimension of the problem. But there was another aspect which was no less important. Only if confronted by a unified Anglo-American stand might the Egyptians be willing to concede a continuing occupation by the forces of a regional defence organization. Making a persuasive case to Eisenhower thus became a transcendent priority.

'My dear Friend', he wrote to the President in February 1953. 'There is no question of our seeking or needing military, physical, or financial aid from you.' The British had sufficient military strength, he assured Eisenhower, 'to prevent a massacre of white people and to rescue them' in both Alexandria and Cairo. Emphasizing a repeated theme, Churchill drove home the point that there was 'no question of our needing your help or to reinforce the 80,000 men we have kept at great expense on tiptoe during the last year.' What he did request, however, was joint action: 'we should present to the dictator Neguib an agreed plan'.[27]

Eisenhower was puzzled at the tone of urgency as well as the course of action urged on him. He drew the letter to the attention of the National Security Council. He stated that he was concerned about the 'somewhat frightening phraseology' used by the Prime Minister.[28] He did nothing to encourage Churchill, who then pursued the matter in the following month. 'My dear Friend', Churchill began again. 'I am very sorry that you do not feel that you can do much to help us about the Canal Zone.' Churchill now spoke of the danger of 'the bear' and of his own determination 'not to be bullied any further by Neguib'. 'I have reached my limit', Churchill wrote.[29] This time Eisenhower responded immediately. 'Dear Winston', he wrote, 'I am a bit puzzled as to the real meaning of your note to me.' He now told Churchill explicitly that the United States would not become involved in the dispute between Britain and Egypt unless invited to do so by the Egyptians.[30]

Churchill was by no means deterred by Eisenhower's studied determination not to become embroiled. He now wrote of the 'unity of the English-speaking world' and the way in which 'Anglo-American unity' might have solved the Canal dispute 'to the general advantage of the free world'. He felt that an opportunity had been missed. 'You have decided', he wrote to the President, 'that unless invited by Neguib, who like all dictators is the servant of the forces behind him, we cannot present a joint proposal.' He warned Eisenhower that many in the Labour opposition held 'that we ought to abandon Egypt altogether'.[31]

Churchill also communicated with General Bedell Smith, now serving as Under-Secretary of State. 'My dear Bedell', he wrote. 'There is a point of detail on which I shall have to insist.' If the British were to agree to withdraw from the Canal Zone, the British military personnel left 'to guard or look after the base' must be permitted to wear British uniforms and carry arms. Otherwise they would remain defenceless and 'at the mercy and good faith of any Egyptian dictator who may jump or crawl into office overnight'.[32] Churchill, moreover, sent a telegram to the Secretary of State, John Foster Dulles, protesting against American military assistance to Egypt. Did Dulles not know, he asked, that 'German Nazis' had been engaged by Neguib to train guerrillas to sabotage the British position in the Zone? 'Do you wish to give them American arms as well at a moment when so much hangs in the balance . . .?'[33]

Eisenhower himself responded to Churchill's telegram about military equipment. He had looked into the matter himself, he reported, and judged it to be only 'a meager quantity of arms'. The Egyptians had pressed hard for military assistance and it had been long delayed. If the United States refused it would be a breach of faith. Why should the British object to the transfer of such items as helmets and jeeps? 'I hope my comments do not offend', he wrote to Winston.[34] Eisenhower was, in fact, alarmed at the deteriorating situation. In May 1953 it looked as if the British and the Egyptians were on collision course. What might happen, he asked the members of the National Security Council, if the Egyptians managed to kick the British out? 'Do we expect the Russians to take over? Would the Russians supply the Egyptians with arms? Would we blockade Egyptian ports to prevent these arms from reaching Egypt?'[35] No-one could answer those questions. But Eisenhower himself had views on how to resolve the Anglo-Egyptian imbroglio. The demands on the Egyptians, he wrote to Churchill in June 1953, should be kept to a minimum. Otherwise the British—and the Americans—would find themselves at odds 'with the very strong nationalist sentiments of the Egyptian Government and people'.[36]

Eisenhower's message constituted a clear warning that it was better to evacuate quickly, thereby retaining as much good will as possible. To Churchill this seemed to embody a defeatist attitude. 'My dear Friend', he wrote to Eisenhower in June shortly before the debilitating stroke. 'We have been disappointed not to receive more support . . .' In Churchill's view the Egyptians were playing the Western partners off

against each other. 'Dictator Neguib', Churchill continued, 'is embold-
ened to translate his threats into action, [with] bloodshed on a scale
difficult to measure . . .'[37] Eisenhower was now genuinely alarmed that
Churchill might go off the deep end. Churchill himself apparently
thought that he had pitched his rhetoric too high because he now
promised to express himself 'less belligerently'.[38] Eisenhower was glad
of that. He confined himself in his response to saying that there were
'certain passages' in Churchill's letter 'which I fail to understand', but
that they could be resolved orally at a meeting planned for late June at
Bermuda. The rendezvous did not take place because of Churchill's illness. Eisenhower welcomed Lord Salisbury's less flamboyant approach.

The Churchill–Eisenhower exchange of views on the Canal Zone
now lapsed until much later in the year. Churchill still believed that
with 'unequivocal American support' the Egyptians would be forced to
yield to the continued presence of at least 'a few thousand British
troops'.[39] He thus returned to the charge in December, relating the
Egyptian issue to other questions and protesting against American economic assistance to Egypt. 'My dear Friend', Churchill began again.
The 'Socialist Opposition' would exploit the issue of American aid to
Egypt as an opportunity 'to press for the inclusion of Red China in
U.N.O.' Would Eisenhower, with his 'immense responsibilities', get
much help on these matters from a socialist government in Britain? It
was something to think about, Churchill suggested.[40] Indeed it was.
Eisenhower decided to respond patiently and firmly issue by issue:

You state that the Socialist Opposition would be bitterly resentful of American
economic aid to Egypt because of American objection to trade with Communist China. It has been my understanding that Britain has continued to
carry on trade in economic non-strategic items with Red China, and we do not
now propose more with respect to Egypt than beginning to help develop its
economy. Consequently, I am at a loss to understand the basis on which the
Socialists could make a logical attack.

You likewise mention that the Opposition would resent any economic aid to
Egypt so bitterly that they would urge you to press for inclusion of Red China
in the UN. By implication this would seem to mean that if we do not extend
economic aid to Egypt, you are prepared to stand firm with us in opposing the
inclusion of the bloody Chinese aggressor into the councils of peaceful nations,
at least until Red China withdraws her invading armies, ceases supporting the
Indo–China war and begins to act like a civilized government. Could you
confirm this to me?[41]

Eisenhower made a tart comment in this letter: 'I assume, of course,
that you are genuinely anxious to arrange a truce with Egypt . . .'

Churchill now attempted to defend his comments about socialists, Egyptians, and Red Communists, but he only made things worse. 'It is always difficult to explain the internal politics of one to another and I have not succeeded this time.' He did not mean, really, what Eisenhower thought he had said about the socialists, or about China. In fact he backed down and, in effect, apologized, thereby acknowledging that he had been wasting the President's time with breezy ideas that had not been clearly thought out. He then made the mistake of resorting to sentiment. He invoked the spirit of the Special Relationship. He mentioned that '50,000 British graves lie in Egypt and its approaches'. If only Britain and the United States had made common cause against the Egyptians 'all might well have been settled six months ago'.[42] Eisenhower was irritated. He asked Dulles whether he had seen 'the latest one' from Winston. Eisenhower had to confess, he told Dulles, that he was 'very annoyed'. He responded briefly but courteously to Churchill by expressing hope that the dispute with the Egyptians would soon come to an end. 'Dear Winston', he wrote, 'I am anxious to find a way for us to conform as far as possible to your views on Egypt.' After a few other platitudes, Eisenhower wished Winston a 'Merry Christmas'.[43] He thereby ended the Churchill–Eisenhower correspondence over Suez at the close of 1953.

By early 1954, Churchill found his military and political advisers as well as the President of the United States urging him to acquiesce in a settlement with the Egyptians. His preference was still to retreat at British convenience, to maintain troops in the Canal Zone in any event, and, if provoked, to break off relations with the Egyptians. It is clear from the historical record that he would have welcomed a fight. He wished to give the Egyptians a military thump, then to redeploy British forces in Libya and Jordan. At one stage it appeared that events might be moving in the direction he preferred. In early 1954 Gamal Abdel Nasser challenged Neguib's control of the Egyptian government, though Nasser did not in fact consolidate his own power until later in the year. 'Neg-wib's gone', Churchill said in his inimitable lisp to Shuckburgh. When it was pointed out that Nasser might not be an improvement, Churchill responded, 'No, no. Much worse. That's the point. Perhaps he will bring it to a head. I have been afraid they [the Egyptians] might agree.' When Shuckburgh reflected on what the Prime Minister meant by Nasser's forcing matters to a head, he concluded that Churchill 'can only mean attacking our troops, so that we have an excuse for fighting'.[44]

One of the issues at stake, which troubled Members of Parliament as
well as the Prime Minister, was the possible decline of British nerve.
Those who protested against caving in to the Egyptians became known
as the 'Suez rebels'. They were led by Captain Charles Waterhouse,
who bitterly opposed withdrawal as evidence of sagging will and failing
confidence in British purpose. Churchill did not publicly support the
extreme right-wing Tories who opposed the evacuation from Egypt,
but privately he encouraged them. 'You keep it up', he said to the son
of Leo Amery, Julian, who was now an MP and the intellectual force in
the 'rebel' movement. 'You're on the right lines.'[45] According to the
younger Amery, British forces could be reduced to 10,000 'teeth troops'
and the Canal Zone held indefinitely. Churchill was attracted to this
point of view. Unfortunately for him, the Chiefs of Staff were not.
They regarded 'teeth troops' as mere 'hostages of fortune'.[46] Churchill
concurred, formally if not in spirit, in their judgement. To Julian
Amery he commented ironically that 'it is not worth while keeping the
Suez Canal when you Amerys have given away India'—a return to the
controversies of the Second World War when Churchill had acrimo-
niously blocked Leo Amery's plan to grant Dominion status to India.[47]

The Leo Amery diaries reveal Churchill's changing moods as well as
the essential questions as seen from the right wing of the Tory Party.
Leo Amery complained that Churchill had never really possessed an
'imperial' or 'Commonwealth' intellect: 'That the Suez Canal might
make all the difference to keeping not only India and Pakistan but also
Australia and New Zealand in the Commonwealth does not fit in with
his mentality.'[48] Thus in Amery's judgement Churchill failed to see
some of the larger issues and was able to justify the withdrawal from
the Canal Zone by arguing the need for 'redeployment'. Both Leo and
Julian Amery regarded redeployment as a misguided venture that
would drive British troops from African pillar to Middle Eastern post
until nothing was left. It would be better to detach the Canal Zone
from Egypt and hold on to it at any cost as an enclave. There was
more than the military issues at stake. 'If only we stand firm now', Leo
Amery wrote in 1953, 'it may be a turning point in the whole psychology of the Empire.'[49]

'Better for us to run our own show', Amery exclaimed, 'than to be
mixed up with the Americans.' Here was a fundamental point of
difference between Churchill and the Amerys. Churchill believed that
the British, at the minimum, would have to gain at least the acquiescence of the United States in any Middle Eastern settlement while Leo

Amery, by contrast, lamented 'sucking up to Ike'.[50] Amery thought, in other words, that it was still possible for Britain to act independently of the United States. Churchill did not, as has been shown in his correspondence with Eisenhower. Of the two points of view, Churchill's was certainly the more realistic, as was to be demonstrated in the Suez crisis. But Amery's instinctive reaction represented a main stream of British thought which resented American ascendancy and Egyptian recalcitrance. 'Will the British worm never turn?', Amery asked.[51] He believed that Britain's position in the Middle East could be reasserted and maintained indefinitely if there were bold leadership and strength of will. Churchill's own stewardship in the spring and summer of 1954 he regarded as 'lamentable'.[52]

The Anglo-Egyptian settlement may have been deplorable from a true-blue Tory point of view, but from Churchill's own perspective it proved to be one of his finest hours. The agreement, it will be recalled, provided for the withdrawal of British troops with the provision of re-entry in the event of war. It might have been humiliating for Churchill to have defended in Parliament such an accord that went against his views on the British Empire and his attitude towards the Egyptians. He managed, however, to twist victory out of potential disaster by availing himself of the opportunity provided by the great debate in the spring of 1954 on the consequences of the hydrogen bomb tested by the Americans on 1 March. No-one who has studied Churchill's letters and speeches at this time can doubt the genuine concern he felt about the 'bloody invention' and the harm it could do 'to society and to the race'.[53] He believed that thermo-nuclear warfare would be a turning-point in the history of mankind. Nevertheless, to those involved in the Suez issue the hydrogen bomb appeared as a *deus ex machina* that allowed Churchill to solve the problem of the Canal Zone in an entirely unexpected way. As Julian Amery put it, 'I cannot help feeling that this mention of the hydrogen bomb was introduced as a political camouflage . . .'[54] In any event Churchill had joined whole-heartedly in the Cabinet consensus that 'our strategic needs in the Middle East had been radically changed by the development of thermo-nuclear weapons. . . . Our withdrawal from Egypt could be presented as a part of a re-deployment of our forces in the Middle East based on a re-assessment of our essential strategic needs in that area.' For his own part Churchill made it clear to his colleagues in the Cabinet, once again, that he regretted 'abandoning the position which we had held in Egypt since 1882'.[55] To those in his immediate circle, his comments had become somewhat sentimental about India as well as Egypt: 'We have thrown away our glorious Empire, our wonderful Indian Empire, we have cast it away'.[56]

The great Parliamentary debate took place in the last week of June 1954. There was considerable uneasiness among Churchill's associates. He was now approaching the age of 80. In March Eden had said: 'he is gaga; he cannot finish his sentences.'[57] This was not a single impression. 'Gaga' was the word used by others as well.[58] How then might he respond in the House of Commons, where he would be under attack by rebels in his own party as well as from leaders of the Opposition? Attlee, for one, had no intention of giving him an easy time. He quoted Churchill's words in 1946 that things had been built up with labour and thrown away with folly. Churchill had previously believed that the only way of keeping open the canal was to station British troops there. Why then had he changed his mind? Attlee thought it was inexcusable to brush away the earlier position with an easy reference to 'his hydrogen bomb'. For years Churchill had thrown about the word 'scuttle'. Now that he was Prime Minister he had to face the realities. There was a great difference, Attlee concluded, in Churchill in and out of office. They now witnessed Churchill having 'to eat humble pie'. He was leading Britain into a new era in the Middle East which had been foreseen almost a decade earlier by the Labour government. Attlee wished it to be clear to everyone that Churchill emerged with little credit.[59]

That view was also shared by the Tories belonging to the Suez group. 'I and my friends had feared that there would be a sell-out', stated Captain Waterhouse. 'This is not a sell-out. It is a give-away. Instead of having physical control of a great base, instead of having troops on the major waterway of the world, we have got this piece of paper in our hands.' With stinging words he went on to say that, if he had foreseen 'this piece of paper' at the time of the last election, he and his colleagues 'would not now be sitting on this side of the House'.[60] In what must be taken as the ultimate rebuke, Waterhouse indicted the Tory government for 'losing our will to rule'. A further speaker made a point that was close to Churchill's own heart. The British should have intervened at the time of the rioting during 'Black Saturday' in January 1952: 'We could have gone into Egypt then and taught the pashas and the very small class of educated Egyptians a lesson which they would not have forgotten for a decade.'[61]

Churchill finally rose to respond. He did so briefly and eloquently by demonstrating that his mind had been open to recent changes. 'I have not in the slightest degree concealed in public speech how much I regretted the course of events in Egypt. But I had not held my mind closed to the tremendous changes that have taken place in the whole strategic position in the world which make the thoughts which were well-founded and well knit together a year ago utterly obsolete, and which have changed the opinions of every competent soldier that I have been able to meet.' He then placed the issue of the Canal Zone in the perspective of larger problems:

I should be prepared . . . to show how utterly out of all proportion to the Suez Canal and the position which we held in Egypt are the appalling developments and the appalling spectacle which imagination raises before us. Merely to try to imagine in outline the first few weeks of a war . . . would, I am sure, convince hon. Gentlemen of the obsolescence of the base and of the sense of proportion which is vitally needed at the present time, not only in military dispositions but in all our attempts to establish human relationships between nation and nation.[62]

Churchill spoke for only four minutes, but he captured the House of Commons. 'It was a triumph', he said the next day. 'If I never speak again in the House I can say I have done nothing better.'[63]

It is ironic that Churchill, having all along objected to the evacuation, deserves large credit for the settlement achieved between Britain and Egypt in 1954. He was acclaimed by all parties for rising to the occasion, even though his critics, of course, continued to disagree with him. Leo Amery, like Julian, believed that the argument about the hydrogen bomb was camouflage to cover up a disagreeable decision. It was a deplorable outcome, Leo noted in his diary. He concluded that the British were 'abdicating our responsibilities in the Middle East'.[64] Nevertheless Amery recognized that Churchill, for all his lapses, continued to demonstrate the qualities of a statesman. 'Balancing pros and cons', Amery wrote later in the year, 'I dare say lack of continuous grip in the Cabinet may be more than offset by his reputation and power of broad statesmanlike utterance when required. What a maturing from the aggressive young political swashbuckler of . . . 50 years ago.'[65]

On the eve of the invasion of Suez in early November 1956, Churchill issued a public statement explaining his reason for supporting the Eden government. Britain's aim, he emphasized, was 'to restore peace and order' in the Middle East. He expressed confidence 'that our American friends will come to realize that, not for the first time, we have acted independently for the common good'.[66] He said later that 'I would never have dared to do it without squaring the Americans, and once I had started I would never have dared stop.'[67] Had he reflected on his exchanges with Eisenhower, he would have known that American co-operation or acquiescence was the one thing he could never have secured. On the other hand, the whole history of Churchill's career certainly bears testimony that he would never have stopped.

28

Churchill: The Government of 1951–1955

ROY JENKINS

RECIDIVIST Prime Ministers have become rare. For the hundred years from 1850 they were more the rule than the exception: Russell, Palmerston, Derby, Disraeli, Gladstone (the only inmate of 10 Downing Street who came back three times), Salisbury, Baldwin, MacDonald, and Churchill. Since 1955 there have been eight Prime Ministers but only Harold Wilson has returned, and his second term was brief and quietist.

For Churchill the risks of a second throw were the greatest. For some others—Palmerston, Disraeli, Salisbury, Baldwin, and MacDonald—their first governments were merely preliminary snatches at Downing Street. With the possible exception of Palmerston they would all have had very thin Prime Ministerial reputations had they not come back for separated second terms. Short terms of office are a fatal bar to being a Prime Minister of the first rank. This is borne out by every brief premiership of the twentieth century. Campbell-Bannerman, Bonar Law, and Eden were brief because of the collapse of their health and, in the case of the last, of his policies as well. Rosebery, Chamberlain, Home, and Callaghan were so due to a collapse of support in one form or another. Balfour and Heath were on the margin between short and medium terms (just over three and a half years in both cases) and on the margin too of major impact on events, Heath probably just over it because of Europe. But none of these nine would be serious contenders for a place amongst the 'greats' if British historians were as inclined to organize concourses about their Prime Ministers as American ones are about their Presidents. The clear British conclusion is that no-one who has not served at least four years in Downing Street can stand near to the front. Many of these who came back therefore needed to do so if they were to give their reputations a chance to grow.

Churchill was in the reverse position. After 1945 he had nowhere to go but down. Had he been a careful guardian of the treasures of his own reputation, he would surely have given up both the leadership of the Opposition and any thought of a return to office. This would not have precluded him from his most notable activities of the late 1940s: writing his memoirs, delivering the Fulton, Zurich, Strasbourg, and other orations, or even chiding the Labour government when he wished to do so. He would not have been a would-be gambler who was afraid to play. No-one even before 1940, let alone after, could ever have accused him of that. He would have been one who had played, and won, for the highest stakes, but who knew when to get up from the tables and cash his winnings.

He was prevented from doing so by his zest for office. In the early years after his defeat in 1945 I do not think this was primarily a question of public duty. In that summer of national victory and personal and party defeat he was lacking a message he wanted to give to the world. His performance from Yalta to Potsdam was peculiarly uncertain. Later, particularly in 1953–5, when he exasperated his Cabinet by staying on from the age of 78 to 80 as much as Gladstone had done by doing so from the age of 83 to 84, he became absorbed by a mission to save the world from confrontation and the hydrogen bomb. But in 1945 it was more the private deprivation of the withdrawal of the props of public office which he felt.

He was always subject to bouts of 'black-dog' depression, the threat of which became greater as his life moved to a stage when windows were more likely to close than to open. The best prophylactic for black dog that he knew was red boxes and the fleet of private secretaries and sense of purpose and power which went with them. But his decision to face a full period in Opposition and, as it turned out, two further general elections before getting back to the enjoyment of these appurtenances was an extraordinarily rash one from the point of view of his reputation. The amazing thing was how well it stood up to the strain put upon it. This was the triumph of the quiet government of 1951–5, although Churchill also had the unprecedented advantage of the solidity of the previous achievement. This was both so substantial and so legendary that it had become an iceberg very difficult to melt.

Nevertheless, it is impossible to re-read the story of Churchill's life as Prime Minister of that second government without feeling that he was gloriously unfit for office. The oxymoron is appropriate to the contradictions in his performance. The splendour of his personality, which infused everything he did with style and interest, was not in doubt. He put on a great show. Indeed there is a constant feeling that he was asking all his interlocutors, the new Queen, President Eisenhower, his age-ing crown prince Anthony Eden, the members of the House of Commons, and various insecure Prime Ministers of the Fourth French Republic to live up to a role which they thought was a little over the top for the beginning of the second half of the twentieth century. With the exception of one issue, that of saving the world from nuclear con-frontation, too much of his attention, in Jean Monnet's distinction, was concentrated on 'being someone' rather than on 'doing something'. The struggle to prolong active life became dominant over any policy issue except for the nuclear one. The most important milestones in his politi-cal year were the occasions when he would endeavour to show the Cabinet or the Americans, the Conservative Conference or the House of Commons, that he was fit to carry on. It was not so much what he said on these occasions, although he maintained his habit of meticulous preparation, as the fact that he was able to keep on his feet for sufficiently long to say it at all. There was even an element of play-act-ing about it. The most vivid moments of the second premiership were in the bustle of his returning to office: putting together the govern-ment, summoning officials, re-creating his staff, sending or acknowledg-ing greetings all over the world. It was at least as much a pageant to commemorate the great days of the first government as it was a realistic preparation for a new period of office.

At this stage no-one contemplated his retaining the premiership for the forty-one months that he in fact achieved. A year or, at most, two was the assumption which he fostered in the minds of others, and maybe in his own too. Then, throughout 1952 and 1953 and 1954, he fought one of the most brilliant delaying actions in history. It was rem-iniscent of the way he had avoided unnecessary risk and Anglo-American carnage by delaying the Second Front until 1944. Had this delay been announced in the summer of 1941 it would have produced a much worse explosion from Stalin than those which actually took place following each successive intimation that a further postponement was necessary. *Mutatis mutandis* Churchill pursued the same tactics with Eden. Delaying until 1955 would have been intolerable in 1951, not only to the heir apparent but to the generality of the Cabinet as well. Little by little it became acceptable, or at any rate unavoidable.

Whether Churchill intended from the beginning to pursue a strategy of relentless delay is difficult to determine. Probably, as with much human activity, his motives were mixed and his intention was not wholly clear, even to himself. As with many great phrase-makers, there was always a danger of the words determining the thought rather than vice versa. His lament to Rab Butler on 12 March 1954 created an unforgettable and poignant image: 'I feel like an aeroplane at the end of its flight, in the dusk, with the petrol running out, in search of a safe landing.'[1] But how resolutely was he seeking the haven, even in 1954 let alone in the previous two years, and how much was he enjoying the cruising in the last minutes of twilight?

Compared with what might have been expected in 1951, his own circumstances made survival more difficult, but external ones made it easier. His health, despite the greater care and medical knowledge which was lavished upon it, was much less good than that of Palmerston and Gladstone, the only two of his predecessors who were in office at comparable ages. Already in February 1952 Churchill had a small arterial spasm, and at a consequent conclave on the consequences between his doctor, his private secretary, and Lord Salisbury, a senior member of the government who was not in competition for the succession, there was general agreement that he had not been functioning adequately even before this minor blow fell. But he rallied quickly and then had a sustained period of buoyancy. To be set against his basically precarious bodily condition there was his unique vigour of spirit. This was interspersed by low depressions, but these mostly occurred when there was neither much pressure of events upon him, nor particular need to assert his will to live. When necessary the adrenalin rarely failed to produce zest and even gaiety.

In early 1953 he was on better form than a year before, even though he was at that time probably running down his own reserves as fast as Chancellor of the Exchequer Butler was temporarily building up those behind sterling. Then in the spring Churchill's hopes of longevity in office received two great fillips. The first was the death of Stalin on 5 March. This gave Churchill the prestige of being the sole survivor of the triumvirate of war leadership. It also aroused the hope of a new fluidity in the world balance, which increased both his desire to continue in office and his excuse for doing so.

The second was the botched operation on Anthony Eden on 12 April 1953. With a false twist of a surgeon's knife, and a remarkable turn up for the book, the 78-year-old Prime Minister emerged as fitter than his 55-year-old Foreign Secretary, who had previously been breathing down his neck with impatient vigour. Eden, who never wholly recovered although he lived for another twenty-six years, was completely out of action for six months.

A third of the way through this period, when Eden was in a Boston clinic undergoing his third dose of surgery, Churchill himself suffered a major stroke. It would have finished anyone without his indomitable spirit and would have forced even his resignation had Eden not been equally incapacitated. As it was, Churchill survived at the head of the government, the seriousness of his condition concealed from the public with a web of subterfuge, through two months of complete incapacity and at least another two months of more convalescence than activity. Never had Britain been nominally governed by two such sick men. Yet it was the compounding of invalidism which made Churchill's continuation possible. The defenders of Eden's right to the succession, fortified by the perhaps larger group of those who did not want to see it usurped by Rab Butler, the only possible alternative of the time, swung to wanting to keep Churchill in office. If this proved impossible, elaborate plans were laid for making Lord Salisbury the acting head of an interim administration while the billet was kept warm for Eden when he returned. This was of doubtful constitutional propriety, and it was much easier to keep Churchill in position. Even so it would not have worked had Butler had the spirit of a usurper. But this was the last attribute he possessed. He was one of nature's intendants. He did the work, presided over no fewer than sixteen consecutive Cabinet meetings, probably had wistful thoughts about the glories of the full position, but did not demand it. As a result Butler set the pattern which enabled him also to be deprived of the premiership in 1957 and 1963. Churchill survived not merely in life but in office, and a most remarkable demonstration was given of the ability of a country to manage without identifiable leadership. Rarely was more appropriate that favourite question of Churchill's friend Beaverbrook: 'Who's in charge of the clattering train?'

Having benefited from Churchill's singular attachment to office over the summer and autumn of 1953, Eden was inevitably in a weak position to force the pace quickly after his return. So, improbable though it would have seemed two and a half years before, Churchill was still stubbornly in Downing Street in the spring of 1954, even if dropping encouraging hints about a retirement in June. Once again his strength, and this time still more his judgement, were manifestly failing. In November 1953, on his reappearance in the House of Commons, he had by general consent secured a great triumph, delivering a long speech which was witty, commanding, and visionary. Then in April 1954 he matched it with a Parliamentary disaster, pettily partisan and as embarrassing to his own side as it was provocative to the other. 'Things didn't go as well as I expected', he rather touchingly told his ever-present and ever-scribbling doctor the following morning.[2]

A harsher view was taken by others. There was a press campaign against him, although it was prevented from being general by his friendship with the important proprietors Camrose, Beaverbrook, and, to a lesser extent, Rothermere. But what the most hostile newspaper, the then powerful *Daily Mirror*, said about him was not as bad as the comments of his colleagues. On 31 March, after 'a terrible Cabinet, slow, waffling and indecisive', Eden's private secretary recorded the Foreign Secretary as saying: 'This simply cannot go on; he is gaga; he cannot finish his sentences.'[3]

By that time Churchill had got a new bit between his teeth. The devastating results of a major US hydrogen bomb test had just become known, and he became as convinced that his last mission was to save mankind from this horror as he was determined to achieve a bilateral meeting with Malenkov, Stalin's short-lived successor. The quest for this blocked off the summer. In a Washington visit at the end of June he surprisingly secured the reluctant acquiescence of Eisenhower to his attempting such a mission. His prestige and even his persuasiveness were still extraordinary. On that visit he and his entourage stayed in the White House for three days, entertained by the President at every meal save one, when Churchill addressed a luncheon on Capitol Hill, and then on the fourth day, when he had retreated to the British Embassy, Eisenhower came there to dine. What visiting head of government could now command such an attention span from a President?

Having got over this high hurdle, Churchill unexpectedly failed at the next one, which was his own Cabinet. A cave, led by Salisbury, which broadened out into a majority prominently including Eden and Macmillan, fought a successful spoiling action throughout July, and by the end of the month, as Martin Gilbert put it: 'Churchill's last great foreign policy initiative was at an end.'[4] So, it might be thought, was his last excuse for staying in office. Instead of bowing under this blow, however, he had a spectacular late summer and early autumn of renewed vigour. He put his colleagues in their place one by one. He wrote a letter to Eden which could be interpreted as meaning that he intended to stay on and fight a general election in November 1955![5] He achieved a triumph, which gave no hint of being a swan-song, at the Conservative Conference. He carried through a major and successful ministerial reshuffle. And he surmounted his 80th birthday on

30 November with gusto for everything except the Parliamentary gift of his portrait by Graham Sutherland.

Then, satisfied as it were by having breached this time barrier and broken free from the advice of over-officious friends, he changed his mind at the beginning of January. He made a narrowly communicated but for the first time firmly embraced and therefore resolute decision to resign at the beginning of the Easter recess, and did so, two days in advance, on 5 April. The penalty he paid for nearly three years of delaying action was that he went in the middle of a national newspaper strike. As a result the most famous and one of the most headline-conscious of Prime Ministers departed from Downing Street surrounded by the heavy padding of journalistic silence.

The second Churchill government was therefore too much dominated by its chief's stubborn battle for survival to be a splendid affair. There was inevitably more of the doggedness of a tired old garrison commander than the dash of a young cavalry subaltern at Omdurman about it. Yet in the circumstances of 1951–5 there was a good deal, but by no means everything, to be said for a spirit of wary caution. Churchill's successor but six, Margaret Thatcher, decided that while two of the intervening Conservative leaders, Eden and Home, could be left undisturbed in amicable obscurity and two, Macmillan and Heath, had to be excoriated for profligate and consensual heresy, the hand of fellowship as a defiant doctrinaire could be extended back to Churchill. On the performance of his second government, this was the strictest nonsense. It could hardly be sustained on the basis of his first government either, with Ernest Bevin, Herbert Morrison, and the great (if portentous) public servant John Anderson (Lord Waverley) in charge of the home front, and John Maynard Keynes as adviser at the Treasury.

The government of 1951–5 was a very consensual one. There were occasional flourishes of partisan rhetoric, but little partisan action. The keynote was struck by Churchill's speech at the beginning of the Parliament:

What the nation needs is several years of quiet steady administration, if only to allow the Socialist legislation to reach its full fruition. What the House needs is a period of tolerant and constructive debating on the merits of the questions without nearly every speech on either side being distorted by the passions of one election or the preparations for another.[6]

He did not entirely succeed in giving it that. This was partly because his non-partisanship was always unreliable. He would lurch, as with the contrast between the November 1953 and the April 1954 speeches, from the heights of statesmanship to the depths of exaggerated party abuse with little notice and less reason. At a more personal level he alternated between a lachrymose generosity towards opponents and a sudden picking of an irrelevant quarrel. His relations with Emmanuel Shinwell, Defence Minister at the end of the Attlee government, were a good example of this. Nor was his attitude to more substantial figures like Attlee, Cripps, and Morrison free of it. Ernest Bevin he came nearest to admiring, although Bevin was dead before the second government was formed, and indeed Cripps, to whom he also accorded an arm's length respect, was *hors de combat*. But he never in these latter days approached a real cross-party friendship.

As a young minister he had notably had such relationships with F. E. Smith (with whom he had founded the Other Club, which was specifically designed to mix opponents, without weakening 'the rancour of party politics', in rumbustious conversation over dinners at which oysters and champagne were ritual), with Lord Hugh Cecil (who was best man at his wedding), and then in the 1920s, when he had become a Tory, with Lloyd George. But he never had a 'crony' amongst any of his wartime Labour ministers. He never got any of them into the Other Club, although in the next generation Wilson and Callaghan both joined. Attlee and co. were too respectable for him. He much preferred those with a touch of bounderism, as Clementine Churchill frequently complained. The list of those whom he chose to have to lunch at Chartwell in his naturally most self-indulgent period after his stroke was illuminating. Some ministers whom he might not have chosen, notably Rab Butler, had to come *ex officio*, but there was never throughout his long convalescent months there and at Chequers a single visit from a member of the Opposition. Beaverbrook, on the other hand, although fairly tiresome to the government particularly on German rearmament, was there within the first three days.

The Labour Party in turn was edgy to deal with during those 1951–5 years. They were convulsed by the Bevanite revolt, which started with health service charges and Aneurin Bevan's resignation in 1951, widened into a complaint against British foreign-policy subservience to America, and continued until the late 1950s. One effect was that the official leadership of Attlee and Morrison, with Gaitskell increasingly strongly in reserve, was simultaneously determined not to trim on major issues, such as basic support for the American leadership of NATO, the need for German rearmament, and the commitment to a

British hydrogen bomb, and resolved to show that it could be at least as anti-Tory as the Bevanites. The result was that great areas of policy were left unmolested while fierce battles were fought over little patches of ground that had in them no profit but the name. Thus in February 1954 the most ludicrous storm broke out over the rifle with which NATO forces should be equipped. But that was a small price to pay for official Labour support for the need for, say, twelve German divisions in Europe or for the ratification of the peace treaty with Japan.

In return Churchill fulminated at the fringes of the legacy of the Labour government of 1945–51 but left the core of its work inviolate. His complaint at the first Lord Mayor's Banquet in the November after his return to office was an almost perfect example of his desire to singe the King of Spain's beard without wounding him more viscerally. He spoke of 'a tangled web of commitments and shortages, the like of which I have never seen before', and hoped his government could have 'the wisdom and strength to cope with them effectively'.[7] Of the nationalization measures he reversed iron and steel, which was hardly implemented, and road haulage, which was manifestly unpopular. But coal, railways, civil aviation, the Bank of England, electricity, gas, and one or two others were left unchallenged. So were the main social security provisions and the National Health Service. So were such constitutional changes as had been introduced under Attlee, from the second Parliament Act, which reduced the Lords' powers of delay to one year, to the abolition of university seats in the House of Commons. On the latter point Churchill had to do some very direct eating of his own words, but this, as he had memorably made clear on an earlier occasion, was an act of mastication which he found acceptable and even healthy.

What this Churchill government essentially did was to give the country a rest from dogma and to relax the acerbities of Crippsian austerity without setting the clock back on most of the work of the Attlee administration. The liberalization worked well. It was cautiously done. Operation Robot, to free sterling and make it fully convertible, was defeated after an epic Cabinet struggle over which Churchill presided with detachment. The reduction in food subsidies was not such as to produce a serious price inflation. The end of the remains of rationing proved to be like the dispersal of a thin layer of mist. Previously shortages had loomed up menacingly but a puff of wind produced bright sunshine and no sinister shapes. It was all much less drastically done than the moves in progress or contemplation in eastern Europe in the early 1990s.

This was perfectly suited to the national mood in the early 1950s. There was no significant support for a counter-revolution and a return to the Britain of Neville Chamberlain. There was support for the knocking off of the rough edges of the previous administration, but not for much more. This was precisely what this Churchill government did. It was an era of massed political armies and committed party loyalties. The 1951 election was one of the most remarkable in British political history: 83 per cent voted and 97 per cent of those voted Conservative or Labour. By 1983 the percentage voting was down to 72.7 per cent and the percentage voting for one or other of the big parties to 69.9 per cent. The art of statesmanship in the 1951 circumstances called for the manœuvring of these vast armies with considerable caution. They were too big to be allowed to maul each other with abandon. The result would have been an unacceptable carnage rather like that in the hidden war between Russia and Austro-Hungary in 1914–17, which destroyed both their regimes. Churchill recoiled from this almost as much as he did from the use of the hydrogen bomb. Indeed it might be held that he stayed his hand too much, particularly against trades union-backed wage claims. The appointment of Walter Monckton as Minister of Labour was like ringing up a signal that all differences would be split, all disputes would be arbitrated, and the seeds of the great inflation would be sown.

This approach was not just based on a general desire for weak compromise. Churchill had an institutional respect for trades union leaders, provided they were patriotic and reasonably responsive to his flattery, although they did not have to be suborned by it. He preferred them on the whole to Labour Parliamentarians. One of his narrownesses was that he could not easily accept upper-middle-class Labour politicians. This was odd, for in his young days as a duke's grandson who had become a radical member of a Liberal government he had been much accused of class betrayal. Yet he was inclined to take the same view of Cripps, Gaitskell, and Crossman. He had something of an anti-Wykehamist obsession, half regarding them as inky-fingered pen-pushers who should be clerks not rulers, and half thinking they ought not to be Labour MPs. When he engaged with one of them in the House of Commons he often fell back on mocking inter-school jokes. This too was odd, for no Wykehamist had ever done him much harm, and several, from Edward Grey to Ronald Tree, his host at Ditchley on wartime moonlit weekends, had done him an appreciable amount of good. By some deficiency of understanding, maybe mixed with a little snobbery, he found it much easier to embrace Arthur Deakin, Bevin's successor as head of the Transport Workers, or Tom O'Brien, a chairman of the TUC whom he had to visit him at Beaverbrook's villa in the South of France, than not only the three Wykehamists but also the Etonian couple, Hugh Dalton and John Strachey. Nor did he ever have close social relations with Attlee, his wartime deputy and post-war *vis-à-vis*. Churchill respected him as a public figure, but found him a little prim for conviviality.

This was unimportant and did not affect the central achievement of the second Churchill government, which was that it excellently restored the balance of British politics. This had been severely upset by two developments. The first was the over-reaction to the financial crisis of 1931. Baldwin, who had worked hard in the 1920s to create a new post-Liberal balance, allowed himself to be pushed into destroying it by creating the National government. MacDonald and Arthur Henderson assisted by going in opposite directions from each other. It looked as though between them they had destroyed Labour as a party of government for a full generation. After fourteen years it sprang back, and the question then became one of whether the Conservative Party could escape from the miasma of pre-war appeasement and mass unemployment to govern convincingly a post-war welfare state Britain. Churchill's second government, much aided by the work of R. A. Butler both on policy in Opposition and at the Treasury in government, settled that issue and put the British two-party system back upon its throne. The late 1940s and the 1950s, even more so than the age of Gilbert and Sullivan, were the time when every child 'That's born into the world alive was either a little Liberal [Labourite] or else a little Conservative'.

Exactly how beneficial this was may be open to question. The present writer imports the scepticism of being a member of a third party, although at the time he was an enthusiastic supporter of one of the two, and that not Churchill's. But even with hindsight he would not deny that the electorate seemed more or less satisfied with their two teams, that the area over which they disputed was sufficiently circumscribed as not to endanger constitutional or other stability, and that it was a classical period, as much so as the age of Gladstone and Disraeli, for the working of the British two-party system.

What emphatically did not occur was the creation of a new national dynamic. About the mid-point in this Churchill premiership Leicester was adjudged on some reputable scale of measurement to be the most prosperous city in Europe. Less than forty years later neither it nor any other British city could be put within the first hundred. That clearly cannot be exclusively blamed on the government under which the country enjoyed the final phase of this relative prosperity. But in those years when austerity had at last been successfully surmounted, but Britain had not satisfactorily carried through the adjustment from its wartime glory to the realities of its post-war position, most of the fallacies which subsequently bedevilled us can be seen floating around in official thinking and uncontradicted by ministerial leadership. But it could hardly have been expected that a second Churchill government, inevitably existing in a glow of nostalgia for the first and greater one, would make the necessary break with the trappings of world power. At least it did not commit the two great errors—not going to the Messina Conference of 1955 which led on to the Treaty of Rome, and plunging into Suez—of its successor.

29

Churchill the Parliamentarian, Orator, and Statesman

ROBERT RHODES JAMES

W INSTON CHURCHILL'S extraordinary life and career, and the astonishing variety of his interests, involvements, and achievements, makes it difficult for the historian to take one particular aspect without unwittingly distorting the whole picture. It is also only too easy to miss the main point about this phenomenon—namely, that he was a human being and a very fallible one. To dehumanize Churchill, to make him an all-wise automaton that poured out speeches, books, articles, and military decrees, does him no service at all. Indeed, it was his very humanity, his failures as well as his triumphs, his weaknesses as well as his strengths, that make him so fascinating.

When I first visited the United States in 1965, I was astonished to find that so many Americans still loathed Franklin D. Roosevelt, one of Britain's great heroes. Similarly, many Americans and Canadians were astonished and shocked to discover that so many in Britain had hated and distrusted Churchill, even during his war leadership. They also found it difficult to accept that his denigrators had any real cause for their hostility, and thought that the fault lay entirely with them, and not with him. But I remember watching a newsreel in an Oxford cinema in 1954 of his eightieth birthday honours by Parliament in Westminster Hall when a large element in the audience booed him. There are those in Australia and New Zealand who will never forgive him for Gallipoli. The survivors of Bomber Command remain bitter that they received no campaign medal and that their Commander-in-Chief was so scurvily treated at the end of the war. There were many who echoed the comment of Churchill's closest friend, Lord Birkenhead, that 'When Winston is right he is unique. When he is wrong—Oh My God!'[1]

When I entitled my study of his life and career up to 1939 *A Study In Failure*,[2] there were many raised eyebrows, but the fact was that in 1939 as he entered his sixty-fifth year he had been out of office for ten years, and that his total following in the House of Commons consisted of Robert Boothby, Brendan Bracken, and his son-in-law Duncan Sandys. Even those most strongly opposed to Chamberlainite appeasement kept well clear of him, so low was his public standing. If he had died in 1939, he would have been written off as another Lord Randolph—a brilliant start and great talents brought to nothing by errors of judgement and character flaws that were more important than the qualities.

This was a very widespread view—indeed, in political circles a virtually universal one. Nor was it unreasonable—although excessively harsh—as his admiring biographers have alleged. To them, he never put a foot wrong throughout his long life. The fact is that he did. His egotism, which was one of his great strengths, was repellent to many. Outside his family he had remarkably few real friends. Working with Churchill, and under him, could be, and often was, a disagreeable experience. His loving daughter Mary Soames has made it clear in her wonderful book about her parents that her father could be impossible at times, even at home.[3]

He was, in short, a genius, and such people are complicated, much larger than life, self-enfolded, hungry for power and fame, passionately ambitious, and often inconsiderate of others. In Churchill's case these aspects were softened by his humanity, kindness, sensitivity, and, above all, a glorious sense of humour and capacity as a conversationalist. Oh, that he had had a Boswell!

Let us have a little glimpse of what we have lost. In 1948 Robert Boothby spent a day with the Churchills in Provence, and recorded the experience immediately afterwards. It was a day of much excellent food and drink, much conversation and argument, and a fair amount of chaos. This was part of Boothby's record:

Lunch was all right: Langouste mayonnaise, soufflé, a couple of bottles of champagne on ice, and a bottle of Volnay, topped up with brandy.

'I find alcohol a great support in life,' he said, 'Sir Alexander Walker, who keeps me supplied with your native brew [whisky] told me that a friend of his, who died the other day, drank a bottle of whisky a day for the last ten years of his life. He was eighty-five.' 'If you ever gave it up,' I replied, 'You'd die.'

Then: 'If I become Prime Minister again, I shall give up cigars. For there will be no more smoking. We cannot afford it.' 'What,' I said, 'None at all?'

'Well, only a small ration for everyone. And then a black market in coupons, organized by the government, so that anyone who couldn't give it up would have to pay through the nose!'

'You'd better not say that before the election!' I said.

'I shan't', he answered.

At the end of this extraordinary day of heat and chaos, Boothby found a bistro where they served beer. To quote Boothby's account again:

'It is cool, but not cold,' Winston said with truth. Two pails of ice immediately appeared. Clemmie ordered a lemonade, and peace was gradually restored. 'I hate the taste of beer,' Clemmie said. 'So do most people, to begin with,' he answered, 'It is, however, a prejudice that many have been able to overcome.'[4]

What always baffled his contemporaries about Churchill, and will continue to mystify his biographers, was that he was a mass of contradictions, in which he closely resembled someone with whom his relations were stormy—Charles de Gaulle. Both were soldiers, men of action of great physical and moral courage. Each regarded himself as a man of destiny who in their person embodied their peoples; they read deeply in the histories of their nations, and others; each seemed to others to be separate, aloof, utterly egotistical, and even ruthless, but de Gaulle dedicated immense time and sensitivity to his adored mentally handicapped daughter, and Churchill was sentimental, and not ashamed of tears. There was a hardness in both, but also gentleness and compassion. Each of them wrote and spoke incomparably. I was present at that unforgettable occasion when de Gaulle came to London on a state visit in 1959. In Westminster Hall, in front of a huge audience of professional speakers, de Gaulle held us enraptured with a faultless delivery, without notes, of a speech of which we all had the text, and, with a grand gesture that rolled away all the disputes and animosities of the past, referred to 'Le Grand Churchill'. Churchill burst into tears, and the entire audience trembled with emotion, knowing that we were present at a great reconciliation between two very great, and pretty impossible, men. They were also, both of them, rather lonely men, who preferred to march alone rather than in company, and who in old age reflected rather more on what they had *not* achieved than on what they had. Both had a strong romantic streak, but also one of melancholy, and both were subject to periods of deep depression and unhappiness. This is, perhaps, the price of genius and greatness.

Both were great war leaders, but also in peacetime shared a vision of

Europe. It was a different vision, it is true, but a vision none the less. Both wanted desperately to be great leaders in peace as in war, and in their way they both succeeded. Where would Britain and France be now if Churchill and de Gaulle had not lived, and not conveyed to their compatriots their own burning faiths in their own peoples? Perhaps Roosevelt was in the same league of national leaders. Perhaps, oddly enough, Hitler was, whereas Stalin and Mao were not, for all their military achievements. Neither Churchill nor de Gaulle underestimated Hitler or the German people, and both assumed the lead after the war in extending the hand of friendship to the latter—which took some political courage, in which neither was lacking.

Both, also, shared the same political fate after victory: in 1945, they were both rejected by their peoples. They fell from power and adulation to impotence and what was thought to be obscurity. Churchill retreated to Chartwell and his memoirs, de Gaulle to Colombey-les-Deux-Eglises (where, to make matters more complicated, there is in fact only *one* church) and *his* memoirs. But both came back: Churchill as Prime Minister again, de Gaulle as President of France, Churchill resolved to deliver mankind from the ghastly shadow of thermo-nuclear war, de Gaulle to deliver France from the nightmares of Algeria and Indo-China.

We, who are *not* great, who are not leaders in peace or in war, should always retain the capacity to recognize greatness—not slavishly, nor in mindless adulation, because that is not the way in democracies, nor should it ever be. Churchill, for all his aristocratic background—and there are those in Britain who do not regard the Churchills as aristocratic at all, but as a bunch of opportunistic adventurers—was a democrat, and believed passionately in democracy. He much preferred to win—and so do we all—but he accepted the verdict of the people. So did de Gaulle.

When Clement Attlee was once asked if Churchill had been a great Parliamentarian, he replied: 'No. He was a great parliamentary figure.'[5] To those outside politics this might seem a fine distinction, and somewhat ungenerous to the author of some of the greatest speeches ever delivered in the history of the House of Commons, but Attlee, as so often, had made a wise comment. Nor was it in any way to Churchill's discredit.

Churchill was not a natural speaker, unlike his father, Lord Randolph Churchill, who was one of the most remarkable opportunists in modern Parliamentary history, or Lloyd George, whose final decisive intervention, in the famous Norway debate of 7–8 May 1940, was unplanned and impromptu. Churchill frankly admitted this defect: 'I had never the practice which comes to young men at the university of speaking in small debating societies impromptu on all sorts of subjects', as he himself wrote, adding that for many years he was unable to say anything in public that he had not prepared and written out beforehand and learned by heart. His Harrow school days may have been scholastically barren, but learning by heart was an attribute at which he had excelled.[6]

What puzzled those who knew him best was that this most articulate man was so totally dependent on detailed prior preparation. Robert Boothby has vividly described the miseries, when he was Churchill's Parliamentary private secretary in the 1920s, of the lengthy preparations for even a minor speech, and the weird organization of the final speaking draft, almost like a musical score, of which Martin Gilbert has reproduced some memorable examples. But, as Boothby noted, 'It can be said of Churchill, as it was of Burns, that his conversation is better than anything he has ever written: and those who have not had the opportunity of listening to it can hardly appreciate the full quality of the man.' Also, virtually all his books and articles were, in whole or in substantial part, dictated. In his own words: 'I lived from mouth to hand.' In a very real sense, he wrote his speeches and spoke his books.[7]

Determined to succeed, the young Churchill dedicated himself to acquiring the art of oratory. In 1897 he wrote an unpublished essay on 'The Scaffolding of Rhetoric'.[8] And in his only novel, *Savrola* (1900), a work strangely neglected by Churchill scholars as it is a very revealing self-portrait, Churchill clearly had himself in mind when he wrote of Savrola: 'He . . . knew that nothing good can be obtained without effort. These impromptu feats of oratory existed only in the minds of the listeners: the flowers of rhetoric were hothouse plants.'[9]

This was certainly true in Churchill's case, but it is significant that he used the word 'rhetoric'. It was as an orator that he aspired to achieve. By sheer diligence, and hours and even days of preparation, he did achieve what Harold Nicolson marvellously described as 'the combination of great flights of oratory with sudden swoops to the intimate and conversational'.[10] But this was written of the older Churchill in his prime. His first major speech in the Commons, on 12 May 1901, took six weeks to prepare. It was a strong denunciation of his government's decision to increase the size of the army, and the eloquent pacifism of his early speeches was notable. Thus:

Europe is now groaning beneath the weight of armies. There is scarcely a single important government whose finances are not embarrassed; there is not a parliament or people from whom the cry of weariness has not been wrung . . . What a pity it would be if, just at the moment when there is good hope of a change, our statesmen were to commit us to the old and vicious policy! Is it not a much more splendid dream that this realm of England should be found bold enough and strong enough to send forth for the wings of honest purpose the message which the Russian Emperor tried vainly to proclaim: that the cruel and clanking struggle of armaments is drawing to a close, and that with the new century has come a clearer and calmer sky?[11]

To an exceptional extent, Churchill's oratory mirrored the real man. As Violet Bonham Carter noted: 'There was nothing false, inflated, artificial in his eloquence. It was his natural idiom. His world was built and fashioned in heroic lines. He spoke its language.'[12] Isaiah Berlin, in what remains one of the most thoughtful and penetrating analyses of Churchill ever written, later wrote: 'Churchill is preoccupied by his own vivid world, and it is doubtful how far he has ever been aware of what actually goes on in the heads or hearts of others. He does not react, he acts: he does not mirror, he affects others and alters them to his own powerful measure.'[13]

This essential feature of Churchill's personality, so clearly reflected in his oratory, was evident from an early age. The war correspondent G. W. Steevens, the first to draw attention publicly to Churchill's extraordinary potential, noted this as early as 1898,[14] and Charles Masterman wrote of the young Churchill:

In nearly every case an idea enters his head from the outside. It then rolls round the hollow of his brain, collecting strength like a snowball. Then, after whirling winds of rhetoric, he becomes convinced that it is right: and denounces every one who criticises it. He is in the Greek sense a rhetorician, the slave of the words which his mind forms about ideas. He sets ideas to rhetoric as musicians set theirs to music. And he can convince himself of almost every truth if it is once allowed thus to start on its wild career through his rhetorical machinery.[15]

In 1921 A. G. Gardiner put it more pithily: 'He does not want to hear your views. He does not want to disturb the beautiful clarity of his thought by the tiresome reminders of the other side. What has he to do with the other side when his side is the right side? He is not arguing with you; he is telling you.'[16]

On 22 April 1904 Churchill had a Parliamentary disaster. Again pretending to be making an impromptu speech, for once his memory let him down. He completely forgot what he was going to say next, and had to resume his seat in a shocked silence. Many members had unforgettable and tragic memories of Lord Randolph's last speeches, and wondered whether there was a fatal and hereditary weakness. Churchill never made a speech without copious notes to hand ever again.[17]

Churchill was not, of course, the only great orator or preacher who has had to write and prepare his speeches meticulously, and then read them out. A classic example was Abraham Lincoln. His Gettysburg Address contained ten sentences, lasted for five minutes, and was the result of many weeks of thought, writing, rewriting, and revising. Lincoln spoke from his text, as Churchill had to do. Before Lincoln, Edward Everett, the great orator of the day, had spoken for two hours, and no-one can remember anything he said. Similarly, great orators like Gladstone and Lloyd George held huge audiences spellbound, but their impact was immediate—and ephemeral. When Richard Sheridan made his great speech at the trial of Warren Hastings, it was regarded by Fox, Burke, and the Younger Pitt as utterly phenomenal, Pitt declaring that 'it passed all the eloquence of ancient and modern times', but who remembers it? Sheridan's enduring fame is as a writer and playwright of genius, and it usually comes as a surprise to his admirers that he was also a formidable politician. The closest comparison with Churchill, however, is Edmund Burke, whose ponderous style and poor diction emptied the House of Commons, but who read out some of the finest speeches in the English language. Read by others, they had an immense impact, but not on his immediate audience—as at Gettysburg.

The great impromptu orator relies on his audience to inspire him. As Gladstone once revealingly remarked: 'I wish you knew the state of total impotence to which I should be reduced if there were no echo to the accents of my own voice.' Lloyd George, also, was temperamentally dependent on his audience. As was remarked of him, 'If he was alone in a room, the room was empty.'

Curiously enough, Churchill's son Randolph was an outstanding natural orator, who could speak impromptu with great eloquence and fervour on almost any subject. This was a fatal defect. He did not have to work at his speeches as his father had to, and only made one memorable remark in his life when he described the ethos of the great press magnates as 'Sonofabitch don't eat sonofabitch'. It all came too easily to Randolph, and too early, with disastrous results.

The trouble with his father's technique in Parliamentary terms is that it is impossible to gauge the mood of the House of Commons in advance. Indeed, that mood can change rapidly from hour to hour, almost from minute to minute. One moment it is relaxed and good-humoured, at the next, it can be angry and venomous, and the House—any House—in this mood is a frightening spectacle, especially for the recipient of its wrath. Churchill had not only to try to antici-pate its varying moods, but to impose his views upon it. This was to lead to some spectacular disasters and, ultimately, to his greatest tri-umphs. Attlee's comment was absolutely true. Churchill would have been incapable of making the epic spontaneous speech that Lloyd George made in May 1940 in the debate that made Churchill Prime Minister. But politics are not about speaking techniques. As Lord Rosebery wrote of Chatham's oratory, 'It is not merely the thing that is said, but the man who says it that counts, the character which breathes through the sentences.'

This was the problem. Churchill's burning personal ambition was manifest. It was believed, probably rightly, that if Arthur Balfour had given him office in 1902 Churchill would not have developed such a burning interest in free trade and joined the Liberals after a series of scathing speeches against his government and party and their leaders. Even before he defected to the Liberal Party in 1904 he was deeply unpopular, even reviled, on the Unionist benches. The experienced political commentator, Henry Lucy, a great admirer of Lord Randolph, wrote tartly that 'Winston Churchill may be safely counted upon to make himself quite as disagreeable on the Liberal side as he did on the Unionist. But he will always be handicapped by the aversion that always pertains to a man who, in whatsoever honourable circumstances, has turned his coat.'[18]

That was putting it very mildly, and there was great pleasure—not confined to the Opposition benches—when his first ministerial speech in 1906 was a celebrated catastrophe. 'The harshness of utterance which in its proper place is one of Winston's assets as a speaker, asserted itself out of season', his new private secretary, Eddie Marsh, sadly noted.[19] The exultant Conservatives claimed that he was finished. They were destined to make the same claim on numerous other occa-sions. They were to find that he was, like Mr Gladstone, 'Terrible on the rebound'. They never liked him, and he never liked them.

This was a classic example of Churchill's fundamental problem as a Parliamentarian. He had got the mood wrong, he knew he had got it wrong, but there was no escape from the carefully prepared text. It was characteristic that he recovered: his next speech was a success, and his outstanding qualities as a minister became recognized. But there was always the lurking fear of a repetition—and repetitions there were to be, the last one as late as 1954.

But it was 'the character breathing through the sentences' that worried the House of Commons, and his friends and colleagues. His egotistical personal ambition was manifest and unconcealed. The flamboyance of his demeanour, the floridity of his oratory, and his great capacity for abuse of his opponents were difficult enough to take. Even before he went to the Admiralty in 1911, there were major questions being asked about his stability and judgement, and not least by his own Prime Minister, H. H. Asquith, and colleagues. There seemed no controversy into which he would not plunge himself with partisan ardour, and the fact that his scathing philippics were known to have been carefully prepared in advance made them all the more difficult to take. Bonar Law was not the only member of Parliament who came not only to distrust Churchill deeply, but actively to loathe him. A more sensitive Parliamentarian would have recognized these very obvious warning signals, but Churchill hurtled on, heedless of them. When he crashed in May 1915 over the Dardanelles, he was genuinely astonished to realize how few political friends he had.[20]

For the rest of his life, Churchill was as obsessed with his role at Gallipoli as he was with the Bolshevik menace (which he had to suppress temporarily between 1941 and 1945). He could not understand why so many blamed him personally for Gallipoli, and when he described it as 'A legitimate war gamble' the relatives of the 46,000 who had perished were incensed. His leading role in the British intervention in the Russian Civil War in 1919–20, and the ferocity of his language, were deeply unwelcome to a nation that had passed through a terrible war and craved for peace and not for more military adventures—and especially one that, again, totally failed. In the Chanak Crisis of 1922 he was all for fighting the Turks over again at the Dardanelles, but the House of Commons, truly reflecting British and Commonwealth public opinion, had had enough of this warlike sword-rattling and latter-day imperialism. The Lloyd George coalition fell, and with it, Churchill. He had fatally misjudged the national mood, and that of the House of Commons. He was astounded by his downfall. No-one else was.

The trouble was that Churchill was only interested in office and power. This was his natural habitat, not the House of Commons. Furthermore, he did not make speeches *to* the House, but *at* it. Also, if the division records for the quite exceptionally severe session of 1911 are any guide, he does not appear to have gone there very much. He certainly did not woo or try to seduce the most jealous institution in the world.

The developing power of his oratory was conceded, but he had over-valued its potency. In his early essay on rhetoric he wrote that 'abandoned by his party, betrayed by his friends, stripped of his offices, whoever can command this power is still formidable'.[21] This was prophetic indeed, but as he was to find in 1915, 1922, and in the terrible 1930s, rhetoric by itself is not enough. He simply did not arouse either affection or trust, and, having forfeited these crucial assets, his political fortunes disintegrated at the first severe test.

The curious feature of all this was that Churchill revered the House of Commons. Boothby, in writing of his outstanding physical and political courage, amounting in both cases on occasion to foolhardiness, remarked that Churchill was frightened of only one thing—the House of Commons.[22] And this was because he was never really at home in it, unlike Lloyd George who, asked on an empty Friday why on earth he was hanging around the House, replied that 'To anyone with politics in his blood, this place is like a pub to a drunkard.'[23] Churchill would have been in his department if in office, at Chartwell if out of it, writing, painting, reorganizing the grounds, or brick-laying, and certainly not wasting his time at the House of Commons.

Churchill's attitude to party did not help much, either. The celebrated jibe that he regarded party rather as a rider regards his horse, not minding much about it provided that it carried him safely and comfortably, had much truth in it. He was in turn Conservative, Liberal, Lloyd George Coalitionist, 'Constitutionalist and Anti-Socialist', a Conservative again, without appearing to care which side he was on provided that it was the winning one. There was enough validity in this charge to harm his already flawed reputation.

Churchill's tenure at the Treasury under Baldwin between 1924 and 1929 was unsuccessful: indeed, it was the only office he did not adorn. His vehement opposition to the granting of a modest degree of Dominion status to India between 1931 and 1935 was not only wrong, but prompted him to use language so excessively offensive about the Indian leaders that when he turned his attention to the infinitely more real menace looming in Europe no-one was listening. His prolonged campaign against the Government of India Act 1935, described as 'Winston's six-year war', not only devalued the language of alarmism, and discredited his judgement, but bored the House of Commons. For once in his career, these lengthy interventions and marathon sessions do not even read very impressively and, unsurprisingly, were in the main delivered to empty benches.[24]

The boredom threshold of any House of Commons is very low, and the one-issue politician empties the chamber with remarkable rapidity. Also, those Conservatives who supported Churchill on this futile enterprise were from the extreme right, and only agreed with him on this issue. Thus, when he began to deliver his warnings about Hitler and the need to rearm, they ignored him, and his personal support was limited to Brendan Bracken and Bob Boothby. He was almost totally isolated. After he had been howled down by an enraged House of Commons over the abdication crisis in December 1936, in itself a colossal Parliamentary misjudgement, his position was so hopeless that even his few supporters were in despair—as was he—and looked elsewhere for their leadership against Chamberlain and appeasement.

The tragedy, of course, was that these were, until 1940, the greatest speeches of his life. When one reads them one asks oneself again and again, 'Why didn't they *listen*?' The easy answer, that he was speaking to a craven audience of wishful thinkers and party hacks (on both sides), contains an element of truth, but it was to be exactly that House of Commons that was to give him such staunch support between 1940 and 1945, and which indeed made him Prime Minister. The harsh reality is that he was so widely distrusted and disliked by his Parliamentary colleagues that they did not believe him. The anti-Chamberlain dissidents in the Conservative Party kept well clear of him, regarding him as a major liability, gravitating to Leo Amery and Anthony Eden. In one of many such cabals it was agreed that Churchill would make a very good minister of supply![25]

Nothing demonstrates Churchill's isolation more graphically than the fact, which to my generation remains astonishing, that the first and virtually unanimous choice as Chamberlain's replacement in May 1940 was not Churchill, but Lord Halifax. This was not a bad example of how politicians can get out of touch not only with reality but with a very changed mood in public opinion. Churchill's appointment as Prime Minister was not well received by the House of Commons. All contemporary accounts testify to the cold reception he had on his first appearance in the Chamber as Prime Minister, compared to the warmth of the response to the deposed Neville Chamberlain.

One aspect of Churchill's oratory that is usually neglected is the fact that he was a poet in prose, using utterly unexpected words and phrases that suddenly transformed a narrative or an argument into something quite different, and the knowledge that this could happen— and usually did—could hold his audience. The wartime speeches in the Commons provide many examples, but by then he had in one respect emulated Cromwell, of whom Clarendon wrote that: 'Yet as he grew in place and authority, his parts seemed to be raised, as if he had concealed faculties, till he had occasion to use them.' But this quality could be seen from the beginning, and one example was his speech in April 1925 at the unveiling of the memorial to the Royal Naval Division, which he had founded, and which had been derided as 'Winston's Private Army'.

We are often tempted to ask ourselves what we gained by the enormous sacrifices made by those to whom this memorial is erected. But this was never the issue with those who marched away. No question of advantage presented itself to their minds. They only saw the light shining on the clear path to duty. They only saw their duty to resist oppression, to protect the weak, to vindicate the profound but unwritten Law of Nations, to testify to truth and justice and mercy among men. They never asked the question 'What shall we gain?' They asked only the question 'Where lies the right?' It was thus that they marched away for ever, and yet from their uncalculating exaltation and devotion, detached from all consideration of material gain, we may be sure that good will come to their countrymen and to this island they guarded in its reputation and safety so faithfully and so well.[26]

Much has often been made of the simplicity of Churchill's oratory, and the use of short words and short sentences. In reality, he had the capacity to take very complex themes and topics, and reduce them not to simplicities and clichés but to terms that others could understand without being talked down to. George Sampson once pondered on that age-old miracle, the power of words arranged in a certain order: 'You take a few words, you put them together, and in a way not explicable, they flash into life, and you have not a sentence but a song, a revelation, a new creation, a joy forever.' And then there is this example of Churchill's poetry in prose:

When great causes are on the move in the world, stirring all men's souls, drawing them from their firesides, casting aside comfort, wealth, and the pursuit of happiness in response to impulses at once awe-striking and irresistible, we learn that we are spirits, not animals, and that something is going on in space and time which, whether we like it or not, spells duty.

But the test of Parliamentary oratory is less its quality, but its persuasive power, and it was in this that, until 1939, Churchill failed. The days of oratory in the Commons had passed. The new style was conversational, give and take, cut and thrust, not the prepared oration reeking of midnight oil. Thus, Churchill's magnificent speech on Munich—'All is over. Silent, mournful, abandoned, broken, Czechoslovakia receded into the darkness'—was a failure. Hardly anyone wanted to hear this, and when he described Munich as a 'total and unmitigated defeat' there was angry uproar.[27] It was only in March 1939 that the British woke up to the grim fact that he had been right, and that the policy of sleep-walking and wishful thinking had led the country to the verge of catastrophe. But, even then, Churchill did not convince the House of Commons. Events had to do that for him. As he told Anthony Eden at 10 Downing Street in June 1940, 'Had it not been for Hitler, neither of us would be in this room.'

But, then, Churchill's weaknesses as a Parliamentarian were totally and marvellously eclipsed by one speech—the brief and unforgettable 'Blood, Toil, Tears and Sweat' speech. Here, he was indeed imposing his views and his character and his resolve on the House of Commons, whether they liked it or not. The effect was electrifying. As he walked out of the chamber he said to his devoted friend and aide, Desmond Morton, 'That got the SODS, didn't it!'[28]

There were to be other great Parliamentary performances during the war, but that was the turning-point. The poet and the patriot in him radiated forth. He was still speaking at the House of Commons, but it was now listening, and cheering. And he was later to write that even at the height of the crises in the war 'I did not begrudge twelve hours preparing a speech to the House of Commons'. The previous defect had become the most wonderful of virtues.

After the war, he was generally considered to have been a poor leader of the Opposition. It was not a chore that he relished, and his performances in the Commons were not highly rated by either side. There were many who wished that he had taken the advice of, among others, his wife, that he had retired in glory in 1945. But in his second premiership, between 1951 and 1955, although the old disadvantages remained obvious, and could cause difficulties, his mere arrival in the chamber caused a ripple of excitement not only in the galleries, but on the floor of the House. His fluency in replying to questions got better and better, and he had a marvellous Indian summer.

Although Churchill always had to prepare his speeches, one of the features of his character and wartime premiership that had come as a surprise to the House of Commons, although not to friends, was his spontaneous sense of humour and wit. In his early years this had been rather ponderous, and smelt of preparation. Now, at ease with himself and the House, the wit came bubbling out—when he was in the mood. There were days when he came in glowering and bad-tempered, and all could see at once what his mood was. There were some quite ugly Parliamentary episodes during that Parliament, but also ones of rocking laughter. His eightieth birthday tributes in Westminster Hall were absolutely genuine and warm, and his own speech of thanks a gentle masterpiece.[29]

But so was his last major speech to the House of Commons, on 1 March 1955, on the nuclear deterrent, in which he expressed the hope that 'Safety will be the sturdy child of terror, and survival the twin brother of annihilation', and ending: 'The day may dawn when fair play, love for one's fellow-man, respect for justice and freedom, will enable tormented generations to march forth serene and triumphant from the hideous epoch in which we have to dwell. Meanwhile, never flinch, never weary, never despair.'[30] This was indeed 'the character breathing through the sentences' again.

Apart from an interlude between November 1922 and October 1924 Churchill had been a Member of Parliament, for various constituencies and various parties, since 1900. After his retirement as Prime Minister in April 1955, which was not as voluntary as was believed at the time, he remained in the Commons until the 1964 general election. Old age and a hard life now exacted their toll, and his appearances were not frequent. He made only one intervention, when Hugh Gaitskell charmingly congratulated him on his birthday. The old man rose, bowed, and expressed his thanks. The entire House glowed.[31]

Towards the end of his membership he was in a wheelchair, but he was invariably cheered as he made his way to his seat below the gangway assisted by a team of Conservative MPs. His mere arrival caused excitement, and a different feeling. Afterwards, he would often be wheeled into the smoking-room, the one place in the Palace of Westminster where he felt at home. Once a new Conservative MP timorously asked him if he would like a cup of tea. Churchill glared at him and said 'No. Don't be a bloody fool. I want a *large* glass of whisky!'[32]

Lady Churchill's role in Churchill's amazing Parliamentary and political career has been marvellously described by their daughter, Lady Soames.[33] What people loved Churchill for, and others hated him for, was his assumption of his own destiny ('Over me beat the invisible wings'). But, love it or hate it, this was an essential aspect of his character, so perfectly described by Isaiah Berlin:

As much as any king conceived by a renaissance dramatist or by a nineteenth century historian or moralist, he thinks it a brave thing to ride in triumph through Persepolis, he knows with an unshakeable certainty what he considers to be big, handsome, noble and worthy of pursuit by someone in high station, and what, on the contrary, he abhors as being dim, grey, thin, likely to lower or destroy the play of colour and movement in the universe.[34]

This inspired many. It repelled many others, who resented their supporting role in the drama. But when the French Resistance came, at their own expense, to raise and lower their banners at his funeral when his coffin passed by, and the notoriously bloody-minded socialist dock workers voluntarily dipped their cranes in homage when the boat carrying him passed by, one had the complete answer. London's East End remembered him. They had never voted for him, but at a terrible time they had stood and suffered together. And so, in a London context, he did indeed ride in triumph through Persepolis. As his funeral train chugged through the Oxfordshire countryside to Bladon there were crowds everywhere, but what his family never forgot was an old man standing alone in a field, in RAF uniform and with his medals, saluting, with tears streaming down his face. Silently, he was speaking for England—and for countless millions of others. He was also saying, in Churchill's own words in another context: 'We are not ashamed to be grateful.'

But let us return to the last words of the prescient *Savrola*:

Those who care to further follow the annals of the republic of Laurania may read how, after the tumults had subsided, the hearts of the people turned again to the illustrious exile who had won them freedom and whom they had deserted in the hour of victory. They may, scoffing at the fickleness of men, read of the return of Savrola and his beautiful escort to the city he had loved so well.

And thus it came to pass.

NOTES

CHAPTER 1

1 C. V. Balsan, *The Glitter and the Gold* (New York, 1952), 72; D. Cannadine, *The Decline and Fall of the British Aristocracy* (London, 1990), 680.

2 C. P. Snow, *Variety of Men* (Harmondsworth, 1969), 125, 131; J. R. Colville, *The Churchillians* (1981), 4, 10, 20.

3 W. S. Churchill, *My Early Life* (New York, 1939 edn.), 62, 151–2, 162–3.

4 R. S. Churchill and M. Gilbert, *Winston S. Churchill* (8 vols., 1966–88, and 5 companion vols. so far), i. 517.

5 This is the general thesis advanced in R. Rhodes James, *Churchill: A Study in Failure, 1900–1939* (Harmondsworth, 1973 edn.).

6 Ibid. 16.

7 R. F. Foster, *Lord Randolph Churchill: A Political Life* (Oxford, 1981), 127.

8 A. L. Rowse, *The Later Churchills* (Harmondsworth, 1971), 237–40, 249–50.

9 P. Magnus, *King Edward VII* (London, 1964), 185–93; P. Churchill and J. Mitchell, *Jennie, Lady Randolph Churchill: A Portrait with Letters* (London, 1974), 87–104; Foster, *Lord Randolph Churchill*, 9–16; Rowse, *Later Churchills*, 274–9.

10 Foster, *Lord Randolph Churchill*, 122–4, 376.

11 R. S. Churchill, *Churchill*, companion vol. ii, part 1, pp. 487–90; M. Ashley, *Churchill as Historian* (London, 1968), 1–5.

12 Balsan, *Glitter and the Gold*, 42–54, 187–212; H. Vickers, *Gladys, Duchess of Marlborough* (1979), 51, 69, 106–7, 134, 172, 213, 223, 225–33; S. Leslie, *Long Shadows* (London, 1966), 236–9; Magnus, *Edward VII*, 497.

13 Foster, *Lord Randolph Churchill*, 24, 30, 59, 96–7, 217–19, 349; R. G. Martin, *Jennie: The Life of Lady Randolph Churchill*, i: *The Romantic Years, 1854–1895* (London, 1969), 56–7, 110–11, 152–3, 177–8, 307–8, 321–35.

14 Magnus, *Edward VII*, 191–3; Rhodes James, *Study in Failure*, 22.

15 Mrs George Cornwallis-West, *The Reminiscences of Lady Randolph Churchill* (New York, 1908), preface, 362–85.

16 R. G. Martin, *Jennie: The Life of Lady Randolph Churchill*, ii: *The Dramatic Years, 1895–1921* (London, 1971), 190–1, 389.

17 M. Soames, *Clementine Churchill* (London, 1979), 1–11, 26–7, 199, 213.

18 *The Times*, 25 Feb. 1947; R. Hough, *Winston and Clementine: The Triumphs and Tragedies of the Churchills* (New York, 1991), 26, 47, 150, 372, 422.

19 R. S. Churchill, *Churchill*, companion vol. ii, part 2, pp. 695–7, 704, 728, 736; J. R. Colville, *The Fringes of Power: Downing Street Diaries, 1939–1955* (London, 1985), 210.

20 Lord Birkenhead, *Churchill, 1872–1922* (London, 1989), 526–52.

21 D. Irving, *Churchill's War*, i: *The Struggle For Power* (Bullsbrook, Western Australia, 1987), 169.

22 Rhodes James, *Study in Failure*, 272; Gilbert, *Churchill*, v. 592–3; B. Roberts, *Randolph: A Study of Churchill's Son* (London, 1984), 130–9, 140–2, 153–6.

23 R. S. Churchill, *Churchill*, companion vol. ii, part 1, pp. 239, 393; Foster, *Lord Randolph Churchill*, 16.

24 J. R. Vincent (ed.), *The Crawford Papers: The Journals of David Lindsay, Twenty-*

Seventh Earl of Crawford, and Tenth Earl of Balcarres, 1871–1940, During the Years 1882–1940 (Manchester, 1984), 73; N. Blewett, *The Peers, the Parties and the People: The General Elections of 1910* (London, 1972), 374–6, 465 n. 1, 478 nn. 68–70; H. Pelling, *Social Geography of British Elections, 1885–1910* (London, 1967), 135–6.

25 *The Times*, 15 June 1939; M. and E. Brock (eds.), *H. H. Asquith: Letters to Venetia Stanley* (Oxford, 1982), 161, 162 n. 2.

26 R. S. Churchill, *Churchill*, companion vol. ii, part 3, p. 1393; Gilbert, *Churchill*, companion vol. iii, part 1, p. 268; Brocks, *Asquith Letters*, 254, 273, 278, 313, 377, 637.

27 T. Cullen, *Maundy Gregory: Purveyor of Honours* (London, 1974), pp. 93–5, 103–5, 107–9; Brocks, *Asquith Letters*, 383.

28 G. Searle, *Corruption in British Politics, 1895–1930* (Oxford, 1987), 382; *The Times*, 29 Apr. 1937.

29 H. M. Hyde, *The Londonderrys: A Family Chronicle* (London, 1979), 109–10, 136–43, 157, 163, 170–9, 208–9, 213, 217–18, 238, 253, 256, 261; R. S. Churchill, *Churchill*, companion vol. ii, part 3, pp. 1382–7.

30 M. Cowling, *The Impact of Hitler: British Politics and British Policy, 1933–1940* (Cambridge, 1975), 240–1; Gilbert, *Churchill*, v. 191–204, 217–18, 635–40, 731–3, 873, 1019–20.

31 Cannadine, *Decline and Fall*, 416–17.

32 Viscount Churchill, *Be All My Sins Remembered* (New York, 1965), 11, 40–3, 51, 85–126, 138–56.

33 A. Leslie, *Mr Frewen of England* (London, 1966), 202; A. Andrews, *The Splendid Pauper* (London, 1968), 215.

34 S. Leslie, *Studies in Sublime Failure* (London, 1932), 247–95.

35 S. Leslie, *The End of a Chapter* (London, 1916), pp. iii, 16, 164–6, 183; idem, *The Irish Tangle for English Readers* (London, 1943), 11–13, 146–52.

36 *Dictionary of National Biography (DNB), 1971–80*, 501–2; S. Leslie, *The Fulness of Memory* (London, 1938), 118–19, 145, 373–6.

37 R. S. Churchill, *Churchill*, companion vol. ii, part 1, pp. 591–4.

38 G. Cornwallis-West, *Edwardian Hey-Days: Or, A Little About a Lot of Things* (London, 1930), 118–27, 158–69; E. Quelch, *Perfect Darling: The Life and Times of George Cornwallis-West* (London, 1972), 81–3, 102–4, 128–9, 144, 149–51, 164–72, 188, 192–6.

39 Cannadine, *Decline and Fall*, 387.

40 M. Harrison, *Lord of London: A Biography of the Second Duke of Westminster* (London, 1966), 1–8, 70–7, 183–91, 212, 224–7; G. D. Phillips, *The Diehards: Aristocratic Society and Politics in Edwardian England* (London, 1979), 91, 107–8; R. Rhodes James (ed.), *'Chips': The Diaries of Sir Henry Channon* (London, 1967), 477.

41 K. Ingram, *Rebel: The Short Life of Esmond Romilly* (London, 1985), 1–3, 9–15, 17–18, 42–6, 64–73, 146–8, 154–5.

42 Hough, *Winston and Clementine*, 4–5.

43 Cannadine, *Decline and Fall*, 550–4; D. Pryce-Jones, *Unity Mitford: A Quest* (London, 1976), 114–15, 169–70, 178; Colville, *Fringes of Power*, 177.

44 Foster, *Lord Randolph Churchill*, 177; Gilbert, *Churchill*, companion vol. iii, part 2, p. 1545; R. Hyam, *Elgin and Churchill at the Colonial Office, 1905–1908: The Watershed of Empire-Commonwealth* (London, 1968), 502.

45 Irving, *Churchill's War*, 33.

CHAPTER 2

1 William Manchester, *The Last Lion* (New York, 1988), i. 424. He was also blithely indifferent to its most basic rules of pronunciation, a fact that during the Second World War gave his references to members of Hitler's party, whom he called 'the Nahzzies', a doubly contemptuous, but also faintly comic, ring.

2 Isaiah Berlin, 'Winston Churchill in 1940', *Personal Impressions* (New York, 1981), 5.

3 Felix Gilbert, *History: Politics or Culture? Reflections on Ranke and Burckhardt* (Princeton, 1990), 28–30.

4 Leopold von Ranke, 'Dialogue on Politics' (1836), in Theodore H. von Laue, *Leopold von Ranke: The Formative Years* (Princeton, 1950), 168, 180.

5 Winston S. Churchill, *The Second World War*, 6 vols. (Boston, 1948 ff.), i. 66 ff.

6 Kaiser Wilhelm II 'was pleased to be sarcastic' about British apprehensions in a conversation with Churchill during the German manœuvres of 1906. Randolph S. Churchill, *Winston S. Churchill*, ii. 191.

7 R. S. Churchill, *Churchill*, ii. 301. On this, and Churchill's social policy in general, see Henry Pelling, *Winston Churchill* (2nd edn., London, 1989), 118–29.

8 Manchester, *The Last Lion*, i. 350.

9 R. S. Churchill, *Churchill*, ii. 493–4.

10 Pelling, *Churchill*, 123.

11 R. S. Churchill, *Churchill*, ii. 219.

12 Gordon A. Craig, *Germany, 1866–1945* (Oxford, 1978), 328 ff.

13 On all of this, see Paul Kennedy, *The Rise of Anglo-German Antagonism, 1860–1914* (London, 1982), 447–50.

14 R. S. Churchill, *Churchill*, ii. 504–5.

15 Ibid. 508–10.

16 Ibid. 542.

17 See E. L. Woodward, *Great Britain and the German Navy* (Oxford, 1935), chs. 18, 19, 20, 23; Lamar Cecil, *Albert Ballin: Business and Politics in Imperial Germany, 1888–1918* (Princeton, 1967), 183–98; R. S. Churchill, *Churchill*, ii. 545, 551 ff.

18 R. S. Churchill, *Churchill*, ii. 561.

19 Pelling, *Churchill*, 230.

20 Lord Newton, *Lord Lansdowne: A Biography* (London, 1929), 468–9.

21 Martin Gilbert, *Winston S. Churchill*, iv. 123.

22 Ibid. 129.

23 Ibid. 123.

24 Gilbert, *Churchill*, iii. 333–4.

25 Gilbert, *Churchill*, iv. 170–1.

26 Winston S. Churchill, *The World Crisis* (London, 1929), iv, 5.

27 Gilbert, *Churchill*, iv. 896.

28 Churchill, *Second World War*, i. 7.

29 Gilbert, *Churchill*, iv. 608–9.

30 Gordon A. Craig and Alexander L. George, *Force and Statecraft: Diplomatic Problems of Our Time* (2nd edn. New York, 1990), 22.

31 Gilbert, *Churchill*, iv. 253, 382.

32 Ibid. 897.

33 Ibid. v. 51.

34 Ibid. 406 ff.

35 *Documents on British Foreign Policy, 1919–1939*, ed. E. L. Woodward and Rohan Butler (London, 1949–), 2nd series, i. 501 n., 517.

36 Gilbert, *Churchill*, v. 408 ff.

37 See *Internationale Beziehungen während der Weltwirtschaftskrise, 1929–1933*, ed. Josef

Becker and Klaus Hildebrand (Munich, 1980), 265 ff.

38 Gaines Post, Jr, *The Civil Military Fabric of the Weimar Republic* (Princeton, 1973), 304 ff.; Michael Salewski, 'Zur deutschen Sicherheitspolitik in der Spätzeit der Weimarer Republik', *Vierteljahrsheft für Zeitgeschichte*, xxii (1974), 135, 140–3.

39 Churchill, *Second World War*, i. 72.

40 Ibid. 75.

41 Dietrich Aigner, *Das Ringen um England. Das deutsche–britische Verhältnis. Die öffentliche Meinung, 1933–1939. Tragödie zweier Völker* (Munich and Esslingen, 1969), 155. See also Aigner, *Winston S. Churchill: Ruhm und Legende* (Göttingen, 1975), and 'Pazifisten und Friedenskampfer am Vorabend des 2. Weltkrieges', *Veröffentlichung der zeitgeschichtlichen Forschungsstelle Ingolstadt*, v (Ingolstadt, 1983).

42 W. M. Jordan, *Great Britain, France, and the German Question 1918–1939* (London, 1943).

43 Martin Gilbert, *Winston Churchill: The Wilderness Years* (Boston, 1982), 154.

44 Joachim C. Fest, *Hitler: Eine Biographie* (Frankfurt am Main, 1973), 5. See also Sebastian Haffner, *Anmerkungen zu Hitler* (Munich, 1978), 54 ff.

45 Fritz Lehmann, *1939–1945. Beobachtungen und Bekenntinisse* (Hamburg, 1946), 40.

46 *Documents on British Foreign Policy*, 3rd series, i. 22, 28, 49, 109, 257, 273, 307, 345; ii. 133, 185; *Documents on German Foreign Policy: From the Archives of the German Foreign Office* (Washington, 1949–), series D, i. 221, 264, 1168. On these points see also Donald Cameron Watt, Ch. 12 in this volume.

47 See Gordon A. Craig, 'Roosevelt and Hitler: The Problem of Perception', in *Deutsche Frage und europäisches Gleichgewicht*, ed. Klaus Hildebrand and Reiner Pommerin (Cologne and Vienna, 1985).

48 David Dilks, '"We must hope for the best and prepare for the worst": The Prime Minister, the Cabinet and Hitler's Germany, 1937–1939', *Proceedings of the British Academy*, lxxiii (1987), 348.

49 John Lukacs, *The Duel: The Struggle between Churchill and Hitler, 10 May–31 July 1940* (New York, 1991), 42–7.

50 *The Second World War Diary of Hugh Dalton, 1940–1945*, ed. Ben Pimlott (London, 1986), 175.

51 Churchill, *Second World War*, v. 330; Lord Moran, *Churchill: Taken from the Diaries of Lord Moran* (Boston, 1966), 152.

52 Gilbert, *Churchill*, vii. 1025.

53 John Colville, *The Fringes of Power: Downing Street Diaries, 1939–1955* (London, 1985), 363.

54 The best book on the subject is Lothar Kettenacker, *Krieg zur Friedenssicherung: Die Deutschlandplanung der britischen Regierung während des Zweiten Weltkrieges* (Göttingen and Zurich, 1989). See also the splendid collection *Dokumente zur Deutschlandpolitik*, 1 Reihe, Bd 3: *1 Januar bis 31 Dezember 1942: Britische Deutschlandpolitik* (2 half-vols.), ed. Rainer Blasius (Frankfurt am Main, 1988).

55 On all of this see Kettenacker, *Krieg zur Friedenssicherung*, 537 ff.

56 On this, see Steven Merritt Miner, *Between Churchill and Stalin: The Soviet Union, Great Britain, and the Origins of the Grand Alliance* (Chapel Hill, 1988).

57 *The War Diaries of Oliver Harvey, 1941–1945*, ed. J. Harvey (London, 1978), 171, cited in *Dokumente zur Deutschlandpolitik*, 1 Reihe, Bd 3, 916 n.

58 Kettenacker, *Krieg zur Friedenssicherung*, 542.

59 Moran, *Diaries*, 190–1.

60 Churchill, *Second World War*, vi. 157.

61 Kettanacker, *Krieg zur Friedenssicherung*, 542.

62 Gilbert, *Churchill*, viii. 265 ff.

63 Ibid. 286 ff. See the arguments of Max Beloff (this volume, Ch. 25), who empha-
sizes that Churchill saw no place for Britain in a new European Union.

CHAPTER 3

1 Robert Rhodes James (ed.), *Winston S. Churchill: His Complete Speeches, 1897–1963*
(London, 1974), vii. 7031.
2 François Kersaudy, *Churchill and de Gaulle* (London, 1981), 372 ff.
3 Charles de Gaulle, *Mémoires: L'Unité* (Paris, 1959), 646; Duff Cooper, *Old Men
Forget* (London, 1953), 334; Kersaudy, *Churchill and de Gaulle*, 357–9.
4 Martin Gilbert, *Winston S. Churchill*, viii. 246–7.
5 Randolph Churchill, *Winston S. Churchill*, i. 154–6, 159–65.
6 S. R. Williamson, *The Politics of Grand Strategy: Britain and France Prepare for
War, 1904–1914* (Cambridge, Mass., 1969); K. I. Hamilton, 'Great Britain and
France, 1911–1914', in F. H. Hinsley (ed.), *British Foreign Policy under Sir Edward
Grey* (Cambridge, 1977); T. Wilson, 'Britain's "Moral Commitment" to France in
August 1914', *History*, 64 (1979); John F. V. Kieger, *France and the Origins of the
First World War* (London, 1983).
7 T. Higgins, *Winston Churchill and the Dardanelles* (London, 1964); C. J. Lowe, 'The
Failure of British Policy in the Balkans', *Canadian Journal of History*, 1969; G. H.
Cassar, *France and the Dardanelles* (London, 1971); J. K. Tannenbaum, *General
Maurice Sarrail 1856–1929* (Chapel Hill, 1974). The minutes of the Dardanelles
Committee are to be found in CAB 22/2/17. See also the unpublished Ph.D. thesis
by David Dutton, 'France, England and the Politics of the Salonika Campaign
(1915–1918)' (University of London, 1974).
8 Douglas Johnson, 'Austen Chamberlain and the Locarno Agreements', *University of
Birmingham Historical Journal*, 8 (1961), is based upon the Austen Chamberlain
papers.
9 Winston S. Churchill, *The Second World War* (London, 1948), i. 441–2.
10 Kersaudy, *Churchill and de Gaulle*; Gaston Palewski and Douglas Johnson, 'De Gaulle,
La Grande Bretagne et la France Libre 1940–1943', *Espoir* (Paris, June 1983).
11 Jean Lacouture, *De Gaulle*, i: *Le Rebelle* (Paris, 1984).
12 See the conversation between Churchill and Mendès France in Pierre Mendès
France, *Œuvres Complètes*, iii: *Gouverner, c'est choisir* (Paris, 1986), 245–8; vi: *Une
vision du monde* (Paris, 1990), 327–34.

CHAPTER 4

1 Martin Gilbert, *Churchill: A Life* (London, 1991), p. xix.
2 Henry Pelling, *Winston Churchill* (London, 1974), 73, quoting from the *Oldham
Standard*, 1 July 1899.
3 Randolph S. Churchill, *Winston S. Churchill*, companion vol. ii, part 1, p. 111. The
review was unpublished and undated.
4 Robert Rhodes James (ed.), *Winston S. Churchill: His Complete Speeches* (New York,
1974), i. 152–3, speech of 12 May 1902.
5 Norman and Jeanne McKenzie (eds.), *The Diary of Beatrice Webb*, ii: *1892–1905*
(London, 1986), 327, diary for 10 June 1904.
6 Rhodes James (ed.), *Complete Speeches*, i. 675–6, speech of 11 Oct. 1906.
7 Peter Clarke, *Lancashire and the New Liberalism* (Cambridge, 1971), 189–91.
8 Churchill to Alexander Murray, Master of Elibank, 28 Sept. 1906, Elibank MSS
8801, National Library of Scotland.

9 Churchill to J. A. Spender, 22 Dec. 1907, BM Add. MSS 46, 388.
10 For the social policy context and the role of the Board of Trade see Roger Davidson, 'Sir Hubert Llewellyn Smith and Labour Policy 1886–1916', Cambridge University Ph.D. thesis (1971); José Harris, *Unemployment and Politics: A Study in English Social Policy 1886–1914* (Oxford, 1972); José Harris, *William Beveridge: A Biography* (Oxford, 1977), ch. 6.
11 Lucy Masterman, *C. F. G. Masterman: A Biography* (London, 1939), 97.
12 For Churchill's impact see Harris, *Unemployment and Politics*, 276–7, 293–4; Bentley B. Gilbert, *The Evolution of National Insurance in Great Britain* (London, 1966), 252–3; Beveridge Papers III/36, Typescript of address to commemorate 50th anniversary of labour exchanges, London School of Economics.
13 Randolph S. Churchill, *Churchill*, companion vol. ii, part 2, p. 863, Churchill to Asquith, 29 Dec. 1908.
14 Harris, *Unemployment and Politics*, 365.
15 Beveridge Papers III/39 Z2, 'Notes on Malingering', 6 June 1909.
16 Sir Leon Radzinovicz and Roger Hood, *A History of English Criminal Law and its Administration from 1750*, v: *The Emergence of Penal Policy* (London, 1986), 770–3; V. A. C. Gatrell, 'Crime, Authority and the Policeman-State', in F. M. L. Thompson (ed.), *The Cambridge Social History of Britain* (Cambridge, 1989), iii. 308–9.
17 PRO HO 45/10631/200605, Memo by Churchill of 8 July 1910.
18 Radzinovicz and Hood, *English Criminal Law*, 677.
19 Quoted in Violet Bonham-Carter, *Winston Churchill as I Knew Him* (London, 1965), 220–1.
20 R. S. Churchill, *Churchill*, ii. 423–4; Michael J. Winstanley, *The Shopkeeper's World* (Manchester, 1983), 96–9.
21 Bonham-Carter, *Winston Churchill*, 164.
22 John M. McEwen (ed.), *The Riddell Diaries 1908–1923* (London, 1986), 71, diary entry for 31 Oct./1 Nov. 1913.
23 Arthur J. Marder, *From the Dreadnought to Scapa Flow: The Royal Navy in the Fisher Era 1904–1919*, i: *The Road to War 1904–1914* (Oxford, 1961), 267; 'Captain X' (Andrew Dewar Gibb), *With Winston Churchill at the Front* (London, 1924), 72–7.
24 Rhodes James (ed.), *Complete Speeches*, iii. 2485–90, speech of 22 Aug. 1916; Martin Gilbert, *Winston S. Churchill*, companion vol. iv, part 1, p. 447, Churchill to Lloyd George, 26 Dec. 1918.
25 PRO CAB 23/10 WC 557, 16 Apr. 1919.
26 Gilbert, *Churchill*, companion vol. iv, part 2, p. 791, Churchill to Lloyd George, 4 Aug. 1919; Mary Elizabeth Short, 'The Politics of Personal Taxation: Budget-Making in Britain 1917–1931', Cambridge University Ph.D. thesis (1985), 83.
27 Kenneth O. Morgan, *Consensus and Disunity: The Lloyd George Coalition Government 1918–1922* (Oxford, 1979), 102–3.
28 W. B. Garside, *British Unemployment 1919–1939* (Cambridge, 1990), 182, 190.
29 Gilbert, *Churchill*, companion vol. iv, part 3, p. 2126, Churchill to Wolfe, 20 Nov. 1922.
30 Rhodes James (ed.), *Complete Speeches*, iv. 3443, speech of 12 Mar. 1924.
31 W. J. Reader, *Architect of Air Power: The Life of the First Viscount Weir of Eastwood 1877–1959* (London, 1968), 117–20; for Churchill on housing see his article in *The Weekly Dispatch*, 13 July 1924, reprinted in Michael Wolff (ed.), *The Collected Essays of Sir Winston Churchill*, ii: *Churchill and Politics* (n.d.), 141–2.
32 P. J. Grigg, *Prejudice and Judgement* (London, 1948), 174.
33 PRO T 171/247, Deputation from National Confederation of Employers Organisations to the Chancellor of the Exchequer on the Social Services, 4 Mar. 1925.

34 Reader, *Architect of Air Power*, 124; David Dilks, *Neville Chamberlain*, i: *Pioneering and Reform 1869–1929* (London, 1984), 424.
35 Gilbert, *Churchill*, companion vol. v, part 1, p. 997, Churchill to Niemeyer, 20 May 1927.
36 *Parliamentary Debates* (Commons), vol. 310, 31 Mar. 1936, col. 1968.
37 *The Scotsman*, 6 Mar. 1931, 13.
38 *Parliamentary Debates* (Commons), vol. 311, 23 Apr. 1936, col. 334.
39 Rhodes James (ed.), *Complete Speeches*, v. 6143, speech of 28 June 1939.
40 John Colville, *The Fringes of Power: Downing Street Diaries, 1939–1955* (London, 1985), 216, diary for 10 Aug. 1940.
41 A. J. P. Taylor (ed.), *W. P. Crozier: Off the Record: Political Interviews 1933–1943* (London, 1973), 212, interview of 12 Mar. 1941.
42 G. S. Harvie-Watt, *Most of My Life* (London, 1980), 117; Rhodes James (ed.), *Complete Speeches*, vii. 6760, broadcast of 21 Mar. 1943.
43 Francis Williams, *A Prime Minister Remembers: The War and Post-War Memoirs of the Rt Hon Earl Attlee* (London, 1961), 57.
44 Kevin Jefferys, *The Churchill Coalition and Wartime Politics, 1940–1945* (Manchester, 1991), 191–2.
45 Rhodes James (ed.), *Complete Speeches*, vii. 7853–4, speech of 28 Sept. 1949.
46 John Ramsden, *The Making of Conservative Party Policy* (London, 1980), 147.
47 Kenneth O. Morgan, *The People's Peace: British History 1945–1979* (Oxford, 1990), 113.
48 Charles Webster, *The Health Services since the War*, i: *Problems of Health Care: The National Health Service before 1957* (London, 1988), 185–94.
49 PRO PREM 11/40, Memorandum on 'External Action' by the Chancellor of the Exchequer attached to letter of R. A. Butler to Churchill of 21 Feb. 1952.
50 PRO PREM 11/137, Cherwell to Churchill, 18 Mar. 1952.
51 *The Times*, 25 July 1952.
52 PRO CAB 11/13. The committee was dissolved in December 1952.
53 Harold Macmillan, *Tides of Fortune 1945–1955* (London, 1969), 411.
54 Robert Rhodes James, *Churchill: A Study in Failure* (Harmondsworth, 1973 edn.), 45; McEwen (ed.), *The Riddell Diaries*, 255, entry for 26 Jan. 1919; Taylor (ed.), *Off the Record*, 323, conversation with Morrison of 28 May 1942.

CHAPTER 5

1 Martin Gilbert, *Winston S. Churchill*, v. 24.
2 Ibid. 59.
3 Henry Pelling, *Winston Churchill* (London, 1974), 298.
4 Winston S. Churchill, 'Parliamentary Government and the Economic Problem', in *Thoughts and Adventures* (1932; London, 1947), 176–7.
5 Mary Short, 'The Politics of Personal Taxation: Budget-Making in Britain, 1917–1931', Ph.D. thesis (Cambridge University, 1985), 176, 209.
6 Sir Bruce Fraser, quoted in Peter Hennessy, *Whitehall* (London, 1989), 397.
7 Susan Howson, *Domestic Monetary Management in Britain, 1919–38* (Cambridge, 1975), 42.
8 P. J. Grigg, *Prejudice and Judgement* (London, 1948), 195.
9 Donald Moggridge and Austin Robinson (eds.), *The Collected Writings of John Maynard Keynes*, 30 vols. (London, 1971–89), ix. 212 (cited hereafter as *JMK*).
10 Donald Moggridge, *British Monetary Policy, 1924–31* (Cambridge, 1972), 76.
11 Ibid. 75 n. 4.
12 Gilbert, *Churchill*, v. 411.

13 Grigg, *Prejudice and Judgement*, 180.
14 Lord Moran, *Winston Churchill: The Struggle for Survival, 1940–1965* (London, 1966; Sphere edn., 1968), 330.
15 Robert Rhodes James (ed.), *Winston S. Churchill: His Complete Speeches, 1897–1963*, 8 vols. (New York, 1974), iv. 3496 (Epping, 24 Oct. 1924).
16 I am drawing here on Peter Clarke, 'The Treasury's Analytical Model of the British Economy between the Wars', in Mary O. Furner and Barry Supple (eds.), *The State and Economic Knowledge* (New York, 1990), 171–207.
17 Committee on Finance and Industry, *Minutes of Evidence*, 2 vols. (London, 1931), Q. 3389.
18 Ibid. Q. 3328.
19 Ibid. Q. 3390.
20 Rhodes James (ed.), *Complete Speeches*, ii. 1365 (Preston, 3 Dec. 1909).
21 Winston S. Churchill, *The People's Rights* (1909; London, 1970), 96.
22 Rhodes James (ed.), *Complete Speeches*, i. 212 (House of Commons, 29 July 1903).
23 Marshall's 'Memorandum on the Fiscal Policy of International Trade' (1903), as printed in W. H. B. Court, *British Economic History, 1870–1914* (Cambridge, 1965), 467–8.
24 Rhodes James (ed.), *Complete Speeches*, i. 238 (Halifax, 21 Dec. 1903).
25 Ibid. i. 315 (Manchester, 15 June 1904).
26 Ibid. i. 872 (Manchester, 21 Jan. 1908).
27 Ibid. ii. 1444; i. 912 (Dundee, 5 Jan. 1910; London, 18 Mar. 1908).
28 Ibid. i. 873 (Manchester, 21 Jan. 1908).
29 Ibid. i. 945 (Manchester, 14 Apr. 1908).
30 *The Second World War Diary of Hugh Dalton*, ed. Ben Pimlott (London, 1986), 578 (7 Apr. 1943).
31 Rhodes James (ed.), *Complete Speeches*, iv. 3596 (House of Commons, 4 May 1925).
32 Moggridge, *British Monetary Policy*, 271.
33 Ibid. 75–6.
34 Rhodes James (ed.), *Complete Speeches*, ii. 1079 (Westminster, 4 Aug. 1908).
35 Moggridge, *British Monetary Policy*, 76.
36 Rhodes James (ed.), *Complete Speeches*, iv. 3598 (House of Commons, 4 May 1925).
37 Ibid. iv. 3744–5 (House of Commons, 5 Aug. 1925).
38 It is printed in full in Moggridge, *British Monetary Policy*, 260–2, from which the Churchill quotations in the next three paragraphs are taken.
39 Ibid. 270.
40 Rhodes James (ed.), *Complete Speeches*, iv. 3744 (5 Aug. 1925).
41 Grigg, *Prejudice and Judgement*, 82.
42 *JMK*, xix. 766.
43 Much of this section is summarized from Peter Clarke, *The Keynesian Revolution in the Making, 1924–36* (Oxford, 1988), ch. 3; see pp. 48–54 for the sources in this paragraph.
44 Ibid. 57.
45 Ibid. 61.
46 Keith Middlemas (ed.), *Thomas Jones: Whitehall Diary, 1916–30*, 2 vols. (London, 1969), ii. 175–6.
47 Clarke, *Keynesian Revolution*, 62–5.
48 Rhodes James (ed.), *Complete Speeches*, v. 4593 (House of Commons, 15 Apr. 1929).
49 Paul Kennedy, *The Rise and Fall of the Great Powers* (London, 1988; Fontana edn., 1989), 197–201.
50 Robert W. D. Boyce, *British Capitalism at the Crossroads, 1919–32* (Cambridge, 1987), 176.

51 Churchill, *Thoughts and Adventures*, 174, 183.
52 Grigg, *Prejudice and Judgement*, 260.

CHAPTER 6

1 Written under the pen-name 'Brutus' for the *North Wales Express* (Nov. 1880).
2 'I will not say but that I eyed the assembly in a spirit similar to that in which William the Conqueror eyed England on his visit to Edward the Confessor, as the region of his future domain.' Diary entry for 12 Nov. 1881, quoted in Herbert du Parcq, *Life of David Lloyd George* (London, 1912), i. 40.
3 Winston S. Churchill, *My Early Life* (London, 1930), ch. XXIX.
4 Randolph S. Churchill, *Winston S. Churchill*, ii. 80.
5 Speech at the Pavilion, Carnarvon, 18 Oct. 1904.
6 Lord Riddell, *More Pages from My Diary, 1908–1914* (London, 1934), 1, entry for 'October 1908'.
7 Churchill to Lloyd George, 29 Aug. 1908 (Earl Lloyd George collection, now in National Library of Wales).
8 Private information from Lady Soames.
9 Violet Bonham-Carter, *Winston Churchill as I Knew Him* (London, 1965), 27.
10 J. Hugh Edwards, *David Lloyd George: The Man and the Statesman* (London, 1930), i. 73; quoting an article in the monthly magazine *Young Wales*, published in 1899, 15 years after the debate described.
11 Unpublished memoir of David Lloyd George in the National Library of Wales, translated from Welsh (for the author) by Dr Prys Morgan.
12 Frances Stevenson, *Lloyd George: A Diary* (London, 1971), entry for 19 May 1915.
13 Clementine S. Churchill to Churchill, 30 Dec. 1915, quoted in Martin Gilbert, *Winston S. Churchill*, iii. 623; Churchill to Clementine S. Churchill, 1 Jan. and 4 Jan. 1916, in Gilbert, *Churchill*, companion vol. iii, part 2, pp. 1351 and 1357.
14 Lloyd George to Churchill, 22 Sept. 1919, quoted in Gilbert, *Churchill*, iv. 333.
15 Boothby, *Recollections of a Rebel* (London, 1978), 51–2.
16 Nicolson, *Diaries and Letters, 1930–39* (London, 1966), 394, entry for 3 Apr. 1939.
17 House of Commons, 28 Mar. 1945.
18 *My Darling Pussy, The Letters of Lloyd George and Frances Stevenson*, ed. A. J. P. Taylor (London, 1975), 7–8, letter dated 7 Apr. 1915.

CHAPTER 7

1 *Oldham Standard*, 1 July 1899.
2 Winston S. Churchill, *My Early Life* (London, 1959 edn.), 366.
3 Henry Pelling, *Winston Churchill* (London, 1974), 85.
4 Ibid.
5 *Dundee Advertiser*, 5 May 1908.
6 WSC in *Parliamentary Debates* (Commons), 24 Nov. 1910, vol. 20, col. 421.
7 J. R. MacDonald in *Parliamentary Debates* (Commons), vol. 21, col. 2297, 22 Aug. 1911.
8 Churchill to King George V, 10 Feb. 1911, and Knollys to V. Nash, 11 Feb. 1911, quoted in Randolph S. Churchill, *Winston S. Churchill*, companion vol. ii, p. 1037.
9 WSC in *Parliamentary Debates* (Commons), 30 May 1911, vol. 26, col. 1022.
10 Churchill to King George V, 27 June 1911, quoted in R. S. Churchill, *Churchill*, companion vol. ii, p. 1094.
11 C. C. Coote, *The Other Club* (London, 1971), 20.

12 W. C. Anderson in *Parliamentary Debates* (Commons), 6 Nov. 1917, vol. 98, col. 2073.

13 *Dundee Advertiser*, 10 and 13 Dec. 1918.

14 K. O. Morgan, *Consensus and Disunity* (Oxford, 1979), 137.

15 Ibid. 218.

16 *The Times*, 18 Jan. 1924.

17 Keith Middlemas (ed.), *Thomas Jones: Whitehall Diary*, 2 vols. (London, 1969), ii. 78 (Sept. 1926).

18 *The Times*, 2 Nov. 1928.

19 *New Statesman*, 19 Mar. 1938.

20 War Cabinet Meetings 140 and 141 (26 and 27 May 1940), Confidential Annexes, PRO CAB 65/13.

21 Winston S. Churchill, *The Second World War* (London, 1949), ii. 211.

22 Figures from *Ministry of Labour Gazette*.

23 *Harold Nicolson, Diaries and Letters, 1939–45*, ed. Nigel Nicolson (London, 1967), 178 (18 July 1941).

24 See especially Gallup Poll, *News Chronicle*, 22 Jan. 1942.

25 Winston S. Churchill, *Victory* (London, 1946), 203 (21 June 1945).

26 J. Stuart, *Within the Fringe* (London, 1967), 147.

27 *The Times*, 1 Nov. 1951.

28 Winston ·S. Churchill, *Stemming the Tide* (London, 1953), 139 (9 Oct. 1951).

29 TUC *Report*, 1952, 291–5.

30 *The Times*, 26 Jan. 1955.

31 *Dundee Advertiser*, 5 May 1908.

CHAPTER 8

1 Martin Gilbert, *Winston S. Churchill*, iii. 31.

2 Ibid.

3 Violet Bonham-Carter, *Winston Churchill as I Knew Him* (London, 1965), 361.

4 Gilbert, *Churchill*, iii. 76.

5 Ibid. 137.

6 Lord Beaverbrook, *Politicians and the War 1914–1916* (London, 1928), i. 31.

7 Arthur J. Marder, *From the Dreadnought to Scapa Flow* (London, 1961), i. 435.

8 This was an interesting forerunner of the various private armies whose formation Churchill was to encourage during the Second World War: 'Layforce', the Chindits, 'Popski's Private Army', the Special Air Service—units whose military utility remains a matter of some debate.

9 The idea originated with Colonel Maurice Hankey, but it is signficant that he should have suggested it to Churchill rather than to Kitchener or Asquith: Maurice Hankey, *The Supreme Command* (London, 1961), i. 195.

10 Marder, *Dreadnought to Scapa Flow* (1965), ii. 176.

11 Ibid. 177.

12 Gilbert, *Churchill*, iii. 236.

13 Arthur J. Marder, *Portrait of an Admiral: The Life and Papers of Sir Herbert Richmond* (London, 1952), 134.

14 Gilbert, *Churchill*, iii. 58.

15 Hankey, *Supreme Command*, i. 203.

16 Ibid. 204.

17 J. E. B. Seeley, *Adventure* (London, 1930), 189.

18 Gilbert, *Churchill*, iii. 111.

19 H. H. *Asquith: Letters to Venetia Stanley*, selected and edited by M. and E. Brock (Oxford, 1982), 263.

20 Earl of Oxford and Asquith, *Memories and Reflections* (London, 1928), ii. 45–6.

21 Winston Churchill, *The World Crisis* (abridged and revised edn., London, 1931), 216.

22 Hankey, *Supreme Command*, ii. 865.

23 Arthur J. Marder (ed.), *Fear God and Dread Nought: The Correspondence of Admiral of the Fleet Lord Fisher of Kilverstone* (London, 1959), iii. 375.

24 The best account of this complex matter is to be found in B. H. Liddell Hart, *The Tanks* (London, 1959), i. 17–43.

25 Gilbert, *Churchill*, iii. 226.

26 Ibid. 220.

27 Ibid. 234.

28 Ibid. 236.

29 Hankey, *Supreme Command*, i. 266.

30 Ibid.

31 The best comprehensive account, giving full weight to the political as well as military factors, is Robert Rhodes James, *Gallipoli* (London, 1965).

32 Gilbert, *Churchill*, iii. 329.

33 Lord Riddell, *War Diary* (London, 1933), 89.

34 Gilbert, *Churchill*, iii. 755.

35 Gilbert, *Churchill*, iv. 17.

36 Lord Beaverbrook, *Men and Power 1917–1918* (London, 1956), 122.

37 Ibid. 139.

38 Ibid. 131.

39 Stephen Roskill, *Hankey: Man of Secrets* (London, 1970), i. 415.

40 Churchill, *World Crisis*, 706.

41 Gilbert, *Churchill*, iv. 42.

42 Ibid. 44.

43 Ibid. 72.

44 Ibid. 146.

45 Ibid. 149.

46 Beaverbrook, *Politicians and the War*, i. 131.

47 Robert Rhodes James, *Churchill: A Study in Failure, 1900–1939* (London, 1970), 87.

CHAPTER 9

1 From his articles, 'Zionism versus Bolshevism', *Illustrated Sunday Herald*, 8 Feb. 1920, in Michael Wolff (ed.), *The Collected Essays of Sir Winston Churchill* (London, 1976), iv. 26–30; and 'Moses', in Churchill, *Thoughts and Adventures* (London, 1932), 283–94.

2 Lord Moran, *Winston Churchill: The Struggle for Survival, 1940–1965* (London, 1968 edn.), 489–90, 682. For his attitude towards the Arabs, Martin Gilbert, *Churchill*, companion vol. v, part 3, pp. 596–617, and Ronald Zweig, *Britain and Palestine During the Second World War* (London, 1986), 174 n. 107. For his feelings towards Indians, see Gilbert, *Churchill*, v. 322 n. 1, and his crusade against the Government of India Act, 1935, in Gilbert, *Churchill*, companion vol. v, part 2, *passim*. Also Paul Addison, 'The Political Beliefs of Winston Churchill', *Transactions of the Royal Historical Society*, 5th series, xxx (London, 1980), 38–41.

3 See Nigel Nicolson (ed.), *Harold Nicolson, Diaries and Letters, 1939–45* (London, 1970 edn), 473. For a look into the Gentile Zionist mind, Josiah Wedgewood, *The Seventh Dominion* (London, 1928), and Norman Rose, *The Gentile Zionists* (London, 1973).

4 In this connection, see below, pp. 150–1.
5 For Lord Randolph and the Jews, see R. F. Foster, *Lord Randolph Churchill* (Oxford, 1981), 30, 217, 349, and Oskar K. Rabinowicz, *Winston Churchill on Jewish Problems* (London, 1956), 85. For the visits to Tring, R. S. Churchill, *Churchill*, companion vol. ii, part 1, pp. 338, 423.
6 This theme was brought to a ludicrous climax by David Irving who, in a fantastic exercise of imaginative writing, depicts Churchill as a drunken reprobate in the pay of a clique of Jewish plutocrats. See his *Churchill's War, i: The Struggle for Power* (Bullsbrook, Western Australia, 1987).
7 For Churchill and Cassel, R. S. Churchill, *Churchill*, companion vol. ii, part 1, pp. 167 *et passim*; Gilbert, *Churchill*, companion vol. iv, part 3, p. 1627; Churchill, *My Early Life* (London, 1983 edn.), 369; Rabinowicz, *Churchill*, 175–84.
8 R. S. Churchill, *Churchill*, companion vol. ii, part 2, p. 976.
9 See R. S. Churchill, *Churchill*, companion vol. ii, part 1, pp. 487–90.
10 Gilbert, *Churchill*, companion vol. iii, part 2, p. 1368.
11 See 'Zionism versus Bolshevism'; and Robert Rhodes James (ed.), *Winston S. Churchill: His Complete Speeches, 1897–1963* (London, 1974), i. 684, 685, 984–5.
12 For the Aliens Bill, see R. S. Churchill, *Churchill*, companion vol. ii, part 1, pp. 354–7; R. S. Churchill, *Churchill*, ii. 410–11; Rhodes James (ed.), *Complete Speeches*, i. 305–6, 345; ibid. ii. 1590; and Rabinowicz, *Churchill*, 49–81.
13 For the South Wales episode, Rabinowicz, *Churchill*, 167–72, and Norman Rose, *Lewis Namier and Zionism* (Oxford, 1980), 9–10.
14 *Parliamentary Debates* (Commons), vol. 63, cols. 1135–1230; Robert Henriques, *Marcus Samuel* (London, 1960), 575–86; and Michael Cohen, *Churchill and the Jews* (London, 1985), 46–9, who takes an unnecessarily harsh, almost perverse, attitude towards Churchill's motives regarding Zionist and Jewish matters, scarcely giving him the benefit of any doubt.
15 From 'Zionism versus Bolshevism'; also Gilbert, *Churchill*, companion vol. iv, part 2, pp. 860, 912, 1010–12; part 3, pp. 1699, 1874. For the background to the article, companion vol. iv, part 3, pp. 1010, 1028–9.
16 R. S. Churchill, *Churchill*, companion vol. ii, part 2, p. 933. Also his essay, 'The Scaffolding of Rhetoric', ibid. 816–21.
17 His comment to Lord Lloyd, minutes of a meeting between Namier and Lloyd, 7 Jan. 1941, Weizmann Archives, Rehovoth; and his speech to the House of Commons, 1 Aug. 1946, Rhodes James (ed.), *Complete Speeches*, vii. 7376.
18 Norman Rose (ed.), *'Baffy': The Diaries of Blanche Dugdale, 1936–1947* (London, 1973), 67.
19 In *Thoughts and Adventures*.
20 Gilbert, *Churchill*, companion vol. iii, part 2, p. 1373.
21 For a compulsive writer, Churchill wrote surprisingly little on these topics. Apart from 'Moses'—a Bible tale retold in Churchillian prose—and 'Zionism versus Bolshevism', composed more under the influence of his anti-Bolshevik obsession than his feelings for Zionism, and a couple of articles in the late 1930s denouncing partition (see below), there is practically nothing. In his *World Crisis* (London, 1923–7) and *Aftermath* (London, 1929), that deal with world events and British policy from 1911 to 1922, there is no mention of Zionism, the Balfour Declaration, the British mandate for Palestine, or Weizmann. This pattern is repeated in the first volume of *The Second World War* (London, 1948), though the remaining volumes do contain material on these topics.
22 *The Letters and Papers of Chaim Weizmann*, Series A: *Letters* (Jerusalem/New Brunswick, NJ, 1972–80), x. 153.
23 For Disraeli's 'The Lord deals with Nations', minutes of meeting between

Churchill and Weizmann, 23 Oct. 1943, Weizmann Archives. Also Eilath to Weizmann, 17 Sept. 1950, Weizmann Archives; Churchill's remarks to the Arab delegation, 28 Mar. 1921, in CAB 24/126, PRO, London; and his comment to the Commons, 26 Jan. 1949, Rhodes James (ed.), *Complete Speeches*, vii. 7777.

24 These affairs may be followed in *Weizmann Letters*, iv. 213, 215–16; ibid. xxi. 180; and Rabinowicz, *Churchill*, 36, 86–8.

25 See Richard Crossman, the last of his Gentile conquests, in *A Nation Reborn* (London, 1960), 41.

26 Minutes of Weizmann–Churchill meeting, 12 Mar. 1941, Weizmann Archives. For Weizmann's fascination, Robert Rhodes James, *Victor Cazalet: A Portrait* (London, 1976), 265. Also *Weizmann Letters*, xxiii. 133–4.

27 John Darwin, *Britain, Egypt and the Middle East: Imperial Policy in the Aftermath of War, 1918–1922* (London, 1981), 204–5.

28 Churchill's offer to Belgium in FO 800/88, no. 320, minute of 18 Mar. 1915; his readiness to reconstitute the Turkish Empire, Gilbert, *Churchill*, companion vol. iv, part 2, pp. 937–9, 1119–20; also companion vol. iv, part 3, pp. 1500–1, where he proposes handing over the mandates for Mesopotamia and Palestine to the United States. For British politicians and relinquishing the Palestine mandate to the United States, see Richard Meinertzhagen, *Middle East Diary, 1917–1956* (London, 1959), 25; Leonard Stein, *The Balfour Declaration* (London, 1961), 605–20, and 'Zionist–Arab–British relations and the Inter-Allied Peace Commission in 1919', in Norman Rose (ed.), *From Palmerston to Balfour: Collected Essays of Mayir Verete* (London, 1992).

29 From 'Zionism versus Bolshevism'.

30 Reducing costs in Palestine, in Rhodes James (ed.), *Complete Speeches*, iv. 3351. For 'hebrophobe' atmosphere in Colonial Office, Meinertzhagen, *Middle East Diary*, 99, and Notes of a Conversation held at Balfour's House, 22 July 1921, Weizmann Archives. Also CAB 24/115, CP 1504, a highly coloured and hostile report of 21 June 1920 by military intelligence regarding imagined Zionist intention; also CAB 24/125, CP 3030.

31 For the press campaign, A. J. P. Taylor, *Beaverbrook* (London, 1972), 200, 206; Chaim Weizmann, *Trial and Error* (London, 1949), 349; and Norman Rose, *Chaim Weizmann* (New York, 1987), 219–21. The activities of the Palestine Arab Delegation may be followed in CO 733/17B, nos. 41298, 43805, and Cmd. 1700; also Gilbert, *Churchill*, companion vol. iv, part 3, pp. 1610–18. Also *Parliamentary Debates* (Lords), 21 June 1922, vol. 50, cols. 994–1034.

32 Weizmann's plea for Transjordan, *Weizmann Letters*, x. 159–62; also Herbert Sidebotham to Weizmann, 28 Apr. 1921, Weizmann Archives. Churchill and Zionist pledges, *Parliamentary Debates* (Commons), 16 June 1921, vol. 143, col. 283. His tiff with Churchill, *Weizmann Letters*, x. 215. Churchill 'astonished' at Balfour's house on 22 July 1921, minutes in Weizmann Archives; and for Weizmann's reaction, *Weizmann Letters*, x. 233–4. Record of Churchill's talks with Arab and Jewish leaders in Jerusalem, 28 Mar. 1921, CAB 24/126, appendix 23; and Report of Discussions at Cairo and Jerusalem, 12–30 Mar. 1921, CP 2866, CAB 24/122, extracts also in Weizmann Archives.

33 See his Cabinet papers in Gilbert, *Churchill*, companion vol. iv, part 3, pp. 1585–90.

34 For Churchill's defence of Zionism, *Parliamentary Debates* (Commons), vol. 143, cols. 266–96; vol. 151, cols. 1547–72; vol. 156, cols. 337–40; and Gilbert, *Churchill*, companion vol. iv, part 3, pp. 1592–1601, 1610–18; also *Complete Speeches*, iii. 3102–9; ibid. iv. 3342–51. See also his firm words to the Arabs in Jerusalem, *Weizmann Letters*, xi. 135. For Salisbury's advice, *Parliamentary Debates* (Commons), vol. 143, col. 287.

35 Churchill's White Paper was inspired and drafted by Sir Herbert Samuel, Palestine's first High Commissioner. See his draft of 24 May 1922, CO 733/34, published as Cmd. 1700; also Gilbert, *Churchill*, companion vol. iv. part 3, p. 1491. For terms of the mandate, Cmd. 1500. And the Rutenberg concession, his speech of 4 July 1922, *Parliamentary Debates* (Commons), vol. 156, cols. 328–40.
36 *Weizmann Letters*, xi. 109.
37 Quoted in Zweig, *Britain and Palestine*, 113.
38 See his speech, *Parliamentary Debates* (Commons), 23 May 1939, vol. 347, cols. 2167–78.
39 Quoted in Zweig, *Britain and Palestine*, 171. For his refusal to recognize the 1939 White Paper, see his paper. 'The American Zionist Organization and His Majesty's Government's Policy in Palestine', 25 Dec. 1939, CAB 67/3. Also Zweig, *Britain and Palestine*, 19, 29, 113; Gabriel Cohen, *Churchill and Palestine, 1939–1942* (Jerusalem, 1976, in Hebrew), 82–96; and Rose, *'Baffy'*, 203–4. Weizmann's 'truce' proposal in *Weizmann Letters*, xix. 207–8.
40 See below, pp. 161–4.
41 Churchill, *The World Crisis* (London, 1938, 2nd edn.), i. 208–9.
42 Quoted in Paul Addison, *The Road to 1945* (London, 1977), 253.
43 Martin Gilbert, *Auschwitz and the Allies* (London, 1981), 160–1.
44 These tortuous negotiations may be followed in Zweig, *Britain and Palestine*; Gabriel Cohen, *The British Cabinet and Palestine, April–July 1943* (Tel Aviv, 1976, in Hebrew); Michael J. Cohen, *Retreat from the Mandate* (London, 1978), and *Churchill and the Jews*; Bernard Wasserstein, *Britain and the Jews of Europe, 1939–1945* (Oxford, 1979); Gilbert, *Churchill*, vi, vii; and Rose, *Lewis Namier*.
45 Quotations in *Weizmann Letters*, xx. 314–15; John Harvey (ed.), *The War Diaries of Oliver Harvey, 1941–1945* (London, 1978), 193–4, 247; and Wasserstein, *Britain and the Jews of Europe*, 34, 351.
46 Minute to Eden, 11 July 1944, FO 371/42809/115, has been quoted in full in Wasserstein, *Britain and the Jews of Europe*, 259; passages have been printed in Churchill, *The Second World War* (London, 1954), vi. 597; also Gilbert, *Auschwitz*, 268. Historians of the Brandt affair are still divided in their evaluation of it; see Michael Marrus, *The Holocaust in History* (London, 1989), 188–9.
47 Note of 7 July 1944 in PREM 4/51/10; also Wasserstein, *Britain and the Jews of Europe*, 311, and Gilbert, *Auschwitz*, 270.
48 The evidence is overwhelming; see Gilbert, *Auschwitz*, 190 *et passim*; Marrus, *The Holocaust in History*, 192–4, Wasserstein, *Britain and the Jews of Europe*, 307–20; and Cohen, *Churchill and the Jews*, 294–305. Also a report in *Jerusalem Post*, 3 Aug. 1990.
49 See Churchill, *The Second World War*, vi, chs. 1–9; also Moran, *Struggle for Survival*, 184–94.
50 From a memorandum by Shertok, 11 July 1944, printed in Wasserstein, *Britain and the Jews of Europe*, 310.
51 See *Weizmann Letters*, xx. 313; xxi. 39; and *The Letters and Papers of Chaim Weizmann*, Series B: *Papers* (Jerusalem/New Brunswick, NJ, 1983–4), ii. 427, 523–4.
52 For Churchill's initial support for the Uganda scheme, R. S. Churchill, *Churchill*, ii, part 1, pp. 495–6; Ronald Hyam, *Elgin and Churchill at the Colonial Office, 1905–1908* (London, 1968), 407; and Rabinowicz, *Churchill*, 194–5; and for his cooling off, Rhodes James (ed.), *Complete Speeches*, i. 858. The letter to Moser is quoted in Martin Gilbert's pamphlet, *Churchill and Zionism* (World Jewish Congress, London, 1974). Also Cohen, *Churchill and the Jews*, 34.
53 In 'Zionism versus Bolshevism'.
54 Notes of a dinner conversation, 8 June 1937, Weizmann Archives. Also John Barnes

and David Nicholson (eds.), *The Empire at Bay: The Leo Amery Diaries, 1929–1945* (London, 1988), 444; Rose, *'Baffy'*, 45; and Rose, *The Gentile Zionists*, 131–3. For further testimonies of Churchill's dislike of partition, see his articles, 'Partition Perils in Palestine', *Evening Standard*, 23 July 1937, and 'Why I Am Against Partition', *Jewish Chronicle*, 30 July 1937. For Churchill's ten-year plan of 24 Nov. 1938, *Parliamentary Debates* (Commons), vol. 341, cols. 2029–39. It was clearly inspired by the 'palliatives' of the Peel Report that also put a political high level on immigration—less generous than Churchill's—of 12,000 a year for five years. See Cmd. 5479, pp. 366–7.

55 Churchill's minute in PREM 4/52/5, part 2; also Record of a Meeting between Weizmann and Churchill. 17 Dec. 1939, Weizmann Archives; and *Weizmann Letters*, xx. 125–6, 370 n. 1.

56 Weizmann's letter in *Weizmann Letters*, xxi. 19–21; and for Churchill's reaction, *The Second World War* (London, 1951), iv. 849. Spears' observation quoted in Zweig, *Britain and Palestine*, 174 n. 107.

57 Memoranda by Churchill, WP(43) 178, Lord Cranborne, WP(43) 187, Oliver Stanley, WP(43) 192, Anthony Eden, WP(43) 214, in CAB 66/36; Richard Casey, WP(43) 246, in CAB 66/37; Oliver Lyttelton, WP(43) 265, Clement Attlee, WP(43) 266, Sir Stafford Cripps, WP(43) 288, in CAB 66/38; and Minutes of Middle East War Council, WP(43) 247, CAB 66/37. Also Barnes and Nicholson, *Amery Diaries*, 896–7.

58 Zweig, *Britain and Palestine*, 174 n. 107. In May 1941 Rashid Alid, premier of a pro-Axis administration in Iraq, invited German intervention. German aircraft and troops entered the country but were eventually crushed by British armed forces. One consequence of Rashid Ali's regime was widespread pogroms against the Iraqi Jewish community.

59 *Amery Diaries*, 896–7.

60 See WP(43) 563, CAB 63/44, for the committee's report of 20 Dec. 1943, and CAB 66/65, for a summary of the committee's discussions and proposals. Also Barnes and Nicholson, *Amery Diaries*, 951, 955; and for cabinet decision of 25 Jan. 1944, CAB 65/45. For Foreign Office discontent with the cabinet committee, Churchill's note to Eden, 11 July 1943, PREM 4/51/1.

61 Quotations in *Amery Diaries*, 897, and *Weizmann Letters*, xxi. 244. For American co-operation and a Middle East settlement, Minutes of Meetings between Churchill and Weizmann, 12 Mar. 1941 and 4 Nov. 1944, Weizmann Archives; also *Weizmann Letters*, xx. 125–6, 301, and *Weizmann Letters*, xxi. 39 and n. 1, 243–6; and Gilbert, *Churchill*, vi. 1090, and vii. 1048–50. Also Gabriel Cohen, *Churchill and Palestine, 1939–1942*, 82–98, which includes five of Churchill's minutes on this topic written between May 1941 and May 1942.

62 Minutes of meeting in Weizmann Archives; also *Weizmann Letters*, xxi. 243–6, and *Weizmann Papers*, ii. 540–3.

63 Cohen, *Churchill and the Jews*, 259.

64 *Parliamentary Debates* (Commons), 17 Nov. 1944, vol. 404 col. 2242.

65 Amery noted presciently on 6 Nov. 1944 that Moyne's murder 'inflicted a possibly fatal injury of their [the Zionists] own cause': *Amery Diaries*, 1018.

66 See Eden's memoranda of 19 Nov. 1937, CAB 24/273, and 'The Case Against Partition', 15 Sept. 1944, CAB 95/14; also PREM 4/52/1 for much of the anti-partition material.

67 Correspondence in *Weizmann Letters*, xxii. 11–12, 20.

68 See Rose, *'Baffy'*, 221–3; minutes of Zionist meetings, 13 and 27 June 1945, Weizmann Archives; and Bartley Crum, *Behind the Silken Curtain* (New York, 1947), 169.

69 *Weizmann Letters*, xxii. 67, 119–20 and n. 9.

70 Quotations in *Weizmann Letters*, xxiii. 15, 196 n. 1; Lord Boothby, *My Yesterday, Your Tomorrow* (London, 1962), 211; Rhodes James (ed.), *Complete Speeches*, vii. 7377.
71 See his speeches to the House of Commons, 1 Aug., 23 Oct. 12 Nov. 1946; 31 Jan., 6 Mar. 1947; 21 Apr., 10 Dec. 1948; and 26 Jan. 1949, in *Complete Speeches*, vii. 7372–9, 7393, 7404, 7421–5, 7445–6, 7627–8, 7766–7, 7774–83; at the Albert Hall, 21 Apr. 1948, and to the Scottish Unionists at Perth, 28 May 1948, *Complete Speeches*, vii. 7627–8, 7654; and *Weizmann Letters*, xxii. 188, 190.

   Like many others, Churchill was deeply critical of Bevin's heavy-handed and insensitive handling of the Palestine problem. Far from resolving this complex issue, Bevin, in deed and word, it made it more acute, dragging Britain's good name and reputation in the mud, particularly in the United States.
72 *Weizmann Letters*, xxiii. 251 n. 4.
73 Carefully recorded in Gilbert, *Churchill*, viii. 557 *et passim*.
74 Ibid. 1093.
75 *Weizmann Papers*, ii. 427, and *Weizmann Letters*, xx. 313.
76 Moshe Pearlman, *Ben Gurion Looks Back* (London, 1965), 99–106.

CHAPTER 10

1 Ronald Hyam, *Elgin and Churchill at the Colonial Office, 1905–1908* (London, 1968), 505.
2 J. Barnes and D. Nicholson (eds.), *The Leo Amery Diaries, 1896–1929* (London, 1980), i. 392.
3 Martin Gilbert, *Winston S. Churchill*, companion vol. iv, part 3: *Documents, April 1921 to November 1922*, pp. 859, 913–15, 1543, 1999–2004, 2043, 2080, 2094; K. Jeffery, 'Sir H. Wilson and the Defence of the British Empire, 1918–1922', *Journal of Imperial and Commonwealth History*, 5 (1977), 270–93.
4 Milner to Buxton, 10 May 1919, Sydney Buxton Papers.
5 Quoted in full in M. Gilbert, *Churchill's Political Philosophy* (Oxford, 1981), 43–4, without acknowledgement, from Hyam, *Elgin and Churchill at the Colonial Office*, 492. See also R. Hyam, 'Winston Churchill before 1914', *Historical Journal*, 12 (1969), 164–73.
6 British Cotton Growing Association, pamphlet nos. 20, 57, and 74 (Manchester, 1907, 1921).
7 Gilbert, *Churchill*, companion vol. iv, part 3, pp. 1474–5.
8 *Parliamentary Debates* (Commons), 14 July 1921, vol. 44, cols. 1620–9.
9 I. Friedman, *The Question of Palestine, 1914–1918: British–Jewish–Arab Relations* (London, 1973), 7, 17–18, 172–3; *Parliamentary Debates* (Commons), 4 July 1922, vol. 156, col. 335.
10 PRO CAB 23/25, no. 45; CAB 23/26, no. 70; CO 733/18, no. 5285.
11 *Parliamentary Debates* (Commons), vol. 156, col. 334; Gilbert, *Churchill*, companion vol. iv, part 3, pp. 1610–18.
12 CAB 24/128, CP 3328; Gilbert, *Churchill*, companion vol. iv, part 3, pp. 1577–80.
13 Gilbert, *Churchill*, companion vol. iv, part 3, pp. 1648, 1701, 1801, 1869; PREM 11/472, D4(53)4.
14 CO 733/6, nos. 50764 and 52088; *Parliamentary Debates* (Commons), vol. 156, cols. 334–5.
15 CO 533/270, no. 40187.
16 CO 533/264, 265, 270, 287, 288, and 291; CO 537/782.
17 CAB 23/29, fols. 223–4, 258.
18 R. Furse, *Aucuparius: Recollections of a Recruiting Officer* (Oxford, 1962), 85.

19 CO 417/664, 681, and 682; CO 537/1182, 1184 and 1203; CAB 23/27, fol. 95.
20 N. Mansergh *et al.* (eds.), *Transfer of Power in India* (London, 1971), iii. 809; W. S. Churchill, *The Second World War* (London, 1951), iv. 824.
21 J. D. B. Miller, *Sir Winston Churchill and the Commonwealth of Nations* (Queensland, 1967).
22 PREM 4/44/1, WP(G)(41)109.
23 PREM 11/1765.
24 PREM 11/472 and 1367; CAB 128/28, CC 15(55)1.
25 C. Thorne, *Allies of a Kind: The United States, Britain and the War against Japan, 1941–1945* (London, 1978), 669, 725, 750.
26 P. Addison, 'The Political Beliefs of Winston Churchill', *Transactions of the Royal Historical Society*, 5th series, xxx (London, 1980), 23–47.
27 Churchill, *Second World War*, iv. 824.
28 W. S. Churchill, *The River War: An Historical Account of the Reconquest of the Soudan* (London, 1899), i. 10.
29 Lord Moran, *Winston Churchill: The Struggle for Survival, 1940–1965: the Diaries* (London, 1966), pp. 449–50.
30 Churchill, *Second World War* (London, 1952), v. 571; PREM 8/180.

CHAPTER 11

1 Martin Gilbert, *Winston S. Churchill*, viii. 570.
2 Brian Loring Villa, *Unauthorised Action: Mountbatten and the Dieppe Raid* (Oxford, 1990), 210.
3 John Colville, *The Fringes of Power: Downing Street Diaries, 1939–1955* (London, 1985), 128.
4 Randolph S. Churchill, *Churchill*, i. 545.
5 Ibid. 336.
6 R. S. Churchill, *Churchill*, ii. 211.
7 Ibid. 94, 185.
8 Philip Magnus, *King Edward VII* (London, 1964), 386.
9 R. S. Churchill, *Churchill*, ii. 327.
10 Magnus, *Edward VII*, 413.
11 Kenneth Rose, *King George V* (London, 1983), 76.
12 Giles St Aubyn, *Edward VII, Prince and King* (London, 1979), 344.
13 Rose, *George V*, 71.
14 Ibid. 160–1.
15 Ibid. 111–12.
16 Ibid. 160.
17 R. S. Churchill, *Churchill*, ii. 670.
18 Ibid. 710.
19 Gilbert, *Churchill*, iii. 454.
20 Philip Ziegler, *King Edward VIII* (London, 1990), 46.
21 Ibid. 78.
22 Gilbert, *Churchill*, iv. 790–1.
23 Ibid. 702.
24 Gilbert, *Churchill*, v. 244.
25 Ziegler, *Edward VIII*, 215.
26 *Diaries and Letters of Marie Belloc Lowndes*, ed. Susan Lowndes (London, 1971), 154–5.
27 Ziegler, *Edward VIII*, 488.
28 Colville, *Fringes of Power*, 716.

29 Ziegler, *Edward VIII*, 316.
30 Ibid.
31 *The Sunday Times*, 24 Apr. 1966.
32 Ziegler, *Edward VIII*, 319.
33 Gilbert, *Churchill*, v. 823.
34 *Parliamentary Debates* (Commons), vol. 318, cols. 2188–91.
35 Harold Nicolson Diary for 6 Apr. 1955: Balliol College, Oxford.
36 John Wheeler-Bennett, *King George VI* (London, 1958), 444.
37 Halifax papers, A.7.8.4, 5 June 1940.
38 Colville, *Fringes of Power*, 211.
39 Ibid. 160.
40 Gilbert, *Churchill*, vi. 453–4.
41 Sarah Bradford, *King George VI* (London, 1989), 340.
42 Ibid. 339.
43 Gilbert, *Churchill*, vii. 159.
44 Ibid. 251.
45 Piers Dixon, *Double Diploma* (London, 1968), 115.
46 Gilbert, *Churchill*, vii. 999.
47 Gilbert, *Churchill*, viii. 114–15.
48 Gilbert, *Churchill*, v. 303.
49 *Parliamentary Debates* (Commons), vol. 495, cols. 958–62.
50 Gilbert, *Churchill*, viii. 1124.
51 Ibid. 1126.
52 Colville, *Fringes of Power*, 709.

CHAPTER 12

1 *The Times*, 16 Nov. 1945.
2 Ibid. 17 Oct. 1938.
3 *Le Figaro*, 19 July 1939, cited in A. de Monzie, *Ci-Devant* (Paris, 1949), diary entry of 19 Aug. 1939.
4 PRO CAB 16/109, DRC 14, 28 Feb. 1934.
5 WSC to Linlithgow, 3 Nov. 1937: Martin Gilbert, *Churchill*, v. 886.
6 *Daily Telegraph*, 6 May 1938.
7 WSC to Chamberlain, 27 Mar. 1939: Gilbert, *Churchill*, v. 1051.
8 Chamberlain to his sister, cited in Gilbert, *Churchill*, v. 1098.
9 See on this Uri Bialer, *The Shadow of the Bomber* (London, 1976), *passim*.
10 K. H. Völker, *Die Deutsche Luftwaffe* (Stuttgart, 1967), 149; Horst Borg, *Die Deutsche Luftwaffeführung, 1935–1945* (Stuttgart, 1982), 93.
11 WSC to Viscount Cecil, 9 Apr. 1936; Gilbert, *Churchill*, v. 721.
12 WSC to Violet Bonham-Carter, 25 May 1936: Gilbert, *Churchill*, v. 740.
13 CAB 27/623, FPC, 18 Mar. 1938.
14 Cited in Gilbert, *Churchill*, v. 971.
15 Ibid. v. 943–65.
16 *Documents on German Foreign Policy, 1918–1945* (hereafter *DGFP*) (Washington), series D, i, no. 19.
17 Ibid. series D, ii, no. 221.
18 D. C. Watt, 'Hitler's Visit to Rome and the May Weekend Crisis. A Study in Hitler's Response to External Stimuli', *Journal of Contemporary History*, 9 (1974).
19 *Trials of the Major War Criminals*, xxxiv, document 175–C.
20 Michael Salewski, *Die deutsche Seekriegsleitung, 1935–1945* (Frankfurt, 1970), i. 76.

Klaus Meier *et al.* (eds.), *Das Deutsche Reich und der Zweite Weltkrieg* (Stuttgart, 1979), ii. 98 n. 44, citing German Naval Archives MA II-M40.

21 J. Dülffer, *Hitler, Weimar und die Marine* (Dusseldorf, 1979), 468.

22 *DGFP*, series D, vii, Appendix ii, (K), no. iv, 27 Jan. 1939.

23 *Führer Naval Conferences*, Raeder memorandum, 3 Sept. 1939.

24 These passages are based on Harold C. Deutsch, *Hitler and His Generals: The Hidden Crisis, January–June 1938* (Minneapolis, 1974); K. J. Mueller, *Das Heer und Hitler* (Stuttgart, 1979); *Armee und Drittes Reich* (Paderborn, 1987); *Ludwig Beck* (Paderborn, 1989); Bodo Scheurig, *Ewald von Kleist-Schmenzin. Ein Konservative gegen Hitler* (Oldenburg, 1968).

25 See D. C. Watt, 'The *Week* That Was', *Encounter* (May 1972).

26 Gilbert, *Churchill*, v. 720.

27 Anthony Adamthwaite, 'The British Government and the Media, 1937–1938', *Contemporary History*, 18 (1983); Bryan Haworth, 'The BBC, Nazi Germany and the Foreign Office, 1933–1936', *Historical Journal of Film, Radio and Television*, 1 (1981); Philip M. Taylor, *A Call to Arms: British Rearmament, Propaganda and Psychological Preparations for World War II* (Leeds, 1985), Nicholas Pronay, 'The First Reality: Film Censorship in Liberal England', in K. R. M. Short (ed.), *Feature Films on History* (London, 1981); Richard Cockett, *Twilight of Truth: Chamberlain, Appeasement and the Manipulation of the Press* (London, 1989).

28 *Documents on British Foreign Policy*, 3rd series, ii. 686–7, Chamberlain to Halifax, 24 Aug. 1938.

CHAPTER 13

1 Martin Gilbert, *Winston S. Churchill*, companion vol. v, part 1, pp. 1054 and 1202.

2 Lord Gainford to The Hon. Vivian Phillipps, 27 Oct. 1925. BBC Written Archives Centre (WAC), R34/534/1, Policy: Politics General 1922–31.

3 See A. Briggs, *The History of Broadcasting in the United Kingdom*, i: *The Birth of Broadcasting* (London, 1961), and J. Reith, *Into the Wind* (London, 1949).

4 See Briggs, *History of Broadcasting*, and P. Scannel and D. Cardiff, *A Social History of British Broadcasting*, i: *1922–1939* (London, 1991).

5 *The Times*, 11 Feb. 1928, 12.

6 MacDonald Papers, PRO 30/69/8/31, MacDonald to Reith, 1 May 1928. Quoted in T. J. Hollins, 'The Presentation of Politics: The Place of Party Publicity, Broadcasting and Film in British Politics 1918–39', 2 vols. (unpublished Ph.D. thesis, University of Leeds, 1981).

7 Gilbert, *Churchill*, companion vol. v, part 2, pp. 119–24.

8 C. Stuart (ed.), *The Reith Diaries* (London, 1975), 59 and 225.

9 Gilbert, *Churchill*, v. 358.

10 Gilbert, *Churchill*, companion vol. v, part 2, pp. 450–2.

11 Ibid. 1053–61.

12 BBC WAC RCONT 1, Winston Churchill, Talks 1926–39. Letter from WSC to C. A. Siepmann, 3 Jan. 1934.

13 Gilbert, *Churchill*, companion vol. v, part 2, p. 581 n.

14 R. Rhodes James (ed.), *Churchill Speaks: Winston S. Churchill in Peace and War. Collected Speeches 1897–1963* (London, 1981), iv. 3528.

15 PRO PREM/1/301, Memorandum by O. S. Cleverly, 20 Apr. 1939.

16 BBC WAC RCONT 1, Winston Churchill, Talks 1926–39, 15 Dec. 1939, internal memo from Edward Shackleton, and comment by Sir Richard Maconachie, Director of Talks.

17 A. Roberts, '*The Holy Fox*': *A Biography of Lord Halifax* (London, 1991) 189; and Gilbert, *Churchill*, vi. 136–40.
18 Entry in Murrow's diary for 30 Nov. 1954; E. Bliss (ed.), *In Search of Light: The Broadcasts of Edward R. Murrow* (London, 1968), 237.
19 J. Colville in J. W. Wheeler-Bennett (ed.), *Action This Day* (London, 1968), 72.
20 G. Wyndham Goldie, *Facing the Nation: Television and Politics 1935–1976* (London, 1977), 173.
21 The four occasions were: (a) April 1928: the BBC was ready to transmit but permission was not given (Stuart, *Reith Diaries*, 99); (b) the BBC prepared to record for subsequent transmission his speech to the House of Commons on Tuesday 20 Aug. 1940; however, the arrangements were quickly cancelled by instructions from Mr L. Wellington of the Ministry of Information (BBC WAC RCONT 1, Winston Churchill, Talks 1940–65); (c) September 1940 (*Parliamentary Debates* (Commons), 19 Sept. 1940, cols. 192–3); (d) January 1942 (*Parliamentary Debates* (Commons), 20 Jan. 1942, cols. 199–202).
22 See Appendix.
23 A Listener Research Report: The Prime Minister's broadcast before the 9 p.m. news, Sunday 15 Feb. 1942, Ref. BBC WAC R/713 Confidential. The workings of the bureau are explained in R. E. Silvey, *Who's Listening* (London, 1974).
24 BBC WAC RCONT 1, Winston Churchill, Talks 1940–65. Memo from Robert Gladwell to Assistant Controller of Talks, 6 Sept. 1956. There is no reply on file; presumably the suggestion was dropped.
25 'After dinner we had a deplorable American film, *Citizen Kane*, based on the personality of William Randolph Hearst. The P.M. was so bored that he walked out before the end.' Diary entry by John Colville for 20 July 1941, in J. Colville, *The Fringes of Power: Downing Street Diaries, 1939–1955* (London, 1985), 416.
26 Projection equipment was installed, first at Ditchley Manor, his safe haven for weekends in 1940–1, later at Chequers, and after the war as a gift from Alexander Korda, at Chartwell. See D. J. Wenden and K. R. M. Short, 'Churchill Film Fan', *Historical Journal of Film Radio and Television* (*H.J.F.R.T.*), 11, 3 (1991).
27 W. S. Churchill, *The River War* (London, 1899), 142–3. This comment is not in the abridged 1933 edition. W. K. L. Dickson, The *Biograph in Battle* (London, 1901); M. Gilbert, *Churchill: A Life* (London, 1991), 106.
28 *The Film in National Life. The Report of the Commission on Educational and Cultural Films* (London, 1932), 10. Letter to Sir Horace Hamilton, 26 Mar. 1926; Gilbert, *Churchill*, companion vol. v, part 1, p. 683.
29 Gilbert, *Churchill*, companion vol. v, part 1, p. 1247.
30 Ibid. 1051–2.
31 WSC is also portrayed in *The Fall of Berlin* (USSR, 1949), *The Unforgettable Year 1919* (USSR, 1952), *The Siege of Sidney Street* (GB, 1960), *Operation Crossbow* (GB, 1965), *The Great Battle* (USSR, 1969), and *The Eagle has Landed* (GB, 1977).
32 Gilbert, *Churchill*, viii. 1204–7.
33 See C. Foreman, *The Screen Play of the Film: Young Winston* (London, 1972). In addition to Anne Bancroft and Simon Ward, the cast reads like a Who's Who of British stage and screen.
34 See J. Richards, *Visions of Yesterday* (London, 1973).
35 He was lampooned in *Soldaten von Morgen* (1941) and vilified in *Il Dottor Churchill* (1941).
36 16 mm. copies of *Ohm Krüger* and the films mentioned in n. 35 can be rented from the Imperial War Museum.
37 Gilbert, *Churchill*, v. 346–9, and companion vol. v, part 2, pp. 83, 96–8, 282, 357, and 394.

38 K. Brownlow, documentary film, *The Unknown Chaplin*.
39 The first shots of Churchill in the National Film Archive (NFA) of the British Film Institute, London, are 1910 Pathé Freres, 110 ft. They show WSC and the General Staff on horseback. Three items dealing with the siege are listed in the NFA Catalogue (London, 1965), N. 323, N. 354, and N. 355. They are available for viewing.
40 In April 1899 during the Dreyfus agitation Jules Guerin, together with other anti-Semitic Derouledistes in their rue de Chabrol offices, defied police and military for 37 days. They were starved into submission without a shot being fired. See *The Times*, 5 Jan. 1911.
41 Ibid. 5 Jan. 1911.
42 *Parliamentary Debates* (Commons), 13 Feb. 1911, col. 843.
43 See G. Aldermann, *The Jewish Community in British Politics* (Oxford, 1983).
44 *Parliamentary Debates* (Commons), 26 June 1911, col. 251.
45 *Parliamentary Debates* (Commons), 6 Feb. 1911, col. 55.
46 See K. Kulick, *Alexander Korda: The Man Who Could Work Miracles* (London, 1975).
47 R. Schickel, *D. W. Griffith and the Birth of Film* (London, 1984), 345.
48 See R. Fielding, *The March of Time, 1935–1951* (New York, 1978).
49 Gilbert, *Churchill*, companion vol. v, part 2, pp. 869–70.
50 Ibid. 876–8, 880–1, 883, 909, 954–5, 962–4, 972–4, 981, 1031–4, 1038–9, 1045–6, 1081. The draft scenario is given on pp. 989–1031.
51 Ibid. 974.
52 Ibid. 1081.
53 D. Garnett (ed.), *The Letters of T. E. Lawrence* (London, 1938), 851.
54 J. Mack, *A Prince of Our Disorder: The Life of T. E. Lawrence* (Boston, 1976), 404.
55 See K. R. M. Short, 'That Hamilton Woman', *H.J.F.R.T.*, 11, 1 (1991).
56 See M. Balcon, *Michael Balcon Presents . . . A Lifetime of Films* (London, 1969), 132–6, and J. Richards, 'War Time British Cinema Audiences and the Class System: The Case of "Ships With Wings" ', *H.J.F.R.T.*, 7 (1987), 129–41.
57 C. Moorehead, *Sidney Bernstein: A Biography* (London, 1984), 148–9.
58 M. Balcon, *Michael Balcon Presents*; C. Coultass, 'British Cinema and the Reality of War', in P. Taylor (ed.), *Britain and the Cinema in the Second World War* (London, 1988), 84–6; and J. Richards, *Thorold Dickinson: The Man and His Films* (London, 1986), 93–105.
59 See D. Badder, 'Powell and Pressburger: The War Years', and I. Christie, 'The Colonel Blimp File', *Sight and Sound*, 48 (1978); I. Christie, *Arrows of Desire: The Films of M. Powell and E. Pressburger* (London, 1985); and M. Powell, *A Life in Movies* (London, 1986).
60 C. Barr, 'War Records', *Sight and Sound*, 58, 4 (1987), 262.
61 Richards, *Dickinson*, 104.
62 T. J. Hollins, 'The Presentation of Politics', 672.
63 See *Researcher's Guide to British Newsreel* and *Researcher's Guide to British Film and Television Collection*, both published by the British Universities Film and Video Council.
64 E. Barrymore, *Ethel Barrymore, Memories* (New York, 1955), 85, 91, 114, 125, 146, 163: H. Alpert, *The Barrymores* (London, 1965), 79; and Randolph S. Churchill, *Churchill*, i. 252.
65 D. Irving, *Churchill's War*, i: *The Struggle for Power* (London, 1987), 313.
66 J. Snagge and M. Barsley, *Those Vintage Years of Radio* (London, 1972), 35–6.
67 Letter from Sally Hine to the *Guardian*, 29 Apr. 1991.
68 Letter to H. Nicolson, 5 June 1940, in *Harold Nicolson, Diaries and Letters 1939–1945*, ed. Nigel Nicolson (London, 1967), 93.

69 Nicolson, *Diaries and Letters*, 97.
70 C. Ponting, *1940: Myth and Reality*, (London, 1990), 158–9.
71 *New Scientist*, 18 May 1991, p. 26.
72 I wish to acknowledge the use of material from the BBC Written Archives Centre, Caversham, Reading, and especially the assistance given by Mr Jeffery Walden, who works for, and Ms Sian Nicholas (Nuffield College) who is researching in, the archives.

CHAPTER 14

1 Winston S. Churchill, *The Second World War* (6 vols., London, 1948–54), i. 526–7.
2 'A Note on the War in 1940', ADM 199/1929 (PRO). The official biography quotes extensively from this memorandum, but without including these sentences. See Martin Gilbert, *Winston S. Churchill*, vi. 111–12.
3 Churchill, *Second World War*, i. 320. Cf. Arthur Marder, '"Winston is Back": Churchill at the Admiralty, 1939–1940', *English Historical Review*, supplement 5 (1972).
4 'The Naval Memoirs of Admiral J. H. Godfrey', vol. v, part 1, p. 63, GDFY I/VI (Churchill College Archive Centre, Cambridge).
5 Letter to Stanley Baldwin, May 1926, in Gilbert, *Churchill*, v. 196.
6 Neville Chamberlain to Hilda Chamberlain, 17 Sept. 1939, Neville Chamberlain papers, NC 18/1/1121 (Birmingham University Library).
7 Treasury, 'A Note on the Financial Situation', 3 July 1939, copy in CAB 23/100, fols. 138–40 (PRO).
8 Neville Chamberlain to Ida Chamberlain, 8 Oct. 1939, Chamberlain papers, NC 18/1/1124.
9 David Dilks, 'The Twilight War and the Fall of France: Chamberlain and Churchill in 1940', *Transactions of the Royal Historical Society*, 5th series, xxviii (1978), 64.
10 Churchill, 'Possible Détente with Italy in the Mediterranean', 18 Oct. 1939, CAB 66/2, WP (39) 92 (PRO).
11 Pound to Churchill, 3 Dec. 1939, ADM 199/1928 (PRO). Accounts of the Baltic strategy include Marder, '"Winston is Back"', esp. 31 ff.; R. A. C. Parker, 'Britain, France and Scandinavia, 1939–40', *History*, 61 (1976), 369–87; François Bédarida, 'France, Britain and the Nordic Countries', and David Dilks, 'Great Britain and Scandinavia in the "Phoney War"', *Scandinavian Journal of History*, 2 (1977), 7–27 and 29–51; and Gilbert, *Churchill*, vi, chs. 6–14.
12 Marder, '"Winston is Back"', 58.
13 WM 10 (40) 1, CA, 12 Jan. 1940, CAB 65/11 (PRO).
14 Churchill to Halifax, 14 Mar. 1940, FO 800/328, Hal/40/11 (PRO).
15 Williamson Murray, 'The Strategy of the "Phoney War": A Re-evaluation', *Military Affairs*, 45 (1981), 13–17.
16 Churchill, *Second World War*, ii. 38. For the rest of this paragraph see fuller detail in David Reynolds, '1940: Fulcrum of the Twentieth Century?', *International Affairs*, 66 (1990), 325–50.
17 Brian Bond, *British Military Policy between the Two World Wars* (Oxford, 1980), 337.
18 Cf. Richard Overy, 'German Air Strength, 1933 to 1939: A Note', *Historical Journal*, 27 (1984), 465–71.
19 P. M. H. Bell, *A Certain Eventuality: Britain and the Fall of France* (Farnborough, Hants, 1974), ch. 2.
20 For full documentation see David Reynolds, 'Churchill and the British "Decision" to Fight On in 1940: Right Policy, Wrong Reasons', in Richard Langhorne (ed.),

Diplomacy and Intelligence during the Second World War (Cambridge, 1985), 147–67.

21 Halifax diary, 27 May 1940, Hickleton papers, A7.8.4, p. 142 (Borthwick Institute, York).

22 WM 142 CA, 27 May 1940, CAB 65/13 (PRO).

23 Gilbert, *Churchill*, vi. 419–21.

24 Quotations from Mallet to FO, 19 June 1940, and Churchill to Halifax, 26 June 1940, FO 800/322, fols. 272 and 277. See also Thomas Munch-Petersen, '"Common Sense not Bravado": The Butler-Prytz Interview of 17 June 1940', *Scandia*, 52 (1986), 73–114.

25 Churchill, *Second World War*, ii. 24.

26 Churchill to Chamberlain, 9 Oct. 1939, PREM 1/395.

27 WM 142 CA, 27 May 1940, CAB 65/13, fol. 180.

28 Robert E. Sherwood, notes of interview with Ismay, 11 July 1946, Sherwood papers, folder 1891 (Houghton Library, Harvard University, Cambridge, Mass.).

29 Memorandum of 3 Sept. 1940, WP (40) 352, CAB 66/11.

30 Cf. Lindsay to Vansittart, 21 Oct. 1929, Vansittart papers, VNST II, 1/2 (Churchill College Archive Centre).

31 Neville Chamberlain to Hilda Chamberlain, 17 Dec. 1937, Chamberlain papers, NC 18/1/1032.

32 Churchill, *Second World War*, ii. 22.

33 WP (40) 168, para. 1, 25 May 1940, CAB 66/7 (PRO).

34 Winston S. Churchill, *Secret Session Speeches*, compiled by Charles Eade (London, 1946), 15. For fuller background see Reynolds, 'Churchill and the British "Decision"', 160–7, and David Reynolds, *The Creation of the Anglo–American Alliance, 1937–1941: A Study in Competitive Co-operation* (London, 1981), chs. 4–5.

35 WM 141 (40) 9, CAB 65/7.

36 Churchill to Ismay, 17 July 1940, PREM 3/475/1.

37 *Parliamentary Debates* (Commons), 5th series, 5 Sept. 1940, vol. 365, col. 39.

38 WM 310 (40) 5, CAB 65/10; Churchill to Halifax, 5 May 1941, FO 371/26148, A3496.

39 *Parliamentary Debates* (Commons), 20 Aug. 1940, vol. 364, col. 1171.

40 Churchill, *Second World War*, ii. 293–7.

41 *The Memoirs of General the Lord Ismay* (London, 1960), 179–80.

42 Sir John Wheeler-Bennett (ed.), *Action This Day: Working with Churchill* (London, 1968), 49.

43 John Colville, *The Fringes of Power: Downing Street Diaries, 1939–1955* (London, 1985), 154, 159.

44 Wheeler-Bennett, *Action This Day*, 162.

45 Christopher Andrew, 'Churchill and Intelligence', *Intelligence and National Security*, 3 (1988), 182.

46 Edward Thomas, 'The Evolution of the JIC System up to and during World War II', in Christopher Andrew and Jeremy Noakes (eds.), *Intelligence and International Relations, 1900–1945* (Exeter, 1987), 228.

47 F. H. Hinsley, with E. E. Thomas, C. F. G. Ransom, and R. C. Knight, *British Intelligence in the Second World War* (London, 1979), i. 176–9.

48 David Dilks (ed.), *The Diaries of Sir Alexander Cadogan O.M., 1938–1945* (London, 1971), 21.

49 Gilbert, *Churchill*, vi. 612.

50 Ismay, *Memoirs*, 183–4.

51 E. Bliss (ed.), *In Search of Light: The Broadcasts of Edward R. Murrow* (London, 1968), 237.

52 Piers Brendon, *Winston Churchill* (London, 1984), 142.

53 Letter of 5 June, in *Harold Nicolson, Diaries and Letters, 1939–1945*, ed. Nigel Nicolson (London, 1967), 93.
54 Churchill, *Second World War*, ii. 198–9.
55 Henry Pelling, *Winston Churchill* (2nd edn., London, 1989), 458–9.
56 Churchill to Chamberlain, 10 May 1940, Chamberlain papers, NC 7/9/80.
57 Wheeler-Bennett, *Action This Day*, 29.
58 David Cannadine (ed.), *Blood, Toil, Tears and Sweat: Winston Churchill's Famous Speeches* (London, 1989), 4.
59 For fuller detail see D. J. Wenden in this volume, Ch. 13.
60 Colville, *Fringes of Power*, 509.
61 J. H. Plumb, 'The Historian', in A. J. P. Taylor *et al.*, *Churchill: Four Faces and the Man* (London, 1969), 149.
62 For an entertainingly apoplectic example see Noel Annan in the *London Review of Books*, 1 Aug. 1985, 5.

CHAPTER 15

1 Martin Gilbert, *Winston S. Churchill*, v. 457.
2 Winston S. Churchill, *Great Contemporaries* (London, 1937), 261.
3 Quoted in Henry Pelling, *Winston Churchill* (London, 1974), 393.
4 R. J. Minney, *The Private Papers of Hore-Belisha* (London, 1960), 130.
5 See D. Cameron Watt, in this volume, Ch. 12.
6 The most accessible source for this is David Cannadine (ed.), *Blood, Toil, Tears and Sweat: Winston Churchill's Famous Speeches* (London, 1989), 130–43.
7 Lord Halifax, *Fulness of Days* (London, 1957), 200.
8 Keith Feiling, *Neville Chamberlain* (London, 1947), 406.
9 Pelling, *Churchill*, 397.
10 Lord Birkenhead, *Halifax* (London, 1965), 454, quoting diary of 9 May 1940.
11 Sir John Anderson (later Lord Waverley), Home Secretary at the time. He was Churchill's recommended choice to the King early in 1945 in the event of both Churchill and Eden being killed.
12 Birkenhead, *Halifax*, 453.
13 Ibid.
14 Where the Labour Party Conference was being held.
15 Birkenhead, *Halifax*, 454.
16 Ibid. 455.
17 Winston Churchill, *The Second World War* (London, 1948), i. 523–4.
18 Lord Moran, *Winston Churchill: The Struggle for Survival, 1940–1965* (London, 1966), 323.
19 C. E. Lysaght, *Brendan Bracken* (London, 1979), 172–3. The references are to A. J. P. Taylor, *Beaverbrook* (London, 1972), 409; L. S. Amery, *My Political Life* (London, 1950), iii. 371; and E. L. Spears, *Prelude to Dunkirk* (London, 1954), 130–1.
20 A largely forgotten figure (1881–1942) who held numerous offices and till then had been a strong supporter of Chamberlain. He was Chancellor of the Exchequer, 1940–2.
21 Lord Avon, *The Reckoning* (London, 1965), 96–7.
22 Taylor, *Beaverbrook*, 409.
23 Amery, *My Political Life*, iii. 371–2.
24 Lysaght, *Bracken*, 173.
25 Kenneth Harris, *Attlee* (London, 1982), 173.

26 Harris, *Attlee*, 173.
27 Ben Pimlott (ed.), *The Political Diary of Hugh Dalton* (London, 1986), 344.
28 John Wheeler-Bennett, *King George VI* (London, 1958), 443–4.
29 Churchill, *Second World War*, i. 525.
30 Sir Archibald Sinclair, Leader of the Liberal Party.
31 Taylor, *Beaverbrook*, 410.
32 John Wheeler-Bennett (ed.), *Action This Day* (London, 1968), 48–9.
33 Taylor, *Beaverbrook*, 410. They spent the afternoon of 12 May together, and Beaverbrook stayed for dinner.
34 Gilbert, *Churchill*, vi. 316.
35 Ibid. 327, quoting Baldwin papers.
36 Ibid., quoting Colville's Diary.
37 Andrew Roberts, '*The Holy Fox*' (London, 1991), 208.
38 Ibid. 209.

CHAPTER 16

1 Adolf Hitler, *Mein Kampf* (Boston, 1971), 158.
2 Winston S. Churchill, *The World Crisis, 1911–1918* (London, 1960), 17.
3 Martin Gilbert, *Winston S. Churchill*, iii. 43.
4 Ibid.
5 Gilbert, *Churchill*, iii. 205.
6 Gilbert, *Churchill*, iv. 607.
7 Ibid.
8 Gilbert, *Churchill*, v. 76.
9 Cabinet Minutes, 17 Mar. 1924, cited in Stephen Roskill, *Hankey: Man of Secrets* (London, 1972), ii. 360.
10 Gilbert, *Churchill*, v. 457.
11 Ibid. 700.
12 P. G. Edwards, *Prime Ministers and Diplomats: The Making of Australian Foreign Policy 1901–1949* (Melbourne, 1983), 63.
13 G. Hermon Gill, *Royal Australian Navy, 1939–1942* (Canberra, 1957), 24.
14 John Colville, *Footprints in Time* (London, 1976), 129.
15 Winston S. Churchill, *The Second World War* (London, 1950), iii. 367.
16 Ibid. 369.
17 Gilbert, *Churchill*, v. 1075.
18 Churchill, *Second World War*, iv. 4.
19 Ibid. 7–8.
20 Ibid. 8.

Chapter 17

1 Craig R. Whitney, *New York Times*, 25 Jan. 1991. For effect, ellipses have not been used. The full quotation reads: 'The war in the Persian Gulf has abruptly halted momentum toward political unity in Europe, breathed new life into the "special relationship" between the United States and Britain and raised widespread concern about pacifism in Germany, diplomats, Government officials and strategic experts here [London] say.'
2 Paul Fussell's *Wartime* (New York, 1989), which attacked the romanticizing of the Second World War, received strong criticism. For an example of Anglo-American tension as headline news see the *New York Times*, 11 July 1984, 1.

3 After hours of poring over wartime photographs of Churchill, I have found only a handful without a cigar—usually taken when he was making a formal speech. Equally intriguing is the rare appearance of any plume of smoke. Averell Harriman claimed that Churchill talked so much during meetings that he had no time to light the cigar. In one picture, what I at first thought to be a curious signet ring turned out to be a cigar band slipped over his ring finger. (Raymond O'Connor to the author, 21 Dec. 1987, recounting an interview with Harriman.) See also Ian Jacob's essay in John Wheeler-Bennett (ed.), *Action This Day* (London, 1968), 182.

4 See, for example, Fraser J. Harbutt, *The Iron Curtain: Churchill, America, and the Origins of the Cold War* (New York, 1986).

5 Much of this paragraph is lifted, with gratitude, from Christopher Hitchens, *Blood, Class, and Nostalgia: Anglo-American Ironies* (New York, 1990), 180–6, although the positioning of the statue in Kansas City is based on my own recollection. Similar information but in an even more sarcastic tone is found in Andrew Sullivan, 'Winstoned! America's Churchill Addiction', *The New Republic*, 7 Dec. 1987, reprinted, with a rejoinder, in *Finest Hour*, no. 58 (winter 1987–8), 16–18.

6 *New York Times Book Review*, 21 Oct. 1984; *Times Literary Supplement*, 8 Feb. 1985; *The New York Review*, 14 Feb. 1985; *Asiaweek*, 31 May 1985; *Newsday*, 9 Sept. 1984; *Baltimore Sun*, 27 Jan. 1985; *Atlantic Magazine*, Oct. 1984.

7 Letters to the editor, *New York Times*, 21 July 1984.

8 For examples of new studies on Anglo-American relations, see the works of David Reynolds: 'A "Special Relationship"? America, Britain and the International Order since the Second World War', *International Affairs*, 62, 1 (winter 1985–6), 1–20, in which n. 2 gives some additional studies; 'Roosevelt, Churchill, and the Wartime Anglo-American Alliance, 1939–1945: Towards a New Synthesis', in Wm. Roger Louis and Hedley Bull (eds.), *The 'Special Relationship'* (Oxford, 1986), 17–41; 'The "Big Three" and the Division of Europe, 1945–1949', *Diplomacy and Statecraft*, 1, 2 (July 1990), 111–36; 'Rethinking Anglo-American Relations', *International Affairs*, 65, 1 (winter 1988–9), 89–111; 'Churchill, the Special Relationship and the Debate about Post-War European Security, 1940–1945' (unpublished paper presented at the American Historical Assoc. meeting, San Francisco, Dec. 1983). Also D. C. Watt, *Succeeding John Bull* (New York, 1984), and the works of Christopher Thorne. A good summary of the recent literature is Peter Boyle, 'The Special Relationship: An Alliance of Convenience?', *Journal of American Studies*, 22 (Dec. 1988), 457–65. Joseph P. Lash described the partnership in the subtitle of his book, *Roosevelt and Churchill, 1939–1941: The Partnership that Saved the West* (New York, 1976).

9 The pages of the Churchill Society publication, *Finest Hour*, provide the best example of the popular view. As for scholars, the wartime volumes of Martin Gilbert's official biography, *Winston S. Churchill* (vols. vi and vii) follow the picture drawn by Churchill in his own history, *The Second World War*, 6 vols. (Boston, 1948–53). Recent examples of Churchill-as-hero-and-saviour are David Jablonsky, *Churchill, The Great Game and Total War* (London, 1991), and John Lukacs, *The Duel: Hitler vs. Churchill: 10 May–31 July 1940* (London, 1990).

10 '"Dr. New Deal": Franklin D. Roosevelt as Commander in Chief', in J. Dawson (ed.), *Commander in Chief: Presidential Wartime Leadership from McKinley to Nixon* (Lawrence: Univ. Press of Kansas, forthcoming).

11 Robert Sherwood, *Roosevelt and Hopkins* (rev. edn.; New York, 1950), 364.

12 Eden is quoted in David Reynolds, *The Creation of the Anglo-American Alliance, 1937–1941* (Chapel Hill, 1982), 266. The Tom Sawyer image is that of Leslie H. Gelb, *Anglo-American Relations, 1945–1949* (Harvard Dissertations in American History and Political Science; New York and London, 1988), 47. A. J. P. Taylor, *English History, 1914–1945* (Oxford, 1965).

13 The Churchill quip is taken from a speech by Anthony Montague Brown, printed in *Finest Hour*, no. 50 (winter 1985–6), 12. Brown asserted that it came in response to a sally by Sir Samuel Hoare: 'Winston has written a huge book all about himself and called it *The World Crisis*.' Brown also pointed out, correctly, that Churchill frequently repeated his best epigrams. The facts-to-phrases confession is quoted by Norman Rose in 'Churchill and Zionism', this volume, Ch. 9. Deakin's characterization is from a speech by Lord Blake, 'Winston Churchill the Historian', printed in *Proceedings of the Churchill Societies, 1988–1989*, ed. Richard M. Langworth (Contoo-cook, NH: Dragonwyck Publ. for the International Churchill Societies, 1990), 21.

Colville's comment is from a diary entry of 1 Jan. 1953, *The Fringes of Power* (New York and London, 1985), 658. That entry includes a summary of comments by Churchill that, if accurate, suggest a quite extraordinary historical memory on Churchill's part: 'Finally he [Churchill] lamented that . . . he could not tell the story of how the United States gave away, to please Russia, vast tracts of Europe . . . If F.D.R. had lived, and had been in good health, he would have seen the red light in time to check American policy: Truman, after all, had only been a novice bewildered by the march of events . . .'

14 McNeill, *America, Britain, and Russia: Their Co-operation and Conflict, 1941–1946* (New York and London, 1970; orig. publ. 1953), 4–5, 151 n. 1.

15 To take but three examples: Wm. Roger Louis, *Imperialism At Bay* (New York, 1977); Christopher Thorne, *Allies of a Kind* (New York, 1978); and Michael Howard, *Grand Strategy, iv: August 1942–September 1943* (British official History of the Second World War; London, 1972), who wrote with special access to British archives.

16 See Reynolds, 'Roosevelt, Churchill, and the Wartime Anglo–American Alliance'. Theodore A. Wilson, *The First Summit: Roosevelt and Churchill at Placentia Bay, 1941* (rev. edn.; Lawrence, KS, 1991), pp. x–xi provides additional comment and citations on this point. An example of how the new documentation has cast doubts on the reliability of Churchill's account is Steven M. Miner, *Between Churchill and Stalin: The Soviet Union, Great Britain, and the Origins of the Grand Alliance* (Chapel Hill, 1988), 196.

17 At a 1986 meeting of the Soviet–American Project on the History of the Second World War, Soviet historians claimed that there was no need to push for access to their archives because Stalin had removed everything of value. Then, lo and behold, three years later Soviet archivists 'found' a copy of the Secret Protocol to the Nazi–Soviet Pact.

Most of the recent Soviet publications of the Second World War era documents are a bit disappointing. Those on Anglo–Soviet and Soviet–American relations ignore the period of the Nazi–Soviet Pact, and are padded with previously published Stalin statements and messages. There are exchanges between Soviet ambassadors and Moscow that offer glimpses into their thinking, but policy formulation remains shrouded. The volumes on Franco–Soviet relations go so far as to include excerpts from Charles de Gaulle's published memoirs. See *Sovetsko-Angliiskie Otnosheniya vo vremya velikoi otechestvennoi voiny, 1941–1945*, 2 vols. (Moscow, 1983); *Sovetsko-Amerikanskie Otnosheniya vo vremya velikoi otechestvennoi voiny, 1941–1945*, 2 vols. (Moscow, 1983). More promising is the collection *God Krizisa [Year of Crisis], 1938–1939: Dokumenty i Materialy* (Moscow, 1990), which prints some of the Soviet analyses of policy options that faced Stalin. Steven Miner of Ohio University is preparing a review of these and other recent documentary collections published by the Soviet government.

18 Robin Edmonds, *The Big Three: Churchill, Roosevelt and Stalin in Peace and War* (New York, 1991), 14.

19 These conferences were: Atlantic (Aug. 1941), 1st Washington (Dec. 1941–Jan. 1942), 2nd Washington (June 1942), Casablanca (Jan. 1943), 3rd Washington (May 1943), 1st Quebec (Aug.–Sept. 1943), 1st Cairo (Nov. 1943), Tehran (Nov.–Dec. 1943), 2nd Cairo (Dec. 1943), 2nd Quebec (Sept. 1944), Malta (Feb. 1945), Yalta (Feb. 1945), Gt Bitter Lake, Egypt (Feb. 1945).

20 The Churchill–Stalin meetings were both in Moscow, in Aug. 1942 and Oct. 1944.

21 That was also the occasion for Burton to characterize the role as depressing, for he found Churchill bloodthirsty and vindictive. He received a thorough scolding from Churchill's contemporaries for his iconoclasm. Burton's feelings are expressed in 'To Play Churchill is to Hate Him', *New York Times*, sec. 2, 24 Nov. 1974.

22 Sherwood, *Roosevelt and Hopkins*, 350–1; Michael Beschloss, *Kennedy and Roosevelt: The Uneasy Alliance* (New York, 1980), 200, 230; Wilson, *The First Summit*, 80–1. See also Harry Hopkins to Felix Frankfurter, 14 Dec. 1948 (Frankfurter papers, Library of Congress, box 102, folder 2112). Churchill's revised recollection of their meeting in his *The Second World War*, i: *The Gathering Storm*, 440.

23 Warren F. Kimball (ed.), *Churchill & Roosevelt: The Complete Correspondence*, 3 vols. (Princeton, 1984), i. 23. The *Marlborough* volume was inscribed: 'With earnest best wishes for the success of the greatest crusade of modern times.' Actually, Churchill was ambivalent about the New Deal, though he staunchly praised the repeal of prohibition. Churchill was re-elected to Parliament in the election of 1929, but lost his Cabinet office when Labour took power.

24 Kimball, *Churchill & Roosevelt*, i. R–ix.

25 Beschloss, *Kennedy and Roosevelt*, 200. When Roosevelt and Canadian Prime Minister Mackenzie King met in April 1940, they spent much of the time gossiping about Churchill's drinking; J. L. Granatstein, *Canada's War* (Toronto, 1975), 117. When Churchill became Prime Minister, Roosevelt commented he 'supposed Churchill was the best man that England had, even if he was drunk half of his time': David Dimbleby and David Reynolds, *An Ocean Apart: The Relationship Between Britain and America in the Twentieth Century* (New York, 1988), 136. Wendell Willkie, asked by Roosevelt in 1941 if Churchill was a drunk, replied that he had as much to drink as Churchill did when they met, 'and no one has ever called me a drunk'. See Warren F. Kimball, *The Juggler: Franklin Roosevelt as Wartime Statesman* (Princeton, 1991), 225–6 n. 6. Churchill's Victorianism is discussed in ibid. 66–7, and seen as an asset by Jablonsky in *Churchill, The Great Game and Total War*.

26 We can speculate as to why F.D.R. did not contact other potential Prime Ministers—perhaps Churchill's hard-nosed anti-Hitler views appealed to F.D.R.? But the available evidence suggests that practical politics, opportunism, was Roosevelt's motive—not any sense of a 'special relationship' with Churchill. The Roosevelt martini is described with distaste by Charles E. Bohlen, *Witness to History, 1929–1969* (New York, 1973), 143. See Sherwood, *Roosevelt and Hopkins*, 115, for some other 'vile' concoctions.

27 Churchill later denied delivering such a line, but there are two sources for the story; Kimball, *The Juggler*, 16.

28 Hugh Dalton Diary, 21 July 1941 (London School of Economics Library); Alexander Cadogan Diaries, 17 July 1941 (Churchill College, Cambridge); David Dilks (ed.), *The Diaries of Sir Alexander Cadogan* (New York, 1972), 21 July 1941, 393; Duff Cooper to Churchill, 22 July 1941, PREM 3/224/2 (Public Record Office, Kew), 69–70.

29 For example, despite a number of written pleas from myself and other historians, a number of PREM 3 files for late 1941 on relations with Japan remain closed. The study by James Rusbridger and Eric Nave, *Betrayal at Pearl Harbor: How Churchill Lured Roosevelt into World War II* (New York, 1991) points to a number of other

still-closed British files that if opened for research could, once and for all, settle this matter.

30 Kimball, *Churchill & Roosevelt*, i. C–103, C–146; iii. C–914; and *The Juggler*, 173–83.

31 Minute by Alexander Cadogan, 25 Jan. 1941, quoted in Lash, *Roosevelt and Churchill*, 282. Kimball, *Churchill & Roosevelt*, i. pp. 3–4 and R–78x.

32 Lord Moran [Charles Wilson], *Churchill: Taken from the Diaries of Lord Moran* (Boston, 1966), entry for 5 Feb. 1945, 240. See also Ted Morgan, *FDR: A Biography* (London, 1986), 759. Averell Harriman claimed that Roosevelt saw Churchill as 'pretty much a nineteenth century colonialist': W. Averell Harriman and Elie Abel, *Special Envoy to Churchill and Stalin, 1941–1946* (New York, 1975), 191. Sherwood describes Churchill's White House quarters; *Roosevelt and Hopkins*, 203. For the concerns of New Dealers see, for example, the diaries of Henry Morgenthau, Jr, at the Franklin D. Roosevelt Library (FDRL: Hyde Park, NY), or the diaries of Assistant Secretary of State Adolf Berle, *Navigating the Rapids, 1918–1971: From the Papers of Adolf A. Berle*, ed. Beatrice Bishop Berle and Travis Beal Jacobs (New York, 1973). See also Harbutt, *The Iron Curtain* esp. 15–19. F.D.R's 'wonderful old Tory' comment is from John Gunther, *Roosevelt in Retrospect* (New York, 1950), 16.

33 A recent study of Churchill's problems with domestic politics during the war is Kevin Jefferys, *The Churchill Coalition and Wartime Politics, 1940–1945* (Manchester and New York, 1991).

34 One Rex Applegate, who had been a bodyguard for F.D.R., recalled 'sitting in earshot when Roosevelt and Churchill met at Shangri-la—you should have heard them cuss each other out!' Found, with thanks to Lloyd Gardner, in Garry Wills, *The Second Civil War* (New York, 1968), 63. Churchill, convalescing in Marrakesh, said of Roosevelt: 'I love that man': Moran, *Diaries*, 243.

35 All these are discussed in Kimball, *Churchill & Roosevelt*, i. 12–13, and in the Churchill–Roosevelt exchanges preceding the Tehran and Yalta conferences. For the TOLSTOY meetings see *The Juggler*, 159–83.

36 Kimball, *Churchill & Roosevelt*, iii. 632; Churchill, *The Second World War*, vi: *Triumph and Tragedy*, 478–80.

37 See Kimball, *Churchill & Roosevelt*, i. 281–324, esp. R–73x, drafts A and B. Pressure for a Pacific-First campaign is discussed in Mark A. Stoler, *The Politics of the Second Front: American Military Planning and Diplomacy in Coalition Warfare, 1941–1943* (Westport, CT, 1977), 25–6, 28–9, 40–1, and 'The "Pacific-First" Alternative in American World War II Strategy', *The International History Review*, 2 (July 1980), 432–52; Robert Dallek, *Franklin D. Roosevelt and American Foreign Policy, 1932–1945* (New York, 1979), 331–4; and Richard W. Steele, *The First Offensive, 1942: Roosevelt, Marshall, and the Making of American Strategy* (Bloomington, 1973), ch. 4. Roosevelt's concerns are obvious from a reading of the Harry Hopkins papers (FDRL), and Sherwood, *Roosevelt and Hopkins*, e.g. 594.

38 See Kimball, *The Juggler*, 'Casablanca: The End of Imperial Romance', 63–81. As Michael Howard has explained in *Grand Strategy*, Churchill did not blindly oppose a Second Front in France—in fact he endorsed it on a number of occasions. But it is equally clear from the Churchill–Roosevelt correspondence that Churchill did not support an American-style, all-or-nothing invasion.

39 See Warren F. Kimball, 'Roosevelt and the Southwest Pacific: "Merely a Facade"?', in David Day (ed.), *The Making of Australian Foreign Policy: The Contribution of Dr H. V. Evatt* (St Lucia, Queensland, forthcoming).

40 Moran, *Diaries*, 218, 221.

41 Robert Garson, 'The Atlantic Alliance, Eastern Europe and the Origins of the Cold War: From Pearl Harbor to Yalta', in H. C. Allen and Roger Thompson (eds.),

Contrast and Connection: Bicentennial Essays in Anglo–American History (London, 1976), 300.

42 That was not, of course, Churchill's reason for retirement, but it did determine the timing. See Gilbert, *Churchill*, viii. 1018–1128. See also the documents in Peter Boyle (ed.), *The Churchill–Eisenhower Correspondence, 1953–1955* (Chapel Hill, 1991).

43 Kimball, *Churchill & Roosevelt*, iii. C-905, 8 Mar. 1945.

44 Quoted in David Carlton, *Anthony Eden* (London, 1981), 254, 255.

45 Theodore A. Wilson, 'The Road to Bretton Woods: Winston Churchill and Imperial Finance', *Proceedings of the Churchill Societies, 1988–1989*, 46; Kimball, *Churchill & Roosevelt*, i. C-165x (not sent); United States, Department of State, *Foreign Relations of the United States* (Washington, 1862–), 1942, i, pp. 534–5. Neville Chamberlain flatly expressed such fears in a letter to his sister, Ida, on 27 Jan. 1940: 'Heaven knows I don't want the Americans to fight for us—we should have to pay too dearly for that if they had a right to be in on the peace terms . . .': as quoted in Dimbleby and Reynolds, *An Ocean Apart*, 135.

46 These issues and others are examined throughout the literature of Anglo-American relations during the war. See the bibliography to Kimball, *The Juggler*, for a start. The American commitment to multilateralism is examined in Randall B. Woods, *A Changing of the Guard: Multilateralism and Internationalism in Anglo-American Relations, 1941–1946* (Chapel Hill, 1989). The civil aviation dispute has finally found its historian in Alan P. Dobson, *Peaceful Air Warfare: The United States, Britain and the Politics of International Aviation* (Oxford, 1991).

47 Gilbert, *Churchill*, vii. 44.

48 Churchill to George VI, 13 Apr. 1945, as quoted in Gilbert, *Churchill*, vii. 1294.

49 See Norman Rose, 'Churchill and Zionism', in this volume, Ch. 9.

50 Harold Macmillan, *War Diaries: Politics and War in the Mediterranean, January 1943–May 1945* (New York, 1984), 10.

51 Kimball, *The Juggler*, 90, 192–3.

52 As quoted in Gelb, *Anglo-American Relations, 1945–1949*, 52.

53 Robin Edmonds has provided a perceptive look at the geopolitics of that developing Cold War relationship in *Setting the Mould: The United States and Britain, 1945–1950* (New York and London, 1986).

54 This follows what I wrote originally in 'Churchill and Roosevelt: The Personal Equation', *Prologue: The Journal of the National Archives*, 6 (Fall 1974), 169–82, and in revised form as the Introduction to *Churchill & Roosevelt*, i. 3–20. For a recent voice again suggesting that the Roosevelt–Churchill relationship was not all sweetness and light, see Richard Lamb, *Churchill as War Leader: Right or Wrong?* (London, 1991).

55 Gunther, *Roosevelt in Retrospect*, 19.

56 This raises the question of whether or not Halifax and other Conservative leaders might have negotiated with Hitler in 1940. See, for example, John Costello, *Ten Days to Destiny: The Secret Story of the Hess Peace Initiative and British Efforts to Strike a Deal with Hitler* (New York, 1991). On 15 Nov. 1991, the Associated Press reported on notes made by author Fulton Oursler concerning a December 1940 message he carried to Roosevelt from the Duke of Windsor. F.D.R. was to offer to intervene for peace which, according to one of the Duke's aides, would bring a statement of support from the Duke and 'start a revolution in England and force peace': *The Star-Ledger* (Newark, NJ), 15 Nov. 1991. However bizarre that proposal, and whatever my doubts that only Churchill-in-charge prevented a compromise with Hitler, the refusal of the British government to grant access to relevant documents that are over 50 years old fuels suspicions that such a 'peace' movement involved prominent people.

57 It is instructive to recognize that, until the presidency of Ronald Reagan, Americans recoiled at the allegation that the United States had an 'empire' after the Second World War. It was Reagan who convinced Americans that an American Empire was a good and moral thing. This is reflected in the historical literature as well. See, for example, John L. Gaddis, *The Long Peace* (New York, 1987).

CHAPTER 18

1 Cited by E. T. Williams in his notice of Churchill in the *Dictionary of National Biography Supplement, 1961–1970* (Oxford, 1981), 214.
2 'Notes on the Present Russian Situation': Cabinet Memorandum of 9 Dec. 1917 by the Foreign Secretary, A. J. Balfour, who wrote of his own recommendation that an open Anglo-Bolshevik breach should be avoided as long as possible: 'If this be drifting, then I am a drifter by deliberate policy'; cited in Richard H. Ullman, *Anglo-Soviet Relations, 1917–1921*, 3 vols. (Princeton, 1961), i. 31.
3 *Dokumenty vneshnei politiki SSSR* (Politizdat, Moscow) (hereafter *DVPS*), i. 401–2.
4 For the subsequent execution of the 26 members of the Baku Soviet, for which Stalin blamed the British, see Ullman, *Anglo-Soviet Relations*, i. 320 ff.
5 FO telegram no. 178 to Balfour (in Paris), 16 Feb. 1919, drafted by Lloyd George and subsequently printed by him in his *The Truth about the Peace Treaties* (London, 1938), i. 370 ff., which also contains his comment about Churchill.
6 FO telegram no. 88 to Peking, 18 Mar. 1920, cited in Ullman, *Anglo-Soviet Relations*, ii. 253.
7 *The Times*, 12 Apr. 1919.
8 Field Marshal Sir Henry Wilson, diary entry for 16 Oct. 1919, cited in Vladimir Truchanovsky, *Uinston Cherchill'*, 4th (Russian) edn., Mezhdunarodnye Otnosheniya (Moscow, 1989), 175.
9 *Illustrated Sunday Herald*, 25 Jan. 1920.
10 Lord Birkenhead to Churchill, 17 Nov. 1920, cited in Martin Gilbert, *Winston S. Churchill*, companion vol. iv, part 2, Documents July 1919–March 1921, pp. 1241–2. The most recent account of 'the great debate' in the Imperial War Cabinet about intervention in Russia and the British government's subsequent *de facto* recognition is that of Sir Curtis Keeble, *Britain and the Soviet Union, 1917–1989* (London, 1990), 50 ff.
11 *DVPS*, xxi, Document 103.
12 Ibid., Document 111.
13 Winston Churchill, *The World Crisis: The Eastern Front* (London, 1931), 7 and 343 ff.
14 *Parliamentary Debates* (Commons), 19 May 1939.
15 Churchill, *The Second World War*, 6 vols. (London, 1948–1954), i. 307; and Dmitrii A. Volkogonov, *I. V. Stalin: Triumf i Tragediya*, 2 vols., 4 parts: ii, part 1 (Moscow, 1989), 20 ff.
16 Quoted in Churchill, *Second World War*, i. 353.
17 For Churchill's 1940 letter to Stalin, see ibid. ii. 119–20; for the 1941 'lightning flash', see ibid. iii. 319; and for Cripps's unprofessional behaviour in delaying the delivery of Churchill's April message by a fortnight, see Gilbert, *Churchill*, vi. 1050–1.
18 Warren F. Kimball (ed.), *Churchill & Roosevelt: The Complete Correspondence*, 3 vols. (Princeton, 1984), i. C-100X.
19 John Colville, *The Fringes of Power: Downing Street Diaries, 1939–1955* (London, 1985), 404.
20 The full text of Churchill's broadcast address on the German invasion of Russia, 22 June 1941, is in *War Speeches by the Right Honourable Winston S. Churchill*, compiled by Charles Eade (London, 1942), 176–80.

21 On Soviet Intelligence in 1941, see e.g. the full-page article in *Pravda*, 8 May 1989, 4. Molotov's telegram is Document 3 in vol. i. of *Sovetsko—Angliiskie Otnosheniya vo vremya velikoi otechestvennoi voiny, 1941–1945*, 2 vols. (Moscow, 1983) (hereafter '*Sov-Angl-O*': the parallel volumes of Soviet–American documents are abbreviated '*Sov-Am-O*').

22 Extracts from Stalin's 'Brothers and Sisters' broadcast form *Sov-Angl-O*, i, Document 10. For the exchanges leading up to the Anglo-Soviet Declaration, see ibid., Documents 1, 15, and 21.

23 *Perepiska predsedatelya soveta ministrov SSSR s prezidentami SShA i premer-ministrami veliko-britanii vo vremya velikoi otechestvennoi voiny, 1941–1945 gg.*, 2 vols. (Moscow, 1986; 2nd edn., 1989), i, Documents 3 and 12; and *Sov-Angl-O*, i, Documents 47–9.

24 *Perepiska*, i. 46–7.

25 *Sov-Angl-O*, i, Document 78.

26 Ibid. 184 ff.; and Churchill, *Second World War*, iii. 394 (the Atlantic Charter) and 559–60. See also *Soviet–Polish Relations, 1939–1945*, 2 vols. (The General Sikorsky Historical Institute, London, 1961), i, Document 160.

27 Kimball, *Churchill & Roosevelt*, i. C-40; *Sov-Angl-O*, i, Documents 107 and 110, and p. 301.

28 *Sov-Angl-O*, i, Documents 112, 123, and 126.

29 Kimball, *Churchill & Roosevelt*, iii. C-126a.

30 The British records are in PREM 3/76A/9 ff. and the Soviet in *Sov-Angl-O*, i. 265 ff. For the incident of the Churchillian philippic, see Gilbert, *Churchill*, vii. 186 (the Soviet records omit Stalin's response).

31 *Sov-Angl-O*, i, Documents 161 and 163.

32 The Jacob Diary in the Jacob Papers at Woodbridge, Suffolk, records Churchill's early decision, which he strongly supported. (Colonel Jacob also provided the Prime Minister with his new, bilingual, interpreter, Major A. H. Birse.) The dramatic record of Clark Kerr's subsequent argument with Churchill, during their walk together, forms part of his manuscript account of Churchill's visit (FO 800/300, not circulated—it included a sketch of Churchill in the nude). Clark Kerr, a man whose vanity was well known, was not with the Prime Minister throughout his visit. See also Gilbert, *Churchill*, iv. 444 ff.

33 Kimball, *Churchill & Roosevelt*, i. C-134; *Sov-Angl-O*, i. 279.

34 Kimball, *Churchill & Roosevelt*, ii. C-263.

35 *Sov-Angl-O*, i, Document 226.

36 Kimball, *Churchill & Roosevelt*, ii. C-309, C-310, and R-289; *Sov-Angl-O*, i, Document 194; and *Foreign Relations of the United States* (Washington, 1955–) (hereafter *FRUS*), *The Teheran Conference*, 3–4.

37 Kimball, *Churchill & Roosevelt*, i. R-123/11 letter.

38 Unless otherwise stated, the accounts of and the quotations from the Tehran, Yalta, and Potsdam Conferences are based on the Bohlen minutes in the relevant volumes of *FRUS*.

39 From the Soviet record, *Sovetskii Soyuz na mezhdunarodnykh konferentsiyach perioda velikoi otechestvennoi voiny, 1941–1945 gg., Sbornik dokumentov*, 6 vols. (Izdatel'stvo politicheskoi literatury, Moscow, 1978–9) (hereafter *SSNMK*), ii. 124. The British record—CAB 120/113—tallies, except for including a remark by Stalin to the effect that it would be very difficult for the Russians, who were 'war weary', to carry on if there were 'no big change in 1944'.

40 *FRUS, The Teheran Conference*, 640–1.

41 Kimball, *Churchill & Roosevelt*, iii. C-740.

42 Ibid. 282 ff., and *Perepiska*, i. 285 ff.

43 British Embassy, Moscow telegram no. 2819 to FO, 12 Oct. 1944, cited in Gilbert, *Churchill*, vii. 1002.

44 British Embassy, Moscow telegram no. 2935 to FO, 15 Oct 1944, cited in ibid. 1010.
45 FO 800/302/227–35; CAB 120/158; and Churchill, *Second World War*, vi. 227–8.
46 Gilbert, *Churchill*, vii. 994 and 998 ff.
47 PREM 3/434/4.
48 Kimball, *Churchill & Roosevelt*, iii. C–894.1.
49 Churchill Papers 2/497, cited in Gilbert, *Churchill*, vii. 1031.
50 Kimball, *Churchill & Roosevelt*, iii. c–894.1.
51 Ibid. C–732 and 733.
52 *SSNMK*, iii. 100–1.
53 In fact the original (State Department) drafters of this document almost certainly conceived it as aimed just as much at events in Greece, for which the British were responsible, as those in Poland: *FRUS, 1945: The Conferences at Malta and Yalta*, 93 ff. As Arthur Schlesinger, Jr, has argued, 'signing the Declaration was from the Soviet point of view a diplomatic blunder': Arthur J. Schlesinger, Jr, 'Roosevelt's Diplomacy at Yalta', in *Yalta: Un mito che resiste* (Rome, 1989), 152.
54 *Parliamentary Debates* (Commons), 27 Feb. 1945.
55 Kimball, *Churchill & Roosevelt*, iii. C–910 and R–742; and see e.g. *Sov-Am-O*, ii. 400.
56 Minute by Sir Orme Sargent, 1 Oct. 1945, FO 371/44557.
57 David Dilks (ed.), *The Diaries of Sir Alexander Cadogan* (London, 1971), 776–8.
58 Churchill, *Second World War*, vi. 583.
59 Churchill to Truman, 6 and 11 May 1945, *FRUS, 1945: The Conference of Berlin*, i. 3 ff; and Richard Hewlett and Oscar Anderson, *History of the United States Atomic Energy Commission* (University Park, PA, 1962), i. 351 ff.
60 Churchill's appeal to Stalin (FO telegram no. 2255 to Moscow, 29 Apr. 1945) is translated in full in *Sov-Angl-O*, ii, Document 250. Stalin's reply, dated 4 May 1945, is Document 258. An example of the Soviet Ambassador's reporting from London at this time is in Document 270; an account of the conversation at lunch at 10 Downing Street on 18 May.
61 Churchill, *Second World War*, vi. 581.
62 Understanding between the Polish Committee of National Liberation and the Government of the USSR regarding the Polish–Soviet state frontier (signed by Molotov and Osóbka-Morawski), Moscow, 27 July 1944: Polish text published in *Dokumenty i materiały do historii stosunków polsko-radzieckich* (Warsaw, 1974), viii.
63 Margaret Gowing, *Britain and Atomic Energy, 1939–1945* (London, 1964), 363.
64 Harry S. Truman, *Year of Decisions, 1945* (New York, 1955), 416; Churchill, *Second World War*, vi. 580; and *SSNMK*, vi. 15.
65 Zhukov's account is in G. K. Zhukov, *Vospominaniya i razmyshleniya* (Moscow, 1969), 732; see also Yu. V. Sirintsev, *I. V. Kurchatov i yadernaya energetika* (Moscow, 1980), 10–11.
66 Memorandum by Stanislaw Mikolajczyk, Appendix A, *FRUS 1945: The Conference of Berlin*.
67 Colville, *Fringes of Power*, 624.
68 A good example is described by Churchill himself in *Second World War*, v. 330. 'Grubost' is a word not easily translated in this context. It means 'rude' and 'vulgar'; and the English-language edition of Roy Medvedev's *Let History Judge* even prefers to render it as 'nasty'.
69 Memorandum by Colin Coote, 27 Jan. 1944, cited in Gilbert, *Churchill*, vii. 664; and Eden diary, 17 July 1945, cited in Robert Rhodes James, *Anthony Eden* (London, 1986), 307.
70 Churchill, *Second World War*, vi. 379.

CHAPTER 19

1 Martin Gilbert, *Churchill*, vi. 1208.
2 J. Wheeler-Bennett (ed.), *Action This Day* (London, 1968), 54.
3 Ibid. 51.
4 Ronald Lewin, *Churchill as Warlord* (London, 1973), 33.
5 Wheeler-Bennett, *Action This Day*, 250.
6 Ibid. 193–5.
7 Ibid. 73.
8 See, *inter alia*, James M. Burns, *Roosevelt: The Soldier of Freedom* (New York, 1970); John Erickson, *The Road to Stalingrad* (London, 1975); David Irving, *Hitler's War* (London, 1977); T. Harry Williams, *Lincoln and His Generals* (New York, 1952).
9 Wheeler-Bennett, *Action This Day*, 195–6.
10 See D. Reynolds, 'Churchill and the British "Decision" to Fight On in 1940: Right Policy, Wrong Reasons', in R. Langhorne (ed.), *Diplomacy and Intelligence during the Second World War* (Cambridge, 1985), 145–67.
11 Gilbert, *Churchill*, vi. 326.
12 Ibid. 667.
13 M. R. D. Foot, *SOE 1940–46* (London, 1984), 19.
14 Werner Rings, *Leben mit dem Feind* (Munich, 1979), ch. 2, *passim*.
15 Gilbert, Churchill, vi. 813.
16 Ibid. 822.
17 The Turkish government allowed 15 RAF observer posts to be set up on its side of the border with Bulgaria at the end of May 1940; Gilbert, *Churchill*, vi. 678.
18 Ibid. 980.
19 Winston Churchill, *The Second World War* (London, 1950), iii. 607–8.
20 Eliot Cohen, 'Churchill and Coalition Strategy in World War II', in Paul Kennedy, *Grand Strategies in War and Peace* (New Haven, 1991), 49.
21 On US war production, see e.g. A. S. Milward, *War, Economy and Society, 1939–45* (London, 1977), 63–74.
22 Irving, *Hitler's War*, 352–4.
23 Stephen Roskill, *Churchill and the Admirals* (London, 1977), 276.
24 For the *Prince of Wales* and *Repulse*, see ibid. 196–201.
25 Ibid. 277.
26 Number of sorties flown against U-boat bases: see Lewin, *Churchill as Warlord*, 185.
27 Maxwell P. Schoenfeld, *The War Ministry of Winston Churchill*, (Ames, Iowa, 1972), 93.
28 Max Hastings, *Bomber Command* (London, 1979), 349.
29 Lewin, *Churchill as Warlord*, 95.
30 Schoenfeld, *War Ministry*, 95.
31 On the Dodecanese, see Gilbert, *Churchill*, vii, chs 31 and 33 *passim*, and Jeffrey Holland, *The Aegean Mission* (New York, 1988).
32 Charles Messenger, *The Commandos* (London, 1985), 26.
33 Christopher Andrew, 'Churchill and Intelligence', in Michael I. Handel (ed.), *Leaders and Intelligence* (London, 1989), 189.
34 Correlli Barnett, *The Audit of War* (London, 1986), esp. ch. 9.
35 Ibid. 180.
36 F. H. Hinsley, *et al.*, *British Intelligence in the Second World War* (London, 1979), vol. iii, part 1, pp. 373 and 448.
37 Wheeler-Bennett, *Action This Day*, 102, 104.
38 Albert Speer, *Inside the Third Reich* (New York, 1970), 231–2.
39 Lewin, *Churchill as Warlord*, 45.

40 On Churchill's dealings with the Dominions and lesser allies, see Cohen, 'Churchill and Coalition Strategy'.
41 Michael Howard, *Grand Strategy*, iv (London, 1972); and *The Mediterranean Strategy in the Second World War* (London, 1968).
42 Quoted in John Keegan, *Six Armies in Normandy* (London, 1982), 35.
43 Ibid. 35.
44 Gilbert, *Churchill*, vii. 152.
45 Keegan, *Six Armies*, 50.
46 Gilbert, *Churchill* vii. 414.
47 Ibid. 563.
48 Keegan, *Six Armies*, 55.
49 On British aid to Russia, see Joan Beaumont, *Comrades in Arms* (London, 1980).
50 Gilbert, *Churchill*, vii. 992–3; see also Robin Edmonds, in this volume, Ch. 18.
51 See Barbara Jelavich, *History of the Balkans*, ii: *Twentieth Century* (Cambridge, 1983), 268.
52 Lewin, *Churchill as Warlord*, 50.

CHAPTER 20

1 Winston S. Churchill, *Marlborough: His Life and Times*, 2 vols. (London, 1947 edn.), i. 568–70.
2 Stephen Roskill, *Churchill and the Admirals* (London, 1977), 184.
3 Ronald Lewin, *The Chief* (London, 1971), 38–9.
4 Martin Gilbert, *Winston S. Churchill*, vi. 1013.
5 Ibid. 1025.
6 Ibid. 1055.
7 Lewin, *The Chief*, 140.
8 Ibid. 141.
9 Winston S. Churchill, *The Second World War*, 6 vols. (London, 1950), iii. 354.
10 Gilbert, *Churchill*, vi. 1144.
11 Ibid. 1150.
12 Lord Ismay, *Memoirs* (London, 1960), 269–71.
13 John Terraine, *The Right of the Line* (London, 1985), 355.
14 Gilbert, *Churchill*, vi. 1227.
15 David Fraser, *Alanbrooke* (London, 1987), 202.
16 Ibid. 531–2.
17 Terraine, *The Right of the Line*, 291.
18 Ibid. 295.
19 Ibid. 297.
20 Lewin, *The Chief*, 164.
21 Churchill, *The Second World War*, iii. 331.
22 Ibid.
23 Ibid. 411.
24 Philip Ziegler, *Mountbatten* (London, 1985), 222.

CHAPTER 21

1 *Winston Churchill as I Knew Him* (London, 1965), 154. For a sceptical assessment of her account, see Randolph Churchill, *Churchill*, ii. 240–2.
2 Then Admiral Sir John Fisher, later Admiral of the Fleet Lord Fisher of Kilverstone.

3 Winston S. Churchill, *The World Crisis* (London, 1923), i. 93.
4 Quoted in Stephen Roskill, *Hankey: Man of Secrets* (London, 1970), i. 102.
5 Richard Ollard, *Fisher and Cunningham: A Study in the Personalities of the Churchill Era* (London, 1991).
6 Arthur Marder, *Fear God and Dread Nought: The Correspondence of Admiral of the Fleet Lord Fisher of Kilverstone*, 2 vols (London, 1961 and 1965), ii. 292.
7 Churchill, *World Crisis*, i. 7.
8 Admiral Sir Peter Gretton, *Former Naval Person: Winston Churchill and the Royal Navy* (London, 1968), 244.
9 *World Crisis*, i. 88.
10 On all this see my *Fisher and Cunningham*, 103–7.
11 Philip Ziegler in his *Mountbatten* (London, 1985), 175–6, records Ismay's disbelief in Churchill's seriousness but by no means dismisses the possibility.
12 The King of course won. She was commissioned as HMS *Valiant*. The story is admirably told in Gretton, *Former Naval Person*, 86–8.
13 *World Crisis*, i. 129 ff. Churchill's letter to Fisher pressing him to preside over the Commission on Fuel & Engines is a virtuoso performance. It is printed in the companion volume of Martin Gilbert and R. S. Churchill's *Churchill*, ii. 1929.
14 Largely printed in Gretton, *Former Naval Person*, 98–102. I have drawn freely on this source.
15 Stephen Roskill, *Admiral of the Fleet Earl Beatty: The Last Naval Hero* (London, 1980), 219–20.
16 Gretton, *Former Naval Person*, 203.
17 Churchill, *World Crisis*, i. 157.
18 See Roskill, *Churchill and the Admirals* (London, 1977), 220–2.
19 Culpeper to Hyde, Clarendon MS 28f. 189, Bodleian Library, Oxford.
20 Lord Selborne, quoted in Gretton, *Former Naval Person*, 197–8.
21 Roskill, *Churchill and the Admirals*, 37.
22 Marder, *Fear God and Dread Nought*, iii. 451–2.
23 E. W. R. Lumby (ed.), *The Mediterranean 1912–1914* (Navy Records Society, 1970), 135 ff.
24 'Rosy' Wemyss, an attractive, able, and conspicuously unselfish officer whom everyone liked, from Beresford and Fisher to King George V. Lady Beatty, jealous of the Wemysses' popularity (and anyway rather mad), had their bed thrown out of the window on to the Horse Guards Parade on moving into the First Lord's quarters (private information).
25 Lloyd George Papers, F/8/3/46, House of Lords Record Office. I am most grateful to Professor B. M. Ranft who is editing the Beatty Papers for the Navy Records Society for allowing me to use his transcript.
26 Correlli Barnett, *Engage the Enemy More Closely: The Royal Navy in the Second World War* (London, 1991), *passim*.
27 On Churchill's part in this important decision see Gretton, *Former Naval Person*, 235 ff., and Roskill, *Churchill and the Admirals*, 86–7.
28 See Roskill, *Churchill and the Admirals*, 90–1.
29 Code-named 'Catherine'. For this see Correlli Barnett, *Engage the Enemy More Closely*.
30 Lindemann's role in this matter is disputed. In his defence see Lord Birkenhead, *The Prof. in Two Worlds* (London, 1961). The contrary view is fully set out in C. P. Snow's *Science and Government* (London, 1961) and its *Postscript* (London, 1962).
31 I infer this from the entry in Cunningham's diary for 26 Dec. 1945 (on the death of Keyes) (BL Add. MS 52578): 'Roger . . . was not much good as C o S to de Robeck at the Dardanelles but he had an offensive spirit which at times undoubtedly clouded his judgement.'

32 For an account see Ollard, *Fisher and Cunningham*, 84 ff.
33 On all this see ibid. 113–15.
34 BL Add. MS 52575.
35 On this disaster and Churchill's responsibility for it see Barnett, *Engage the Enemy More Closely.*
36 Cunningham's diary, 19 Feb. 1946, BL Add. MS 52579.
37 Ibid., 13 Apr. 1945, BL Add. MS 52578.
38 Gretton, *Former Naval Person*, 264–5.
39 Quoted in ibid. 260.

CHAPTER 22

1 Eisenhower diary, 1 June 1953. The diary is in the Eisenhower Library, Abilene, Kansas.
2 Ibid., 7 July 1942.
3 Ibid., 30 May 1943.
4 Memorandum, Eisenhower to George Marshall and Ernest King, 19 July 1942, Eisenhower Library.
5 Harry Butcher diary, 23 Aug. 1942, Eisenhower Library.
6 Eisenhower to Marshall, 21 Sept. 1942.
7 Dwight D. Eisenhower, *At Ease: Stories I Tell to Friends* (Garden City, NY, 1967), 273.
8 Sir Arthur Tedder, *With Prejudice* (London, 1966), 528–30.
9 Eisenhower to British Chiefs, 6 Mar. 1944, Eisenhower Library.
10 Eisenhower, *At Ease*, 275.
11 Butcher diary, 13 May 1944.
12 Ibid.
13 Dwight D. Eisenhower, *Crusade in Europe* (Garden City, NY, 1948), 281.
14 Eisenhower to Marshall, 5 Aug. 1944, Eisenhower Library.
15 Ibid.
16 Eisenhower to Marshall, 11 Aug. 1944; Eisenhower to Churchill, 11 Aug. 1944, Eisenhower Library.
17 Eisenhower to Churchill, 11 Aug. 1944, Eisenhower Library; Eisenhower, *Crusade*, 281–3.
18 Winston S. Churchill, *The Second World War* (Boston, 1953), vi. 463–5.
19 Quoted in Stephen E. Ambrose, *Eisenhower and Berlin: The Decision to halt at the Elbe* (New York, 1967), 64–5.
20 Eisenhower to Marshall, 7 Apr. 1945, Eisenhower Library.
21 Eisenhower to Marshall, 16 Aug. 1944, Eisenhower Library.
22 Eisenhower, *Crusade*, 62.
23 Eisenhower to Swede Hazlett, 8 Dec. 1954, Eisenhower Library.

CHAPTER 23

1 Christopher Andrew, 'Churchill and Intelligence', *Intelligence and National Security*, 3 (1988), 181, 187.
2 F. H. Hinsley *et al.*, *British Intelligence in the Second World War* (London, 1979), i, p. 160 and Appendix 6.
3 Ibid. 296–8.
4 Ibid. 294–5.
5 Ibid. 295.

6 Ibid.
7 Christopher Andrew, 'Secret Intelligence and British Foreign Policy, 1900–1939', in Christopher Andrew and Jeremy Noakes (eds.), *Intelligence and International Relations, 1900–1945* (Exeter, 1987), 18–19.
8 Hinsley *et al.*, *British Intelligence*, i. 91.
9 Ibid. i. 295; ii. 4.
10 Andrew, 'Secret Intelligence and British Foreign Policy', 16.
11 Andrew, 'Churchill and Intelligence', 184.
12 Hinsley *et al.*, *British Intelligence*, i. 296–8; ii. 4–5.
13 Ibid. i. 299–302.
14 Martin Gilbert, *Churchill*, vi. 630–1.
15 Hinsley et al., *British Intelligence*, i. 154–8.
16 Ibid. 255–8.
17 Ibid. 351–63; Winston S. Churchill, *The Second World War* (London, 1950), iii. 63, 68, 83–94;) F. de Guingand, *Generals at War* (London, 1964), 24.
18 Hinsley *et al.*, *British Intelligence*, i. 388–9.
19 Ibid. 395.
20 Ibid. 396–7; Ralph Bennett, *Ultra and Mediterranean Strategy* (London, 1989), 38–46.
21 Hinsley *et al.*, *British Intelligence*, i. 366–8, 409–14.
22 Ibid. 411–12, 415–19, 422–4.
23 Ibid. 371, 429–30, 450–2.
24 Ibid. 453–74; Churchill, *Second World War*, iii. 318–19, 326.
25 Hinsley *et al.*, *British Intelligence*, ii. 59–60, 73, 109–10, 644–7.
26 Ibid. 286–7, 494–5.
27 Ibid. ii. 150; iii (part 1). 324.
28 Ibid. ii. 279, 290–304.
29 Ibid. 351–6.
30 Ibid. 456, 459.
31 Ibid. iii (part 1). 120, 125–6, 131.
32 Ibid. 26–7; iii (part 2). 316–18.
33 Ibid. iii (part 1). 399, 415, 449, 569–71; iii (part 2). 578–80.
34 Ibid. iii (part 2). 502.
35 Ibid. 369, 380–2.

CHAPTER 24

1 Winston S. Churchill, *My Early Life* (London, 1959 edn.), 34.
2 Ibid. 49.
3 Violet Bonham-Carter, *Winston Churchill as I Knew Him* (London, 1965), 106.
4 Ibid. 262.
5 In the course of his military career, Churchill served as a regimental officer in no fewer than eight regiments: 4th Hussars, 31st Punjaubis (Churchill's spelling), 21st Lancers, South African Light Horse, Oxfordshire Yeomanry, Grenadier Guards, Royal Scots Fusiliers, Oxfordshire Artillery.
6 Martin Gilbert, *Churchill*, iii. 639.
7 R. V. Jones, *Biographical Memoirs of Fellows of the Royal Society* (London, 1966), xii. 61.
8 *Parliamentary Debates* (Commons) (appreciation of Stalin), Sept. 1942.
9 Randolph Churchill, *Churchill*, ii. 704.
10 Gilbert, *Churchill*, v. 126.

11 Mary Soames, *Clementine Churchill* (London, 1979), 229.
12 Gilbert, *Churchill*, v. 443.
13 Jones, *Biographical Memoirs*, 66.
14 According to Martin Gilbert the 'German' was Lindemann (*Churchill*, iv. 51). This was Churchill's sole acknowledgement in the article, and it can hardly have given pleasure to Lindemann in so describing him, for as Lord Birkenhead recorded in his official biography of Lindemann he had a grievance against his mother because she went from England to Baden-Baden shortly before he was born and 'the fact that she knew her time was drawing near and yet gave birth to him on German territory was a source of life-long annoyance to Lindemann': *The Prof. in Two Worlds* (London, 1961), 16.
15 Winston S. Churchill, *Thoughts and Adventures* (London, 1947 edn.), 188.
16 Jones, *Biographical Memoirs*, 67.
17 Ibid. 68.
18 Churchill, *Thoughts and Adventures*, 208.
19 Jones, *Biographical Memoirs*, 69.
20 Lord Cherwell, *Chemistry and Industry* (London, 1954), 940–3.
21 Churchill, *Second World War* (London, 1948), i. 62.
22 *Parliamentary Debates* (Commons), 7 June 1935.
23 Gilbert, *Churchill*, v. 947.
24 Churchill, *Second World War*, i. 325.
25 Ibid.
26 Gilbert, *Churchill*, v. 1076.
27 Gilbert, *Churchill*, vi. 310.
28 Churchill, *Second World War*, ii. 338.
29 Ibid. 346.
30 Jones, *Biographical Memoirs*, 79.
31 David Irving, *Churchill's War* (London, 1987), 395.
32 Julian Lewis, *Changing Direction* (London, 1988), 388–405.
33 Notably Robert Harris on BBC 'Newsnight' programme of 1 May 1981, effectively refuted by Julian Lewis in *Changing Direction*, Appendix 8. The BBC never apologized for this discreditable smear.
34 Margaret Gowing, *Britain and Atomic Energy, 1939–1945* (London, 1964), 106.
35 Jones, *Biographical Memoirs*, 88.
36 Randolph Churchill (ed), *The Unwritten Alliance: Speeches 1953–59 by Winston Churchill* (London, 1961), 226.
37 Ibid. 230.
38 *Parliamentary Debates* (Commons), 7 Nov. 1945.
39 Churchill, *My Early Life*, 209.
40 Jones, *Biographical Memoirs*, 90.
41 Ibid. 92.
42 Ibid.
43 *Parliamentary Debates* (Commons), 18 June 1940.
44 Churchill, Speech at Fulton, Missouri, 5 Mar. 1946.
45 John Colville, 'A Brief Account of the Establishment of Churchill College' (July 1959), Archives of Churchill College, Cambridge.
46 Ibid. I was able to give some minor sidelights in *Reflections on Intelligence* (London, 1989).
47 *The Unwritten Alliance*, 329–30.

CHAPTER 25

1 Martin Gilbert has shown how Churchill's time in opposition after 1945 was divided between the writing of *The Second World War* and intermittent political activity: Martin Gilbert, *Churchill: A Life* (London, 1991), ch. 37.

2 Ibid. 81.

3 Winston S. Churchill, *The World Crisis* (London, 1923), 14.

4 Winston S. Churchill, *Marlborough: His Life and Times*, 4 vols. (London, 1933–8, edn.).

5 Max Beloff, 'The Anglo-French Project of June 1940', reprinted from *Mélanges Pierre Renouvin* (Paris, 1966) in Max Beloff, *The Intellectual in Politics* (London, 1970).

6 For a recent discussion of moves towards settlement with Germany after the Fall of France, see Andrew Roberts, *'The Holy Fox': A Biography of Lord Halifax* (London, 1991), chs. 24 and 25.

7 The most vivid account of the triangular relationship between Britain, France, and the USA is that in Jean Lacouture, *De Gaulle*, i: *Le Rebelle* (Paris, 1984).

8 The study of the all-important Churchill–Roosevelt relationship free of the inhibitions that guided Churchill in his own memoirs has been renewed by Robin Edmonds in *The Big Three: Churchill, Roosevelt and Stalin in Peace and War* (New York and London, 1991).

9 John Colville, *The Fringes of Power: Downing Street Diaries*, i: *1939–October 1941* (London, 1985), 371.

10 John Harvey (ed.), *The War Diaries of Oliver Harvey* (London, 1978), 175–6.

11 '"Morning Thoughts": Note on Post War Security by the Prime Minister', 1 Feb. 1943, printed as Appendix V in Michael Howard, *Grand Strategy*, iv: *August 1942–September 1943* (London, 1972), 637–9.

12 Memorandum of a luncheon at the British Embassy, Washington, 22 May 1943, in W. F. Kimball (ed.), *Churchill & Roosevelt: The Complete Correspondence* (Princeton, 1984), ii. 222–6.

13 'The United Nations Plan for Organizing Peace', circulated to the Cabinet by the Foreign Office on 7 July 1943; printed in Sir Llewellyn Woodward, *British Foreign Policy in the Second World War* (London, 1976), v. 50–61.

14 Martin Gilbert, *Winston S. Churchill*, viii. 243.

15 Ibid. 265–6.

16 Ibid. 285–7. The relations between Churchill and de Gaulle provide an essential backdrop to Churchill's successive positions on European unity. For a study of this relationship see François Kersaudy, *De Gaulle et Churchill* (Paris, 1982).

17 John Colville in John Wheeler-Bennett (ed.), *Action This Day* (London, 1968), 98. Colville adds that Churchill remained closer in his thinking to de Gaulle than to Spaak, Monnet, and Schuman.

18 Gilbert, *Churchill*, viii. 321.

19 Ibid. 337.

20 Ibid. 407.

21 Gilbert, *Churchill: A Life*, 880.

22 Gilbert, *Churchill*, viii. 354–5.

23 Ibid. 535–7.

24 Gilbert, *Churchill: A Life*, 487.

25 Ibid. 892.

26 Gilbert, *Churchill*, viii. 535–7.

27 Robert Rhodes James, *Anthony Eden* (London, 1986), 333 and 347–51.

28 Anthony Selden, *Churchill's Indian Summer: The Conservative Government, 1951–1955* (London, 1981), 413–14.

29 On American policy in respect of European integration, see Max Beloff, *The United States and the Unity of Europe* (Washington, 1963).

30 Gilbert, *Churchill: A Life*, 900.

31 Colville, *The Fringes of Power*, i. 323 and 349–50.

32 Ibid. 327.

33 Speech in London at a meeting of the European Movement, 28 Nov. 1949, in R. S. Churchill (ed.), *In the Balance: Speeches by Winston S. Churchill 1949–50* (London, 1951).

34 See ch. 5 in this volume by Peter Clarke, 'Churchill's Economic Ideas'.

35 Speech at Brighton, 4 Oct. 1947, in Randolph Churchill (ed.), *Europe Unite* (London, 1950).

36 Gilbert, *Churchill*, viii. 263–5.

37 Speech at the Hague, 7 May 1948, in Randolph Churchill, *Europe Unite*, 313.

38 Speech in the House of Commons, 23 Jan. 1948.

39 See ch. 3 in this volume by Douglas Johnson, 'Churchill and France'.

CHAPTER 26

1 Winston Churchill, *My Early Life* (London, 1930), 101–2; Randolph S. Churchill, *Winston S. Churchill*, i. 297.

2 See Churchill to Curzon, 22 Aug. 1905: Curzon Papers, India Office Library, MSS Eur. F. 111, vol. clxxxiii, part 1, no. 134a.

3 Martin Gilbert, *Winston S. Churchill*, iv. 404–12.

4 Robert Rhodes James, *Churchill: A Study in Failure, 1900–1939* (London, 1970), 186.

5 W. S. Churchill,*The Second World War* (London, 1948), i. 31; Carl Bridge, *Holding India to the Empire* (Delhi, 1986), 43.

6 Churchill to Baldwin, 24 Sept. 1930, and Baldwin to J. C. C. Davidson, 13 Nov. 1930, both quoted in J. Barnes and D. Nicholson (eds.), *The Empire at Bay: The Leo Amery Diaries, 1929–1945* (London, 1988), 92 and 97 respectively.

7 Duff Cooper, *Old Men Forget* (London, 1953), 103; A. Horne, *Macmillan* (London, 1988), i. 110.

8 Carl Bridge, 'Churchill and Indian Political Freedom; The Diehards and the 1935 Act', *Indo-British Review* (July–December 1987), 26–30.

9 Churchill's speech at the West Essex Unionist Association, 23 Feb.: *The Times*, 24 Feb. 1931.

10 Churchill to Irwin, 24 Mar. 1931, cited in Bridge, *Holding India to the Empire*, 65.

11 Speech in the House of Commons, 12 Mar. 1931.

12 Speech at the Indian Empire Society, 18 Mar.: *The Times*, 19 Mar. 1931.

13 Clare Sheridan (Churchill's cousin), 'The Great Little Mahatma', in S. Radhakrishnan (ed.), *Mahatma Gandhi* (London, revised edn., 1949), 274.

14 W. S. Churchill, 'The New Phase in India', *Evening Standard*, 16 Apr. 1937.

15 R. J. Moore, *Churchill, Cripps and India 1939–1945* (Oxford, 1979), 21–3, 28; Bridge, *Holding India to the Empire*, 153.

16 For Halifax's comment, see Amery's diary entry for 26 July 1940, in Barnes and Nicholson, *Amery Diaries*, 636; and for Amery's own views, diary entries for 12 July 1940 and 24 Nov. 1941, ibid. 633 and 750.

17 See Churchill to Roosevelt, 9 Aug. 1942: Gilbert, *Churchill*, vi. 1164.

18 R. Coupland, *The Cripps Mission* (Oxford, 1942), 22.

19 Lord Glendevon, *The Viceroy at Bay* (London, 1971), 208–12.

20 Churchill to Attlee from Washington, 7 Jan. 1942: N. Mansergh (ed.), *The Transfer of Power 1942–1947* (London, 1970), i, no. 6; Churchill to Chiang Kai-shek, 3 Feb. 1942: ibid., no. 62; Averell Harriman's report of conversation with Churchill, 26

Feb. 1942, quoted in M. S. Venkatramani and B. K. Shrivastava, *Roosevelt, Gandhi, Churchill* (Delhi, 1983), 16–17.

21 To Amery, 8 Mar. 1942: Barnes and Nicholson, *Amery Diaries*, 785–6.

22 For the details of the Cripps mission, see the documents in *Transfer of Power*, i; General G. N. Molesworth, *Curfew on Olympus* (London, 1965), 220; Moore, *Churchill, Cripps and India*, 104–26; S. Gopal, *Jawaharlal Nehru* (London, 1975), i. 278–87.

23 Churchill to Hopkins, Apr. 1942: Venkatramani and Shrivastava, *Roosevelt, Gandhi, Churchill*, 33–4.

24 Churchill to Amery, 9 Sept. 1942: Barnes and Nicholson, *Amery Diaries*, 832.

25 Record of Churchill's talk with A. R. Mudaliar and others, 10 Sept. 1942: *Transfer of Power*, iii, document 2 enclosure; Churchill to Amery, 12 Nov. 1942: Barnes and Nicholson, *Amery Diaries*, 842.

26 Speech at the Mansion House, 10 Nov. 1942.

27 Churchill to Viceroy and Amery to Viceroy, both 8 Feb. 1943: *Transfer of Power*, iii, nos. 424 and 437.

28 Record by Phillips of interview with Churchill, 22 May 1943: Venkatramani and Shrivastava, *Roosevelt, Gandhi, Churchill*, 156.

29 27 July 1943: P. Moon (ed.), *Wavell: The Viceroy's Journal* (Oxford, 1973), 12.

30 6 Oct. 1943: *Transfer of Power*, iv, no. 164.

31 Gandhi to Churchill, 17 July 1944: *Transfer of Power*, v, no. 20, enclosure 5.

32 Wavell to Churchill, 24 Oct. 1944: *Transfer of Power*, v, no. 64.

33 Amery's diary entry for 24 Sept. 1943: Barnes and Nicholson, *Amery Diaries*, 943; Wavell to Amery, 25 Feb. 1944: *Transfer of Power*, iv, no. 401; C. B. A. Behrens, *Merchant Shipping and the Demands of War* (London, 1955), 359 and 434–5.

34 Mountbatten to Wavell, 7 Sept. 1944: Moon, *Wavell: The Viceroy's Journal*, 89; Mountbatten to the author, 28 May 1970.

35 4 Aug. 1944: Barnes and Nicholson, *Amery Diaries*, 993.

36 Amery to Linlithgow, 30 Oct. 1942: *Transfer of Power*, iii, no. 128.

37 Amery to Linlithgow, 1 Sept. 1942 and to Wavell, 9 Aug. 1944: *Transfer of Power*, ii, no. 673, and iv, no. 634 respectively.

38 R. A. Butler's report to Samuel Hoare of conversation with Churchill, 27 Nov. 1942: quoted in Moore, *Churchill, Cripps and India*, 137.

39 18 Mar. 1942: *Transfer of Power*, i, no. 346.

40 King George VI's diary, 28 July 1942: J. Wheeler-Bennett, *King George VI, His Life and Reign* (London, 1953), 703.

41 Churchill to Chiang Kai-shek, 26 Aug. 1942: *Transfer of Power*, ii, no. 637.

42 21 June 1943: Barnes and Nicholson, *Amery Diaries*, 895.

43 Record by W. Phillips of conversation with Churchill, 11 Dec. 1942: Venkatramani and Shrivastava, *Roosevelt, Gandhi, Churchill*, 70–1; minute of Churchill, 9 Dec. 1944: *Transfer of Power*, v, no. 146; R. A. Butler, *The Art of the Possible* (London, 1971), 111.

44 Churchill to Jinnah, 3 Aug. 1946: Gilbert, *Churchill*, viii. 248.

45 Lord Pethick-Lawrence's record of talk with R. A. Butler, 27 Nov. 1946: *Transfer of Power*, ix, no. 105; Butler to Wavell, 5 Dec. 1946: Moon, *Wavell: The Viceroy's Journal*, 390.

46 'The New Phase in India', *Evening Standard*, 16 Apr. 1937.

47 J. Nehru, *The Discovery of India* (Calcutta, 1945), 439.

48 Amery to Linlithgow, 14 Nov. 1940: Linlithgow Papers, India Office Library, MSS Eur. F. 125, vol. ix.

49 See Churchill's speech in the House of Commons, 6 Mar. 1947.

50 Churchill in House of Commons, 12 Dec. 1946. In fact there had been no occasion for Nehru to give any such order.

51 Churchill in the House of Commons, 6 Mar. 1947.
52 Record of Mountbatten's interview with Churchill, 22 May 1947: *Transfer of Power*, x, no. 513.
53 Churchill's message to Mountbatten, 8 July 1947: *Transfer of Power*, xii, no. 26.
54 19 Nov. 1947: P. Ziegler, *Mountbatten* (London, 1985), 461.
55 Churchill to Eden, 12 Sept. 1948: Gilbert, *Churchill*, viii, 431.
56 V. K. Krishna Menon, High Commissioner of India in London, to Nehru, 11 Mar. 1949, Nehru Papers.
57 Nehru's report of the conversation, in J. S. Mehta, *The Nehru We Loved to Serve* (mimeo paper, University of Texas, Austin).
58 Dictation notes, 2 May 1949: Gilbert, *Churchill*, viii. 743.
59 Quoted in H. Tinker, *Separate and Unequal* (London, 1976), 388.
60 K. Natwar Singh, 'Jawaharlal Nehru and Winston Churchill', *Secular Democracy* (Delhi), August–September 1989.
61 Telegram forwarded by British High Commissioner in Delhi, 1 July 1953, Nehru Papers.
62 Churchill to Nehru, 21 Feb. and 30 June 1955: ibid.
63 Lord Moran, *Winston Churchill: The Struggle for Survival* (London, 1966), 630–1.
64 Quoted in F. Kersaudy, *Churchill and de Gaulle* (Fontana edn., 1990), 200.
65 T. Paulin, 'Into the Heart of Englishness', *Times Literary Supplement*, 20–6 July 1990.
66 Report of J. F. Dulles on the Bermuda conference, 4–8 Dec. 1953, Eisenhower Papers, Dwight D. Eisenhower Library, Abilene, Kansas.
67 Memorandum of Dulles on a conversation at dinner with Churchill, 12 Apr. 1954, ibid.
68 I owe this reference to Dr Anita Inder Singh.

CHAPTER 27

1 D. E. Butler, *The British General Election of 1951* (London, 1952), 55; Martin Gilbert, *Winston S. Churchill*, viii. 643.
2 Churchill to Eden, 'Private and Personal', 30 Jan. 1952, PREM 11/91.
3 Raymond A. Callahan, *Churchill: Retreat from Empire* (Wilmington, Delaware, 1984), is an excellent survey of Churchill's early life and career with the imperial theme as the focus.
4 *Parliamentary Debates* (Commons), 6 Mar. 1947, col. 678.
5 Ibid., 7 May 1946, col. 895.
6 Ibid., 30 July 1951, col. 981.
7 Minute by Churchill, 26 Aug. 1952, PREM 11/392.
8 Shuckburgh Diaries, 16 Dec. 1951. References are to unpublished Shuckburgh Diaries (privately held) unless the excerpt appears in the published version, Evelyn Shuckburgh, *Descent to Suez: Diaries 1951–56* (London, 1986).
9 Churchill to Eden, 15 Feb. 1952, PREM 11/91.
10 Minute by Churchill, 19 Aug. 1952, PREM 11/392.
11 Shuckburgh, *Descent to Suez*, 76.
12 *Parliamentary Debates* (Commons), 7 May 1946, cols. 781 and 894.
13 Minute by Churchill, 24 Mar. 1952, FO 371/96928.
14 Churchill to Eden, 'Private and Personal', 30 Jan. 1952, PREM 11/91.
15 Minute by Churchill, 19 Aug. 1952, PREM 11/392.
16 Minute by Churchill, 19 Oct. 1952, PREM 11/398.
17 Minute by Churchill, 20 Feb. 1953, PREM 11/392.
18 Diary entry, no date but probably December 1951, Shuckburgh Diaries.
19 Shuckburgh, *Descent to Suez*, 75.

20 Ibid. 95.
21 Memorandum by Hankey, 'Secret', 22 May 1953, FO 371/102765.
22 Ibid.
23 Hankey to Roger Allen (head of the African Department of the Foreign Office), 'Confidential', 24 Sept. 1953, FO 371/102706.
24 Minute by Salisbury, 9 Sept. 1953, FO 371/102816.
25 Shuckburgh, *Descent to Suez*, 112 and 121.
26 *Churchill: Taken from the Diaries of Lord Moran: The Struggle for Survival, 1940–1965* (Boston, 1966), 513.
27 Churchill to Eisenhower, 'Private and Confidential', 18 Feb. 1953: *Foreign Relations of the United States 1952–1954*, ix, part 2, p. 1990. The significant exchanges have been published in *Foreign Relations*, which I cite for convenience. I follow, however, the punctuation, spelling, and form in the originals in the PREM series.
28 24 Feb. 1953: ibid. 1997–8. Eisenhower had written a month earlier in his diary: 'He talks very animatedly about certain . . . international problems, especially Egypt and its future. But so far as I can see, he has developed an almost childlike faith that all of the answers are to be found merely in British–American partnership'. Robert H. Ferrell (ed.), *The Eisenhower Diaries* (New York, 1981), 223.
29 18 Mar. 1953: *Foreign Relations 1952–1954*, ix, part 2, p. 2026.
30 19 Mar. 1953: ibid. 2027–8.
31 5 Apr. 1953: ibid. 2042–3.
32 15 Apr. 1953: ibid. 2049.
33 8 May 1953: ibid. 2060–1.
34 8 May 1953: ibid. 2061–2.
35 20 May 1953: ibid. 2076.
36 10 June 1953: ibid. 2089.
37 15 June 1953: ibid. 2095.
38 17 June 1953: ibid. 2096.
39 Cabinet Conclusions (53) 72, 26 Nov. 1953, CAB 128/26.
40 19 Dec. 1953: *Foreign Relations 1952–1954*, ix, part 2, p. 2177.
41 20 Dec. 1953: ibid. 2178–9.
42 22 Dec. 1953: ibid. 2183.
43 22 Dec. 1953: ibid. 2184.
44 25 Feb. 1954: Shuckburgh, *Descent to Suez*, 136.
45 Brian Lapping, *End of Empire* (London, 1985), 255.
46 See e.g. minutes of Meeting of Ministers, 8 Feb. 1954, PREM 11/701.
47 Leo Amery Diaries (privately held), 16 Nov. 1953.
48 Ibid.
49 Ibid., 12 May 1953.
50 Ibid., 15 Jan. 1954.
51 Ibid., 10 Mar. 1953.
52 Ibid., 27 July 1954.
53 26 Mar. 1954: Moran, *Struggle for Survival*, 566.
54 *Parliamentary Debates* (Commons), 29 July 1954, col. 780.
55 Cabinet Conclusions, 22 June 1954, CAB 128/27.
56 Shuckburgh, *Descent to Suez*, 173.
57 31 Mar. 1954: Shuckburgh, *Descent to Suez*, 157. 'We are under the dictatorship of an old dotard . . .': Shuckburgh Diary, 6 July 1954.
58 See Gilbert, *Churchill*, viii. 961.
59 *Parliamentary Debates* (Commons), 29 July 1954, cols. 731–7.
60 Ibid., cols. 739–40.
61 Ibid., col. 748.

62 Ibid., col. 750.
63 30 July 1954: Moran, *Struggle for Survival*, 622; Gilbert, *Churchill*, viii. 1037.
64 Amery Diary, 27 July 1954.
65 Ibid., 18 Oct. 1954.
66 Gilbert, *Churchill*, viii. 1220–1.
67 Ibid. 1222 n. 2. Another version of this remark is 'I am not sure I should have dared to start; but I am sure I should not have dared to stop': Hugh Thomas, *The Suez Affair* (London, 1986 edn.), 182–3.

CHAPTER 28

1 R. A. Butler, *The Art of the Possible: The Memoirs of Lord Butler* (London, 1971), 173.
2 Lord Moran, *Winston Churchill: The Struggle for Survival, 1940–1965* (London, 1966), 538.
3 Evelyn Shuckburgh, *Descent to Suez* (London, 1986), 157.
4 Martin Gilbert, *Winston S. Churchill*, viii. 1036.
5 Ibid. 1049–51.
6 *Parliamentary Debates* (Commons), 4 Nov. 1951.
7 Quoted in Gilbert, *Churchill*, viii. 660.

CHAPTER 29

1 The comment has several different versions: e.g. John Campbell, *F. E. Smith: First Earl of Birkenhead* (London, 1983), 792: 'Often right, "but my God when he's wrong"!!'
2 Robert Rhodes James, *Churchill: A Study in Failure, 1900–1939* (Cleveland, 1970).
3 Mary Soames, *Clementine Churchill* (London, 1979), 441.
4 Robert Rhodes James, *Bob Boothby* (London, 1991), 342–4.
5 BBC Radio interview, March 1965.
6 Winston S. Churchill, *My Early Life* (London, 1930), 18.
7 Rhodes James, *Study in Failure*, 26.
8 Randolph S. Churchill, *Winston S. Churchill*, companion vol. ii, pp. 816–21.
9 Winston S. Churchill, *Savrola* (London, 1900).
10 Rhodes James, *Study in Failure*, 28.
11 Speech on Army Reform, House of Commons, 12 May 1901: Robert Rhodes James (ed.), *Winston S. Churchill: His Complete Speeches, 1897–1963*, 8 vols. (London, 1974), i. 76–86.
12 Violet Bonham-Carter, *Winston Churchill as I Knew Him* (New York, 1965), 18.
13 Isaiah Berlin, *Personal Impressions* (New York, 1981), 13.
14 G. W. Steevens, 'The Youngest Man in Europe', in Charles Eade (ed.), *Churchill by His Contemporaries* (London, 1953), 61–6.
15 Rhodes James, *Study in Failure*, 29.
16 Ibid.
17 Speech on Trades Dispute Bill, House of Commons, 22 Apr. 1904: Rhodes James (ed.), *Complete Speeches*, i. 274–6.
18 R. S. Churchill, *Churchill*, i, ch. 2.
19 Edward Marsh, *A Number of People* (London, 1939), 151.
20 Rhodes James, *Study in Failure*, 88.
21 Churchill, 'The Scaffolding of Rhetoric'.
22 Robert Boothby, *Recollections of a Rebel* (London, 1978), 46.

23 Ibid. 157.
24 Rhodes James, *Study in Failure*, 230–2, 237–8.
25 Norman A. Rose (ed.), *'Baffy': The Diaries of Blanche Dugdale, 1936–1947* (London, 1973), 91.
26 Speech at Royal Naval Division Memorial, 25 Apr. 1925: Rhodes James (ed.), *Complete Speeches*, iv. 3554–6.
27 Speech on 'A Total and Unmitigated Defeat', House of Commons, 5 Oct. 1938: Rhodes James (ed.), *Complete Speeches*, vi. 6004–13.
28 Speech on 'Blood, Toil, Tears and Sweat', House of Commons, 13 May 1940: Rhodes James (ed.), *Complete Speeches*, vi. 6218–20. Private information from the late Sir Desmond Morton.
29 'Eightieth Birthday', 30 Nov. 1954: Rhodes James (ed.), *Complete Speeches*, viii. 8607–9.
30 Speech on 'The Deterrent—Nuclear Warfare', 1 Mar. 1955: Rhodes James (ed.), *Complete Speeches*, viii. 8625–33.
31 Personal recollection.
32 Personal information from Julian Critchley, MP.
33 Soames, *Clementine Churchill*.
34 Isaiah Berlin, *Personal Impressions*, 7.

INDEX